INTRODUCTION TO PROGRAMMING WITH C++,
Second Edition

Student
Access Card

S0-BCX-507

Thank you for purchasing a new copy of *Introduction to Programming with C++*, Second Edition, by Y. Daniel Liang. The information below provides instruction on how to access Liang's VideoNotes and Bonus Chapters.

VideoNotes are Pearson's new visual tool for teaching C++ programming concepts and techniques. Step-by-step video tutorials demonstrate how to solve programming problems from design through coding. VideoNotes allow for self-paced instruction with easy navigation including the ability to play, rewind, fast-forward, and stop within each VideoNote exercise.

 – Margin icons in your textbook let you know that a VideoNotes tutorial is available for a particular concept or representative homework problem.

In addition to VideoNotes, the access code below gives access to the following Bonus Chapters:
- ➢ Chapter 21 Binary Search Trees
- ➢ Chapter 22 STL Containers
- ➢ Chapter 23 STL Algorithms
- ➢ Chapter 24 Graphs and Applications
- ➢ Chapter 25 Weighted Graphs and Applications
- ➢ Chapter 26 AVL Trees and Splay Trees

To access VideoNotes and the Bonus Chapters for Liang, 2e, please follow these steps:
1. Go to www.prenhall.com/liang
2. Click on the title *Introduction to Programming with C++*, Second Edition.
3. Click on the link to VideoNotes or the Bonus Chapters. There you can register as a First-Time User and Returning User.
4. Use a coin to scratch off the coating below and reveal your student access code.
   ****Do not use a knife or other sharp object as it may damage the code.*

5. On the registration page, enter your student access code. Do not type the dashes. You can use lower or uppercase letters.
6. Follow the on-screen instructions. If you need help during the online registration process, simply click on Need Help?
7. Once your personal Login Name and Password are confirmed, you can begin viewing your VideoNotes or Bonus Chapter

To login to VideoNotes or to access the Bonus Chapters for the first time after you've registered:
Follow steps 1 and 2 to return to the VideoNotes or Bonus Chapters links. Then, follow the prompts for "Returning Users" to enter your Login Name and Password.
Note to Instructors: For access to the Instructor Resource Center, contact your Pearson Representative.

IMPORTANT: The access code on this page can only be used once to establish a subscription to the Liang, *Introduction to Programming with C++*, Second Edition VideoNotes and the Bonus Chapters.. If this access code has already been scratched off, it may no longer be valid. If this is the case, you can purchase a subscription by going to the *www.prenhall.com/liang* website, selecting *Introduction to Programming with C++ 2e*, clicking on login or register under VideoNotes, and then selecting "Get Access."

PEARSON

www.pearsonhighered.com

For help with registration or technical support, visit http://247pearsoned.custhelp.com

INTRODUCTION TO
PROGRAMMING
WITH

Second Edition

Y. Daniel Liang

Armstrong Atlantic State University

Prentice Hall

Upper Saddle River   Boston   Columbus   San Francisco   New York
Indianapolis   London   Toronto   Sydney   Singapore   Tokyo   Montreal
Dubai   Madrid   Hong Kong   Mexico City   Munich   Paris   Amsterdam   Cape Town

Vice President and Editorial Director, ECS: Marcia J. Horton
Executive Editor: Tracy Dunkelberger
Assistant Editor: Melinda Haggerty
Director of Team-Based Project Management: Vince O'Brien
Senior Managing Editor: Scott Disanno
Production Liaison: Irwin Zucker
Production Editor: Haseen Khan, Laserwords
Senior Operations Specialist: Alan Fischer
Operations Specialist: Lisa McDowell
Marketing Manager: Erin Davis
Marketing Assistant: Mack Patterson
Art Director: Kenny Beck
Cover Image: Charles and Josette Lenars/CORBIS
Art Editor: Greg Dulles
Media Editor: Daniel Sandin
Media Project Manager: John M. Cassar
Composition/Full-Service Project Management: Laserwords, Inc.

Library of Congress Cataloging-in-Publication Data
Liang, Y. Daniel.
  Introduction to programming with C++ / Y. Daniel Liang. -- 2nd ed.
     p. cm.
  Includes bibliographical references and index.
  ISBN 0-13-609720-0 (alk. paper)
  1. C++ (Computer program language) I. Title.
  QA76.73.C153L5 2009
  005.13'3--dc22
                          2009004380

Prentice Hall
is an imprint of

www.pearsonhighered.com

10 9 8 7 6 5 4 3 2 1

ISBN-13: 978-0-13-609720-4
ISBN-10:   0-13-609720-0

To Samantha, Michael, and Michelle

PREFACE

Two years ago we published the first edition of *Introduction to Programming with C++*. The book has been well received. Our fundamentals-first approach and clear and concise writing style strike a chord with the readers. We have built upon our successful approach with the following major improvements:

- This edition includes a wide variety of interesting new examples and exercises in business, game, simulation, math, and science with different levels of difficulty to better motivate students. Half of the examples and exercises are new.

what's new?

- Chapter 5, "Functions," has been split into two chapters to enable instructors to cover basic features and advanced features separately.

- Chapter 6, "Arrays," has been split into two chapters, enabling instructors to skip two-dimensional arrays.

- Chapters in the OOP part have been reorganized. The new organization introduces simple concepts early.

- The new Chapter 10 focuses on class design and explores the differences between the procedural and object-oriented paradigms. This chapter helps students to progress from the procedural to the object-oriented programming.

- Pointers and dynamic memory management are introduced along with copy constructors and destructors in a new Chapter 11, enabling instructors to cover these related topics in one chapter.

- To take the advantage of the powerful C++ `string` class, all examples involving strings now use the `string` class rather than the legacy C-strings.

- All advanced and nonessential language features such as multiple inheritance, function parameters, and enumerated types are moved to the companion Website, so that students can focus on problem solving and fundamental programming techniques.

- Brand-new Chapter 18, "Algorithm Efficiency," uses many concrete examples to introduce how to design efficient algorithms. Brand-new bonus Chapters 24–26 introduce graph algorithms and applications and AVL trees. Bonus chapters are available from the companion Website.

- The companion Website has been renovated to provide more useful supporting materials, including a brand-new *LiveLab*.

Teaching Strategies

Several strategies are used in teaching programming. This book adopts the *fundamentals-first* strategy. We proceed at a steady pace through all the necessary and important basic concepts, then move on to object-oriented programming and the use of the object-oriented approach to build interesting applications with exception handling, I/O, and data structures.

fundamentals-first

My own experience, confirmed by the experiences of many colleagues, demonstrates that new programmers in order to succeed must learn basic logic and *fundamental programming techniques* like loops and stepwise refinement. Students who cannot write code in procedural programming are not able to learn object-oriented programming. A good introduction to primitive data types, control statements, functions, and arrays prepares students to learn object-oriented programming.

fundamental programming techniques

The fundamentals-first approach presents the procedural solutions and then demonstrates how to improve upon them using the object-oriented programming (OOP) approach. Students learn when and how to apply OOP effectively.

using OOP effectively

Problem-Driven

Programming is more than just syntax, classes, or objects—it is *problem solving*.

This book uses the problem-driven approach to teach problem solving. Interesting and practical examples are used not only to illustrate syntax but also to teach problem solving and programming. Each chapter is introduced with representative problems to give the reader an overview what to expect from the chapter. A wide variety of problems at various levels of difficulty are presented, covering many application areas in gaming, math, business, science, and simulation. Some representative problems are described below.

Example 1: Chapter 2 introduces a simple problem of computing a circle's area given its radius (§2.2, "Writing Simple Programs"). To solve this problem, we introduce variables for storing data and data types for declaring variables. We also introduce expressions for computing area. Initially, the input value for radius is coded in the program. This is not convenient. We show next how to prompt the user to enter data at runtime from the console (§2.3).

Example 2: The selection statements are introduced with the birth-date guessing game (Listing 3.2) and the `SubtractionQuiz` game (Listing 3.5). The guessing game finds one's birth date by asking five questions, and the `SubtractionQuiz` game automatically generates a subtraction question (i.e., `firstNumber – secondNumber`) and grades the user's answer.

Example 3: The `SubtractionQuiz` game generates just one question. To repeatedly generate random questions, you have to use loops. In Chapter 4, we revise `SubtractionQuiz` to generate ten questions in `SubtractionQuizLoop` (Listing 4.3).

Example 4: The `GreatestCommonDivisor` program (Listing 4.8) computes the greatest common divisor (gcd) of two numbers. Because all the code is in the main function, this program is not reusable. To make it modular and reusable, we revise the program to create a function for computing gcd in Listing 5.4.

Example 5: Listing 3.3, ComputeBMI.cpp, gives a program for computing Body Mass Index. Suppose you want to store the user's information. The program is difficult to expand in the procedural paradigm. In §10.9, "Object-Oriented Thinking," we redesign the program using classes, and we use this problem to demonstrate the advantages of the object-oriented over the procedural paradigm.

Learning Strategies

A programming course is quite different from other courses. You learn from examples, from practice, and from mistakes. You need to devote a lot of time to writing programs, testing them, and fixing errors.

For first-time programmers, learning C++ is like learning any high-level programming language. The aim is to learn to formulate programmatic solutions for real problems and translate them into programs using selection statements, loops, functions, and arrays.

Once you learn to write programs using loops, functions, and arrays, you can begin to learn object-oriented programming for developing large projects using class encapsulation and class inheritance.

Pedagogical Features

The Liang Series promotes *teaching by example and learning by doing*. Basic features are explained by example so that students can learn by doing. This book uses the following elements to get the most from the material:

- **Objectives** list what students should have learned from the chapter. This will help them to determine whether they have met the objectives after completing the chapter.

- **Introduction** opens the discussion with representative problems to give the reader an overview of what to expect from the chapter.

- **Examples**, carefully chosen and presented in an easy-to-follow style, teach programming concepts. The book uses many small, simple, and stimulating examples to demonstrate important ideas.

- **Chapter Summary** reviews the important subjects that students should understand and remember. It helps them to reinforce the key concepts they have learned in the chapter.

- **Review Questions** are grouped by sections to help students track their progress and evaluate their learning.

- **Programming Exercises** are grouped by sections to provide students with opportunities to apply on their own the new skills they have learned. The level of difficulty is rated easy (no asterisk), moderate (*), hard (**), or challenging (***). The trick of learning programming is practice, practice, and practice. To that end, this book provides a great many exercises.

- **Notes**, **Tips**, and **Cautions** are inserted throughout the text to offer valuable advice and insight on important aspects of program development.

 Note
Provides additional information on the subject and reinforces important concepts.

 Tip
Teaches good programming style and practice.

 Caution
Helps students steer away from the pitfalls of programming errors.

Flexible Chapter Orderings

The book provides flexible chapter orderings, as shown in the following diagram:

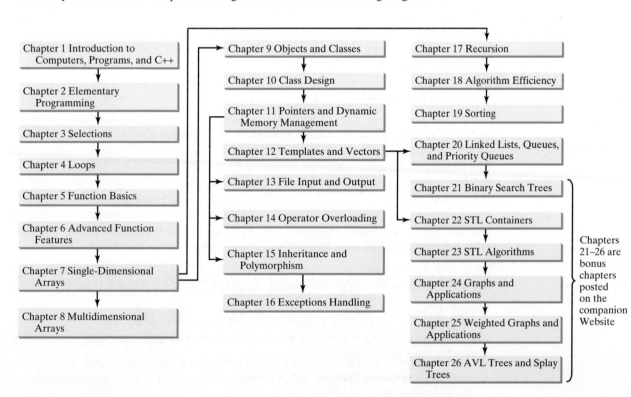

Organization of the Book

The chapters can be grouped into three parts, which together form a solid introduction to problem solving and programming using C++.

Part I: Fundamentals of Programming (Chapters 1–8)

The first part of the book is a stepping stone, preparing you to embark on the journey of learning programming with C++. You will begin to know C++ (Chapter 1) and will learn elementary programming techniques with primitive data types, expressions, and operators (Chapter 2), control statements (Chapters 3–4), functions (Chapters 5–6), and arrays (Chapters 7–8).

Part II: Object-Oriented Programming (Chapters 9–16)

This part introduces object-oriented programming. C++ is an object-oriented programming language that uses abstraction, encapsulation, inheritance, and polymorphism to provide great flexibility, modularity, and reusability in developing software. You will learn programming with objects and classes (Chapter 9), design classes (Chapter 10), explore pointers and dynamic memory management (Chapter 11), develop generic classes using templates (Chapter 12), use IO classes for file input and output (Chapter 13), use operators to simplify functions (Chapter 14), derive classes from base classes (Chapter 15), and make your programs robust using exception handling (Chapter 16).

Part III: Algorithms and Data Structures (Chapters 17–20)

This part introduces the main subjects in a typical data structures course. Chapter 17 introduces recursion to write functions for solving inherently recursive problems. Chapter 18 introduces how to measure algorithm efficiency in order to choose an appropriate algorithm for applications. You will learn how to design and implement linked lists, queues, and priority queues in Chapter 20.

Part III: Algorithms and Data Structures Online Bonus Chapters (Chapters 21–26)

Bonus Chapters 21–26 are located on the book's website at www.prenhall.com/liang. A valid student access code is required to access this premium content. Instructions on how to obtain an access code are available at www.prenhall.com/liang.

Chapter 21 introduces binary search trees. Chapters 22 and 23 cover the standard template library in C++. Chapters 24 and 25 introduce graph algorithms and applications. Chapter 26 introduces balanced binary search trees.

C++ Development Tools

You can use a text editor, such as the Windows Notepad or WordPad, to create C++ programs, and you can compile and run the programs from the command window. You can also use a C++ development tool, such as Visual C++ or Dev-C++. These tools support an integrated development environment (IDE) for rapidly developing C++ programs. Editing, compiling, building, executing, and debugging programs are integrated in one graphical user interface. Using these tools effectively will greatly increase your programming productivity. How to create, compile, and run programs using Visual C++ and Dev-C++ is introduced in Chapter 1. The programs in this book have been tested on Visual C++ and the GNU C++ compiler. A DVD containing the Microsoft Visual C++® 2008 Express Edition is included with this book.

LiveLab (Web-Based Course Assessment and Grade Management System)

This book is accompanied by a Web-based course assessment and management system. The system has three main components:

■ **Automatic Grading System:** All of the programs featured in the book are available in the web-based automatic grading system.

- **Quiz Creation/Submission/Grading System:** It enables instructors to create/modify quizzes and let students take them and be graded automatically.
- **Tracking grades, attendance, etc.:** The system enables students to track grades and enables instructors to view the grades of all students and track attendance.

The main features of the Automatic Grading System are as follows:

- Allows students to compile, run and submit exercises online. (Students can find out whether their program runs correctly with student test cases and can continue to run and submit the program before the due date.)
- Allows instructors to review submissions, run programs with instructor test cases, correct them online, and provide feedback to students online.
- Allows instructors to create/modify their own programming exercises, create public and secret test cases, assign exercises, and set due dates for the whole class or for individuals.
- Allows instructors to sort and filter all exercises and check grades (by time frame, student, date, and/or exercise).
- Allows instructors to delete students from the system.
- Allows students and instructors to track grades on programming exercises.

The main features of the Quiz System are as follows:

- Allows instructors to create/modify quizzes from test bank or from a text file, or to create complete new tests online.
- Allows instructors to assign the quizzes to students and to set a due date and test time limit for the whole class or for individuals.
- Allows students and instructors to review submitted quizzes.
- Allows students and instructors to track grades on quizzes.

VideoNotes

VideoNotes are Pearson's new visual tool designed for teaching students key programming concepts and techniques. These short step-by-step videos demonstrate how to solve problems from design through coding. VideoNotes allow for self-paced instruction with easy navigation including the ability to select, play, rewind, fast-forward, and stop within each VideoNote exercise.

VideoNote margin icons in your textbook let you know when a VideoNotes video is available for a particular concept or homework problem.

VideoNotes are free with the purchase of a new book. To *purchase* access to VideoNotes, go to www.prenhall.com/liang and click on the VideoNotes under *Student Resources*.

Student Resource Website

Resources associated with this book can be accessed via www.prenhall.com/liang or directly at www.cs.armstrong.edu/liang/cpp2e.

- Answers to review questions
- Solutions to even-numbered programming exercises
- Source code for the examples in the book
- Interactive Self-Test (organized by sections for each chapter)

- LiveLab
- Supplements
- Resource links
- Errata

Supplements

The text covers the essential subjects. The supplements extend the text to introduce additional topics that might be of interest to readers. The following supplements are available from the companion Website.

Supplements for Introduction to Programming with C++, 2E

Part I General Supplements
  A Glossary
  B Installing and Configuring C++ Compiler
  C Compiling and Running C++ from the Command Window
  D Compiling and Running C++ from the Unix
  E C++ Coding Style Guidelines

Part II IDE Supplements
  A Visual C++ 2008 Tutorial
  B Learning C++ Effectively with Visual C++
  C Dev-C++ Tutorial
  D C++Builder Tutorial
  E Learning C++ Effectively with C++Builder
  F Compiling and Linking Object Files in g++

Part III Preprocessor
  A Preprocessor Directives

Part IV Advanced C++ Topics
  A Multiple Inheritance
  B Namespaces
  C Operator Keywords
  D Default Arguments in Constructors and Functions
  E Constructor Initializer Lists
  F Immutable Classes and Objects
  G Passing Functions as Parameters
  H Enumerated Types
  I Nested Classes

Part V Legacy Topics
  A Redirecting Input/Output
  B Using Command-Line Argument
  C C goto Statements
  D C printf Statements
  E Structures
  F C-Strings

Instructor Resource Website

The Instructor Resource Website is accessible from www.cs.armstrong.edu/liang/cpp2e. Contact your local Pearson Sales Rep for the username and password required to access the site. The Instructor Resource Website includes:

- Microsoft PowerPoint Slides: Slides have interactive buttons to view full-color, syntax-highlighted source code, and to run programs without leaving the slides.

- Sample Exams: In general, each exam has four parts:

  1. Multiple-choice and Short-Answer Questions

2. Correct programming errors

3. Trace programs

4. Write programs

- Instructor Solutions Manual: Includes solutions to all exercises.

- Web-based Quiz Generator: Instructors can choose chapters and generate quizzes from a database of more than 800 questions.

Some readers have requested the materials from the Instructor Resource Website. Please understand that these are for instructors only. Such requests will not be answered.

Acknowledgments

I would like to thank Armstrong Atlantic State University for enabling me to teach what I write and for supporting me in writing what I teach. Teaching is the source of inspiration for continuing to improve the book. I am grateful to the instructors and students who have offered comments, suggestions, bug reports, and praise.

This book was greatly enhanced thanks to outstanding reviews for this and previous editions. The reviewers are: Waleed Farag (Indiana University of Pennsylvania), Max I. Fomitchev (Penn State University), Brian Linard (University of California, Riverside), Dan Lipsa (Armstrong Atlantic State University), Jon Hanrath (Illinois Institute of Technology), Hui Liu (Missouri State University), Ronald Marsh (University of North Dakota), Peter Maurer (Baylor University), Jay D. Morris (Old Dominion University), Charles Nelson (Rock Valley College), Martha Sanchez (University of Texas at Dallas), Kate Stewart (Tallahassee Community College), Ronald Taylor (Wright State University), Margaret Tseng (Montgomery College), and Barbara Tulley (Elizabethtown College).

It is a great pleasure, honor, and privilege to work with Prentice Hall. I would like to thank Marcia Horton, Tracy Dunkelberger, Margaret Waples, Erin Davis, Jake Warde, Melinda Haggerty, Scott Disanno, Irwin Zucker, Haseen Khan and their colleagues for organizing, producing, and promoting this project, and Robert Lentz for copy editing.

As always, I am indebted to my wife, Samantha, for her love, support, and encouragement.

Y. Daniel Liang
y.daniel.liang@gmail.com
www.cs.armstrong.edu/liang/cpp2e

BRIEF CONTENTS

The following bonus chapters are on book's website at www.prenhall.com/liang. Access to this premium content requires a valid student access code. Instructions on how to obtain an access code are provided on the book's website.

CONTENTS

PART 1

FUNDAMENTALS OF PROGRAMMING

The first part of the book is a stepping stone that will prepare you to embark on the journey of learning C++. You will begin to know C++ and will develop fundamental programming skills. Specifically, you will learn elementary programming, control statements, functions, and arrays.

Prerequisites for Part I

This book does not require any prior programming experience, or any mathematics, other than elementary high school algebra and basic computer skills such as using Windows, Web browsing, and word processing.

You may cover Chapter 17, "Recursion," Chapter 18, "Algorithm Efficiency," and Chapter 19, "Sorting," after Chapter 7, "Single-Dimensional Arrays."

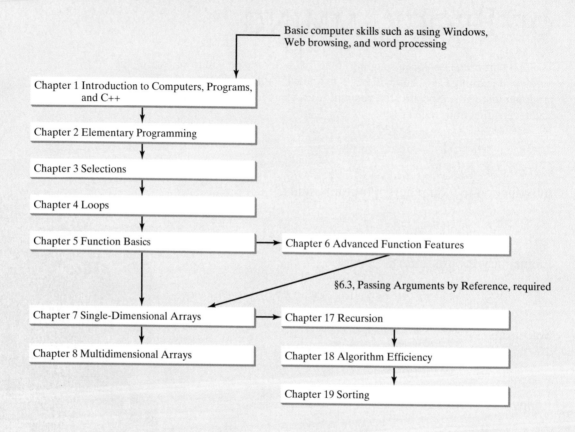

CHAPTER 1

INTRODUCTION TO COMPUTERS, PROGRAMS, AND C++

Objectives

- To review computer basics, programs, and operating systems (§§1.2–1.4).
- To know the history of C++ (§1.5).
- To write a simple C++ program for console output (§1.6).
- To understand the C++ program-development cycle (§1.7).
- To develop C++ using Visual C++ (§1.8).
- To develop C++ using Dev-C++ (§1.9).
- To develop C++ using command-line tools on Windows (§1.10).
- To develop C++ using command-line tools on UNIX (§1.11).

1.1 Introduction

You use word processors to write documents, Web browsers to explore the Internet, and email programs to send email over the Internet. Word processors, browsers, and email programs are all examples of software that runs on computers. Software is developed using programming languages. Among programming languages, a popular and powerful one is C++. Most application software, such as word processors, browsers, and email programs, is developed using C++. This book will introduce you to developing programs using C++.

You are about to begin an exciting journey, learning a powerful programming language. Before you begin, it is helpful to review computer basics, programs, and operating systems. If you are familiar with such terms as CPU, memory, disks, operating systems, and programming languages, you may skip the review in §§1.2–1.4.

1.2 What Is a Computer?

A computer is an electronic device that stores and processes data. A computer includes both *hardware* and *software*. In general, hardware is the physical aspect of the computer that can be seen, and software is the invisible instructions that control the hardware and make it perform specific tasks. Computer programming consists of writing instructions for computers to perform. You can learn a programming language without knowing computer hardware, but you will be better able to understand the effect of the instructions in the program if you do. This section gives a brief introduction to computer hardware components and their functionality.

A computer consists of the following major hardware components, as shown in Figure 1.1.

- Central processing unit (CPU)

- Memory (main memory)

- Storage devices (e.g, disks, CDs, tapes)

- Input and output devices (e.g, monitors, keyboards, mice, printers)

- Communication devices (e.g, modems and network interface cards (NICs))

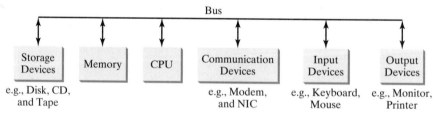

FIGURE 1.1   A computer consists of CPU, memory, storage devices, input and output devices, and communication devices.

The components are connected through a subsystem called a *bus* that transfers data between the components.

1.2.1 Central Processing Unit

The *central processing unit* (CPU) is the computer's brain. It retrieves instructions from memory and executes them. The CPU usually has two components: a *control unit* and an *arithmetic/logic unit*. The control unit controls and coordinates the actions of the other components. The arithmetic and logic unit performs numeric operations (addition, subtraction, multiplication, division) and logical operations (comparisons).

(margin notes: hardware, software, bus, CPU)

Today's CPU is built on a small silicon semiconductor chip with millions of transistors. The CPU's *speed* is determined mainly by an internal clock. The clock emits electronic pulses at a constant rate, and these are used to control and synchronize the pace of operations. The faster the clock speed, the more instructions are executed in a given period of time. The unit of measurement is the *hertz* (Hz), with 1 hertz equaling 1 pulse per second. The clock speed of computers is usually measured in *megahertz* (MHz) (1 MHz is 1 million Hz). The speed of the CPU has been improved continuously. At the time of this writing, you can get an "Intel Core 2" at up to 3.2 *gigahertz* (GHz) (1 GHz is 1000 MHz).

speed

hertz

megahertz

gigahertz

1.2.2   Memory

Digital devices have two stable states, referred to by convention as *zero* and *one*. Accordingly, computers use zeros and ones to store and transmit data. Data of various kinds, such as numbers, characters, and strings, are encoded as a series of *bits* (*bi*nary dig*its*: zeros and ones). *Memory* stores data and program instructions for the CPU to execute. A memory unit is an ordered sequence of *bytes*, each holding eight bits, as shown in Figure 1.2.

bit

byte

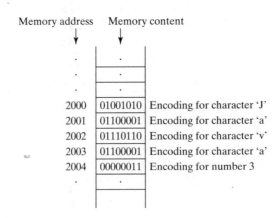

FIGURE 1.2   Memory stores data and program instructions.

The programmer need not to be concerned about the encoding and decoding of data, which the system performs automatically based on the encoding scheme. Encoding schemes vary. In the popular ASCII encoding, for example, character 'J' is represented by 01001010 in one byte. A small number such as 3 can be stored in a single byte. If a computer needs to store a large number that cannot fit into a single byte, it uses several adjacent bytes. A byte is the minimum storage unit. No two data items can share or split the same byte.

Before it can be executed, a program must be brought to memory. A memory byte is never empty, but its initial content may be meaningless to your program. The current content of a memory byte is lost whenever new information is placed in it.

Every byte has a unique address, which is used to locate the byte for storing and retrieving data. Since bytes can be accessed in any order, the memory is also referred to as *RAM* (random-access memory). Today's personal computers usually have at least 1 gigabyte of RAM. Computer storage size is measured in bytes, kilobytes (KB), megabytes (MB), gigabytes (GB), and terabytes (TB). A *kilobyte* is $2^{10} = 1024$ (about 1000) bytes, a *megabyte* is $2^{20} = 1048576$ (about 1 million) bytes, a *gigabyte* is about 1 billion bytes, and a *terabyte* is about 1000 gigabytes. Like the CPU, memory is built on silicon semiconductor chips containing thousands of transistors embedded on their surface. Memory chips are less complicated than CPU chips, slower, and less expensive.

RAM

megabyte

1.2.3   Storage Devices

Memory is volatile, because information is lost when the power is turned off. Programs and data are permanently stored on *storage devices* and are moved to memory when the computer actually uses them. The reason is that operations occur much faster on memory than on storage devices.

There are four main types of storage devices:

- Disk drives
- CD drives (CD-R, CD-RW, and DVD)
- Tape drives
- USB flash drives

drive

Drives are devices for operating a medium, such as disks, CDs, and tapes.

Disks

hard disk

Each computer has at least one hard disk drive (also called simply a hard drive). Hard disks are for permanently storing data and programs. The hard disks of the latest PCs store from 80 to 250 gigabytes. Often they are encased inside the computer. Removable hard disks are also available.

CDs and DVDs

CD-R

CD-RW

CD stands for compact disc. There are two types of CD drives: CD-R and CD-RW. A *CD-R* is for read-only permanent storage, and the user cannot modify its contents, once they are recorded. A CD-RW can be used like a hard disk, and thus can be both read and rewritten. A single CD can hold up to 700MB. Most software is distributed through CD-ROMs. Most new PCs are equipped with a CD-RW drive that can work with both CD-R and CD-RW.

DVD stands for digital versatile disc. DVDs and CDs look alike. You can store data using either a CD or a DVD. A DVD can hold more information than a CD. Standard DVD storage capacity is 4.7GB.

Tapes

Tapes are used mainly for backing up data and programs. Unlike disks and CDs, tapes store information sequentially. The computer must retrieve information in the order it was stored. Tapes are very slow. It would take one to two hours to back up a 1GB hard disk on tape. Tapes are becoming obsolete.

USB Flash Drives

USB flash drives are popular new devices for storing and transporting data. They are small— about the size of a pack of gum. They act like a portable hard disk that can be plugged into the USB port of your computer. USB flash drives are currently available with up to 32GB storage capacity.

1.2.4   Input and Output Devices

Input and output devices let the user communicate with the computer. The common input devices are *keyboards* and *mice*. The common output devices are *monitors* and *printers*.

The Keyboard

A computer *keyboard* looks like a typewriter keyboard with extra keys for certain special functions.

function key

Function keys are located at the top of the keyboard and are labeled with prefix F. Their use depends on the software.

A *modifier key* is special key (e.g., *Shift*, *Alt*, *Ctrl*) that modifies the normal action of another key when the two are pressed in combination.

modifier key

The *numeric keypad,* located on the right-hand corner of the keyboard, is a separate set of number keys for quick input of numbers.

numeric keypad

Arrow keys, located between the main keypad and the numeric keypad, are used to move the cursor up, down, left, and right.

The *Insert, Delete, Page Up,* and *Page Down keys*, located above the arrow keys, are used in word processing to perform insert, delete, page up, and page down.

The Mouse

A *mouse* is a pointing device. It is used to move an electronic pointer called a *cursor* around the screen or to click on an object on the screen to trigger it to respond.

The Monitor

The *monitor* displays information (text and graphics). The resolution and dot pitch determine the quality of the display.

The *resolution* specifies the number of *pixels* per square inch. Pixels (short for "picture elements") are tiny dots that form an image on the screen. A common resolution for a 17-inch screen, for example, is 1024 pixels wide and 768 pixels high. The resolution can be set manually. The higher the resolution, the sharper and clearer the image.

screen resolution

The *dot pitch* is the amount of space between pixels. Typically, it has a range from 0.21 to 0.81 millimeters. The smaller the dot pitch, the better the display.

dot pitch

1.2.5 Communication Devices

Computers can be networked through communication devices. Those that are commonly used are the dialup modem, DSL, cable modem, and network interface card. A dialup *modem* uses a phone line and can transfer data at a speed up to 56,000 bps (bits per second). A *DSL* (digital subscriber line) also uses a phone line and can transfer data twenty times faster than a dialup modem. A cable modem uses the TV cable line maintained by the cable company. A cable modem is as fast as DSL. A *network interface card (NIC)* is a device that connects a computer to a *local area network (LAN)*. The LAN is commonly used in business, universities, and government organizations. A typical NIC called *10BaseT* can transfer data at 10 *mbps* (*million bits per second*).

modem
DSL

NIC
LAN
mbps

1.3 Programs

Computer *programs*, known as *software*, are instructions to the computer. You use programs to tell a computer what to do. Without programs, a computer is an empty machine.

software

Computers do not understand human languages, so you need to use computer languages to communicate with them. A computer's native language or *machine language* is a set of primitive instructions built into it. Machine languages differ among computers. Machine-language instructions are in the form of binary code, so you have to enter binary codes for various instructions. Programming using a native machine language is a tedious process. Moreover, the programs are highly difficult to read and modify. For example, to add two numbers, you might have to write an instruction in binary like this:

machine language

```
1101101010011010
```

Assembly language is a low-level programming language using mnemonics to represent machine-language instructions. For example, to add two numbers, you might write an instruction in assembly code like this:

assembly language

```
ADDF3 R1, R2, R3
```

assembler

Assembly languages were developed to make programming easy. Since the computer cannot understand assembly language, however, a program called *assembler* is used to convert assembly-language programs into machine code, as shown in Figure 1.3.

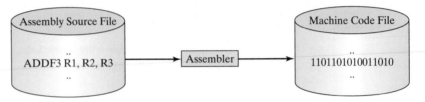

FIGURE 1.3 Assembler translates assembly-language instructions to machine code.

Since assembly language is machine dependent, an assembly program can be executed only on a particular kind of machine. The high-level languages were developed in order to overcome the platform-specific problem and make programming easier.

high-level language

The *high-level languages* are English-like and easy to learn and program. Here, for example, is a high-level language statement that computes the area of a circle with radius 5:

```
area = 5 * 5 * 3.1415;
```

There are over one hundred high-level languages. The popular ones are:

- COBOL (COmmon Business Oriented Language)
- FORTRAN (FORmula TRANslation)
- BASIC (Beginner's All-purpose Symbolic Instruction Code)
- Pascal (named for Blaise Pascal)
- Ada (named for Ada Lovelace)
- Visual Basic (BASIC-like visual language developed by Microsoft)
- Delphi (Pascal-like visual language developed by Borland)
- C (developed by the designer of the B language)
- C++ (an object-oriented language, based on C)
- Java
- C# (a Java-like language developed by Microsoft)

Each of these languages was designed for a specific purpose. COBOL was designed for business applications and is used primarily for business data processing. FORTRAN was designed for mathematical computations and is used mainly for numeric computations. BASIC was designed to be learned and used easily. Ada was developed for the Department of Defense and is used mainly in defense projects. Visual Basic and Delphi are used in developing graphical user interfaces and in rapid application development. C combines the power of an assembly language with the ease of use and portability of a high-level language. C++ is popular for system software projects such as writing compilers and operating systems. The Microsoft Windows operating system was coded using C++. Java, developed by Sun Microsystems, is widely used for developing Internet applications. C# (pronounced C sharp) is a new language developed by Microsoft for developing applications based on the Microsoft .NET platform.

source program
compiler

A program written in a high-level language is called a *source program*. Since a computer cannot understand a source program, a program called a *compiler* is used to translate it into a machine-language program. The machine-language program is often then linked with other supporting library code to form an executable file. The executable file can be executed on the machine, as shown in Figure 1.4. On Windows, executable files have extension .exe.

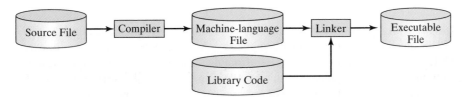

FIGURE 1.4 A source program is compiled into a machine-language file, which is then linked with the system library to form an executable file.

1.4 Operating Systems

The *operating system (OS)*, the most important program that runs on a computer, enables it to manage and control its activities. Application programs, such as a Web browser or a word processor, cannot run without an operating system. On your personal computer you are probably using Microsoft Windows (currently the most popular PC operating system), Mac OS, or Linux. The interrelationship of hardware, operating system, application software, and the user is shown in Figure 1.5.

OS

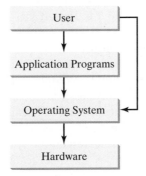

FIGURE 1.5 The operating system is the software that controls and manages the system.

The major tasks of the operating systems are:

- Controlling and monitoring system activities
- Allocating and assigning system resources
- Scheduling operations

1.4.1 Controlling and Monitoring System Activities

Operating systems are responsible for security, ensuring that unauthorized users do not access the system. Operating systems perform basic tasks, such as recognizing input from the keyboard, sending output to the monitor, keeping track of files and directories on the disk, and controlling peripheral devices, such as disk drives and printers. Operating systems also make sure that different programs and users running at the same time do not interfere with each other.

1.4.2 Allocating and Assigning System Resources

The OS is responsible for determining what computer resources (CPU, memory, disks, input and output devices) a program needs and for allocating and assigning them to run the program.

1.4.3 Scheduling Operations

The OS is responsible for scheduling programs to use the system resources efficiently. Many of today's operating systems support such techniques as *multiprogramming*, *multithreading*, or *multiprocessing* to increase system performance.

multiprogramming

Multiprogramming allows multiple programs to run simultaneously by sharing the CPU. The CPU is much faster than the other components. As a result, it is often idle—for example, while waiting for data to be transferred from the disk or from other sources. A multiprogramming OS takes advantage of this by allowing multiple programs to use the CPU when it would otherwise be idle. For example, you may use a word processor to edit a file while the Web browser is downloading a file.

multithreading

Multithreading allows concurrency within a program, so that its subunits can run at the same time. For example, a word-processing program allows users to simultaneously edit text and save it to a file. In this example, editing and saving are two tasks within the same application. These two tasks may run on separate threads concurrently.

multiprocessing

Multiprocessing, or parallel processing, uses two or more processors together to perform a task. It is like a surgical operation where several doctors work together on one patient.

1.5 History of C++

C, C++, Java, and C# are related. C++ evolved from C. Java was modeled after C++. C# is a subset of C++ with some features similar to Java. If you know one of these languages, it is easy to learn the others.

BCPL

C evolved from the B language, which evolved from the BCPL (Basic Combined Programming Language). Martin Richards developed BCPL in the mid-1960s for writing operating systems and compilers. Ken Thompson incorporated many features from BCPL in his

B

B language and used it to create early versions of the UNIX operating system at Bell Laboratories in 1970 on a DEC PDP-7 computer. Both BCPL and B are typeless—that is, every data item occupies a fixed-length "word" or "cell" in memory. How a data item is treated—for example, as a number or as a string—is the responsibility of the programmer. Dennis Ritchie extended the B language by adding types and other features in 1971 to develop the UNIX

C

operating system on a DEC PDP-11 computer. Today, C is portable and hardware independent. It is widely used for developing operating systems.

C++

C++ is an extension of C, developed by Bjarne Stroustrup at Bell Labs during 1983–1985. C++ added a number of features that improved the C language. Most important, it added the support of using classes for object-oriented programming. Object-oriented programming can make programs easy to develop and easy to maintain. C++ could be considered a superset of C. The features of C are supported by C++. C programs can be compiled using C++ compilers. After learning C++, you will be able to read and understand C programs as well.

ANSI standard

An international standard for C++ was created by the American National Standards Institute (ANSI) in 1998. The ANSI standard is an attempt to ensure that C++ is portable—that is, your programs compiled using one vendor's compiler can be compiled without errors from any other vendor's on any platform. Since the standard has been around for a while, all the major vendors now support the ANSI standard. Nevertheless, the C++ compiler vendors may add proprietary features into the compiler. So, it is possible that your program may compile fine by one compiler but may need to be modified in order to be compiled by a different compiler.

Video Note
Your first C++ program

what is console?

1.6 A Simple C++ Program

Let us begin with a simple C++ program that displays the message "Welcome to C++!" on the console. (*Console* refers to a computer's text entry and display device.) The program is shown in Listing 1.1.

LISTING 1.1 Welcome.cpp

```
 1 #include <iostream>                               include library
 2 using namespace std;                              using namespace
 3
 4 int main()                                         main function
 5 {
 6   // Display Welcome to C++ to the console         comment
 7   cout << "Welcome to C++!" << endl;               output
 8
 9   return 0;                                        successful return
10 }
```

```
Welcome to C++!
```

The line numbers are not part of the program but are displayed for reference purposes. So, don't type line numbers in your program.

line numbers

The first line in the program

```
#include <iostream>
```

is a compiler *preprocessor directive* that tells the compiler to include the `iostream` library in this program, which is needed to support console input and output. The library like `iostream` is called a *header file* in C++, because it is usually included at the head of a program.

preprocessor directive

header file

The statement in line 2

```
using namespace std;
```

namespace

tells the compiler to find the names in the standard library. The names `cout` and `endl` in line 7 are defined in the standard library. You can use them in your program.

Every C++ program is executed from a main function. A function is a construct that contains statements. The main function defined in lines 4–10 contains two statements. They are enclosed in a block that starts with a left brace, {, (line 5) and ends with a right brace, } (line 10). Every statement in C++ must end with a semicolon (;), known as the *statement terminator*.

main function

The statement in line 7 displays a message to the console. `cout` stands for *console output*. The `<<` operator, referred to as the *stream insertion operator*, sends a string to the console. A string must be enclosed in quotation marks. The statement in line 7 first outputs the string `"Welcome to C++!"` to the console, then outputs `endl`. Note that `endl` stands for *end line*. Sending `endl` to the console outputs a new line and flushes the output buffer to ensure that the output is displayed immediately.

console output

stream insertion operator

The statement (line 9)

```
return 0;
```

is placed at the end of every main function to exit the program. The value `0` indicates that the program has terminated successfully.

successful exit

Line 6 is a *comment* that documents what the program is and how it is constructed. Comments help programmers to communicate and understand the program. They are not programming statements and thus are ignored by the compiler. In C++, a comment is preceded by two slashes (`//`) on a line, called a *line comment*, or enclosed between `/*` and `*/` on one or several lines, called a *paragraph comment*. When the compiler sees `//`, it ignores all text after `//` on the same line. When it sees `/*`, it scans for the next `*/` and ignores any text between `/*` and `*/`.

comment

line comment

paragraph comment

Here are examples of the two types of comments:

```
// This application program prints Welcome to C++!
/* This application program prints Welcome to C++! */
/* This application program
   prints Welcome to C++! */
```

keyword

Keywords, or *Reserved words,* have a specific meaning to the compiler and cannot be used in the program for other purposes. In this program there are four keywords: `using`, `namespace`, `int`, and `return`.

Note

You are probably wondering about such points as why the main function is declared this way and why `cout << "Welcome to C++!" << endl` is used to display a message to the console. Your questions cannot be fully answered yet. For the time being, simply accept that this is how things are done. You will find the answers in subsequent chapters.

Note

syntax rules

Like any other programming language, C++ has its own rules of grammar, called *syntax*, and you need to write code that obeys the syntax rules. If your program violates these rules, the C++ compiler will report syntax errors. Pay close attention to the punctuation. The redirection symbol `<<` is two consecutive <'s. Every statement in the function ends with a semicolon (`;`).

Caution

directives are not statements

Preprocessor directives are not C++ statements. So, don't put semicolons at the end of preprocessor directives. Doing so may cause subtle errors.

Caution

case sensitive

C++ source programs are case sensitive. It would be wrong, for example, to replace `main` in the program with `Main`.

The program in Listing 1.1 displays one message. Once you understand the program, it is easy to extend it to display more messages. For example, you can rewrite the program to display three messages, as shown in Listing 1.2.

LISTING 1.2   Welcome1.cpp

include library

main function

output

successful return

```
 1 #include <iostream>
 2 using namespace std;
 3
 4 int main()
 5 {
 6   cout << "Programming is fun!" << endl;
 7   cout << "Fundamentals First" << endl;
 8   cout << "Problem Driven" << endl;
 9
10   return 0;
11 }
```

```
Programming is fun!
Fundamentals First
Problem Driven
```

Further, you can perform mathematical computations and display the result to the console. Listing 1.3 gives such an example.

LISTING 1.3 ComputeExpression.cpp

```
 1 #include <iostream>
 2 using namespace std;
 3
 4 int main()
 5 {
 6   cout << "(10.5 + 2 * 3) / (45 - 3.5) = ";
 7   cout << (10.5 + 2 * 3) / (45 - 3.5) << endl;
 8
 9   return 0;
10 }
```

include library

main function

computing expression

successful return

```
(10.5 + 2 * 3) / (45 - 3.5) = 0.39759036144578314
```

The multiplication operator in C++ is *. As you see, it is a straightforward process to translate an arithmetic expression to a C++ expression. We will discuss C++ expressions further in Chapter 2.

You can combine multiple outputs in a single statement. For example, the following statement performs the same function as lines 6–7.

```
cout << "(10.5 + 2 * 3) / (45 - 3.5) = "
     << (10.5 + 2 * 3) / (45 - 3.5) << endl;
```

1.7 C++ Program-Development Cycle

You have to create your program and compile it before it can be executed. This process is repetitive, as shown in Figure 1.6. If your program has compilation errors, you have to modify it to fix them and then recompile it. If your program has runtime errors or does not produce the correct result, you have to modify the program, recompile it, and execute it again.

Note

A C++ source file typically ends with the extension .cpp. Some compilers may accept other filename extensions (e.g., .c, .cp, or .c), but you should stick with the .cpp extension to be compliant with all ANSI C++ compilers.

.cpp source file

Note

The C++ compiler command performs three tasks in sequence: *preprocessing, compiling,* and *linking*. The compiler first processes the directives. The directives start with the # sign. For example, the `include` statement in line 1 of Listing 1.1 is a directive to tell the compiler to include a library. The compiler then translates the source code into a machine-code file called an object file, and finally it links the object file with supporting library files to form an executable file. On Windows, the object file is stored on disk with an .obj extension, and the executable files are stored with an .exe extension. On UNIX, the object file has an `.o` extension and the executable files do not have file extensions.

compiler command

You can develop a C++ program from a command line or from an IDE. An IDE is software that provides an *integrated development environment (IDE)* for rapidly developing C++ programs. Editing, compiling, building, debugging, and online help are integrated in one graphical user interface. Just enter source code or open an existing file in a window, then click a button, menu item, or function key to compile and run the program. Examples of popular IDEs are Microsoft Visual C++, Borland C++Builder, and Dev-C++.

IDE

The sections that follow introduce how to develop a C++ program using Visual C++, Dev-C++, the Windows command prompt, and the UNIX console.

Source code (developed by the programmer)

```cpp
#include <iostream>
using namespace std;

int main()
{
    // Display Welcome to C++ to the console
    cout << "Welcome to C++!" << endl;

    return 0;
}
```

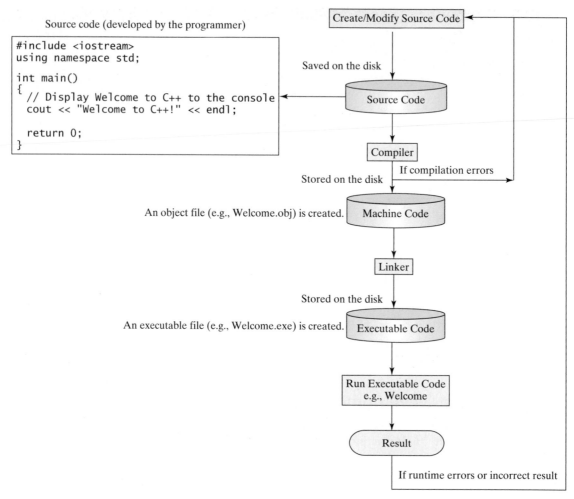

FIGURE 1.6 The C++ program-development process consists of creating/modifying source code, compiling, linking and executing programs.

1.8 Developing C++ Programs Using Visual C++

Visual C++ is a component of Microsoft Visual Studio .NET for developing C++ programs. A free version named *Visual C++ 2008 Express Edition* is included in this book's Companion CD-ROM. This section introduces how to create a project, create a program, and compile and run the program in Visual C++ Express 2008 Edition.

1.8.1 Getting Started with Visual C++

Visual C++ is easy to install. If you need help with installation, please refer to Supplement II.A on the Companion Website.

Suppose you have installed Visual C++ 2008 Express Edition. You can launch Visual C++ from the Windows Start button by choosing *All Programs, Visual C++ 9.0 Express Edition, Microsoft Visual C++ 2008 Express Edition*. The Visual C++ 2008 Express Edition user interface appears, as shown in Figure 1.7.

1.8.2 Creating a Project

To create C++ programs in Visual C++, you have to first create a project. A project is like a holder that ties all the files together. Here are the steps to create a project:

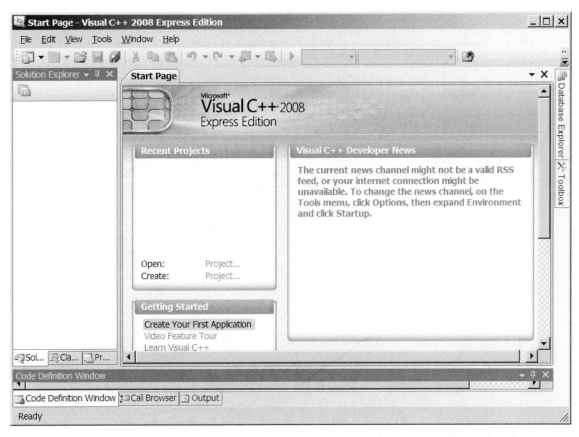

FIGURE 1.7   The Visual C++ user interface is a single window that performs editing, compiling, debugging, and running programs.

1. Choose *File*, *New*, *Project* to display the New Project window, as shown in Figure 1.8.

2. Choose *Win32* in the Project types column and *Win32 Console Application* in the Templates column. Type `bookexample` in the Name field and `c:\smith` in the Location field. Click *OK* to display the Win32 Application Wizard window, as shown in Figure 1.9.

FIGURE 1.8   You need to create a project before creating programs.

3. Click *Next* to display the application settings window, as shown in Figure 1.10.

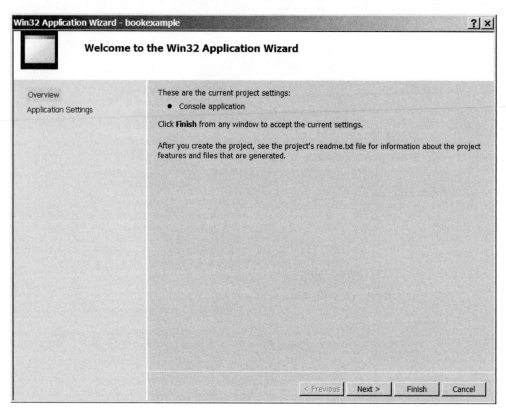

FIGURE 1.9 Win32 Application Wizard creates a project for Win32 applications.

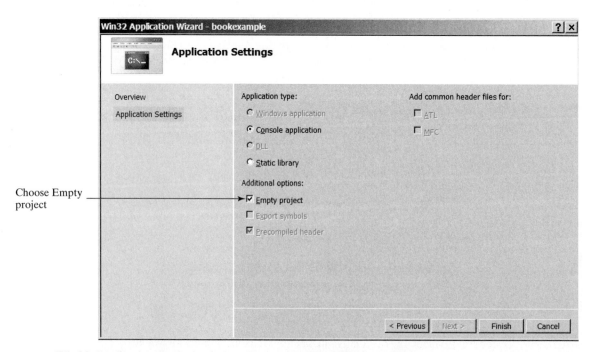

Choose Empty project

FIGURE 1.10 Win32 Application Settings window lets you set the application type.

4. Select *Console application* in the Application type section and check *Empty project* in the Additional options section. Click *Finish* to create a project. You will see the project named `bookexample` in the Solution Explorer, as shown in Figure 1.11.

Solution
Explorer shows
the files in the
project

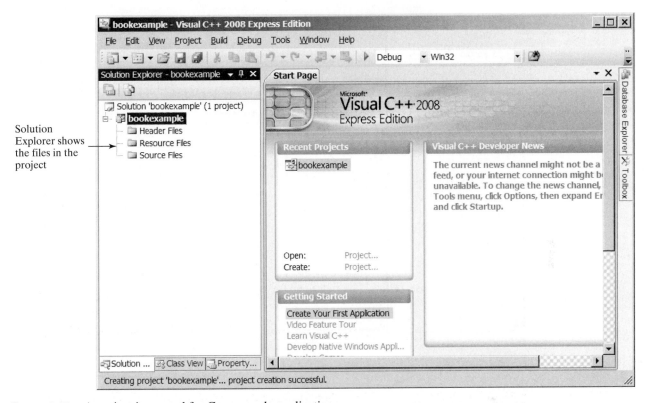

FIGURE 1.11   A project is created for C++ console applications.

1.8.3   Creating a C++ Program

After you create a project, you can create programs in it. Here are the steps to create a C++ program for Listing 1.1:

1. Choose *Add, Add New Item* from the context menu of the bookexample project (see Figure 1.12) to display the Add New Item window, as shown in Figure 1.13.

2. Choose Code in the Categories column and C++ File (.cpp) in the Templates column. Enter `Welcome` in the Name field and `c:\smith\bookexample\bookexample` in the Location field. Click *Add* to create the file, as shown in Figure 1.14.

3. Enter the code for Welcome.cpp exactly from Listing 1.1, as shown in Figure 1.15.

1.8.4   Compiling a C++ Program

After you create a program, you can compile it. You may do so by choosing *Build, Compile*, or press *Ctrl+F7*, or choose *Compile* in the context menu for Welcome.cpp, as shown in Figure 1.16.

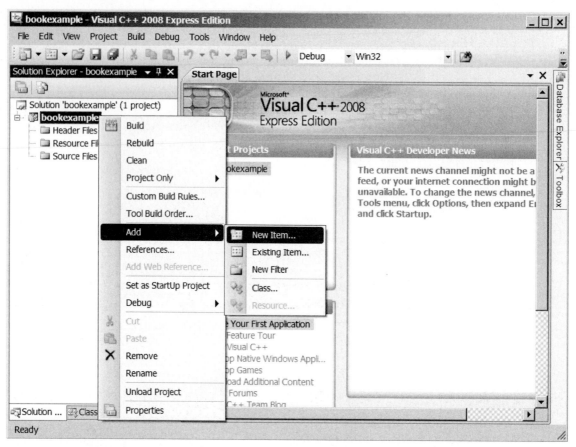

FIGURE 1.12 You can open the Add New Item window from the project's context menu.

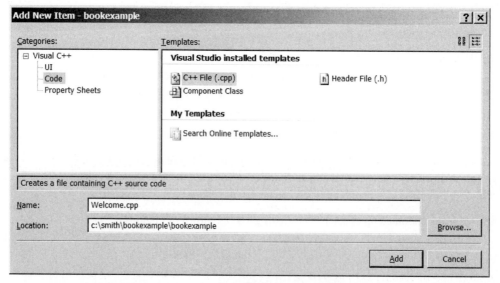

FIGURE 1.13 You can specify the file type, name, and location to create a file.

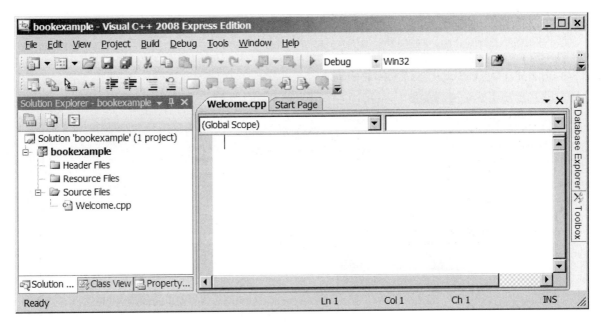

FIGURE 1.14   Welcome.cpp is created in the project.

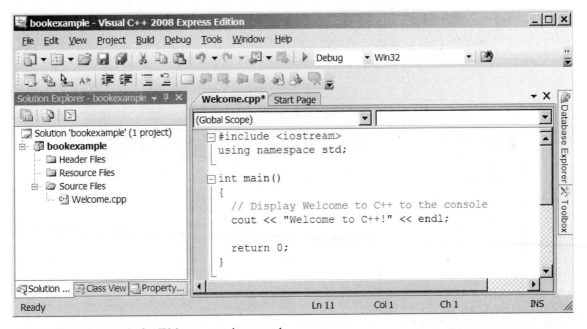

FIGURE 1.15   The source code for Welcome.cpp is entered.

1.8.5   Running a C++ Program

To run the program, choose *Debug*, *Start Without Debugging*, or press *Ctrl+F5*. You will see
the output displayed in a DOS window, as shown in Figure 1.17.

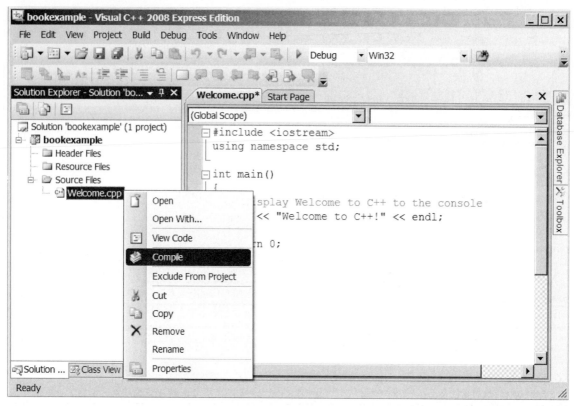

FIGURE 1.16 Choose the Compile command to compile the program.

FIGURE 1.17 The output is displayed in a DOS window.

Note

compile and run

The *Run* command invokes the *Compile* command if the program is not compiled or was modified after the last compilation.

Note

one main function

Each project can have only one file that contains a main function. If you need to create another file with a main function, you have two options:

■ Remove the current file that contains a main function from the project by choosing *Remove* from the context menu of the program, as shown in Figure 1.18. (Note that you can add an existing file to the project by choosing *File, Add Existing Item.*)

■ Create a new project for the new program.

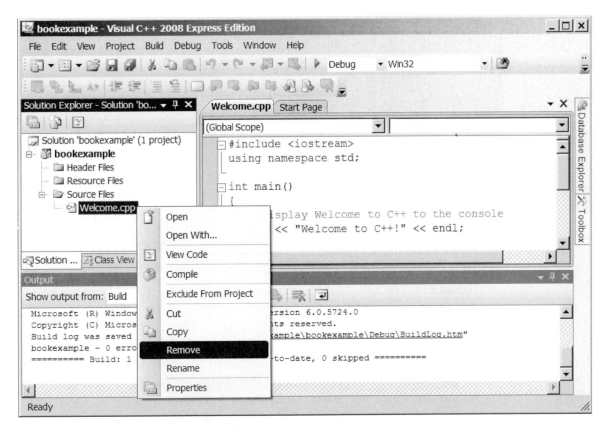

FIGURE 1.18   You can remove a file from a project.

1.9 Developing C++ Programs Using Dev-C++

Dev-C++ is a free C++ IDE, which can be downloaded from http://www.bloodshed.net/dev/devcpp.html. Visual C++ is much more powerful than Dev-C++. But new IDE users will find Dev-C++ simpler and easier to use. Another benefit of Dev-C++ is that it runs fine on older machines with less system resource.

1.9.1   Getting Started with Dev-C++

Dev-C++ is easy to install. If you need help with installation, please refer to Supplement II.B on the Companion Website.

Suppose you have installed Dev-C++. You can launch it from the Windows Start button by choosing *All Programs*, *Bloodshed Dev-C++*, *Dev-C++*. The Dev-C++ user interface appears, as shown in Figure 1.19.

1.9.2   Creating a Program

To create a C++ program in Dev-C++, follow the steps below:

1. Choose *File*, *New*, *Source File*. An untitled file appears in the content pane, as shown in Figure 1.20.

2. Type the code from Listing 1.1 exactly into the content pane, as shown in Figure 1.21.

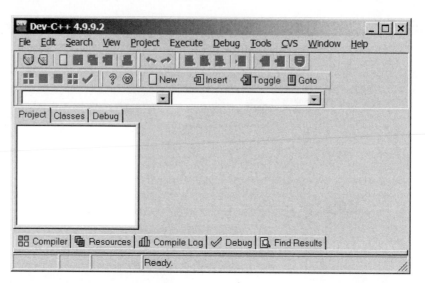

FIGURE 1.19 The Dev-C++ user interface is a single window that performs functions for editing, compiling, debugging, and running programs.

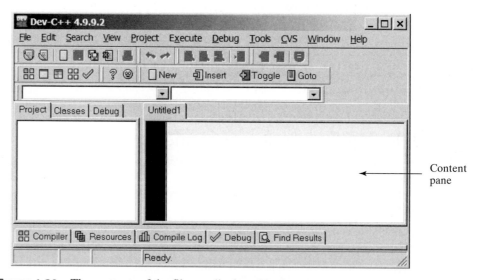

FIGURE 1.20 The contents of the file are displayed in the content pane.

3. Choose *File, Save* to display the Save File dialog box, as shown in Figure 1.22. Enter `Welcome.cpp` in the File name field and click *Save* to save the file into `Welcome.cpp`. (*Note:* You may change the directory in the Save in field to save the file in any directory.)

4. After you save the file, you will see the Welcome.cpp tab appear in the content pane, as shown in Figure 1.23.

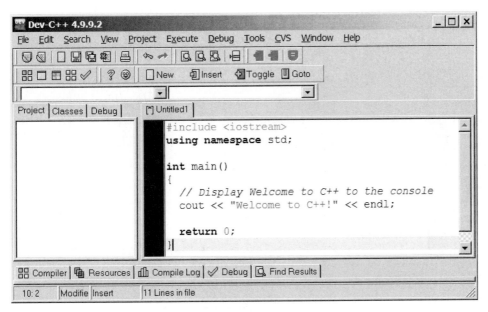

FIGURE 1.21 The code is entered in the content pane.

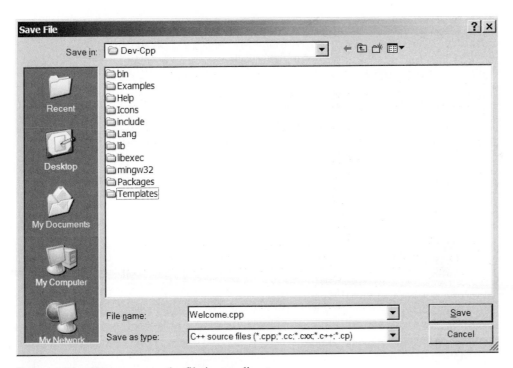

FIGURE 1.22 You may save the file in any directory.

1.9.3 Compiling a C++ Program

After you create a program, you can compile it. To do so, choose *Execute*, *Compile*, or press *Ctrl+F9*, or choose the *Compile* toolbar button (🖽), as shown in Figure 1.24. The compilation status is displayed in a dialog box, as shown in Figure 1.25. You may close this dialog box now.

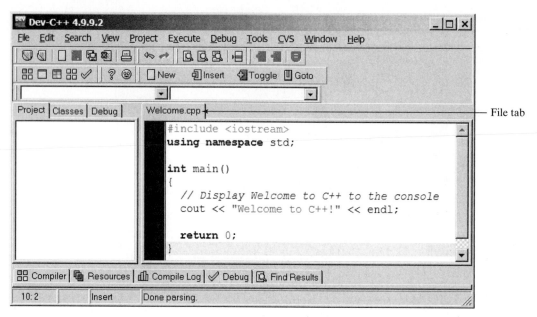

FIGURE 1.23 The Welcome.cpp tab appears in the content pane.

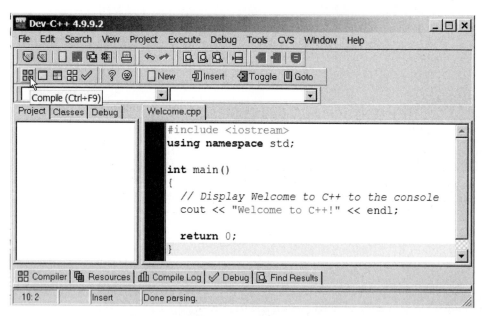

FIGURE 1.24 You can click a tool button to compile the program.

1.9.4 Running a C++ Program

To run the program, choose *Execute, Run*, or press *F9*, or click the *Run* toolbar button ( ). A Windows command window is displayed, then disappears. You can barely see the command window. To see it, you have to add the following statement before the **return** statement, as shown in Figure 1.26.

```
system("PAUSE");
```

This statement pauses the execution and prompts the user to enter any key to continue.

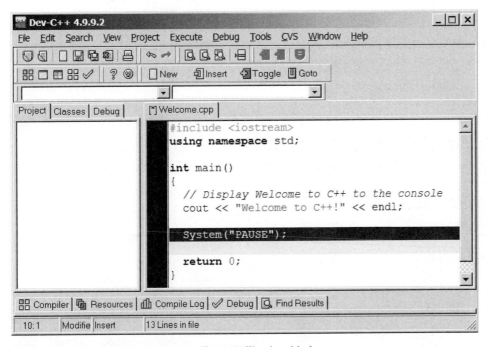

FIGURE 1.25 The compilation status is displayed.

FIGURE 1.26 The statement `system("PAUSE");` is added.

Recompile and run the program. You will see the command window displayed, as shown in Figure 1.27.

FIGURE 1.27 The command window displays the console output.

 Tip

You may compile and run the program using one command by choosing *Execute, Compile & Run*, or pressing *F9*, or clicking the *Compile & Run* toolbar button (🔲).

compile and run

multiple programs

Note

If you have multiple programs in the content pane, choose the one you want to run from the file tab and use the *Compile & Run* command to run it.

1.10 Developing C++ Programs from the Command Prompt on Windows

DOS commands

Note

To develop programs from the Windows command line, you need to know how to use DOS commands. Please see Supplement I.C, "Compiling and Running C++ from the Command Window," on how to use basic DOS commands. All the supplements are accessible from the Companion Website.

compilers

When you install Dev-C++ as in the previous section, a popular compiler, known as the GNU C++ compiler, is automatically installed in c:\dev-cpp\bin\g++.exe. GNU is an organization devoted to developing open-source software (see www.gnu.org). To use the compiler directly from the command line, you have to add c:\dev-cpp\bin into PATH environment variable. Here are the steps to add the new paths in Windows 2000 and Windows XP:

1. Choose Systems from the Windows Control Panel to display the System Properties dialog, as shown in Figure 1.28(a).

2. Choose the *Advanced* tab and click *Environment Variables* to display the Environment Variables dialog as shown in Figure 1.28(b).

3. Choose *Path* in the System variables section and click *Edit* to add the paths.

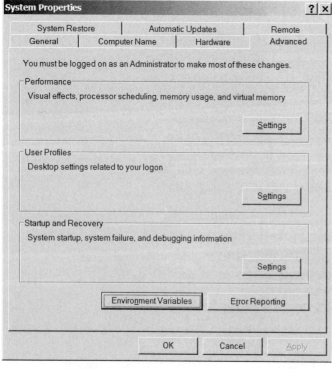

(a)

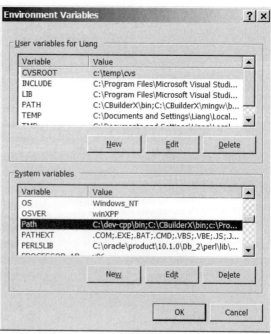

(b)

FIGURE 1.28 You need to add compilers in the environment path.

You can use any text editor to create and edit a C++ source-code file. Figure 1.29 shows how to use Notepad to create and edit the source-code file.

To compile Welcome.cpp using the GNU C++ compiler, type the command **g++ Welcome.cpp -o Welcome**, as shown in Figure 1.30. If there are no syntax errors, an executable file named Welcome.exe is created. You can run it by typing **Welcome**.

text editor

g++ compiler

```
Welcome.cpp - Notepad
File  Edit  Format  View  Help
#include <iostream>
using namespace std;

int main()
{
  // Display Welcome to C++ to the console
  cout << "Welcome to C++!" << endl;

  return 0;
}
```

FIGURE 1.29 You can create a C++ source-code file using Windows Notepad.

GNU C++ compiler →
```
C:\Dev-Cpp>g++ Welcome.cpp -o Welcome
```
Run →
```
C:\Dev-Cpp>Welcome
Welcome to C++!

C:\Dev-Cpp>
```

FIGURE 1.30 You can compile using the GNU C++ compiler.

1.11 Developing C++ Programs on UNIX

Note
To develop programs on UNIX, you need to know how to use UNIX commands. Please see Supplement I.D, "Compiling and Running C++ from UNIX," on how to use basic UNIX commands.

UNIX commands

By default, a GNU C++ compiler is automatically installed on UNIX. You can use the **vi** or **emacs** editor to create a C++ source-code file. Figure 1.31(a) shows how to use the **vi** editor to create and edit the source-code file named Welcome.cpp (using the command vi Welcome.cpp).

compilers

To compile Welcome.cpp using the GNU compiler, type the command **g++ Welcome.cpp -o Main**, as shown in Figure 1.31(b). If there are no syntax errors, an executable file named **Main** is created. You can run it by typing **./Main**, as shown in Figure 1.31(b).

GNU compiler

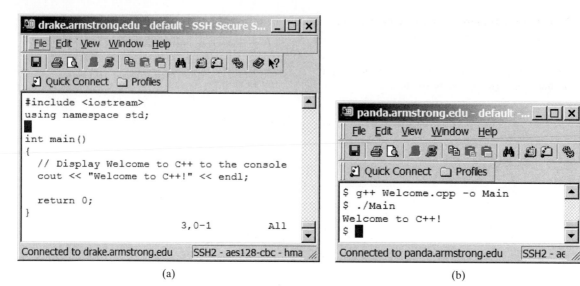

FIGURE 1.31 (a) You can create a C++ source file using the vi editor. (b) You can compile a C++ source file using the GNU compiler.

KEY TERMS

assembly language 7
bit 5
byte 5
bus 4
cable modem 7
central processing unit (CPU) 4
comment 11
compiler 8
console 10
cout 11
Dev-C++ 21
dot pitch 7
DSL (digital subscriber line) 7
hardware 4
high-level programming language 8
Integrated Development Environment
    (IDE) 13

keyword (or reserved word) 12
machine language 7
main function 11
memory 5
modem 7
network interface card (NIC) 7
operating system (OS) 9
pixel 7
preprocessor directive 11
resolution 7
software 4
storage devices 6
statement terminator 11
stream insertion operator ($<<$) 11
Visual C++ 14

CHAPTER SUMMARY

1. A computer is an electronic device that stores and processes data.

2. A computer includes both *hardware* and *software*.

3. *Hardware* is the physical aspect of the computer that can be seen.

4. Computer *programs*, known as *software*, are the invisible instructions that control the hardware and make it perform tasks.

5. Computer programming is the writing of instructions (i.e., code) for computers to perform.

6. The central processing unit (CPU) is the computer's brain. It retrieves instructions from memory and executes them.

7. Computers use zeros and ones because digital devices have two stable states, referred to by convention as zero and one.

8. A bit is a binary digit 0 or 1.

9. A byte is a sequence of 8 bits.

10. A kilobyte is about 1000 bytes, a megabyte about 1 million bytes, a gigabyte about 1 billion bytes, and a terabyte about 1000 gigabytes.

11. Memory stores data and program instructions for the CPU to execute.

12. A memory unit is an ordered sequence of bytes.

13. Memory is volatile, because information is lost when the power is turned off.

14. Programs and data are permanently stored on storage devices and are moved to memory when the computer actually uses them.

15. The machine language is a set of primitive instructions built into every computer.

16. Assembly language is a low-level programming language in which a mnemonic is used to represent each machine-language instruction.

17. High-level languages are English-like and easy to learn and program.

18. A program written in a high-level language is called a source program.

19. A compiler is software that translates the source program into a machine-language program.

20. An operating system (OS) is a program that manages and controls a computer's activities.

21. C++ is an extension of C. C++ added a number of features that improved the C language. Most important, it added the support of using classes for object-oriented programming.

22. C++ source files end with the .cpp extension.

23. `#include` is a preprocessor directive. All preprocessor directives begin with the symbol #.

24. The `cout` object along with the stream insertion operator (<<) can be used to display a string on the console.

25. Every C++ program is executed from a main function. A function is a construct that contains statements.

26. Every statement in the C++ must end with a semicolon (;), known as the *statement terminator*.

27. In C++, a comment is preceded by two slashes (//) on a line, called a *line comment*, or enclosed between /* and */ on one or several lines, called a paragraph comment.

28. Keywords, or reserved words, have a specific meaning to the compiler and cannot be used in the program for other purposes.

29. `using`, `namespace`, `int`, and `return` are examples of keywords.

30. C++ source programs are case sensitive.

31. You can develop C++ applications from the command line or by using an IDE such as Visual C++ or Dev-C++.

REVIEW QUESTIONS

 Note
Answers to review questions are on the Companion Website.

Sections 1.2–1.4

1.1   Define hardware and software.

1.2   Define machine language, assembly language, and high-level programming language.

1.3   What is an operating system?

Sections 1.5–1.11

1.4   Describe the history of C++. Can C++ run on any machine? What is needed to compile and run C++ programs?

1.5   What are the input and output of a C++ compiler?

1.6   List some C++ development tools. Are tools such as Visual C++ and Dev-C++ different languages from C++, or are they dialects or extensions of C++?

1.7   What is the relationship between C, C++, Java, and C#?

1.8   Explain the C++ keywords. List some C++ keywords you learned in this chapter.

1.9   Is C++ case sensitive? What is the case for C++ keywords?

1.10   What is the C++ source file-name extension, and what is the C++ executable file-name extension on Windows?

1.11   What is a comment? What is the syntax for a comment in C++? Is the comment ignored by the compiler?

1.12   What is the statement to display a string on the console?

1.13   Identify and fix the errors in the following code:

```
1 include <iostream>;
2 using namespace std;
3
4 int main
5 {
6   // Display Welcome to C++ to the console
7   cout << Welcome to C++! << endl;
8
9   return 0;
10 }
```

1.14   What is the command to compile a C++ program using the GNU compiler? What is the command to run a C++ application on Windows and on UNIX?

1.15   Show the output of the following code:

```
#include <iostream>
using namespace std;

int main()
{
  cout << "3.5 * 4 / 2 - 2.5 = " << (3.5 * 4 / 2 - 2.5) << endl;

  return 0;
}
```

1.16   Show the output of the following code:

```
#include <iostream>
using namespace std;

int main()
{
  cout << "C++" << "Java"  << endl;
  cout << "C++" << endl << "Java"  << endl;

  return 0;
}
```

PROGRAMMING EXERCISES

Note
(*Note:* Solutions to even-numbered exercises are on the Companion Website. Solutions to all exercises are on the Instructor Resource Website. The level of difficulty is rated easy (no star), moderate (*), hard (**), or challenging (***)).

level of difficulty

1.1   (*Displaying three messages*) Write a program that displays Welcome to C++, Welcome to Computer Science, and Programming is fun.

1.2   (*Displaying five messages*) Write a program that displays Welcome to C++ five times.

Video Note
display five messages

1.3*   (*Displaying a pattern*) Write a program that displays the following pattern:

```
  CCCC     +         +
  C        +         +
  C      +++++++  +++++++
  C        +         +
  CCCC     +         +
```

1.4   (*Printing a table*) Write a program that displays the following table:

```
a        a^2      a^3
1        1        1
2        4        8
3        9        27
4        16       64
```

1.5   (*Computing expressions*) Write a program that displays the result of
$$\frac{9.5 \times 4.5 - 2.5 \times 3}{45.5 - 3.5}.$$

1.6   (*Summation of a series*) Write a program that displays the result of $1 + 2 + 3 + 4 + 5 + 6 + 7 + 8 + 9$.

1.7   (*Approximating* π) π can be computed using the following formula:

$$\pi = 4 \times \left(1 - \frac{1}{3} + \frac{1}{5} - \frac{1}{7} + \frac{1}{9} - \frac{1}{11} + \frac{1}{13} + \cdots \right)$$

Write a program that displays the result of $4 \times \left(1 - \frac{1}{3} + \frac{1}{5} - \frac{1}{7} + \frac{1}{9} - \frac{1}{11} + \frac{1}{13} \right)$. Use `1.0` instead of `1` in your program.

CHAPTER 2

ELEMENTARY PROGRAMMING

Objectives

- To write C++ programs to perform simple calculations (§2.2).
- To read input from the keyboard (§2.3).
- To use identifiers to name elements in the program (§2.4).
- To use variables to store data (§§2.5-2.6).
- To program with assignment statements and assignment expressions (§2.6).
- To name constants using the `const` keyword and `#define` directive (§2.7).
- To declare variables using numeric data types (§2.8).
- To use operators to write numeric expressions (§2.8).
- To convert numbers to a different type using casting (§2.9).
- To represent character using the `char` type (§2.10).
- To program computations using three examples (ComputeLoan, ComputeChange, ShowCurrentTime) (§2.11).
- To become familiar with C++ documentation, programming style, and naming conventions (§2.12).
- To distinguish syntax errors, runtime errors, and logic errors (§2.13).
- To debug logic errors (§2.14).

2.1 Introduction

In Chapter 1 you learned how to create, compile, and run a C++ program. Now you will learn how to solve practical problems programmatically. In doing so, you will learn elementary programming using primitive data types, variables, constants, operators, expressions, and input and output.

2.2 Writing Simple Programs

problem

To begin, let's look at a simple program that computes the area of a circle. The program reads in a circle's radius and displays its area. It will use variables to store the radius and the area and will use an expression to compute the area.

algorithm

Writing a program involves designing algorithms and translating algorithms into programming codes. An *algorithm* describes how a problem is solved in terms of the actions to be executed, and it specifies the order in which they should be executed. Algorithms can help the programmer plan a program before writing it in a programming language. The algorithm for this program can be described as follows:

1. Read in the radius.

2. Compute the area using the following formula:

$$\text{area} = \text{radius} \times \text{radius} \times \pi$$

3. Display the area.

Many of the problems you will encounter when taking an introductory course in programming can be described with simple, straightforward algorithms. As your education progresses, and you take courses on data structures or on algorithm design and analysis, you will encounter complex problems that require sophisticated solutions. In order to solve such problems, you will need to design correct, efficient algorithms with appropriate data structures.

primitive data types

Data structures involve data representation and manipulation. C++ provides simple data types for representing integers, *floating-point numbers* (i.e., numbers with a decimal point), characters, and Boolean types. These are known as *primitive data types*, or *fundamental types*. C++ also supports arrays and some advanced data types, such as `string` and `vector`. You can also define your own data types.

To novice programmers, coding is a daunting task. When you *code*, you translate an algorithm into a programming language understood by the computer. You already know that every C++ program begins its execution from the main function. The outline of the main function would look like this:

```cpp
int main()
{
  // Step 1: Read in radius

  // Step 2: Compute area

  // Step 3: Display the area
}
```

The program needs to read the radius entered by the user from the keyboard. This raises two important issues:

■ Reading the radius.

■ Storing the radius in the program.

Let's address the second issue first. In order to store the radius, the program needs to declare a symbol called a *variable*. Variables are used to store data and computational results in the program.

variable

Rather than using x and y, choose descriptive names—in this case, radius for radius and area for area. To let the compiler know what they are, specify their data types, whether integer, floating-point number, or something else. Declare radius and area as double-precision floating-point numbers. Now the program can be expanded as follows:

descriptive names

```
int main()
{
  double radius;
  double area;

  // Step 1: Read in radius

  // Step 2: Compute area

  // Step 3: Display the area
}
```

The program declares radius and area as variables. The reserved word double indicates that they are double-precision floating-point values stored in the computer.

The first step is to read in radius. You will learn how to do so later. For the time being, let us assign a fixed value to radius in the program.

The second step is to compute area by assigning the result of the expression radius * radius * 3.14159 to area.

In the final step, display area on the console by using cout << area.

The complete program is shown in Listing 2.1.

LISTING 2.1 ComputeArea.cpp

```
 1 #include <iostream>
 2 using namespace std;
 3
 4 int main()
 5 {
 6   double radius;
 7   double area;
 8
 9   // Step 1: Assign a radius
10   radius = 20;
11
12   // Step 2: Compute area
13   area = radius * radius * 3.14159;
14
15   // Step 3: Display the area
16   cout << "The area is " << area << endl;
17
18   return 0;
19 }
```

include library

declare variable

assign value

```
The area is 1256.64
```

Variables such as radius and area correspond to memory locations. Every variable has a name, a type, a size, and a value. Line 6 declares that radius can store a double value. The value is not defined until you assign a value. Line 10 assigns 20 into radius. Similarly, line 7 declares variable area and line 13 assigns a value into area. If you comment out line 10, the program will compile and run, but the result is unpredictable, because radius is not assigned

declaring variable

assigning value

a proper value. The table below shows the value in the memory for `area` and `radius` when the program is executed. Each row in the table shows the values of variables after the statement in the corresponding line in the program is executed. Hand trace is helpful for understanding how a program works, and it is also a useful tool for finding errors in the program.

line#	radius	area
6	undefined value	
7		undefined value
10	20	
13		1256.64

Line 16 sends a string `"The area is "` to the console. It also sends the value in variable `area` to the console. Note that quotation marks are not placed around `area`. If they were, the string `"area"` would be sent to the console.

Tip

This example consists of three steps. It is a good approach to develop and test these steps *incrementally* by adding one step at a time. You should apply this approach to all the programs, although for many programs in this book the problem-solving steps are not explicitly stated.

incremental development
and testing

2.3 Reading Input from the Keyboard

In Listing 2.1, the radius is fixed in the source code. To use a different radius, you have to modify the source code and recompile it. Obviously, this is not convenient. You can use the `cin` object to read input from the keyboard, as shown in Listing 2.2.

LISTING 2.2 ComputeAreaWithConsoleInput.cpp

```cpp
1 #include <iostream>
2 using namespace std;
3
4 int main()
5 {
6   // Step 1: Read in radius
7   double radius;
8   cout << "Enter a radius: ";
9   cin >> radius;
10
11  // Step 2: Compute area
12  double area = radius * radius * 3.14159;
13
14  // Step 3: Display the area
15  cout << "The area is " << area << endl;
16
17  return 0;
18 }
```

input

```
Enter a radius: 2.5  ⏎Enter
The area is 19.6349
```

```
Enter a radius: 2  ⏎Enter
The area is 12.5664
```

Line 8 displays a string `"Enter a radius: "` to the console. This is known as a *prompt*, because it directs the user to enter an input. Your program should always tell the user what to enter when expecting input from the keyboard.

prompt

Line 9 uses the `cin` object to read a value from the keyboard. Note that `cin` stands for *console input*. The `>>` symbol, referred to as the *stream extraction operator*, assigns an input to a variable. As shown in the sample output, the program displays the prompting message `"Enter a radius: "`; the user then enters number `2`, which is assigned to variable `radius`. The `cin` object causes a program to wait until data is typed at the keyboard and the *Enter* key is pressed. C++ automatically converts the data read from the keyboard to the data type of the variable.

console input
stream extraction operator

Note that the `>>` operator is the opposite of the `<<` operator. The `>>` indicates that the data flows from `cin` to a variable. The `<<` shows that the data flows from a variable or a string to `cout`.

You can use a single statement to read multiple values. For example, the following statement reads three values into variables `x1`, `x2`, and `x3`:

multiple input

```
cin >> x1 >> x2 >> x3;
```

Listing 2.3 gives an example of reading three numbers and displaying their average.

LISTING 2.3 ComputeAverage.cpp

Video Note
Obtain input

```cpp
1  #include <iostream>
2  using namespace std;
3
4  int main()
5  {
6    // Prompt the user to enter three numbers
7    double number1, number2, number3;
8    cout << "Enter three numbers: ";
9    cin >> number1 >> number2 >> number3;
10
11   // Compute average
12   double average = (number1 + number2 + number3) / 3;
13
14   // Display result
15   cout << "The average of " << number1 << " " << number2
16        << " " << number3 << " is " << average << endl;
17
18   return 0;
19 }
```

reading three numbers

```
Enter three numbers: 1 2 3  ↵Enter
The average of 1 2 3 is 2
```

```
Enter three numbers: 10.5  ↵Enter
11  ↵Enter
11.5  ↵Enter
The average of 10.5 11 11.5 is 11
```

Line 8 prompts the user to enter three numbers. The numbers are read in line 9. You may enter three numbers separated by spaces, then press the *Enter* key, or enter each number followed by the *Enter* key, as shown in the sample runs of this program.

2.4 Identifiers

identifier naming rules

As you see in Listing 2.3, `main`, `number1`, `number2`, `number3`, and so on are the names of things that appear in the program. Such names are called *identifiers*. All identifiers must obey the following rules:

- An identifier is a sequence of characters that consists of letters, digits, and underscores (_).

- An identifier must start with a letter or an underscore. It cannot start with a digit.

- An identifier cannot be a reserved word. (See Appendix A, "C++ Keywords," for a list of reserved words.)

- An identifier can be of any length, but your C++ compiler may impose some restrictions. Use identifiers of 31 characters or fewer to ensure portability.

For example, `area` and `radius` are legal identifiers, whereas `2A` and `d+4` are illegal because they do not follow the rules. The compiler detects illegal identifiers and reports syntax errors.

case sensitive

 Note
Since C++ is case sensitive, `area`, `Area`, and `AREA` are all different identifiers.

descriptive names

 Tip
Identifiers are used for naming variables, functions, and other things in a program. Descriptive identifiers make programs easy to read.

2.5 Variables

why called variables?

As you see from the programs in the preceding sections, variables are used to store values so that these values can be used later in a program. They are called variables because their values can be changed. In the program in Listing 2.2, `radius` and `area` are variables of double-precision, floating-point type. You can assign any numerical value to `radius` and `area`, and the values of `radius` and `area` can be reassigned. For example, you can write the code shown below to compute the area for different radii:

```
// Compute the first area
radius = 1.0;
area = radius * radius * 3.14159;
cout << area;

// Compute the second area
radius = 2.0;
area = radius * radius * 3.14159;
cout << area;
```

Variables are for representing data of a certain type. To use a variable, you declare it by telling the compiler its name and what type of data it represents. This is called a *variable declaration*. It tells the compiler to allocate appropriate memory space for the variable based on its data type. Here is the syntax for declaring a variable:

```
datatype variableName;
```

declaring variable

Here are some examples of variable declarations:

```
int count;          // Declare count to be an integer variable
double radius;      // Declare radius to be a double variable
double interestRate; // Declare interestRate to be a double variable
char ch;            // Declare ch to be a character variable
```

The examples use the data types `int`, `double`, and `char`. Later in this chapter you will learn more about data types.

If variables are of the same type, they can be declared together, as follows:

```
datatype variable1, variable2, ..., variablen;
```

The variables are separated by commas. For example,

```
int i, j, k; // Declare i, j, and k as int variables
```

Note

By convention, variable names are in lowercase. If a name consists of several words, concatenate all of them and capitalize the first letter of each word except the first. Examples of variables are `radius` and `interestRate`.

naming variables

Variables often have initial values. You can declare a variable and initialize it in one step. Consider, for instance, the following code:

initializing variables

```
int count = 1;
```

This is equivalent to the next two statements:

```
int count;
count = 1;
```

You can also use a shorthand form to declare and initialize variables of the same type together. For example,

```
int i = 1, j = 2;
```

Tip

A variable must be declared before it can be assigned a value. A variable declared in a function must be assigned a value. Otherwise, the variable is called *uninitialized* and its value is unpredictable. Whenever possible, declare a variable and assign its initial value in one step. This will make the program easy to read and avoid programming errors.

uninitialized variable

Note

C++ allows an alternative syntax for declaring and initializing variables, as shown in the following example:

```
int i(1), j(2);
```

which is equivalent to

```
int i = 1, j = 2;
```

2.6 Assignment Statements and Assignment Expressions

After a variable is declared, you can assign it a value by using an *assignment statement*. In C++, the equal sign (=) is used as the *assignment operator*. The syntax for assignment statements is as follows:

assignment statement
assignment operator

```
variable = expression;
```

expression

An *expression* represents a computation involving values, variables, and operators that together evaluate to a value. For example, consider the following code:

```
int x = 1;                 // Assign 1 to variable x
double radius = 1.0;       // Assign 1.0 to variable radius
x = 5 * (3 / 2) + 3 * 2;   // Assign the value of the expression to x
x = y + 1;                 // Assign the addition of y and 1 to x
area = radius * radius * 3.14159; // Compute area
```

A variable can appear in both sides of the assignment operator. For example,

```
x = x + 1;
```

In this assignment statement, the result of `x + 1` is assigned to `x`. If `x` is `1` before the statement is executed, it becomes `2` after the statement is executed.

In assigning a value to a variable, the variable name must be on the left of the assignment operator. Thus, `1 = x` would be wrong.

 Note

In mathematics, $x = 2 * x + 1$ denotes an equation. However, in C++, $x = 2 * x + 1$ is an assignment statement that evaluates the expression $2 * x + 1$ and assigns the result to x.

assignment expression

In C++, an assignment statement is essentially an expression that evaluates to the value to be assigned to the variable on the left-hand side of the assignment operator. For this reason, an assignment statement is also known as an *assignment expression*. For example, the following statement is correct:

```
cout << (x = 1);
```

which is equivalent to

```
x = 1;
cout << x;
```

The following statement is also correct:

```
i = j = k = 1;
```

which is equivalent to

```
k = 1;
j = k;
i = j;
```

2.7 Named Constants

constant

The value of a variable may change during the execution of a program, but a *named constant* or simply *constant* represents permanent data that never changes. In our `ComputeArea` program, π is a constant. If you use it frequently, you don't want to keep typing `3.14159`; instead, you can name a constant for π. Here is the syntax for naming a constant:

```
const datatype CONSTANTNAME = VALUE;
```

A constant must be declared and initialized in the same statement. `const` is a C++ keyword for declaring a constant. For example, you may declare π as a constant and rewrite Listing 2.2 as in Listing 2.4.

LISTING 2.4 ComputeAreaWithConstant.cpp

```
1 #include <iostream>
2 using namespace std;
3
```

```
 4 int main()
 5 {
 6   const double PI = 3.14159;
 7
 8   // Step 1: Read in radius
 9   double radius;
10   cout << "Enter a radius: ";
11   cin >> radius;
12
13   // Step 2: Compute area
14   double area = radius * radius * PI;
15
16   // Step 3: Display the area
17   cout << "The area is ";
18   cout << area << endl;
19
20   return 0;
21 }
```

constant PI

Caution

By convention, constants are named in uppercase: `PI`, not `pi` or `Pi`.

naming constants

Note

There are three benefits of using constants: (1) you don't have to repeatedly type the same value; (2) if you have to change the constant value (e.g., from `3.14` to `3.14159` for `PI`), you need change it only in a single location in the source code; (3) descriptive constant names make the program easy to read.

benefits of constants

Another way to specify constants is to use the `#define` *directive* with the following syntax:

#define directive

```
#define name value
```

For example, you can rewrite Listing 2.4 to define `PI` using the `#define` directive in Listing 2.5:

LISTING 2.5 ComputeArea5.cpp

```
 1 #include <iostream>
 2 #define PI 3.14159
 3 using namespace std;
 4
 5 int main()
 6 {
 7   // Step 1: Read in radius
 8   double radius;
 9   cout << "Enter a radius: ";
10   cin >> radius;
11
12   // Step 2: Compute area
13   double area = radius * radius * PI;
14
15   // Step 3: Display the area
16   cout << "The area is ";
17   cout << area << endl;
18
19   return 0;
20 }
```

constant PI

no semicolon

The compiler directives are not C++ statements. So, don't put a semicolon (;) at the end of the directive line. When the compiler sees identifier `PI` in the program, it replaces `PI` with `3.14159`. If you mistakenly put a semicolon in the directive as shown below:

```
                        ——should have no semicolon
#define PI 3.14159;
```

`PI` in the program is replaced by `3.14159;` with the semicolon.

#define vs. **const**

You can define a constant using the `#define` directive or use the `const` to declare a constant. How do they differ, and which one should you use? When you define a constant using the `#define` directive, the constant is not stored in memory. The constant will be replaced with a value by the compiler. When you declare a constant using the `const` keyword, the constant is stored in memory just like a variable. If a constant is used in multiple programs, use the `#define` directive to define it in a header file so it can be included in other programs. If a constant is used only in one program, using `const` to declare it is more efficient.

2.8 Numeric Data Types and Operations

Every *data type* has a range of values. The compiler allocates memory space to store each variable or constant according to its data type. C++ provides primitive data types for numeric values, characters, and Boolean values. This section introduces numeric data types. Table 2.1 lists the numeric data types with their typical ranges and storage sizes.

TABLE 2.1 Numeric Data Types

Name	Synonymn	Range	Storage Size
short	short int	-2^{15} ($-32,768$) to $2^{15}-1$ (32,767)	16-bit signed
unsigned short	unsigned short int	0 to $2^{16}-1$ (65535)	16-bit unsigned
int		-2^{31} (-2147483648) to $2^{31}-1$ (2147483647)	32-bit signed
unsigned	unsigned int	0 to $2^{32}-1$ (4294967295)	32-bit unsigned
long	long int	-2^{31} (-2147483648) to $2^{31}-1$ (2147483647)	32-bit signed
unsigned long	unsigned long int	0 to $2^{32}-1$ (4294967295)	32-bit unsigned

float		Negative range:
		  $-3.4028235E+38$ to $-1.4E-45$
		Positive range:
		  $1.4E-45$ to $3.4028235E+38$
			32-bit IEEE 754

double		Negative range:
		  $-1.7976931348623157E+308$ to $-4.9E-324$
		Positive range:
		  $4.9E-324$ to $1.7976931348623157E+308$
			64-bit IEEE 754

long double		Negative range:
		  $-1.18E+4932$ to $-3.37E-4932$
		Positive range:
		  $3.37E-4932$ to $1.18E+4932$
		Significant decimal digits: 19
			80-bit

C++ uses three types for integers: `short`, `int`, and `long`. Each integer type comes in two flavors: *signed* and *unsigned*. Half of the numbers represented by a signed short are negative and the other half are positive. All the numbers represented by an unsigned short are non-negative. Because you have the same storage size for both, the largest number you can store in an unsigned integer is twice as big as the largest positive number you can store in a signed integer. If you know the value stored in a variable is always nonnegative, declare it as unsigned.

Note

short int is synonymous with `short`. unsigned short int is synonymous with `unsigned short`. unsigned int is synonymous with `unsigned`. long int is synonymous with `long`. unsigned long int is synonymous with `unsigned long`. For example,

```
short int i = 2;
```

is the same as

```
short i = 2;
```

signed vs. unsigned

synonymous types

The size of the data types may vary depending on the compiler and computer you are using. Typically, `int` and `long` have the same size. On some systems, `long` requires 8 bytes.

size may vary

Tip

You can use the `sizeof` function to find the size of a type. For example, the following statement displays the size of `int`, `long`, and `double` on your machine.

```
cout << sizeof(int) << " " << sizeof(long) << " " << sizeof(double);
```

`sizeof` function

C++ uses three types for floating-point numbers: `float`, `double`, and `long double`. The `double` *type* is usually twice as big as `float`. So, the `double` is known as double precision, while `float` is single precision. The `long double` is even bigger than `double`. For most applications, using the `double` type is desirable.

floating-point

2.8.1   Numeric Literals

A *literal* is a constant value that appears directly in a program. In the following statements, for example, `34` and `0.305` are literals:

literal

```
int i = 34;
double footToMeters = 0.305;
```

By default, an integer literal is a decimal number. To denote an octal integer literal, use a leading *0* (zero), and to denote a hexadecimal integer literal, use a leading *0x* or *0X* (zero x). For example, the following code displays the decimal value `65535` for hexadecimal number FFFF and decimal value 8 for octal number 10.

octal and hex literals

```
cout << 0xFFFF << " " << 010;
```

Hexadecimal numbers, binary numbers, and octal numbers are introduced in Appendix D, "Number Systems."

Floating-point literals are written with a decimal point. `2.0` is a floating-point number, but `2` is an integer. Floating-point literals can also be specified in scientific notation. For example, `1.23456e+2`, the same as `1.23456e2`, is equivalent to $1.23456 \times 10^2 = 123.456$, and 1.23456e−2 is equivalent to $1.23456 \times 10^{-2} = 0.0123456$. `E` (or `e`) represents an exponent and can be in either lowercase or uppercase.

floating-point literals
scientific notation

why called floating-point?

Note

The `float` and `double` types are used to represent numbers with a decimal point. Why are they called *floating-point numbers*? These numbers are stored in scientific notation. When a number such as `50.534` is converted into scientific notation, such as `5.0534e+1`, its decimal point is moved (i.e., floated) to a new position.

2.8.2 Numeric Operators

operators +, -, *, /, %

The *operators* for numeric data types include the standard arithmetic operators: addition (+), subtraction (−), multiplication (*), division (/), and modulus (%), as shown in Table 2.2.

TABLE 2.2 Numeric Operators

Operator	Name	Example	Result
+	Addition	34 + 1	35
−	Subtraction	34.0 − 0.1	33.9
*	Multiplication	300 * 30	9000
/	Division	1.0 / 2.0	0.5
%	Modulus	20 % 3	2

integer division

When both operands of a division are integers, the result of the division is an integer. The fractional part is truncated. For example, `5 / 2` yields `2`, not `2.5`, and `-5 / 2` yields `-2`, not `-2.5`. To perform regular mathematical division, one of the operands must be a floating-point number. For example, `5.0 / 2` yields `2.5`.

integer modulus

The modulus (%) operator works only with integer operands and yields the remainder after division. The left-hand operand is the dividend and the right-hand operand the divisor. Therefore, `7 % 3` yields `1`, `12 % 4` yields `0`, `26 % 8` yields `2`, and `20 % 13` yields `7`.

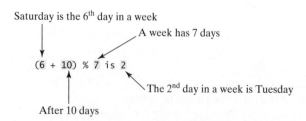

The % operator is often used with positive integers but also can be used with negative integers. The remainder is negative only if the dividend is negative. For example, `-7 % 3` yields `-1`, `-12 % 4` yields `0`, `-26 % -8` yields `-2`, and `20 % -13` yields `7`. In C++, the % operator is for integers only.

Modulus is very useful in programming. For example, an even number % `2` is always `0` and an odd number % `2` is always `1`. So you can use this property to determine whether a number is even or odd. If today is Saturday, it will be Saturday again in 7 days. Suppose you and your friends are going to meet in 10 days. What day is in 10 days? You can find that day is Tuesday using the following expression:

Listing 2.6 gives a program that obtains minutes and remaining seconds from an amount of time in seconds. For example, 500 seconds contains 8 minutes and 20 seconds.

LISTING 2.6 `DisplayTime.cpp`

```cpp
1 #include <iostream>
2 using namespace std;
3
4 int main()
5 {
6   // Prompt the user for input
7   int seconds;
8   cout << "Enter an integer for seconds: ";
9   cin >> seconds;
10  int minutes = seconds / 60;
11  int remainingSeconds = seconds % 60;
12  cout << seconds << " seconds is " << minutes <<
13    " minutes and " << remainingSeconds << " seconds " << endl;
14
15  return 0;
16 }
```

```
Enter an integer for seconds: 500  ↵Enter
500 seconds is 8 minutes and 20 seconds
```

line#	seconds	minutes	remainingSeconds
6	500		
7		8	
8			20

Line 9 reads an integer for seconds. Line 10 obtains the minutes using seconds / 60. Line 11 (seconds % 60) obtains the remaining seconds after taking away minutes.

The + and – operators can be both unary and binary. A *unary* operator has only one operand; a *binary* operator has two. For example, the – operator in -5 can be considered a unary operator to negate number 5, whereas the – operator in 4 – 5 is a binary operator for subtracting 5 from 4.

unary operator
binary operator

 Note

C++ allows you to assign an integer value to a floating-point variable and a floating-point value to an integer variable. When assigning a floating-point value to an integer variable, the fraction part of the floating-point value is truncated (*not rounded*). For example:

floating-point to integer

```cpp
int i = 34.7;   // i becomes 34
float f = i;    // f is now 34
float g = 34.3; // g becomes 34.3
long j = g;     // j is now 34
```

 Caution

When a variable is assigned a value too large in size to be stored, it causes *overflow*. For example, executing the following statement causes *overflow*, because the largest value that can be stored in a variable of the short type is 32767. 32768 is too large.

what is overflow?

```cpp
short value = 32767 + 1; // value will actually be -32768
```

Likewise, executing the following statement causes *overflow*, because the smallest value that can be stored in a variable of the **short** type is −32768. The value −32769 is too large to be stored in a **short** variable.

```
short value = -32768 - 1; // value will actually be 32767
```

C++ does not report warnings or errors on overflow. So be careful when working with numbers close to the maximum or minimum range of a given type.

When a floating-point number is too small (i.e., too close to zero) to be stored, it causes *underflow*. C++ approximates it to zero. So, normally you need not be concerned with underflow.

what is underflow?

2.8.3 Arithmetic Expressions

Writing numeric expressions in C++ involves a straightforward translation of an arithmetic expression using C++ operators. For example, the arithmetic expression

$$\frac{3 + 4x}{5} - \frac{10(y - 5)(a + b + c)}{x} + 9\left(\frac{4}{x} + \frac{9 + x}{y}\right)$$

can be translated into a C++ expression as

```
(3 + 4 * x) / 5 - 10 * (y - 5) * (a + b + c) / x +
9 * (4 / x + (9 + x) / y)
```

The numeric operators are applied in a C++ expression the same way as in an arithmetic expression. Operators contained within pairs of parentheses are evaluated first. Parentheses can be nested, in which case the expression in the inner parentheses is evaluated first. Multiplication, division, and modulus operators are applied next. If an expression contains several multiplication, division, and modulus operators, they are applied from left to right. Addition and subtraction operators are applied last. If an expression contains several addition and subtraction operators, they are applied from left to right.

Listing 2.7 gives a program that converts Fahrenheit degrees to Celsius using the formula $celsius = \left(\frac{5}{9}\right)(fahrenheit - 32)$.

LISTING 2.7 FahrenheitToCelsius.cpp

```
1 #include <iostream>
2 using namespace std;
3
4 int main()
5 {
6    // Enter a degree in Fahrenheit
7    double fahrenheit;
8    cout << "Enter a degree in Fahrenheit: ";
9    cin >> fahrenheit;
10
11   // Obtain a Celsius degree
12   double celsius = (5.0 / 9) * (fahrenheit - 32);
13
14   // Display result
15   cout << "Fahrenheit " << fahrenheit << " is " <<
16       celsius << " in Celsius" << endl;
17
18   return 0;
19 }
```

input fahrenheit

compute celsius

display result

```
Enter degrees in Fahrenheit: 100  ⏎ Enter
Fahrenheit 100 is 37.7778 in Celsius
```

line#	fahrenheit	celsius
7	undefined	
9	100	
12		37.7778

Be careful when applying division. In C++, division of two integers yields an integer. In line 12, $\frac{5}{9}$ is translated to `5.0 / 9` instead of `5 / 9`, because `5 / 9` yields `0` in C++.

integer vs. decimal division

2.8.4 Shorthand Assignment Operators

Very often the current value of a variable is used, modified, and then reassigned back to the same variable. For example, the following statement adds the current value of `i` with value `8` and assigns the result back to `i`:

```
i = i + 8;
```

C++ allows you to combine assignment and addition operators using a shorthand operator. For example, the preceding statement can be written as:

shorthand operator

```
i += 8;
```

The `+=` is called the *addition assignment operator*. Other shorthand operators are shown in Table 2.3.

TABLE 2.3 Shorthand Operators

Operator	Name	Example	Equivalent
+=	Addition assignment	i += 8	i = i + 8
-=	Subtraction assignment	i -= 8	i = i - 8
*=	Multiplication assignment	i *= 8	i = i * 8
/=	Division assignment	i /= 8	i = i / 8
%=	Modulus assignment	i %= 8	i = i % 8

Note

Like the assignment operator (`=`), the operators (`+=`, `-=`, `*=`, `/=`, `%=`) can be used to form an assignment statement as well as an expression. For example, in the following code, `x += 2` is a statement in the first line and an expression in the second line.

```
x += 2; // Statement
cout << (x += 2); // Expression
```

If a statement is used as an expression, it is called an *expression statement*.

expression statement

Caution

There are no spaces in the shorthand operators. For example, `+ =` should be `+=`.

2.8.5 Increment and Decrement Operators

There are two more shorthand operators for incrementing and decrementing a variable by 1. This is handy, because that's often how much the value needs to be changed. These two operators are ++ and --. For example, the following code increments i by 1 and decrements j by 1.

```
int i = 3, j = 3;
i++; // i becomes 4
j--; // j becomes 2
```

The ++ and -- operators can be used in prefix or suffix mode, as shown in Table 2.4.

TABLE 2.4   Increment and Decrement Operators

Operator	Name	Description	Example (assume i = 1)
++var	preincrement	Increment var by 1 and use the new var value	int j = ++i; // j is 2, i is 2
var++	postincrement	Increment var by 1, but use the original var value	int j = i++; // j is 1, i is 2
--var	predecrement	Decrement var by 1 and use the new var value	int j = --i; // j is 0, i is 0
var--	postdecrement	Decrement var by 1 and use the original var value	int j = ++i; // j is 1, i is 0

If the operator is *before* (prefixed to) the variable, the variable is incremented or decremented by 1, then the *new* value of the variable is returned. If the operator is *after* (suffixed to) the variable, the original *old* value of the variable is returned, then the variable is incremented or decremented by 1. Therefore, the prefixes ++x and --x are referred to, respectively, as the *preincrement operator* and the *predecrement operator*; and the suffixes x++ and x-- are referred to, respectively, as the *postincrement operator* and the *postdecrement operator*. The prefix form of ++ (or --) and the suffix form of ++ (or --) are the same if they are used in isolation, but they cause different effects when used in an expression. The following code illustrates this:

preincrement, predecrement

postincrement, postdecrement

```
int i = 10;                         Same effect as    int newNum = 10 * i;
int newNum = 10 * i++;         ───────────────▶      i = i + 1;
```

In this case, i is incremented by 1, then the *old* value of i is returned and used in the multiplication. So newNum becomes 100. If i++ is replaced by ++i, as follows:

```
int i = 10;                         Same effect as    i = i + 1;
int newNum = 10 * (++i);      ───────────────▶      int newNum = 10 * i;
```

i is incremented by 1, and the new value of i is returned and used in the multiplication. Thus newNum becomes 110.

Here is another example:

```
double x = 1.0;
double y = 5.0;
double z = x-- + (++y);
```

After all three lines are executed, y becomes 6.0, z becomes 7.0, and x becomes 0.0.

The *increment operator* ++ and the *decrement operator* -- can be applied to all integer and floating-point types. These operators are often used in loop statements. A *loop statement* is a structure that controls how many times an operation or a sequence of operations is performed in succession. This structure, along with the topic of loop statements, is introduced in Chapter 4, "Loops."

Caution

For most binary operators, C++ does not specify the operand evaluation order. Normally, you assume that the left operand is evaluated before the right operand. This is not guaranteed in C++. For example, suppose i is 1; then the expression

operand evaluation order

```
++i + i
```

evaluates to 4 (2 + 2) if the left operand (++i) is evaluated first and evaluates to 3 (2 + 1) if the right operand (i) is evaluated first.

Since C++ cannot guarantee the operand evaluation order, you should not write code that depends on the operand evaluation order.

2.9 Numeric Type Conversions

Can you perform binary operations with two operands of different types? Yes. If an integer and a floating-point number are involved in a binary operation, C++ automatically converts the integer to a floating-point value. So, 3 * 4.5 is same as 3.0 * 4.5.

C++ also allows you to manually convert a value from one type to another using a *casting* operator. The syntax is

type casting

```
static_cast<type>(value)
```

where value is a variable, a literal, or an expression and type is the type you wish to convert the value to.

For example, the following statement

```
cout << static_cast<int>(1.7);
```

displays 1. When a double value is cast into an int value, the fractional part is truncated. The following statement

```
cout << static_cast<double>(1) / 2;
```

displays 0.5, because 1 is cast to 1.0 first, then 1.0 is divided by 2. However, the statement

```
cout << 1 / 2;
```

displays 0, because 1 and 2 are both integers and the resulting value should also be an integer.

Note

It is worth mentioning that static casting can also be done using the (type) syntax—that is, giving the target type in parentheses, followed by a variable, a literal, or an expression. This is called the *C-style cast*. For example,

C-style cast

```
int i = (int)5.4;
```

This is the same as

```
int i = static_cast<int>(5.4);
```

The C-style cast has been replaced by the C++ static_cast operator.

widening a type
narrowing a type
loss of precision

Casting a variable of a type with a small range to a variable of a type with a larger range is known as *widening a type*. Casting a variable of a type with a large range to a variable of a type with a smaller range is known as *narrowing a type*. Narrowing a type, such as assigning a `double` value to an `int` variable, may cause loss of precision. Lost information might lead to inaccurate results. The GNU and Visual C++ compilers give a warning when you narrow a type, unless you use `static_cast` to make the conversion explicit.

 Note

Casting does not change the variable being cast. For example, **d** is not changed after casting in the following code:

```
double d = 4.5;
int i = static_cast<int>(d);  // d is not changed
```

Listing 2.8 gives a program that displays the sales tax with two digits after the decimal point.

LISTING 2.8 SalesTax.cpp

```cpp
1 #include <iostream>
2 using namespace std;
3
4 int main()
5 {
6   // Enter purchase amount
7   double purchaseAmount;
8   cout << "Enter purchase amount: ";
9   cin >> purchaseAmount;
10
11  double tax = purchaseAmount * 0.06;
12  cout << "Sales tax is " << static_cast<int>(tax * 100) / 100.0;
13
14  return 0;
15 }
```

```
Enter purchase amount: 197.55  ↵Enter
Sales tax is 11.85
```

line#	purchaseAmount	tax	output
7	undefined		
9	197.55		
11		11.853	
12			Sales tax is 11.85

formatting numbers

Variable `purchaseAmount` stores the purchase amount entered by the user (lines 7–9). Suppose the user entered 197.55. The sales tax is 6% of the purchase, so the `tax` is evaluated as `11.853` (line 11). The statement in line 12 displays the tax `11.85` with two digits after the decimal point. Note that

```
tax * 100 is 1185.3
static_cast<int>(tax * 100) is 1185
static_cast<int>(tax * 100) / 100.0 is 11.85
```

2.10 Character Data Type and Operations

The character data type, `char`, is used to represent a single character. A character literal is enclosed in single quotation marks. Consider the following code:

char type

```
char letter = 'A';
char numChar = '4';
```

The first statement assigns character `A` to the `char` variable `letter`. The second statement assigns the digit character `4` to the `char` variable `numChar`.

Caution

A string literal must be enclosed in quotation marks. A character literal is a single character enclosed in single quotation marks. So `"A"` is a string, but `'A'` is a character.

char literal

Computers use binary numbers internally. A character is stored in a computer as a sequence of 0s and 1s. Mapping a character to its binary representation is called *encoding*. There are different ways to encode a character, as defined by an *encoding scheme*.

character encoding

Most computers use *ASCII* (*American Standard Code for Information Interchange*), a 7-bit encoding scheme for representing all uppercase and lowercase letters, digits, punctuation marks, and control characters. See Appendix B, "The ASCII Character Set," for a list of ASCII characters and their decimal and hexadecimal codes. On most systems, the size of the `char` type is 1 byte.

ASCII

Note

The increment and decrement operators can also be used on `char` variables to get the next or preceding character. For example, the following statements display character `b`:

char increment and decrement

```
char ch = 'a';
cout << ++ch;
```

To read a character from the keyboard, use

read character

```
cout << "Enter a character: ";
char ch;
cin >> ch; // Read a character
cout << "The character read is " << ch << endl;
```

2.10.1 Escape Sequences for Special Characters

C++ allows you to use escape sequences to represent special characters, as shown in Table 2.5. An escape sequence begins with the *backslash* character (\) followed by a character that has a special meaning to the compiler.

TABLE 2.5 Character Escape Sequences

Character Escape Sequence	Name	ASCII Code
\b	Backspace	8
\t	Tab	9
\n	Linefeed	10
\f	Formfeed	12
\r	Carriage Return	13
\\	Backslash	92
\'	Single Quote	39
\"	Double Quote	34

Suppose you want to print the quoted message shown below:

He said "C++ is powerful"

Here is how to write the statement:

cout << "He said \"C++ is powerful\"";

Note

whitespace

The characters ' ', '\t', '\f', '\r', and '\n' are known as the *whitespace* characters.

Note

\n vs. **endl**

The following two statements both display a string and move the cursor to the next line.

cout << "Welcome to C++\n";
cout << "Welcome to C++" << endl;

However, using **endl** ensures that the output is displayed immediately on all platforms.

2.10.2 Casting between `char` and Numeric Types

A `char` can be cast into any numeric type, and vice versa. When an integer is cast into a `char`, only its lower 8 bits of data are used (assume that your system stores a char in 8 bits); the other part is ignored. For example:

char c = 0XFF41; // The lower 8 bits hex code 41 is assigned to c
cout << c;   // c is character A

When a floating-point value is cast into a `char`, the floating-point value is first cast into an `int`, which is then cast into a `char`.

char c = 65.25; // 65 is assigned to c
cout << c;   // c is character A

When a `char` is cast into a numeric type, the character's ASCII is cast into the specified numeric type. For example:

int i = 'A';   // The ASCII code of character A is assigned to i
cout << i;   // i is 65

Note

numeric operators on characters

The `char` type is treated as if it were an integer of the byte size. All numeric operators can be applied to `char` operands. A `char` operand is automatically cast into a number if the other operand is a number or a character. For example, the following statements

int i = '2' + '3'; // (int)'2' is 50 and (int)'3' is 51
cout << "i is " << i << endl; // i is decimal 101

int j = 2 + 'a'; // (int)'a' is 97
cout << "j is " << j << endl;
cout << j << " is the ASCII code for character " <<
  static_cast<char>(j) << endl;

display

i is 101
j is 99
99 is the ASCII code for character c

Note

It is worthwhile to note that the ASCII codes for lowercase letters are consecutive integers starting from the code for 'a', then that for 'b', 'c', ..., and 'z'. The same is true for the uppercase letters. Furthermore, the ASCII code for `'a'` is greater than the code for `'A'`. So `'a'` – `'A'` is the same as `'b'` – `'B'`. For a lowercase letter *ch*, its corresponding uppercase letter is `static_cast<char>('A' + (ch - 'a'))`.

2.11 Case Studies

In the preceding sections, you learned about variables, constants, primitive data types, operators, and expressions. You are now ready to use them to write interesting programs. This section presents three problems: computing loan payments, breaking a sum of money down into smaller units, and displaying the current time.

2.11.1 Problem: Computing Loan Payments

The problem is to write a program that computes loan payments. The loan can be a car loan, a student loan, or a home mortgage loan. The program lets the user enter the interest rate, number of years, and loan amount, and displays the monthly and total payments.

The formula to compute the monthly payment is as follows:

$$\frac{loanAmount \times monthlyInterestRate}{1 - \dfrac{1}{(1 + monthlyInterestRate)^{numberOfYears \times 12}}}$$

You don't have to know how this formula is derived. Nonetheless, given the monthly interest rate, number of years, and loan amount, you can use it to compute the monthly payment.

Here are the steps in developing the program:

1. Prompt the user to enter the annual interest rate, number of years, and loan amount.

2. Obtain the monthly interest rate from the annual interest rate.

3. Compute the monthly payment using the preceding formula.

4. Compute the total payment, which is the monthly payment multiplied by `12` and multiplied by the number of years.

5. Display the monthly payment and total payment.

In the formula, you have to compute $(1 + monthlyInterestRate)^{numberOfYears \times 12}$. C++ contains the `pow(a, b)` function in the `cmath` library, which can be used to compute a^b. For example,

```
cout << pow(2.0, 3);
```

pow(a, b) function

displays `8`. Note that C++ requires that either `a` or `b` in `pow(a, b)` be a decimal value. Here we use `2.0` rather than `2`.

$(1 + monthlyInterestRate)^{numberOfYears \times 12}$ can be computed using `pow(1 + monthly-InterestRate, numberOfYears * 12)`.

Listing 2.9 gives the complete program.

Video Note

Program computations

include **cmath** library

LISTING 2.9 ComputeLoan.cpp

```
1 #include <iostream>
2 #include <cmath>
3 using namespace std;
4
5 int main()
6 {
```

enter interest rate

```
 7    // Enter yearly interest rate
 8    cout << "Enter yearly interest rate, for example 8.25: ";
 9    double annualInterestRate;
10    cin >> annualInterestRate;
11
12    // Obtain monthly interest rate
13    double monthlyInterestRate = annualInterestRate / 1200;
14
15    // Enter number of years
16    cout << "Enter number of years as an integer, for example 5: ";
17    int numberOfYears;
18    cin >> numberOfYears;
19
20    // Enter loan amount
21    cout << "Enter loan amount, for example 120000.95: ";
22    double loanAmount;
23    cin >> loanAmount;
24
25    // Calculate payment
26    double monthlyPayment = loanAmount * monthlyInterestRate / (1
27      - 1 / pow(1 + monthlyInterestRate, numberOfYears * 12));
28    double totalPayment = monthlyPayment * numberOfYears * 12;
29
30    // Display results
31    cout << "The monthly payment is " << monthlyPayment <<
32      "\nThe total payment is " << totalPayment << endl;
33
34    return 0;
35  }
```

monthlyPayment (at line 26)

totalPayment (at line 28)

display result (at line 35)

```
Enter yearly interest rate, for example 8.25: 5.75  ↵Enter
Enter number of years as an integer, for example 5: 15  ↵Enter
Enter loan amount, for example 120000.95: 250000  ↵Enter
The monthly payment is 2076.03
The total payment is 373685
```

variable \ line#	10	13	18	23	26	28
annualInterestRate	5.75					
monthlyInterestRate		0.00479				
numberOfYears			15			
loanAmount				250000		
monthlyPayment					2076.03	
totalPayment						373685

To use the pow(a, b) function, you have to include the cmath library in the program (line 2) in the same way you include the iostream library (line 1).

The program prompts the user to enter annualInterestRate, numberOfYears, and loanAmount in lines 7–23. If you entered an input other than a numeric value, a runtime error would occur. In Chapter 16, "Exception Handling," you will learn how to handle the exception so that the program can continue to run.

Choose the most appropriate data type for the variable. For example, `numberOfYears` is better declared as `int` (line 17), although it could be declared as `long`, `float`, or `double`. Note that `unsigned short` might be the most appropriate for `numberOfYears`. For simplicity, however, the examples in this book will use `int` for integer and `double` for floating-point values.

The formula for computing the monthly payment is translated into C++ code in lines 26–27.

2.11.2 Problem: Counting Monetary Units

Suppose you want to develop a program that classifies a given amount of money into smaller monetary units. The program lets the user enter an amount as a `double` value representing a total in dollars and cents, and outputs a report listing the monetary equivalent in dollars, quarters, dimes, nickels, and pennies, as shown in the sample output.

Your program should report the maximum number of dollars, then the maximum number of quarters, and so on, in this order.

Here are the steps in developing the program:

1. Prompt the user to enter the amount as a decimal number, such as `11.56`.

2. Convert the amount (e.g., `11.56`) into cents (`1156`).

3. Divide the cents by `100` to find the number of dollars. Obtain the remaining cents using the cents remainder `100`.

4. Divide the remaining cents by `25` to find the number of quarters. Obtain the remaining cents using the remaining cents remainder `25`.

5. Divide the remaining cents by `10` to find the number of dimes. Obtain the remaining cents using the remaining cents remainder `10`.

6. Divide the remaining cents by `5` to find the number of nickels. Obtain the remaining cents using the remaining cents remainder `5`.

7. The remaining cents are the pennies.

8. Display the result.

The complete program is given in Listing 2.10.

LISTING 2.10   ComputeChange.cpp

```
1 #include <iostream>
2 using namespace std;
3
4 int main()
5 {
6   // Receive the amount
7   cout << "Enter an amount in double, for example 11.56: ";
8   double amount;
9   cin >> amount;
10
11  int remainingAmount = static_cast<int>(amount * 100);
12
13  // Find the number of one dollars
14  int numberOfOneDollars = remainingAmount / 100;          dollars
15  remainingAmount = remainingAmount % 100;
16
17  // Find the number of quarters in the remaining amount
18  int numberOfQuarters = remainingAmount / 25;             quarters
```

dimes

nickels

pennies

display result

```
19      remainingAmount = remainingAmount % 25;
20
21      // Find the number of dimes in the remaining amount
22      int numberOfDimes = remainingAmount / 10;
23      remainingAmount = remainingAmount % 10;
24
25      // Find the number of nickels in the remaining amount
26      int numberOfNickels = remainingAmount / 5;
27      remainingAmount = remainingAmount % 5;
28
29      // Find the number of pennies in the remaining amount
30      int numberOfPennies = remainingAmount;
31
32      // Display results
33      cout << "Your amount " << amount << " consists of \n" <<
34        "\t" << numberOfOneDollars << " dollars\n" <<
35        "\t" << numberOfQuarters << " quarters\n" <<
36        "\t" << numberOfDimes << " dimes\n" <<
37        "\t" << numberOfNickels << " nickels\n" <<
38        "\t" << numberOfPennies << " pennies";
39
40      return 0;
41 }
```

Enter an amount in double, for example 11.56: **11.56** ⏎ Enter
Your amount 11.56 consists of
   11 dollars
   2 quarters
   0 dimes
   1 nickels
   1 pennies

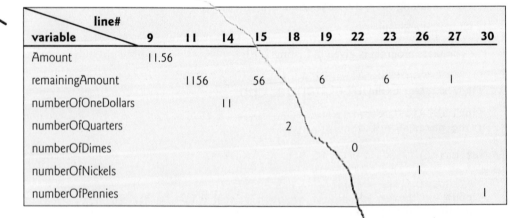

variable \ line#	9	11	14	15	18	19	22	23	26	27	30
Amount	11.56										
remainingAmount		1156		56		6		6		1	
numberOfOneDollars			11								
numberOfQuarters					2						
numberOfDimes							0				
numberOfNickels									1		
numberOfPennies											1

The variable amount stores the amount entered from the keyboard (lines 7–9). This variable should not be changed, because the amount has to be used at the end of the program to display the results. The program introduces the variable remainingAmount (line 11) to store the changing remainingAmount.

The variable amount is a double decimal representing dollars and cents. It is converted to an int variable remainingAmount, which represents all the cents. For instance, if amount is 11.56, then the initial remainingAmount is 1156. The division operator yields the integer part of the division. So `1156 / 100` is `11`. The remainder operator obtains the remainder of the division. So `1156 % 100` is `56`.

The program extracts the maximum number of singles from the total amount and obtains the remaining amount in the variable `remainingAmount` (lines 14–15). It then extracts the maximum number of quarters from `remainingAmount` and obtains a new `remainingAmount` (lines 18–19). Continuing the same process, the program finds the maximum number of dimes, nickels, and pennies in the remaining amount.

One serious problem with this example is the possible loss of precision when casting a `double` amount to an `int remainingAmount`. This could lead to an inaccurate result. If you try to enter the amount `10.03`, then `10.03 * 100` becomes `1002.9999999999999`. You will find that the program displays `10` dollars and `2` pennies. To fix the problem, enter the amount as an integer value representing cents (see Exercise 2.9).

loss of precision

As shown in the sample output, `0` dimes, `1` nickels, and `1` pennies are displayed in the result. It would be better not to display `0` dimes, and to display `1` nickel and `1` penny using the singular forms of the words. You will learn how to use selection statements to modify this program in the next chapter (see Exercise 3.4).

2.11.3 Problem: Displaying the Current Time

The problem is to develop a program that displays the current time in GMT (Greenwich Mean Time) in the format hour:minute:second, such as 13:19:8.

The `time(0)` function, in the `ctime` header file, returns the current time in seconds elapsed since the time 00:00:00 on January 1, 1970 GMT, as shown in Figure 2.1. This time is known as the *UNIX epoch* because 1970 was the year when the UNIX operating system was formally introduced.

`time(0)` function

UNIX epoch

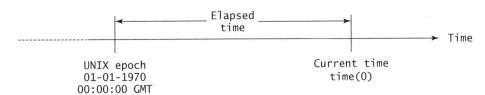

FIGURE 2.1 Invoking `time(0)` returns the number of seconds since the UNIX epoch.

You can use this function to obtain the current time, and then compute the current second, minute, and hour as follows.

1. Obtain the total seconds since midnight, January 1, 1970, in `totalSeconds` by invoking `time(0)` (e.g., 1103203148 seconds).

2. Compute the current second from `totalSeconds % 60` (e.g., 1103203148 seconds % 60 = 8, which is the current second).

3. Obtain the total minutes `totalMinutes` by dividing `totalSeconds` by 60 (e.g., 1103203148 seconds/60 = 18386719 minutes).

4. Compute the current minute from `totalMinutes % 60` (e.g., 18386719 minutes % 60 = 19, which is the current minute).

5. Obtain the total hours `totalHours` by dividing `totalMinutes` by 60 (e.g., 18386719 minutes/60 = 306445 hours).

6. Compute the current hour from `totalHours % 24` (e.g., 306445 hours % 24 = 19, which is the current hour).

Listing 2.11 shows the complete program followed by a sample run.

LISTING 2.11 ShowCurrentTime.cpp

```cpp
 1 #include <iostream>
 2 #include <ctime>
 3 using namespace std;
 4
 5 int main()
 6 {
 7   // Obtain the total seconds since the midnight, Jan 1, 1970
 8   int totalSeconds = time(0);
 9
10   // Compute the current second in the minute in the hour
11   int currentSecond = totalSeconds % 60;
12
13   // Obtain the total minutes
14   int totalMinutes = totalSeconds / 60;
15
16   // Compute the current minute in the hour
17   int currentMinute = totalMinutes % 60;
18
19   // Obtain the total hours
20   int totalHours = totalMinutes / 60;
21
22   // Compute the current hour
23   int currentHour = totalHours % 24;
24
25   // Display results
26   cout << "Current time is " << currentHour << ":"
27     << currentMinute << ":" << currentSecond << " GMT" << endl;
29
30   return 0;
31 }
```

totalSeconds

currentSecond

totalMinutes

currentMinute

totalHours

currentHour

preparing output

Current time is 17:31:26 GMT

Line#	8	11	14	17	20	23
totalSeconds	1203183086					
currentSecond		26				
totalMinutes			20053051			
currentMinute				31		
totalHours					334217	
currentHour						17

When `time(0)` (line 8) is invoked, it returns the difference, measured in seconds, between the current GMT and midnight, January 1, 1970 GMT.

2.12 Programming Style and Documentation

programming style

Programming style deals with what programs look like. A program could compile and run properly even if you wrote it on only one line, but writing it that way would be bad programming style because it would be hard to read. *Documentation* is the body of explanatory remarks and comments pertaining to a program. Programming style and documentation are as important as coding. Good programming style and appropriate documentation reduce the chance of errors and make programs easy to read. So far you have learned some good programming styles. This section summarizes them and gives several guidelines. More detailed guidelines on programming style and documentation can be found in Supplement I.E, "C++ Coding Style Guidelines," on the Companion Website.

2.12.1   Appropriate Comments and Comment Styles

Include a summary at the beginning of the program to explain what the program does, its key features, its supporting data structures, and any unique techniques it uses. In a long program, you should also include comments that introduce each major step and explain anything that is difficult to read. It is important to make comments concise so that they do not crowd the program or make it difficult to read.

2.12.2   Naming Variables and Constants

Make sure that you choose descriptive names with straightforward meanings for the variables, constants, and functions in your program. Names are case sensitive. Follow the conventions adopted in this book for naming variables and constants.

Avoid using abbreviations for identifiers. Using complete words is more descriptive. For example, `numberOfStudents` is better than `numStuds`, `numOfStuds`, or `numOfStudents`.

2.12.3   Proper Indentation and Spacing

A consistent indentation style makes programs clear and easy to read, debug, and maintain. *Indentation* is used to illustrate the structural relationships between a program's components or statements. C++ compiler can read the program even if all the statements are in a straight line, but properly aligned code is easier to read and maintain. Indent each subcomponent or statement *two* spaces more than the structure within which it is nested.

indent code

A single space should be added on both sides of a binary operator, as shown below:

```
int i = 3+4 * 4;        ◄──── Bad style
int i = 3 + 4 * 4;      ◄──── Good style
```

A single line of space should be used to separate segments of the code to make the program easier to read.

2.13 Programming Errors

Programming errors are unavoidable, even for experienced programmers. Errors can be categorized into three types: syntax errors, runtime errors, and *logic errors*.

2.13.1   Syntax Errors

Errors that occur during compilation are called *syntax errors* or *compilation errors*. Syntax errors result from errors in code construction, such as mistyping a keyword, omitting some necessary punctuation, or using an opening brace without a corresponding closing brace. These errors are usually easy to detect, because the compiler tells you where they are and what caused them. For example, compiling the following program results in a syntax error, as shown in Figure 2.2.

syntax errors

```
// ShowSyntaxErrors.cpp: The program contains syntax errors
#include <iostream>
using namespace std;

int main()
{
  i = 30;
  cout << i + 4;
}
```

```
Command Prompt                                                    _ □ ×
C:\example>g++ ShowSyntaxErrors.cpp
ShowSyntaxErrors.cpp: In function `int main()':
ShowSyntaxErrors.cpp:7: `i' undeclared (first use this function)
ShowSyntaxErrors.cpp:7: (Each undeclared identifier is reported only once for
   each function it appears in.)

C:\example>
```

FIGURE 2.2   The compiler reports syntax errors.

Three lines of errors are reported. All are the result of not declaring variable i. Since a single error will often display many lines of compilation errors, it is a good practice to start debugging from the top line and work downward. Fixing errors that occur earlier in the program may also fix additional errors that occur later.

2.13.2 Runtime Errors

runtime errors

Runtime errors cause a program to terminate abnormally. They occur while an application is running if the environment detects an operation that is impossible to carry out. Input errors are typical runtime errors.

An *input error* occurs when the user enters an unexpected input value that the program cannot handle. For instance, if the program expects to read in a number, but instead the user enters a string, this causes data-type errors to occur in the program. To prevent input errors, the program should prompt the user to enter values of the correct type. It may display a message like `"Please enter an integer"` to prompt the user for entering an integer.

2.13.3 Logic Errors

Logic errors occur when a program does not perform the way it was intended to. Errors of this kind occur for many different reasons. For example, suppose you wrote the following program to add `number1` to `number2`:

```
// ShowLogicErrors.cpp: The program contains a logic error
#include <iostream>
using namespace std;

int main()
{
  int number1 = 3;
  int number2 = 3;
  number2 += number1 + number2;
  cout << "number2 is " << number2 << endl;

  return 0;
}
```

The program does not have syntax errors or runtime errors, but it does not print the correct result for `number2`. See if you can find the error.

2.14 Debugging

In general, syntax errors are easy to find and easy to correct, because the compiler gives indications as to where the errors came from and why they are wrong. Runtime errors are not difficult to find, either, since the operating system displays them on the console when the program aborts. Finding logic errors, on the other hand, can be very challenging.

Logic errors are called *bugs*. The process of finding and correcting errors is called *debugging*. A common approach to debugging is to use a combination of methods to narrow down to the part of the program where the bug is located. You can *hand-trace* the program (i.e., catch errors by reading the program), or you can insert print statements in order to show the values of the variables or the execution flow of the program. This approach might work for a short, simple program. But for a large, complex program, the most effective way to debug is to use a *debugger* utility.

The C++ IDE tools, such as Visual C++ and C++Builder, include integrated debuggers. The debugger utilities let you follow the execution of a program. They vary from one system to another, but they all support most of the following helpful features:

- **Executing a single statement at a time:** The debugger allows you to execute one statement at a time so that you can see its effect.

- **Tracing into or stepping over a function:** If a function is being executed, you can ask the debugger to enter it and execute one statement at a time. If you know that the function works, you can ask the debugger to step over it. For example, always step over system-supplied functions, such as `pow(a, b)`.

- **Setting breakpoints:** You can also set a breakpoint at a specific statement. Your program pauses when it reaches a breakpoint and displays the line with the breakpoint. You can set as many breakpoints as you want. Breakpoints are particularly useful when you know where your programming error starts. You can set a breakpoint at that line and have the program execute until it reaches the breakpoint.

- **Displaying variables:** The debugger lets you select several variables and display their values. As you trace through a program, the content of a variable is continuously updated.

- **Displaying call stacks:** The debugger lets you trace all the function calls and lists all pending functions. This feature is helpful when you need to see a large picture of the program-execution flow.

- **Modifying variables:** Some debuggers enable you to modify the value of a variable when debugging. This is convenient when you want to test a program with different samples but do not want to leave the debugger.

[margin notes: bugs, debugging, hand-traces]

Tip

If you use Microsoft Visual C++, please refer to *Learning C++ Effectively with* Microsoft Visual C++ in the supplement on the Companion Website. The supplement shows you how to use a debugger to trace programs and how debugging can help you learn C++ effectively.

[margin note: debugging in IDE]

KEY TERMS

algorithm   34
assignment operator (=)   39
assignment statement   39
backslash (\)   51
C-style cast   49
casting   49
char type   51
cin   36
const   40
constant   40
data type   42
debugger   61
debugging   61
declaration   38
decrement operator (−−)   49
#define directive   41
double type   43
encoding   51
float type   42
floating-point number   34
expression   40
expression statement   47

identifier   38
increment operator (++)   49
incremental development
   and testing   36
indentation   59
int type   42
literal   43
logic error   59
long type   42
narrowing (of types)   50
operator   44
overflow   45
primitive data type   34
runtime error   60
short type   42
stream extraction operator (>>)   37
syntax error   59
underflow   46
UNIX epoch   57
variable   35
widening (of types)   50
whitespace   52

CHAPTER SUMMARY

1. The cin object along with the stream extraction operator (>>) can be used to read an input from the console.

2. Identifiers are names for things in a program.

3. An identifier is a sequence of characters that consists of letters, digits, and underscores (_).

4. An identifier must start with a letter or an underscore. It cannot start with a digit.

5. An identifier cannot be a reserved word.

6. Choosing descriptive identifiers can make programs easy to read.

7. Declaring a variable tells the compiler what type of data a variable can hold.

8. In C++, the equal sign (=) is used as the *assignment operator*.

9. A variable declared in a function must be assigned a value. Otherwise, the variable is called *uninitialized* and its value is unpredictable.

10. A *named constant* or *simply constant* represents permanent data that never changes.

11. A named constant is declared by using the keyword const.

12. A named constant can also be defined using the #define directive in C++.

13. By convention, constants are named in uppercase.

14. C++ provides integer types (`short`, `int`, `long`, `unsigned short`, `unsigned int`, and `unsigned long`) that represent signed and unsigned integers of various sizes.

15. Unsigned integers are nonnegative integers.

16. C++ provides floating-point types (`float`, `double`, and `long double`) that represent floating-point numbers of various precisions.

17. C++ provides operators that perform numeric operations: + (addition), – (subtraction), * (multiplication), / (division), and % (modulus).

18. Integer arithmetic (/) yields an integer result.

19. In C++, the % operator is for integers only.

20. The numeric operators in a C++ expression are applied the same way as in an arithmetic expression.

21. The increment operator (++) and the decrement operator (--) increment or decrement a variable by 1.

22. C++ provides shorthand operators += (addition assignment), -= (subtraction assignment), *= (multiplication assignment), /= (division assignment), and %= (modulus assignment).

23. When evaluating an expression with values of mixed types, C++ automatically converts the operands to appropriate types.

24. You can explicitly convert a value from one type to the other using the `<static_cast>(type)` notation or the legacy c-style `(type)` notation.

25. Character type (`char`) represents a single character.

26. The character \ is called the escape character.

27. C++ allows you to use escape sequences to represent special characters such as `'\t'` and `'\n'`.

28. The characters `' '`, `'\t'`, `'\f'`, `'\r'`, and `'\n'` are known as the whitespace characters.

29. In computer science, midnight of January 1, 1970 is known as the *UNIX epoch.*

30. Programming errors can be categorized into three types: syntax errors, runtime errors, and logic errors.

31. Errors that occur during compilation are called *syntax errors* or *compilation errors.*

32. *Runtime errors* are those that cause a program to terminate abnormally.

33. *Logic errors* occur when a program does not perform the way it was intended to.

REVIEW QUESTIONS

Sections 2.2–2.7

2.1   Which of the following identifiers are valid? Which are C++ keywords?

```
x, X, a++, --a, 4#R, $4, #44, apps
main, int, count, radius
```

2.2 Translate the following algorithm into C++ code:

- Step 1: Declare a `double` variable named `miles` with initial value `100`;
- Step 2: Declare a `double` constant named `MILE_TO_KILOMETER` with value `1.609`;
- Step 3: Declare a `double` variable named `kilometer`, multiply `miles` and `MILE_TO_KILOMETER` and assign the result to `kilometer`.
- Step 4: Display `kilometer` to the console.

2.3 What are the benefits of using constants? Declare an `int` constant `SIZE` with value `20` using the `const` keyword. Declare an `int` constant `SIZE` with value `20` using the `#define` directive. What is the wrong in the following code?

```
#include <iostream>
#define PI 3.14159;
using namespace std;

int main()
{
  double temp = PI * 5;
  cout << temp << endl;
  return 0;
}
```

Section 2.8

2.4 Assume that `int a = 1` and `double d = 1.0`, and that each expression is independent. What are the results of the following expressions?

```
a = 46 / 9;
a = 46 % 9 + 4 * 4 - 2;
a = 45 + 43 % 5 * (23 * 3 % 2);
a %= 3 / a + 3;
d = 4 + d * d + 4;
d += 1.5 * 3 + (++a);
d -= 1.5 * 3 + a++;
```

2.5 Show the results of the following expressions.

```
56 % 6
78 % -4
-34 % 5
-34 % -5
5 % 1
1 % 5
```

2.6 If today is Tuesday, what will be the day in 100 days?

2.7 Find the size of `short`, `int`, `long`, `float`, and `double` on your machine.

2.8 What is the result of `25 / 4`? How would you rewrite the expression if you wished the result to be a floating-point number?

2.9 Show the output of the following statements.

```
cout << "25 / 4 is " << 25 / 4 << endl;
cout << "25 / 4.0 is " << 25 / 4.0 << endl;
cout << "3 * 2 / 4 is " << 3 * 2 / 4 << endl;
cout << "3.0 * 2 / 4 is " << 3.0 * 2 / 4 << endl;
```

2.10 How would you write the following arithmetic expression in C++?

(a) $\dfrac{4}{3(r + 34)} - 9(a + bc) + \dfrac{3 + d(2 + a)}{a + bd}$

(b) $5.5 \times (r + 2.5)^{2.5+t}$

2.11 Which of these statements are true?

(a) Any expression can be used as a statement in C++.
(b) The expression x++ can be used as a statement.
(c) The statement x = x + 5 is also an expression.
(d) The statement x = y = x = 0 is illegal.

2.12 Which of the following are correct literals for floating-point numbers?

```
12.3, 12.3e+2, 23.4e-2, -334.4, 20, 39F, 40D
```

2.13 Identify and fix the errors in the following code:

```
1 #include <iostream>
2 using namespace std;
3
4 int Main()
5 {
6     int i = k + 1;
7     cout << i++ << << endl;
8
9     int i = 1;
10    cout << i++ << << endl;
11
12    return 0;
13 }
```

Section 2.9

2.14 Can numeric values of different types be used together in a computation?

2.15 What does an explicit conversion from a **double** to an **int** do with the fractional part of the *double* value? Does casting change the variable being cast?

2.16 Show the following output.

```
double f = 12.5F;
int i = f;
cout << "f is " << f << endl;
cout << "i is " << i << endl;
```

Section 2.10

2.17 Use print statements to find out the ASCII code for '1', 'A', 'B', 'a', 'b'. Use print statements to find out the character for the decimal code 40, 59, 79, 85, 90. Use print statements to find out the character for the hexadecimal code 40, 5A, 71, 72, 7A.

2.18 Which of the following are correct literals for characters?

```
'1', '\t', '&', '\b', '\n'
```

2.19 How do you display characters \ and "?

2.20 Evaluate the following:

```
int i = '1';
int j = '1' + '2';
int k = 'a';
char c = 90;
```

2.21 Can the following conversions involving casting be allowed? If so, find the converted result.

```
char c = 'A';
int i = c;

float f = 1000.34f;
int i = f;

double d = 1000.34;
int i = d;

int i = 97;
char c = i;
```

2.22 Show the output of the following program:

```
#include <iostream>
using namespace std;

int main()
{
  char x = 'a';
  char y = 'c';

  cout << ++x << endl;
  cout << y++ << endl;
  cout << (x - y) << endl;

  return 0;
}
```

Sections 2.11–2.14

2.23 How do you obtain the current minute?

2.24 How do you denote a comment line and a comment paragraph?

2.25 What are the naming conventions for constants and variables? Which of the following items can be a constant or a variable according to the naming conventions?

MAX_VALUE, Test, read, readInt

2.26 Reformat the following program according to the programming style and documentation guidelines.

```
#include <iostream>
using namespace std;

int main()
{
cout << "2 % 3 = "<<2%3;
  return 0;
}
```

2.27 Describe syntax errors, runtime errors, and logic errors.

PROGRAMMING EXERCISES

 Note

The compiler usually gives a reason for a syntax error. If you don't know how to correct it, compare your program closely with similar examples in the text character by character.

learn from examples

Sections 2.2–2.9

2.1   (*Converting Celsius to Fahrenheit*) Write a program that reads a Celsius degree in double, converts it to Fahrenheit, and displays the result. The formula for the conversion is as follows:

```
fahrenheit = (9 / 5) * celsius + 32
```

(*Hint:* In C++, 9 / 5 is 1, so you need to write 9.0 / 5 in the program to obtain the correct result.)

Here is a sample run:

```
Enter a degree in Celsius: 43  ↵Enter
Fahrenheit degree is 109.4
```

2.2   (*Computing the volume of a cylinder*) Write a program that reads in the radius and length of a cylinder and computes volume using the following formulas:

```
area = radius * radius * π
volume = area * length
```

Here is a sample run:

```
Enter the radius and length of a cylinder: 5.5 12  ↵Enter
The area is 95.0331
The volume is 1140.4
```

2.3   (*Converting feet into meters*) Write a program that reads a number in feet, converts it to meters, and displays the result. One foot is 0.305 meter. Here is a sample run:

```
Enter a value for feet: 16  ↵Enter
The meter is 4.88
```

2.4   (*Converting pounds into kilograms*) Write a program that converts pounds into kilograms. The program prompts the user to enter a number in pounds, converts it to kilograms, and displays the result. One pound is 0.454 kilogram. Here is a sample run:

```
Enter a number in pounds: 55.5  ↵Enter
The kilograms is 25.197
```

2.5* (*Financial application: calculating tips*) Write a program that reads the subtotal and the gratuity rate and computes the gratuity and total. For example, if the user enters 10 for subtotal and 15 percent for gratuity rate, the program displays $1.5 as gratuity and $11.5 as total.

Here is a sample run:

```
Enter the subtotal and a gratuity rate: 15.69 15  ↵Enter
The gratuity is 2.3535 and total is 18.0435
```

2.6** (*Summing the digits in an integer*) Write a program that reads an integer between 0 and 1000 and adds all the digits in the integer. For example, if an integer is 932, the sum of all its digits is 14.

(*Hint:* Use the % operator to extract digits, and use the / operator to remove the extracted digit. For instance, 932 % 10 = 2 and 932 / 10 = 93.)

Here is a sample run:

```
Enter a number between 0 and 1000: 999  ↵Enter
The sum of the digits is 27
```

Section 2.10

2.7* (*Converting an uppercase letter to lowercase*) Write a program that prompts the user to enter an uppercase letter and converts it to a lowercase letter.

(*Hint:* In the ASCII table (see Appendix B), uppercase letters appear before lowercase letters. The offset between any uppercase letter and its corresponding lowercase letter is the same. So you can find a lowercase letter from its corresponding uppercase letter, as shown below.)

```
int offset = 'a' - 'A';
char lowercase = (char)(uppercase + offset);
```

Here is a sample run:

```
Enter an uppercase letter: T  ↵Enter
The lowercase letter is t
```

2.8* (*Finding the character of an ASCII code*) Write a program that receives an ASCII code (an integer between 0 and 128) and displays its character. For example, if the user enters 97, the program displays character a. Here is a sample run:

```
Enter an ASCII code: 69  ↵Enter
The character is E
```

Section 2.11

2.9* (*Financial application: monetary units*) Rewrite Listing 2.10, ComputeChange.cpp, to fix the possible loss of accuracy when converting a double value to an int value. Enter the input as an integer whose last two digits represent the cents. For example, the input 1156 represents 11 dollars and 56 cents.

2.10 (*Financial application: calculating interests*) If you know the balance and annual percentage interest rate, you can compute the interest on the next monthly payment using the following formula:

```
interest = balance × (annualInterestRate / 1200)
```

Write a program that reads the balance and annual percentage interest rate in this order and displays the interest for the next month. Here is a sample run:

```
Enter balance and interest rate (e.g., 3 for 3%): 1000 3.5  ↵Enter
The interest is 2.91667
```

2.11* (*Financial application: calculating the future investment value*) Write a program that reads in investment amount, annual interest rate, and number of years in this order, and displays the future investment value using the following formula:

$$\text{accumulatedValue} = \text{investmentAmount} \times (1 + \text{monthlyInterestRate})^{\text{numberOfYears}*12}$$

(*Hint:* Use the **pow(a, b)** function to compute **a** raised to the power of **b**.)

Here is a sample run:

```
Enter investment amount: 1000  ↵Enter
Enter monthly interest rate: 4.25  ↵Enter
Enter number of years: 1  ↵Enter
Accumulated value is 1043.34
```

2.12** (*Financial application: compound value*) Suppose you save $100 *each* month into a savings account with annual interest rate 5%. So, the monthly interest rate is 0.05 / 12 = 0.00417. After the first month, the value in the account becomes

```
100 * (1 + 0.00417) = 100.417
```

After the second month, the value in the account becomes

```
(100 + 100.417) * (1 + 0.00417) = 201.252
```

After the third month, the value in the account becomes

```
(100 + 201.252) * (1 + 0.00417) = 302.507
```

and so on.

Write a program to display the account value after the sixth month. (In Exercise 4.30, you will use a loop to simplify the code and display the account value for any month.)

2.13* (*Health application: computing BMI*) Body Mass Index (BMI) is a measure of health on weight. It can be calculated by taking your weight in kilograms and dividing by the square of your height in meters. Write a program that prompts the

Video Note
Computing BMI

user to enter a weight in pounds and height in inches and display the BMI. Note that one pound is 0.45359237 kilogram and one inch is 0.0254 meter. Here is a sample run:

```
Enter weight in pounds: 95.5  ↵Enter
Enter height in inches: 50  ↵Enter
BMI is 26.8573
```

2.14 (*Science: calculating energy*) Write a program that calculates the energy needed to heat water from an initial temperature to a final temperature. Your program should prompt the user to enter the water amount in kilograms and its initial and final temperatures. The formula to compute the energy is

```
Q = M * (final temperature – initial temperature) * 4184
```

where M is the weight of water in kilograms, temperatures are in degrees Celsius, and energy Q is measured in joules. Here is a sample run:

```
Enter the amount of water in kilograms: 55.5  ↵Enter
Enter the initial temperature: 3.5  ↵Enter
Enter the final temperature: 10.5  ↵Enter
The energy needed is 1.62548e+06
```

2.15* (*Science: wind-chill temperature*) How cold is it outside? We need to know more than the temperature alone. Other factors, including wind speed, relative humidity, and sunshine, play important roles in determining coldness outside. In 2001, the National Weather Service (NWS) implemented the new wind-chill temperature to measure the coldness using temperature and wind speed. The formula is

$$t_{wc} = 35.74 + 0.6215t_a - 35.75v^{0.16} + 0.4275t_av^{0.16}$$

where t_a is the outside temperature in degrees Fahrenheit and v is the speed in miles per hour. t_{wc} is the wind-chill temperature. The formula cannot be used for wind speeds below 2 mph or temperatures below −58°F or above 41°F.

Write a program that prompts the user to enter a temperature between −58°F and 41°F and a wind speed greater than or equal to 2 and displays the wind-chill temperature. Use pow(a, b) to compute $v^{0.16}$. Here is a sample run:

```
Enter the temperature in Fahrenheit: 5.3  ↵Enter
Enter the wind speed miles per hour: 6
The wind-chill index is -5.56707
```

2.16 (*Printing a table*) Write a program that displays the following table:

a	b	pow(a, b)
1	2	1
2	3	8
3	4	81
4	5	1024
5	6	15625

2.17 (*Geometry: distance of two points*) Write a program that prompts the user to enter two points (x1, y1) and (x2, y2) and displays their distances. The formula for computing the distance is $\sqrt{(x_2 - x_1)^2 + (y_2 - y_1)^2}$. Note that you can use pow(a, 0.5) to compute $\sqrt{a}$. Here is a sample run:

```
Enter x1 and y1: 1.5 -3.4  ↵Enter
Enter x2 and y2: 4 5  ↵Enter
The distance of the two points is 8.764131445842194
```

2.18 (*Geometry: area of a hexagon*) Write a program that prompts the user to enter the side of a hexagon and displays its area. The formula for computing the area of a hexagon is $Area = \dfrac{3\sqrt{3}}{2}s^2$, where s is the length of a side and $\sqrt{3} = 1.732$. Here is a sample run:

```
Enter the side: 5.5  ↵Enter
The area of the hexagon is 78.5895
```

2.19* (*Geometry: area of a triangle*) Write a program that prompts the user to enter three points (x1, y1), (x2, y2), (x3, y3) of a triangle and displays its area. The formula for computing the area of a triangle is

$$s = (side1 + side2 + side3)/2;$$

$$area = \sqrt{s(s - side1)(s - side2)(s - side3)}$$

Here is a sample run:

```
Enter three points for a triangle: 1.5 -3.4 4.6 5 9.5 -3.4  ↵Enter
The area of the triangle is 33.6
```

2.20 (*Physics: acceleration*) Average acceleration is defined as the change of velocity divided by the time taken to make the change, as shown in the following formula:

$$a = \frac{v_1 - v_0}{t}$$

Write a program that prompts the user to enter the starting velocity v_0 in meters/second, ending velocity v_1 in meters/second, and the time span t in seconds, and displays the average acceleration. Here is a sample run:

```
Enter v0, v1, and t: 5.5 50.9 4.5  ↵Enter
The average acceleration is 10.0889
```

2.21 (*Physics: finding runway length*) Given an airplane's acceleration a and take-off speed v, you can compute the minimum runway length needed for the airplane to take off using the following formula:

$$length = \frac{v^2}{2a}$$

Write a program that prompts the user to enter v in meters/second and acceleration a in meters/seconds^2 and displays the minimum runway length. Here is a sample run:

```
Enter v and a: 60 3.5 ↵Enter
The minimum runway length for this airplane is 514.286
```

The program
ible by 5 (lines

3.4 Probl

You can find out
question asks wl

1	3
9	11
17	19
25 27	

Set

FIGURE 3.2 The

The birth date
ple, if the birth d
sets are 1, 2, and
The way the
numbers in each
in binary. If a da
Setk. For examp
binary 1 + 10
11111, so it appe
+ 10000 = 111
Listing 3.2 gi
(lines 10–16), in
Set5 (lines 58–6
to date (lines 19

LISTING 3.2

```
1  #include <i
2  using names
3
4  int main()
5  {
6     int date
7     char answ
8
9     // Prompt
10    cout << '
11    cout << '
12           "
13           "
14           "
15    cout << "
16    cin >> an
17
18    if (answe
19      date +=
20
```

cou
display

N
Ir
a
b

b
b
b

3.3 One-Way if Statements

The pr
with si
which

A o
tax for

```
if
{

}
```

The

FIGURE
true.

If th
As an e

```
if (
{
    ar
    co

}
```

CHAPTER 3

SELECTIONS

Objectives

- To declare `bool` type and write Boolean expressions using comparison operators (§3.2).
- To implement selection control using one-way `if` statements (§3.3)
- To program the `GuessBirthDate` game using one-way `if` statements (§3.4).
- To implement selection control using two-way `if` statements (§3.5).
- To implement selection control using nested `if` statements (§3.6).
- To avoid common errors in `if` statements (§3.7).
- To program using selection statements for a variety of examples (`BMI`, `ComputeTax`, `SubtractionQuiz`) (§§3.8–3.10).
- To generate random numbers using the `rand` function and set a seed using the `srand` function (§3.10).
- To combine conditions using logical operators (`&&`, `||`, and `!`) (§3.11).
- To program using selection statements with combined conditions (`LeapYear`, `Lottery`) (§§3.12–3.13).
- To implement selection control using `switch` statements (§3.14).
- To write expressions using the conditional operator (§3.15).
- To format output using stream manipulators (§3.16).
- To examine the rules governing operator precedence and operator associativity (§3.17).

problem

pseudoco

```
if i > 0
{
   cout << "
}
```

comparis

```
if (i > 0)
{
   cout << '
}
```

compare

enter input

check 5

check even

== vs. =

Boolean

in Set2?

in Set3?

in Set4?

in Set5?

```
21   // Prompt the user for Set2
22   cout << "\nIs your birth date in Set2?" << endl;
23   cout << " 2  3  6  7\n" <<
24           "10 11 14 15\n" <<
25           "18 19 22 23\n" <<
26           "26 27 30 31" << endl;
27   cout << "Enter N for No and Y for Yes: ";
28   cin >> answer;
29
30   if (answer == 'Y')
31     date += 2;
32
33   // Prompt the user for Set3
34   cout << "\nIs your birth date in Set3?" << endl;
35   cout << " 4  5  6  7\n" <<
36           "12 13 14 15\n" <<
37           "20 21 22 23\n" <<
38           "28 29 30 31" << endl;
39   cout << "Enter N for No and Y for Yes: ";
40   cin >> answer;
41
42   if (answer == 'Y')
43     date += 4;
44
45   // Prompt the user for Set4
46   cout << "\nIs your birth date in Set4?" << endl;
47   cout << " 8  9 10 11\n" <<
48           "12 13 14 15\n" <<
49           "24 25 26 27\n" <<
50           "28 29 30 31"   << endl;
51   cout << "Enter N for No and Y for Yes: ";
52   cin >> answer;
53
54   if (answer == 'Y')
55     date += 8;
56
57   // Prompt the user for Set5
58   cout << "\nIs your birth date in Set5?" << endl;
59   cout << "16 17 18 19\n" <<
60           "20 21 22 23\n" <<
61           "24 25 26 27\n" <<
62           "28 29 30 31" << endl;
63   cout << "Enter N for No and Y for Yes: ";
64   cin >> answer;
65
66   if (answer == 'Y')
67     date += 16;
68
69   cout << "Your birth date is " << date << endl;
70
71   return 0;
72 }
```

```
Is your birth date in Set1?
 1  3  5  7
 9 11 13 15
17 19 21 23
25 27 29 31
Enter N for No and Y for Yes: Y ↵Enter
```

```
Is your birth date in Set2?
 2   3   6   7
10 11 14 15
18 19 22 23
26 27 30 31
Enter N for No and Y for Yes: Y  ⏎Enter

Is your birth date in Set3?
 4   5   6   7
12 13 14 15
20 21 22 23
28 29 30 31
Enter N for No and Y for Yes: N  ⏎Enter

Is your birth date in Set4?
 8   9  10 11
12 13 14 15
24 25 26 27
28 29 30 31
Enter N for No and Y for Yes: N  ⏎Enter

Is your birth date in Set5?
16 17 18 19
20 21 22 23
24 25 26 27
28 29 30 31
Enter N for No and Y for Yes: Y  ⏎Enter
Your birth date is 19
```

line#	date	answer	output
6	0		
7		undefined value	
16		y	
19	1		
28		y	
31	3		
40		N	
52		N	
64		y	
67	19		
69			Your birth date is 19

3.5 if . . . else Statements

A one-way `if` statement performs an action if the specified condition is `true`. If the condition is `false`, nothing is done. But what if you want to perform an alternative action when the condition is `false`? You can use a *two-way* `if` statement. A two-way `if` statement specifies different actions, depending on whether the condition is `true` or `false`.

Here is the syntax for a two-way statement:

```
if (booleanExpression)
{
    statement(s)-for-the-true-case;
}
else
{
    statement(s)-for-the-false-case;
}
```

The flow chart of the statement is shown in Figure 3.3.

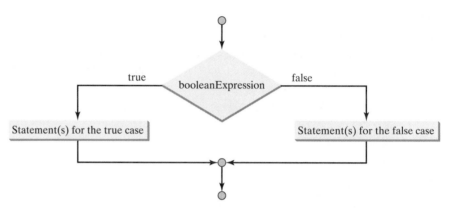

FIGURE 3.3 An `if ... else` statement executes statements for the true case if the `booleanExpression` evaluates to `true`; otherwise, it executes statements for the false case.

If the `booleanExpression` evaluates to `true`, the statement(s) for the true case is executed; otherwise, the statement(s) for the false case is executed. For example, consider the following code:

two-way if statement

```
if (radius >= 0)
{
    area = radius * radius * PI;
    cout << "The area for the circle of radius " <<
        radius << " is " << area;
}
else
{
    cout << "Negative radius";
}
```

If `radius >= 0` is `true`, `area` is computed and displayed; if it is `false`, the message `"Negative radius"` is displayed.

As usual, the braces can be omitted if they enclose only one statement. In the preceding example, therefore, the braces enclosing the `cout << "Negative radius"` statement can be omitted.

Here is another example of the use of the `if ... else` statement. The example checks whether a number is even or odd, as follows:

```
if (number % 2 == 0)
    cout << number << " is even.";
else
    cout << number << " is odd.";
```

3.6 Nested **if** Statements

The statement in an `if` or `if ... else` statement can be any legal C++ statement, including another `if` or `if ... else` statement. The inner `if` statement is said to be *nested* inside the outer `if` statement. The inner `if` statement can contain another `if` statement; in fact, there is no limit to the depth of the nesting. For example, the following is a nested `if` statement:

```
if (i > k)
{
  if (j > k)
    cout << "i and j are greater than k";
}
else
  cout << "i is less than or equal to k";
```

nested if statement

The `if (j > k)` statement is nested inside the `if (i > k)` statement.

The nested `if` statement can be used to implement multiple alternatives. The statement given in Figure 3.4(a), for instance, assigns a letter grade to the variable `grade` according to the score, with multiple alternatives.

```
if (score >= 90.0)
  grade = 'A';
else
  if (score >= 80.0)
    grade = 'B';
  else
    if (score >= 70.0)
      grade = 'C';
    else
      if (score >= 60.0)
        grade = 'D';
      else
        grade = 'F';
```

(a)

Equivalent

This is better

```
if (score >= 90.0)
  grade = 'A';
else if (score >= 80.0)
  grade = 'B';
else if (score >= 70.0)
  grade = 'C';
else if (score >= 60.0)
  grade = 'D';
else
  grade = 'F';
```

(b)

FIGURE 3.4 A preferred format for multiple alternative `if` statements is shown in (b).

The execution of this `if` statement proceeds as follows. The first condition (`score >= 90.0`) is tested. If it is `true`, the grade becomes `'A'`. If it is `false`, the second condition (`score >= 80.0`) is tested. If the second condition is `true`, the grade becomes `'B'`. If that condition is `false`, the third condition and the rest of the conditions (if necessary) continue to be tested until a condition is met or all the conditions prove to be `false`. In the latter case, the grade becomes `'F'`. Note that a condition is tested only when all the conditions that come before it are `false`.

The `if` statement in Figure 3.4(a) is equivalent to the `if` statement in Figure 3.4(b). In fact, Figure 3.4(b) is the preferred writing style for multiple-alternative `if` statements. This style avoids deep indentation and makes the program easy to read.

Note

The `else` clause matches the most recent unmatched `if` clause in the same block. For example, the statement in (a) below is equivalent to the statement in (b).

*matching **else** with **if***

```
int i = 1; j = 2; k = 3;

if (i > j)
  if (i > k)
    cout << "A";
else
    cout << "B";
```

(a)

Equivalent

This is better with correct indentation

```
int i = 1, j = 2, k = 3;

if (i > j)
  if (i > k)
    cout << "A";
  else
    cout << "B";
```

(b)

Since `(i > j)` is false, the statement in (a) and (b) displays nothing. To force the `else` clause to match the first `if` clause, you must add a pair of braces:

```
int i = 1, j = 2, k = 3;

if (i > j)
{
  if (i > k)
    cout << "A";
}
else
  cout << "B";
```

This statement displays B.

Tip

assign **bool** variable

Often new programmers write as in (a) the code that assigns a test condition to a **bool** variable:

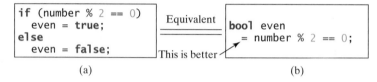

(a)   (b)

The code can be simplified by assigning the test value directly to the variable, as shown in (b).

3.7 Common Errors in Selection Statements

The following errors are common among new programmers.

Common Error 1: Forgetting Necessary Braces

The braces can be omitted if the block contains a single statement. However, forgetting the braces when they are needed for grouping multiple statements is a common programming error. If you modify the code by adding new statements in an `if` statement without braces, you will have to insert the braces. For example, the following code in (a) is wrong. It should be written with braces to group multiple statements as in (b).

```
if (radius >= 0)
  area = radius * radius * PI;
  cout << "The area "
    << " is " << area;
```

```
if (radius >= 0)
{
  area = radius * radius * PI;
  cout << "The area "
    << " is " << area;
}
```

(a) Wrong   (b) Correct

Common Error 2: Wrong Semicolon at the `if` Line

Adding a semicolon at the `if` line, as shown in (a) below, is a common mistake.

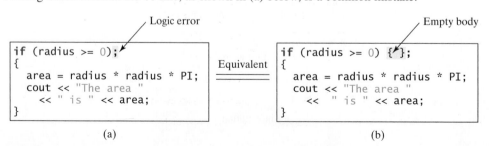

(a)   (b)

This mistake is hard to find, because it is neither a compilation error nor a runtime error; it is a logic error. The code in (a) is equivalent to that in (b) with an empty block.

Common Error 3: Mistakenly Using = for ==

The equality comparison operator is two equal signs (==). In C++, if you mistakenly use = for ==, it will lead a logic error. Consider the following code:

```
if (count = 1)
  cout << "count is zero" << endl;
else
  cout << "count is not zero" << endl;
```

It always displays "count is zero", because count = 1 assigns 1 to count and the assignment expression is evaluated to 1, which is true. Recall that any nonzero value evaluates true and zero value evaluates false.

Common Error 4: Redundant Testing of Boolean Values

To test whether a bool variable is true or false in a test condition, it is redundant to use the equality comparison operator like the code in (a):

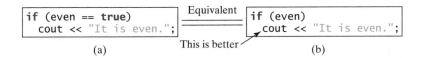

```
if (even == true)
  cout << "It is even.";
```
(a)

Equivalent
— This is better

```
if (even)
  cout << "It is even.";
```
(b)

Instead, it is better to use the bool variable directly, as in (b). Another good reason for doing this is to avoid errors that are difficult to detect. Using the = operator instead of the == operator to compare equality of two items in a test condition is a common error. It could lead to the following erroneous statement:

```
if (even = true)
  cout << "It is even.";
```

This statement does not have syntax errors. It assigns true to even so that even is always true.

3.8 Problem: Computing Body Mass Index

Body Mass Index (BMI) is a measure of health on weight. It can be calculated by taking your weight in kilograms and dividing by the square of your height in meters. BMI for people 16 years or older is interpreted as follows:

BMI	Interpretation
below 16	seriously underweight
16-18	underweight
18-24	normal weight
24-29	overweight
29-35	seriously overweight
above 35	gravely overweight

Write a program that prompts the user to enter a weight in pounds and height in inches and displays the BMI. Note that one pound is 0.45359237 kilograms and one inch is 0.0254 meters. Listing 3.3 gives the program.

LISTING 3.3 ComputeBMI.cpp

```cpp
1  #include <iostream>
2  using namespace std;
3
4  int main()
5  {
6    // Prompt the user to enter weight in pounds
7    cout << "Enter weight in pounds: ";
8    double weight;
9    cin >> weight;
10
11   // Prompt the user to enter height in inches
12   cout << "Enter height in inches: ";
13   double height;
14   cin >> height;
15
16   const double KILOGRAMS_PER_POUND = 0.45359237; // Constant
17   const double METERS_PER_INCH = 0.0254; // Constant
18
19   // Compute BMI
20   double weightInKilogram = weight * KILOGRAMS_PER_POUND;
21   double heightInMeter = height * METERS_PER_INCH;
22   double bmi = weightInKilogram /
23     (heightInMeter * heightInMeter);
24
25   // Display result
26   cout << "Your BMI is " << bmi << endl;
27   if (bmi < 16)
28     cout << "You are seriously underweight" << endl;
29   else if (bmi < 18)
30     cout << "You are underweight" << endl;
31   else if (bmi < 24)
32     cout << "You are normal weight" << endl;
33   else if (bmi < 29)
34     cout << "You are overweight" << endl;
35   else if (bmi < 35)
36     cout << "You are seriously overweight" << endl;
37   else
38     cout << "You are gravely overweight" << endl;
39
40   return 0;
41 }
```

input weight — (line 9)

input height — (line 14)

compute bmi — (line 22)

display output — (line 26)

```
Enter weight in pounds: 146  ⏎Enter
Enter height in inches: 70  ⏎Enter
Your BMI is 20.9486
You are normal weight
```

line#	weight	height	weightInKilogram	heightInMeters	bmi	output
9	146					
14		70				

line#	weight	height	weightInKilogram	heightInMeters	bmi	output
20			66.22448602			
21				1.778		
22					20.9486	
26						Your BMI is 20.95
32						You are normal weight

Two constants `KILOGRAMS_PER_POUND` and `METERS_PER_INCH` are defined in lines 16–17. Using constants here makes the program easy to read.

You should enter the input that covers all possible cases for BMI to ensure that the program works for all cases.   test all cases

3.9 Problem: Computing Taxes

The United States federal personal income tax is calculated based on filing status and taxable income. There are four filing statuses: single filers, married filing jointly, married filing separately, and head of household. The tax rates vary every year. Table 3.2 shows the rates for 2002. If you are, say, single with a taxable income of $10,000, the first $6,000 is taxed at 10% and the other $4,000 is taxed at 15%. So, your tax is $1,200.

TABLE 3.2 2002 U.S. Federal Personal Tax Rates

Tax Rate	Single Filers	Married Filing Jointly or Qualifying window/widower	Married Filing Separately	Head of Household
10%	Up to $6,000	Up to $12,000	Up to $6,000	Up to $10,000
15%	$6,001–$27,950	$12,001–$46,700	$6,001–$23,350	$10,001–$37,450
27%	$27,951–$67,700	$46,701–$112,850	$23,351–$56,425	$37,451–$96,700
30%	$67,701–$141,250	$112,851–$171,950	$56,426–$85,975	$96,701–$156,600
35%	$141,251–$307,050	$171,951–$307,050	$85,976–$153,525	$156,601–$307,050
38.6%	$307,051 or more	$307,051 or more	$153,526 or more	$307,051 or more

You are to write a program to compute personal income tax. Your program should prompt the user to enter the filing status and taxable income and should then compute the tax. Enter 0 for single filers, 1 for married filing jointly, 2 for married filing separately, and 3 for head of household.

Your program computes the tax for the taxable income based on the filing status. The filing status can be determined using `if` statements, outlined as follows:

```
if (status == 0)
{
  // Compute tax for single filers
}
else if (status == 1)
{
  // Compute tax for married file jointly
}
```

```
    else if (status == 2)
    {
      // Compute tax for married file separately
    }
    else if (status == 3)
    {
      // Compute tax for head of household
    }
    else
    {
      // Display wrong status
    }
```

For each filing status, there are six tax rates. Each rate is applied to a certain amount of taxable income. For example, of a taxable income of $400,000 for single filers, $6,000 is taxed at 10%, (27,950–6,000) at 15%, (67,700–27,950) at 27%, (141,250–67,700) at 30%, (307,050–141,250) at 35%, and (400,000–307,050) at 38.6%.

Listing 3.4 gives the solution to compute taxes for single filers. The complete solution is left as exercise.

LISTING 3.4 ComputeTax.cpp

```cpp
 1 #include <iostream>
 2 using namespace std;
 3
 4 int main()
 5 {
 6   // Prompt the user to enter filing status
 7   cout << "Enter the filing status\n"
 8        << "(0-single filer, 1-married jointly,\n"
 9        << "2-married separately, 3-head of household): ";
10   int status;
11   cin >> status;
12
13   // Prompt the user to enter taxable income
14   cout << "Enter the taxable income: ";
15   double income;
16   cin >> income;
17
18   // Compute tax
19   double tax = 0;
20
21   if (status ==  0)
22   {
23     // Compute tax for single filers
24     if  (income <= 6000)
25       tax = income * 0.10;
26     else if (income <= 27950)
27       tax = 6000 * 0.10 + (income - 6000) * 0.15;
28     else if (income <= 67700)
29       tax = 6000 * 0.10 + (27950 - 6000) * 0.15 +
30         (income - 27950) * 0.27;
31     else if (income <= 141250)
32       tax = 6000 * 0.10 + (27950 - 6000) * 0.15 +
33         (67700 - 27950) * 0.27 + (income - 67700) * 0.30;
34     else if (income <= 307050)
35       tax = 6000 * 0.10 + (27950 - 6000) * 0.15 +
36         (67700 - 27950) * 0.27 + (141250 - 67700) * 0.30 +
37         (income - 141250) * 0.35;
```

enter status

enter income

compute tax

```
38    else
39       tax = 6000 * 0.10 + (27950 - 6000) * 0.15 +
40          (67700 - 27950) * 0.27 + (141250 - 67700) * 0.30 +
41          (307050 - 141250) * 0.35 + (income - 307050) * 0.386;
42    }
43    else if (status == 1)
44    {
45       // Compute tax for married filing jointly
46       // Left as exercise
47    }
48    else if (status == 2)
49    {
50       // Compute tax for married filing separately
51       // Left as an exercise
52    }
53    else if (status == 3)
54    {
55       // Compute tax for head of household
56       // Left as an exercise
57    }
58    else
59    {
60       cout << "Error: invalid status";
61       return 0;
62    }
63
64    // Display the result
65    cout << "Tax is" << static_cast<int>(tax * 100) / 100.0 << endl;    display tax
66
67    return 0;
68 }
```

```
Enter the filing status
(0-single filer, 1-married jointly,
2-married separately, 3-head of household): 0 ⏎Enter
Enter the taxable income: 400000 ⏎Enter
Tax is 130599
```

line#	status	income	tax	output
11	0			
16		400000		
19			0	
39			130599	
65				Tax is 130599

The program receives the filing status and taxable income. The multiple alternative `if` statements (lines 21, 43, 48, 53, 58) check the filing status and compute the tax based on it.

To test a program, you should provide input that covers all cases. For this program, your input should cover all statuses (0, 1, 2, 3). For each status, test the tax for each of the six brackets. So, there are 24 cases altogether.

test all cases

Tip

incremental development and testing

For all programs, write a small amount of code and test it before adding more code. This approach, called *incremental development and testing*, makes debugging easier, because the errors are likely to be in the new code you just added.

3.10 Problem: A Math Learning Tool

Suppose you are to develop a program to let a first-grader practice subtractions. The program randomly generates two single-digit integers, number1 and number2, with number1 > number2, and displays to the student a question such as "What is 9 − 2?" After the student types the answer, the program displays a message indicating whether the answer is correct.

rand function

To generate a random number, use the rand() function in the cstdlib header file. This function returns a random integer between 0 and RAND_MAX. RAND_MAX is platform-dependent constant. In Visual C++, RAND_MAX is 32767.

pseudorandom

The numbers rand() produces are pseudorandom. That is, every time it is executed on the same system, rand() produces the same sequence of numbers. On the author's machine, for example, executing these three statements will always produce the numbers 130, 10982, and 1090.

```
cout << rand() << endl << rand() << endl << rand() << endl;
```

Why? The reason is that the rand() function's algorithm uses a value called the *seed* to control how to generate the numbers. By default the seed value is 1. If you change the seed to a different value, the sequence of random numbers will be different. To change the seed, use the srand(seed) function in the cstdlib header file. To ensure that the seed value is different each time you run the program, use time(0). As discussed in §2.11.3, "Problem: Displaying the Current Time," invoking time(0) returns the current time in seconds elapsed since the time 00:00:00 on January 1, 1970 GMT. So, the following code will display a random integer every second you run it on any machine.

srand function

```
srand(time(0));
cout << rand() << endl;
```

To obtain a random integer between 0 and 9, use

```
rand() % 10
```

The program may be set up to work as follows:

- **Step 1:** Generate two single-digit integers into number1 and number2.
- **Step 2:** If number1 < number2, swap number1 with number2.
- **Step 3:** Prompt the student to answer "What is number1 – number2?"
- **Step 4:** Check the student's answer and display whether it is correct.

The complete program is shown in Listing 3.5.

LISTING 3.5 SubtractionQuiz.cpp

include **ctime**
include **cstdlib**

```
1 #include <iostream>
2 #include <ctime>    // for time function
3 #include <cstdlib> // for rand and srand functions
4 using namespace std;
5
```

```
 6 int main()
 7 {
 8   // 1. Generate two random single-digit integers
 9   srand(time(0));                                              set a seed
10   int number1 = rand() % 10;                                   random number1
11   int number2 = rand() % 10;                                   random number2
12
13   // 2. If number1 < number2, swap number1 with number2
14   if (number1 < number2)
15   {
16     int temp = number1;                                        swap numbers
17     number1 = number2;
18     number2 = temp;
19   }
20
21   // 3. Prompt the student to answer "What is number1 - number2?"
22   cout << "What is " << number1 << " - " << number2 << "? ";
23   int answer;                                                  enter answer
24   cin >> answer;
25
26   // 4. Grade the answer and display the result
27   if (number1 - number2 == answer)                             display result
28     cout << "You are correct!";
29   else
30     cout << "Your answer is wrong.\n" << (number1 << " - " << number2)
31          << " should be " << (number1 - number2) << endl;
32
33   return 0;
34 }
```

```
What is 5 - 2? 3  ↵Enter
You are correct!
```

```
What is 4 - 2? 1  ↵Enter
Your answer is wrong.
4 - 2 should be 2
```

line#	number1	number2	temp	answer	output
10	2				
11		4			
16			2		
17	4				
18		2			
24				1	
30					Your answer is wrong 4 – 2 should be 2

To swap two variables `number1` and `number2`, a temporary variable `temp` (line 16) is used to first hold the value in `number1`. The value in `number2` is assigned to `number1` (line 17) and the value in `temp` is assigned to `number2` (line 18).

3.11 Logical Operators

Sometimes, a combination of several conditions determines whether a statement is executed. You can use logical operators to combine these conditions. *Logical operators*, also known as *Boolean operators*, operate on Boolean values to create a new Boolean value. Table 3.3 gives a list of Boolean operators. Table 3.4 defines the not (!) operator. The not (!) operator negates true to false and false to true. Table 3.5 defines the and (&&) operator. The and (&&) of two Boolean operands is true if and only if both operands are true. Table 3.6 defines the or (||) operator. The or (||) of two Boolean operands is true if at least one of the operands is true.

TABLE 3.3 Boolean Operators

Operator	Name	Description
!	not	logical negation
&&	and	logical conjunction
||	or	logical disjunction

TABLE 3.4 Truth Table for Operator !

p	!p	Example (*assume age = 24, gender = 'F'*)
true	false	!(age > 18) is false, because (age > 18) is true.
false	true	!(gender == 'M') is true, because (grade == 'M') is false.

TABLE 3.5 Truth Table for Operator &&

p1	p2	p1 && p2	Example (*assume age = 24, gender = 'F'*)
false	false	false	(age > 18) && (gender == 'F') is true, because (age
false	true	false	> 18) and (gender == 'F') are both true.
true	false	false	(age > 18) && (gender != 'F') is false, because
true	true	true	(gender != 'F') is false.

TABLE 3.6 Truth Table for Operator ||

p1	p2	p1 || p2	Example (*assume age = 24, gender = 'F'*)
false	false	false	(age > 34) || (gender == 'F') is true, because
false	true	true	(gender == 'F') is true.
true	false	true	(age > 34) || (gender == 'M') is false, because (age
true	true	true	> 34) and (gender == 'M') are both false.

Listing 3.6 gives a program that checks whether a number is divisible by 2 and 3, by 2 or 3, and by 2 or 3 but not both:

LISTING 3.6 TestBooleanOperators.cpp

```
1 #include <iostream>
2 using namespace std;
3
4 int main()
5 {
6   int number;
7   cout << "Enter an integer: ";                                          enter input
8   cin >> number;
9
10  if (number % 2 == 0 && number % 3 == 0)                                &&
11    cout << number << " is divisible by 2 and 3." << endl;
12
13  if (number % 2 == 0 || number % 3 == 0)                                ||
14    cout << number << " is divisible by 2 or 3." << endl;
15
16  if ((number % 2 == 0 || number % 3 == 0) &&
17      !(number % 2 == 0 && number % 3 == 0))
18    cout << number << " divisible by 2 or 3, but not both." << endl;
19
20  return 0;
21 }
```

```
Enter an integer: 4 ↵Enter
4 is divisible by 2 or 3.
4 divisible by 2 or 3, but not both.
```

```
Enter an integer: 18 ↵Enter
18 is divisible by 2 and 3.
18 is divisible by 2 or 3.
```

(number % 2 == 0 && number % 3 == 0) (line 10) checks whether the number is divisible by 2 and 3. (number % 2 == 0 || number % 3 == 0) (line 13) checks whether the number is divisible by 2 or 3. So, lines 16–17

```
((number % 2 == 0 || number % 3 == 0) &&
  !(number % 2 == 0 && number % 3 == 0))
```

check whether the number is divisible by 2 or 3 but not both.

Caution

In mathematics, the expression   incompatible operands

```
1 <= numberOfDaysInAMonth <= 31
```

is correct. However, it is incorrect in C++, because `1 <= numberOfDaysInAMonth` is evaluated to a `bool` value, and then a `bool` value (`1` for `true` and `0` for `false`) is compared with `31`, which would lead to a logic error. The correct expression is

```
(1 <= numberOfDaysInAMonth) && (numberOfDaysInAMonth <= 31)
```

De Morgan's law

 Note

De Morgan's law, named after Indian-born British mathematician and logician Augustus De Morgan (1806–1871), can be used to simplify Boolean expressions. The law states

```
!(condition1 && condition2)  is same as  !condition1 || !condition2
!(condition1 || condition2)  is same as  !condition1 && !condition2
```

So, line 17 in the preceding example,

```
!(number % 2 == 0 && number % 3 == 0)
```

can be simplified using an equivalent expression

```
(number % 2 != 0 || number % 3 != 0)
```

As another example,

```
!(n == 2 || n == 3)
```

is better written as

```
n != 2 && n != 3
```

If one of the operands of an **&&** operator is `false`, the expression is `false`; if one of the operands of an **||** operator is `true`, the expression is `true`. C++ uses these properties to improve the performance of these operators. When evaluating **p1 && p2**, C++ evaluates **p1** and, if it is true, evaluates **p2**; otherwise it does not evaluate **p2**. When evaluating **p1 || p2**, C++ evaluates **p1** and, if it is `false`, evaluates **p2**; otherwise it does not evaluate **p2**. Therefore, we refer to **&&** as the *conditional* or *short-circuit AND* operator and to **||** as the *conditional* or *short-circuit OR* operator.

short-circuit operator

3.12 Problem: Determining Leap Year

leap year

A year is a *leap year* if it is divisible by 4 but not by 100 or if it is divisible by 400. So, you can use the following Boolean expressions to check whether a year is a leap year:

```cpp
// A leap year is divisible by 4
bool isLeapYear = (year % 4 == 0);

// A leap year is divisible by 4 but not by 100
isLeapYear = isLeapYear && (year % 100 != 0);

// A leap year is divisible by 4 but not by 100 or divisible by 400
isLeapYear = isLeapYear || (year % 400 == 0);
```

or you can combine all these expressions into one:

```cpp
isLeapYear = (year % 4 == 0 && year % 100 != 0) || (year % 400 == 0)
```

Listing 3.7 gives a program that lets the user enter a year and checks whether it is a leap year.

LISTING **3.7** LeapYear.cpp

```cpp
1 #include <iostream>
2 using namespace std;
3
```

```
 4 int main()
 5 {
 6   cout << "Enter a year: ";
 7   int year;
 8   cin >> year;
 9
10   // Check whether the year is a leap year
11   bool isLeapYear =
12     (year % 4 == 0 && year % 100 != 0) || (year % 400 == 0);
13
14   // Display the result
15   if (isLeapYear)
16     cout << year << " is a leap year.";
17   else
18     cout << year << " is not a leap year.";
19
20   return 0;
21 }
```

leap year?

if statement

```
Enter a year: 2008 ↵Enter
2008 is a leap year.
```

```
Enter a year: 2002 ↵Enter
2002 is not a leap year.
```

3.13 Problem: Lottery

Suppose you are to develop a program to play lottery. The program randomly generates a lottery of a two-digit number, prompts the user to enter a two-digit number, and determines whether the user wins according to the following rule:

1. If the user input matches the lottery in exact order, the award is $10,000.

2. If the user input matches the lottery, the award is $3,000.

3. If one digit in the user input matches a digit in the lottery, the award is $1,000.

The complete program is shown in Listing 3.8.

LISTING 3.8 Lottery.cpp

```
 1 #include <iostream>
 2 #include <ctime> // for time function
 3 #include <cstdlib> // for rand and srand functions
 4 using namespace std;
 5
 6 int main()
 7 {
 8   // Generate a lottery
 9   srand(time(0));
10   int lottery = rand() % 100;
11
12   // Prompt the user to enter a guess
13   cout << "Enter your lottery pick (two digits): ";
```

generate a lottery

enter a guess

```cpp
14    int guess;
15    cin >> guess;
16
17    // Get digits from lottery
18    int lotteryDigit1 = lottery / 10;
19    int lotteryDigit2 = lottery % 10;
20
21    // Get digits from guess
22    int guessDigit1 = guess / 10;
23    int guessDigit2 = guess % 10;
24
25    cout << "The lottery number is " << lottery << endl;
26
27    // Check the guess
28    if (guess == lottery)
29      cout << "Exact match: you win $10,000" << endl;
30    else if (guessDigit2 == lotteryDigit1
31        && guessDigit1 == lotteryDigit2)
32      cout << "Match all digits: you win $3,000" << endl;
33    else if (guessDigit1 == lotteryDigit1
34          || guessDigit1 == lotteryDigit2
35          || guessDigit2 == lotteryDigit1
36          || guessDigit2 == lotteryDigit2)
37      cout << "Match one digit: you win $1,000" << endl;
38    else
39      cout << "Sorry, no match" << endl;
40
41    return 0;
42  }
```

exact match?

match all digits?

match one digit?

```
Enter your lottery pick (two digits): 45  ↵Enter
The lottery number is 12
Sorry, no match
```

```
Enter your lottery pick: 23  ↵Enter
The lottery number is 34
Match one digit: you win $1,000
```

line# variable	10	15	18	19	22	23	37
lottery	34						
guess		23					
lotteryDigit1			3				
lotteryDigit2				4			
guessDigit1					2		
guessDigit2						3	
output							Match one digit: you win $1,000

The program generates a lottery using the `rand()` function (line 10) and prompts the user to enter a guess (line 15). Note that `guess % 10` obtains the last digit from `guess`, and `guess / 10` obtains the first digit from `guess`, since `guess` is a two-digit number (lines 22–23).

The program checks the guess against the lottery number in this order:

1. First check whether the guess matches the lottery exactly (line 28).

2. If not, check whether the reversal of the guess matches the lottery (lines 30–31).

3. If not, checks whether one digit is in the lottery (lines 33–36).

4. If not, nothing matches.

3.14 **switch** Statements

The `if` statement in Listing 3.4, ComputeTax.cpp, makes selections based on a single `true` or `false` condition. There are four cases for computing taxes, which depend on the value of `status`. To fully account for all the cases, nested `if` statements were used. Overuse of nested `if` statements makes a program difficult to read. C++ provides a `switch` statement to handle multiple cases efficiently. You may write the following `switch` statement to replace the nested `if` statement in Listing 3.4:

```
switch (status)
{
  case 0:  compute taxes for single filers;
           break;
  case 1:  compute taxes for married filing jointly;
           break;
  case 2:  compute taxes for married filing separately;
           break;
  case 3:  compute taxes for head of household;
           break;
  default: cout << "Errors: invalid status" << endl;
}
```

The flow chart of the preceding `switch` *statement* is shown in Figure 3.5.

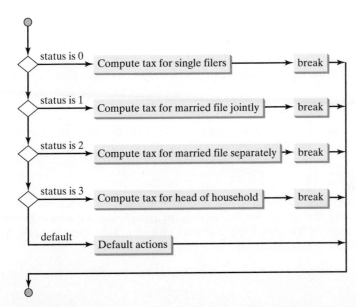

FIGURE 3.5 The `switch` statement checks all cases and executes the statements in the matched case.

This statement checks to see whether the status matches the value 0, 1, 2, or 3, in that order. If matched, the corresponding tax is computed; if not matched, a message is displayed. Here is the full syntax for the switch statement:

switch statement

```
switch (switch-expression)
{
  case value1: statement(s)1;
               break;
  case value2: statement(s)2;
               break;
  ...
  case valueN: statement(s)N;
               break;
  default:     statement(s)-for-default;
}
```

The switch statement observes the following rules:

- The switch-expression must yield an integral value and must always be enclosed in parentheses.

- The value1, ..., and valueN are integral constant expressions, meaning that they cannot contain variables, such as 1 + x.

- When the value in a case statement matches the value of the switch-expression, the statements *starting from this case* are executed until either a break statement or the end of the switch statement is reached.

- The keyword break is optional. The break statement immediately ends the switch statement.

- The default case, which is optional, can be used to perform actions when none of the specified cases matches the switch-expression.

- The case statements are checked in sequential order, but the order of the cases (including the default case) does not matter. However, it is good programming style to follow the logical sequence of the cases and place the default case at the end.

Note

integral value

In C++, a char or bool value is treated as an integral. So, this type of value can be used in a switch statement as a switch expression or case value.

Caution

without **break**

Do not forget to use a break statement when one is needed. Once a case is matched, the statements starting from the matched case are executed until a break statement or the end of the switch statement is reached. This phenomenon is referred to as *fall-through* behavior. For example, the following code displays character a three times if ch is 'a':

fall-through behavior

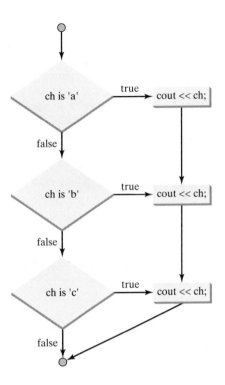

```
switch (ch)
{
    case 'a': cout << ch;
    case 'b': cout << ch;
    case 'c': cout << ch;
}
```

Tip
To avoid programming errors and improve code maintainability, it is a good idea to put a comment in a case clause if break is purposely omitted.

3.15 Conditional Expressions

You might want to assign a variable a value that is restricted by certain conditions. For example, the following statement assigns 1 to y if x is greater than 0, and –1 to y if x is less than or equal to 0.

```
if (x > 0)
    y = 1;
else
    y = -1;
```

Alternatively, as in the next example, you can use a conditional expression to achieve the same result:

```
y = (x > 0) ? 1 : -1;
```

Conditional expressions have a completely different structure and do not include an explicit if. The syntax is shown below:

```
booleanExpression ? expression1 : expression2;
```

conditional expression

The result of this *conditional expression* is `expression1` if `booleanExpression` is `true`; otherwise the result is `expression2`.

Suppose you want to assign the larger number between variable `num1` and `num2` to `max`. You can simply write a statement using the conditional expression:

```
max = (num1 > num2) ? num1 : num2;
```

As another example, the following statement displays the message `"num is even"` if `num` is even, and otherwise displays `"num is odd."`

```
cout << ((num % 2 == 0) ? "num is even" : "num is odd");
```

Note

The symbols `?` and `:` appear together in a conditional expression. They form a conditional operator. It is called a *ternary operator* because it uses three operands. It is the only ternary operator in C++.

3.16 Formatting Output

If you wish to display only two digits after the decimal point in a floating-point value, you may write the code like this:

```
double x = 2.0 / 3;
cout << "x is " << static_cast<int>(x * 100) / 100.0;
```

```
x is 0.66
```

However, a better way to accomplish this task is to format the output using stream manipulators. You already know how to display console output using the `cout` object. C++ provides additional functions for formatting how a value is displayed. These functions are called *stream manipulators* and are included in the `iomanip` header file. Table 3.7 summarizes several useful stream manipulators.

stream manipulator

TABLE 3.7 Frequently Used Stream Manipulators

Operator	Description
`setprecision(n)`	sets the precision of a floating-point number
`fixed`	displays floating-point numbers in fixed-point notation
`showpoint`	causes a floating-point number to be displayed with a decimal point with trailing zeros even if it has no fractional part
`setw(width)`	specifies the width of a print field
`left`	justifies the output to the left
`right`	justifies the output to the right

3.16.1 `setprecision(n)` Manipulator

You can specify the total number of digits displayed for a floating-point number using the `setprecision(n)` manipulator, where n is the number of significant digits (i.e., the total number of digits that appear before and after the decimal point). If a number to be displayed has more digits than the specified precision, it will be rounded. For example, the code

```
double number = 12.34567;
cout << setprecision(3) << number << " "
     << setprecision(4) << number << " "
     << setprecision(5) << number << " "
     << setprecision(6) << number << endl;
```

displays

    12.3☐12.35☐12.346☐12.3457

where the square box (☐) denotes a blank space.

The value of number is displayed using precision 3, 4, 5, and 6, respectively. Using precision 3, 12.34567 is rounded to 12.3. Using precision 4, 12.34567 is rounded to 12.35. Using precision 5, 12.34567 is rounded to 12.346. Using precision 6, 12.34567 is rounded to 12.3457.

The setprecision manipulator remains in effect until the precision is changed. So,

```
double number = 12.34567;
cout << setprecision(3) << number << " " << endl;
cout << 9.34567 << " " << 121.3457 << " " << 0.2367 << endl;
```

displays

    12.3☐9.35☐121☐0.237

The precision is set to 3 for the first value, and it remains effective for the next two values, because it has not been changed.

If the width is not sufficient for an integer, the setprecision manipulator is ignored. For example,

```
cout << setprecision(3) << 23456 << endl;
```

displays

    23456

3.16.2 `fixed` Manipulator

Sometimes, the computer automatically displays a large floating-point number in scientific notation. On the Windows machine, for example, the statement

```
cout << 232123434.357;
```

displays

    2.32123e+08

You can use the `fixed` manipulator to force the number to be displayed in nonscientific notation with a fixed number of digits after the decimal point. For example,

```
cout << fixed << 232123434.357;
```

displays

    232123434.357000

By default, the fixed number of digits after the decimal point is 6. You can change it using the `fixed` manipulator along with the `setprecision` manipulator. When it is used after the `fixed` manipulator, the `setprecision` manipulator specifies the number of digits after the decimal point. For example,

```
double monthlyPayment = 345.4567;
double totalPayment = 78676.887234;
cout << fixed << setprecision(2)
     << monthlyPayment << endl
     << totalPayment << endl;
```

displays

```
345.46
78676.89
```

3.16.3 `showpoint` Manipulator

By default, floating-point numbers that do not have a fractional part are not displayed with a decimal point. You can use the `fixed` manipulator to force the floating-point numbers to be displayed with a decimal point and a fixed number of digits after the decimal point. Alternatively, you can use the `showpoint` manipulator together with the `setprecision` manipulator.

For example,

```
cout << setprecision(6);
cout << 1.23 << endl;
cout << showpoint << 1.23 << endl;
cout << showpoint << 123.0 << endl;
```

displays

```
1.23
1.23000
123.000
```

The `setprecision(6)` function sets the precision to 6. So, the first number 1.23 is displayed as 1.23. Because the `showpoint` manipulator forces the floating-point number to be displayed with a decimal point and trailing zeros if necessary to fill in the positions, the second number 1.23 is displayed as 1.23000 with trailing zeros, and the third number 123.0 is displayed as 123.000 with a decimal point and trailing zeros.

3.16.4 `setw(width)` Manipulator

By default, `cout` uses just the number of the positions needed for an output. You can use `setw(width)` to specify the minimum number of columns for an output. For example,

```
cout << setw(8) << "C++" << setw(6) << 101 << endl;
cout << setw(8) << "Java" << setw(6) << 101 << endl;
cout << setw(8) << "HTML" << setw(6) << 101 << endl;
```

displays

```
□□□□□C++□□□101
□□□□Java□□□101
□□□□HTML□□□101
```

The output is right-justified within the specified columns. In line 1, `setw(8)` specifies that "C++" is displayed in eight columns. So, there are five spaces before C++. `setw(6)` specifies that 101 is displayed in six columns. So, there are three spaces before 101.

Notice that the `setw` manipulator affects only the next output. For example,

```
cout << setw(8) << "C++" << 101 << endl;
```

displays

◻◻◻◻◻C++101

The `setw(8)` manipulator affects only the next output "C++", not 101.

Note that the argument n for `setw(n)` and `setprecision(n)` can be an integer variable, expression, or constant.

3.16.5 `left` and `right` Manipulators

Note that the `setw` manipulator uses right justification by the default. You can use the `left` manipulator to left-justify the output and use the `right` manipulator to right-justify the output. For example,

```
cout << right;
cout << setw(8) << 1.23 << endl;
cout << setw(8) << 351.34 << endl;
```

displays

◻◻◻◻1.23
◻◻◻351.34

```
cout << left;
cout << setw(8) << 1.23 << endl;
cout << setw(8) << 351.34 << endl;
```

displays

1.23
351.34

3.17 Operator Precedence and Associativity

Operator precedence and associativity determine the order in which operators are evaluated. Suppose that you have this expression:

```
3 + 4 * 4 > 5 * (4 + 3) - 1
```

What is its value? How does the compiler know the execution order of the operators? The expression in the parentheses is evaluated first. (Parentheses can be nested, in which case the expression in the inner parentheses is executed first.) When evaluating an expression without parentheses, the compiler applies the operators according to the *precedence* rule and the associativity rule. The precedence rule defines precedence for operators, as shown in Table 3.8, which displays the operators you have learned so far. Operators are listed in decreasing order of precedence from top to bottom. Operators with the same precedence appear in the same group. (See Appendix C, "Operator Precedence Chart," for a complete list of C++ operators and their precedence.)

precedence

If operators with the same precedence are next to each other, their *associativity* determines the order of evaluation. All binary operators except assignment operators are *left-associative*.

associativity

TABLE 3.8 Operator Precedence Chart

Precedence	Operator
	`var++` and `var--` (postfix), `static_cast<type>()` (cast)
	+, - (Unary plus and minus), `++var` and `--var` (prefix)
	! (Not)
	*, /, % (Multiplication, division, and modulus)
	+, - (Binary addition and subtraction)
	<, <=, >, >= (Comparison)
	==, != (Equality)
	&& (AND)
	|| (OR)
	=, +=, -=, *=, /=, %= (Assignment operator)

For example, since + and − are of the same precedence and are left-associative, we have the equivalence

$$a - b + c - d \overset{equivalent}{=\!=\!=} ((a - b) + c) - d$$

Assignment operators are *right-associative*. Therefore, we have the equivalence

$$a = b += c = 5 \overset{equivalent}{=\!=\!=} a = (b += (c = 5))$$

Suppose a, b, and c are 1 before the assignment. After the whole expression is evaluated, a becomes 6, b becomes 6, and c becomes 5. Note that left associativity for the assignment operator would not make sense.

Applying the operator precedence and associativity rule, we evaluate the expression 3 + 4 * 4 > 5 * (4 + 3) - 1 as follows:

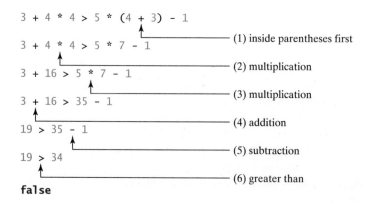

```
3 + 4 * 4 > 5 * (4 + 3) - 1
                                        (1) inside parentheses first
3 + 4 * 4 > 5 * 7 - 1
                                        (2) multiplication
3 + 16 > 5 * 7 - 1
                                        (3) multiplication
3 + 16 > 35 - 1
                                        (4) addition
19 > 35 - 1
                                        (5) subtraction
19 > 34
                                        (6) greater than
false
```

Tip
You can use parentheses to force an evaluation order as well as to make a program easy to read. Use of redundant parentheses does not slow down the execution of the expression.

KEY TERMS

Boolean expression   74
Boolean value   74
`bool` type   74
`break` statement   96
conditional operator   98
fall-through behavior   96

one-way if statement   75
operator associativity   101
operator precedence   101
short-circuit operator   92
switch statement   95
two-way if statement   79

CHAPTER SUMMARY

1. The relational operators (<, <=, ==, !=, >, >=) work with numbers and characters and yield a Boolean value.

2. The equality comparison operator is two equal signs (==), not a single equal sign (=). The latter symbol is for assignment.

3. Internally, C++ uses 1 to represent `true` and 0 for `false`.

4. If you display a `bool` value to the console, 1 is displayed if the value is `true` and 0 if the value is `false.`

5. In C++, you can assign a numeric value to a `bool` variable. Any nonzero value evaluates `true` and zero value evaluates `false`.

6. Selection statements incorporate conditions for executing statements.

7. There are several types of selection statements: one-way `if` statements, two-way `if` statements, nested `if` statements, `switch` statements, and conditional expressions.

8. A one-way `if` statement executes an action if and only if the condition is `true`. The syntax for a one-way selection statement is shown below:

```
if (booleanExpression)
{
    statement(s);
}
```

9. A two-way `if` statement uses the following syntax:

```
if (booleanExpression)
{
    statement(s)-for-the-true-case;
}
else
{
    statement(s)-for-the-false-case;
}
```

If the `booleanExpression` evaluates to `true`, the statement(s) for the true case is executed; otherwise, the statement(s) for the false case is executed.

10. The Boolean operators &&, ||, and ! operate with Boolean values and variables.

11. When evaluating **p1 && p2**, C++ first evaluates **p1** and then, if it is **true**, evaluates **p2**; otherwise it does not evaluate **p2**. && is referred to as the *short-circuit AND* operator,

12. When evaluating **p1 || p2**, C++ first evaluates **p1** and then, if it is **false** evaluates **p2**; otherwise it does not evaluate **p2**. || is referred to as the *short-circuit OR* operator.

13. The **switch** statement makes control decisions based on a switch expression of type **char**, **byte**, **short**, or **int**.

14. The keyword **break** is optional in a **switch** statement, but it is normally used at the end of each case in order to terminate the remainder of the **switch** statement. If the **break** statement is not present, the next **case** statement will be executed.

15. The operators in arithmetic expressions are evaluated in the order determined by the rules of parentheses, operator precedence, and associativity.

16. Parentheses can be used to force the order of evaluation to occur in any sequence.

17. Operators with higher precedence are evaluated earlier. For operators of the same precedence, their associativity determines the order of evaluation

18. All binary operators except assignment operators are left-associative, and assignment operators are right-associative.

REVIEW QUESTIONS

Section 3.2

3.1 List six comparison operators.

3.2 Assuming that x is 1, show the result of the following Boolean expressions.

```
(x > 0)
(x < 0)
(x != 0)
(x >= 0)
(x != 1)
```

Sections 3.3–3.10

3.3 What is wrong in the following code?

```
if radius >= 0
{
  area = radius * radius * PI;
  cout << "The area for the circle of " <<
    " radius " << radius << " is " << area;
}
```

3.4 What is the output of the code in (a) and (b) below if **number** is **30** and **35**, respectively?

```
if (number % 2 == 0)
   cout << number << " is even." << endl;

cout << number << " is odd." << endl;
```

(a)

```
if (number % 2 == 0)
   cout << number << " is even." << endl;
else
   cout << number << " is odd." << endl;
```

(b)

3.5 Can the following conversions involving casting be allowed? If so, find the converted result.

```cpp
bool b = true;
int i = b;

i = 1;
b = i;
```

3.6 Suppose x = 3 and y = 2. Show the output, if any, of the code below. What is the output if x = 3 and y = 4? If x = 2 and y = 2? Draw a flow chart of the following code.

```cpp
if (x > 2)
{
  if (y > 2)
  {
    int z = x + y;
    cout << "z is " << z << endl;
  }
}
else
  cout << "x is " << x << endl;
```

3.7 Which of the following statements are equivalent? Which ones are correctly indented?

(a)	(b)	(c)	(d)

`if (i > 0) if`
`(j > 0)`
`x = 0; else`
`if (k > 0) y = 0;`
`else z = 0;`
	`if (i > 0) {`
	`  if (j > 0)`
	`    x = 0;`
	`  else if (k > 0)`
	`    y = 0;`
	`}`
	`else`
	`  z = 0;`
		`if (i > 0)`
		`  if (j > 0)`
		`    x = 0;`
		`  else if (k > 0)`
		`    y = 0;`
		`  else`
		`    z = 0;`
			`if (i > 0)`
			`  if (j > 0)`
			`    x = 0;`
			`  else if (k > 0)`
			`    y = 0;`
			`else`
			`  z = 0;`

3.8 Suppose x = 2 and y = 3. Show the output, if any, of the following code. What is the output if x = 3 and y = 2? What is the output if x = 3 and y = 3? (*Hint:* Indent the statement correctly first.)

```cpp
if (x > 2)
  if (y > 2)
  {
    int z = x + y;
    cout << "z is " << z << endl;
  }
else
  cout << "x is " << x << endl;
```

3.9 (a) Write an if statement that increases pay by 3% if score is greater than 90.
(b) Write an if statement that increases pay by 3% if score is greater than 90, otherwise increases pay by 1%.

3.10 What is wrong in the following code?

```cpp
if (score >= 60.0)
  grade = 'D';
```

```
        else if (score >= 70.0)
          grade = 'C';
        else if (score >= 80.0)
          grade = 'B';
        else if (score >= 90.0)
          grade = 'A';
        else
          grade = 'F';
```

3.11 Are the following two statements equivalent?

```
if (income <= 10000)
  tax = income * 0.1;
else if (income <= 20000)
  tax = 1000 +
    (income - 10000) * 0.15;
```

```
if (income <= 10000)
  tax = income * 0.1;
else if (income > 10000 &&
          income <= 20000)
  tax = 1000 +
    (income - 10000) * 0.15;
```

3.12 Which of the following is a possible output from invoking `rand()`?

```
323.4, 5, 34, 1, 0.5, 0.234
```

3.13 How do you generate a random integer i such that $0 \le i < 20$?
How do you generate a random integer i such that $10 \le i < 20$?
How do you generate a random integer i such that $10 \le i \le 50$?
Find out what RAND_MAX is on your machine.

Sections 3.11–3.13

3.14 Assuming that x is 1, show the result of the following Boolean expressions:

```
(true) && (3 > 4)
!(x > 0) && (x > 0)
(x > 0) || (x < 0)
(x != 0) || (x == 0)
(x >= 0) || (x < 0)
(x != 1) == !(x == 1)
```

3.15 Write a Boolean expression that evaluates to `true` if a number stored in variable num is between 1 and 100.

3.16 Write a Boolean expression that evaluates to `true` if a number stored in variable num is between 1 and 100 or the number is negative.

3.17 Assume that x and y are `int` type. Which of the following are correct expressions?

```
x > y > 0
x = y && y
x /= y
x or y
x and y
(x != 0) || (x = 0)
```

3.18 Suppose that x is 1. What is x after the evaluation of the following expressions?

```
(a) (x > 1) && (x++ > 1)
(b) (x >= 1) && (x++ > 1)
```

3.19 What is the value of the expression ch >= 'A' && ch <= 'Z' if ch is 'A', 'p', 'E', or '5'?

3.20 Suppose that, when you run the program, you enter input 2 3 6 from the console. What is the output?

```cpp
#include <iostream>
using namespace std;

int main()
{
  double x, y, z;
  cin >> x >> y >> z;

  cout << "(x < y && y < z) is " << (x < y && y < z) << endl;
  cout << "(x < y || y < z) is " << (x < y || y < z) << endl;
  cout << "!(x < y) is " << !(x < y) << endl;
  cout << "(x + y < z) is " << (x + y < z) << endl;
  cout << "(x + y < z) is " << (x + y < z) << endl;

  return 0;
}
```

Section 3.14

3.21 What data types are required for a switch variable? If the keyword break is not used after a case is processed, what statement is executed next? Can you convert a switch statement to an equivalent if statement, or vice versa? What are the advantages of using a switch statement?

3.22 What is y after the following switch statement is executed?

```cpp
x = 3; y = 3;
switch (x + 3)
{
  case 6:  y = 1;
   default: y += 1;
}
```

3.23 Use a switch statement to rewrite the following if statement and draw the flow chart for the switch statement:

```cpp
if (a == 1)
  x += 5;
else if (a == 2)
  x += 10;
else if (a == 3)
  x += 16;
else if (a == 4)
  x += 34;
```

Section 3.15

3.24 Rewrite the following if statement using the conditional operator:

```cpp
if (count % 10 == 0)
  cout << count << "\n";
else
  cout << count << " ";
```

Section 3.16

3.25 To use stream manipulators, which header file must you include?

3.26 Show the output of the following statements.

```
cout << setw(10) << "C++" << setw(6) << 101 << endl;
cout << setw(8) << "Java" << setw(5) << 101 << endl;
cout << setw(6) << "HTML" << setw(4) << 101 << endl;
```

3.27 Show the output of the following statements:

```
double number = 93123.1234567;
cout << setw(10) << setprecision(5) << number;
cout << setw(10) << setprecision(4) << number;
cout << setw(10) << setprecision(3) << number;
cout << setw(10) << setprecision(8) << number;
```

3.28 Show the output of the following statements:

```
double monthlyPayment = 1345.4567;
double totalPayment = 866.887234;

cout << setprecision(7);
cout << monthlyPayment << endl;
cout << totalPayment << endl;

cout << fixed << setprecision(2);
cout << setw(8) << monthlyPayment << endl;
cout << setw(8) << totalPayment << endl;
```

3.29 Show the output of the following statements:

```
cout << right;
cout << setw(6) << 21.23 << endl;
cout << setw(6) << 51.34 << endl;
```

3.30 Show the output of the following statements.

```
cout << left;
cout << setw(6) << 21.23 << endl;
cout << setw(6) << 51.34 << endl;
```

Section 3.17

3.31 List the precedence order of the Boolean operators. Evaluate the following expressions:

```
true || true && false
true && true || false
```

3.32 Show and explain the output of the following code:

```
(a) int i = 0;
    i = i + (i = 1);
    cout << i << endl;

(b) int i = 0;
    i = (i = 1) + i;
    cout << i << endl;
```

3.33 Assume that `int a = 1` and `double d = 1.0`, and that each expression is independent. What are the results of the following expressions?

```
a = (a = 3) + a;
a = a + (a = 3);
a += a + (a = 3);
a = 5 + 5 * 2 % a--;
a = 4 + 1 + 4 * 5 % (++a + 1);
d += 1.5 * 3 + (++d);
d -= 1.5 * 3 + d++;
```

3.34 Is `(x > 0 && x < 10)` the same as `((x > 0) && (x < 10))`? Is `(x > 0 || x < 10)` the same as `((x > 0) || (x < 10))`? Is `(x > 0 || x < 10 && y < 0)` the same as `(x > 0 || (x < 10 && y < 0))`?

PROGRAMMING EXERCISES

 Pedagogical Note
For each exercise, students should carefully analyze the problem requirements and design strategies for solving the problem before coding.

think before coding

 Pedagogical Note
Instructors may ask students to document analysis and design for selected exercises. Students should use their own words to analyze the problem, including the input, output, and what needs to be computed, and describe how to solve the problem using pseudocode.

document analysis and design

 Debugging Tip
Before you ask for help, read and explain the program to yourself, and trace it using several representative inputs by hand or using an IDE debugger. By debugging your own mistakes, you learn how to program

learn from mistakes

Sections 3.2–3.10

3.1* (*Algebra: solving linear equations*) You can use Cramer's rule to solve the following 2 × 2 system of linear equation:

$$ax + by = e \qquad x = \frac{ed - bf}{ad - bc} \qquad y = \frac{af - ec}{ad - bc}$$
$$cx + dy = f$$

Write a program that prompts the user to enter a, b, c, d, e, and f, and display the result. If $ad - bc$ is 0, report that `"The equation has no solution."`

```
Enter a, b, c, d, e, f: 9.0 4.0 3 -5 -6 -21 ↵Enter
x is -2.0 and y is 3.0
```

```
Enter a, b, c, d, e, f: 1.0 2.0 2 4 4 5 ↵Enter
The equation has no solution
```

3.2 (*Checking whether a number is even*) Write a program that reads an integer and checks whether it is even. Here are the sample runs of this program:

```
Enter an integer: 25 ↵Enter
Is 25 an even number? false
```

```
Enter an integer: 2000 ↵Enter
Is 2000 an even number? true
```

3.3* (*Algebra: solving quadratic equations*) The two roots of a quadratic equation $ax^2 + bx + c = 0$ can be obtained using the following formula:

$$r_1 = \frac{-b + \sqrt{b^2 - 4ac}}{2a} \text{ and } r_2 = \frac{-b - \sqrt{b^2 - 4ac}}{2a}$$

$b^2 - 4ac$ is called the discriminant of the quadratic equation. If it is positive, the equation has two real roots. If it is zero, the equation has one root. If it is negative, the equation has no real roots.

Write a program that prompts the user to enter values for a, b, and c and displays the result based on the discriminant. If the discriminant is positive, display two roots. If the discriminant is 0, display one root. Otherwise, display "The equation has no real roots".

Note you can use **Math.pow(x, 0.5)** to compute $\sqrt{x}$. Here is a sample run.

```
Enter a, b, c: 1.0 3 1 ↵Enter
The roots are -0.381966 and -2.61803
```

```
Enter a, b, c: 1 2.0 1 ↵Enter
The root is -1
```

```
Enter a, b, c: 1 2 3 ↵Enter
The equation has no real roots
```

3.4 (*Financial application: monetary units*) Modify Listing 2.10, ComputeChange.cpp, to display only the nonzero denominations, using singular words for single units such as 1 dollar and 1 penny, and plural words for more than one unit such as 2 dollars and 3 pennies.

3.5* (*Sorting three integers*) Write a program that sorts three integers. The integers are entered from the console and stored in variables **num1**, **num2**, and **num3**, respectively. The program sorts the numbers so that $num1 \leq num2 \leq num3$.

3.6 (*Random character*) Write a program that displays a random uppercase letter.

3.7 (*Financial application: computing taxes*) Listing 3.4, ComputeTax.cpp, gives the source code to compute taxes for single filers. Complete Listing 3.4 to give the complete source code. Your program should prompt the user to enter filing status and then the income. If a wrong filing status is entered, the program should display "Error: invalid status".

3.8 (*Science: day of the week*) Zeller's congruence is an algorithm developed by Christian Zeller to calculate the day of the week. The formula is

$$h = \left(q + \left\lfloor \frac{26(m + 1)}{10} \right\rfloor + k + \left\lfloor \frac{k}{4} \right\rfloor + \left\lfloor \frac{j}{4} \right\rfloor + 5j \right) \% 7$$

where

■ h is the day of the week (0: Saturday, 1: Sunday, 2: Monday, 3: Tuesday, 4: Wednesday, 5: Thursday, 6: Friday).

- q is the day of the month.
- m is the month (3: March, 4: April, ..., 12: December). January and February are counted as months 13 and 14 of the previous year.
- j is the century (i.e., $\left\lfloor \dfrac{year}{10} \right\rfloor$).
- k is the year of the century (i.e., *year* % 7).

Write a program that prompts the user to enter a year, month, and day of the month, and displays the name of the day of the week. Here are some sample

```
Enter year: (e.g., 2008): 2002 ↵Enter
Enter month: 1-12: 3 ↵Enter
Enter the day of the month: 1-31: 26 ↵Enter
Day of the week is Tuesday
```

```
Enter year: (e.g., 2008): 2008 ↵Enter
Enter month: 1-12: 1 ↵Enter
Enter the day of the month: 1-31: 1 ↵Enter
Day of the week is Tuesday
```

runs: (*Hint:* $\lfloor n \rfloor$ = *static_cast* <int> *n* for a positive *n*. January and February are counted as **13** and **14** in the formula. So, you need to convert the user input **1** to **13** and **2** to **14** for the month and change the year to the previous year.)

3.9* (*Game: addition quiz*) Listing 3.5, SubtractionQuiz.cpp, randomly generates a subtraction question. Revise the program to randomly generate an addition question with two integers less than **100**. p 88

3.10* (*Game: addition for three numbers*) Listing 3.5, SubtractionQuiz.cpp, randomly generates a subtraction question. Revise the program to randomly generate an addition question with three integers less than **100**.

3.11* (*Game: head or tail*) Write a program that lets the user guess the coin's head or tail. The program randomly generates an integer **0** or **1**, which represents the head or the tail. The program prompts the user to enter a guess and reports whether the guess is correct or incorrect.

3.12* (*Health application: BMI*) Revise Listing 3.3, ComputeBMI.cpp, to let the user enter weight, feet, and inches. For example, if a person is **5** feet and **10** inches, you will enter **5** for feet and **10** for inches.

Sections 3.11–3.17

3.13*** (*Game: lottery*) Revise Listing 3.8, Lottery.cpp, to generate a lottery of a three-digit number. The program prompts the user to enter a three-digit number and determines whether the user wins according to the following rules: p 93

1. If the user input matches the lottery in exact order, the award is $10,000.
2. If the user input matches the lottery, the award is $3,000.
3. If one digit in the user input matches a digit in the lottery, the award is $1,000.

3.14* (*Science: wind-chill temperature*) Exercise 2.15 gives a formula to compute the wind-chill temperature. The formula is valid for temperatures in the range between −58°F and 41°F and wind speed greater than or equal to **2**. Write a program that prompts the user to enter a temperature and a wind speed. If the input is valid, the program displays the wind-chill temperature; otherwise, it displays a message indicating whether the temperature and/or wind speed is invalid.

3.15* (*Game: scissor, rock, paper*) Write a program that plays the popular scissor–rock–paper game. (A scissor can cut a paper, a rock can knock a scissor, and a paper can wrap a rock.) The program randomly generates a number **0**, **1**, or **2** representing scissor, rock, or paper. It prompts the user to enter a number **0**, **1**, or **2** and displays a message indicating whether the user or the computer wins or draws.

3.16 (*Computing the perimeter of a triangle*) Write a program that reads three edges for a triangle and computes the perimeter if the input is valid. Otherwise, display that the input is invalid. The input is valid if the sum of any two edges is greater than the third edge.)

3.17** (*Business: checking ISBN*) An **ISBN** (International Standard Book Number) consists of 10 digits $d_1d_2d_3d_4d_5d_6d_7d_8d_9d_{10}$. The last digit d_{10} is a checksum, which is calculated from the other nine digits using the following formula:

$$(d_1 \times 1 + d_2 \times 2 + d_3 \times 3 + d_4 \times 4 + d_5 \times 5 + d_6 \times 6 + d_7 \times 7$$
$$+ d_8 \times 8 + d_9 \times 9) \% 11$$

According to the ISBN convention, if the checksum is **10**, the last digit is denoted X. Write a program that prompts the user to enter the first 9 digits and displays the 10-digit ISBN (including leading zeros). Your program should read the input as an integer.

3.18** (*Finding the number of days in a month*) Write a program that prompts the user to enter the year and month in this order, and displays the number of days in the month. For example, if the user entered month 2 and year 2000, the program should display that February 2000 has 29 days. If the user entered month 3 and year 2005, the program should display that March 2005 has 31 days.

3.19** (*Geometry: point in a circle?*) Write a program that prompts the user to enter a point (**x**, **y**) and checks whether the point is within the circle centered at (**0**, **0**) with radius **10**. For example, (**4**, **5**) is inside the circle and (**9**, **9**) is outside the circle, as shown in Figure 3.6(a).

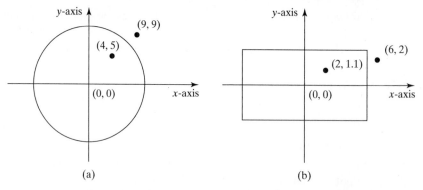

FIGURE 3.6 (a) Points inside and outside the circle; (b) points inside and outside the rectangle.

(*Hint:* A point is in the circle if its distance to (**0**, **0**) is less than or equal to **10**. The formula for computing the distance is $\sqrt{(x_2 - x_1)^2 + (y_2 - y_1)^2}$.) Here are two sample runs:

```
Enter a point with two coordinates: 4 5  Enter
Point (4.0, 5.0) is in the circle
```

```
Enter a point with two coordinates: 9 9 ↵Enter
Point (9.0, 9.0) is not in the circle
```

3.20**(*Geometry: point in a rectangle?*) Write a program that prompts the user to enter a point (x, y) and checks whether it is within the rectangle centered at (0, 0) with width 10 and height 5. For example, (2, 1.1) is inside the rectangle and (6, 2) is outside the circle, as shown in Figure 3.6(b). (*Hint:* A point is in the rectangle if its horizontal distance to (0, 0) is less than or equal to 10 / 2 and its vertical distance to (0, 0) is less than or equal to 5 / 2.) Here are two sample runs:

```
Enter a point with two coordinates: 2 1.1 ↵Enter
Point (2.0, 1.1) is in the rectangle
```

```
Enter a point with two coordinates: 6 2 ↵Enter
Point (6.0, 2.0) is not in the rectangle
```

3.21**(*Game: picking a card*) Write a program that simulates picking a card from a deck of 52 cards. For each card your program should display the rank (Ace, 2, 3, 4, 5, 6, 7, 8, 9, 10, Jack, Queen, King) and suit (Clubs, Diamonds, Hearts, Spades). Here is a sample run of the program:

```
The card you picked is Jack of Hearts
```

3.22 (*Using the && and || operators*) Write a program that prompts the user to enter an integer and determines whether it is divisible by 5 and 6, whether it is divisible by 5 or 6, and whether it is divisible by 5 or 6 but not both. Here is a sample run of this program:

```
Enter an integer: 10 ↵Enter
Is 10 divisible by 5 and 6? false
Is 10 divisible by 5 or 6? true
Is 10 divisible by 5 or 6, but not both? true
```

3.23* (*Validating triangles*) Write a program that reads three edges for a triangle and determines whether the input is valid. The input is valid if the sum of any two edges is greater than the third edge. Here are the sample runs of this program:

```
Enter three edges: 1 2.5 1 ↵Enter
Can edges 1, 2.5, and 1 form a triangle? false
```

```
Enter three edges: 2.5 2 1 ↵Enter
Can edges 2.5, 2, and 1 form a triangle? true
```

3.24* (*Phone key pads*) The international standard letter/number mapping found on the telephone is shown below:

1	2 ABC	3 DEF
4 GHI	5 JKL	6 MNO
7 PQRS	8 TUV	9 WXYZ
	0	

Write a program that prompts the user to enter an uppercase letter and displays its corresponding number.

```
Enter an uppercase letter: A  ↵Enter
The corresponding number is 2
```

```
Enter an uppercase letter: t  ↵Enter
Invalid input
```

3.25** (*Geometry: points in triangle?*) Suppose a right triangle is placed in a two-dimensional plain as shown below.

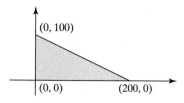

The right angle point is placed at (0, 0), and the other two points are placed at (200, 0), and (0, 100). Write a program that prompts the user to enter a point with *x*- and *y*-coordinates and determines whether the point is inside the triangle. Here are the sample runs:

```
Enter a point's x- and y-coordinates: 100.5 25.5  ↵Enter
The point is in the triangle
```

```
Enter a point's x- and y-coordinates: 100.5 50.5  ↵Enter
The point is not in the triangle
```

CHAPTER 4

LOOPS

Objectives

- To write programs for executing statements repeatedly using a `while` loop (§4.2).
- To develop programs for `GuessNumber` and `SubtractionQuizLoop` (§§4.2.1–4.2.2).
- To control a loop with the user confirmation (§4.2.3).
- To control a loop with a sentinel value (§4.2.4).
- To obtain large input from a file using input redirection rather than typing from the keyboard (§4.2.5).
- To write loops using `do-while` statements (§4.3).
- To write loops using `for` statements (§4.4).
- To discover the similarities and differences of three types of loop statements (§4.5).
- To write nested loops (§4.6).
- To learn the techniques for minimizing numerical errors (§4.7).
- To learn loops from a variety of examples (`GCD`, `FutureTuition`, `PrintPyramid`, `PrimeNumber`) (§§4.8, 4.10).
- To implement program control with `break` and `continue` (§4.9).

4.1 Introduction

Suppose that you need to print a string (e.g., `"Welcome to C++!"`) a hundred times. It would be tedious to write a hundred times:

```
cout << "Welcome to C++!\n";
```

problem

why loop?

So, how do you solve this problem?

C++ provides a powerful control structure called a *loop*, which controls how many times in succession an operation or a sequence of operations is performed. Using a loop statement, you don't have to code the print statement a hundred times; you simply tell the computer to print a string a hundred times.

Loops are structures that control repeated executions of a block of statements. The concept of looping is fundamental to programming. C++ provides three types of loop statements: `while` loops, `do-while` loops, and `for` loops.

4.2 The `while` Loop

The syntax for the `while` loop is:

while loop

```
while (loop-continuation-condition)
{
  // Loop body
  Statement(s);
}
```

loop body

iteration

Figure 4.1(a) shows the `while`-loop flow chart. The part of the loop that contains the statements to be repeated is the *loop body*. A single execution of a loop body is an *iteration of the loop*. Each loop contains a `loop-continuation-condition`, a Boolean expression that controls the body's execution. It is always evaluated beforehand. If its evaluation is true, the loop body is executed; otherwise the entire loop terminates and the program control turns to the statement that follows the `while` loop. For example, the following `while` loop prints `Welcome to C++!` a hundred times.

(a)   (b)

FIGURE 4.1 The `while` loop repeatedly executes the statements in the loop body when the `loop-continuation-condition` evaluates to `true`.

```cpp
int count = 0;
while (count < 100)
{
  cout << "Welcome to C++!\n";
  count++;
}
```

The flow chart of the preceding statement is shown in Figure 4.1(b). The variable count is initially 0. The loop checks whether (count < 100) is true. If so, it executes the loop body to print the message Welcome to C++! and increments count by 1. It repeatedly executes the loop body until (count < 100) becomes false (i.e., when count reaches 100). At this point the loop terminates and the next statement after the loop statement is executed.

In this example, you know exactly how many times the loop body needs to be executed. So a control variable count is used to count the executions. A loop of this type is a *counter-controlled loop*.

counter-controlled loop

Note

The loop-continuation-condition always must appear inside the parentheses. The braces enclosing the loop body can be omitted only if the loop body contains a single statement or none.

Caution

Make sure that the loop-continuation-condition eventually becomes false so that the program will terminate. A common programming error involves *infinite loops*. For instance, if you forgot to increase count (count++) in the code, the program would not stop. To terminate the program, press *Ctrl+C*.

infinite loop

Here is another example illustrating how a loop works.

```cpp
int sum = 0, i = 1;
while (i < 10)
{
  sum = sum + i;
  i++;
}

cout << "sum is " << sum; // sum is 45
```

If i < 10 is true, the program adds i to sum. Variable i is initially set to 1, then incremented to 2, 3, and up to 10. When i is 10, i < 10 is false, the loop exits. So sum is 1 + 2 + 3 + ... + 9 = 45.

Suppose the loop is mistakenly written as follows:

```cpp
int sum = 0, i = 1;
while (i < 10)
{
  sum = sum + i;
}
```

This loop is infinite, because i is always 1 and i < 10 will always be true.

4.2.1   Problem: Guessing Numbers

The problem is to guess what a number a computer has in mind. You will write a program that randomly generates an integer between 0 and 100, inclusive. The program prompts the user to enter a number continuously until it matches the randomly generated number. For each user input, the program reports whether it is too low or too high, so the user can choose the next input intelligently. Here is a sample run:

```
Guess a magic number between 0 and 100

Enter your guess: 50  ↵Enter
Your guess is too high

Enter your guess: 25  ↵Enter
Your guess is too high

Enter your guess: 12  ↵Enter
Your guess is too high

Enter your guess: 6  ↵Enter
Your guess is too low

Enter your guess: 9  ↵Enter
Your guess is too high

Enter your guess: 7  ↵Enter
Your guess is too low

Enter your guess: 8  ↵Enter
Yes, the number is 8
```

intelligent guess

The magic number is between 0 and 100. To minimize the number of guesses, enter 50 first. If your guess is too high, the magic number is between 0 and 49. If your guess is too low, the magic number is between 51 and 100. So, after one guess, you can eliminate half the numbers from further consideration.

think before coding

How do you write this program? Do you immediately begin coding? No. It is important to *think before coding*. Think how you would solve the problem without writing a program. You need first generate a random number between 0 and 100, inclusive, and then prompt the user to enter a guess, and compare the guess with the random number.

code incrementally

It is a good practice to *code incrementally* one step at a time. For programs involving loops, if you don't know how to write a loop right away, you may first write the code for executing the code once, and then figure out how to execute it repeatedly in a loop. For this program, you may create an initial draft, as shown in Listing 4.1:

Video Note
guessing number

LISTING 4.1 GuessNumberOneTime.cpp

```cpp
1 #include <iostream>
2 #include <cstdlib>
3 #include <ctime>
4 using namespace std;
5
6 int main()
7 {
8   // Generate a random number to be guessed
9   srand(time(0));
10  int number = rand() % 101;
11
12  cout << "Guess a magic number between 0 and 100";
13
14  // Prompt the user to guess the number
15  cout << "\nEnter your guess: ";
16  int guess;
```

generate a number

```
17    cin >> guess;
18
19    if (guess == number)
20      cout << "Yes, the number is " << number << endl;
21    else if (guess > number)
22      cout << "Your guess is too high" << endl;
23    else
24      cout << "Your guess is too low" << endl;
25
26    return 0;
27 }
```

enter a guess

correct guess?

too high?

too low?

When this program runs, it prompts the user to enter a guess only once. To let the user enter a guess repeatedly, you may put the code in lines 15–24 in a loop, as follows:

```
while (true)
{
  // Prompt the user to guess the number
  cout << "\nEnter your guess: ";
  cin >> guess;

  if (guess == number)
    cout << "Yes, the number is " << number << endl;
  else if (guess > number)
    cout << "Your guess is too high" << endl;
  else
    cout << "Your guess is too low" << endl;
} // End of loop
```

This loop repeatedly prompts the user to enter a guess. However, this loop is not correct, because it never terminates. When **guess** matches **number**, the loop should end. So, revise the loop as follows:

```
while (guess != number)
{
  // Prompt the user to guess the number
  cout << "\nEnter your guess: ";
  cin >> guess;

  if (guess == number)
    cout << "Yes, the number is " << number << endl;
  else if (guess > number)
    cout << "Your guess is too high" << endl;
  else
    cout << "Your guess is too low" << endl;
} // End of loop
```

The complete code is given in Listing 4.2.

LISTING 4.2 GuessNumber.cpp

```
1 #include <iostream>
2 #include <cstdlib>
3 #include <ctime>
4 using namespace std;
5
6 int main()
7 {
8   // Generate a random number to be guessed
9   srand(time(0));
```

Video Note
guessing number

generate a number

```
10    int number = rand() % 101;
11
12    cout << "Guess a magic number between 0 and 100";
13
14    int guess = -1;
15    while (guess != number)
16    {
17      // Prompt the user to guess the number
18      cout << "\nEnter your guess: ";
19      cin >> guess;
20
21      if (guess == number)
22        cout << "Yes, the number is " << number << endl;
23      else if (guess > number)
24        cout << "Your guess is too high" << endl;
25      else
26        cout << "Your guess is too low" << endl;
27    } // End of loop
28
29    return 0;
30  }
```

enter a guess

too high?

too low?

line#	number	guess	output
10	8		
14		-1	
19		50	
24			Your guess is too high
19		25	
24			Your guess is too high
19		12	
24			Your guess is too high
19		6	
26			Your guess is too low
19		9	
24			Your guess is too high
19		7	
26			Your guess is too low
19		8	
22			Yes, the number is 8

The program generates the magic number in line 10 and prompts the user to enter a guess continuously in a loop (lines 15–27). For each guess, the program checks whether it is correct, too high, or too low (lines 21–26). When the guess is correct, the program exits the loop (line 15). Note that **guess** is initialized to -1. Initializing it to a value between 0 and 100 would be wrong, because that could be the number to be guessed.

4.2.2 Problem: An Improved Math Learning Tool

The subtraction quiz program in Listing 3.5, SubtractionQuiz.cpp, generates just one question for each run. You can use a loop to generate questions repeatedly. Listing 4.3 gives a program that generates five questions and, after a student answers all of them, reports the number of correct answers. The program also displays the time spent on the test, as shown in the sample output.

LISTING 4.3 SubtractionQuizLoop.cpp

```cpp
 1 #include <iostream>
 2 #include <ctime> // for time function
 3 #include <cmath> // for the srand and rand functions
 4 using namespace std;
 5
 6 int main()
 7 {
 8   int correctCount = 0;// Count the number of correct answers
 9   int count = 0;// Count the number of questions
10   long startTime = time(0);
11   const int NUMBER_OF_QUESTIONS = 5;
12
13   while (count < NUMBER_OF_QUESTIONS)
14   {
15     // 1. Generate two random single-digit integers
16     srand(time(0));
17     int number1 = rand() % 10;
18     int number2 = rand() % 10;
19
20     // 2. If number1 < number2, swap number1 with number2
21     if (number1 < number2)
22     {
23       int temp = number1;
24       number1 = number2;
25       number2 = temp;
26     }
27
28     // 3. Prompt the student to answer "what is number1 - number2?"
29     cout << "What is " << number1 << " - " << number2 << "? ";
30     int answer;
31     cin >> answer;
32
33     // 4. Grade the answer and display the result
34     if (number1 - number2 == answer)
35     {
36       cout << "You are correct!\n";
37       correctCount++;
38     }
39     else
40       cout << "Your answer is wrong.\n" << number1 << " - " <<
41         number2 << " should be " << (number1 - number2) << endl;
42
43     // Increase the count
44     count++;
45   }
46
47   long endTime = time(0);
48   long testTime = endTime - startTime;
49
```

Video Note
multiple subtraction quiz

correct count
total count
get start time

loop

display a question

grade an answer

increase correct count

increase control variable

get end time
test time

display result

```
50    cout << "Correct count is " << correctCount << "\nTest time is "
51          << testTime << " seconds\n";
52
53    return 0;
54 }
```

```
What is 1 - 1? 0  [↵Enter]
You are correct!

What is 7 - 2? 5  [↵Enter]
You are correct!

What is 9 - 3? 4  [↵Enter]
Your answer is wrong.
9 - 3 should be 6

What is 6 - 6? 0  [↵Enter]
You are correct!

What is 9 - 6? 2  [↵Enter]
Your answer is wrong.
9 - 6 should be 3

Correct count is 3
Test time is 58 seconds
```

The program uses the control variable `count` to control the execution of the loop. `count` is initially `0` (line 9) and is increased by `1` in each iteration (line 44). A subtraction question is displayed and processed in each iteration. The program obtains the time before the test starts in line 10, the time after the test ends in line 47, and computes the test time in line 48.

4.2.3 Controlling a Loop with User Confirmation

confirmation

The preceding example executes the loop five times. If you want the user to decide whether to take another question, you can offer a user *confirmation*. The template of the program can be coded as follows:

```
char continueLoop = 'Y';
while (continueLoop == 'Y')
{
    // Execute the loop body once
    ...
    // Prompt the user for confirmation
    cout << "Enter Y to continue and N to quit: ";
    cin >> continueLoop;
}
```

You can rewrite Listing 4.3 with user confirmation to let the user decide whether to advance to the next question.

Video Note
input from file
sentinel value
sentinel-controlled loop

4.2.4 Controlling a Loop with a Sentinel Value

Another common technique for controlling a loop is to designate a special input value, known as a *sentinel value*, which signifies the end of the loop. A loop using a sentinel value in this way is a *sentinel-controlled loop*.

Listing 4.4 writes a program that reads and calculates the sum of an unspecified number of integers. The input **0** signifies the end of the input. Do you need to declare a new variable for each input value? No. Just use a variable named **data** (line 8) to store the input value and use a variable named **sum** (line 12) to store the total. Whenever a value is read, assign it to **data** (lines 9, 20) and add it to **sum** (line 15) if it is not zero.

LISTING 4.4 SentinelValue.cpp

```
 1 #include <iostream>
 2 using namespace std;
 3
 4 int main()
 5 {
 6   cout << "Enter an int value (the program exits " <<
 7     "if the input is 0): ";
 8   int data;
 9   cin >> data;                                              input data
10
11   // Keep reading data until the input is 0
12   int sum = 0;
13   while (data != 0)                                         loop
14   {
15     sum += data;
16
17     // Read the next data
18     cout << "Enter an int value (the program exits " <<
19       "if the input is 0): ";
20     cin >> data;
21   }
22
23   cout << "The sum is " << sum << endl;                     output result
24
25   return 0;
26 }
```

```
Enter an int value (the program exits if the input is 0): 2 ↵Enter
Enter an int value (the program exits if the input is 0): 3 ↵Enter
Enter an int value (the program exits if the input is 0): 4 ↵Enter
Enter an int value (the program exits if the input is 0): 0 ↵Enter
The sum is 9
```

line#	data	sum	output
9	2		
12		0	
15		2	
20	3		
15		5	
20	4		
17		9	
20	0		
23			The sum is 9

If **data** is not **0**, it is added to the **sum** (line 15) and the next items of input data are read (lines 18–20). If **data** is **0**, the loop body is no longer executed and the **while** loop terminates. The input value **0** is the sentinel value for this loop. Note that if the first input read is **0**, the loop body never executes, and the resulting sum is **0**.

numeric error

 Caution

Don't use floating-point values for equality checking in a loop control. Since they are approximated, it could lead to imprecise counter values. This example uses **int** value for **data**. If a floating-point type value is used for **data**, (**data != 0**) may be **true** even though **data** is **0**. For example:

```
double data = pow(pow(2.0, 0.5), 2) - 2;
if (data == 0)
  cout << "data is zero";
else
  cout << "data is not zero";
```

The variable **data** in the above code should be zero, but it is not, because of rounding-off errors.

Video Note
input from file

4.2.5 Input and Output Redirections

In the preceding example, if you have a lot of data to enter, it would be cumbersome to type from the keyboard. You may store the data separated by whitespaces in a text file, say input.txt, and run the program using the following command:

```
SentinelValue.exe < input.txt
```

input redirection

This command is called *input redirection*. Rather than having the user to type the data from the keyboard, the program takes the input from the file input.txt. Suppose the file contains

```
2 3 4 5 6 7 8 9 12 23 32
23 45 67 89 92 12 34 35 3 1 2 4 0
```

The program should get **sum** to be **518**. Note that SentinelValue.exe can be obtained using the command-line compiler command:

```
g++ SentinelValue.cpp -o SentinelValue.exe
```

Similarly, output redirection can send the output to a file rather than displaying output on the console. The command for *output redirection* is:

```
Program.exe > output.txt
```

Input and output redirection can be used in the same command. For example, the following command gets input from input.txt and sends output to output.txt:

```
SentinelValue.exe < input.txt > output.txt
```

Please run the program and see what contents are in output.txt.

4.3 The **do-while** Loop

The **do-while** loop is a variation of the **while** loop. Its syntax is given below:

do-while loop

```
do
{
  // Loop body;
  Statement(s);
} while (loop-continuation-condition);
```

Its execution flow chart is shown in Figure 4.2.

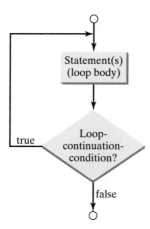

FIGURE 4.2   The **do-while** loop executes the loop body first, then checks the **loop-continuation-condition** to determine whether to continue or terminate the loop.

The loop body is executed first. Then the **loop-continuation-condition** is evaluated. If the evaluation is **true**, the loop body is executed again; otherwise, the **do-while** loop terminates. The major difference between a **while** and a **do-while** loop is the order in which the **loop-continuation-condition** is evaluated and the loop body executed. The **while** and **do-while** loops have equal expressive power. Sometimes one is a more convenient choice than the other. For example, you can rewrite the **while** loop in Listing 4.4 using a **do-while** loop, as shown in Listing 4.5.

LISTING 4.5   TestDoWhile.cpp

```
 1 #include <iostream>
 2 using namespace std;
 3
 4 int main()
 5 {
 6   // Keep reading data until the input is 0
 7   int sum = 0;
 8   int data = 0;
 9
10   do
11   {                                                               loop
12     sum += data;
13
14     // Read the next data
15     cout << "Enter an int value (the program exits " <<
16       "if the input is 0): ";
17     cin >> data;                                                  input
18   }
19   while (data != 0);
20
21   cout << "The sum is " << sum << endl;
22
23   return 0;
24 }
```

What would happen if **sum** and **data** were not initialized to **0**? Would it cause a syntax error? No. It would cause a logic error, because **sum** and **data** could be initialized to any value.

> **Tip**
> Use the `do-while` loop if you have statements inside the loop that must be executed at least once, as in the case of the `do-while` loop in the preceding TestDoWhile program. These statements must appear before the loop as well as inside the loop if you use a `while` loop.

4.4 The **for** Loop

Often you write a loop in the following common form:

```
i = initialValue;  // Initialize loop-control variable
while (i < endValue)
{
  // Loop body
  ...
  i++; // Adjust loop-control variable
}
```

A **for** loop can be used to simplify the above loop:

```
for (i = initialValue; i < endValue; i++)
{
  // Loop body
  ...
}
```

In general, the syntax of a **for** loop is as shown below:

for loop

```
for (initial-action; loop-continuation-condition;
     action-after-each-iteration)
{
  // Loop body;
  Statement(s);
}
```

The flow chart of the **for** loop is shown in Figure 4.3(a).

The **for**-loop statement starts with the keyword **for**, followed by a pair of parentheses enclosing `initial-action`, `loop-continuation-condition`, and `action-after-each-iteration`, followed by the loop body enclosed inside braces. `initial-action`, `loop-continuation-condition`, and `action-after-each-iteration` are separated by semicolons.

control variable

A **for** loop generally uses a variable to control how many times the loop body is executed and when the loop terminates. This is called a *control variable*. The `initial-action` often initializes a control variable, the `action-after-each-iteration` usually increments or decrements the control variable, and the `loop-continuation-condition` tests whether the control variable has reached a termination value. For example, the following **for** loop prints Welcome to C++! a hundred times:

```
int i;
for (i = 0; i < 100; i++)
{
  cout << "Welcome to C++!\n";
}
```

The flow chart of the statement is shown in Figure 4.3(b). The **for** loop initializes i to 0, then repeatedly executes the statement to display a message and evaluates i++ while i is less than 100.

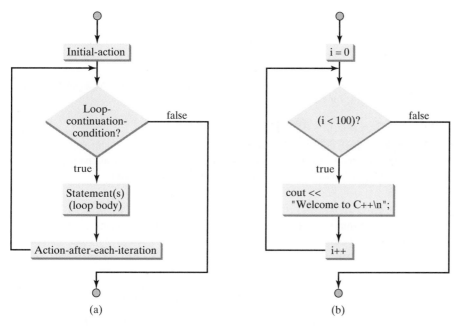

(a)   (b)

FIGURE 4.3   A `for` loop performs an initial action once, then repeatedly executes the statements in the loop body, performing an action after an iteration when the `loop-continuation-condition` evaluates to `true`.

The `initial-action`, `i = 0`, initializes the control variable, `i`. The `loop-continuation-condition`, `i < 100`, is a Boolean expression. The expression is evaluated right after the initialization and at the beginning of each iteration. If this condition is `true`, the loop body is executed. If it is `false`, the loop terminates and the program control turns to the line following the loop.

The `action-after-each-iteration`, `i++`, is a statement that adjusts the control variable. This statement is executed after each iteration. It increments the control variable. Eventually, the value of the control variable should force the `loop-continuation-condition` to become `false`. Otherwise the loop is infinite.

The loop control variable can be declared and initialized in the for loop. Here is an example:

```
for (int i = 0; i < 100; i++)
{
  cout << "Welcome to C++!\n";
}
```

If there is only one statement in the loop body, as in this example, the braces can be omitted.

Tip

The control variable must be declared inside the control structure of the loop or before the loop. If the loop-control variable is used only in the loop, and not elsewhere, it is better to declare it in the `initial-action` of the `for` loop. If the variable is declared inside the loop-control structure, it cannot be referenced outside the loop. For example, you cannot reference `i` outside the `for` loop in the preceding code, because it is declared inside the `for` loop.

Note

The `initial-action` in a `for` loop can be a list of zero or more comma-separated variable declaration statements or assignment expressions. For example,

```
for (int i = 0, j = 0; (i + j < 10); i++, j++)
{
  // Do something
}
```

The **action-after-each-iteration** in a **for** loop can be a list of zero or more comma-separated statements. For example,

```
for (int i = 1; i < 100; cout << i, i++);
```

This example is correct, but it is a bad example, because it makes the code difficult to read. Normally, you declare and initialize a control variable as an **initial-action** and increment or decrement the control variable as an **action-after-each-iteration**.

 Note

If the **loop-continuation-condition** in a **for** loop is omitted, it is implicitly **true**. Thus the statement given below in (a), which is an infinite loop, is correct. To avoid confusion, though, it is better to use the equivalent loop in (b):

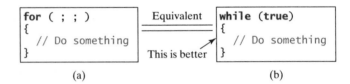

```
for ( ; ; )
{
  // Do something
}
```

Equivalent

This is better

```
while (true)
{
  // Do something
}
```

(a)   (b)

4.5 Which Loop to Use?

pretest loop
posttest loop

The **while** loop and **for** loop are called *pretest loops* because the continuation condition is checked before the loop body is executed. The **do-while** loop is called *posttest loop* because the condition is checked after the loop body is executed. The three forms of loop statements, **while**, **do-while**, and **for**, are expressively equivalent; that is, you can write a loop in any of these three forms. For example, a **while** loop in (a) in the following figure can always be converted into the **for** loop in (b):

```
while (loop-continuation-condition)
{
  // Loop body
}
```

Equivalent

```
for ( ; loop-continuation-condition; )
{
  // Loop body
}
```

(a)   (b)

The **for** loop in (a) in the next figure can generally be converted into the **while** loop in (b) except in certain special cases (see Review Question 4.17 for such a case):

```
for (initial-action;
     loop-continuation-condition;
     action-after-each-iteration)
{
  // Loop body;
}
```

Equivalent

```
initial-action;
while (loop-continuation-condition)
{
  // Loop body;
  action-after-each-iteration;
}
```

(a)   (b)

Use the loop statement that is most intuitive to you. In general, a **for** loop may be used if the number of repetitions is known in advance—for example, when you need to print a message a hundred times. A **while** loop may be used if the number of repetitions is not fixed, as when reading numbers until the input is 0. A do-while loop can be used to replace a while loop if the loop body has to be executed before the continuation condition is tested.

 Caution

Adding a semicolon at the end of the for clause before the loop body is a common mistake, as shown below. In (a), the semicolon signifies the end of the loop prematurely. The loop body is actually empty, as shown in (b). (a) and (b) are equivalent.

Error

```
for (int i = 0; i < 10; i++);
{
  cout << "i is " << i << endl;
}
```

(a)

Empty Body

```
for (int i = 0; i < 10; i++) { };
{
  cout << "i is " << i << endl;
}
```

(b)

Similarly, the loop in (c) is also wrong. (c) is equivalent to (d).

Error

```
int i = 0;
while (i < 10);
{
  cout << "i is " << i << endl;
  i++;
}
```

(c)

Empty Body

```
int i = 0;
while (i < 10) { };
{
  cout << "i is " << i << endl;
  i++;
}
```

(d)

In the case of the do-while loop, the semicolon is needed to end the loop.

```
int i = 0;
do
{
  cout << "i is " << i << endl;
  i++;
} while (i < 10);        Correct
```

4.6 Nested Loops

Nested loops consist of an outer loop and one or more inner loops. Each time the outer loop is repeated, the inner loops are reentered and started anew.

Listing 4.6 is a program that uses nested for loops to print a multiplication table.

LISTING 4.6 TestMultiplicationTable.cpp

```
 1 #include <iostream>
 2 #include <iomanip>
 3 using namespace std;
 4
 5 int main()
 6 {
 7   cout << "         Multiplication Table\n";        table title
 8   cout << "--------------------------------------\n";
 9
10   // Display the number title
11   cout << "   | ";
12   for (int j = 1; j <= 9; j++)
13     cout << setw(3) << j;
14
```

```
15      cout << "\n";
16
17      // Print table body
18      for (int i = 1; i <= 9; i++)
19      {
20        cout << i << " | ";
21        for (int j = 1; j <= 9; j++)
22        {
23          // Display the product and align properly
24          cout << setw(3) << i * j;
25        }
26        cout << "\n";
27      }
28
29      return 0;
30 }
```

table body

nested loop

```
          Multiplication Table
     ----------------------------
        | 1   2   3   4   5   6   7   8   9
     1  | 1   2   3   4   5   6   7   8   9
     2  | 2   4   6   8  10  12  14  16  18
     3  | 3   6   9  12  15  18  21  24  27
     4  | 4   8  12  16  20  24  28  32  36
     5  | 5  10  15  20  25  30  35  40  45
     6  | 6  12  18  24  30  36  42  48  54
     7  | 7  14  21  28  35  42  49  56  63
     8  | 8  16  24  32  40  48  56  64  72
     9  | 9  18  27  36  45  54  63  72  81
```

The program displays a title (line 7) on the first line and dashes (-) (line 8) on the second line. The first **for** loop (lines 12–13) displays the numbers **1** through **9** on the third line.

The next loop (lines 18–27) is a nested **for** loop with the control variable i in the outer loop and j in the inner loop. For each i, the product $i * j$ is displayed on a line in the inner loop, with j being 1, 2, 3, ..., 9. The **setw(3)** manipulator (line 24) specifies the width for each number to be displayed.

4.7 Minimizing Numerical Errors

Numeric errors involving floating-point numbers are inevitable. This section discusses in terms of an example how to minimize such errors.

Listing 4.7 presents an example that sums a series that starts with **0.01** and ends with **1.0**. The numbers in the series will increment by **0.01**, as follows: **0.01 + 0.02 + 0.03** and so on.

LISTING 4.7 TestSum.cpp

```
1 #include <iostream>
2 using namespace std;
3
4 int main()
5 {
6   // Initialize sum
7   double sum = 0;
8
```

```
 9    // Add 0.01, 0.02, ..., 0.99, 1 to sum
10    for (double i = 0.01; i <= 1.0; i = i + 0.01)                loop
11      sum += i;
12
13    // Display result
14    cout << "The sum is " << sum;
15
16    return 0;
17 }
```

```
The sum is 49.5
```

The result is **49.5**, but the correct result should be **50.5**. What went wrong? For each iter-   numeric error
ation in the loop, **i** is incremented by **0.01**. When the loop ends, the **i** value is slightly larger
than **1** (not exactly **1**). This causes the last **i** value not to be added into **sum**. The fundamental
problem is that the floating-point numbers are represented by approximation.

To fix the problem, use an integer count to ensure that all the numbers are added to **sum**.
Here is the new loop:

```
double currentValue = 0.01;

for (int count = 0; count < 100; count++)
{
  sum += currentValue;
  currentValue += 0.01;
}
```

After this loop, **sum** is **50.5**.

4.8 Case Studies

Loops are fundamental in programming. The ability to write loops is essential in learning programming. *If you can write programs using loops, you know how to program!* For this reason,
this section presents three additional examples of solving problems using loops.

4.8.1 Problem: Finding the Greatest Common Divisor

The greatest common divisor of two integers **4** and **2** is **2**. The greatest common divisor of   gcd
two integers **16** and **24** is **8**. How do you find the greatest common divisor? Let the two input
integers be **n1** and **n2**. You know that number **1** is a common divisor, but it may not be the
greatest common divisor. So you can check whether **k** (for **k** = **2**, **3**, **4**, and so on) is a common divisor for **n1** and **n2**, until **k** is greater than **n1** or **n2**. Store the common divisor in a
variable named **gcd**. Initially, **gcd** is **1**. Whenever a new common divisor is found, it becomes
the new **gcd**. When you have checked all the possible common divisors from **2** up to **n1** or
n2, the value in variable **gcd** is the greatest common divisor. The idea can be translated into
the following loop:

```
int gcd = 1;
int k = 2;

while (k <= n1 && k <= n2)
{
  if (n1 % k == 0 && n2 % k == 0)
    gcd = k;
```

```
        k++;
    }
```

```
    // After the loop, gcd is the greatest common divisor for n1 and n2
```

Listing 4.8 presents the program that prompts the user to enter two positive integers and finds their greatest common divisor.

LISTING 4.8 GreatestCommonDivisor.cpp

```
 1  #include <iostream>
 2  using namespace std;
 3
 4  int main()
 5  {
 6      // Prompt the user to enter two integers
 7      cout << "Enter first integer: ";
 8      int n1;
 9      cin >> n1;
10
11      cout << "Enter second integer: ";
12      int n2;
13      cin >> n2;
14
15      int gcd = 1;
16      int k = 2;
17      while (k <= n1 && k <= n2)
18      {
19          if (n1 % k == 0 && n2 % k == 0)
20              gcd = k;
21          k++;
22      }
23
24      cout << "The greatest common divisor for " << n1 << " and "
25          << n2 << " is " << gcd;
26
27      return 0;
28  }
```

input (line 9)
input (line 13)
gcd (line 15)
output (line 24)

```
Enter first integer: 125  ⏎Enter
Enter second integer: 2525  ⏎Enter
The greatest common divisor for 125 and 2525 is 25
```

think before you type

How did you write this program? Did you immediately begin to write the code? No. It is important to *think before you type*. Thinking enables you to generate a logical solution for the problem without wondering how to write the code. Once you have a logical solution, type the code to translate the solution into a program. The translation is not unique. For example, you could use a **for** loop to rewrite the code as follows:

```
for (int k = 2; k <= n1 && k <= n2; k++)
{
    if (n1 % k == 0 && n2 % k == 0)
        gcd = k;
}
```

multiple solutions

A problem often has multiple solutions. The GCD problem can be solved in many ways. Exercise 4.15 suggests another solution. A more efficient solution is to use the classic Euclidean algorithm. See http://www.cut-the-knot.org/blue/Euclid.shtml for more information.

You might think that a divisor for a number `n1` cannot be greater than `n1 / 2`. So, you would attempt to improve the program using the following loop: ·erroneous solutions

```
for (int k = 2; k <= n1 / 2 && k <= n2 / 2; k++)
{
  if (n1 % k == 0 && n2 % k == 0)
    gcd = k;
}
```

This revision is wrong. Can you find the reason? See Review Question 4.14 for the answer.

4.8.2 Problem: Predicating the Future Tuition

Suppose that the tuition for a university is $10,000 this year and increases 7% every year. In how many years will the tuition have doubled?

Before you attempt to write a program, first consider how to solve this problem by hand. The tuition for the second year is the tuition for the first year * 1.07. The tuition for a future year is the tuition of its preceding year * 1.07. So, the tuition for each year can be computed as follows:

```
double tuition = 10000;    int year = 1  // Year 1
tuition = tuition * 1.07; year++;        // Year 2
tuition = tuition * 1.07; year++;        // Year 3
tuition = tuition * 1.07; year++;        // Year 4
...
```

Keep computing tuition for a new year until it is at least 20000. By then you will know how many years it will take for the tuition to be doubled. You can now translate the logic into the following loop:

```
double tuition = 10000;    // Year 1
int year = 1;
while (tuition < 20000)
{
  tuition = tuition * 1.07;
  year++;
}
```

The complete program is shown in Listing 4.9.

LISTING 4.9 FutureTuition.cpp

```
 1 #include <iostream>
 2 using namespace std;
 3
 4 int main()
 5 {
 6   double tuition = 10000;    // Year 1
 7   int year = 1;
 8   while (tuition < 20000)                                          loop
 9   {
10     tuition = tuition * 1.07;                                      next year's tuition
11     year++;
12   }
13
14   cout << "Tuition will be doubled in " << year << " years" << endl;
15
16   return 0;
17 }
```

> Tuition will be doubled in 12 years

The `while` loop (lines 8–12) is used to repeatedly compute the tuition for a new year. The loop terminates when tuition is greater than or equal to `20000`.

4.8.3 Problem: *Monte Carlo Simulation*

Monte Carlo simulation uses random numbers and probability to solve problems. It has a wide range of applications in computational mathematics, physics, chemistry, and finance. We now look at an example of using Monte Carlo simulation for estimating π.

First, draw a circle with its bounding square.

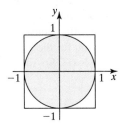

Assume the radius of the circle is 1. So, the circle area is π and the square area is 4. Randomly generate a point in the square. The probability that the point falls in the circle is `circleArea / squareArea = ` π `/ 4`.

Write a program that randomly generates `1000000` points that fall in the square and let `numberOfHits` denote the number of points that fall in the circle. So, `numberOfHits` is approximately `1000000 * (`π `/ 4)`. π can be approximated as `4 * numberOfHits / 1000000`. The complete program is shown in Listing 4.10.

LISTING 4.10 MonteCarloSimulation.cpp

```
1 #include <iostream>
2 using namespace std;
3
4 int main()
5 {
6   const int NUMBER_OF_TRIALS = 1000000;
7   int numberOfHits = 0;
8   srand(time(0));
9
10   for (int i = 0; i < NUMBER_OF_TRIALS; i++)
11   {
12     double x = rand() * 2.0 / RAND_MAX - 1;
13     double y = rand() * 2.0 / RAND_MAX - 1;
14     if (x * x + y * y <= 1)
15       numberOfHits++;
16   }
17
18   double pi = 4.0 * numberOfHits / NUMBER_OF_TRIALS;
19   cout << "PI is " << pi << endl;
20
21   return 0;
22 }
```

generate random points

check inside circle

estimate pi

> PI is 3.14124

The program repeatedly generates a random point (x, y) in the square in lines 12–13:

```
double x = rand() * 2.0 / RAND_MAX - 1;
double y = rand() * 2.0 / RAND_MAX - 1;
```

If $x^2 + y^2 \leq 1$, the point is inside the circle and numberOfHits is incremented by 1. π is approximately 4 * numberOfHits / NUMBER_OF_TRIALS (line 18).

4.9 Keywords *break* and *continue*

Pedagogical Note

Two keywords, break and continue, can be used in loop statements to provide additional controls. In some cases this can simplify programming. However, overusing or improperly using break and continue can make programs difficult to read and debug. Instructors may choose to skip this section without affecting the rest of the book.

You have used the keyword break in a switch statement. You can also use break in a loop to immediately terminate a loop. Listing 4.11 presents a program to demonstrate the effect of using break in a loop.

break

LISTING 4.11 TestBreak.cpp

```
 1 #include <iostream>
 2 using namespace std;
 3
 4 int main()
 5 {
 6     int sum = 0;
 7     int number = 0;
 8
 9     while (number < 20)
10     {
11         number++;
12         sum += number;
13         if (sum >= 100)
14             break;
15     }
16
17     cout << "The number is " << number << endl;
18     cout << "The sum is " << sum << endl;
19
20     return 0;
21 }
```

break

```
The number is 14
The sum is 105
```

The program adds integers from 1 to 20 in this order to sum until sum is greater than or equal to 100. Without lines 13–14 this program would calculate the sum of the numbers from 1 to 20. But with lines 13–14 the loop terminates when sum becomes greater than or equal to 100. Without lines 13–14 the output would be:

```
The number is 20
The sum is 210
```

continue

You can also use the `continue` keyword in a loop. When it is encountered, it ends the current iteration. Program control goes to the end of the loop body. In other words, `continue` breaks out of an iteration, while the `break` keyword breaks out of a loop. The program in Listing 4.12 shows the effect of using `continue` in a loop.

LISTING 4.12 TestContinue.cpp

```cpp
1 #include <iostream>
2 using namespace std;
3
4 int main()
5 {
6   int sum = 0;
7   int number = 0;
8
9   while (number < 20)
10  {
11    number++;
12    if (number == 10 || number == 11)
13      continue;
14    sum += number;
15  }
16
17  cout << "The sum is " << sum;
18
19  return 0;
20 }
```

continue

```
The sum is 189
```

The program adds all the integers from 1 to 20 except 10 and 11 to `sum`. The `continue` statement is executed when `number` becomes 10 or 11. The `continue` statement ends the current iteration so that the rest of the statement in the loop body is not executed; therefore, `number` is not added to `sum` when it is 10 or 11.

Without lines 12–13 the output would be as follows:

```
The sum is 210
```

In this case, all the numbers are added to `sum`, even when `number` is 10 or 11. Therefore, the result is 210.

Note

The `continue` statement is always inside a loop. In the `while` and `do-while` loops, the `loop-continuation-condition` is evaluated immediately after the `continue` statement. In the `for` loop, the `action-after-each-iteration` is performed, then the `loop-continuation-condition` is evaluated, immediately after the `continue` statement.

You can always write a program without using `break` or `continue` in a loop. See Review Question 4.18. In general, it is appropriate to use `break` and `continue` if their use simplifies coding and makes programs easy to read.

Listing 4.2 gives a program for guessing a number. You can rewrite it using a `break` statement, as shown in Listing 4.13.

LISTING 4.13 GuessNumberUsingBreak.cpp

```
1 #include <iostream>
2 #include <ctime>
3 #include <cstdlib>
4 using namespace std;
5
6 int main()
7 {
8    // Generate a random number to be guessed
9    srand(time(0));
10   int number = rand() % 101;                              generate a number
11
12   cout << "Guess a magic number between 0 and 100";
13
14   while (true)                                            loop continuously
15   {
16      // Prompt the user to guess the number
17      cout << "\nEnter your guess: ";
18      int guess;
19      cin >> guess;                                        enter a guess
20
21      if (guess == number)
22      {
23         cout << "Yes, the number is " << number << endl;
24         break;                                            break
25      }
26      else if (guess > number)
27         cout << "Your guess is too high" << endl;
28      else
29         cout << "Your guess is too low" << endl;
30   } // End of loop
31
32   return 0;
33 }
```

Using the **break** statement makes the program simpler and easier to read. Use **break** and **continue** with caution, however. Too many **break** and **continue** statements will produce a loop with many exit points and make the program difficult to read.

Note

The C language has a **goto** statement. You can also use it in C++. However, using it will make your program vulnerable to errors. The **goto** statement can transfer the control anywhere in the program indiscriminately, whereas the **break** and **continue** statements operate only in a loop or a switch statement.

goto statement

4.10 Example: Displaying Prime Numbers

This section presents a program that displays the first fifty prime numbers in five lines, each containing ten numbers. An integer greater than 1 is *prime* if its only positive divisor is 1 or itself. For example, 2, 3, 5, and 7 are prime numbers, but 4, 6, 8, and 9 are not.

The problem can be broken into the following tasks:

- Determine whether a given number is prime.
- For number = 2, 3, 4, 5, 6, ..., test whether the number is prime.
- Count the prime numbers.
- Print each prime number, and print ten numbers per line.

Obviously, you need to write a loop and repeatedly test whether a new number is prime. If the number is prime, increase the count by 1. The count is 0 initially. When it reaches 50, the loop terminates.

Here is the algorithm for the problem:

```
Set the number of prime numbers to be printed as
   a constant NUMBER_OF_PRIMES;
Use count to track the number of prime numbers and
   set an initial count to 0;
Set an initial number to 2;

while (count < NUMBER_OF_PRIMES)
{
  Test if number is prime;

  if (number is prime)
  {
    Print the prime number and increase the count;
  }

  Increment number by 1;
}
```

To test whether a number is prime, check whether it is divisible by 2, 3, 4, up to number/2. If a divisor is found, the number is not a prime. The algorithm can be described as follows:

```
Use a Boolean variable isPrime to denote whether
   the number is prime; Set isPrime to true initially;

for (int divisor = 2; divisor <= number / 2; divisor++)
{
  if (number % divisor == 0)
  {
    Set isPrime to false
    Exit the loop;
  }
}
```

The complete program is given in Listing 4.14.

LISTING 4.14   PrimeNumber.cpp

```
 1 #include <iostream>
 2 #include <iomanip>
 3 using namespace std;
 4
 5 int main()
 6 {
 7   const int NUMBER_OF_PRIMES = 50; // Number of primes to display
 8   const int NUMBER_OF_PRIMES_PER_LINE = 10; // Display 10 per line
 9   int count = 0;  // Count the number of prime numbers
10   int number = 2; // A number to be tested for primeness
11
12   cout << "The first 50 prime numbers are \n";
13
14   // Repeatedly find prime numbers
15   while (count < NUMBER_OF_PRIMES)
16   {
17     // Assume the number is prime
18     bool isPrime = true; // Is the current number prime?
19
```

count prime numbers

check primeness

```
20      // Test if number is prime
21      for (int divisor = 2; divisor <= number / 2; divisor++)
22      {
23        if (number % divisor == 0)
24        {
25          // If true, the number is not prime
26          isPrime = false; // Set isPrime to false
27          break; // Exit the for loop                               exit loop
28        }
29      }
30
31      // Print the prime number and increase the count
32      if (isPrime)                                                  print if prime
33      {
34        count++; // Increase the count
35
36        if (count % NUMBER_OF_PRIMES_PER_LINE == 0)
37        {
38          // Print the number and advance to the new line
39          cout << setw(4) << number << endl;
40        }
41        else
42          cout << setw(4) << number << " ";
43      }
44
45      // Check if the next number is prime
46      number++;
47    }
48
49    return 0;
50 }
```

```
The first 50 prime numbers are
    2    3    5    7   11   13   17   19   23   29
   31   37   41   43   47   53   59   61   67   71
   73   79   83   89   97  101  103  107  109  113
  127  131  137  139  149  151  157  163  167  173
  179  181  191  193  197  199  211  223  227  229
```

This is a complex example for novice programmers. The key to developing a programmatic solution to this problem, and to many other problems, is to break it into subproblems   subproblem
and develop solutions for each of them in turn. Do not attempt to develop a complete solution
in the first trial. Instead, begin by writing the code to determine whether a given number is
prime, then expand the program to test whether other numbers are prime in a loop.

To determine whether a number is prime, check whether it is divisible by a number
between 2 and number/2 inclusive. If so, it is not a prime number; otherwise, it is a prime
number. For a prime number, display it. If the count is divisible by 10, advance to a new line.
The program ends when the count reaches 50.

The program uses the break statement in line 27 to exit the for loop as soon as the number is found to be a nonprime. You can rewrite the loop (lines 21–29) without using the break
statement, as follows:

```
for (int divisor = 2; divisor <= number / 2 && isPrime;
     divisor++)
{
  // If true, the number is not prime
  if (number % divisor == 0)
```

```
          {
              // Set isPrime to false, if the number is not prime
              isPrime = false;
          }
      }
```

However, using the `break` statement makes the program simpler and easier to read in this case.

KEY TERMS

`break` statement 135	`loop-continuation-condition` 116
`continue` statement 135	loop body 116
infinite loop 117	nested loop 129
input redirection 124	output redirection 124
iteration 116	sentinel value 122
loop 116	

CHAPTER SUMMARY

1. There are three types of repetition statements: the `while` loop, the `do-while` loop, and the `for` loop.

2. The part of the loop that contains the statements to be repeated is called the *loop body*.

3. A one-time execution of a loop body is referred to as an *iteration of the loop*.

4. An infinite loop is a loop statement that executes infinitely.

5. In designing loops, you need to consider both the loop-control structure and the loop body.

6. The `while` loop checks the `loop-continuation-condition` first. If the condition is `true`, the loop body is executed; otherwise the loop terminates.

7. The `do-while` loop resembles the `while` loop but executes the loop body first and then checks the `loop-continuation-condition` to decide whether to continue or to terminate.

8. Since the `while` loop and the `do-while` loop contain the `loop-continuation-condition`, which is dependent on the loop body, the number of repetitions is determined by the loop body. The `while` loop and the `do-while` loop often are used when the number of repetitions is unspecified.

9. A *sentinel value* is a special value that signifies the end of the loop.

10. The `for` loop generally is used to execute a loop body a predictable number of times; this number is not determined by the loop body.

11. The `for`-loop control has three parts. The first part is an initial action that often initializes a control variable. The second part, the `loop-continuation-condition`, determines whether the loop body is to be executed. The third part is executed after

each iteration and is often used to adjust the control variable. Usually, the loop-control variables are initialized and changed in the control structure.

12. The `while` and `for` loops are called *pretest loops* because the continuation condition is checked before the loop body is executed.

13. The `do-while` loop is called a *posttest loop* because the condition is checked after the loop body is executed.

14. Two keywords, `break` and `continue`, can be used in a loop.

15. The `break` keyword immediately ends the innermost loop, which contains the break.

16. The `continue` keyword ends only the current iteration.

REVIEW QUESTIONS

Sections 4.2–4.8

4.1 Analyze the following code. Is `count < 100` always `true`, always `false`, or sometimes `true` or sometimes `false` at Point A, Point B, and Point C?

```cpp
int count = 0;
while (count < 100)
{
  // Point A
  cout << "Welcome to C++!\n";
  count++;
  // Point B
}
// Point C
```

4.2 What is wrong if `guess` is initialized to `0` in line 14 in Listing 4.2?

4.3 How many times is the following loop body repeated? What is the printout of the loop?

```cpp
int i = 1;
while (i < 10)
  if (i % 2 == 0)
    cout << i << endl;
```
(a)

```cpp
int i = 1;
while (i < 10)
  if (i % 2 == 0)
    cout << i++ << endl;
```
(b)

```cpp
int i = 1;
while (i < 10)
  if ((i++) % 2 == 0)
    cout << i << endl;
```
(c)

4.4 What are the differences between a `while` loop and a `do-while` loop? Convert the following `while` loop into a `do-while` loop.

```cpp
int sum = 0;
int number;
cin >> number;
while (number != 0)
{
  sum += number;
  cin >> number;
}
```

4.5 Do the following two loops result in the same value in `sum`?

```
for (int i = 0; i < 10; ++i)
{
  sum += i;
}
```

(a)

```
for (int i = 0; i < 10; i++)
{
  sum += i;
}
```

(b)

4.6 What are the three parts of a `for`-loop control? Write a `for` loop that prints the numbers from 1 to 100.

4.7 What does the following statement do?

```
for ( ; ; )
{
  do something;
}
```

4.8 If a variable is declared in the `for`-loop control, can it be used after the loop exits?

4.9 Suppose the input is 2 3 4 5 0. What is the output of the following code?

```cpp
#include <iostream>
using namespace std;

int main()
{
  int number, max;
  cin >> number;
  max = number;

  while (number != 0)
  {
    cin >> number;
    if (number > max)
      max = number;
  }

  cout << "max is ".<< max << endl;
  cout << "number " << number << endl;

  return 0;
}
```

4.10 Suppose the input is 2 3 4 5 0. What is the output of the following code?

```cpp
#include <iostream>
using namespace std;

int main()
{
  int number, sum = 0, count;

  for (count = 0; count < 5; count++)
  {
    cin >> number;
    sum += number;
  }
```

```
    cout << "sum is " << sum << endl;
    cout << "count is " << count << endl;

    return 0;
}
```

4.11   Suppose the input is 2 3 4 5 0. What is the output of the following code?

```cpp
#include <iostream>
using namespace std;

int main()
{
  int number, max;
  cin >> number;
  max = number;

  do
  {
    cin >> number;
    if (number > max)
      max = number;
  } while (number != 0);

  cout << "max is " << max << endl;
  cout << "number " << number << endl;

  return 0;
}
```

4.12   Can you convert a **for** loop to a **while** loop? List the advantages of using **for** loops.

4.13   Convert the following **for** loop statement to a **while** loop and to a **do-while** loop:

```cpp
long sum = 0;
for (int i = 0; i <= 1000; i++)
  sum = sum + i;
```

4.14   Will the program work if **n1** and **n2** are replaced by **n1 / 2** and **n2 / 2** in line 17 in Listing 4.8?

Section 4.9

4.15   What is the keyword **break** for? What is the keyword **continue** for? Will the following program terminate? If so, give the output.

```cpp
int balance = 1000;
while (true)
{
  if (balance < 9)
    break;
  balance = balance - 9;
}

cout << "Balance is " <<
  balance << endl;
```
(a)

```cpp
int balance = 1000;
while (true)
{
  if (balance < 9)
    continue;
  balance = balance - 9;
}

cout << "Balance is "
  << balance << endl;
```
(b)

4.16 Can you always convert a `while` loop into a `for` loop? Convert the following `while` loop into a `for` loop.

```
int i = 1;
int sum = 0;
while (sum < 10000)
{
  sum = sum + i;
  i++;
}
```

4.17 The `for` loop on the left is converted into the `while` loop on the right. What is wrong? Correct it.

```
for (int i = 0; i < 4; i++)
{
  if (i % 3 == 0) continue;
  sum += i;
}
```
Converted →
Wrong conversion
```
int i = 0;
while (i < 4)
{
  if (i % 3 == 0) continue;
  sum += i;
  i++;
}
```

4.18 Rewrite the programs `TestBreak` and `TestContinue` in Listings 4.11 and 4.12 without using `break` and `continue` statements.

Comprehensive

4.19 Identify and fix the syntax errors in (a) and the logic errors in (b).

```
for (int i = 0; i < 10; i++);
  sum += i;

if (i < j);
  cout << i
else
  cout << j;

while (j < 10);
{
  j++;
};

do
{
  j++;
} while (j < 10)
```
(a)

```
int total = 0, num = 0;

do
{
  // Read the next data
  cout << "Enter an int value, " <<
    "\nexit if the input is 0: ";
  int num;
  cin >> num;

  total += num;
} while (num != 0);

cout << "Total is " << total << endl;
```
(b)

4.20 Show the output of the following programs. (*Tip:* Draw a table and list the variables in the columns to trace these programs.)

```
for (int i = 1; i < 5; i++)
{
  int j = 0;
  while (j < i)
  {
    cout << j << " ";
    j++;
  }
}
```
(a)

```
int i = 0;
while (i < 5)
{
  for (int j = i; j > 1; j--)
    cout << j << " ";
  cout << "****" << endl;
  i++;
}
```
(b)

```
int i = 5;
while (i >= 1)
{
  int num = 1;
  for (int j = 1; j <= i; j++)
  {
    cout << num << "xxx";
    num *= 2;
  }

  cout << endl;
  i--;
}
```
(c)

```
int i = 1;
do
{
  int num = 1;
  for (int j = 1; j <= i; j++)
  {
    cout << num << "G";
    num += 2;
  }

  cout << endl;
  i++;
} while (i <= 5);
```
(d)

4.21 What is the output of the following program? Explain the reason.

```
int x = 80000000;

while (x > 0)
  x++;

cout << "x is " << x << endl;
```

4.22 Count the number of iterations in the following loops.

```
int count = 0;
while (count < n)
{
  count++;
}
```
(a)

```
for (int count = 0;
  count < n; count++)
{
}
```
(b)

```
int count = 5;
while (count < n)
{
  count++;
}
```
(c)

```
int count = 5;
while (count < n)
{
  count = count + 3;
}
```
(d)

PROGRAMMING EXERCISES

Pedagogical Note

For each problem, read it several times until you understand it. Think how to solve the problem before coding. Translate your logic into a program.   read and think before coding

A problem often can be solved in many different ways. Students are encouraged to explore   explore solutions
various solutions.

Sections 4.2–4.7

4.1* (*Counting positive and negative numbers and computing the average of numbers*)
Write a program that reads an unspecified number of integers, determines how
many positive and negative values have been read, and computes the total and average of the input values (not counting zeros). Your program ends with the input 0.
Display the average as a floating-point number. Here is a sample run:

```
Enter an int value, the program exits if the input is 0:
 1 2 -1 3 0
The number of positives is 3
The number of negatives is 1
The total is 5
The average is 1.25
```

4.2 (*Repeating additions*) Listing 4.3, SubtractionQuizLoop.cpp, generates five random subtraction questions. Revise the program to generate ten random addition questions for two integers between 1 and 15. Display the correct count and test time.

4.3 (*Conversion from kilograms to pounds*) Write a program that displays the following table (note that 1 kilogram is 2.2 pounds):

```
Kilograms        Pounds

1                2.2
3                6.6
...
197              433.4
199              437.8
```

4.4 (*Conversion from miles to kilometers*) Write a program that displays the following table (note that 1 mile is 1.609 kilometers):

```
Miles        Kilometers

1            1.609
2            3.218
...
9            14.481
10           16.090
```

4.5* (*Conversion from kilograms to pounds*) Write a program that displays the following two tables side by side (note that 1 kilogram is 2.2 pounds):

```
Kilograms   Pounds    |    Pounds    Kilograms

1           2.2       |    20        9.09
3           6.6       |    25        11.36
...
197         433.4     |    510       231.82
199         437.8     |    515       234.09
```

4.6* (*Conversion from miles to kilometers*) Write a program that displays the following two tables side by side (note that 1 mile is 1.609 kilometers):

```
Miles       Kilometers  |  Kilometers    Miles

1           1.609       |  20            12.430
2           3.218       |  25            15.538
...
9           14.481      |  60            37.290
10          16.090      |  65            40.398
```

4.7** (*Financial application: computing future tuition*) Suppose that the tuition for a university is $10,000 this year and increases 5% every year. Write a program that computes the tuition in ten years and the total cost of four years' worth of tuition starting ten years from now.

4.8   (*Finding the highest score*) Write a program that prompts the user to enter the number of students and each student's score, and displays the highest score.

4.9*   (*Finding the two highest scores*) Write a program that prompts the user to enter the number of students and each student's score, and displays the highest and second-highest scores.

4.10   (*Finding numbers divisible by 5 and 6*) Write a program that displays, ten numbers per line, all the numbers from 100 to 1000 that are divisible by 5 and 6.

4.11   (*Finding numbers divisible by 5 or 6, but not both*) Write a program that displays, ten numbers per line, all the numbers from 100 to 200 that are divisible by 5 or 6, but not both.

4.12   (*Finding the smallest n such that n^2 > 12000*) Use a `while` loop to find the smallest integer n such that n^2 is greater than 12,000.

4.13   (*Finding the largest n such that n^3 < 12000*) Use a `while` loop to find the largest integer n such that n^3 is less than 12,000.

4.14*   (*Displaying the ACSII character table*) Write a program that prints the characters in the ASCII character table from `'!'` to `'~'`. Print ten characters per line.

Section 4.8

4.15*   (*Computing the greatest common divisor*) For Listing 4.8, another solution to find the greatest common divisor of two integers `n1` and `n2` is as follows: First find **d** to be the minimum of `n1` and `n2`, then check whether **d**, **d–1**, **d–2**, ..., **2**, or **1** is a divisor for both `n1` and `n2` in this order. The first such common divisor is the greatest common divisor for `n1` and `n2`.

4.16**   (*Finding the factors of an integer*) Write a program that reads an integer and displays all its smallest factors, also known as *prime factors*. For example, if the input integer is 120, the output should be as follows: 2, 2, 2, 3, 5.

4.17**   (*Displaying pyramid*) Write a program that prompts the user to enter an integer from 1 to 15 and displays a pyramid, as shown in the following sample output:

```
Enter the number of lines: 7 ↵Enter
                  1
                2 1 2
              3 2 1 2 3
            4 3 2 1 2 3 4
          5 4 3 2 1 2 3 4 5
        6 5 4 3 2 1 2 3 4 5 6
      7 6 5 4 3 2 1 2 3 4 5 6 7
```

4.18*   (*Printing four patterns using loops*) Use nested loops that print the following patterns in four separate programs:

```
Pattern I       Pattern II      Pattern III       Pattern IV

1               1 2 3 4 5 6               1      1 2 3 4 5 6
1 2             1 2 3 4 5               2 1        1 2 3 4 5
1 2 3           1 2 3 4               3 2 1          1 2 3 4
1 2 3 4         1 2 3               4 3 2 1            1 2 3
1 2 3 4 5       1 2             5 4 3 2 1                1 2
1 2 3 4 5 6     1             6 5 4 3 2 1                  1
```

4.19** *(Printing numbers in a pyramid pattern)* Write a nested `for` loop that prints the following output:

```
                              1
                          1   2   1
                      1   2   4   2   1
                  1   2   4   8   4   2   1
              1   2   4   8  16   8   4   2   1
          1   2   4   8  16  32  16   8   4   2   1
      1   2   4   8  16  32  64  32  16   8   4   2   1
  1   2   4   8  16  32  64 128  64  32  16   8   4   2   1
```

Hint

Here is the pseudocode solution:

```
for the row from 0 to 7
{
  Pad leading blanks in a row using a loop like this:
  for the column from 1 to 7-row
    cout << "    ";

  Print left half of the row for numbers 1, 2, 4, up to
    2^row using a loop like this:
  for the column from 0 to row
    cout << "     " << pow(2, column);

  Print the right half of the row for numbers
    2^row-1, 2^row-2, ..., 1 using a loop like this:
  for (int column = row - 1; column >= 0; column--)
    cout << "     " << pow(2, column);

  Start a new line
  cout << endl;
}
```

You need to figure out how many spaces to print before the number. This depends on the number. If a number is a single digit, print four spaces. If a number has two digits, print three spaces. If a number has three digits, print two spaces.

The `pow()` function was introduced in Listing 2.9, ComputeLoan.cpp. Can you write this program without using it?

4.20* *(Printing prime numbers between 2 and 1000)* Modify Listing 4.14 to print all the prime numbers between 2 and 1000, inclusive. Display eight prime numbers per line.

Comprehensive

4.21**(*Financial application: comparing loans with various interest rates*) Write a program that lets the user enter the loan amount and loan period in number of years and displays the monthly and total payments for each interest rate starting from 5% to 8%, with an increment of 1/8. Here is a sample run:

```
Loan Amount: 10000 ↵Enter
Number of Years: 5 ↵Enter

Interest Rate              Monthly Payment    Total Payment
5%                         188.71             11322.74
5.125%                     189.28             11357.13
```

5.25%	189.85	11391.59
...		
7.85%	202.16	12129.97
8.0%	202.76	12165.83

For the formula to compute monthly payment, see Listing 2.9, ComputeLoan.cpp.

4.22**(*Financial application: loan amortization schedule*) The monthly payment for a given loan pays the principal and the interest. The monthly interest is computed by multiplying the monthly interest rate and the balance (the remaining principal). The principal paid for the month is therefore the monthly payment minus the monthly interest. Write a program that lets the user enter the loan amount, number of years, and interest rate, then displays the amortization schedule for the loan. Here is a sample run:

Video Note
displaying loan schedule

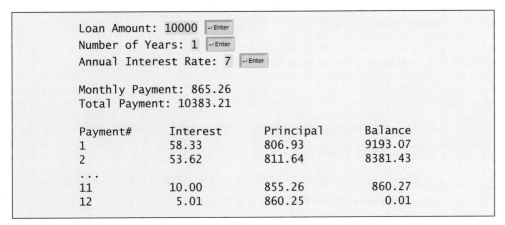

Note
The balance after the last payment may not be zero. If so, the last payment should be the normal monthly payment plus the final balance.

Hint
Write a loop to print the table. Since the monthly payment is the same for each month, it should be computed before the loop. The balance is initially the loan amount. For each iteration in the loop, compute the interest and principal and update the balance. The loop may look like this:

```
for (i = 1; i <= numberOfYears * 12; i++)
{
  interest = monthlyInterestRate * balance;
  principal = monthlyPayment - interest;
  balance = balance - principal;
  cout << i << "\t\t" << interest
    << "\t\t" << principal << "\t\t" << balance << endl;
}
```

4.23* (*Demonstrating cancellation errors*) A cancellation error occurs when you are manipulating a very large number with a very small number. The large number may cancel out the smaller number. For example, the result of 100000000.0 + 0.000000001 is equal to 100000000.0. To avoid cancellation errors and obtain more accurate results, carefully select the order of computation. For example, in computing the following series, you will obtain more accurate results by computing from right to left rather than from left to right:

$$1 + \frac{1}{2} + \frac{1}{3} + \ldots + \frac{1}{n}$$

Write a program that compares the results of the summation of the preceding series, computing from left to right and from right to left with n = 50000.

4.24* (*Summing a series*) Write a program to sum the following series:

$$\frac{1}{3} + \frac{3}{5} + \frac{5}{7} + \frac{7}{9} + \frac{9}{11} + \frac{11}{13} + \ldots + \frac{95}{97} + \frac{97}{99}$$

4.25** (*Computing* π) You can approximate π by using the following series:

$$\pi = 4\left(1 - \frac{1}{3} + \frac{1}{5} - \frac{1}{7} + \frac{1}{9} - \frac{1}{11} + \frac{1}{13} - \ldots - \frac{1}{2i-1} + \frac{1}{2i+1}\right)$$

Write a program that displays the π value for i = 10000, 20000, ..., and 100000.

4.26** (*Computing* e) You can approximate e by using the following series:

$$e = 1 + \frac{1}{1!} + \frac{1}{2!} + \frac{1}{3!} + \frac{1}{4!} + \ldots + \frac{1}{i!}$$

Write a program that displays the e value for i = 10000, 20000, ..., and 100000. (*Hint:* Since $i! = i \times (i-1) \times \ldots \times 2 \times 1$, then $\frac{1}{i!}$ is $\frac{1}{i(i-1)!}$. Initialize e and item to be 1 and keep adding a new item to e. The new item is the previous item divided by i for i = 2, 3, 4, ...)

4.27 (*Displaying leap years*) Write a program that displays, ten per line, all the leap years in the twenty-first century (from year 2001 to 2100).

4.28** (*Displaying the first days of each month*) Write a program that prompts the user to enter the year and first day of the year, and displays the first day of each month in the year on the console. For example, if the user entered year 2005, and 6 for Saturday, January 1, 2005, your program should display the following output:

```
January 1, 2005 is Saturday
...
December 1, 2005 is Thursday
```

4.29** (*Displaying calendars*) Write a program that prompts the user to enter the year and first day of the year and displays on the console the calendar table for the year. For example, if the user entered year 2005, and 6 for Saturday, January 1, 2005, your program should display the calendar for each month in the year, as follows:

January 2005						
Sun	Mon	Tue	Wed	Thu	Fri	Sat
						1
2	3	4	5	6	7	8
9	10	11	12	13	14	15
16	17	18	19	20	21	22
23	24	25	26	27	28	29
30	31					

...

December 2005

Sun	Mon	Tue	Wed	Thu	Fri	Sat
				1	2	3
4	5	6	7	8	9	10
11	12	13	14	15	16	17
18	19	20	21	22	23	24
25	26	27	28	29	30	31
30	31					

4.30* (*Financial application: compound value*) Suppose you save $100 *each* month into a savings account with the annual interest rate 5%. So, the monthly interest rate is 0.05 / 12 = 0.00417. After the first month, the value in the account becomes

$$100 * (1 + 0.00417) = 100.417$$

After the second month, the value in the account becomes

$$(100 + 100.417) * (1 + 0.00417) = 201.252$$

After the third month, the value in the account becomes

$$(100 + 201.252) * (1 + 0.00417) = 302.507$$

and so on.

Write a program that prompts the user to enter an amount (e.g., 100), the annual interest rate (e.g., 5), and the number of months (e.g., 6), and displays the amount in the savings account after the given month.

4.31* (*Financial application: computing CD value*) Suppose you put $10000 into a CD with an annual percentage yield of 5.75%. After one month, the CD is worth

$$10000 + 10000 * 5.75 / 1200 = 10047.91$$

After two months, the CD is worth

$$10047.91 + 10047.91 * 5.75 / 1200 = 10096.06$$

After three months, the CD is worth

$$10096.06 + 10096.06 * 5.75 / 1200 = 10144.43$$

and so on.

Write a program that prompts the user to enter an amount (e.g., 10000), the annual percentage yield (e.g., 5.75), and the number of months (e.g., 18), and displays a table as shown in the sample output.

```
Enter the initial deposit amount: 10000  ↵Enter
Enter annual percentage yield: 5.75  ↵Enter
Enter maturity period (number of months): 18  ↵Enter

MonthCD Value
110047.91
210096.06
...
1710846.56
1810898.54
```

4.32** (*Perfect number*) A positive integer is called a *perfect number* if it is equal to the sum of all of its positive divisors, excluding itself. For example, **6** is the first perfect number, because **6** = **3** + **2** + **1**. The next is **28** = **14** + **7** + **4** + **2** + **1**. There are four perfect numbers less than **10000**. Write a program to find these four numbers.

4.33** (*Game: lottery*) Revise Listing 3.8, Lottery.cpp, to generate a lottery of a two-digit number. The two digits in the number are distinct. (*Hint:* Generate the first digit. Use a loop to continuously generate the second digit until it is different from the first digit.)

4.34*** (*Game: scissor, rock, paper*) Exercise 3.15 gives a program that plays the scissor–rock–paper game. Revise the program to let the user continuously play until either the user or the computer wins more than two times.

4.35* (*Summation*) You can prove that the following summation is **24**.

$$\frac{1}{1 + \sqrt{2}} + \frac{1}{\sqrt{2} + \sqrt{3}} + \frac{1}{\sqrt{3} + \sqrt{4}} + \ldots + \frac{1}{\sqrt{624} + \sqrt{625}}$$

Write a program to verify your result.

4.36** (*Checking ISBN*) Use loops to simplify Exercise 3.17.

4.37* (*Financial application: finding the sales amount*) You have just started a sales job in a department store. Your pay consists of a base salary and a commission. The base salary is $5,000. The scheme shown below is used to determine the commission rate.

Sales Amount	Commission Rate
$0.01–$5,000	8 percent
$5,000.01–$10,000	10 percent
$10,000.01 and above	12 percent

Your goal is to earn $30,000 a year. Write a program that finds out the minimum amount of sales you have to generate in order to make $30,000.

4.38 (*Simulation: head or tail*) Write a program that simulates flipping a coin one million times and displays the number of heads and tails.

4.39** (*Occurrence of max numbers*) Write a program that reads integers, finds the largest of them, and counts its occurrences. Assume that the input ends with number **0**. Suppose that you entered **3 5 2 5 5 5 0**; the program finds that the largest is **5** and the occurrence count for **5** is **4**. (*Hint:* Maintain two variables, **max** and **count**. **max** stores the current max number, and **count** stores its occurrences. Initially, assign the first number to **max** and **1** to **count**. Compare each subsequent number with **max**. If the number is greater than **max**, assign it to **max** and reset **count** to **1**. If the number is equal to **max**, increment **count** by **1**.)

```
Enter numbers: 3 5 2 5 5 5 0  ↵Enter
The largest number is 5
The occurrence count of the largest number is 4
```

4.40* (*Financial application: finding the sales amount*) Rewrite Exercise 4.37 as follows:

- Use a `for` loop instead of a `do-while` loop.
- Let the user enter `COMMISSION_SOUGHT` instead of fixing it as a constant.

4.41* (*Simulation: clock countdown*) Write a program that prompts the user to enter the number of seconds, then displays a message every second and terminates when the time expires. Here is a sample run:

```
Enter the number of second: 3 ↵Enter
2 seconds remaining
1 second remaining
Stopped
```

4.42** (*Monte Carlo simulation: clock countdown*) A square is divided into four smaller regions as shown below in (a). If you throw a dart into the square 1000000 times, what is the probability for a stone to fall into the odd region? Write a program to simulate the process and display the result.

(*Hint:* Place the center of the square in the center of a coordinate system, as shown in (b). Randomly generate a point in the square and count the number of times for a point to fall in the odd region.)

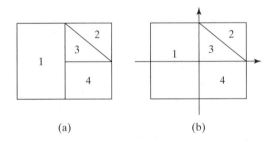

(a)   (b)

CHAPTER 5

FUNCTION BASICS

Objectives

- To define functions (§5.2).
- To invoke value-returning functions (§5.3).
- To invoke void functions (§5.4).
- To pass arguments (§5.5).
- To develop reusable code that is modular, easy to read, easy to debug, and easy to maintain (§5.6).
- To use function overloading and understand ambiguous overloading (§5.7).
- To use function prototypes for function headers (§5.8).
- To create header files for reusing functions (§5.9).
- To separate function headers from implementation (§5.10).
- To develop functions for generating random characters (§5.11).
- To develop applications using the C++ mathematical functions (§5.12).
- To develop applications using the C++ character functions (§5.13).

why function?

5.1 Introduction

A *function* is a construct for grouping statements together to perform a task. Using a function, you can write the code once to perform the task in a program and then reuse it in many other programs. For example, often you need to find the larger of two numbers. To perform this operation, you have to write the following code:

```
int result;

if (num1 > num2)
    result = num1;
else
    result = num2;
```

If you define a function to perform this task, you don't have to repeatedly write the same code. You define it just once and then reuse it in other programs.

A function is a collection of statements grouped together to perform an operation. In earlier chapters, you learned about such functions as `pow(a, b)`, `rand()`, `srand(seed)`, `time(0)`, and `main()`. When you call the `pow(a, b)` function, for example, the system actually executes the statements in the function and returns the result. In this chapter, you will learn how to create functions and apply function abstraction to solve complex problems.

5.2 Defining a Function

The syntax for defining a function is as follows:

```
returnValueType functionName(list of parameters)
{
    // Function body;
}
```

Let's look at a function created to find which of two integers is bigger. This function, named `max`, has two `int` parameters, `num1` and `num2`, the larger of which is returned by the function. Figure 5.1 illustrates the components of this function.

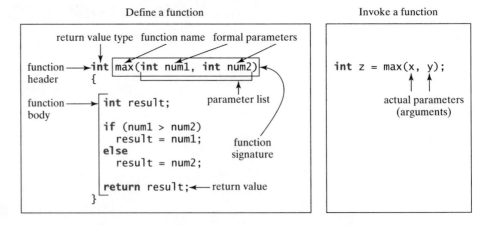

FIGURE 5.1 You can define a function and invoke it with arguments.

function header

The function header specifies the function's *return value type*, *function name*, and *parameters*.

A function may return a value. The `returnValueType` is the data type of that value. Some functions perform desired operations without returning a value. In this case, the `returnValueType` is the keyword `void`. For example, the `returnValueType` in the `srand` function is `void`. The function that returns a value is called a *value-returning function* and the function that does not return a value is called a *void function*.

value-returning function
void function

The variables declared in the function header are known as *formal parameters* or simply *parameters*. A parameter is like a placeholder. When a function is invoked, you pass a value to the parameter. This value is referred to as an *actual parameter or argument*. The *parameter list* refers to the type, order, and number of the parameters of a function. The function name and the parameter list together constitute the *function signature*. Parameters are optional; that is, a function may contain no parameters. For example, the `rand()` function has no parameters.

parameter
argument
parameter list
function signature

The function body contains a collection of statements that define what the function does. The function body of the `max` function uses an `if` statement to determine which number is larger and return the value of that number. A return statement using the keyword `return` is *required* for a *value-returning* function to return a result. The function terminates when a return statement is executed.

Caution

In the function header, you need to declare a separate data type for each parameter. For instance, `max(int num1, int num2)` is correct, but `max(int num1, num2)` is wrong.

Note

We say "*define* a function" and "*declare* a variable." Is there any particular reason for this? Yes. There is a subtle difference. A definition specifies what the defined item is, but a declaration usually involves allocating memory to store data for the declared item. Recall that the `#define` directive defines a constant and the `const` keyword declares a constant. The `#define` directive is like defining an alias for a value, but the `const` keyword allocates memory to store the constant.

define vs. declare

5.3 Calling a Function

In creating a function, you define what it is to do. To use a function, you have to *call* or *invoke* it. There are two ways to call a function, depending on whether or not it returns a value.

If the function returns a value, a call to that function is usually treated as a value. For example,

```
int larger = max(3, 4);
```

calls `max(3, 4)` and assigns the result of the function to the variable `larger`. Another example of a call that is treated as a value is

```
cout << max(3, 4);
```

which prints the return value of the function call `max(3, 4)`.

Note

A value-returning function also can be invoked as a statement in C++. In this case, the caller simply ignores the return value. This is rare but is permissible if the caller is not interested in the return value.

When a program calls a function, program control is transferred to the called function. A called function returns control to the caller when its return statement is executed or when its function-ending closing brace is reached.

Listing 5.1 shows a complete program that is used to test the `max` function.

define max function

main function

invoke max

LISTING 5.1 TestMax.cpp

```cpp
1 #include <iostream>
2 using namespace std;
3
4 // Return the max between two numbers
5 int max(int num1, int num2)
6 {
7   int result;
8   if (num1 > num2)
9     result = num1;
10  else
11    result = num2;
12
13    return result;
14 }
15
16 int main()
17 {
18   int i = 5;
19   int j = 2;
20   int k = max(i, j);
21   cout << "The maximum between " << i <<
22     " and " << j << " is " << k;
23
24   return 0;
25 }
```

```
The maximum between 5 and 2 is 5
```

line#	i	j	k	num1	num2	result
18	5					
19		2				
20				5	2	
6						undefined
9						5
20			5			

main function

order of functions

max function

This program contains the `max` function and the `main` function. The latter is just like any other function except that it is invoked by the operating system to execute the program.

A function must be defined before it is invoked. Since the `max` function is invoked by the `main` function, it must be defined before the main function.

When the `max` function is invoked (line 20), variable `i`'s value `5` is passed to `num1`, and variable `j`'s value `2` is passed to `num2` in the `max` function. The flow of control transfers to the `max` function. The `max` function is executed. When the `return` statement in the `max` function is executed, the `max` function returns the control to its caller (in this case the caller is the `main` function). This process is illustrated in Figure 5.2.

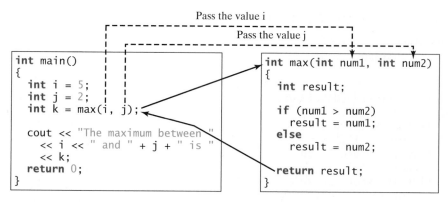

```
int main()                            int max(int num1, int num2)
{                                     {
   int i = 5;                            int result;
   int j = 2;
   int k = max(i, j);                    if (num1 > num2)
                                            result = num1;
   cout << "The maximum between "        else
      << i << " and " + j + " is "          result = num2;
      << k;
   return 0;                             return result;
}                                     }
```

Pass the value i

Pass the value j

FIGURE 5.2 When the `max` function is invoked, the flow of control transfers to the `max` function. Once the `max` function is finished, it returns the control back to the caller.

5.3.1 Call Stacks

Each time a function is invoked, the system stores its arguments and variables in an area of memory, known as a *stack*, which stores elements in last-in, first-out fashion. When a function calls another function, the caller's stack space is kept intact, and new space is created to handle the new function call. When a function finishes its work and returns to its caller, its associated space is released.

stack

Understanding call stacks helps us comprehend how functions are invoked. The variables defined in the `main` function are `i`, `j`, and `k`. The variables defined in the `max` function are `num1`, `num2`, and `result`. The variables `num1` and `num2` are defined in the function signature and are parameters of the function. Their values are passed through function invocation. Figure 5.3 illustrates the variables in the stack.

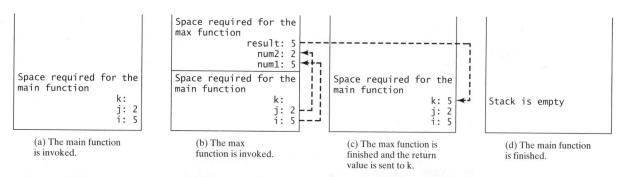

FIGURE 5.3 When the `max` function is invoked, the flow of control transfers to the `max` function. Once the `max` function is finished, it returns the control back to the caller.

Tip

If you use Visual C++, please refer to Supplement II.B, "*Learning C++ Effectively with Visual C++.NET*," in the supplements. It shows you how to use a debugger to trace function calls.

debugging in IDE

5.4 void Functions

The preceding section gives an example of a value-returning function. This section shows how to define and invoke a void function. Listing 5.2 gives a program that defines a function named `printGrade` and invokes it to print the grade for a given score.

Video Note
void function vs. value-return function

printGrade function

LISTING 5.2 TestVoidFunction.cpp

```cpp
1 #include <iostream>
2 using namespace std;
3
4 // Print grade for the score
5 void printGrade(double score)
6 {
7   if (score >= 90.0)
8     cout << 'A';
9   else if (score >= 80.0)
10     cout << 'B';
11   else if (score >= 70.0)
12     cout << 'C';
13   else if (score >= 60.0)
14     cout << 'D';
15   else
16     cout << 'F';
17 }
18
19 int main()
20 {
21   cout << "Enter a score: ";
22   double score;
23   cin >> score;
24
25   cout << "The grade is ";
26   printGrade(score);
27
28   return 0;
29 }
```

main function

invoke **printGrade**

```
Enter a score: 78.5  ⏎ Enter
The grade is C
```

invoke void function

The **printGrade** function is a void function. It does not return any value. A call to a void function must be a statement. So, it is invoked as a statement in line 26 in the main function. Like any C++ statement, it is terminated with a semicolon.

Note

return in void function

A **return** statement is not needed for a void function, but it can be used for terminating the function and returning control to the function's caller. The syntax is simply

```cpp
return;
```

This is rare but sometimes is useful for circumventing the normal flow of control in a void function. For example, the following code has a return statement to terminate the function when the score is invalid.

```cpp
// Print grade for the score
void printGrade(double score)
{
  if (score < 0 || score > 100)
  {
    cout << "Invalid score";
    return;
  }
```

```
    if (score >= 90.0)
      cout << 'A';
    else if (score >= 80.0)
      cout << 'B';
    else if (score >= 70.0)
      cout << 'C';
    else if (score >= 60.0)
      cout << 'D';
    else
      cout << 'F';
  }
```

To see the differences between a void and a value-returning function, let us redesign the **printGrade** function to return a value. We call the new function that returns the grade, as shown in Listing 5.3, **getGrade**.

LISTING 5.3 TestReturnGradeFunction.cpp

```
1 #include <iostream>
2 using namespace std;
3
4 // Return the grade for the score
5 char getGrade(double score)
6 {
7   if (score >= 90.0)
8     return 'A';
9   else if (score >= 80.0)
10    return 'B';
11  else if (score >= 70.0)
12    return 'C';
13  else if (score >= 60.0)
14    return 'D';
15  else
16    return 'F';
17 }
18
19 int main()
20 {
21   cout << "Enter a score: ";
22   double score;
23   cin >> score;
24
25   cout << "The grade is ";
26   cout << getGrade(score) << endl;
27
28   return 0;
29 }
```

Video Note
void function vs. value-return function

getGrade function

main function

invoke **getGrade**

```
Enter a score: 78.5  ⏎Enter
The grade is C
```

The **getGrade** function defined in lines 5–17 returns a character grade based on the numeric score value. The caller invokes this function in line 26.

The **getGrade** function can be invoked by a caller wherever a character may appear. The **printGrade** function does not return any value. It must be invoked as a statement.

5.5 Passing Arguments

The power of a function is its ability to work with parameters. You can use `max` to find the maximum between any two `int` values. When calling a function, you need to provide arguments, which must be given in the same order as their respective parameters in the function specification. This is known as *parameter order association*. For example, the following function prints a character `n` times:

parameter order association

```cpp
void nPrintln(char ch, int n)
{
  for (int i = 0; i < n; i++)
    cout << ch;
}
```

You can use `nPrintln('a', 3)` to print `'a'` three times. The `nPrintln('a', 3)` statement passes the actual `char` parameter, `'a'`, to the parameter, `ch`; passes `3` to `n`; and prints `'a'` three times. However, the statement `nPrintln(3, 'a')` has a different meaning. It passes `3` to `ch` and `'a'` to `n`.

 Caution

The arguments must match the parameters in *order*, *number*, and *compatible type*, as defined in the function signature. Compatible type means that you can pass an argument to a parameter without explicit casting, such as passing an `int` value argument to a `double` value parameter.

5.6 Modularizing Code

Functions can be used to reduce redundant code and enable code reuse. Functions can also be used to modularize code and improve the program's quality.

Listing 4.8, GreatestCommonDivisor.cpp, gives a program that prompts the user to enter two integers and displays their greatest common divisor. You can rewrite the program using a function, as shown in Listing 5.4.

Video Note
modularizing code

compute **gcd**

LISTING 5.4 GreatestCommonDivisorFunction.cpp

```cpp
1 #include <iostream>
2 using namespace std;
3
4 /** Return the gcd of two integers */
5 int gcd(int n1, int n2)
6 {
7   int gcd = 1; // Initial gcd is 1
8   int k = 2;   // Possible gcd
9
10   while (k <= n1 && k <= n2)
11   {
12     if (n1 % k == 0 && n2 % k == 0)
13       gcd = k; // Update gcd
14     k++;
15   }
16
17   return gcd; // Return gcd
18 }
19
20 int main()
21 {
22   // Prompt the user to enter two integers
23   cout << "Enter first integer: ";
```

return **gcd**

```
24    int n1;
25    cin >> n1;
26
27    cout << "Enter second integer: ";
28    int n2;
29    cin >> n2;
30
31    cout << "The greatest common divisor for " << n1 <<
32      " and " << n2 << " is " << gcd(n1, n2);
33
34    return 0;
35 }
```

invoke **gcd**

```
Enter first integer: 45 [↵Enter]
Enter second integer: 75 [↵Enter]
The greatest common divisor for 45 and 75 is 15
```

By enclosing the code for obtaining the gcd in a function, this program has several advantages:

1. It isolates the problem for computing the gcd from the rest of the code in the main function. Thus, the logic becomes clear and the program is easier to read.

2. The errors on computing gcd are confined in the **gcd** function, which narrows the scope of debugging.

3. The **gcd** function now can be reused by other programs.

Listing 5.5 applies the concept of code modularization to improve Listing 4.14, PrimeNumber.cpp. The program defines two new functions **isPrime** and **printPrimeNumbers**. The **isPrime** function checks whether a number is prime and the **printPrimeNumbers** function prints prime numbers.

LISTING 5.5 PrimeNumberFunction.cpp

```
 1 #include <iostream>
 2 #include <iomanip>
 3 using namespace std;
 4
 5 /** Check whether number is prime */
 6 bool isPrime(int number)
 7 {
 8   for (int divisor = 2; divisor <= number / 2; divisor++)
 9   {
10     if (number % divisor == 0)
11     {
12       // If true, number is not prime
13       return false; // number is not a prime
14     }
15   }
16
17   return true; // number is prime
18 }
19
20 void printPrimeNumbers(int numberOfPrimes)
21 {
22   const int NUMBER_OF_PRIMES = 50; // Number of primes to display
```

isPrime function

printPrimeNumbers
function

```
23    const int NUMBER_OF_PRIMES_PER_LINE = 10; // Display 10 per line
24    int count = 0; // Count the number of prime numbers
25    int number = 2; // A number to be tested for primeness
26
27    // Repeatedly find prime numbers
28    while (count < numberOfPrimes)
29    {
30      // Print the prime number and increase the count
31      if (isPrime(number))
32      {
33        count++; // Increase the count
34
35        if (count % NUMBER_OF_PRIMES_PER_LINE == 0)
36        {
37          // Print the number and advance to the new line
38          cout << setw(4) << number << endl;
39        }
40        else
41          cout << setw(4) << number << " ";
42      }
43
44      // Check if the next number is prime
45      number++;
46    }
47  }
48
49  int main()
50  {
51    cout << "The first 50 prime numbers are \n";
52    printPrimeNumbers(50);
53
54    return 0;
55  }
```

invoke **isPrime** (line 31)

invoke **printPrimeNumbers** (line 52)

```
The first 50 prime numbers are
 2    3    5    7   11   13   17   19   23   29
31   37   41   43   47   53   59   61   67   71
73   79   83   89   97  101  103  107  109  113
127  131  137  139  149  151  157  163  167  173
179  181  191  193  197  199  211  223  227  229
```

We divided a large problem into two subproblems. As a result, the new program is easier to read and easier to debug. Moreover, the functions printPrimeNumbers and isPrime can be reused by other programs.

5.7 Overloading Functions

The max function that was used earlier works only with the int data type. But what if you need to determine which of two floating-point numbers has the larger value? The solution is to create another function with the same name but different parameters, as shown in the following code:

```
double max(double num1, double num2)
{
  if (num1 > num2)
    return num1;
  else
    return num2;
}
```

If you call `max` with `int` parameters, the `max` function that expects `int` parameters will be invoked; if you call `max` with `double` parameters, the `max` function that expects `double` parameters will be invoked. This is referred to as *function overloading*; that is, two functions have the same name but different parameter lists within one file. The C++ compiler determines which function is used based on the function signature.

function overloading

Listing 5.6 is a program that creates three functions. The first finds the maximum integer, the second finds the maximum double, and the third finds the maximum among three double values. All three functions are named `max`.

LISTING 5.6 TestFunctionOverloading.cpp

```
 1 #include <iostream>
 2 using namespace std;
 3
 4 // Return the max between two int values
 5 int max(int num1, int num2)                              max function
 6 {
 7   if (num1 > num2)
 8     return num1;
 9   else
10     return num2;
11 }
12
13 // Find the max between two double values
14 double max(double num1, double num2)                     max function
15 {
16   if (num1 > num2)
17     return num1;
18   else
19     return num2;
20 }
21
22 // Return the max among three double values
23 double max(double num1, double num2, double num3)        max function
24 {
25   return max(max(num1, num2), num3);
26 }
27
28 int main()                                               main function
29 {
30   // Invoke the max function with int parameters
31   cout << "The maximum between 3 and 4 is " << max(3, 4) << endl;   invoke max
32
33   // Invoke the max function with the double parameters
34   cout << "The maximum between 3.0 and 5.4 is "
35     << max(3.0, 5.4) << endl;                            invoke max
36
37   // Invoke the max function with three double parameters
38   cout << "The maximum between 3.0, 5.4, and 10.14 is "
39     << max(3.0, 5.4, 10.14) << endl;                     invoke max
40
41   return 0;
42 }
```

When calling `max(3, 4)` (line 31), the `max` function for finding the maximum of two integers is invoked. When calling `max(3.0, 5.4)` (line 35), the `max` function for finding the maximum of two doubles is invoked. When calling `max(3.0, 5.4, 10.14)` (line 39), the `max` function for finding the maximum of three double values is invoked.

Can you invoke the `max` function with an `int` value and a `double` value, such as `max(2, 2.5)`? If you can, which of the `max` functions is invoked? The answer to the first question is yes. The answer to the second is that the `max` function for finding the maximum of two `double` values is invoked. The argument value 2 is automatically converted into a `double` value and passed to this function.

You may be wondering why the function `max(double, double)` is not invoked for the call `max(3, 4)`. Both `max(double, double)` and `max(int, int)` are possible matches for `max(3, 4)`. The C++ compiler finds the most specific function for a function invocation. Since the function `max(int, int)` is more specific than `max(double, double)`, `max(int, int)` is used to invoke `max(3, 4)`.

Tip

Overloading functions can make programs clearer and more readable. Functions that perform closely related tasks should be given the same name.

Note

Overloaded functions must have different parameter lists. You cannot overload functions based on different return types.

ambiguous invocation

Sometimes there are two or more possible matches for an invocation of a function, but the compiler cannot determine the most specific match. This is referred to as *ambiguous invocation*. Ambiguous invocation causes a compilation error. Consider the following code:

```cpp
#include <iostream>
using namespace std;

int maxNumber(int num1, double num2)
{
  if (num1 > num2)
    return num1;
  else
    return num2;
}

double maxNumber(double num1, int num2)
{
  if (num1 > num2)
    return num1;
  else
    return num2;
}

int main()
{
  cout << maxNumber(1, 2) << endl;

  return 0;
}
```

Both `maxNumber(int, double)` and `maxNumber(double, int)` are possible candidates to match `maxNumber(1, 2)`. Since neither is more specific than the other, the invocation is ambiguous, resulting in a compilation error.

If you change `maxNumber(1, 2)` to `maxNumber(1, 2.0)`, it will match the first `maxNumber` function. So, there will be no compilation error.

5.8 Function Prototypes

Before a function is called, it must be defined. One way to ensure this is to place the definition before all function calls. Another approach is to define a function prototype before the function is called. A function prototype is a function header without implementation. The implementation can be given later in the program.

Listing 5.7 rewrites TestFunctionOverloading.cpp in Listing 5.6 using function prototypes. Three `max` function prototypes are defined in lines 5–7. These functions are called later in the `main` function. The functions are implemented in lines 27, 36, and 45.

LISTING 5.7 TestFunctionPrototype.cpp

```
1 #include <iostream>
2 using namespace std;
3
4 // Function prototype
5 int max(int num1, int  num2);                      function prototype
6 double max(double num1, double num2);              function prototype
7 double max(double num1, double num2, double num3); function prototype
8
9 int main()                                         main function
10 {
11   // Invoke the max function with int parameters
12   cout << "The maximum between 3 and 4 is " <<
13     max(3, 4) << endl;                             invoke max
14
15   // Invoke the max function with the double parameters
16   cout << "The maximum between 3.0 and 5.4 is "
17     << max(3.0, 5.4) << endl;                      invoke max
18
19   // Invoke the max function with three double parameters
20   cout << "The maximum between 3.0, 5.4, and 10.14 is "
21     << max(3.0, 5.4, 10.14) << endl;               invoke max
22
23   return 0;
24 }
25
26 // Return the max between two int values
27 int max(int num1, int num2)                        function implementation
28 {
29   if (num1 > num2)
30     return num1;
31   else
32     return num2;
33 }
34
35 // Find the max between two double values
36 double max(double num1, double num2)               function implementation
37 {
38   if (num1 > num2)
39     return num1;
40   else
41     return num2;
42 }
43
```

function implementation

```
44 // Return the max among three double values
45 double max(double num1, double num2, double num3)
46 {
47    return max(max(num1, num2), num3);
48 }
```

Note

omitting parameter names

In the prototype you need not list the parameter names, only the parameter types. C++ compiler ignores the parameter names. The prototype tells the compiler the name of the function, its return type, the number of parameters, and each parameter's type. So, lines 5–7 can be replaced by

```
int max(int, int);
double max(double, double);
double max(double, double, double);
```

5.9 Reuse of Functions by Different Programs

One benefit of functions is that you can reuse them. In the preceding sections, you defined functions and used them from the same program. To make them available for other programs to use, you need to place the functions in a separate file, called the *header file*. By convention, the file has a .h extension. Programs use #include preprocessor directives to include header files in order to reuse the functions defined in those files.

Listing 5.8 creates a header file named MyLib.h. This file defines a function named isEven(number) that returns true if the number is even.

LISTING 5.8 MyLib.h

isEven

```
1 bool isEven(int number)
2 {
3    return (number % 2 == 0);
4 }
```

Listing 5.9 creates a file named UseMyLib.cpp. This file contains a main function for testing the isEven function.

LISTING 5.9 UseMyLib.cpp

include MyLib.h

```
1 #include <iostream>
2 #include "MyLib.h"
3
4 using namespace std;
5
6 int main()
7 {
```
invoke **isEven**
invoke **isEven**
```
8    cout << (isEven(4) ? "true" : "false") << endl;
9    cout << (isEven(5) ? "true" : "false") << endl;
10
11    return 0;
12 }
```

```
true
false
```

The program includes two header files, iostream (line 1) and MyLib.h (line 2). iostream is a header file defined in the C++ library and MyLib.h is user defined. Enclose a user-defined header file in double quotation marks (" ") and a C++ library header file in angle brackets (< >).

user-defined header file
library header file

Header files can be placed anywhere on the disk. For example, if MyLib.h is placed under the c:\ root directory on Windows, you can include it using the absolute file name as follows:

placing header file

```
#include "c:\\MyLib.h"
```

This makes your code dependent on Windows. To fix the problem, you may place the header file in or under the same directory with the program that includes it, or you may compile the program using the –I option to specify the location for the header file:

```
g++ UseMyLib.cpp -I c:\ -o Main
```

Caution

Header files are designed for reuse by other programs that likely have a main function. Because one program cannot have two main functions, you should not write a main function in a header file.

*no **main** in header file*

5.10 Separating Function Headers from Implementation

If you are a software vendor, you wish to hide the source code from the client. You can separate function headers and implementation into two files. The header file simply lists all the function prototypes. The implementation file implements the functions. Both files should have the same name, but with an .h extension for the header file and .cpp for the implementation file, as shown in Listings 5.10 and 5.11.

LISTING 5.10 MyLib.h

```
1 bool isEven(int number);
```

function prototype

LISTING 5.11 MyLib.cpp

```
1 bool isEven(int number)
2 {
3    return (number % 2 == 0);
4 }
```

implement function

For the client to use MyLib, you need only provide the header file and object code generated from MyLib.cpp. You don't need to provide MyLib.cpp. This protects the software vendor's intellectual property.

5.11 Case Study: Generating Random Characters

Computer programs process numeric data and characters. You have seen many examples involving numeric data. It is also important to understand characters and how to process them. This section gives an example of generating random characters.

As introduced in §2.11, every character has a unique ASCII code between 0 and 127. To generate a random character is to generate a random integer between 0 and 127. You learned in §3.10 how to generate a random number. Recall that you can use the srand(seed) function to set a seed and use rand() to return a random integer. You can use it to write a simple expression to generate random numbers in any range. For example,

rand() % 10   ⟶   Returns a random integer between 0 and 9.

50 + rand() % 50   ⟶   Returns a random integer between 50 and 99.

In general,

a + rand() % b   ⟶   Returns a random number between a and a + b, excluding a + b.

So, you can use the following expression to generate a random integer between 0 and 127:

```
rand() % 128
```

Now let us consider how to generate a random lowercase letter. The ASCII codes for lowercase letters are consecutive integers starting with the code for 'a', then that for 'b', 'c', ..., and 'z'. The code for 'a' is

```
static_cast<int>('a')
```

So a random integer between static_cast<int>('a') and static_cast<int>('z') is

```
static_cast<int>('a') +
    rand() % (static_cast<int>('z') - static_cast<int>('a') + 1)
```

As discussed in §2.10.2, all numeric operators can be applied to the char operands. The char operand is cast into a number if the other operand is a number or a character. Thus the preceding expression can be simplified as follows:

```
'a' + rand() % ('z' - 'a' + 1)
```

and a random lowercase letter is

```
static_cast<char>('a' + rand() % ('z' - 'a' + 1))
```

To generalize the foregoing discussion, a random character between any two characters ch1 and ch2 with ch1 < ch2 can be generated as follows:

```
static_cast<char>(ch1 + rand() % (ch2 - ch1 + 1))
```

This is a simple but useful discovery. In Listing 5.12 we create a header file named Random-Character.h with five overloaded functions to get a certain type of character randomly. You can use these functions in your future projects.

LISTING 5.12   RandomCharacter.h

```cpp
 1  #include <cstdlib>
 2  using namespace std;
 3
 4  // Generate a random character between ch1 and ch2
 5  char getRandomCharacter(char ch1, char ch2)
 6  {
 7    return static_cast<char>(ch1 + rand() % (ch2 - ch1 + 1));
 8  }
 9
10  // Generate a random lowercase letter
11  char getRandomLowerCaseLetter()
12  {
13    return getRandomCharacter('a', 'z');
14  }
15
16  // Generate a random uppercase letter
17  char getRandomUpperCaseLetter()
18  {
19    return getRandomCharacter('A', 'Z');
20  }
21
22  // Generate a random digit character
23  char getRandomDigitCharacter()
24  {
25    return getRandomCharacter('0', '9');
```

```
26 }
27
28 // Generate a random character
29 char getRandomCharacter()
30 {
31   return getRandomCharacter(0, 127);
32 }
```

Listing 5.13 is a test program that displays 100 random lowercase letters.

LISTING 5.13 TestRandomCharacter.cpp

```
1 #include <iostream>
2 #include "RandomCharacter.h"
3 using namespace std;
4
5 int main()
6 {
7   const int NUMBER_OF_CHARS = 175;                                    constants
8   const int CHARS_PER_LINE = 25;
9
10  srand(time(0)); // Set a new seed for random function              new seed
11
12  // Print random characters between '!' and '~', 25 chars per line
13  for (int i = 0; i < NUMBER_OF_CHARS; i++)
14  {
15    char ch = getRandomLowerCaseLetter();                            lowercase letter
16    if ((i + 1) % CHARS_PER_LINE == 0)
17      cout << ch << endl;
18    else
19      cout << ch;
20  }
21
22  return 0;
23 }
```

```
gmjsohezfkgtazqgmswfclrao
pnrunulnwmaztlfjedmpchcif
lalqdgivxkxpbzulrmqmbhikr
lbnrjlsopfxahssqhwuuljvbe
xbhdotzhpehbqmuwsfktwsoli
cbuwkzgxpmtzihgatdslvbwbz
bfesoklwbhnooygiigzdxuqni
```

Line 2 includes RandomCharacter.h, since the program invokes the function defined in this header file.

The getRandomLowerCaseLetter() function utilizes the rand() function to obtain a random character. To ensure that you get a sequence of different random numbers, srand(time(0)) is invoked in line 10 to set a new seed for the random-number-generator algorithm.

Note that the function getRandomLowerCaseLetter() does not have any parameters, but you still have to use the parentheses when defining and invoking it.   parentheses required

5.12 The Math Functions

C++ contains the functions needed to perform basic mathematical operations. In Listing 2.9, ComputeLoan.cpp, you used the pow(a, b) function to compute a^b. This section introduces other useful mathematical functions, summarized in Table 5.1.

TABLE 5.1   Mathematical Functions

Function	Description	Example
abs(x)	Returns the absolute value of the argument.	abs(-2) is 2
ceil(x)	Rounds x up to its nearest integer and returns this integer.	ceil(2.1) is 3 ceil(-2.1) is -2
floor(x)	Rounds x down to its nearest integer and returns this integer.	floor(2.1) is 2 floor(-2.1) is -3
exp(x)	Returns the exponential function of x (e^x).	exp(1) is 2.71828
pow(x, y)	Returns x raised to power y (x^y).	pow(2.0, 3) is 8
log(x)	Returns the natural logarithm of x.	log(2.71828) is 1.0
log10(x)	Returns the base-10 logarithm of x.	log10 (10.0) is 1
sqrt(x)	Returns the square root of x.	sqrt(4.0) is 2
sin(x)	Returns the sine of x. x represents an angle in radians.	sin(3.14159 / 2) is 1 sin(3.14159) is 0
cos(x)	Returns the cosine of x. x represents an angle in radians.	cos(3.14159 / 2) is 0 cos(3.14159) is -1
tan(x)	Returns the tangent of x. x represents an angle in radians.	tan(3.14159 / 4) is 1 tan(0.0) is 0
fmod(x, y)	Returns the remainder of x/y as double.	fmod(2.4, 1.3) is 1.1
rand()	Returns a random number.	
srand(seed)	Sets a new seed for random number generator.	srand(300)
max(a, b)	Returns the maximum between the two numbers.	max(5, 6)
min(a, b)	Returns the minimum between the two numbers.	min(5, 6)

 Note

The argument x is double. The functions **abs**, **rand**, and **srand** are in the **cstdlib** header and all others are in the **cmath** header.

Listing 5.14 is a program to test some math functions.

LISTING 5.14   MathFunctions.cpp

```
 1 #include <iostream>
 2 #include <cmath>
 3 using namespace std;
 4
 5 int main()
 6 {
 7    const double PI = 3.14159;
 8
 9    // Test trigonometric functions
10    cout << "sin(PI / 2) = " << sin(PI / 2) << endl;
11    cout << "cos(PI / 2) = " << cos(PI / 2) << endl;
12    cout << "tan(PI / 2) = " << tan(PI / 2) << endl;
13
14    // Test algebraic functions
15    cout << "exp(1.0) = " << exp(1.0) << endl;
16    cout << "log(2.78) = " << log(2.78) << endl;
17    cout << "log10(10.0) = " << log10(10.0) << endl;
18    cout << "sqrt(4.0) = " << sqrt(4.0) << endl;
```

include **cmath**

const **PI**

sin
cos
tan

exp
log
log10
sqrt

<!-- -->

```
19    cout << "pow(2.5, 2.5) = " << pow(2.5, 2.5) << endl;
20
21    return 0;
22 }
```

pow

```
sin(PI / 2) = 1
cos(PI / 2) = 1.32679e-06
tan(PI / 2) = 753696
exp(1.0) = 2.71828
log(2.78) = 1.02245
log10(10.0) = 1
sqrt(4.0) = 2
pow(2.5, 2.5) = 9.88212
```

Caution

Math functions are overloaded in the `<cmath>` header file. For example, there are three over-loaded functions for `sin`:

float sin(**float**)
double sin(**double**)
long double sin(**long double**)

If you invoke `sin(2)`, you will get an ambiguous overloading error, because the compiler cannot decide which function matches this call for an `int` argument.

ambiguous overloading

5.13 Character Functions

C++ provides several functions for testing a character in the `<cctype>` header file, as shown in Table 5.2. These functions test a single character and return `true` or `false`. Note that they actually return an `int` value. A nonzero integer corresponds to `true` and zero to `false`. C++ also provides two functions for converting cases, as shown in Table 5.3.

TABLE 5.2 Character Test Functions

Function	Description	Example
isdigit(c)	Returns true if c is a digit.	isdigit('7') is true isdigit('a') is false
isalpha(c)	Returns true if c is a letter.	isalpha('7') is false isalpha('a') is true
isalnum(c)	Returns true if c is a letter or a digit.	isalnum('7') is true isalnum('a') is true
islower(c)	Returns true if c is a lowercase letter.	islower('7') is false islower('a') is true
isupper(c)	Returns true if c is an uppercase letter.	isupper('a') is false isupper('A') is true
isspace(c)	Returns true if c is a whitespace character.	isspace('\t') is true isspace('A') is false
isprint(c)	Returns true if c is a printable character including space ' '.	isprint(' ') is true isprint('A') is true
isgraph(c)	Returns true if c is a printable character excluding space ' '.	isgraph(' ') is false isgraph('A') is true

TABLE 5.2 Character Test Functions *(Continued)*

Function	Description	Example
ispunct(c)	Returns true if c is a printable character other than a digit, letter, or space.	ispunct('*') is true ispunct(',') is true ispunct('A') is false
iscntrl(c)	Returns true if c is a control character such as '\n', '\f', '\v', '\a', and '\b'.	iscntrl('*') is false iscntrl('\n') is true iscntrl('\f') is true

TABLE 5.3 Case Conversion Functions

Function	Description	Example
tolower(c)	Returns the lowercase equivalent of c, if c is an uppercase letter. Otherwise, returns c itself.	tolower('A') returns 'a' tolower('a') returns 'a' tolower('\t') returns '\t'
toupper(c)	Returns the uppercase equivalent of c, if c is a lowercase letter. Otherwise, returns c itself.	toupper('A') returns 'A' toupper('a') returns 'A' toupper('\t') returns '\t'

Listing 5.15 is a program to test character functions.

LISTING 5.15 CharacterFunctions.cpp

```cpp
 1 #include <iostream>
 2 #include <cctype>
 3 using namespace std;
 4
 5 int main()
 6 {
 7   cout << "Enter a character: ";
 8   char ch;
 9   cin >> ch;
10
11   cout << "You entered " << ch << endl;
12
13   if (islower(ch))
14   {
15     cout << "It is a lowercase letter " << endl;
16     cout << "Its equivalent uppercase letter is " <<
17       static_cast<char>(toupper(ch)) << endl;
18   }
19   else if (isupper(ch))
20   {
21     cout << "It is an uppercase letter " << endl;
22     cout << "Its equivalent lowercase letter is " <<
23       static_cast<char>(tolower(ch)) << endl;
24   }
25   else if (isdigit(ch))
26   {
27     cout << "It is a digit character " << endl;
28   }
29
30   return 0;
31 }
```

input character

is lowercase?

convert to uppercase

is uppercase?

convert to lowercase

is digit?

```
Enter a character: a  ↵Enter
You entered a
It is a lowercase letter
Its equivalent uppercase letter is A
```

```
Enter a character: T  ↵Enter
You entered T
It is an uppercase letter
Its equivalent lowercase letter is t
```

```
Enter a character: 8  ↵Enter
You entered 8
It is a digit character
```

KEY TERMS

actual parameter 157	function prototype 167
ambiguous invocation 166	function signature 157
argument 157	header file 168
formal parameter (i.e., parameter) 157	parameter 157
function 156	return type 156
function overloading 165	return value 157

CHAPTER SUMMARY

1. Making programs modular and reusable is one of the central goals in software engineering.

2. Functions can be used to develop modular and reusable code.

3. The function header specifies the *return value type*, *function name*, and *parameters* of the function.

4. A function may return a value. The `returnValueType` is the data type of the value that the function returns.

5. If the function does not return a value, the `returnValueType` is the keyword `void`.

6. The *parameter list* refers to the type, order, and number of the parameters of a function.

7. The arguments that are passed to a function should have the same number, type, and order as the parameters in the function definition.

8. The function name and the parameter list together constitute the *function signature*.

9. Parameters are optional; that is, a function may contain no parameters.

10. A value-returning function must return a value when the function is finished.

11. A return statement also can be used in a void function for terminating the function and returning control to the function's caller.

12. When a program calls a function, program control is transferred to the called function.

13. A called function returns control to the caller when its return statement is executed or its function-ending closing brace is reached.

14. A value-returning function also can be invoked as a statement in C++. In this case, the caller simply ignores the return value.

15. Each time a function is invoked, the system stores its arguments, local variables, and system registers in a space known as a *stack*.

16. When a function calls another function, the caller's stack space is kept intact, and new space is created to handle the new function call.

17. When a function finishes its work and returns to its caller, its associated space is released.

18. A function can be overloaded. This means that two functions can have the same name as long as their function parameter lists differ.

19. Math functions such as `sin`, `cos`, `pow`, `sqrt`, `exp`, and `log` are provided in the `cmath` header.

20. C++ provides useful functions for testing characters and converting letters in the `<cctype>` header file: `isdigit(c)`, `isalpha(c)`, `isalnum(c)`, `islower(c)`, `isupper(c)`, `isspace(c)`, `isprint(c)`, `isgraph(c)`, `ispunct(c)`, and `iscntrl(c)`.

REVIEW QUESTIONS

Sections 5.2–5.6

5.1 What are the benefits of using a function? How do you define a function? How do you invoke a function? What is the subtle difference between "defining a function" and "declaring a variable"?

5.2 What is the `return` type of a `main` function?

5.3 Can you use the conditional operator to simplify the `max` function in Listing 5.1?

5.4 True or false? A call to a function with a `void` return type is always a statement itself, but a call to a value-returning function is always a component of an expression.

5.5 What would be wrong with not writing a `return` statement in a value-returning function? Can you have a `return` statement in a `void` function, such as the following?

```
void p()
{
  int i;
  while (true)
  {
    // Prompt the user to enter an integer
    cout << "Enter an integer: ";
    cin >> i;
```

```
      if (i == 0)
        return;
      cout << "i is " << i << endl;
  }
}
```

Does the `return` statement in the following function cause syntax errors?

```
void p(double x, double y)
{
  cout << x << " " << y << endl;
  return x + y;
}
```

5.6 Describe the terms *parameter*, *argument*, and *function signature*.

5.7 Write a function header for the following functions:

- Computing a sales commission, given the sales amount and the commission rate.
- Printing the calendar for a month, given the month and year.
- Computing a square root.
- Testing whether a number is even, and returning `true` if it is.
- Printing a character a specified number of times.
- Computing the monthly payment, given the loan amount, number of years, and annual interest rate.
- Finding the corresponding uppercase letter, given a lowercase letter.

5.8 Identify and correct the errors in the following program:

```
1 int function1(int n)
2 {
3   cout << n;
4 }
5
6 function2(int n, m)
7 {
8   n += m;
9   function1(3.4);
10 }
```

Sections 5.7–5.11

5.9 What is function overloading? Can we define two functions that have the same name but different parameter types? Can we define two functions in one program that have identical function names and parameter lists but different return value types?

5.10 What is wrong in the following program?

```
void p(int i)
{
  cout << i << endl;
}

int p(int j)
{
  cout << j << endl;
}
```

Section 5.12

5.11 True or false? The argument for trigonometric functions represents an angle in radians.

5.12 Write an expression that returns a random integer between 34 and 55. Write an expression that returns a random integer between 0 and 999. Write an expression that returns a random lowercase letter.

5.13 If you replace the arguments with an `int` value for functions `sin`, `cos`, `tan`, `exp`, `log`, `log10`, `sqrt`, and `pow`, what will happen? Explain the reason.

5.14 Assume PI is 3.14159 and E is 2.71828. Evaluate the following function calls:

```
A. sqrt(4.0)          J. floor(-2.5)
B. sin(2 * PI)        K. abs(-2.5f)
C. cos(2 * PI)        L. log10(100.0)
D. pow(2, 2)          M. cos(PI)
E. log(E)             N. ceil(2.5)
F. exp(1.0)           O. floor(2.5)
G. max(2, min(3, 4))  P. pow(2.0, 4)
H. fmod(2.5, 2.3)     Q. fmod(4.2, 3.5)
I. ceil(-2.5)         R. ceil(abs(-2.5))
```

Section 5.13

5.15 Which function do you use to test whether a character is a digit? a letter? a lowercase letter? an uppercase letter? a digit or a letter?

5.16 Which function do you use to convert a letter to lowercase or to uppercase?

PROGRAMMING EXERCISES

Sections 5.2–5.11

5.1 (*Math: pentagonal numbers*) A pentagonal number is defined as n(3n-1)/2 for n = 1, 2,..., and so on. So, the first few numbers are 1, 5, 12, 22, ... Write the following function that returns a pentagonal number:

```
int getPentagonalNumber(int n)
```

Write a test program that displays the first 100 pentagonal numbers with 10 numbers on each line.

5.2* (*Summing the digits in an integer*) Write a function that computes the sum of the digits in an integer. Use the following function header:

```
int sumDigits(long n)
```

For example, `sumDigits(234)` returns 2 + 3 + 4 = 9. Write a test program that prompts the user to enter an integer and displays the sum of all its digits.

 Hint

Use the % operator to extract a digit and the / operator to remove the extracted digit. For instance, to extract 4 from 234, use 234 % 10 (=4). To remove 4 from 234, use 234 / 10 (=23). Use a loop to repeatedly extract and remove a digit until all the digits are extracted.

5.3* (*Displaying an integer reversed*) Write the following function to display an integer in reverse order:

```
void reverse(int number)
```

For example, `reverse(3456)` displays 6543. Write a test program that prompts the user to enter an integer and displays its reversal.

5.4** (*Returning an integer reversed*) Write the following function to return an integer reversed:

```
int reverse(int number)
```

For example, reverse(3456) returns 6543. Write a test program that prompts the user to enter an integer and displays its reversal.

5.5* (*Palindrome number*) A positive integer is a palindrome if its reversal is the same as itself. Write the following function to check whether an integer is a palindrome:

```
bool isPalindrome(int number)
```

For example, isPalindrome(53435) returns true. Write a test program that prompts the user to enter an integer and reports whether the integer is a palindrome.

5.6* (*Displaying patterns*) Write the following function to display a pattern:

```
void displayPattern(int n)
```

```
        1
      2 1
    3 2 1
...
n n-1 ... 3 2 1
```

5.7 (*Conversions between Celsius and Fahrenheit*) Write a header file that contains the following two functions:

```
/* Converts from Celsius to Fahrenheit */
double celsiusToFahrenheit(double celsius)
```

```
/* Converts from Fahrenheit to Celsius */
double fahrenheitToCelsius(double fahrenheit)
```

The formula for the conversion is:

```
fahrenheit = (9.0 / 5) * celsius + 32
```

Implement the header file and write a test program that invokes these functions to display the following tables:

Celsius	Fahrenheit			Fahrenheit	Celsius
40.0	104.0			120.0	48.89
39.0	102.2			110.0	43.33
...					
32.0	89.6			40.0	4.44
31.0	87.8			30.0	-1.11

5.8 (*Conversions between feet and meters*) Write a header file that contains the following two functions:

```
/* Converts from feet to meters */
double footToMeter(double foot)
```

```
/* Converts from meters to feet */
double meterToFoot(double meter)
```

The formula for the conversion is:

```
meter = 0.305 * foot
```

Implement the header file and write a test program that invokes these functions to display the following tables:

Feet	Meters		Meters	Feet
1.0	0.305		20.0	65.574
2.0	0.61		25.0	81.967
...				
9.0	2.745		60.0	196.721
10.0	3.05		65.0	213.115

5.9 (*Using the* `isPrime` *Function*) Listing 5.5, PrimeNumberFunction.cpp, provides the `isPrime(int number)` function for testing whether a number is prime. Use this function to find the number of prime numbers less than `10000`.

5.10 (*Financial application: computing commissions*) Use the scheme in Exercise 4.37 to write a function that computes the commission. The header of the function is:

```
double computeCommission(double salesAmount)
```

Write a test program that displays the following table:

SalesAmount	Commission
10000	900.0
15000	1500.0
...	
95000	11100.0
100000	11700.0

5.11 (*Displaying characters*) Write a function that prints characters using the following header:

```
void printChars(char ch1, char ch2, int numberPerLine)
```

This function prints the characters between `ch1` and `ch2` with the specified number of characters per line. Write a test program that prints ten characters per line from `'1'` and `'Z'`.

5.12* (*Summing series*) Write a function to compute the following series:

$$m(i) = \frac{1}{2} + \frac{2}{3} + \ \dots \ + \frac{i}{i+1}$$

Write a test program that displays the following table:

i	m(i)
1	0.5
2	1.1667
...	
19	16.4023
20	17.3546

5.13* (*Computing series*) Write a function to compute the following series:

$$m(i) = 4\left(1 - \frac{1}{3} + \frac{1}{5} - \frac{1}{7} + \frac{1}{9} - \frac{1}{11} + \frac{1}{13} - \ \dots \ - \frac{1}{2i-1} + \frac{1}{2i+1}\right)$$

5.14* (*Financial application: printing a tax table*) Listing 3.4, ComputeTax.cpp, is a program to compute tax. Write a function for computing tax using the following header:

```
double computetax(int status, double taxableIncome)
```

Use this function to write a program that prints a tax table for taxable income from $50,000 to $60,000 with intervals of $50 for all four statuses, as follows:

taxable Income	Single	Married Joint	Married Separate	Head of a House
50000	9846	7296	10398	8506
50050	9860	7310	10412	8520
...				
59950	12533	9983	13190	11193
60000	12546	9996	13205	11206

5.15* *(Number of days in a year)* Write a function that returns the number of days in a year using the following header:

```
int numberOfDaysInAYear(int year)
```

Write a test program that displays the number of days in year **2000**, . . . , and **2010**.

5.16* *(Displaying matrix of 0s and 1s)* Write a function that displays an *n*-by-*n* matrix using the following header:

```
void printMatrix(int n)
```

Each element is 0 or 1, which is generated randomly. Write a test program that prints a 3-by-3 matrix that may look like this:

```
0 1 0
0 0 0
1 1 1
```

Section 5.12

5.17* *(Generating random characters)* Use the functions defined in Listing 5.12, RandomCharacter.h, to print 100 uppercase letters and then 100 single digits, and print ten per line.

Section 5.12

5.18 *(Using the sqrt function)* Write a program that prints the following table using the sqrt function:

Number	SquareRoot
0	0.0000
2	1.4142
...	
18	4.2426
20	4.4721

5.19* *(The MyTriangle header file)* Create a header file named MyTriangle.h that contains the following two functions:

```
/* Returns true if the sum of any two sides is
 * greater than the third side. */
bool isValid(double side1, double side2, double side3)

/* Returns the area of the triangle. */
double area(double side1, double side2, double side3)
```

The formula for computing the area is given in Exercise 2.19. Implement the header file and write a test program that reads three sides for a triangle and computes the area if the input is valid. Otherwise, display that the input is invalid.

5.20 (*Using trigonometric functions*) Print the following table to display the `sin` value and `cos` value of degrees from 0 to 360 with increments of 10 degrees. Round the value to keep four digits after the decimal point.

Degree	Sin	Cos
0	0.0000	1.0000
10	0.1736	0.9848
...		
350	-0.1736	0.9848
360	0.0000	1.0000

5.21**(*Financial application: computing mean and standard deviation*) In business applications, you are often asked to compute the mean and standard deviation of data. The mean is simply the average of the numbers. The standard deviation is a statistic that tells you how tightly all the various data in a set are clustered around the mean. For example, what is the average age of the students in a class? How close are the ages? If all the students are the same age, the deviation is 0. Write a program that prompts the user to enter 10 numbers and computes the mean and standard deviation of these numbers using the following formulas:

$$mean = \frac{\sum_{i=1}^{n} x_i}{n} = \frac{x_1 + x_2 + \ldots + x_n}{n} \qquad deviation = \sqrt{\frac{\sum_{i=1}^{n} x_i^2 - \frac{\left(\sum_{i=1}^{n} x_i\right)^2}{n}}{n-1}}$$

Here is a sample run:

```
Enter ten numbers: 1 2 3 4.5 5.6 6 7 8 9 10  ↵Enter
The mean is 5.61
The standard deviation is 2.99794
```

5.22* (*Financial application: computing the future investment value*) Write a function that computes future investment value at a given interest rate for a specified number of years. The future investment is determined using the formula in Exercise 2.11. Use the following function header:

```
double futureInvestmentValue(
    double investmentAmount, double monthlyInterestRate, int years)
```

For example, `futureInvestmentValue(10000, 0.05/12, 5)` returns 12833.59.

Write a test program that prompts the user to enter the investment amount (e.g., 1000) and the interest rate (e.g., 9%), and prints a table that displays future value for the years from 1 to 30, as shown below:

```
The amount invested: 1000  ↵Enter
Annual interest rate: 9  ↵Enter
Years       Future Value
  1           1093.8
  2           1196.41
...
 29          13467.25
 30          14730.57
```

CHAPTER 6

ADVANCED FUNCTION FEATURES

Objectives

- To pass arguments by value (§6.2).

- To pass arguments by reference (§6.3).

- To understand the differences between pass-by-value and pass-by-reference (§§6.2–6.3).

- To declare const parameters to prevent the parameters' being modified accidentally (§6.4).

- To determine the scope of local and global variables (§6.5).

- To improve runtime efficiency for short functions using inline functions (§6.6).

- To define functions with default arguments (§6.7).

- To design and implement functions using stepwise refinement (§6.8).

6.1 Introduction

In the preceding chapter, you learned how to define and invoke functions, how to create header files for functions, and how to use math functions and character functions. This chapter will introduce several advanced topics on pass-by-value, pass-by-reference, constant parameters, global and static variables, inline functions, default arguments, and the design of programs using functions for stepwise refinement.

6.2 Passing Arguments by Values

pass-by-value

When you invoke a function with a parameter, as described in the preceding chapter, the value of the argument is passed to the parameter. This is referred to as *pass-by-value*. If the argument is a variable rather than a literal value, the value of the variable is passed to the parameter. The variable is not affected, regardless of the changes made to the parameter inside the function. As shown in Listing 6.1, the value of x (1) is passed to the parameter n to invoke the increment function (line 14). n is incremented by 1 in the function (line 6), but x is not changed no matter what the function does.

LISTING 6.1   Increment.cpp

```cpp
1  #include <iostream>
2  using namespace std;
3
4  void increment(int n)
5  {
6    n++;
7    cout << "\tn inside the function is " << n << endl;
8  }
9
10 int main()
11 {
12   int x = 1;
13   cout << "Before the call, x is " << x << endl;
14   increment(x);
15   cout << "after the call, x is " << x << endl;
16
17   return 0;
18 }
```

increment **n**

invoke increment

```
Before the call, x is 1
   n inside the function is 2
after the call, x is 1
```

6.3 Passing Arguments by References

limitations of pass-by-value

Pass-by-value has serious limitations. Listing 6.2 illustrates these. The program creates a function for swapping two variables. The swap function is invoked by passing two arguments. However, the values of the arguments are not changed after the function is invoked.

LISTING 6.2   TestPassByValue.cpp

```cpp
1  #include <iostream>
2  using namespace std;
3
```

Video Note
pass-by-value vs. pass-by-reference

```
4  // Attempt to swap two variables does not work!
5  void swap(int n1, int n2)                                          swap function
6  {
7    cout << "\tInside the swap function" << endl;
8    cout << "\tBefore swapping n1 is " << n1 <<
9      " n2 is " << n2 << endl;
10
11   // Swap n1 with n2
12   int temp = n1;
13   n1 = n2;
14   n2 = temp;
15
16   cout << "\tAfter swapping n1 is " << n1 <<
17     " n2 is " << n2 << endl;
18 }
19
20 int main()                                                          main function
21 {
22   // Declare and initialize variables
23   int num1 = 1;
24   int num2 = 2;
25
26   cout << "Before invoking the swap function, num1 is "
27     << num1 << " and num2 is " << num2 << endl;
28
29   // Invoke the swap function to attempt to swap two variables
30   swap(num1, num2);                                                 false swap
31
32   cout << "After invoking the swap function, num1 is " << num1 <<
33     " and num2 is " << num2 << endl;
34
35   return 0;
36 }
```

```
Before invoking the swap function, num1 is 1 and num2 is 2
    Inside the swap function
    Before swapping n1 is 1 n2 is 2
    After swapping n1 is 2 n2 is 1
After invoking the swap function, num1 is 1 and num2 is 2
```

Before the swap function is invoked (line 30), num1 is 1 and num2 is 2. After the swap function is invoked, num1 is still 1 and num2 is still 2. Their values have not been swapped. As shown in Figure 6.1, the values of the arguments num1 and num2 are passed to n1 and n2, but n1 and n2 have their own memory locations independent of num1 and num2. Therefore, changes in n1 and n2 do not affect the contents of num1 and num2.

Another twist is to change the parameter name n1 in swap to num1. What effect does this have? No change occurs, because it makes no difference whether the parameter and the argument have the same name. The parameter is a variable in the function with its own memory space. The variable is allocated when the function is invoked, and it disappears when the function is returned to its caller.

The swap function attempts to swap two variables. After the function is invoked, though, the values of the variables are not swapped, because the values of variables are passed to the arguments. The original variables and arguments are independent. Even though the values in the called function are changed, the values in the original variables are not.

So, can we write a function to swap two variables? Yes. The function can accomplish this by passing the reference of the variables. C++ provides a special type of variable—a

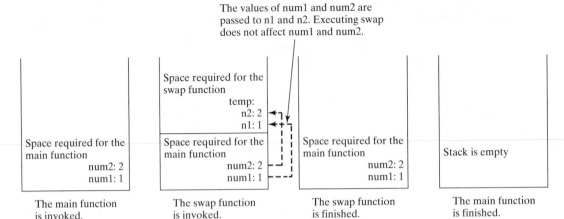

FIGURE 6.1 The values of the variables are passed to the parameters of the function.

reference variable

reference variable—which can be used as a function parameter to reference the original variable. A reference variable is an alias for another variable. Any changes made through the reference variable are actually performed on the original variable. To declare a reference for a variable, place the ampersand (&) in front of the variable. For example, see Listing 6.3.

Video Note

pass-by-value vs. pass-by-reference

LISTING 6.3 TestReferenceVariable.cpp

```
 1  #include <iostream>
 2  using namespace std;
 3
 4  int main()
 5  {
 6    int count = 1;
 7    int &aliasForcount = count;
 8    cout << "count is " << count << endl;
 9    cout << "aliasForcount is " << aliasForcount << endl;
10
11    aliasForcount++;
12    cout << "count is " << count << endl;
13    cout << "aliasForcount is " << aliasForcount << endl;
14
15    count = 10;
16    cout << "count is " << count << endl;
17    cout << "aliasForcount is " << aliasForcount << endl;
18
19    return 0;
20  }
```

declare reference variable

using reference variable

change **count**

```
count is 1
aliasForcount is 1
count is 2
aliasForcount is 2
count is 10
aliasForcount is 10
```

Line 7 declares a reference variable named aliasForcount that is merely an alias for count. As shown in Figure 6.2(a), aliasForcount and count reference the same value. Line 11 increments aliasForcount, which in effect increments count, since they share the same value, as shown in Figure 6.2(b).

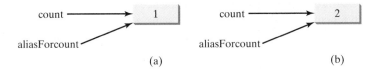

FIGURE 6.2 `aliasForcount` and `count` share the same value.

Line 15 assigns `10` to `count`. Any change made to `count` will also be made to `aliasForcount`, and vice versa. Both `count` and `aliasForcount` are now `10`.

 Note

The following notations for declaring reference variables are equivalent: equivalent notation

```
int &refVar;
int & refVar;
int& refVar;
```

For consistency, the first notation is used throughout this book.

You can use a reference variable as a parameter in a function and pass a regular variable to invoke the function. The parameter becomes an alias for the original variable. This is known as *pass-by-reference*. When you change the value through the reference variable, the original value is actually changed. To demonstrate the effect of pass-by-reference, let us rewrite the `increment` function in Listing 6.1 as in Listing 6.4.

pass-by-reference

LISTING 6.4 `IncrementWithPassByReference.cpp`

```
 1 #include <iostream>
 2 using namespace std;
 3
 4 void increment(int &n)
 5 {
 6    n++;                                                    increment n
 7    cout << "The address of n is " << &n << endl;
 8    cout << "n inside the function is " << n << endl;
 9 }
10
11 int main()
12 {
13    int x = 1;
14    cout << "The address of x is " << &x << endl;
15    cout << "Before the call, x is " << x << endl;
16    increment(x);                                           invoke increment
17    cout << "After the call, x is " << x << endl;
18
19    return 0;
20 }
```

```
The address of x is 0013FF60
Before the call, x is 1
  The address of n is 0013FF60
  n inside the function is 2
After the call, x is 2
```

Invoking `increment(x)` in line 16 passes the reference of variable x to the parameter &n in the `increment` function. Now n and x have the same address 0013FF60, as shown in the output. Incrementing n in the function (line 6) is the same as incrementing x. So, before the function is invoked, x is 1, and afterward, x becomes 2.

Pass-by-value and pass-by-reference are two ways of passing arguments to the parameters of a function. Pass-by-value passes the value to an independent variable and pass-by-reference shares the same variable. Semantically pass-by-reference can be described as *pass-by-sharing*.

pass-by-sharing

Now you can use reference parameters to implement a correct **swap** function, as shown in Listing 6.5.

LISTING 6.5 TestPassByReference.cpp

reference variables

main function

swap

```
1 #include <iostream>
2 using namespace std;
3
4 // Swap two variables
5 void swap(int &n1, int &n2)
6 {
7    cout << "\tInside the swap function" << endl;
8    cout << "\tBefore swapping n1 is " << n1 <<
9       " n2 is " << n2 << endl;
10
11   // Swap n1 with n2
12   int temp = n1;
13   n1 = n2;
14   n2 = temp;
15
16   cout << "\tAfter swapping n1 is " << n1 <<
17      " n2 is " << n2 << endl;
18 }
19
20 int main()
21 {
22   // Declare and initialize variables
23   int num1 = 1;
24   int num2 = 2;
25
26   cout << "Before invoking the swap function, num1 is "
27      << num1 << " and num2 is " << num2 << endl;
28
29   // Invoke the swap function to attempt to swap two variables
30   swap(num1, num2);
31
32   cout << "After invoking the swap function, num1 is " << num1 <<
33      " and num2 is " << num2 << endl;
34
35   return 0;
36 }
```

```
Before invoking the swap function, num1 is 1 and num2 is 2
   Inside the swap function
   Before swapping n1 is 1 n2 is 2
   After swapping n1 is 2 n2 is 1
After invoking the swap function, num1 is 2 and num2 is 1
```

Before the `swap` function is invoked (line 30), `num1` is `1` and `num2` is `2`. After the `swap` function is invoked, `num1` becomes `2` and `num2` becomes `1`. Their values have been swapped. As shown in Figure 6.3, the addresses of `num1` and `num2` are passed to `&n1` and `&n2`, so `n1` and `num1` point to the same memory location and `n2` and `num2` point to the same memory location. Swapping values between `n1` and `n2` is the same as swapping values between `num1` and `num2`, since `n1` is an alias for `num1` and `n2` is an alias for `num2`.

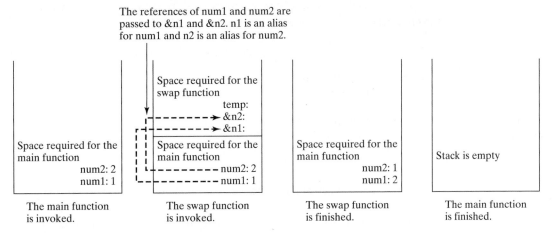

FIGURE 6.3 The references of the variables are passed to the parameters of the function.

When you pass an argument by reference, the formal parameter and the argument must have the same type. For example, in the following code, the reference of variable `x` is passed to the function, which is fine. However, the reference of variable `y` is passed to the function, which is wrong, since `y` and `n` are of different types.

requires same type

```cpp
#include <iostream>
using namespace std;

void increment(double &n)
{
  n++;
}

int main()
{
  double x = 1;
  int y = 1;

  increment(x);
  increment(y); // Cannot invoke increment(y) with an int argument

  cout << "x is " << x << endl;
  cout << "y is " << y << endl;

  return 0;
}
```

When you pass an argument by reference, the argument must be a variable. When you pass an argument by value, the argument can be a literal, a variable, an expression, or even the return value of another function.

requires variable

6.4 Constant Reference Parameters

const

constant reference parameter

If your program uses a call-by-reference parameter and the parameter is not changed in the function, you should mark it constant to tell the compiler that the parameter should not be changed. To do so, place the `const` keyword before the parameter in the function declaration. Such a parameter is known as *constant reference parameter*. For example, `num1` and `num2` are declared as constant reference parameters in the following function.

```cpp
// Return the max between two numbers
int max(const int &num1, const int &num2)
{
  int result;

  if (num1 > num2)
    result = num1;
  else
    result = num2;

  return result;
}
```

In pass-by-value, the actual parameter and its formal parameter are independent variables. In pass-by-reference, the actual parameter and its formal parameter refer to the same variable. Pass-by-reference is more efficient than pass-by-value. However, the difference is negligible for parameters of primitive types such `int` and `double`. So, *if a primitive data type parameter is not changed in the function, you should simply declare it as pass-by-value parameter.*

Later in the book we will introduce arrays and objects. It makes sense to use call-by-reference rather than call-by-value parameters to improve efficiency for arrays and objects, because arrays and objects can take a lot of memory.

6.5 Local, Global, and Static Local Variables

scope

local variable

global variable

The *scope of a variable* is the part of the program where the variable can be referenced. A variable defined inside a function is referred to as a *local variable*. C++ also allows you to use *global variables*. They are declared outside all functions and are accessible to all functions in their scope. Local variables do not have default values, but global variables are defaulted to zero.

A variable must be declared before it can be used. The scope of a local variable starts from its declaration and continues to the end of the block that contains the variable. The scope of a global variable starts from its declaration and continues to the end of the program.

parameter

A parameter is actually a local variable. The scope of a function parameter covers the entire function.

Listing 6.6 demonstrates the scope of local and global variables.

LISTING 6.6 VariableScopeDemo.cpp

function prototype

```cpp
1 #include <iostream>
2 using namespace std;
3
4 void t1(); // Function prototype
5 void t2(); // Function prototype
6
7 int main()
8 {
9   t1();
10   t2();
11
```

```
12    return 0;
13 }
14
15 int y; // Global variable, default to 0
16
17 void t1()
18 {
19   int x = 1;
20   cout << "x is " << x << endl;
21   cout << "y is " << y << endl;
22   x++;
23   y++;
24 }
25
26 void t2()
27 {
28   int x = 1;
29   cout << "x is " << x << endl;
30   cout << "y is " << y << endl;
31 }
```

global variable

local variable

increment **x**
increment **y**

local variable

```
x is 1
y is 0
x is 1
y is 1
```

A global variable y is declared in line 15 with default value 0. This variable is accessible in functions t1 and t2, but not in the main function, because the main function is declared before y is declared.

When the main function invokes t1() in line 9, the global variable y is incremented (line 23) and becomes 1 in t1. When the main function invokes t2() in line 10, the global variable y is now 1.

A local variable x is declared in t1 in line 19 and another is declared in t2 in line 28. Although they are named the same, these two variables are independent. So, incrementing x in t1 does not affect the variable x defined in t2.

If a function has a local variable with the same name as a global variable, only the local variable can be seen from the function.

Note

If a local variable name is the same as a global variable name, you can access the global variable using `::globalVariable`. The `::` operator is known as the *unary scope resolution*. For example, the following code

unary scope resolution

```
#include <iostream>
using namespace std;

int v1 = 10;

int main()
{
  int v1 = 5;
  cout << "local variable v1 is " << v1 << endl;
  cout << "global variable v1 is " << ::v1 << endl;

  return 0;
}
```

displays

```
local variable v1 is 5
global variable v1 is 10
```

Tip

avoid global variables

It is tempting to declare a variable globally once and then use it in all functions without redeclaring it. However, this is a bad practice, because modifying the global variables could lead to errors hard to debug. Avoid using global variables. Using global constants is fine, since constants are never changed.

6.5.1   The Scope of Variables in a `for` Loop

for loop control variable

A variable declared in the initial-action part of a `for`-loop header has its scope in the entire loop. But a variable declared inside a `for`-loop body has its scope limited in the loop body from its declaration to the end of the block that contains the variable, as shown in Figure 6.4.

multiple declarations

It is commonly acceptable to declare a local variable with the same name in different nonnesting blocks in a function, as shown in Figure 6.5(a), but it is not a good practice to declare a local variable twice in nested blocks, even though it is allowed in C++, as shown in Figure 6.5(b). In this case, `i` is declared in the function block and also in the `for` loop. The

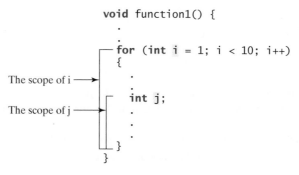

FIGURE 6.4   A variable declared in the initial-action part of a `for`-loop header has its scope in the entire loop.

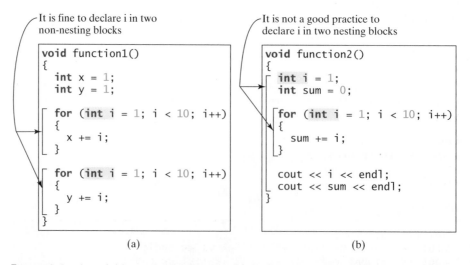

FIGURE 6.5   A variable can be declared multiple times in nonnesting blocks, but you should avoid declaring them in nesting blocks.

program can compile and run, but it is easy to make mistakes. So, you should avoid declaring the same variable in nested blocks.

Caution

Do not declare a variable inside a block and then attempt to use it outside the block. Here is an example of a common mistake:

```
for (int i = 0; i < 10; i++)
{
}

cout << i;
```

The last statement would cause a syntax error, because variable i is not defined outside the for loop.

6.5.2 Static Local Variables

After a function completes its execution, all its local variables are destroyed. These variables are also known as *automatic variables*. Sometimes it is desirable to retain the values stored in local variables so that they can be used in the next call. C++ allows you to declare static local variables. Static local variables are permanently allocated in the memory for the lifetime of the program. To declare a static variable, use the keyword `static`.

automatic variable
static variable

Listing 6.7 demonstrates using static local variables.

LISTING 6.7 StaticVariableDemo.cpp

```
 1 #include <iostream>
 2 using namespace std;
 3
 4 void t1(); // Function prototype
 5
 6 int main()
 7 {
 8   t1();
 9   t1();
10
11   return 0;
12 }
13
14 void t1()
15 {
16   static int x = 1;
17   int y = 1;
18   x++;
19   y++;
20   cout << "x is " << x << endl;
21   cout << "y is " << y << endl;
22 }
```

function prototype

invoke **t1**

static local variable
local variable
increment **x**
increment **y**

```
x is 2
y is 2
x is 3
y is 2
```

A static local variable x is declared in line 16 with initial value 1. The initialization of static variables happens only once in the first call. When t1() is invoked for the first time in line 8, static variable x is initialized to 1 (line 16). x is incremented to 2 (line 18). Since x is a static local variable, x is retained in memory after this call. When t1() is invoked again in line 9, x is 2 and is incremented to 3 (line 18).

A local variable y is declared in line 17 with initial value 1. When t1() is invoked for the first time in line 8, y is incremented to 2 (line 19). Since y is a local variable, it is destroyed after this call. When t1() is invoked again in line 9, y is initialized to 1 and is incremented to 2 (line 19).

6.6 Inline Functions

efficiency

Implementing a program using functions makes the program easy to read and easy to maintain, but function calls involve runtime overhead (i.e., pushing arguments and CPU registers into the stack and transferring control to and from a function). C++ provides *inline functions* to avoid function calls. Inline functions are not called; rather, the compiler copies the function code *in line* at the point of each invocation. To specify an inline function, precede the function declaration with the inline keyword, as shown in Listing 6.8.

LISTING 6.8 InlineDemo.cpp

inline function

```cpp
1 #include <iostream>
2 using namespace std;
3
4 inline void f(int month, int year)
5 {
6     cout << "month is " << month << endl;
7     cout << "year is " << year << endl;
8 }
9
10 int main()
11 {
12     int month = 10, year = 2008;
13     f(month, year); // Invoke inline function
14     f(9, 2010); // Invoke inline function
15
16     return 0;
17 }
```

invoke inline function
invoke inline function

```
month is 10
year is 2008
month is 9
year is 2010
```

As far as programming is concerned, inline functions are the same as regular functions, except in being preceded with the inline keyword. However, behind the scenes, the C++ compiler expands the inline function call by copying the inline function code. So, Listing 6.8 is essentially equivalent to Listing 6.9.

LISTING 6.9 InlineDemo1.cpp

```cpp
1 #include <iostream>
2 using namespace std;
3
```

```
4 int main()
5 {
6    int month = 10, year = 2008;
7    cout << "month is " << month << endl;
8    cout << "year is " << year << endl;
9    cout << "month is " << 9 << endl;
10   cout << "year is " << 2010 << endl;
11
12   return 0;
13 }
```

← Inline function expanded

```
month is 10
year is 2008
month is 9
year is 2010
```

 Note
Inline functions are desirable for short functions but not for long ones that are called in multiple places in a program, because making multiple copies will dramatically increase the executable code size. For this reason, C++ allows the compilers to ignore the **inline** keyword if the function is too long. So, the **inline** keyword is merely a request, and it is up to the compiler to decide whether to honor or ignore it.

for short functions
not for long functions
compiler decision

6.7 Default Arguments

C++ allows you to declare functions with default argument values for pass-by-value parameters. The default values are passed to the parameters when a function is invoked without the arguments.

Listing 6.10 demonstrates how to declare functions with default argument values and how to invoke such functions.

LISTING 6.10 DefaultArgumentDemo.cpp

```
1 #include <iostream>
2 using namespace std;
3
4 // Display area of a circle
5 void printArea(double radius = 1)
6 {
7    double area = radius * radius * 3.14159;
8    cout << "area is " << area << endl;
9 }
10
11 int main()
12 {
13   printArea();
14   printArea(4);
15
16   return 0;
17 }
```

default argument

invoke with default
invoke with argument

```
area is 3.14159
area is 50.2654
```

Line 5 declares the `printArea` function with the parameter `radius`. `radius` has a default value `1`. Line 13 invokes the function without passing an argument. In this case, the default value `1` is assigned to `radius`.

default arguments last

When a function contains a mixture of parameters with and without default values, those with default values must be defined last. For example, the following declarations are illegal:

```
void t1(int x, int y = 0, int z); // Illegal
void t2(int x = 0, int y = 0, int z); // Illegal
```

However, the following declarations are fine:

```
void t3(int x, int y = 0, int z = 0); // Legal
void t4(int x = 0, int y = 0, int z = 0); // Legal
```

When an argument is left out of a function, all arguments that come after it must be left out as well. For example, the following calls are illegal:

```
t3(1,  , 20);
t4(,  , 20);
```

but the following calls are fine:

```
t3(1); // Parameters y and z are assigned a default value
t4(1, 2); // Parameter z is assigned a default value
```

Video Note

stepwise refinement

function abstraction

information hiding

6.8 Function Abstraction and Stepwise Refinement

The key to developing software is to apply the concept of abstraction. You will learn many levels of abstraction from this book. *Function abstraction* is achieved by separating the use of a function from its implementation. The client can use a function without knowing how it is implemented. The details of the implementation are encapsulated in the function and hidden from the client who invokes the function. This is known as *information hiding* or *encapsulation*. If you decide to change the implementation, the client program will not be affected, provided that you do not change the function signature. The implementation of the function is hidden from the client in a "black box," as shown in Figure 6.6.

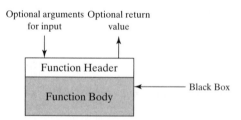

FIGURE 6.6 The function body can be thought of as a black box that contains the detailed implementation for the function.

You have already used the `rand()` function to return a random number, the `time(0)` function to obtain the current time, and the `max` function to find the maximum number. You know how to write the code to invoke these functions in your program, but as a user of these functions, you are not required to know how they are implemented.

divide and conquer

stepwise refinement

The concept of function abstraction can be applied to the process of developing programs. When writing a large program, you can use the "*divide-and-conquer*" strategy, also known as *stepwise refinement*, to decompose it into subproblems. The subproblems can be further decomposed into smaller, more manageable ones.

Header ————→

October 2009						
— —						
Sun	Mon	Tue	Wed	Thu	Fri	Sat
				1	2	3
4	5	6	7	8	9	10
11	12	13	14	15	16	17
18	19	20	21	22	23	24
25	26	27	28	29	30	31

Body ————→

FIGURE 6.7 After prompting the user to enter the year and the month, the program displays the calendar for that month.

Suppose you write a program that displays the calendar for a given month of the year. The program prompts the user to enter the year and the month, then displays the entire calendar for the month, as shown in Figure 6.7.

Let us use this example to demonstrate the divide-and-conquer approach.

6.8.1 Top-Down Design

How would you get started on such a program? Would you immediately start coding? Beginning programmers often start by trying to work out the solution to every detail. Although details are important in the final program, concern for detail in the early stages may block the problem-solving process. To make problem solving flow as smoothly as possible, this example begins by using function abstraction to isolate details from design; only later does it implement the details.

For this example, the problem is first broken into two subproblems: get input from the user, and print the calendar for the month. At this stage, you should be concerned with what the subproblems will achieve, not with how to get input and print the calendar for the month. You can draw a structure chart to help visualize the decomposition of the problem (see Figure 6.8(a)).

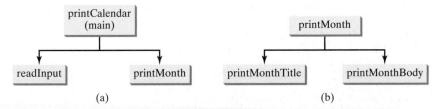

(a)   (b)

FIGURE 6.8 (a) The structure chart shows that the `printCalendar` problem is divided into two subproblems, `readInput` and `printMonth`. (b) and that `printMonth` is divided into two smaller subproblems, `printMonthTitle` and `printMonthBody`.

You can use the `cin` object to read input for the year and the month. The problem of printing the calendar for a given month can be broken into two subproblems: print the month title, and print the month body, as shown in Figure 6.8(b). The month title consists of three lines: month and year, a dashed line, and the names of the seven days of the week. You need to get the month name (e.g., January) from the numeric month (e.g., 1). This is accomplished in `printMonthName` (see Figure 6.9(a)).

In order to print the month body, you need to know which day of the week is the first day of the month (`getStartDay`) and how many days the month has (`getNumberOf-DaysInMonth`), as shown in Figure 6.9(b). For example, October 2009 has thirty-one days, and the first of the month is Thursday, as shown in Figure 6.7.

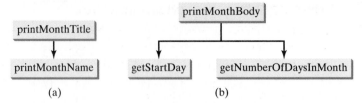

FIGURE 6.9 (a) To accomplish `printMonthTitle`, you need `printMonthName`. (b) The `printMonthBody` problem is refined into several smaller problems.

How would you get the start day for a month? There are several ways to find it. Assume that you know that the start day (`startDay1800 = 3`) for January 1, 1800, was Wednesday. You could compute the total number of days (`totalNumberOfDays`) between January 1, 1800, and the start day of the calendar month. The computation is `(totalNumberOfDays + startDay1800) % 7`, since every week has seven days. So the `getStartDay` problem can be further refined as `getTotalNumberOfDays`, as shown in Figure 6.10(a).

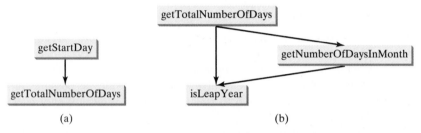

FIGURE 6.10 (a) To accomplish `getStartDay`, you need `getTotalNumberOfDays`. (b) The `getTotalNumberOfDays` problem is refined into two smaller problems.

To get the total number of days, you need to know whether a year is a leap year and how many days are in each month. So `getTotalNumberOfDays` is further refined into two subproblems: `isLeapYear` and `getNumberOfDaysInMonth`, as shown in Figure 6.10(b). The complete structure chart is shown in Figure 6.11.

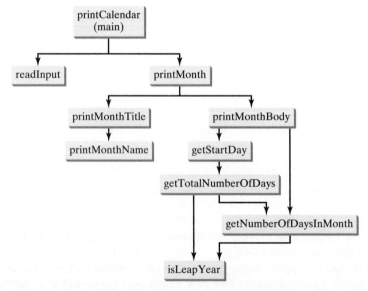

FIGURE 6.11 The structure chart shows the hierarchical relationship of the subproblems in the program.

6.8.2 Top-Down or Bottom-Up Implementation

Now we turn our attention to implementation. In general, a subproblem corresponds to a function in the implementation, although some subproblems are so simple that this is unnecessary. You would need to decide which modules to implement as functions and which to combine in other functions. Such decisions should be based on whether the overall program will be easier to read as a result of your choice. In this example, the subproblem `readInput` can be simply implemented in the `main` function.

You can use either a "*top-down*" or a "*bottom-up*" approach. The top-down approach implements one function in the structure chart at a time from the top to the bottom. Stubs can be used for the functions waiting to be implemented. A *stub* is a simple but incomplete version of a function. The use of stubs enables you to test invoking the function from a caller. Implement the `main` function first, then use a stub for the `printMonth` function. For example, let `printMonth` display the year and the month in the stub. Thus, your program may begin like this:

top-down approach
bottom-up approach
stub

```cpp
#include <iostream>
#include <iomanip>
using namespace std;

void printMonth(int year, int month);
void printMonthTitle(int year, int month);
void printMonthName(int month);
void printMonthBody(int year, int month);
int getStartDay(int year, int month);
int getTotalNumberOfDays(int year, int month);
int getNumberOfDaysInMonth(int year, int month);
bool isLeapYear(int year);

int main()
{
  // Prompt the user to enter year
  cout << "Enter full year (e.g., 2001): ";
  int year;
  cin >> year;

  // Prompt the user to enter month
  cout << "Enter month in number between 1 and 12: ";
  int month;
  cin >> month;

  // Print calendar for the month of the year
  printMonth(year, month);

  return 0;
}

void printMonth(int year, int month)
{
  cout << month << "  " << year << endl;
}
```

Compile and test the program and fix any errors. You can now implement the `printMonth` function. For functions invoked from the `printMonth` function, you can again use stubs.

The bottom-up approach implements one function in the structure chart at a time from the bottom to the top. For each function implemented, write a test program to test it. The top-down and bottom-up approaches are both fine. Both approaches implement functions incrementally, help to isolate programming errors, and make debugging easy. Sometimes they can be used together.

6.8.3 Implementation Details

The `isLeapYear(int year)` function can be implemented using the following code:

```
return (year % 400 == 0 || (year % 4 == 0 && year % 100 != 0));
```

Use the following fact to implement `getTotalNumberOfDaysInMonth(int year, int month)`:

- January, March, May, July, August, October, and December have 31 days.

- April, June, September, and November have 30 days.

- February has 28 days during a regular year and 29 days during a leap year. A regular year, therefore, has 365 days, whereas a leap year has 366.

To implement `getTotalNumberOfDays(int year, int month)`, you need to compute the total number of days (`totalNumberOfDays`) between January 1, 1800, and the first day of the calendar month. You could find the total number of days between the year 1800 and the calendar year and then figure out the total number of days prior to the calendar month in the calendar year. The sum of these two totals is `totalNumberOfDays`.

To print a body, first add some space before the start day and then print the lines for every week, as shown for October 2009 (see Figure 6.7).

The complete program is given in Listing 6.11.

LISTING 6.11 PrintCalendar.cpp

```cpp
1 #include <iostream>
2 #include <iomanip>
3 using namespace std;
4
5 // Function prototypes
6 void printMonth(int year, int month);
7 void printMonthTitle(int year, int month);
8 void printMonthName(int month);
9 void printMonthBody(int year, int month);
10 int getStartDay(int year, int month);
11 int getTotalNumberOfDays(int year, int month);
12 int getNumberOfDaysInMonth(int year, int month);
13 bool isLeapYear(int year);
14
15 int main()
16 {
17   // Prompt the user to enter year
18   cout << "Enter full year (e.g., 2001): ";
19   int year;
20   cin >> year;
21
22   // Prompt the user to enter month
23   cout << "Enter month in number between 1 and 12: ";
24   int month;
25   cin >> month;
26
27   // Print calendar for the month of the year
28   printMonth(year, month);
29
30   return 0;
31 }
32
```

function prototype

main function

input year

input month

print calendar

```
33  // Print the calendar for a month in a year
34  void printMonth(int year, int month)
35  {
36    // Print the headings of the calendar
37    printMonthTitle(year, month);
38
39    // Print the body of the calendar
40    printMonthBody(year, month);
41  }
42
43   // Print the month title, e.g., May, 1999
44  void printMonthTitle(int year, int month)
45  {
46    printMonthName(month);
47    cout << " " << year << endl;
48    cout << "-------------------------------" << endl;
49    cout << " Sun Mon Tue Wed Thu Fri Sat" << endl;
50  }
51
52  // Get the English name for the month
53  void printMonthName(int month)
54  {
55    switch (month)
56    {
57      case 1:
58        cout << "January";
59        break;
60      case 2:
61        cout << "February";
62        break;
63      case 3:
64        cout << "March";
65        break;
66      case 4:
67        cout << "April";
68        break;
69      case 5:
70        cout << "May";
71        break;
72      case 6:
73        cout << "June";
74        break;
75      case 7:
76        cout << "July";
77        break;
78      case 8:
79        cout << "August";
80        break;
81      case 9:
82       cout << "September";
83        break;
84      case 10:
85        cout << "October";
86        break;
87      case 11:
88        cout << "November";
89        break;
```

print month

print month title

print month body

get start day

getTotalNumberOfDays

```
 90     case 12:
 91       cout << setw(16) << "December";
 92   }
 93 }
 94
 95 // Print month body
 96 void printMonthBody(int year, int month)
 97 {
 98   // Get start day of the week for the first date in the month
 99   int startDay = getStartDay(year, month);
100
101   // Get number of days in the month
102   int numberOfDaysInMonth = getNumberOfDaysInMonth(year, month);
103
104   // Pad space before the first day of the month
105   int i = 0;
106   for (i = 0; i < startDay; i++)
107     cout << "    ";
108
109   for (i = 1; i <= numberOfDaysInMonth; i++)
110   {
111     cout << setw(4) << i;
112
113     if ((i + startDay) % 7 == 0)
114       cout << endl;
115   }
116 }
117
118 // Get the start day of the first day in a month
119 int getStartDay(int year, int month)
120 {
121   // Get total number of days since 1//1//1800
122   int startDay1800 = 3;
123   int totalNumberOfDays = getTotalNumberOfDays(year, month);
124
125   // Return the start day
126   return (totalNumberOfDays + startDay1800) % 7;
127 }
128
129 // Get the total number of days since January 1, 1800
130 int getTotalNumberOfDays(int year, int month)
131 {
132   int total = 0;
133
134   // Get the total days from 1800 to year - 1
135   for (int i = 1800; i < year; i++)
136     if (isLeapYear(i))
137       total = total + 366;
138     else
139       total = total + 365;
140
141   // Add days from Jan to the month prior to the calendar month
142   for (int i = 1; i < month; i++)
143     total = total + getNumberOfDaysInMonth(year, i);
144
145   return total;
146 }
147
```

```
148  // Get the number of days in a month
149  int getNumberOfDaysInMonth(int year, int month)
150  {
151    if (month == 1 || month == 3 || month == 5 || month == 7 ||
152        month == 8 || month == 10 || month == 12)
153      return 31;
154
155    if (month == 4 || month == 6 || month == 9 || month == 11)
156      return 30;
157
158    if (month == 2) return isLeapYear(year) ? 29 : 28;
159
160    return 0; // If month is incorrect
161  }
162
163  // Determine if it is a leap year
164  bool isLeapYear(int year)
165  {
166    return year % 400 == 0 || (year % 4 == 0 && year % 100 != 0);
167  }
```

getNumberOfDaysInMonth

isLeapYear

```
Enter full year (e.g., 2001): 2009 ⏎Enter
Enter month in number between 1 and 12: 7 ⏎Enter

        July 2009
-----------------------------
Sun Mon Tue Wed Thu Fri Sat
              1   2   3   4
  5   6   7   8   9  10  11
 12  13  14  15  16  17  18
 19  20  21  22  23  24  25
 26  27  28  29  30  31
```

The program does not validate user input. For instance, if the user entered a month not in the range between 1 and 12, or a year before 1800, the program would display an erroneous calendar. To avoid this error, add an `if` statement to check the input before printing the calendar.

This program prints calendars for a month but could easily be modified to print calendars for a whole year. Although it can only print months after January 1800, it could be modified to trace the day of a month before 1800.

Note

Function abstraction modularizes programs in a neat, hierarchical manner. Programs written as collections of concise functions are easier to write, debug, maintain, and modify than would otherwise be the case. This writing style also promotes function reusability.

Tip

When implementing a large program, use the top-down or bottom-up approach. Do not write the entire program at once. This approach seems to take more time for coding (because you are repeatedly compiling and running the program), but it actually saves time and makes debugging easier.

KEY TERMS

CHAPTER SUMMARY

1. Pass-by-value passes the value of the argument to the parameter.

2. Pass-by-reference passes the reference of the argument.

3. If you change the value of a call-by-value argument in a function, the value is not changed in the called function after the function finishes.

4. If you change the value of a call-by-reference argument in a function, the value is also changed in the called function after the function finishes.

5. A *constant reference parameter* is specified using the `const` keyword to tell the compiler that its value cannot be changed in the function.

6. The *scope of a variable* is the part of the program where the variable can be referenced.

7. Global variables are defined outside all functions and are accessible to all functions in their scope.

8. Local variables are defined inside a function. After a function completes its execution, all of its local variables are destroyed.

9. Local variables are also called automatic variables.

10. Static local variables can be defined to retain the local variables for use by the next function call.

11. C++ provides *inline functions* to avoid function calls.

12. Inline functions are not called; rather, the compiler copies the function code *in line* at the point of each invocation.

13. To specify an inline function, precede the function declaration with the `inline` keyword.

14. C++ allows you to declare functions with default argument values for pass-by-value parameters.

15. The default values are passed to the parameters when a function is invoked without the arguments.

16. *Function abstraction* is achieved by separating the use of a function from its implementation.

17. Programs written as collections of concise functions are easier to write, debug, maintain, and modify than would otherwise be the case.

18. When implementing a large program, use the top-down or bottom-up coding approach.

19. Do not write the entire program at once. This approach seems to take more time for coding (because you are repeatedly compiling and running the program), but it actually saves time and makes debugging easier.

REVIEW QUESTIONS

Sections 6.2–6.4

6.1 What is pass-by-value? What is pass-by-reference? Show the result of the following programs:

```cpp
#include <iostream>
using namespace std;

void maxValue(int value1, int value2, int max)
{
  if (value1 > value2)
    max = value1;
  else
    max = value2;
}

int main()
{
  int max = 0;
  maxValue(1, 2, max);
  cout << "max is " << max << endl;

  return 0;
}
```

(a)

```cpp
#include <iostream>
using namespace std;

void maxValue(int value1, int value2, int &max)
{
  if (value1 > value2)
    max = value1;
  else
    max = value2;
}

int main()
{
  int max = 0;
  maxValue(1, 2, max);
  cout << "max is " << max << endl;

  return 0;
}
```

(b)

```cpp
#include <iostream>
using namespace std;

void f(int i, int num)
{
  for (int j = 1; j <= i; j++)
  {
    cout << num << " ";
    num *= 2;
  }

  cout << endl;
}

int main()
{
  int i = 1;
  while (i <= 6)
  {
    f(i, 2);
    i++;
  }

  return 0;
}
```

(c)

```cpp
#include <iostream>
using namespace std;

void f(int &i, int num)
{
  for (int j = 1; j <= i; j++)
  {
    cout << num << " ";
    num *= 2;
  }

  cout << endl;
}

int main()
{
  int i = 1;
  while (i <= 6)
  {
    f(i, 2);
    i++;
  }

  return 0;
}
```

(d)

6.2   For (a) in the preceding question, show the contents of the stack just before the function `maxValue` is invoked, just entering `maxValue`, just before `maxValue` is returned, and right after `maxValue` is returned.

6.3   Show the output of the following code.

```cpp
#include <iostream>
using namespace std;

void f(double &p)
{
  p += 2;
}

int main()
{
  double x = 10;
  int y = 10;

  f(x);
  f(y);

  cout << "x is " << x << endl;
  cout << "y is " << y << endl;

  return 0;
}
```

6.4   What is wrong in the following program?

```cpp
#include <iostream>
using namespace std;

void p(int &i)
{
  cout << i << endl;
}

int p(int j)
{
  cout << j << endl;
}

int main()
{
  int k = 5;
  p(k);
  return 0;
}
```

Section 6.5

6.5   A student wrote the following function to find the minimum and maximum number between two values **a** and **b**. What is wrong in the program?

```cpp
#include <iostream>
using namespace std;

void minMax(double a, double b, double &min, double &max)
{
  if (a < b)
```

```cpp
    {
      double min = a;
      double max = b;
    }
    else
    {
      double min = b;
      double max = a;
    }
  }

int main()
{
  double a = 5, b = 6, min, max;
  minMax(a, b, min, max);

  cout << "min is " << min << " and max is " << max;

  return 0;
}
```

6.6 Identify global and local variables in the following program. Does a global variable have a default value? Does a local variable have a default value? What will be the output of the code?

```cpp
#include <iostream>
using namespace std;

int j;

int main()
{
  int i;
  cout << "i is " << i << endl;
  cout << "j is " << j << endl;
}
```

6.7 Identify global variables, local variables and static local variables in the following program. What will be the output of the code?

```cpp
#include <iostream>
using namespace std;

int j = 40;

void p()
{
  int i = 5;
  static int j = 5;
  i++;
  j++;

  cout << "i is " << i << endl;
  cout << "j is " << j << endl;
}

int main()
{
  p();
  p();
}
```

6.8 Identify and correct the errors in the following program:

```
1 void p(int i)
2 {
3   int i = 5;
4
5   cout << "i is " << i << endl;
6 }
```

Section 6.6

6.9 What is an inline function? How do you define an inline function?

Section 6.7

6.10 Which of the following function declarations are illegal?

```
void t1(int x, int y = 0, int z);
void t2(int x = 0, int y = 0, int z);
void t3(int x, int y = 0, int z = 0);
void t4(int x = 0, int y = 0, int z = 0);
```

PROGRAMMING EXERCISES

6.1* (*Sorting three numbers*) Write the following function to sort three numbers in increasing order:

void sort(**double** &num1, **double** &num2, **double** &num3)

6.2* (*Algebra: solving quadratic equations*) The two roots of a quadratic equation $ax^2 + bx + c = 0$ can be obtained using the following formula:

$$r_1 = \frac{-b + \sqrt{b^2 - 4ac}}{2a} \quad \text{and} \quad r_2 = \frac{-b - \sqrt{b^2 - 4ac}}{2a}$$

Write a function with the following header

void solveQuadraticEquation(**double** a, **double** b, **double** c, **double** &discriminant, **double** &r1, **double** &r2)

$b^2 - 4ac$ is called the discriminant of the quadratic equation. If the discriminant is less than 0, the equation has no roots. In this case, ignore the value in r1 and r2.

Write a test program that prompts the user to enter values for *a*, *b*, and *c* and displays the result based on the discriminant. If the discriminant is greater than or equal to 0, display the two roots. If the discriminant is equal to 0, display the one root. Otherwise, display "the equation has no roots." See Programming Exercise 3.3 for sample runs.

6.3* (*Algebra: solving 2 × 2 linear equations*) You can use Cramer's rule to solve the following 2 × 2 system of linear equation:

$$\begin{array}{ll} ax + by = e \\ cx + dy = f \end{array} \qquad x = \frac{ed - bf}{ad - bc} \qquad y = \frac{af - ec}{ad - bc}$$

Write a function with the following header:

void solveEquation(**double** a, **double** b, **double** c, **double** d, **double** e, **double** f, **double** &x, **double** &y, **bool** &isSolvable)

If $ad - bc$ is 0, the equation has no solution and isSolvable should be false. Write a program that prompts the user to enter a, b, c, d, e, and f and displays the result. If $ad - bc$ is 0, report that `"The equation has no solution."` See Programming Exercise 3.1 for sample runs.

6.4*** (*Displaying current date and time*) Listing 2.11, ShowCurrentTime.cpp, displays the current time. Improve this example to display the current date and time. The calendar example in §6.8 should give you some ideas on how to find the year, month, and day.

6.5** (*Math: Emirp*) An *emirp* (prime spelled backward) is a prime number whose reversal is also a prime. For example, 17 is a prime and 71 is a prime. So 17 and 71 are emirps. Write a program that displays the first 100 emirps. Display 10 numbers per line and align the numbers properly, as follows:

Video Note
finding emirp prime

```
    2     3     5     7    11    13    17    31    37    71
   73    79    97   101   107   113   131   149   151   157
...
```

6.6** (*Math: Palindromic prime*) A *palindromic prime* is a prime number and also palindromic. For example, 131 is a prime and also a palindromic prime. So are 313 and 757. Write a program that displays the first 100 palindromic prime numbers. Display 10 numbers per line and align the numbers properly, as follows:

```
    2     3     5     7    11   101   131   151   181   191
  313   353   373   383   727   757   787   797   919   929
..
```

6.7** (*Game: craps*) Craps is a popular dice game played in casinos. Write a program to play a variation of the game, as follows:

> Roll two dice. Each die has six faces representing values $1, 2, \ldots,$ and 6, respectively. Check the sum of the two dice. If the sum is 2, 3, or 12 (called *craps*), you lose; if the sum is 7 or 11 (called *natural*), you win; if the sum is another value (i.e., 4, 5, 6, 8, 9, or 10), a *point* is established. Continue until you roll either a 7 (you lose) or the same point value (you win).

Your program acts as a single player. Here are some sample runs.

```
You rolled 5 + 6 = 11
You win
```

```
You rolled 1 + 2 = 3
You lose
```

```
You rolled 4 + 4 = 8
point is 8
You rolled 6 + 2 = 8
You win
```

```
You rolled 3 + 2 = 5
point is 5
You rolled 2 + 5 = 7
You lose
```

6.8** (*Mersenne prime*) A prime number is called a *Mersenne prime* if it can be written in the form of $2^p - 1$ for some positive integer p. Write a program that finds all Mersenne primes with $p \leq 31$ and displays the output as follows:

```
p           2^p - 1

2               3
3               7
5              31
. . .
```

6.9** (*Game: chance of winning at craps*) Revise Exercise 6.7 to run it **10000** times and display the number of winning games.

6.10** (*Math: twin primes*) Twin primes are a pair of prime numbers that differ by **2**. For example, **3** and **5** are twin primes, as are **5** and **7**, and **11** and **13**. Write a program to find all twin primes less than **1000**. Display the output as follows:

```
(3, 5)
(5, 7)
. . .
```

6.11** (*Printing calendar*) Exercise 3_18 uses Zeller's congruence to calculate the day of the week. Simplify Listing 6.11, PrintCalendar.cpp, using Zeller's algorithm to get the start day of the month.

6.12 (*Geometry: area of a pentagon*) The area of a pentagon can be computed using the following formula:

$$area = \frac{5 \times s^2}{4 \times \tan\left(\dfrac{\pi}{5}\right)}$$

Write a program that prompts the user to enter the side of a pentagon and displays the pentagon's area.

6.13* (*Geometry: area of a regular polygon*) A regular polygon is an *n*-sided polygon in which all sides are of the same length and all angles have the same degree (i.e., the polygon is both equilateral and equiangular). The formula for computing the area of a regular polygon is

$$area = \frac{n \times s^2}{4 \times \tan\left(\dfrac{\pi}{n}\right)}.$$

Write a function that returns the area of a regular polygon using the following header:

```
double area(int n, double side)
```

Write a main function that prompts the user to enter the number of sides and the side of a regular polygon, and displays its area.

6.14** (*Approximating the square root*) Implement the sqrt function. The square root of a number, num, can be approximated by repeatedly performing a calculation using the following formula:

```
nextGuess = (lastGuess + (num / lastGuess)) / 2
```

The initial guess can be any positive value (e.g., **1**). This value will be the starting value for lastGuess. If the difference between nextGuess and lastGuess is less than a very small number, such as `0.0001`, you can claim that `nextGuess` is the approximated square root of `num`. If not, `nextGuess` becomes the `lastGuess` and the approximation process continues.

6.15** (*Geometry: intersection*) Suppose two line segments intersect. The two endpoints for the first line segment are ($x1$, $y1$) and ($x2$, $y2$) and for the second line segment are ($x3$, $y3$) and ($x4$, $y5$). Write a program that prompts the user to enter these four endpoints and displays the intersecting point. (*Hint:* Use the function for solving 2 × 2 linear equations.)

Video Note
finding intersecting point of two lines

```
Enter the endpoints of the first line segment: 2.0 2.0 0 0  ↵Enter
Enter the endpoints of the second line segment: 0 2.0 2.0 0  ↵Enter
The intersecting point is: (1, 1)
```

CHAPTER 7

SINGLE-DIMENSIONAL ARRAYS

Objectives

- To describe why an array is necessary in programming (§7.1).

- To declare arrays (§7.2.1).

- To access array elements using indexed variables (§7.2.2).

- To initialize the values in an array (§7.2.3).

- To program common array operations (displaying arrays, summing all elements, finding min and max elements, random shuffling, shifting elements) (§7.2.4).

- To apply arrays in the `LottoNumbers` and `DeckOfCards` problems (§§7.3–7.4).

- To develop and invoke functions with array arguments (§§7.5–7.6).

- To develop functions involving array parameters in the `CountLettersInArray` problem (§7.7).

- To search elements using the linear (§7.8.1) or binary search algorithm (§7.8.2).

- To sort an array using the selection sort (§7.9.1)

- To sort an array using the insertion sort (§7.9.2).

- To process strings using C-strings (§7.10).

7.1 Introduction

why array?

Often during the execution of a program you will have to store a large number of values. Suppose, for instance, that you want to read 100 numbers, compute their average, and find out how many numbers are above the average. Your program first reads the numbers and computes their average, then compares each number with the average to determine whether it is above the average. So that this task can be accomplished, the numbers all must be stored in variables. You have to declare 100 variables and repeatedly write almost identical code 100 times. From the standpoint of practicality, it is impossible to write a program this way. So, how do you solve this problem?

what is an array?

An efficient, organized approach is needed. C++ and most other high-level languages provide a data structure, the *array*, which stores a fixed-size sequential collection of elements of the same type. In the example problem here, you can store all 100 numbers into an array and access them through a single array name. This chapter introduces single-dimensional arrays. The next chapter will introduce two-dimensional and multidimensional arrays.

7.2 Array Basics

An array is used to store a collection of data, but often it is more useful to think of an array as a collection of variables of the same type. Instead of declaring individual variables, such as `number0`, `number1`, ..., and `number99`, you create one array with a name such as `numbers` and use `numbers[0]`, `numbers[1]`, ..., and `numbers[99]` to represent individual variables. This section introduces how to declare arrays and process arrays using indexed variables.

7.2.1 Declaring Arrays

element type

To declare an array, you need to specify its *element type* and size using the following syntax:

```
elementType arrayName[arraySize];
```

The `arraySize` must be an integer greater than zero. The `elementType` can be any data type, and all elements in the array will have the same data type. For example, the following statement declares an array of ten `double` elements:

```
double myList[10];
```

arbitrary initial values

The compiler allocates the space for ten `double` elements for array `myList`. When an array is declared, its elements are assigned arbitrary values. To assign values we use the syntax:

```
arrayName[index] = value;
```

For example, the following code initializes the array.

```
myList[0] = 5.6;
myList[1] = 4.5;
myList[2] = 3.3;
myList[3] = 13.2;
myList[4] = 4.0;
myList[5] = 34.33;
myList[6] = 34.0;
myList[7] = 45.45;
myList[8] = 99.993;
myList[9] = 111.23;
```

The array is pictured in Figure 7.1.

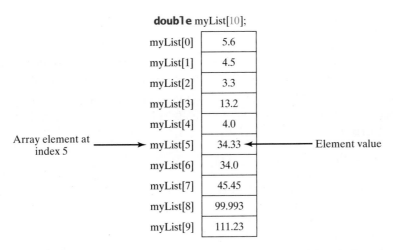

FIGURE 7.1 The array `myList` has ten elements of `double` type and `int` indices from `0` to `9`.

Note

C++ requires that the array size used to declare an array be a constant expression. For example, the following code is illegal:

```
int size = 4;
double myList[size]; // Wrong
```

But it is all right if `SIZE` is a constant as follows:

```
const int SIZE = 4;
double myList[SIZE]; // Correct
```

constant size

Tip

If arrays have the same element type, they can be declared together, as follows:

declaring together

```
elementType arrayName1[size1], arrayName2[size2], ...,
  arrayNamen[sizen];
```

The arrays are separated by commas. For example,

```
double list1[10], list2[25];
```

7.2.2 Array Indexed Variables

The array elements are accessed through the integer index. Array indices are *0-based*; that is, they run from 0 to `arraySize-1`. In the example in Figure 7.1, `myList` holds ten `double` values, and the indices are from `0` to `9`.

array index
0-based

Each element in the array is represented using the following syntax, known as an *indexed variable*:

indexed variables

```
arrayName[index];
```

For example, `myList[9]` represents the last element in the array `myList`.

Caution

Some languages use parentheses to reference an array element, as in `myList(9)`. But C++ uses brackets, as in `myList[9]`.

out-of-bounds error

Caution

Accessing array elements using subscripts beyond the boundaries (e.g., `myList[-1]` and `myList[10]`) causes out-of-bounds error. Out of bounds is a serious error. Unfortunately, the C++ compiler does not report it. Be careful to ensure that array subscripts are within the bounds.

After an array is declared, an indexed variable can be used in the same way as a regular variable. For example, the following code adds the values in `myList[0]` and `myList[1]` to `myList[2]`.

```
myList[2] = myList[0] + myList[1];
```

The following loop assigns 0 to `myList[0]`, 1 to `myList[1]`, ..., and 9 to `myList[9]`:

```
for (int i = 0; i < 10; i++)
{
  myList[i] = i;
}
```

7.2.3   Array Initializers

array initializer

C++ has a shorthand notation, known as the *array initializer*, which both declares and initializes an array in a single statement, using the following syntax:

```
elementType arrayName[arraySize] = {value0, value1, ..., valuek};
```

For example,

```
double myList[4] = {1.9, 2.9, 3.4, 3.5};
```

This statement declares and initializes the array `myList` with four elements, making it equivalent to the statements shown below:

```
double myList[4];
myList[0] = 1.9;
myList[1] = 2.9;
myList[2] = 3.4;
myList[3] = 3.5;
```

Caution

Using an array initializer, you have to declare and initialize the array all in one statement. Splitting it would cause a syntax error. Thus the next statement is wrong:

```
double myList[4];
myList = {1.9, 2.9, 3.4, 3.5};
```

Note

implicit size

C++ allows you to omit the array size when declaring and creating an array using an initializer. For example, the following declaration is fine:

```
double myList[] = {1.9, 2.9, 3.4, 3.5};
```

C++ automatically figures out how many elements are in the array.

Note

C++ allows you to initialize a part of the array. For example, the following statement assigns values 1.9, 2.9 to the first two elements of the array. The other two elements will be set to zero.

Note that if an array is declared, but not initialized, all its elements will contain "garbage," like all other local variables.

partial initialization

```
double myList[4] = {1.9, 2.9};
```

7.2.4 Processing Arrays

When processing array elements, you will often use a `for` loop—for two reasons:

- All of the elements in an array are of the same type. They are evenly processed in the same fashion by repeatedly using a loop.

- Since the size of the array is known, it is natural to use a `for` loop.

Assume the array is declared as follows:

```
const int ARRAY_SIZE = 10;
double myList[ARRAY_SIZE];
```

Here are some examples of processing arrays:

1. (*Initializing arrays with random values*) The following loop initializes the array `myList` with random values between 0 and 99:

```
for (int i = 0; i < ARRAY_SIZE; i++)
{
  myList[i] = rand() % 100;
}
```

2. (*Printing arrays*) To print an array, you have to print each element in it, using a loop like the following:

```
for (int i = 0; i < ARRAY_SIZE; i++)
{
  cout << myList[i] << " ";
}
```

3. (*Copying arrays*) Suppose you have two arrays, `list` and `myList`. Can you copy `myList` to `list` using a syntax like the following?

```
list = myList;
```

This is not allowed in C++. You have to copy individual elements from one array to the other as follows:

```
for (int i = 0; i < ARRAY_SIZE; i++)
{
  list[i] = myList[i];
}
```

4. (*Summing all elements*) Use a variable named `total` to store the sum. Initially, `total` is 0. Add each element in the array to `total` using a loop like this:

```
double total = 0;
for (int i = 0; i < ARRAY_SIZE; i++)
{
  total += myList[i];
}
```

5. (*Finding the largest element*) Use a variable named `max` to store the largest element. Initially `max` is `myList[0]`. To find the largest element in the array `myList`, compare each element in it with `max`, then update `max` if the element is greater than `max`.

```
double max = myList[0];
for (int i = 1; i < ARRAY_SIZE; i++)
{
  if (myList[i] > max) max = myList[i];
}
```

6. (*Finding the smallest index of the largest element*) Often you need to locate the largest element in an array. If an array has more than one largest element, find the smallest index of such an element. Suppose the array myList is {1, 5, 3, 4, 5, 5}. So, the largest element is 5 and the smallest index for 5 is 1. Use a variable named max to store the largest element and a variable named indexOfMax to denote the index of the largest element. Initially max is myList[0] and indexOfMax is 0. Compare each element in myList with max. If the element is greater than max, update max and indexOfMax.

```
double max = myList[0];
int indexOfMax = 0;

for (int i = 1; i < ARRAY_SIZE; i++)
{
  if (myList[i] > max)
  {
    max = myList[i];
    indexOfMax = i;
  }
}
```

What is the consequence if (myList[i] > max) is replaced by (myList[i] >= max)?

7. (*Random shuffling*) In many applications, you need to randomly reorder the elements in an array. This is called *shuffling*. To accomplish this, swap the element in the array with another element with a randomly generated index, as follows:

```
srand(time(0));

for (int i = 0; i < ARRAY_SIZE; i++)
{
  // Generate an index randomly
  int index = rand() % ARRAY_SIZE;

  // Swap myList[i] with myList[index]
  double temp = myList[i];
  myList[i] = myList[index];
  myList[index] = temp;
}
```

8. (*Shifting elements*) Sometimes you need to shift the elements left or right. For example, you may shift the elements one position to the left and fill the last element with the first element:

```
double temp = myList[0]; // Retain the first element

// Shift elements left
for (int i = 1; i < ARRAY_SIZE; i++)
{
  myList[i - 1] = myList[i];
}

// Move the first element to fill in the last position
myList[ARRAY_SIZE - 1] = temp;
```

Caution

Programmers often mistakenly reference the first element in an array with index 1. This is called the *off-by-one error*.

It is a common error in a loop to use <= where < should be used. For example, the following loop is wrong:

```cpp
for (int i = 0; i <= ARRAY_SIZE; i++)
  cout << list[i] << " ";
```

The <= should be replaced by <.

Tip

Since C++ does not check array's boundary, you should pay special attention to ensure that the subscripts are within the range. Check the first and the last iteration in a loop to see whether the subscripts are in the permissible range.

7.3 Problem: Lotto Numbers

Your grandma likes to play the Pick-10 lotto. Each ticket has 10 unique numbers ranging from 1 to 99. Whenever she plays, she buys a lot of tickets. She likes to have her tickets cover all numbers from 1 to 99. Write a program that reads the ticket numbers from a file and checks whether all numbers are covered. Assume the last number in the file is 0. Suppose the file contains the numbers

```
80  3 87 62 30 90 10 21 46 27
12 40 83  9 39 88 95 59 20 37
80 40 87 67 31 90 11 24 56 77
11 48 51 42  8 74  1 41 36 53
52 82 16 72 19 70 44 56 29 33
54 64 99 14 23 22 94 79 55  2
60 86 34  4 31 63 84 89  7 78
43 93 97 45 25 38 28 26 85 49
47 65 57 67 73 69 32 71 24 66
92 98 96 77  6 75 17 61 58 13
35 81 18 15  5 68 91 50 76
0
```

Your program should display

```
The tickets cover all numbers
```

Suppose the file contains the numbers

```
11 48 51 42  8 74  1 41 36 53
52 82 16 72 19 70 44 56 29 33
0
```

Your program should display

```
The tickets don't cover all numbers
```

How do you mark a number as covered? You can create an array with 99 **bool** elements. Each element in the array can be used to mark whether a number is covered. Let the array be **isCovered**. Initially, each element is **false**, as shown in Figure 7.2(a). Whenever a number is read, its corresponding element is set to **true**. Suppose the numbers entered are 1, 2, 3, 99, 0. When number 1 is read, **isCovered[0]** is set to **true** (see Figure 7.2(b)). When number 2 is read, **isCovered[2 - 1]** is set to **true** (see Figure 7.2(c)). When number 3 is read,

	isCovered (a)	isCovered (b)	isCovered (c)	isCovered (d)	isCovered (e)
[0]	false	true	true	true	true
[1]	false	false	true	true	true
[2]	false	false	false	true	true
[3]	false	false	false	false	false
.					
.					
.					
[97]	false	false	false	false	false
[98]	false	false	false	false	true

FIGURE 7.2 If number i appears in a Lotto ticket, isCovered[i-1] is set to true.

isCovered[3 - 1] is set to true (see Figure 7.2(d)). When number 99 is read, set isCovered[98] to true (see Figure 7.2(e)).

The algorithm for the program can be described as follows:

```
for each number k read from the file,
  mark number k as covered by setting isCovered[k - 1] true;

if every isCovered[i] is true
  The tickets cover all numbers
else
  The tickets don't cover all numbers
```

The complete program is given in Listing 7.1.

Video Note
Lotto numbers

LISTING 7.1 LottoNumbers.cpp

```cpp
1  #include <iostream>
2  using namespace std;
3
4  int main()
5  {
6    bool isCovered[99];
7    int number; // number read from a file
8
9    // Initialize the array
10   for (int i = 0; i < 99; i++)
11     isCovered[i] = false;
12
13   // Read each number and mark its corresponding element covered
14   cin >> number;
15   while (number != 0)
16   {
17     isCovered[number - 1] = true;
18     cin >> number;
19   }
20
21   // Check if all covered
22   bool allCovered = true; // Assume all covered initially
23   for (int i = 0; i < 99; i++)
```

declare array

initialize array

read number

mark number covered

read number

```
24    if (!isCovered[i])                                                check allCovered?
25    {
26        allCovered = false; // Find one number is not covered
27        break;
28    }
29
30    // Display result
31    if (allCovered)
32       cout << "The tickets cover all numbers" << endl;
33    else
34       cout << "The tickets don't cover all numbers" << endl;
35
36    return 0;
37 }
```

Suppose you have created a text file named LottoNumbers.txt that contains the input data 2 5
6 5 4 3 23 43 2 0. You can run the program using the following command:

```
LottoNumbers.exe < LottoNumbers.txt
```

The program can be traced as follows:

line#	Representative elements in array isCovered							number	allCovered
	[1]	[2]	[3]	[4]	[5]	[22]	[42]		
11	false	false	false	false	false	false	false		
14								2	
17	true								
18								5	
17					true				
18								6	
17						true			
18								5	
17					true				
18								4	
17				true					
18								3	
17			true						
18								23	
17						true			
18								43	
17							true		
18								2	
17	true								
18								0	
22									true
24(i=0)									false

The program declares an array of `99 bool` elements (line 6) and initializes each element to `false` (lines 10–11). It reads the first number from the file (line 14). The program then repeats the following operations in a loop:

- If the number is not zero, set its corresponding value in array `isCovered` to `true` (line 17);

- Read the next number (line 18).

When the input is `0`, the input ends. The program checks whether all numbered are covered in lines 22–28 and displays the result in lines 31–34.

7.4 Problem: Deck of Cards

The problem is to write a program that picks four cards randomly from a deck of `52` cards. All the cards can be represented using an array named `deck`, filled with initial values `0` to `52`, as follows:

```
int deck[52];

// Initialize cards
for (int i = 0; i < NUMBER_OF_CARDS; i++)
  deck[i] = i;
```

`deck[0]` to `deck[12]` are Clubs, `deck[13]` to `deck[25]` are Diamonds, `deck[26]` to `deck[38]` are Hearts, and `deck[39]` to `deck[51]` are Spades. Listing 7.2 gives the solution to the problem.

LISTING 7.2 **DeckOfCards.cpp**

```
 1 #include <iostream>
 2 #include <ctime>
 3 using namespace std;
 4
 5 const int NUMBER_OF_CARDS = 52;
 6
 7 void displayRank(int rank)
 8 {
 9   if (rank == 0)
10     cout << "Ace of ";
11   else if (rank == 10)
12     cout << "Jack of ";
13   else if (rank == 11)
14     cout << "Queen of ";
15   else if (rank == 12)
16     cout << "King of ";
17   else
18     cout << rank << " of ";
19 }
20
21 void displaySuit(int suit)
22 {
23   if (suit == 0)
24     cout << "Clubs" << endl;
25   else if (suit == 1)
26     cout << "Diamonds" << endl;
27   else if (suit == 2)
28     cout << "Hearts" << endl;
```

display rank

display suit

```
29   else if (suit == 3)
30     cout << "Spades" << endl;
31 }
32
33 int main()
34 {
35   int deck[NUMBER_OF_CARDS];                              create array deck
36
37   // Initialize cards
38   for (int i = 0; i < NUMBER_OF_CARDS; i++)
39     deck[i] = i;                                          initialize deck
40
41   // Shuffle the cards
42   srand(time(0));
43   for (int i = 0; i < NUMBER_OF_CARDS; i++)               shuffle deck
44   {
45     // Generate an index randomly
46     int index = rand() % NUMBER_OF_CARDS;
47     int temp = deck[i];
48     deck[i] = deck[index];
49     deck[index] = temp;
50   }
51
52   // Display the first four cards
53   for (int i = 0; i < 4; i++)
54   {
55     displayRank(deck[i] % 13);                            display rank
56     displaySuit(deck[i] / 13);                            display suit
57   }
58
59   return 0;
60 }
```

```
4 of Clubs
Ace of Diamonds
6 of Hearts
Jack of Clubs
```

The program defines an array **deck** for 52 cards (line 35). The **deck** is initialized with values **0** to **51** in lines 38–39. A deck value **0** represents card Ace of Clubs, **1** represents card 2 of Clubs, **13** represents card Ace of Diamonds, **14** represents card 2 of Diamonds.

Lines 42–50 randomly shuffle the deck. After a deck is shuffled, **deck[i]** contains an arbitrary value. **deck[i] / 13** is **0, 1, 2,** or **3,** which determines a suit (line 56). **deck[i] % 13** is a value between **0** and **12,** which determines a rank (line 55).

7.5 Passing Arrays to Functions

Just as you can pass single values to a function, you also can pass an entire array to a function. Listing 7.3 gives an example to demonstrate how to declare and invoke this type of function.

LISTING 7.3 PassArrayDemo.cpp

```
1 #include <iostream>
2 using namespace std;
3
4 void printArray(int list[], int arraySize); // Function prototype    function prototype
5
```

```
 6 int main()
 7 {
 8    int numbers[5] = {1, 4, 3, 6, 8};
 9    printArray(numbers, 5); // Invoke the function
10
11    return 0;
12 }
13
14 void printArray(int list[], int arraySize)
15 {
16    for (int i = 0; i < arraySize; i++)
17    {
18       cout << list[i] << " ";
19    }
20 }
```

declare array
invoke function

function implementation

```
1 4 3 6 8
```

In the function header (line 14), `int list[]` indicates that the parameter is an integer array of any size. So you can pass any integer array to invoke this function (line 9).

Note that the parameter names in function prototypes can be omitted. So the function prototype may be declared without the parameter names `list` and `arraySize` as follows:

```
void printArray(int [], int); // Function prototype
```

 Note

passing size along with array

Normally when you pass an array to a function, you should also pass its size in another argument, so that the function knows how many elements are in the array. Otherwise, you will have to hard code this into the function or declare it in a global variable. Neither is flexible or robust.

You can pass a primitive data type variable or an array to a function. However, there are important differences between them.

pass-by-value

■ Passing a variable of a primitive type means that the variable's value is passed to a formal parameter. Changing the value of the local parameter inside the function does not affect the value of the variable outside the function. This is *pass-by-value*.

pass-by-reference

■ Passing an array means that the starting address of the array is passed to the formal parameter. The parameter inside the function references to the same array that is passed to the function. No new arrays are created. This is *pass-by-reference*.

Listing 7.4 gives an example that demonstrates the differences between pass-by-value and pass-by-reference.

LISTING 7.4 PassByReferenceDemo.cpp

function prototype

```
 1 #include <iostream>
 2 using namespace std;
 3
 4 void m(int, int []);
 5
 6 int main()
 7 {
 8    int x = 1; // x represents an int value
 9    int y[10]; // y represents an array of int values
10    y[0] = 1; // Initialize y[0]
```

```
11
12  m(x, y); // Invoke m with arguments x and y                          pass array y
13
14  cout << "x is " << x << endl;
15  cout << "y[0] is " << y[0] << endl;
16
17  return 0;
18 }
19
20 void m(int number, int numbers[])
21 {
22   number = 1001; // Assign a new value to number
23   numbers[0] = 5555; // Assign a new value to numbers[0]               modify array
24 }
```

```
x is 1
y[0] is 5555
```

You will see that after function m is invoked, x remains 1, but y[0] is 5555. This is because the value of x is copied to number, and x and number are independent variables, but y and numbers reference to the same array. numbers can be considered as an alias for array y.

Passing arrays by reference makes sense for performance reasons. If an array is passed by value, all its elements must be copied into a new array. For large arrays, it could take some time and additional memory space. However, passing arrays by reference could lead to errors if your function changed the array accidentally. To prevent this, you can put the const keyword before the array parameter to tell the compiler that the array cannot be changed. The compiler will report errors if the code in the function attempts to modify the array.

const array

Listing 7.5 gives an example that declares a const array argument list in the function p (line 4). In line 7 the function attempts to modify the first element in the array. This error is detected by the compiler, as shown in the sample output.

LISTING 7.5 ConstArrayDemo.cpp

```
 1 #include <iostream>
 2 using namespace std;
 3
 4 void p(const int list[], int arraySize)                              const array argument
 5 {
 6   // Modify array accidentally
 7   list[0] = 100; // Compile error!                                   attempt to modify
 8 }
 9
10 int main()
11 {
12   int numbers[5] = {1, 4, 3, 6, 8};
13   p(numbers, 5);
14
15   return 0;
16 }
```

Compiled using
Visual C++

```
error C2166: l-value specifies const object
```

Compiled using
GNU C++

```
ConstArrayDemo.cpp:7: error: assignment of read-only location
```

L-value

R-value

Both Visual C++ and the GNU compiler report the error. *L-value* or *Lvalue* is a term in C++ that refers to anything that can appear on the left–hand side of an assignment operator (=). The opposite term, *R-value* (or *Rvalue*), refers to anything that can appear on the right-hand side of an assignment operator (=). Since the L-value is declared `const`, it cannot be changed.

Note

cascading **const** parameters

If you define a `const` parameter in a function `f1` and this parameter is passed to another function `f2`, then the corresponding parameter in function `f2` should be declared `const` for consistency. Consider the following code:

```
void f2(int list[], int size)
{
  // Do something
}
```

```
void f1(const int list[], int size)
{
  // Do something
  f2(list, size);
}
```

The compiler reports an error, because `list` is `const` in `f1` and it is passed to `f2`, but it is not `const` in `f2`. The function declaration for `f2` should be

```
void f2(const int list[], int size)
```

7.6 Returning Arrays from Functions

You can declare a function to return a primitive type value. For example,

```
// Return the sum of the elements in the list
int sum(int list[], int size)
```

Can you return an array from a function using a similar syntax? For example, you may attempt to declare a function that returns a new array that is a reversal of an array, as follows:

```
// Return the reversal of list
int[] reverse(const int list[], int size)
```

This is not allowed in C++. However, you can circumvent this restriction by passing two array arguments in the function:

```
// newList is the reversal of list
void reverse(const int list[], int newList[], int size)
```

The program is given in Listing 7.6.

LISTING 7.6 ReverseArray.cpp

```
1 #include <iostream>
2 using namespace std;
3
```

Video Note
reversing array

```
 4  // newList is the reversal of list
 5  void reverse(const int list[], int newList[], int size)          reverse function
 6  {
 7    for (int i = 0, j = size - 1; i < size; i++, j--)
 8    {
 9      newList[j] = list[i];                                          reverse to newList
10    }
11  }
12
13  void printArray(const int list[], int size)                       print array
14  {
15    for (int i = 0; i < size; i++)
16      cout << list[i] << " ";
17  }
18
19  int main()
20  {
21    int size = 6;
22    int list[] = {1, 2, 3, 4, 5, 6};                                declare original array
23    int newList[6];                                                 declare new array
24                                                                    invoke reverse
25    reverse(list, newList, size);
26                                                                    print original array
27    cout << "The original array: ";
28    printArray(list, 6);
29    cout << endl;
30                                                                    print reversed array
31    cout << "The reversed array: ";
32    printArray(newList, 6);
33    cout << endl;
34
35    return 0;
36  }
```

```
The original array: 1 2 3 4 5 6
The reversed array: 6 5 4 3 2 1
```

The **reverse** function (lines 5–11) uses a loop to copy the first element, second, ..., and so on in the original array to the last element, second last, ..., in the new array, as shown in the following diagram.

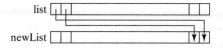

To invoke this function (line 25), you have to pass three arguments. The first argument is the original array, whose contents are not changed in the function. The second argument is the new array, whose contents are changed in the function. The third argument indicates the size of the array.

7.7 Problem: Counting the Occurrences of Each Letter

This section presents a program that counts the occurrences of each letter in an array of characters. The program does the following:

1. Generate 100 lowercase letters randomly and assign them to an array of characters, as shown in Figure 7.3(a). You can obtain a random letter by using the **getRandomLow-erCaseLetter()** function in the RandomCharacter.h header file in Listing 5.12.

2. Count the occurrences of each letter in the array. To do so, create an array, say **counts** of 26 **int** values, each of which counts the occurrences of a letter, as shown in Figure 7.3(b). That is, **counts[0]** counts the number of **a**'s, **counts[1]** counts the number of **b**'s, and so on.

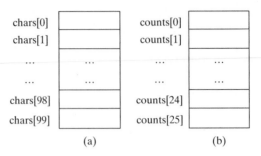

(a)   (b)

FIGURE 7.3 The **chars** array stores **100** characters and the **counts** array stores **26** counts, each counting the occurrences of a letter.

Listing 7.7 gives the complete program.

LISTING 7.7 CountLettersInArray.cpp

```cpp
1 #include <iostream>
2 #include <ctime>
3 #include "RandomCharacter.h"
4 using namespace std;
5
6 const int NUMBER_OF_RANDOM_LETTERS = 100;
7 void createArray(char []);
8 void displayArray(const char []);
9 void countLetters(const char [], int []);
10 void displayCounts(const int []);
11
12 int main()
13 {
14    // Declare and create an array
15    char chars[NUMBER_OF_RANDOM_LETTERS];
16
17    // Initialize the array with random lowercase letters
18    createArray(chars);
19
20    // Display the array
21    cout << "The lowercase letters are: " << endl;
22    displayArray(chars);
23
24    // Count the occurrences of each letter
25    int counts[26];
26
27    // Count the occurrences of each letter
28    countletters(chars, counts);
29
30    // Display counts
31    cout << "\nThe occurrences of each letter are: " << endl;
32    displayCounts(counts);
33
34    return 0;
35 }
36
```

include header file

hundred letters
function prototypes

chars array

assign random letters

display array

counts array

count letters

display counts

```
37  // Create an array of characters
38  void createArray(char chars[])                                    initialize array
39  {
40    // Create lowercase letters randomly and assign
41    // them to the array
42    srand(time(0));                                                 set a new seed
43    for (int i = 0; i < NUMBER_OF_RANDOM_LETTERS; i++)
44      chars[i] = getRandomLowerCaseLetter();                        random letter
45  }
46
47  // Display the array of characters
48  void displayArray(const char chars[])
49  {
50    // Display the characters in the array 20 on each line
51    for (int i = 0; i < NUMBER_OF_RANDOM_LETTERS; i++)
52    {
53      if ((i + 1) % 20 == 0)
54        cout << chars[i] << " " << endl;
55      else
56        cout << chars[i] << " ";
57    }
58  }
59
60  // Count the occurrences of each letter
61  void countLetters(const char chars[], int counts[])               count letter
62  {
63    // Initialize the array
64    for (int i = 0; i < 26; i++)
65     counts[i] = 0;
66
67    // For each lowercase letter in the array, count it
68    for (int i = 0; i < NUMBER_OF_RANDOM_LETTERS; i++)
69      counts[chars[i] - 'a'] ++;
70  }
71
72  // Display counts
73  void displayCounts(const int counts[])
74  {
75    for (int i = 0; i < 26; i++)
76    {
77      if ((i + 1) % 10 == 0)
78        cout << counts[i] << " " << static_cast<char>(i + 'a') << endl;   cast to char
79      else
80        cout << counts[i] << " " << static_cast<char>(i + 'a') << " ";
81    }
82  }
```

```
The lowercase letters are:
p y a o u n s u i b t h y g w q l b y o
x v b r i g h i x w v c g r a s p y i z
n f j v c j c a c v l a j r x r d t w q
m a y e v m k d m e m o j v k m e v t a
r m o u v d h f o o x d g i u w r i q h

The occurrences of each letter are:
6 a 3 b 4 c 4 d 3 e 2 f 4 g 4 h 6 i 4 j
2 k 2 l 6 m 2 n 6 o 2 p 3 q 6 r 2 s 3 t
4 u 8 v 4 w 4 x 5 y 1 z
```

The `createArray` function (lines 38–45) generates an array of 100 random lowercase letters and assigns them in array `chars`. Invoking `getRandomLowerCaseLetter()` (line 44) returns a random lowercase letter. This function is defined in the `RandomCharacter` header file in Listing 5.12. This header file is included in line 3.

The `countLetters` function (lines 61–70) counts the occurrence of letters in `chars` and stores the counts in the array `counts`. Each element in `counts` stores the number of occurrences of a letter. The function processes each letter in the array and increases its count by one. A brute-force approach to count the occurrences of each letter might be as follows:

```
for (int i = 0; i < NUMBER_OF_LETTERS; i++)
  if (chars[i] == 'a')
    counts[0]++;
  else if (chars[i] == 'b')
    counts[1]++;
  ...
```

But a better solution is given in lines 68–69.

```
for (int i = 0; i < NUMBER_OF_LETTERS; i++)
  counts[chars[i] - 'a']++;
```

If the letter (`chars[i]`) is `'a'`, the corresponding count is `counts['a' - 'a']` (i.e., `counts[0]`). If the letter is `'b'`, the corresponding count is `counts['b' - 'a']` (i.e., `counts[1]`) since the ASCII code of `'b'` is one more than that of `'a'`. If the letter is `'z'`, the corresponding count is `counts['z' - 'a']` (i.e., `counts[25]`) since the ASCII code of `'z'` is 25 more than that of `'a'`.

7.8 Searching Arrays

Searching is the process of looking for a specific element in an array—for example, discovering whether a certain score is included in a list of scores. Searching is a common task in computer programming. Many algorithms and data structures are devoted to searching. This section discusses two commonly used approaches: *linear search* and *binary search*.

linear search

binary search

7.8.1 The Linear Search Approach

The linear search approach compares the key element `key` sequentially with each element in the array. The function continues to do so until the key matches an element in the array or the array is exhausted. If a match is made, the linear search returns the index of the element in the array that matches the key. Otherwise, the search returns -1. The `linearSearch` function in Listing 7.8 gives the solution:

LISTING 7.8 LinearSearch.h

```
 1 int linearSearch(const int list[], int key, int arraySize)
 2 {
 3   for (int i = 0; i < arraySize; i++)
 4   {
 5     if (key == list[i])
 6       return i;
 7   }
 8
 9   return -1;
10 }
```

[0] [1] [2] ...

list

key Compare key with list[i] for i = 0, 1, ...

Please trace the function using the following statements:

```
int list[] = {1, 4, 4, 2, 5, -3, 6, 2};
int i = linearSearch(list, 4, 8);  // Returns 1
int j = linearSearch(list, -4, 8); // Returns -1
int k = linearSearch(list, -3, 8); // Returns 5
```

The linear search function compares the key with each element in the array. The elements in the array can be in any order. On average, the algorithm will have to compare half of the elements before finding the key if it exists. Since the execution time of a linear search increases linearly as the number of array elements increases, linear search is inefficient for a large array.

7.8.2 The Binary Search Approach

Binary search is the other common search approach for a list of values. It requires that the elements in the array already be ordered. Assume that the array is in ascending order. The binary search first compares the key with the element in the middle of the array. Consider the following three cases:

- If the key is less than the middle element, you only need to continue to search in the first half of the array.

- If the key is equal to the middle element, the search ends with a match.

- If the key is greater than the middle element, you only need to continue to search in the second half of the array.

Clearly, the binary search function eliminates at least half of the array after each comparison. Sometimes you eliminate half of the elements, and sometimes you eliminate half plus one. Suppose that the array has n elements. For convenience, let n be a power of 2. After the first comparison, $n/2$ elements are left for further search; after the second comparison, $(n/2)/2$ elements are left for further search. After the kth comparison, $n/2^k$ elements are left for further search. When $k = \log_2 n$, only one element is left in the array, and you need only one more comparison. In the worst case, therefore, when using the binary search approach, you need $\log_2 n + 1$ comparisons to find an element in the sorted array. In the worst case, for a list of 1024 (2^{10}) elements, binary search requires only eleven comparisons whereas a linear search requires 1024.

The portion of the array being searched shrinks by half after each comparison. Let `low` and `high` denote, respectively, the first index and last index of the array that is currently being searched. Initially, `low` is 0 and `high` is `listSize-1`. Let `mid` denote the index of the middle element. So `mid` is `(low + high)/2`. Figure 7.4 shows how to find key 11 in the list {2, 4, 7, 10, 11, 45, 50, 59, 60, 66, 69, 70, 79} using binary search.

The binary search returns the index of the search key if it is contained in the list. Otherwise, it returns -1.

You know how the binary approach works. The task now is to implement it in C++, as shown in Listing 7.9.

LISTING 7.9 BinarySearch.h

```
1 int binarySearch(const int list[], int key, int arraySize)
2 {
3    int low = 0;
4    int high = arraySize - 1;
5
```

```
 6  while (high >= low)
 7  {
 8    int mid = (low + high) / 2;
 9    if (key < list[mid])
10      high = mid - 1;
11    else if (key == list[mid])
12      return mid;
13    else
14      low = mid + 1;
15  }
16
17  return -1;
18 }
```

match found

no match

key is 11   low   mid   high

key < 50   [0] [1] [2] [3] [4] [5] [6] [7] [8] [9] [10][11][12]

              list | 2   4   7 10 11 45 **50** 59 60 66 69 70 79 |

                 low   mid   high

                 [0] [1] [2] [3] [4] [5]

key > 7   list | 2   4   7   10   11   45 |

                      low   mid   high

                      [3] [4] [5]

key == 11   list | 10   11   45 |

FIGURE 7.4   Binary search eliminates half of the list from further consideration after each comparison.

You start to compare the key with the middle element in the list whose low index is 0 and high index is listSize-1. If key < list[mid], set the high index to mid-1; if key == list[mid], a match is found and return mid; if key > list[mid], set the low index to mid+1. Continue the search until low > high or a match is found. If low > high, return -1, which indicates that the key is not in the list.

What happens if (high >= low) in line 6 is replaced by (high > low)? The search would miss a possible matching element. Consider a list with just one element. The search would miss the element, because high and low are both 0 in this case.

Does the function still work if there are duplicate elements in the list? Yes, as long as the elements are sorted in increasing order. The function returns the index of one of the matching elements if the element is in the list.

To understand this function better, trace it with the following statements and identify low and high when the function returns.

```
int list[] = {2, 4, 7, 10, 11, 45, 50, 59, 60, 66, 69, 70, 79};
int i = binarySearch(list, 2, 13); // Returns 0
int j = binarySearch(list, 11, 13); // Returns 4
int k = binarySearch(list, 12, 13); // Returns -1
int l = binarySearch(list, 1, 13); // Returns -1
int m = binarySearch(list, 3, 13); // Returns -1
```

Here is the table that lists the `low` and `high` values when the function exits and the value returned from invoking the function.

Function	low	high	Value Returned
binarySearch(list, 2, 13)	0	1	0
binarySearch(list, 11, 13)	3	5	4
binarySearch(list, 12, 13)	5	4	−1
binarySearch(list, 1, 13)	0	−1	−1
binarySearch(list, 3, 13)	1	0	−1

Note

Linear search is useful for finding an element in a small array or an unsorted array, but for large arrays it is inefficient. Binary search is more efficient, but it requires that the array be presorted.

binary search benefits

7.9 Sorting Arrays

Sorting, like searching, is a common task in computer programming. Many different algorithms have been developed for sorting. This section introduces two simple, intuitive sorting algorithms: *selection sort* and *insertion sort*.

Video Note
selection sort

7.9.1 Selection Sort

Suppose that you want to sort a list in ascending order. Selection sort finds the smallest number in the list and places it first. It then finds the smallest number remaining and places it next to first, and so on, until only a single number remains. Figure 7.5 shows how to sort the list {2, 9, 5, 4, 8, 1, 6} using selection sort.

You know how the selection sort approach works. The task now is to implement it in C++. For beginners, it is difficult to develop a complete solution on the first attempt. You may start to write the code for the first iteration to find the smallest element in the list and swap it with the first element, and then observe what would be different for the second iteration, the third, and so on. The insight this gives will enable you to write a loop that generalizes all the iterations.

The solution can be described as follows:

```
for (int i = 0; i < listSize; i++)
{
  select the smallest element in list[i..listSize-1];
  swap the smallest with list[i], if necessary;
  // list[i] is in its correct position.
  // The next iteration apply on list[i+1..listSize-1]
}
```

Listing 7.10 implements the solution.

LISTING 7.10 SelectionSort.h

```
1 void selectionSort(double list[], int listSize)
2 {
3   for (int i = 0; i < listSize; i++)
4   {
5     // Find the minimum in the list[i..listSize-1]
6     double currentMin = list[i];
```

```
7      int currentMinIndex = i;
8
9      for (int j = i + 1; j < listSize; j++)
10     {
11       if (currentMin > list[j])
12       {
13         currentMin = list[j];
14         currentMinIndex = j;
15       }
16     }
17
18     // Swap list[i] with list[currentMinIndex] if necessary;
19     if (currentMinIndex != i)
20     {
21       list[currentMinIndex] = list[i];
22       list[i] = currentMin;
23     }
24   }
25 }
```

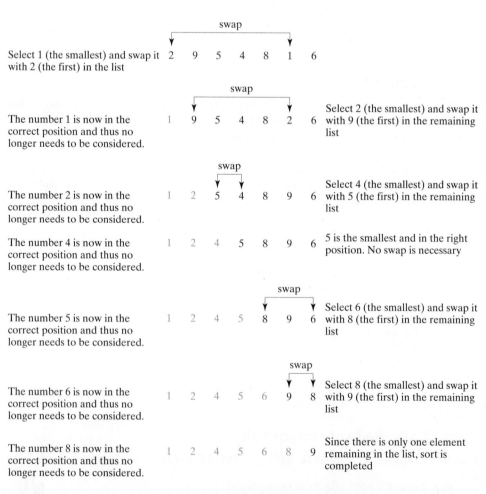

Select 1 (the smallest) and swap it with 2 (the first) in the list

The number 1 is now in the correct position and thus no longer needs to be considered.

The number 2 is now in the correct position and thus no longer needs to be considered.

The number 4 is now in the correct position and thus no longer needs to be considered.

The number 5 is now in the correct position and thus no longer needs to be considered.

The number 6 is now in the correct position and thus no longer needs to be considered.

The number 8 is now in the correct position and thus no longer needs to be considered.

Select 2 (the smallest) and swap it with 9 (the first) in the remaining list

Select 4 (the smallest) and swap it with 5 (the first) in the remaining list

5 is the smallest and in the right position. No swap is necessary

Select 6 (the smallest) and swap it with 8 (the first) in the remaining list

Select 8 (the smallest) and swap it with 9 (the first) in the remaining list

Since there is only one element remaining in the list, sort is completed

FIGURE 7.5 Selection sort repeatedly selects the smallest number and swaps it with the first number in the remaining list.

The `selectionSort(double list[], int listSize)` function sorts any array of double elements. The function is implemented with a nested `for` loop. The outer loop (with the loop-control variable `i`) (line 3) is iterated in order to find the smallest element in the list, which ranges from `list[i]` to `list[listSize - 1]`, and exchange it with `list[i]`.

The variable `i` is initially `0`. After each iteration of the outer loop, `list[i]` is in the right place. Eventually, all the elements are put in the right place; therefore, the whole list is sorted.

To understand this function better, trace it with the following statements:

```
double list[] = {1, 9, 4.5, 6.6, 5.7, -4.5};
selectionSort(list, 6);
```

7.9.2 Insertion Sort

Suppose that you want to sort a list in ascending order. The insertion-sort algorithm sorts a list of values by repeatedly inserting a new element into a sorted sublist until the whole list is sorted. Figure 7.6 shows how to sort the list {2, 9, 5, 4, 8, 1, 6} using insertion sort.

The algorithm can be described as follows:

```
for (int i = 1; i < listSize; i++)
{
    insert list[i] into a sorted sublist list[0..i-1] so that
    list[0..i] is sorted.
}
```

To insert `list[i]` into `list[0..i-1]`, save `list[i]` into a temporary variable, say `currentElement`. Move `list[i-1]` to `list[i]` if `list[i-1] > currentElement`, move `list[i-2]` to `list[i-1]` if `list[i-2] > currentElement`, and so on, until

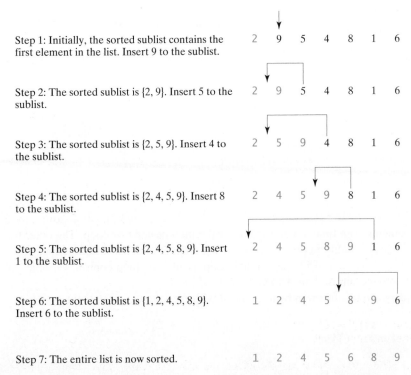

Step 1: Initially, the sorted sublist contains the first element in the list. Insert 9 to the sublist.

Step 2: The sorted sublist is {2, 9}. Insert 5 to the sublist.

Step 3: The sorted sublist is {2, 5, 9}. Insert 4 to the sublist.

Step 4: The sorted sublist is {2, 4, 5, 9}. Insert 8 to the sublist.

Step 5: The sorted sublist is {2, 4, 5, 8, 9}. Insert 1 to the sublist.

Step 6: The sorted sublist is {1, 2, 4, 5, 8, 9}. Insert 6 to the sublist.

Step 7: The entire list is now sorted.

FIGURE 7.6 Insertion sort repeatedly inserts a new element into a sorted sublist.

`list[i-k] <= currentElement`. Assign `currentElement` to `list[i-k+1]`. For example, to insert 4 into {2, 5, 9} in Step 3 in Figure 7.7, move `list[2]` (9) to `list[3]` since 9 > 4, move `list[1]` (5) to `list[2]` since 5 > 4. Finally move `currentElement` (4) to `list[1]`, as shown in Figure 7.7.

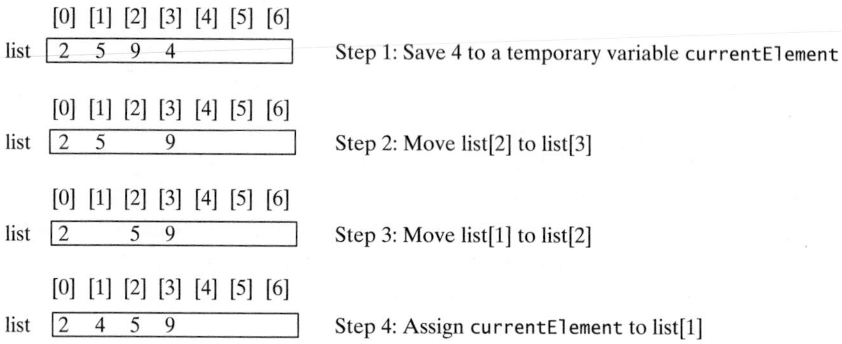

FIGURE 7.7 A new element is inserted into a sorted sublist.

The algorithm is implemented in Listing 7.11.

LISTING 7.11 InsertionSort.h

```
1 void insertionSort(double list[], int listSize)
2 {
3   for (int i = 1; i < listSize; i++)
4   {
5     /* Insert list[i] into a sorted sublist list[0..i-1] so that
6        list[0..i] is sorted. */
7     double currentElement = list[i];
8     int k;
9     for (k = i - 1; k >= 0 && list[k] > currentElement; k--)
10    {
11      list[k + 1] = list[k];
12    }
13
14    // Insert the current element into list[k+1]
15    list[k + 1] = currentElement;
16  }
17 }
```

The `insertionSort(double list[], int listSize)` function sorts any array of double elements. The function is implemented with a nested **for** loop. The outer loop (with the loop-control variable `i`) (line 3) is iterated in order to obtain a sorted sublist, which ranges from `list[0]` to `list[i]`. The inner loop (with the loop-control variable `k`) inserts `list[i]` into the sublist from `list[0]` to `list[i-1]`.

To understand this function better, trace it with the following statements:

```
double list[] = {1, 9, 4.5, 6.6, 5.7, -4.5};
insertionSort(list, 6);
```

7.10 C-Strings

Pedagogical Note

C-string is popular in the C language, but it has been replaced by a more robust, convenient, and useful **string** type in C++. For this reason, the **string** type, to be introduced in Chapter 10, "Class Design," will be used to process strings in this book. The purpose of introducing C-strings in this section is to give additional examples and exercises using arrays and to prepare for the introduction of the **string** type. You will see the benefits of object-oriented programming by contrasting C-strings with the **string** type.

*C-strings vs. **string** type*

A C-string is an array of characters ending with the *null terminator* (`'\0'`), which indicates where a string terminates in memory. Recall that a character that begins with the backslash symbol (\) is an escape character. The symbols \ and 0 together represent one character. This character is the first character in the ASCII table.

C-string
null terminator

Every string literal is a C-string. You can declare an array initialized with a string literal. For example, the following statement creates an array for a C-string that contains characters `'D'`, `'a'`, `'l'`, `'l'`, `'a'`, `'s'`, and `'\0'`, as shown in Figure 7.8.

```
char city[7] = "Dallas";
```

'D'	'a'	'l'	'l'	'a'	's'	'\0'
city[0]	city[1]	city[2]	city[3]	city[4]	city[5]	city[6]

FIGURE 7.8   A character array can be initialized with a C-string.

Note that the size of the array is 7 and the last character in the array is `'\0'`.

There is a subtle difference between a C-string and an array of characters. For example, the following two statements are different:

```
char city1[] = "Dallas"; // C-string
char city2[] = {'D', 'a', 'l', 'l', 'a', 's'}; // Not a C-string
```

The former is a C-string and the latter is just an array of characters. The former has **7** characters including the last null terminator and the latter has **6** characters.

7.10.1   Input and Output of C-Strings

To output a C-string is simple. Suppose s is an array for a C-string. To display it to the console, simply use

```
cout << s;
```

You can read a C-string from the keyboard just as you do a number. For example, consider the following code:

```
1 char city[7];
2 cout << "Enter a city: ";
3 cin >> city; // Read to array city
4 cout << "You entered " << city << endl;
```

declare an array

read C-string

When you read a string to an array, make sure to leave room for the null terminator character. Since `city` has a size 7, your input should not exceed **6** characters.

input size

This approach to reading a string is simple, but there is a problem. The input ends with a whitespace character. You cannot read a string that contains a space. Suppose you want to enter New York; then you have to use an alternative approach. C++ provides the cin.getline function in the iostream header file, which reads a string into an array. The syntax of the function is:

```
cin.getline(char array[], int size, char delimitChar)
```

The function stops reading characters when the delimiter character is encountered or when the size - 1 number of characters have been read. The last character in the array is reserved for the null terminator ('\0'). If the delimiter is encountered, it is read but is not stored in the array. The third argument delimitChar has a default value ('\n').

The following code uses the cin.getline function to read a string:

declare array

string to array

```
1 char city[30];
2 cout << "Enter a city: "; // i.e., New York
3 cin.getline(city, 30, '\n'); // Read to array city
4 cout << "You entered " << city << endl;
```

Since the default value for the third argument in the cin.getline function is '\n', line 3 can be replaced by

```
cin.getline(city, 30); // Read to array city
```

7.10.2   C-string Functions

processing C-string

Given that a C-string ends with a null terminator, C++ can utilize this fact to process C-strings efficiently. When you pass a C-string to a function, you don't have to pass its length, because the length can be obtained by counting all characters from left to right in the array until the null terminator character is reached. Here is the function for obtaining the length of a C-string.

```
unsigned int strlen(char s[])
{
  int i = 0;
  for ( ; s[i] != '\0'; i++);
  return i;
}
```

In fact, strlen and several other functions are provided in the C++ library for processing C-strings, as shown in Table 7.1.

To use these functions, your program needs to include the cstring header file.

copying strings

strcpy

Function strcpy can be used to copy a source string in the second argument to a target string in the first argument. The target string must have already been allocated sufficient memory for the function to work.

A common mistake is to copy a C-string using code like this:

```
char city[30] = "Chicago";
city = "New York"; // Copy New York to city. Wrong!
```

In order to copy "New York" to city, you have to use

```
strcpy(city, "New York");
```

TABLE 7.1 String Functions

Function	Description
size_t strlen(char s[])	Returns the length of the string, i.e., the number of the characters before the null terminator.
strcpy(char s1[], const char s2[])	Copies string s2 to string s1.
strcat(char s1[], const char s2[])	Appends string s2 to s1. The first character of s2 overwrites the null terminator in s1.
int strcmp(char s1[], const char s2[])	Returns a value greater than 0, 0, or less than 0 if s1 is greater than, equal to, or less than s2 based on the numeric code of the characters.
int atoi(char s[])	Converts the string to an int value.
double atof(char s[])	Converts the string to a double value.
long atol(char s[])	Converts the string to a long value.
void itoa(int value, char s[], int radix)	Converts the value to a string based on specified radix.

 Note

size_t is a C++ type. For most compilers, it is the same as unsigned int.   type **size_t**

Function strcat can be used to append the string in the second argument to the string in   combining strings
the first argument. The first string must have already been allocated sufficient memory for the   **strcat**
function to work. For example, the following code works fine to append s2 into s1.

```
char s1[7] = "abc";
char s2[4] = "def";
strcat(s1, s2);
```

However, the following code does not work, because there is no space to add s2 into s1.

```
char s1[4] = "abc";
char s2[4] = "def";
strcat(s1, s2);
```

Function strcmp can be used to compare two strings. How do you compare two strings?   comparing strings
You compare their corresponding characters according to their numeric codes. Most compil-   **strcmp**
ers use the ASCII code for characters.

The function returns the value 0 if s1 is equal to s2, a value less than 0 if s1 is less than
s2, and a value greater than 0 if s1 is greater than s2. For example, suppose s1 is "abc" and
s2 is "abg", and strcmp(s1, s2) returns a negative value. The first two characters (a vs. a)
from s1 and s2 are compared. Because they are equal, the second two characters (b vs. b) are
compared. Because they are also equal, the third two characters (c vs. g) are compared. Since
the character c is 4 less than g, the comparison returns a negative value. Exactly what value is
returned depends on the compiler. Visual C++ and GNU compilers return -1, but Borland
C++ compiler returns -4 since the character c is 4 less than g.

Listing 7.12 is a program to demonstrate these functions.

LISTING 7.12 CStringFunctionDemo.cpp

```
1 #include <iostream>
2 #include <cstring>
```
   include **cstring** header

declare three strings

```
3 using namespace std;
4
5 int main()
6 {
7   char s1[20];
8   char s2[] = "Texas, USA"; // Let C++ figure out the size of s2
9   char s3[] = "Dallas"; // Let C++ figure out the size of s3
10
```

copy **s2** to **s1**

```
11  strcpy(s1, s2); // Copy s2 to s1
12  cout << "The string in s1 is " << s1 << endl;
13
```

length of **s1**

```
14  cout << "The length of string s1 is " << strlen(s1) << endl;
15
```

combine strings

```
16  strcat(strcat(s1, ", "), s2);
17
18  cout << "The string in s1 is " << s1 << endl;
19  cout << "The string in s2 is " << s2 << endl;
20
```

compare strings

```
21  cout << "strcmp(s2, s3) is " << strcmp(s2, s3) << endl;
22
```

convert to number

```
23  // Conversion functions
24  cout << atoi("42") + atoi("56") << endl;
25  cout << atof("3.5") + atof("5.5") << endl;
26
27  char s[10];
```

convert to string

```
28  itoa(42, s, 2); // Radix 2 (binary)
29  cout << "42 is " << s << " in binary" << endl;
30
31  itoa(42, s, 10); // Radix 10
32  cout << s << endl;
33
34  itoa(42, s, 16); // Radix 16 (hexadecimal)
35  cout << "42 is " << s << " in hex" << endl;
36
37  return 0;
38 }
```

```
The string in s1 is Texas, USA
The length of string s1 is 10
The string in s1 is Texas, USA, Texas, USA
The string in s2 is Texas, USA
strcmp(s2, s3) is 16
98
9
42 is 101010 in binary
42
42 is 2a in hex
```

Three strings s1, s2, and s3 are declared in lines 7–9. Line 11 copies s2 to s1 using the strcpy function. Line 14 uses the strlen function to obtain the length of string s1.

Line 16 invokes strcat twice. First, strcat(s1, ", ") appends ", " to s1 and returns the new s1. Second, strcat(strcat(s1, ", "), s2) appends s2 to the new s1. So, s1 is Dallas, Texas, USA.

Line 21 invokes strcmp(s1, s2), which returns 16, because 'T' - 'D' is 16. With some compilers, function strcmp(s1, s2) always return 1, 0, or -1, if s1 is greater than, equal to, or less than s2.

atoi
atof
itoa

Invoking atoi("42") returns an int value 42 in line 24. Invoking atof("3.5") returns a double value 3.5 in line 25. Invoking itoa(42, s, 2) converts an int value 42 to a string using radix `2` in line 28. Invoking `itoa(42, s, 10)` converts an `int` value `42` to a string using radix `10` in line 31. Invoking `itoa(42, s, 16)` converts an `int` value `42` to a string using radix `16` in line 34.

KEY TERMS

array   214
array index   215
array initializer   216
binary search   230
const array   225
C-string   237

indexed variable   215
insertion sort   233
linear search   230
null terminator (`'\0'`)   237
selection sort   233

CHAPTER SUMMARY

1. An array stores a list of value of the same type.

2. An array is created using the syntax

    `elementType arrayName[size]`

3. Each element in the array is represented using the syntax `arrayName[index]`, known as an indexed variable.

4. An index must be an integer or an integer expression.

5. Array index is 0-based, meaning that the index for the first element is 0.

6. Programmers often mistakenly reference the first element in an array with index `1` rather than `0`. This is called the *index off-by-one error*.

7. Accessing array elements using subscripts beyond the boundaries using causes out-of-bounds error.

8. Out of bounds is a serious error, but it is not checked automatically by the C++ compiler.

9. C++ has a shorthand notation, known as the *array initializer*, which creates and initializes an array in a single statement using the syntax:

    `elementType arrayName[] = {value0, value1, ..., valuek};`

10. Array arguments are passed by reference in C++.

11. When you pass an array argument to a function, often you also should pass the size in another argument, so the function knows how many elements are in the array.

12. You can specify `const` array parameters to prevent arrays from being accidentally modified.

13. An array of characters that ends with a null terminator is called a C-string.

14. A string literal is a C-string.

15. C++ provides several functions for processing C-strings.

16. You can obtain a C-string length using the `strlen` function.

17. You can copy a C-string to another C-string using the `strcpy` function.

18. You can compare two C-strings using the `strcmp` function.

19. You can use the `itoa` function to convert an integer to a C-string, and use `atoi` to convert a string to an integer.

REVIEW QUESTIONS

Sections 7.2–7.4

7.1 How do you declare and create an array?

7.2 How do you access elements of an array? Can you copy an array `a` to `b` using `b = a`?

7.3 Is memory allocated when an array is declared? Do the elements in the array have default values? What happens when the following code is executed?

```
int numbers[30];
cout << "numbers[0] is " << numbers[0] << endl;
cout << "numbers[29] is " << numbers[29] << endl;
cout << "numbers[30] is " << numbers[30] << endl;
```

7.4 Indicate true or false for the following statements:

- Every element in an array has the same type.
- The array size is fixed after it is created.
- The array size used to declare an array must be a constant expression.
- The array elements are initialized when an array is created.

7.5 Which of the following statements are valid array declarations?

```
double d[30];
char[30] r;
int i[] = (3, 4, 3, 2);
float f[] = {2.3, 4.5, 6.6};
```

7.6 What is the array index type? What is the lowest index? What is the representation of the third element in an array named `a`?

7.7 Write C++ statements to do the following:

(a) Create an array to hold `10` double values.
(b) Assign value `5.5` to the last element in the array.
(c) Display the sum of the first two elements.
(d) Write a loop that computes the sum of all elements in the array.
(e) Write a loop that finds the minimum element in the array.
(f) Randomly generate an index and display the element of this index in the array.
(g) Use an array initializer to create another array with initial values `3.5`, `5.5`, `4.52`, and `5.6`.

7.8 What happens when your program attempts to access an array element with an invalid index?

7.9 Identify and fix the errors in the following code:

```
1 int main()
2 {
3   double[100] r;
4
```

```
5    for (int i = 0; i < 100; i++);
6      r(i) = rand() % 100;
7 }
```

Sections 7.5- 7.7

7.10   When an array is passed to a function, a new array is created and passed to the function. Is this true?

7.11   Show the output of the following two programs:

```
#include <iostream>
using namespace std;

void m(int x, int y[])
{
    x = 3;
    y[0] = 3;
}

int main()
{
    int number = 0;
    int numbers[1];

    m(number, numbers);

    cout << "number is " << number
        << " and numbers[0] is " << numbers[0];

    return 0;
}
```

(a)

```
#include <iostream>
using namespace std;

void reverse(int list[], int size)
{
    for (int i = 0; i < size / 2; i++)
    {
        int temp = list[i];
        list[i] = list[size - 1 - i];
        list[size - 1 - i] = temp;
    }
}

int main()
{
    int list[] = {1, 2, 3, 4, 5};
    int size = 5;
    reverse(list, size);
    for (int i = 0; i < size; i++)
        cout << list[i] << " ";

    return 0;
}
```

(b)

7.12   How do you prevent the array from being modified accidentally in a function?

Sections 7.8–7.9

7.13   Use Figure 7.4 as an example to show how to apply the binary search approach to search for key 10 and key 12 in list {2, 4, 7, 10, 11, 45, 50, 59, 60, 66, 69, 70, 79}.

7.14   Use Figure 7.5 as an example to show how to apply the selection-sort approach to sort {3.4, 5, 3, 3.5, 2.2, 1.9, 2}.

7.15   Use Figure 7.6 as an example to show how to apply the insertion-sort approach to sort {3.4, 5, 3, 3.5, 2.2, 1.9, 2}.

7.16   How do you modify the `selectionSort` function in Listing 7.10 to sort numbers in decreasing order?

7.17   How do you modify the `insertionSort` function in Listing 7.11 to sort numbers in decreasing order?

Section 7.10

7.18   What are the differences between the following two arrays?

```
char s1[] = {'a', 'b', 'c'};
char s2[] = "abc";
```

7.19 Suppose s1 and s2 are defined as follows:

```
char s1[] = "abc";
char s2[] = "efg";
```

Are the following expressions/statements correct?

(a) s1 = "good"
(b) s1 < s2
(c) s1[0]
(d) s1[0] < s2[0]
(e) strcpy(s1, s2);
(f) strcmp(s1, s2)
(g) strlen(s1)

PROGRAMMING EXERCISES

Sections 7.2–7.4

7.1 (*Analyzing input*) Write a program that reads ten numbers, computes their average, and finds out how many numbers are above the average. Here is a sample run of the program:

```
Enter ten numbers: 1 2.7 3 4 5 6 7 8 9 10  ↵Enter
The average is 5.57
The number of values greater than the average is 5
```

7.2 (*Reversing the numbers entered*) Write a program that reads ten integers and displays them in the reverse of the order in which they were read.

7.3* (*Counting occurrence of numbers*) Write a program that reads the integers between **1** and **100** and counts the occurrence of each number. Assume the input ends with **0**. Here is a sample run of the program:

```
Enter the integers between 1 and 100: 2 5 6 5 4 3 23 43 2 0  ↵Enter
2 occurs 2 times
3 occurs 1 time
4 occurs 1 time
5 occurs 2 times
6 occurs 1 time
23 occurs 1 time
43 occurs 1 time
```

Note that if a number occurs more than one time, the plural word "times" is used in the output.

7.4 (*Analyzing scores*) Write a program that reads an unspecified number of scores and determines how many are above or equal to the average and how many are below the average. Enter a negative number to signify the end of the input. Assume that the maximum number of scores is **100**.

7.5** (*Printing distinct numbers*) Write a program that reads in ten numbers and displays distinct numbers (i.e., if a number appears multiple times, it is displayed only once). (*Hint:* Read a number and store it to an array if it is new. If the number is already in the array, discard it. After the input, the array contains the distinct numbers.) Here is a sample run of the program:

```
Enter ten numbers: 1 2 3 2 1 6 3 4 5 2 ↵Enter
The distinct numbers are: 1 2 3 6 4 5
```

7.6* (*Revising Listing 4.14, PrimeNumber.cpp*) Listing 4.14 determines whether a number **n** is prime by checking whether **2**, **3**, **4**, **5**, **6**, ..., **n/2** is a divisor. If a divisor is found, **n** is not prime. A more efficient approach to determine whether **n** is prime is to check whether any of the prime numbers less than or equal to $\sqrt{n}$ can divide **n** evenly. If not, **n** is prime. Rewrite Listing 4.14 to display the first **50** prime numbers using this approach. You need to use an array to store the prime numbers and later use them to check whether they are possible divisors for **n**.

7.7* (*Counting single digits*) Write a program that generates one hundred random integers between **0** and **9** and displays the count for each number. (*Hint:* Use **rand()** **% 10** to generate a random integer between **0** and **9**. Use an array of ten integers, say **counts**, to store the counts for the number of **0**'s, **1**'s, ..., **9**'s.)

Sections 7.5–7.7

7.8 (*Averaging an array*) Write two overloaded functions that return the average of an array with the following headers:

```
int average(const int array[], int size);
double average(const double array[], int size);
```

Write a test program that prompts the user to enter ten double values, invokes this function, and displays the average value.

7.9 (*Finding the smallest element*) Write a function that finds the smallest element in an array of integers using the following header:

```
double min(double array[], int size)
```

Write a test program that prompts the user to enter ten numbers, invokes this function, and displays the minimum value. Here is a sample run of the program:

```
Enter ten numbers: 1.9 2.5 3.7 2 1.5 6 3 4 5 2 ↵Enter
The minimum number is: 1.5
```

7.10 (*Finding the index of the smallest element*) Write a function that returns the index of the smallest element in an array of integers. If there are more such elements than one, return the smallest index. Use the following header:

```
int indexOfSmallestElement(double array[], int size)
```

Write a test program that prompts the user to enter ten numbers, invokes this function to return the index of the smallest element, and displays the index.

7.11* (*Computing deviation*) Exercise 5.21 computes the standard deviation of numbers. This exercise uses a different but equivalent formula to compute the standard deviation of **n** numbers.

Video Note
finding points nearest to each other

$$mean = \frac{\displaystyle\sum_{i=1}^{n} x_i}{n} = \frac{x_1 + x_2 + \ldots + x_n}{n} \qquad deviation = \sqrt{\frac{\displaystyle\sum_{i=1}^{n} (x_i - mean)^2}{n - 1}}$$

To compute deviation with this formula, you have to store the individual numbers using an array, so that they can be used after the mean is obtained.

Your program should contain the following functions:

```
/** Compute the mean of an array of double values */
double mean(const double x[], int size)

/** Compute the deviation of double values */
double deviation(const double x[], int size)
```

Write a test program that prompts the user to enter ten numbers and displays the mean and deviation, as shown in the following sample run:

```
Enter ten numbers: 1.9 2.5 3.7 2 1 6 3 4 5 2  ↵Enter
The mean is 3.11
The standard deviation is 1.55738
```

7.12*   (*Assigning grades*) Write a program that reads student scores, gets the best score, and then assigns grades based on the following scheme:

Grade is A if score is $>=$ best $-$ 10;

Grade is B if score is $>=$ best $-$ 20;

Grade is C if score is $>=$ best $-$ 30;

Grade is D if score is $>=$ best $-$ 40;

Grade is F otherwise.

The program prompts the user to enter the total number of students, then prompts the user to enter all of the scores, and concludes by displaying the grades. Here is a sample run:

```
Enter the number of students: 4  ↵Enter
Enter 4 scores: 40 55 70 58  ↵Enter
Student 0 score is 40 and grade is C
Student 1 score is 55 and grade is B
Student 2 score is 70 and grade is A
Student 3 score is 58 and grade is B
```

Sections 7.8–7.9

7.13   (*Financial application: finding the sales amount*) Rewrite Programming Exercise 4.37 using the binary search approach. Since the sales amount is between 1 and COMMISSION_SOUGHT/0.08, you can use a binary search to improve the solution.

7.14   (*Timing execution*) Write a program that randomly generates an array of 100000 integers and a key. Estimate the execution time of invoking the linearSearch function in Listing 7.8. Sort the array and estimate the execution time of invoking the binarySearch function in Listing 7.9. You may use the following code template to obtain the execution time:

```
long startTime = time(0);
perform the task;
long endTime = time(0);
long executionTime = endTime - startTime;
```

7.15* (*Game: locker puzzle*) A school has 100 lockers and 100 students. All lockers are closed on the first day of school. As the students enter, the first student, denoted S1, opens every locker. Then the second student, S2, begins with the second locker, denoted L2, and closes every other locker. Student S3 begins with the third locker and changes every third locker (closes it if it was open, and opens it if it was closed). Student S4 begins with locker L4 and changes every fourth locker. Student S5 starts with L5 and changes every fifth locker, and so on until student S100 changes L100.

After all the students have passed through the building and changed the lockers, which lockers are open? Write a program to find your answer.

(*Hint:* Use an array of **100** elements, each of which stores the number of the times a locker has changed. If a locker changes an even number of times, it is closed; otherwise, it is open.)

7.16** (*Bubble sort*) Write a sort function that uses the bubble-sort algorithm. The algorithm makes several passes through the array. On each pass, successive neighboring pairs are compared. If a pair is in decreasing order, its values are swapped; otherwise, the values remain unchanged. The technique is called a *bubble sort* or *sinking sort* because the smaller values gradually "bubble" their way to the top and the larger values sink to the bottom.

The algorithm can be described as follows:

```
bool changed = true;
do
{
  changed = false;
  for (int j = 0; j < listSize - 1; j++)
    if (list[j] > list[j + 1])
    {
      swap list[j] with list[j + 1];
      changed = true;
    }
} while (changed);
```

Clearly, the list is in increasing order when the loop terminates. It is easy to show that the **do** loop executes at most `listSize - 1` times.

Write a test program that reads in an array of ten double numbers, invokes the function, and displays the sorted numbers.

7.17*** (*Game: bean machine*) The bean machine, also known as a quincunx or the Galton box, is a device for statistic experiments named after English scientist Sir Francis Galton. It consists of an upright board with evenly spaced nails (or pegs) in a triangular form, as shown in Figure 7.13.

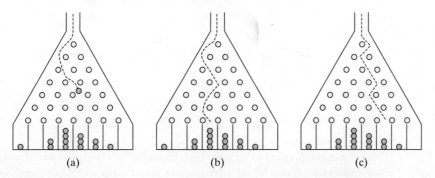

(a)   (b)   (c)

FIGURE 7.13   Each ball takes a random path and falls into a slot.

Balls are dropped from the opening of the board. Every time a ball hits a nail, it has a 50% chance to fall to the left and a 50% chance to fall to the right. The piles of balls are accumulated in the slots at the bottom of the board.

Write a program that simulates the bean machine. Your program should prompt the user to enter the number of the balls and the number of the slots (maximum 50) in the machine. Simulate the falling of each ball by printing its path. For example, the path for the ball in Figure 7.13(b) is LLRRLLR and the path for the ball in Figure 7.13(c) is RLRRLRR. Display the final buildup of the balls in the slots in a histogram. Here is a sample run of the program:

```
Enter the number of balls to drop: 5 ↵Enter
Enter the number of slots in the bean machine: 7 ↵Enter

LRLRLRR
RRLLLRR
LLRLLRR
RRLLLLL
LRLRRLR


    0
    0
  000
```

(*Hint:* Create an array named `slots`. Each element in `slots` stores the number of balls in a slot. Each ball falls into a slot via a path. The number of R's in a path is the position of the slot where the ball falls. For example, for the path LRL-RLRR, the ball falls into `slots[4]`, and for the path RRLLLLL, the ball falls into `slots[2]`.)

7.18 (*Revising selection sort*) In §7.9.1, you used selection sort to sort an array. The selection-sort function repeatedly finds the smallest number in the current array and swaps it with the first. Rewrite this example by finding the largest number and swapping it with the last number in the array. Write a test program that reads in an array of ten double numbers, invokes the function, and displays the sorted numbers.

7.19*** (*Game: Eight Queens*) The classic Eight Queens puzzle is to place eight queens on a chessboard such that no two can attack each other (i.e., no two queens are on the same row, same column, or same diagonal). There are many possible solutions. Write a program that displays one such solution. A sample output is shown below:

7.20*** (*Game: multiple Eight Queens solutions*) Exercise 7.19 finds one solution for the Eight Queens problem. Write a program to count all possible solutions for the Eight Queens problem and displays all solutions.

7.21** (*Simulation: coupon collector's problem*) Coupon collector is a classic statistic problem with many practical applications. The problem is to pick objects from a set of objects repeatedly and find out how many picks are needed for all the objects to be picked at least once. A variation of the problem is to pick cards from a shuffled deck of 52 cards repeatedly and find out how many picks are needed before you see one of each suit. Write a program to simulate the number of picks needed to get four cards from each suit and display the four cards picked (it is possible a card may be picked twice). Here is a sample run of the program:

```
Queen of Spades
5 of Clubs
Queen of Hearts
4 of Diamonds
Number of picks: 12
```

Section 7.10

7.22* (*Checking substrings*) Write the following function to check whether string `s1` is a substring of string `s2`. The function returns the first index in `s2` if there is a match. Otherwise, return `-1`.

```
int indexOf(const char s1[], const char s2[])
```

Write a test program that reads two strings and checks whether the first string is a substring of the second. Here is a sample run of the program:

```
Enter the first string: welcome  ↵Enter
Enter the second string: We welcome you!  ↵Enter
indexOf("welcome", "We welcome you!") is 3
```

```
Enter the first string: welcome  ↵Enter
Enter the second string: We invite you!  ↵Enter
indexOf("welcome", "We invite you!") is -1
```

7.23* (*Occurrences of a specified character*) Write a function that finds the number of occurrences of a specified character in the string using the following header:

```
int count(const char s[], char a)
```

For example, `count("Welcome", 'e')` returns `2`. Write a test program that reads a string and a character and displays the number of occurrences of the character in the string. Here is a sample run of the program:

```
Enter a string: Welcome to C++  ↵Enter
Enter a character: o  ↵Enter
o appears in Welcome to C++ 2 times
```

7.24* (*Counting the letters in a string*) Write a function that counts the number of letters in the string using the following header:

```
int countLetters(const char s[])
```

Write a test program that reads a string and displays the number of letters in the string. Here is a sample run of the program:

```
Enter a string: 2010 is coming  ↵Enter
The number of letters in 2010 is coming is 8
```

7.25* (*Counting occurrence of each letter in a string*) Write a function that counts the occurrence of each letter in the string using the following header:

void count(**const char** s[], **int** counts[], **int** size)

where size is the size of the counts array. In this case, it is 26. Letters are not case-sensitive, i.e., letter A and a are counted the same as a.

Write a test program that reads a string, invokes the count function, and displays the non-zero counts. Here is a sample run of the program:

```
Enter a string: Welcome to New York!  ↵Enter
c: 1 times
e: 3 times
k: 1 times
l: 1 times
m: 1 times
n: 1 times
o: 3 times
r: 1 times
t: 1 times
w: 2 times
y: 1 times
```

7.26* (*Common prefix*) Write a function that finds the common prefix of two strings. For example, the common prefix of "distance" and "disjoint" is "dis". The header of the function is as follows:

void prefix(**const char** s1[], **const char** s2[], **char** commonPrefix[])

Write a test program that prompts the user to enter two strings and displays their common prefix. Here is a sample run of the program:

```
Enter a string s1: abc  ↵Enter
Enter a string s2: abd  ↵Enter
The common prefix is ab
```

7.27* (*Phone key pads*) Exercise 3.24 gives a program that converts an uppercase letter to a number. Write a function that returns a number given an uppercase letter as follows:

int getNumber(**char** uppercaseLetter)

Write a test program that prompts the user to enter a phone number as a string. The input number may contain letters. The program translates a letter (upper- or lower-case) to a digit and leaves all other characters intact. Here is a sample run of the program:

```
Enter a string: 1-800-Flowers ⏎Enter
1-800-3569377
```

```
Enter a string: 1800flowers
18003569377
```

CHAPTER 8

MULTIDIMENSIONAL ARRAYS

Objectives

- To give examples of representing data using two-dimensional arrays (§8.1).

- To declare two-dimensional arrays and access array elements in a two-dimensional array using row and column indexes (§8.2).

- To process two-dimensional arrays (§8.3).

- To pass two-dimensional arrays to functions (§8.4).

- To write a program for grading multiple-choice questions using two-dimensional arrays (§8.5).

- To solve the closest-pair problem using two-dimensional arrays (§8.6).

- To solve the Sudoku problem using two-dimensional arrays (§8.7).

- To declare multidimensional arrays (§8.8).

8.1 Introduction

The preceding chapter introduced how to use one-dimensional arrays to model linear collections of elements. You can use a two-dimensional array to represent a matrix or a table. For example, the following table that describes the distances between the cities can be represented using a two-dimensional array.

Distance Table (in miles)

	Chicago	*Boston*	*New York*	*Atlanta*	*Miami*	*Dallas*	*Houston*
Chicago	0	983	787	714	1375	967	1087
Boston	983	0	214	1102	1763	1723	1842
New York	787	214	0	888	1549	1548	1627
Atlanta	714	1102	888	0	661	781	810
Miami	1375	1763	1549	661	0	1426	1187
Dallas	967	1723	1548	781	1426	0	239
Houston	1087	1842	1627	810	1187	239	0

8.2 Declaring Two-Dimensional Arrays

The syntax for declaring a two-dimensional array is

```
elementType arrayName[ROW_SIZE][COLUMN_SIZE];
```

As an example, here is how you would declare a two-dimensional array `matrix` of `int` values:

```
int matrix[5][5];
```

Two subscripts are used in a two-dimensional array, one for the row and the other for the column. As in a one-dimensional array, the index for each subscript is of the `int` type and starts from `0`, as shown in Figure 8.1(a).

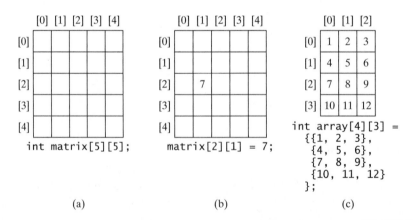

(a)   (b)   (c)

FIGURE 8.1 The index of each subscript of a two-dimensional array is an `int` value starting from `0`.

To assign the value `7` to a specific element at row `2` and column `1`, as shown in Figure 8.1(b), you can use the following:

```
matrix[2][1] = 7;
```

Caution

It is a common mistake to use `matrix[2, 1]` to access the element at row 2 and column 1. In C++, each subscript must be enclosed in a pair of square brackets.

You also can use an array initializer to declare and initialize a two-dimensional array. For example, the code in (a) below declares an array with the specified initial values, as shown in Figure 8.1(c). This is equivalent to the code in (b).

```
int array[4][3] =
  {{1, 2, 3},
   {4, 5, 6},
   {7, 8, 9},
   {10, 11, 12}
};
```

Equivalent

```
int array[4][3];
array[0][0] = 1; array[0][1] = 2; array[0][2] = 3;
array[1][0] = 4; array[1][1] = 5; array[1][2] = 6;
array[2][0] = 7; array[2][1] = 8; array[2][2] = 9;
array[3][0] = 10; array[3][1] = 11; array[3][2] = 12;
```

(a)   (b)

8.3 Processing Two-Dimensional Arrays

Suppose an array `matrix` is declared as follows:

```
const int ROW_SIZE = 10;
const int COLUMN_SIZE = 10;
int matrix[ROW_SIZE][COLUMN_SIZE];
```

Here are some examples of processing two-dimensional arrays:

Video Note
Processing arrays

1. (*Initializing arrays with random values*) The following loop initializes the array with random values between 0 and 99:

```
for (int row = 0; row < ROW_SIZE; row++)
{
  for (int column = 0; column < COLUMN_SIZE; column++)
  {
    matrix[row][column] = rand() % 100;
  }
}
```

2. (*Displaying arrays*) To display a two-dimensional array, you have to display each element in the array using a loop like the following:

```
for (int row = 0; row < ROW_SIZE; row++)
{
  for (int column = 0; column < COLUMN_SIZE; column++)
  {
    cout << matrix[row][column] << " ";
  }

  cout << endl;
}
```

3. (*Summing all elements*) Use a variable named `total` to store the sum. Initially `total` is 0. Add each element in the array to `total` using a loop like this:

```
int total = 0;
for (int row = 0; row < ROW_SIZE; row++)
{
  for (int column = 0; column < COLUMN_SIZE; column++)
  {
    total += matrix[row][column];
  }
}
```

4. (*Summing elements by column*) For each column, use a variable named `total` to store its sum. Add each element in the column to `total` using a loop like this:

```
for (int column = 0; column < COLUMN_SIZE; column++)
{
  int total = 0;
  for (int row = 0; row < ROW_SIZE; row++)
    total += matrix[row][column];
  cout << "Sum for column " << column << " is " << total << endl;
}
```

5. (*Which row has the largest sum?*) Use variables `maxRow` and `indexOfMaxRow` to track the largest sum and index of the row. For each row, compute its sum and update `maxRow` and `indexOfMaxRow` if the new sum is greater.

```
int maxRow = 0;
int indexOfMaxRow = 0;

// Get sum of the first row in maxRow
for (int column = 0; column < COLUMN_SIZE; column++)
  maxRow += matrix[0][column];

for (int row = 1; row < ROW_SIZE; row++)
{
  int totalOfThisRow = 0;
  for (int column = 0; column < COLUMN_ SIZE; column++)
    totalOfThisRow += matrix[row][column];

  if (totalOfThisRow > maxRow)
  {
    maxRow = totalOfThisRow;
    indexOfMaxRow = row;
  }
}

cout << "Row " << indexOfMaxRow
     << " has the maximum sum" << " of " << maxRow << endl;
```

8.4 Passing Two-Dimensional Arrays to Functions

You can pass a two-dimensional array to a function; however, C++ requires that the column size be specified in the function definition. Listing 8.1 gives an example with a function that returns the sum of all the elements in a matrix.

Video Note
Array arguments

fixed column size

LISTING 8.1 PassTwoDimensionalArray.cpp

```
1 #include <iostream>
2 using namespace std;
3
4 const int COLUMN_SIZE = 3;
5
6 int sum(const int a[][COLUMN_SIZE], int rowSize)
7 {
8   int total = 0;
9   for (int row = 0; row < rowSize; row++)
10  {
11    for (int column = 0; column < COLUMN_SIZE; column++)
```

```
12      {
13         total += a[row][column];
14      }
15   }
16
17   return total;
18 }
19
20 int main()
21 {
22   int m[4][3] =
23   {
24     {1, 2, 3},
25     {4, 5, 6},
26     {7, 8, 9},
27     {10, 11, 12}
28   };
29
30   cout << "Sum of all elements is " << sum(m, 4) << endl;        pass array
31   return 0;
32 }
```

```
Sum of all elements is 78
```

The function sum (line 6) has two arguments. The first specifies a two-dimensional array with a fixed column size. The second specifies the row size for the two-dimensional array.

8.5 Problem: Grading a Multiple-Choice Test

The problem is to write a program that grades multiple-choice tests. Suppose there are eight students and ten questions, and the answers are stored in a two-dimensional array. Each row records a student's answers to the questions. For example, the following array stores the test.

Students' Answers to the Questions:

	0	1	2	3	4	5	6	7	8	9
Student 0	A	B	A	C	C	D	E	E	A	D
Student 1	D	B	A	B	C	A	E	E	A	D
Student 2	E	D	D	A	C	B	E	E	A	D
Student 3	C	B	A	E	D	C	E	E	A	D
Student 4	A	B	D	C	C	D	E	E	A	D
Student 5	B	B	E	C	C	D	E	E	A	D
Student 6	B	B	A	C	C	D	E	E	A	D
Student 7	E	B	E	C	C	D	E	E	A	D

The key is stored in a one-dimensional array, as follows:

Key to the Questions:

	0	1	2	3	4	5	6	7	8	9
key	D	B	D	C	C	D	A	E	A	D

Your program grades the test and displays the result. The program compares each student's answers with the key, counts the number of correct answers, and displays it. Listing 8.2 gives the program.

LISTING 8.2 GradeExam.cpp

```cpp
1 #include <iostream>
2 using namespace std;
3
4 int main()
5 {
6   const int NUMBER_OF_STUDENTS = 8;
7   const int NUMBER_OF_QUESTIONS = 10;
8
9   // Students' answers to the questions
10  char answers[NUMBER_OF_STUDENTS][NUMBER_OF_QUESTIONS] =
11  {
12    {'A', 'B', 'A', 'C', 'C', 'D', 'E', 'E', 'A', 'D'},
13    {'D', 'B', 'A', 'B', 'C', 'A', 'E', 'E', 'A', 'D'},
14    {'E', 'D', 'D', 'A', 'C', 'B', 'E', 'E', 'A', 'D'},
15    {'C', 'B', 'A', 'E', 'D', 'C', 'E', 'E', 'A', 'D'},
16    {'A', 'B', 'D', 'C', 'C', 'D', 'E', 'E', 'A', 'D'},
17    {'B', 'B', 'E', 'C', 'C', 'D', 'E', 'E', 'A', 'D'},
18    {'B', 'B', 'A', 'C', 'C', 'D', 'E', 'E', 'A', 'D'},
19    {'E', 'B', 'E', 'C', 'C', 'D', 'E', 'E', 'A', 'D'}
20  };
21
22  // Key to the questions
23  char keys[] = {'D', 'B', 'D', 'C', 'C', 'D', 'A', 'E', 'A', 'D'};
24
25  // Grade all answers
26  for (int i = 0; i < NUMBER_OF_STUDENTS; i++)
27  {
28    // Grade one student
29    int correctCount = 0;
30    for (int j = 0; j < NUMBER_OF_QUESTIONS; j++)
31    {
32      if (answers[i][j] == keys[j])
33        correctCount++;
34    }
35
36    cout << "Student " << i << "'s correct count is " <<
37      correctCount << endl;
38  }
39
40  return 0;
41 }
```

(marginal note beside line 10) two-dimensional array

(marginal note beside line 23) array

```
Student 0's correct count is 7
Student 1's correct count is 6
Student 2's correct count is 5
Student 3's correct count is 4
Student 4's correct count is 8
Student 5's correct count is 7
Student 6's correct count is 7
Student 7's correct count is 7
```

The statement in lines 10–20 declares and initializes a two-dimensional array of characters. The statement in line 23 declares and initializes an array of **char** values.

Each row in the array **answers** stores a student's answer, which is graded by comparing it with the key in the array **keys**. Immediately after an answer is graded, the result is displayed.

8.6 Problem: Finding the Closest Pair

The GPS navigation system is becoming increasingly popular. The system uses the graph and geometric algorithms to calculate distances and map a route. This section presents a geometric problem for finding a closest pair of points.

Given a set of points, the closest-pair problem is to find the two points that are nearest to each other. In Figure 8.2, for example, points **(1, 1)** and **(2, 0.5)** are closest to each other. There are several ways to solve this problem. An intuitive approach is to compute the distances between all pairs of points and find the pair with the minimum distance, as implemented in Listing 8.3.

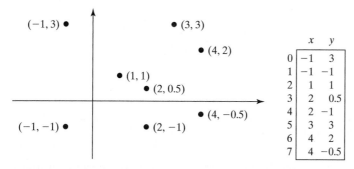

FIGURE 8.2   Points can be represented in a two-dimensional array.

LISTING 8.3   FindNearestPoints.cpp

```
1 #include <iostream>
2 #include <cmath>
3 using namespace std;
4
5 /** Compute the distance between two points (x1, y1) and (x2, y2) */
6 double getDistance(double x1, double y1, double x2, double y2)
7 {
8   return sqrt((x2 - x1) * (x2 - x1) + (y2 - y1) * (y2 - y1));
9 }
10
11 int main()
12 {
13   const int NUMBER_OF_POINTS = 8;
14
15   // Each row in points represents a point
16   double points[NUMBER_OF_POINTS][2];
17
18   cout << "Enter " << NUMBER_OF_POINTS << " points: ";
19   for (int i = 0; i < NUMBER_OF_POINTS; i++)
20     cin >> points[i][0] >> points[i][1];
21
22   // p1 and p2 are the indices in the points array
23   int p1 = 0, p2 = 1; // Initial two points
24   double shortestDistance = getDistance(points[p1][0], points[p1][1],
25     points[p2][0], points[p2][1]); // Initialize shortestDistance
26
27   // Compute distance for every two points
28   for (int i = 0; i < NUMBER_OF_POINTS; i++)
```

Video Note
Nearest points

distance between two points

2-D array

read all points

track **shortestDistance**

for each point **i**

```
29    {
30      for (int j = i + 1; j < NUMBER_OF_POINTS; j++)
31      {
32        double distance = getDistance(points[i][0], points[i][1],
33          points[j][0], points[j][1]); // Find distance
34
35        if (shortestDistance > distance)
36        {
37          p1 = i; // Update p1
38          p2 = j; // Update p2
39          shortestDistance = distance; // Update shortestDistance
40        }
41      }
42    }
43
44    // Display result
45    cout << "The closest two points are " <<
46      "(" << points[p1][0] << ", " << points[p1][1] << ") and (" <<
47      points[p2][0] << ", " << points[p2][1] << ")";
48
49    return 0;
50 }
```

for each point **j** (line 30)

distance between **i** and **j** (lines 32–33)

update **shortestDistance** (line 35)

Enter 8 points: -1 3 -1 -1 1 1 2 0.5 2 -1 3 3 4 2 4 -0.5 ⏎Enter
The closest two points are (1, 1) and (2, 0.5)

The points are read from the console and stored in a two-dimensional array named **points** (lines 19–20). The program uses variable **shortestDistance** (line 24) to store the distance between two nearest points, and the indices of these two points in the **points** array are stored in **p1** and **p2** (line 23).

For each point at index **i**, the program computes the distance between **points[i]** and **points[j]** for all **j** > **i** (lines 28–42). Whenever a shorter distance is found, the variable **shortestDistance**, **p1**, and **p2** are updated (lines 37–39).

The distance between two points (**x1**, **y1**) and (**x2**, **y2**) can be computed using the formula $\sqrt{(x_2 - x_1)^2 + (y_2 - y_1)^2}$ in function **getDistance** (lines 6–9).

The program assumes that the plain has at least two points. You can easily modify the program to handle the case if the plain has one point or none.

multiple closest pairs

Note that there might be more than one closest pair of points with the same minimum distance. The program finds one such pair. You may modify the program to find all closest pairs in Programming Exercise 8.10.

Tip

input file

It is cumbersome to enter all points from the keyboard. You may store the input in a file, say Find-NearestPoints.txt, and compile and run the program using the following command:

g++ FindNearestPoints.cpp –o FindNearestPoints.exe
FindNearestPoints.exe < FindNearestPoints.txt

8.7 Problem: Sudoku

This book teaches you how to program using a wide variety of problems with various levels of difficulty. We use simple, short, and stimulating examples to introduce programming and problem-solving techniques and use interesting and challenging examples to motivate students in programming. This section presents an interesting problem of a sort that appears in the newspaper every day. It is a number-placement puzzle, commonly known as *Sudoku*. This is a very challenging problem. Feel free to skip it at this time if you wish.

8.7.1 Problem Description

Sudoku is a 9 × 9 grid divided into smaller 3 × 3 boxes (also called regions or blocks), as shown in Figure 8.3(a). Some cells, called *fixed cells*, are populated with numbers from 1 to 9. The objective is to fill the empty cells, also called *free cells*, with numbers 1 to 9 so that every row, every column, and every 3 × 3 box contains the numbers 1 to 9, as shown in Figure 8.3(b).

fixed cells
free cells

5	3			7				
6			1	9	5			
	9	8					6	
8				6				3
4			8		3			1
7				2				6
	6							
			4	1	9			5
				8			7	9

(a) Input

Solution ⟶

5	3	4	6	7	8	9	1	2
6	7	2	1	9	5	3	4	8
1	9	8	3	4	2	5	6	7
8	5	9	7	6	1	4	2	3
4	2	6	8	5	3	7	9	1
7	1	3	9	2	4	8	5	6
9	6	1	5	3	7	2	8	4
2	8	7	4	1	9	6	3	5
3	4	5	2	8	6	1	7	9

(b) Output

FIGURE 8.3 (b) is the solution to the Sudoku puzzle in (a).

For convenience, we use value 0 to indicate a free cell, as shown in Figure 8.4(a). The grid can be naturally represented using a two-dimensional array, as shown in Figure 8.4(b).

representing a grid

5	3	0	0	7	0	0	0	0
6	0	0	1	9	5	0	0	0
0	9	8	0	0	0	0	6	0
8	0	0	0	6	0	0	0	3
4	0	0	8	0	3	0	0	1
7	0	0	0	2	0	0	0	6
0	6	0	0	0	0	0	0	0
0	0	0	4	1	9	0	0	5
0	0	0	0	8	0	0	7	9

(a)

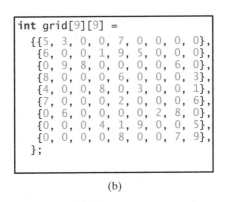

```
int grid[9][9] =
  {{5, 3, 0, 0, 7, 0, 0, 0, 0},
   {6, 0, 0, 1, 9, 5, 0, 0, 0},
   {0, 9, 8, 0, 0, 0, 0, 6, 0},
   {8, 0, 0, 0, 6, 0, 0, 0, 3},
   {4, 0, 0, 8, 0, 3, 0, 0, 1},
   {7, 0, 0, 0, 2, 0, 0, 0, 6},
   {0, 6, 0, 0, 0, 0, 2, 8, 0},
   {0, 0, 0, 4, 1, 9, 0, 0, 5},
   {0, 0, 0, 0, 8, 0, 0, 7, 9},
  };
```

(b)

FIGURE 8.4 A grid can be represented using a two-dimensional array.

8.7.2 Problem-Solving Strategy

How do you solve this problem? An intuitive approach is to employ the following three rules:

Rule 1: Fill in free cells from the first to the last.

Rule 2: Fill in a smallest number possible.

Rule 3: If no number can fill in a free cell, backtrack.

For example, you can fill 1 into `grid[0][2]`, 2 into `grid[0][3]`, 4 into `grid[0][5]`, 8 into `grid[0][6]`, and 9 into `grid[0][7]`, as shown in Figure 8.5(a).

Now look at `grid[0][8]`. There is no possible value to fill in this cell. You need to backtrack to the previous free cell at `grid[0][7]` and reset its value. Since `grid[0][7]` is already 9, no new value is possible. So you have to backtrack to its previous free cell at `grid[0][6]` and change its value to 9. Continue to move forward to set `grid[0][7]` to 8, as shown in Figure 8.5(b). Now there is still no possible value for `grid[0][8]`. Backtrack to

backtrack

(a)

5	3	1	2	7	4	8	9	
6			1	9	5			
	9	8				6		
8				6				3
4			8		3			1
7				2				6
	6							
			4	1	9			5
				8			7	9

(b)

5	3	1	2	7	4	9	8	
6			1	9	5			
	9	8				6		
8				6				3
4			8		3			1
7				2				6
	6							
			4	1	9			5
				8			7	9

FIGURE 8.5   The program attempts to fill in free cells.

`grid[0][7]`: no possible new value for this cell. Backtrack to `grid[0][6]`: no possible new value for this cell. Backtrack to `grid[0][5]` and change it to `6`. Now continue to move forward.

The search moves forward and backward continuously until one of the following two cases arises:

- All free cells are filled. A solution is found.

- The search is backtracked to the first free cell with no new possible value. The puzzle has no solution.

Pedagogical Note

Sudoku animation

Follow the link www.cs.armstrong.edu/liang/animation/SudokuAnimation.html to see how the search progresses. As shown in Figure 8.6(a), number **1** is placed in the first row and last column. This number is invalid, so the next value **2** is placed in Figure 8.6(b). This number is still invalid, so the next value **3** is placed in Figure 8.6(c). The simulation displays all the search steps.

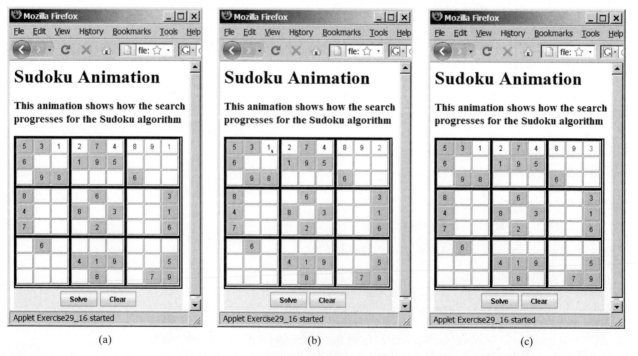

(a)   (b)   (c)

FIGURE 8.6   The animation tool enables you to observe how the search works for solving a Sudoku puzzle.

8.7.3   Program Design

The program can be designed as shown in (a) and further refined with functions as in (b):

```
Read the input for a puzzle;
if (the grid is not valid)
  Report the grid not valid;
else
{
  Search for a solution;
  if (solution found)
    Display the solution;
  else
    Report no solution;
}
```

(a)

Refined ⟶

```
int grid[9][9];
readAPuzzle(grid);
if (!isValid(grid))
  Report the grid not valid;
else
{
  if (search(grid))
    prindGrid(grid);
  else
    Report no solution;
}
```

(b)

The `readAPuzzle` function reads a Sudoku puzzle from the console into `grid`. The `printGrid` function displays the contents in `grid` to the console. The `isValid` function checks whether the grid is valid. These functions are easy to implement. We now turn our attention to the `search` function.

8.7.4   Search Algorithm

To better facilitate search on free cells, the program stores free cells in a two-dimensional array, as shown in 8.7. Each row in the array has two columns, which indicate the subscripts of the free cells in the grid. For example, { `freeCellList[0][0]`, `freeCellList[0][1]`} (i.e., {0, 2}) is the subscript for the first free cell `grid[0][2]` in the grid and { `freeCellList[25][0]`, `freeCellList[25][1]`} (i.e., {4, 4}) is the subscript for free cell `grid[4][4]` in the grid, as shown in Figure 8.7.

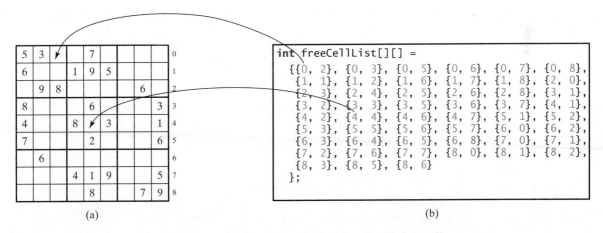

(a)

```
int freeCellList[][] =
  {{0, 2}, {0, 3}, {0, 5}, {0, 6}, {0, 7}, {0, 8},
   {1, 1}, {1, 2}, {1, 6}, {1, 7}, {1, 8}, {2, 0},
   {2, 3}, {2, 4}, {2, 5}, {2, 6}, {2, 8}, {3, 1},
   {3, 2}, {3, 3}, {3, 5}, {3, 6}, {3, 7}, {4, 1},
   {4, 2}, {4, 4}, {4, 6}, {4, 7}, {5, 1}, {5, 2},
   {5, 3}, {5, 5}, {5, 6}, {5, 7}, {6, 0}, {6, 2},
   {6, 3}, {6, 4}, {6, 5}, {6, 8}, {7, 0}, {7, 1},
   {7, 2}, {7, 6}, {7, 7}, {8, 0}, {8, 1}, {8, 2},
   {8, 3}, {8, 5}, {8, 6}
  };
```

(b)

FIGURE 8.7   `freeCellList` is a two-dimensional array representation for the free cells.

The search starts from the first free cell with $k = 0$, where k is the index of the current free cell being considered in the free-cell list, as shown in Figure 8.8. It fills a valid value in the current free cell and then moves forward to consider the next. If no valid value can be found for the current free cell, the search backtracks to the preceding free cell. This process continues until all free cells are filled with valid values (a solution is found) or the search backtracks to the first free cell with no solution.

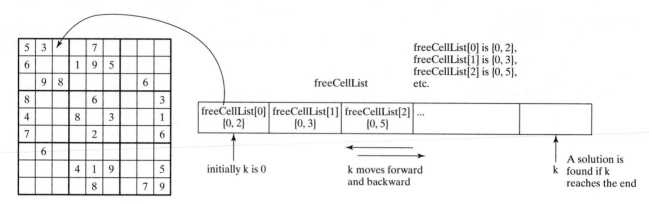

FIGURE 8.8 The search attempts to fill free cells with appropriate values.

The `search` algorithm can be described as follows:

■ Step 1: (Initialization) Obtain a `freeCellList` from a grid, as shown in Figure 8.7. Let `k` denote the index in `freeCellList` with `k` initially 0, as shown in Figure 8.8.

Repeatedly perform Steps 2–4 until search ends with a solution or no solution
{

■ Step 2: Let `grid[i][j]` be the current free cell being considered, where `i = freeCellList[k][0]` and `j = freeCellList[k][1]`.

■ Step 3: If `grid[i][j]` is `0`, fill it with `1`.

■ Step 4: Consider three cases:

solution found

Case 1: `grid[i][j]` is valid. If `k` is the last index in `freeCellList`, *a solution is found*. Otherwise, search moves forward with `k = k + 1`.

Case 2: `grid[i][j]` is invalid and `grid[i][j]` < 9. Set a new value for the free cell with `grid[i][j] = grid[i][j] + 1`.

no solution

Case 3: `grid[i][j]` is invalid and `grid[i][j]` is 9. If `k = 0`, *search ends with no solution*. Otherwise backtrack with `k = k – 1`, reset `i = freeCellList[k][0]` and `j = freeCellList[k][1]`, and continue to backtrack if `grid[i][j]` is 9. When `grid[i][j]` < 9, set `grid[i][j] = grid[i][j] + 1`.

}

8.7.5 Implementation

Listing 8.4 gives the source code for the program.

LISTING 8.4 Sudoku.cpp

```cpp
1 #include <iostream>
2 using namespace std;
3
4 void readAPuzzle(int grid[][9]);
5 bool search(int grid[][9]);
6 int getFreeCellList(const int grid[][9], int freeCellList[][2]);
7 void printGrid(const int grid[][9]);
8 bool isValid(int i, int j, const int grid[][9]);
9 bool isValid(const int grid[][9]);
10
11 int main()
12 {
13   // Read a Sudoku puzzle
```

```
14    int grid[9][9];
15    readAPuzzle(grid);                                    read input
16
17    if (!isValid(grid))                                   input valid?
18      cout << "Invalid input" << endl;
19    else if (search(grid))                                search
20    {
21      cout << "The solution is found:" << endl;
22      printGrid(grid);                                    display result
23    }
24    else
25      cout << "No solution" << endl;
26
27    return 0;
28 }
29
30 /** Read a Sudoku puzzle from the keyboard */
31 void readAPuzzle(int grid[][9])                           read input
32 {
33    // Create a Scanner
34    cout << "Enter a Sudoku puzzle:" << endl;
35    for (int i = 0; i < 9; i++)
36      for (int j = 0; j < 9; j++)
37        cin >> grid[i][j];
38 }
39
40 /** Obtain a list of free cells from the puzzle */
41 int getFreeCellList(const int grid[][9], int freeCellList[][2])    get free-cell list
42 {
43    // 81 is the maximum number of free cells
44    int numberOfFreeCells = 0;
45
46    for (int i = 0; i < 9; i++)
47      for (int j = 0; j < 9; j++)
48        if (grid[i][j] == 0)
49        {
50          freeCellList[numberOfFreeCells][0] = i;
51          freeCellList[numberOfFreeCells][1] = j;
52          numberOfFreeCells++;
53        }
54
55    return numberOfFreeCells;
56 }
57
58 /** Display the values in the grid */
59 void printGrid(const int grid[][9])                       display grid
60 {
61    for (int i = 0; i < 9; i++)
62    {
63      for (int j = 0; j < 9; j++)
64        cout << grid[i][j] << " ";
65      cout << endl;
66    }
67 }
68
69 /** Search for a solution */
70 bool search(int grid[][9])                                search for a solution
71 {
72    int freeCellList[81][2]; // Declare freeCellList
73    int numberOfFreeCells = getFreeCellList(grid, freeCellList);
```

```
74    if (numberOfFreeCells == 0)
75      return true; // No free cells
76
77    int k = 0; // Start from the first free cell
78    while (true)
79    {
80      int i = freeCellList[k][0];
81      int j = freeCellList[k][1];
82      if (grid[i][j] == 0)
83        grid[i][j] = 1; // Fill the free cell with number 1
84
85      if (isValid(i, j, grid))
86      {
87        if (k + 1 == numberOfFreeCells)
88        { // No more free cells
89          return true; // A solution is found
90        }
91        else
92        { // Move to the next free cell
93          k++;
94        }
95      }
96      else if (grid[i][j] < 9)
97      {
98        // Fill the free cell with the next possible value
99        grid[i][j] = grid[i][j] + 1;
100       }
101       else
102       { // grid[i][j] is 9, backtrack
103         while (grid[i][j] == 9)
104         {
105           if (k == 0)
106           {
107             return false;  // No possible value
108           }
109           grid[i][j] = 0; // Reset to free cell
110           k--; // Backtrack to the preceding free cell
111           i = freeCellList[k][0];
112           j = freeCellList[k][1];
113         }
114
115         // Fill the free cell with the next possible value,
116         // search continues from this free cell at k
117         grid[i][j] = grid[i][j] + 1;
118       }
119     }
120
121     return true; // A solution is found
122 }
123
124 /** Check whether grid[i][j] is valid in the grid */
125 bool isValid(int i, int j, const int grid[][9])
126 {
127   // Check whether grid[i][j] is valid at the i's row
128   for (int column = 0; column < 9; column++)
129     if (column != j && grid[i][column] == grid[i][j])
130       return false;
131
132   // Check whether grid[i][j] is valid at the j's column
133   for (int row = 0; row < 9; row++)
```

continuous search

start with 1

is valid?

found

to next free cell

increase cell value

no solution

reset cell value
backtrack

check valid

check row

check column

```
134      if (row != i && grid[row][j] == grid[i][j])
135        return false;
136
137    // Check whether grid[i][j] is valid in the 3-by-3 box
138    for (int row = (i / 3) * 3; row < (i / 3) * 3 + 3; row++)          check box
139      for (int col = (j / 3) * 3; col < (j / 3) * 3 + 3; col++)
140        if (row != i && col != j && grid[row][col] == grid[i][j])
141          return false;
142
143    return true; // The current value at grid[i][j] is valid
144  }
145
146  /** Check whether the fixed cells are valid in the grid */
147  bool isValid(const int grid[][9])                                    valid grid?
148  {
149    for (int i = 0; i < 9; i++)
150      for (int j = 0; j < 9; j++)
151        if (grid[i][j] < 0 || grid[i][j] > 9 ||
152            (grid[i][j] != 0 && !isValid(i, j, grid)))
153          return false;
154    return true; // The fixed cells are valid
155  }
```

```
Enter a puzzle:
0 6 0 1 0 4 0 5 0  ↵Enter
0 0 8 3 0 5 6 0 0  ↵Enter
2 0 0 0 0 0 0 0 1  ↵Enter
8 0 0 4 0 7 0 0 6  ↵Enter
0 0 6 0 0 0 3 0 0  ↵Enter
7 0 0 9 0 1 0 0 4  ↵Enter
5 0 0 0 0 0 0 0 2  ↵Enter
0 0 7 2 0 6 9 0 0  ↵Enter
0 4 0 5 0 8 0 7 0  ↵Enter

The solution is found:
9 6 3 1 7 4 2 5 8
1 7 8 3 2 5 6 4 9
2 5 4 6 8 9 7 3 1
8 2 1 4 3 7 5 9 6
4 9 6 8 5 2 3 1 7
7 3 5 9 6 1 8 2 4
5 8 9 7 1 3 4 6 2
3 1 7 2 4 6 9 8 5
6 4 2 5 9 8 1 7 3
```

The program invokes the **readAPuzzle()** function (line 15) to read a Sudoku puzzle in a two-dimensional array **grid**. There are three possible outputs from the program:

■ The input is invalid (line 17).

■ A solution is found (line 19).

■ No solution is found (line 24).

The **getFreeCellList** function (lines 41–56) returns a two-dimensional array storing   **getFreeCellList** function
the free-cell positions. **freeCellList[i][j]** indicates a free cell at row index **i** and column index **j**.

search function

The `search` function invokes `getFreeCellList` to find all free cells (line 72). It then starts search from the first free cell with `k = 0` (line 77), where `k` is the position of the current free cell being considered in the free-cell list, as shown in Figure 8.8.

The value in a free cell starts with `1` (line 83). If the value is valid, the next cell is considered (line 93). If the value is not valid, its next value is considered (line 99). If the value is already `9`, the search is backtracked (lines 103–113). All the backtracked cells become free again and their values are reset to `0` (line 109). If the search backtracks to the free-cell list at position `k` and the current free-cell value is not `9`, increase the value by `1` (line 117) and continue the search.

The `search` function returns `true` when the search advances but no more free cells are left (line 89). A solution is found.

The search returns `false` when the search is backtracked to the first cell (line 107) and all possible values are exhausted for the cell. No solution can be found.

isValid function

The `isValid(i, j, grid)` function checks whether the current value at `grid[i][j]` is valid. It checks whether `grid[i][j]` appears more than once at row `i` (lines 128–130), at column `j` (lines 133–135), and in the 3 × 3 box (lines 138–141).

How do you locate all the cells in the same box? For any `grid[i][j]`, the starting cell of the 3 × 3 box that contains it is `grid[(i / 3) * 3][(j / 3) * 3]`, as illustrated in Figure 8.9.

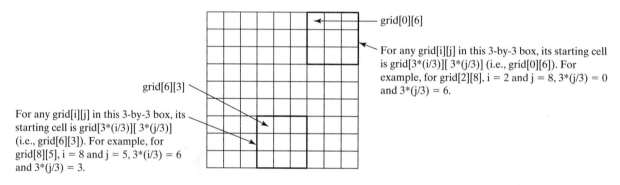

FIGURE 8.9   The location of the first cell in a 3 × 3 box determines the locations of other cells in the box.

With this observation, you can easily identify all the cells in the box. Suppose `grid[r][c]` is the starting cell of a 3 × 3 box; the cells in the box can be traversed in a nested loop as follows:

```
// Get all cells in a 3 by 3 box starting at grid[r][c]
for (int row = r; row < r + 3; row++)
  for (int col = c; col < c + 3; col++)
    // grid[row][col] is in the box
```

find one solution

Note that there may be multiple solutions for an input. The program will find one such solution. You may modify the program to find all solutions in Programming Exercise 8.17.

input file

It is cumbersome to enter 81 numbers from the keyboard. You may store the input in a file, say sudoku.txt, and compile and run the program using the following command:

```
g++ Sudoku.cpp -o Sudoku.exe
Sudoku.exe < sudoku.txt
```

8.8 Multidimensional Arrays

In the preceding section, you used a two-dimensional array to represent a matrix or a table. Occasionally, you will need to represent *n*-dimensional data structures. In C++, you can create *n*-dimensional arrays for any integer *n*.

Declaring a two-dimensional array can be generalized to declaring an *n*-dimensional array for *n* >= 3. For example, the following syntax declares a three-dimensional array `data`.

```
double data[10][24][2];
```

8.8.1   Problem: Daily Temperature and Humidity

Suppose a meteorology station records the temperature and humidity at each hour of every day and stores the data for the past ten days in a text file named weather.txt. Each line of the file consists of four numbers that indicate the day, hour, temperature, and humidity. The contents of the file may appear as in (a):

```
1 1 76.4 0.92
1 2 77.7 0.93
...
10 23 97.7 0.71
10 24 98.7 0.74
```

```
10 24 98.7 0.74
1 2 77.7 0.93
...
10 23 97.7 0.71
1 1 76.4 0.92
```

(a)   (b)

Note that the lines in the file are not necessary in order. For example, the file may appear as shown in (b).

Your task is to write a program that calculates the average daily temperature and humidity for the **10** days. You can use the input redirection to read the data from the file and store them in a three-dimensional array, named `data`. The first index of `data` in the range from **0** to **9** represents **10** days, the second index from **0** to **23** represents **24** hours, and the third index from **0** to **1** represents temperature and humidity, respectively. Note that the days are numbered from **1** to **10** and hours are numbered from **1** to **24** in the file. Since the array index starts from **0**, `data[0][0][0]` stores the temperature in day **1** at hour **1** and `data[9][23][1]` stores the humidity in day **10** at hour **24**.

The program is given in Listing 8.5.

LISTING 8.5   Weather.cpp

```
 1 #include <iostream>
 2 using namespace std;
 3
 4 int main()
 5 {
 6     const int NUMBER_OF_DAYS = 10;
 7     const int NUMBER_OF_HOURS = 24;
 8     double data[NUMBER_OF_DAYS][NUMBER_OF_HOURS][2];
 9
10     // Read input using input redirection from a file
11     int day, hour;
12     double temperature, humidity;
13     for (int k = 0; k < NUMBER_OF_DAYS * NUMBER_OF_HOURS; k++)
14     {
15         cin >> day >> hour >> temperature >> humidity;
16         data[day - 1][hour - 1][0] = temperature;
17         data[day - 1][hour - 1][1] = humidity;
18     }
19
20     // Find the average daily temperature and humidity
21     for (int i = 0; i < NUMBER_OF_DAYS; i++)
22     {
23         double dailyTemperatureTotal = 0, dailyHumidityTotal = 0;
```

three-dimensional array

```
24      for (int j = 0; j < NUMBER_OF_HOURS; j++)
25      {
26        dailyTemperatureTotal += data[i][j][0];
27        dailyHumidityTotal += data[i][j][1];
28      }
29
30      // Display result
31      cout << "Day  " << i << "'s average temperature is "
32        << dailyTemperatureTotal / NUMBER_OF_HOURS << endl;
33      cout << "Day  " << i << "'s average humidity is "
34        << dailyHumidityTotal / NUMBER_OF_HOURS << endl;
35    }
36
37    return 0;
38 }
```

```
Day  0's average temperature is 77.7708
Day  0's average humidity is 0.929583
Day  1's average temperature is 77.3125
Day  1's average humidity is 0.929583
...
Day  9's average temperature is 79.3542
Day  9's average humidity is 0.9125
```

You can use the following command to compile the program:

g++ Weather.cpp –o Weather

Use the following command to run the program:

Weather.exe < Weather.txt

A three-dimensional array **data** is declared in line 8. The loop in lines 13–18 reads the input to the array. You could enter the input from the keyboard, but it would be awkward. For convenience, we store the data in a file and use the input redirection to read the data from the file. The loop in lines 24–28 adds all temperatures for each hour in a day to **dailyTemperatureTotal** and all humidity for each hour to **dailyHumidityTotal**. The average daily temperature and humidity are displayed in lines 31–34.

8.8.2 Problem: Guessing Birth Dates

Listing 3.2, GuessBirthDate.cpp, gives a program that guesses a birth date. The program can be simplified by storing the numbers in five sets in a three-dimensional array and prompting the user for the answers using a loop, as shown in Listing 8.6.

LISTING 8.6 GuessBirthDateUsingArray.cpp

```
1 #include <iostream>
2 #include <iomanip>
3 using namespace std;
4
5 int main()
6 {
7    int date = 0; // Date to be determined
8    char answer;
9
10   int dates[5][4][4] = {
11     {{ 1,  3,  5,  7},
12      { 9, 11, 13, 15},
```

three-dimensional array

```
13          {17, 19, 21, 23},
14          {25, 27, 29, 31}},
15         {{ 2,  3,  6,  7},
16          {10, 11, 14, 15},
17          {18, 19, 22, 23},
18          {26, 27, 30, 31}},
19         {{ 4,  5,  6,  7},
20          {12, 13, 14, 15},
21          {20, 21, 22, 23},
22          {28, 29, 30, 31}},
23         {{ 8,  9, 10, 11},
24          {12, 13, 14, 15},
25          {24, 25, 26, 27},
26          {28, 29, 30, 31}},
27         {{16, 17, 18, 19},
28          {20, 21, 22, 23},
29          {24, 25, 26, 27},
30          {28, 29, 30, 31}}};
31
32    for (int i = 0; i < 5; i++)
33    {
34      cout << "Is your birth date in Set" << (i + 1) << "?" << endl;      Set 1, 2, 3, 4, 5?
35      for (int j = 0; j < 4; j++)
36      {
37        for (int k = 0; k < 4; k++)
38          cout << setw(3) << dates[i][j][k] << " ";
39        cout << endl;
40      }
41      cout << "\nEnter N for No and Y for Yes: ";
42      cin >> answer;
43      if (answer == 'Y')
44        date += dates[i][0][0];
45    }
46
47    cout << "Your birth date is " << date << endl;
48
49    return 0;
50 }
```

A three-dimensional array dates is created in Lines 10–30. This array stores five sets of numbers. Each set is a 4-by-4 two-dimensional array.

The loop starting from line 32 displays the numbers in each set and prompts the user to answer whether the date is in the set (lines 37–38). If it is, the first number (dates[i][0][0]) in the set is added to variable date (line 44).

CHAPTER SUMMARY

1. A two-dimensional array can be used to store a table.

2. A two-dimensional array can be created using the syntax: elementType array-Name[ROW_SIZE][COLUMN_SIZE]

3. Each element in a two-dimensional array is represented using the syntax: arrayName[rowIndex][columnIndex].

4. You can create and initialize a two-dimensional array using an array initializer with the syntax: elementType arrayName[][COLUMN_SIZE] = {{row values}, ..., {row values}}

5. You can pass a two-dimensional array to a function; however, C++ requires that the column size be specified in the function declaration.

6. You can use arrays of arrays to form multidimensional arrays. For example, a three-dimensional array is declared as an array of arrays using the syntax `elementType arrayName[size1][size2][size3]`.

REVIEW QUESTIONS

8.1 Declare and create a 4×5 `int` matrix.

8.2 What is the output of the following code?

```cpp
int array[5][6];
int x[] = {1, 2};
array[0][1] = x[1];
cout << "array[0][1] is " << array[0][1];
```

8.3 What is the output of the following code?

```cpp
#include <iostream>
using namespace std;

int main()
{
  int matrix[4][4] =
    {{1, 2, 3, 4},
     {4, 5, 6, 7},
     {8, 9, 10, 11},
     {12, 13, 14, 15}};

  int sum = 0;

  for (int i = 0; i < 4; i++)
    sum += matrix[i][i];

  cout << sum << endl;

  return 0;
}
```

8.4 What is the output of the following code?

```cpp
#include <iostream>
using namespace std;

int main()
{
  int matrix[4][4] =
    {{1, 2, 3, 4},
     {4, 5, 6, 7},
     {8, 9, 10, 11},
     {12, 13, 14, 15}};

  int sum = 0;

  for (int i = 0; i < 4; i++)
    cout << matrix[i][1] << " ";

  return 0;
}
```

8.5 Which of the following statements are valid array declarations?

```
int r[2];

int x[];

int y[3][];
```

8.6 Which of the following function declarations are wrong?

```
int f(int[][] a, int rowSize, int columnSize);
int f(int a[][], int rowSize, int columnSize);
int f(int a[][3], int rowSize);
```

8.7 True or false? Every valid Sudoku input has a solution. If false, give an example.

8.8 Declare and create a $4 \times 6 \times 5$ int array.

PROGRAMMING EXERCISES

8.1* (*Summing all the numbers in a matrix*) Write a function that sums all the integers in a matrix of integers using the following header:

```
const int SIZE = 4;
double sumMatrix(const double m[][SIZE], int rowSize, int
  columnSize);
```

Write a test program that reads a 4-by-4 matrix and displays the sum of all its elements. Here is a sample run:

```
Enter a 4-by-4 matrix row by row:
1 2 3 4  ↵Enter
5 6 7 8  ↵Enter
9 10 11 12  ↵Enter
13 14 15 16  ↵Enter
Sum of the matrix is 136
```

8.2* (*Summing the major diagonal in a matrix*) Write a function that sums all the integers in the major diagonal in an $n \times n$ matrix of integers using the following header:

```
#define SIZE 4
double sumMajorDiagonal(const double m[][SIZE]);
```

Write a test program that reads a 4-by-4 matrix and displays the sum of all its elements on the major diagonal. Here is a sample run:

```
Enter a 4 by 4 matrix row by row:
1 2 3 4  ↵Enter
5 6 7 8  ↵Enter
9 10 11 12  ↵Enter
13 14 15 16  ↵Enter
Sum of the elements in the major diagonal is 34
```

8.3* (*Sorting students on grades*) Rewrite Listing 8.2, GradeExam.cpp, to display the students in increasing order of the number of correct answers.

8.4* (*Computing the weekly hours for each employee*) Suppose the weekly hours for all employees are stored in a two-dimensional array. Each row records an employee's seven-day work hours with seven columns. For example, the following array stores the work hours for eight employees. Write a program that displays employees and their total hours in decreasing order of the total hours.

	Su	M	T	W	Th	F	Sa
Employee 0	2	4	3	4	5	8	8
Employee 1	7	3	4	3	3	4	4
Employee 2	3	3	4	3	3	2	2
Employee 3	9	3	4	7	3	4	1
Employee 4	3	5	4	3	6	3	8
Employee 5	3	4	4	6	3	4	4
Employee 6	3	7	4	8	3	8	4
Employee 7	6	3	5	9	2	7	9

8.5 (*Algebra: adding two matrices*) Write a function to add two matrices a and b and save the result in c. The header of the function is

```
#define N 3

void addMatrix(const double a[][N],
  const double b[][N], double c[][N])
```

Each element c_{ij} is $a_{ij} + b_{ij}$. Write a test program that prompts the user to enter two 3×3 matrices and displays their addition. Here is a sample run:

```
Enter matrix1: 1 2 3 4 5 6 7 8 9  ↵Enter
Enter matrix2: 0 2 4 1 4.5 2.2 1.1 4.3 5.2  ↵Enter
The multiplication of the matrices is
1 2 3      0 2 4        1 4 7
4 5 6    + 1 4.5 2.2  = 5 9.5 8.2
7 8 9      1.1 4.3 5.2   8.1 12.3 14.2
```

8.6** (*Financial application: computing tax*) Rewrite Listing 3.4, ComputeTax.cpp, using arrays. For each filing status, there are six tax rates. Each rate is applied to a certain amount of taxable income. For example, from the taxable income of $400,000 for a single filer, $6,000 is taxed at 10%, $(27950 - 6000)$ at 15%, $(67700 - 27950)$ at 27%, $(141250 - 67700)$ at 30%, $(307050 - 141250)$ at 35%, and $(400000 - 307050)$ at 38.6%. The six rates are the same for all filing statuses, which can be represented in the following array:

```
double rates[] = {0.10, 0.15, 0.27, 0.30, 0.35, 0.386};
```

The brackets for each rate for all the filing statuses can be represented in a two-dimensional array as follows:

```
int brackets[4][5] = {
  {6000, 27950, 67700, 141250, 307050},   // Single filer
  {12000, 46700, 112850, 171950, 307050}, // Married jointly
  {6000, 23350, 56425, 85975, 153525},    // Married separately
  {10000, 37450, 96700, 156600, 307050}   // Head of household
};
```

Suppose the taxable income is $400,000 for single filers; the tax can be computed as follows:

```
tax = brackets[0][0] * rates[0] +
  (brackets[0][1] - brackets[0][0]) * rates[1] +
  (brackets[0][2] - brackets[0][1]) * rates[2] +
  (brackets[0][3] - brackets[0][2]) * rates[3] +
  (brackets[0][4] - brackets[0][3]) * rates[4] +
  (400000 - brackets[0][4]) * rates[5]
```

8.7** (*Checkerboard*) Write a program that randomly fills 0s and 1s into an 8 × 8 checkerboard, displays the board, and finds the rows, columns, or diagonals with all 0s or 1s. Use a two-dimensional array to represent a checkerboard. Here is a sample run of the program:

```
10101000
10100001
11100011
10100001
11100111
10000001
10100111
00100001
All 0's on subdiagonal
```

8.8*** (*Playing a TicTacToe game*) In a game of TicTacToe, two players take turns marking an available cell in a 3 × 3 grid with their respective tokens (either X or O). When one player has placed three tokens in a horizontal, vertical, or diagonal row on the grid, the game is over and that player has won. A draw (no winner) occurs when all the cells on the grid have been filled with tokens and neither player has achieved a win. Create a program for playing TicTacToe, as follows:

1. The program prompts the first player to enter an X token, and then prompts the second player to enter an O token. Whenever a token is entered, the program refreshes the board and determines the status of the game (win, draw, or unfinished).
2. To place a token, prompt the user to enter the row and the column for the token.

8.9** (*Algebra: multiplying two matrices*) Write a function to multiply two matrices a and b and save the result in c. The header of the function is

```
#define N 3
```

```
void multiplyMatrix(const double a[][N],
  const double b[][N], double c[][N])
```

Each element c_{ij} is $a_{i1} \times b_{1j} + a_{i2} \times b_{2j} + a_{i3} \times b_{3j}$.

Write a test program that prompts the user to enter two 3 × 3 matrices and displays their product. Here is a sample run:

```
Enter matrix1: 1 2 3 4 5 6 7 8 9 ↵Enter
Enter matrix2: 0 2 4 1 4.5 2.2 1.1 4.3 5.2 ↵Enter
The multiplication of the matrices is
1 2 3       0 2.0 4.0       5.3 23.9 24
4 5 6   *   1 4.5 2.2   =   11.6 56.3 58.2
7 8 9       1.1 4.3 5.2     17.9 88.7 92.4
```

8.10** (*All closest pairs*) Listing 8.3, FindNearestPoints.cpp, finds one closest pair. Revise the program to find all closest pairs if multiple closest pairs exist.

8.11** (*Game: nine heads and tails*) Nine coins are placed in a 3-by-3 matrix with some face up and some face down. You can represent the state of the coins using a 3-by-3 matrix with values 0 (head) and 1 (tail). Here are some examples:

```
0 0 0     1 0 1     1 1 0     1 0 1     1 0 0
0 1 0     0 0 1     1 0 0     1 1 0     1 1 1
0 0 0     1 0 0     0 0 1     1 0 0     1 1 0
```

Each state can also be represented using a binary number. For example, the preceding matrices correspond to the numbers

000010000 101001100 110100001 101110100 100111110

The total number of possibilities is 512. So you can use decimal numbers 0, 1, 2, 3, ..., and 511 to represent all states of the matrix. Write a program that prompts the user to enter a number between 0 and 511 and displays the corresponding matrix with characters H and T. Here is a sample output:

```
Enter a number between 0 and 511: 7  ↵Enter
H H H
H H H
T T T
```

The user entered 7, which corresponds to 000000111. Since 0 stands for H and 1 for T, the output is correct.

Video Note
Finding points nearest to each other

8.12* (*Points nearest to each other*) Listing 8.3, FindNearestPoints.cpp, is a program that finds two points in a two-dimensional space nearest to other. Revise the program that finds two points in a three-dimensional space nearest to other. Use a two-dimensional array to represent the points. Test the program using the following points:

```
double points[][3] = {{-1, 0, 3}, {-1, -1, -1}, {4, 1, 1},
  {2, 0.5, 9}, {3.5, 2, -1}, {3, 1.5, 3}, {-1.5, 4, 2},
  {5.5, 4, -0.5}};
```

The formula for computing the distance between two points (x1, y1, z1) and (x2, y2, z2) is $\sqrt{(x_2 - x_1)^2 + (y_2 - y_1)^2 + (z_2 - z_1)^2}$.

8.13* (*Sorting two-dimensional array*) Write a function to sort a two-dimensional array using following header:

```
void sort(int m[][2], int numberOfRows)
```

The function performs a primary sort on rows and a secondary sort on columns. For example, the array $\{\{4, 2\}, \{1, 7\}, \{4, 5\}, \{1, 2\}, \{1, 1\}, \{4, 1\}\}$ will be sorted to $\{\{1, 1\}, \{1, 2\}, \{1, 7\}, \{4, 1\}, \{4, 2\}, \{4, 5\}\}$. Write a test program that prompts the user to enter ten points, invokes this function, and displays the sorted points.

8.14* (*Game: TicTacToe board*) Write a program that randomly fills 0s and 1s into a Tic-TacToc board, displays the board, and finds the rows, columns, or diagonals with all 0s or 1s. Use a two-dimensional array to represent a TicTacToe board. Here is a sample run of the program:

```
001
001
```

```
111
All 1's on row 2
All 1's on column 2
```

8.15* (*Algebra: 2 × 2 matrix inverse*) The inverse of a square matrix A is denoted A^{-1}, such that $A \times A^{-1} = I$, where I is the identity matrix with all 1s on the diagonal and 0 on all other cells. For example, the inverse of matrix $\begin{bmatrix} 1 & 2 \\ 3 & 4 \end{bmatrix}$ is $\begin{bmatrix} -0.5 & 1 \\ 1.5 & 0 \end{bmatrix}$, i.e.,

$$\begin{bmatrix} 1 & 2 \\ 3 & 4 \end{bmatrix} \times \begin{bmatrix} -0.5 & 1 \\ 1.5 & 0 \end{bmatrix} = \begin{bmatrix} 1 & 0 \\ 0 & 1 \end{bmatrix}$$

The inverse of a 2 × 2 matrix A can be obtained using the following formula if ad − bc != 0:

$$A = \begin{bmatrix} a & b \\ c & d \end{bmatrix} \qquad A^{-1} = \frac{1}{ad - bc} \begin{bmatrix} d & -b \\ -c & a \end{bmatrix}$$

Implement the following function to obtain an inverse of the matrix:

void inverse(**const double** A[][2], **double** inverseOfA[][2])

Write a test program that prompts the user to enter a, b, c, d for a matrix, and displays its inverse matrix. Here is a sample run:

```
Enter a, b, c, d: 1 2 3 4  ↵Enter
-2.0 1.0
1.5 -0.5
```

```
Enter a, b, c, d: 0.5 2 1.5 4.5  ↵Enter
-6.0 2.6666666666666665
2.0 -0.6666666666666666
```

8.16* (*Geometry: same line?*) Suppose a set of points are given. Write a program to check whether all the points are on the same line. Use the following sets to test your program:

```
double set1[][2] = {{1, 1}, {2, 2}, {3, 3}, {4, 4}};
double set2[][2] = {{0, 1}, {1, 2}, {4, 5}, {5, 6}};
double set3[][2] = {{0, 1}, {1, 2}, {4, 5}, {4.5, 4}};
```

8.17*** (*Multiple Sudoku solutions*) A Sudoku problem may have multiple solutions. Modify Listing 8.4, Sudoku.cpp, to display the total number of solutions. If multiple solutions exist, display three of them.

8.18* (*Algebra: 3 × 3 matrix inverse*) The inverse of a square matrix A is denoted A^{-1}, such that $A \times A^{-1} = I$, where I is the identity matrix with all 1s on the diagonal and **0** on all other cells. For example, the inverse of matrix $\begin{bmatrix} 1 & 2 & 1 \\ 2 & 3 & 1 \\ 4 & 5 & 3 \end{bmatrix}$ is $\begin{bmatrix} -2 & 0.5 & 0.5 \\ 1 & 0.5 & -0.5 \\ 1 & -1.5 & 0.5 \end{bmatrix}$, i.e.,

$$\begin{bmatrix} 1 & 2 & 1 \\ 2 & 3 & 1 \\ 4 & 5 & 3 \end{bmatrix} \times \begin{bmatrix} -2 & 0.5 & 0.5 \\ 1 & 0.5 & -0.5 \\ 1 & -1.5 & 0.5 \end{bmatrix} = \begin{bmatrix} 1 & 0 & 0 \\ 0 & 1 & 0 \\ 0 & 0 & 1 \end{bmatrix}$$

The inverse of a 3×3 matrix $A = \begin{bmatrix} a_{11} & a_{12} & a_{13} \\ a_{21} & a_{22} & a_{23} \\ a_{31} & a_{32} & a_{33} \end{bmatrix}$ can be obtained using the following formula if $|A| \neq 0$:

$$A^{-1} = \frac{1}{|A|} \begin{bmatrix} a_{22}a_{33} - a_{23}a_{32} & a_{13}a_{32} - a_{12}a_{33} & a_{12}a_{23} - a_{13}a_{22} \\ a_{23}a_{31} - a_{21}a_{33} & a_{11}a_{33} - a_{13}a_{31} & a_{13}a_{21} - a_{11}a_{23} \\ a_{21}a_{32} - a_{22}a_{31} & a_{12}a_{31} - a_{11}a_{32} & a_{11}a_{22} - a_{12}a_{21} \end{bmatrix}$$

$$|A| = \begin{vmatrix} a_{11} & a_{12} & a_{13} \\ a_{21} & a_{22} & a_{23} \\ a_{31} & a_{32} & a_{33} \end{vmatrix} = a_{11}a_{22}a_{33} + a_{31}a_{12}a_{23} + a_{13}a_{21}a_{32}$$
$$- a_{13}a_{22}a_{31} - a_{11}a_{23}a_{32} - a_{33}a_{21}a_{12}.$$

Implement the following function to obtain an inverse of the matrix:

void inverse(**const double** A[][3], **double** inverseOfA[][3])

Write a test program that prompts the user to enter $a_{11}, a_{12}, a_{13}, a_{21}, a_{21}, a_{23}, a_{31}, a_{32}, a_{33}$, for a matrix, and displays its inverse matrix. Here is a sample run:

```
Enter a11, a12, a13, a21, a22, a23, a31, a32, a33:
  1 2 1 2 3 1 4 5 3  ↵Enter
-2 0.5 0.5
1 0.5 -0.5
1 -1.5 0.5
```

```
Enter a11, a12, a13, a21, a22, a23, a31, a32, a33:
  1 4 2 2 5 8 2 1 8  ↵Enter
2.0 -1.875 1.375
0.0 0.25 -0.25
-0.5 0.4375 -0.1875
```

8.19* (*Financial tsunami*) Banks loan money to each other. In tough economic times, if a bank goes bankrupt, it may not be able to pay back the loan. A bank's total asset is its current balance plus its loans to other banks. Figure 8.10 is a diagram that shows five banks. The banks' current balances are **25, 125, 175, 75,** and **181** million dollars, respectively. The directed edge from node 1 to node 2 indicates that bank 1 loans **40** million dollars to bank 2.

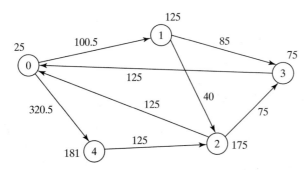

FIGURE 8.10 Banks loan money to each other.

If a bank's total asset is under a certain limit, the bank is unsafe. If a bank is unsafe, the money it borrowed cannot be returned to the lender, and the lender cannot count the loan in its total asset. Consequently, the lender may also be unsafe, if its total asset is under the limit. Write a program to find all unsafe banks. Your program reads the input as follows. It first reads two integers n and limit, where n indicates the number of banks and limit is the minimum asset for keeping a bank safe. It then reads n lines that describe the information for n banks with id from 0 to n-1. The first number in the line is the bank's balance, the second number indicates the number of banks that borrowed money from the bank, and the rest are pairs of two numbers. Each pair describes a borrower. The first number in the pair is the borrower's id and the second is the amount borrowed. Assume that the maximum number of the banks is 100. For example, the input for the five banks in Figure 8.10 is as follows (the limit is 201):

```
5 201
25 2 1 100.5 4 320.5
125 2 2 40 3 85
175 2 0 125 3 75
75 1 0 125
181 1 2 125
```

The total asset of bank 3 is (75 + 125), which is under 201. So bank 3 is unsafe. After bank 3 becomes unsafe, the total asset of bank 1 becomes 125 + 40. So bank 1 is also unsafe. The output of the program should be

```
Unsafe banks are 3 1
```

(*Hint:* Use a two-dimensional array borrowers to represent loans. loan[i][j] indicates the loan the bank i loans to bank j. Once bank j becomes unsafe, loan[i][j] should be set to 0.)

PART 2

OBJECT-ORIENTED PROGRAMMING

In Part I, "Fundamentals of Programming," you learned how to write simple C++ programs using primitive data types, control statements, functions, and arrays. All of these are commonly available in procedural programming languages. In C++, which is an object-oriented programming language, you will also use abstraction, encapsulation, inheritance, and polymorphism, which provide great flexibility, modularity, and reusability for developing software. In this part of the book you will learn how to define, extend, and work with classes and their objects.

Prerequisites for Part 2

flexible order

Chapters 12, 13, 14, and 15 can be covered in flexible order.

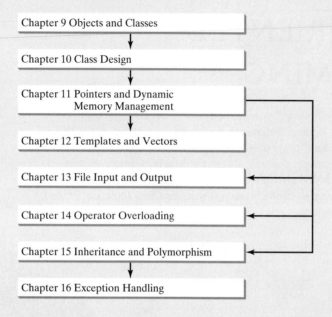

CHAPTER 9

OBJECTS AND CLASSES

Objectives

- To describe objects and classes, and to use classes to model objects (§9.2).

- To use UML graphical notations to describe classes and objects (§9.2).

- To create objects using constructors (§9.3).

- To access data fields and invoke functions using the object member access operator (.) (§9.4).

- To separate a class declaration from a class implementation (§9.5).

- To prevent multiple declarations using the `#ifndef` inclusion guard directive (§9.6).

- To know what inline functions in a class are (§9.7).

- To declare private data fields with appropriate `get` and `set` functions for data field encapsulation and make classes easy to maintain (§9.8).

- To understand the scope of data fields (§9.9).

- To apply class abstraction to develop software (§§9.10–9.11).

9.1 Introduction

why OOP?

Having learned the material in earlier chapters, you are able to solve many programming problems using selections, loops, functions, and arrays. However, these features are not sufficient for developing large-scale software systems. This chapter begins the introduction of object-oriented programming, which will enable you to develop large-scale software systems effectively.

9.2 Defining Classes for Objects

object

Object-oriented programming (OOP) involves programming using objects. An *object* represents an entity in the real world that can be distinctly identified. For example, a student, a desk, a circle, a rectangle, a button, and even a loan can all be viewed as objects. An object has a unique identity, state, and behaviors.

state

■ The *state* of an object is represented by *data fields* (also known as *properties*) with their current values.

behavior

■ The *behavior* of an object is defined by a set of functions. Invoking a function on an object is to ask the object to perform a task.

A circle object, for example, has a data field, `radius`, which is the property that characterizes a circle. One behavior of a circle is that its area can be computed using the function `getArea()`.

Objects of the same type are defined using a common class. A class is a blueprint that defines what an object's data fields and functions will be. An object is an instance of a class.

instantiation
object
instance

You can create many instances of a class. Creating an instance is referred to as *instantiation*. The terms *object* and *instance* are often interchangeable. The relationship between classes and objects is analogous to the relationship between apple pie recipes and apple pies. You can make as many apple pies as you want from a single recipe. Figure 9.1 shows a class named `Circle` and its three objects.

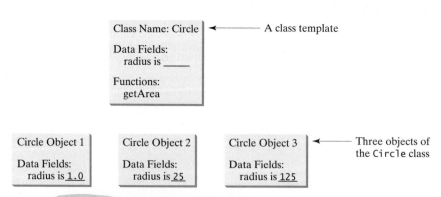

FIGURE 9.1 A class is a blueprint for creating objects.

class
data field
function
constructor

A C++ *class* uses variables to define *data fields* and *functions* to define behaviors. Additionally, a class provides functions of a special type, known as *constructors*, which are invoked when a new object is created. A constructor is a special kind of function. Constructors can perform any action, but they are designed to perform initializing actions, such as initializing the data fields of objects. Figure 9.2 shows an example of the class for `Circle` objects.

```
class Circle
{
public:
  // The radius of this circle
  double radius;          ◄——————— Data field

  // Construct a circle object
  Circle()
  {
    radius = 1;
  }
                                    ◄——————— Constructors
  // Construct a circle object
  Circle(double newRadius)
  {
    radius = newRadius;
  }

  // Return the area of this circle
  double getArea()        ◄——————— Function
  {
    return radius * radius * 3.14159;
  }
};
```

FIGURE 9.2 A class is a blueprint that defines objects of the same type.

The illustration of class and objects in Figure 9.1 can be standardized using UML (*Unified Modeling Language*) notation, as shown in Figure 9.3. This is called a *UML class diagram*, or simply *class diagram*. The data field is denoted as   class diagram

dataFieldName: dataFieldType

The constructor is denoted as

ClassName(parameterName: parameterType)

The function is denoted as

functionName(parameterName: parameterType): returnType

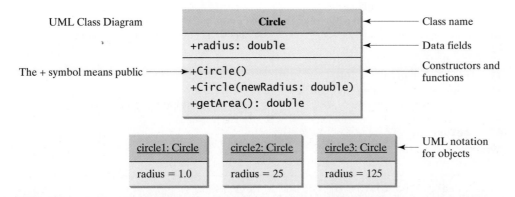

FIGURE 9.3 Classes and objects can be represented using UML notations.

Listing 9.1 is a program that demonstrates classes and objects. It constructs three circle objects with radius 1.0, 25, and 125 and displays the radius and area of each. Change the radius of the second object to 100 and display its new radius and area.

LISTING 9.1 TestCircle.cpp

Video Note
using classes

define class

data field

no-arg constructor

second constructor

function

don't omit ;!

main function

creating object
creating object
creating object

accessing radius
invoking getArea

modify radius

```cpp
 1 #include <iostream>
 2 using namespace std;
 3
 4 class Circle
 5 {
 6 public:
 7   // The radius of this circle
 8   double radius;
 9
10   // Construct a default circle object
11   Circle()
12   {
13     radius = 1;
14   }
15
16   // Construct a circle object
17   Circle(double newRadius)
18   {
19     radius = newRadius;
20   }
21
22   // Return the area of this circle
23   double getArea()
24   {
25     return radius * radius * 3.14159;
26   }
27 };   // Must place a semicolon here
28
29 int main()
30 {
31   Circle circle1(1.0);
32   Circle circle2(25);
33   Circle circle3(125);
34
35   cout << "The area of the circle of radius "
36     << circle1.radius << " is " << circle1.getArea() << endl;
37   cout << "The area of the circle of radius "
38     << circle2.radius << " is " << circle2.getArea() << endl;
39   cout << "The area of the circle of radius "
40     << circle3.radius << " is " << circle3.getArea() << endl;
41
42   // Modify circle radius
43   circle2.radius = 100;
44   cout << "The area of the circle of radius "
45     << circle2.radius << " is " << circle2.getArea() << endl;
46
47   return 0;
48 }
```

```
The area of the circle of radius 1 is 3.14159
The area of the circle of radius 25 is 1963.49
The area of the circle of radius 125 is 49087.3
The area of the circle of radius 100 is 31415.9
```

ending class declaration

The class is defined in lines 4–27. Don't forget that the semicolon (;) in line 27 is required.

The **public** keyword in line 6 denotes that all data fields, constructors, and functions can be accessed from the objects of the class. If you don't use the **public** keyword, the visibility is *private* by default. Private visibility will be introduced in §9.8, "Data Field Encapsulation."

public

private by default

The main function creates three objects named **circle1**, **circle2**, and **circle3** with radius **1.0**, **25**, and **125**, respectively (lines 31–33). These objects have different radii but the same functions. Therefore, you can compute their respective areas by using the **getArea()** function. The data fields can be accessed via the object using **circle1.radius**, **circle2.radius**, and **circle3.radius**, respectively. The functions are invoked using **circle1.getArea()**, **circle2.getArea()**, and **circle3.getArea()**, respectively.

These three objects are independent. The radius of **circle2** is changed to **100** in line 43. The object's new radius and area are displayed in lines 44–45.

This example has given you a glimpse of classes and objects. You may have many questions about constructors and objects, accessing data fields and invoking objects' functions. The sections that follow discuss these issues in detail.

9.3 Constructors

Constructors are a special kind of function, with three peculiarities:

- Constructors must have the same name as the class itself.

constructor's name

- Constructors do not have a return type—not even **void**.

no return type

- Constructors are invoked when an object is created. Constructors play the role of initializing objects.

invoke constructor

The constructor has exactly the same name as the defining class. Like regular functions, constructors can be overloaded (i.e., multiple constructors with the same name but different signatures), making it easy to construct objects with different sets of data values.

overloading constructors

It is a common mistake to put the **void** keyword in front of a constructor. For example,

no **void**

```
void Circle()
{
}
```

Most C++ compilers will report an error, but some will treat this as a regular function, not as a constructor.

Constructors are for initializing data fields. The data field **radius** does not have an initial value, so it must be initialized in the constructor (lines 13 and 19 in Listing 9.1). Note that a variable (local or global) can be declared and initialized in one statement, but as a class member, a data field cannot be initialized when it is declared. For example, it would be wrong to replace line 8 in Listing 9.1 by

initialize data field

```
double radius = 5; // Wrong for data field declaration
```

A class normally provides a constructor without arguments (e.g., **Circle()**). Such constructor is called a *no-arg* or *no-argument constructor*.

no-arg constructor

A class may be defined without constructors. In this case, a no-arg constructor with an empty body is implicitly defined in the class. Called *a default constructor,* it is provided automatically *only if no constructors are explicitly defined in the class*.

default constructor

Data fields may be initialized in the constructor using an initializer list in the following syntax:

initializer list

```
ClassName(parameterList)
  : datafield1(value1), datafield2(value2) // Initializer list
{
  // Additional statements if needed
}
```

The initializer list initializes `datafield1` with `value1` and `datafield2` with `value2`. For example,

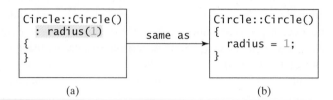

| (a) | | (b) |

Constructor (b), which does not use an initializer list, is actually more intuitive than (a). However, using an initializer list is necessary to initialize object data fields that don't have a no-arg constructor. This is an advanced topic covered in Supplement IV.E, "*Constructor Initializer Lists*," on the companion Website.

9.4 Constructing and Using Objects

constructing objects

A constructor is invoked when an object is created. The syntax to create an object using the no-arg constructor is

invoking no-arg constructor

```
ClassName objectName;
```

For example, the following declaration creates an object named `circle1` by invoking the `Circle` class's no-arg constructor.

```
Circle circle1;
```

The syntax to create an object using a constructor with arguments is

constructing with args

```
ClassName objectName(arguments);
```

For example, the following declaration creates an object named `circle2` by invoking the `Circle` class's constructor with a specified radius `5.5`.

```
Circle circle2(5.5);
```

member access operator

Newly created objects are allocated in the memory. After an object is created, its data can be accessed and its functions invoked using the *dot operator* (`.`), also known as the *object member access operator*:

- `objectName.dataField` references a data field in the object.

- `objectName.function(arguments)` invokes a function on the object.

For example, `circle1.radius` references the radius in `circle1`, and `circle1.getArea()` invokes the `getArea` function on `circle1`. Functions are invoked as operations on objects.

instance variable

The data field `radius` is referred to as an *instance member variable* or simply *instance variable*, because it is dependent on a specific instance. For the same reason, the function `getArea` is referred to as an *instance member function* or simply *instance function*, because you can invoke it only on a specific instance. The object on which an instance function is invoked is called a *calling object*.

instance function

calling object

 Note

class naming convention

object naming convention

When you define a custom class, capitalize the first letter of each word in a class name—for example, the class names `Circle`, `Rectangle`, and `Desk`. The class names in the C++ library are named in lowercase. The objects are named like variables.

The following points on classes and objects are worth noting:

■ You can use primitive data types to define variables. You can also use class names to declare object names. In this sense, a class is also a data type.

class is a type

■ In C++, you can use the assignment operator = to copy the contents from one object to the other. By default, each data field of one object is copied to its counterpart in the other object. For example,

memberwise copy

```
circle2 = circle1;
```

copies the `radius` in `circle1` to `circle2`. After the copy, `circle1` and `circle2` are still two different objects but have the same radius.

■ Object names are like array names. Once an object name is declared, it represents an object. It cannot be reassigned to represent another object. In this sense, an object name is a constant, though the contents of the object may change. Memberwise copy can change an object's contents but not its name.

constant object name

■ An object contains data and may invoke functions. This may lead you to think that an object is quite large. It isn't, though. Data are physically stored in an object, but functions are not. Since functions are shared by all objects of the same class, the compiler creates just one copy for sharing. You can find out the actual size of an object using the `sizeof` function. For example, the following code displays the size of objects `circle1` and `circle2`. Their size is `8`, since the data field radius is `double`, which takes `8` bytes.

object size

```
Circle circle1;
Circle circle2(5.0);

cout << sizeof(circle1) << endl;
cout << sizeof(circle2) << endl;
```

Usually you create a named object and later access its members through its name. Occasionally you may create an object and use it only once. In this case, you don't have to name it. Such objects are called *anonymous objects*.

anonymous objects

The syntax to create an anonymous object using the no-arg constructor is

```
ClassName()
```

The syntax to create an anonymous object using the constructor with arguments is

```
ClassName(arguments)
```

For example,

```
circle1 = Circle();
```

creates a `Circle` object using the no-arg constructor and copies its contents to `circle1`.

```
circle1 = Circle(5);
```

creates a `Circle` object with radius `5` and copies its contents to `circle1`.

For example, the following code creates `Circle` objects and invokes their `getArea()` function.

```
cout << "Area is " << Circle().getArea() << endl;
cout << "Area is " << Circle(5).getArea() << endl;
```

As you see from these examples, you may create an anonymous object if it will not be referenced later.

no-arg constructor

Caution

Please note that in C++, to create an anonymous object using the *no-arg constructor*, you have to add parentheses after the constructor name (e.g., `Circle()`). To create a named object using the no-arg constructor, you cannot use the parentheses after the constructor name (e.g., you use `Circle circle1` rather than `Circle circle1()`). This is the required syntax, which you just have to accept.

9.5 Separating Declaration from Implementation

Video Note
separating declaration

C++ allows you to separate class declaration from implementation. The class declaration describes the *contract* of the class and the class implementation carries out the contract. The class declaration simply lists all the data fields, constructor prototypes, and function prototypes. The class implementation provides full definitions of the constructors and functions. The class declaration and implementation may be in two separate files. Both files should have the same name but different extension names. The class declaration file has an extension name `.h` and the class implementation file an extension name `.cpp`.

Listings 9.2 and 9.3 present the `Circle` class declaration and implementation.

LISTING 9.2 Circle.h

```
1 class Circle
2 {
3 public:
4    // The radius of this circle
5    double radius;
6
7    // Construct a default circle object
8    Circle();
9
10   // Construct a circle object
11   Circle(double);
12
13   // Return the area of this circle
14   double getArea();
15 };
```

data field — line 5
no-arg constructor — line 8
second constructor — line 11
function prototype — line 14
semicolon required — line 15 `};` ← Semicolon required

don't omit semicolon

Caution

It is a common mistake to omit the semicolon (`;`) at the end of the header file.

LISTING 9.3 Circle.cpp

include class declaration

```
1 #include "Circle.h"
2
3 // Construct a default circle object
4 Circle::Circle()
5 {
6    radius = 1;
7 }
8
9 // Construct a circle object
10 Circle::Circle(double newRadius)
11 {
12    radius = newRadius;
13 }
14
15 // Return the area of this circle
```

implement constructor — line 4
implement constructor — line 10

```
16 double Circle::getArea()
17 {
18   return radius * radius * 3.14159;
19 }
```

implement function

The `::` symbol, known as the *binary scope resolution operator*, specifies the scope of a class member in a class.

binary scope resolution operator

Here, `Circle::` preceding each constructor and function in the `Circle` class tells the compiler that these constructors and functions are defined in the `Circle` class.

Listing 9.4 is a *client* program that uses the `Circle` class.

LISTING 9.4 TestCircleWithDeclaration.cpp

```
1 #include <iostream>
2 #include "Circle.h"
3 using namespace std;
4
5 int main()
6 {
7   Circle circle1;
8   Circle circle2(5.0);
9
10   cout << "The area of the circle of radius "
11     << circle1.radius << " is " << circle1.getArea() << endl;
12   cout << "The area of the circle of radius "
13     << circle2.radius << " is " << circle2.getArea() << endl;
14
15   // Modify circle radius
16   circle2.radius = 100;
17   cout << "The area of the circle of radius "
18     << circle2.radius << " is " << circle2.getArea() << endl;
19
20   return 0;
21 }
```

include class declaration

construct circle
construct circle

set a new radius

```
The area of the circle of radius 1 is 3.14159
The area of the circle of radius 5 is 78.5397
The area of the circle of radius 100 is 31415.9
```

There are at least two reasons for separating a class declaration from implementation.

why separation?

- First, it hides implementation from declaration. You can feel free to change the implementation. The client program that uses the class does not need to change as long as the declaration is not changed.

- Second, as a software vendor, you can just provide the customer with the header file and class object code without revealing the source code for implementing the class. This protects the software vendor's intellectual property.

Note

To compile a main program from the command line, you need to add all its supporting files in the command. For example, to compile TestCircleWithDeclaration.cpp using a GNU C++ compiler, the command is

compiling from command line

```
g++ Circle.cpp TestCircleWithDeclaration.cpp -o Main
```

compiling from IDE

Note

If the main program uses other programs, all of these program source files must be present in the project pane in the IDE. Otherwise, you may get linking errors. For example, to run TestCircleWithDeclaration.cpp, you need to place TestCircleWithDeclaration.cpp, Circle.cpp, and Circle.h in the project pane in Visual C++, as shown in Figure 9.4.

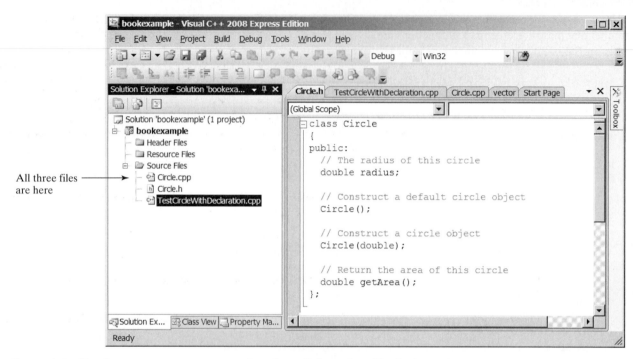

All three files are here

FIGURE 9.4 For the program to run, you need to place all dependent files in the project pane.

9.6 Preventing Multiple Declarations

It is a common mistake to include, inadvertently, the same header file in a program multiple times. Suppose Head1.h includes Circle.h and TestHead1.cpp includes both Head1.h and Circle.h, as shown in Listings 9.5 and 9.6.

LISTING 9.5 Head1.h

include Circle.h

```
1 #include "Circle.h"
2 // Other code in Head1.h omitted
```

LISTING 9.6 TestHead1.cpp

include Circle.h
include Head1.h

```
1 #include "Circle.h"
2 #include "Head1.h"
3
4 int main()
5 {
6    // Other code in TestHead1.cpp omitted
7 }
```

If you compile TestHead1.cpp, you will get a compile error indicating that there are multiple declarations for Circle. What is wrong here? Recall that the C++ preprocessor inserts the contents of the header file at the position where the header is included. Circle.h is included in line 1. Since the header file for `Circle` is also included in `Head1.h` (see line 1 in Listing 9.5), the preprocessor will add the declaration for the `Circle` class another time as result of including Head1.h in TestHead1.cpp, which causes the multiple-declaration errors.

The C++ `#ifndef` directive can be used to prevent a header file from being included multiple times. This is known as *inclusion guard*. To make this work, you have to add three lines to the header file. The three lines are highlighted in Listing 9.7.

inclusion guard

LISTING 9.7 Circle1.h

```
1  #ifndef CIRCLE_H
2  #define CIRCLE_H
3
4  class Circle
5  {
6  public:
7    // The radius of this circle
8    double radius;
9
10   // Construct a default circle object
11   Circle();
12
13   // Construct a circle object
14   Circle(double);
15
16   // Return the area of this circle
17   double getArea();
18 }; ←── Semicolon required
19
20 #endif
```

test constant
define constant

end of `#ifndef`

Recall that the statements preceded by the pound sign (#) are preprocessor directives. They are interpreted by the C++ preprocessor. The preprocessor *directive* `#ifndef` stands for "*if not def*ined." Line 1 tests whether constant `CIRCLE_H` is already defined. If not, define the constant in line 2 and include the header file; otherwise, skip the header file. The `#endif` directive is needed to indicate the end of header file.

If you replace Circle.h by Circle1.h in Listings 9.5 and 9.6, the program will not have the multiple-declaration error.

9.7 Inline Functions in Classes

§6.6, "Inline Functions," introduced how to improve function efficiency using inline functions. Inline functions play an important role in class declarations. When a function is implemented inside a class declaration, it automatically becomes an inline function. This is also known as *inline declaration*. For example, in the following declaration for class `A`, the constructor and function `f1` are automatically inline functions, but function `f2` is not.

inline declaration

```
class A
{
public:
  A()
  {
    // Do something;
  }

  double f1()
  {
    // Return a number
  }
```

```
    double f2();
};
```

There is another way to define inline functions for classes. You may define inline functions in the class's implementation file. For example, to define function `f2` as an inline function, precede the inline keyword in the function header as follows:

```
// Implement function as inline
inline double A::f2()
{
    // Return a number
}
```

As noted in §6.6, short functions are good candidates for inline functions, but long functions are not.

9.8 Data Field Encapsulation

The data fields `radius` in the `Circle` class in Listing 9.1 can be modified directly (e.g., `circle1.radius = 5`). This is not a good practice—for two reasons:

- First, data may be tampered with.
- Second, it makes the class difficult to maintain and vulnerable to bugs. Suppose you want to modify the `Circle` class to ensure that the radius is nonnegative after other programs have already used the class. You have to change not only the `Circle` class, but also the programs that use the `Circle` class. This is because the clients may have modified the radius directly (e.g., `myCircle.radius = -5`).

data field encapsulation

To prevent direct modifications of properties, you should declare the data field private, using the `private` keyword. This is known as *data field encapsulation*. Making the radius data field private in the `Circle` class, you can define the class as follows:

```
class Circle
{
public:
    Circle();
    Circle(double);
    double getArea();

private:
    double radius;
};
```

A private data field cannot be accessed by an object through a direct reference outside the class that defines the private field. But often a client needs to retrieve and/or modify a data field. To make a private data field accessible, provide a *get* function to return the field's value. To enable a private data field to be updated, provide a *set* function to set a new value.

 Note

accessor

mutator

Colloquially, a `get` function is referred to as a *getter* (or *accessor*), and a `set` function is referred to as a *setter* (or *mutator*).

A `get` function has the following signature:

`returnType getPropertyName()`

bool accessor

If the `returnType` is `bool`, by convention the `get` function should be defined as follows:

`bool isPropertyName()`

A set function has the following signature:

```
void setPropertyName(dataType propertyValue)
```

Let us create a new circle class with a private data field radius and its associated accessor and *mutator functions*. The class diagram is shown in Figure 9.5. The new circle class is defined in Listing 9.8.

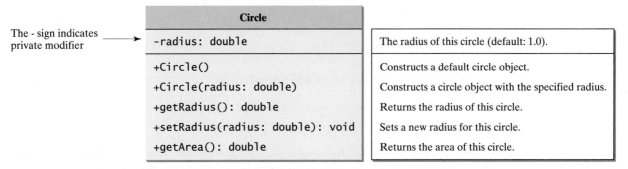

The - sign indicates private modifier →

Circle
-radius: double
+Circle()
+Circle(radius: double)
+getRadius(): double
+setRadius(radius: double): void
+getArea(): double

The radius of this circle (default: 1.0).
Constructs a default circle object.
Constructs a circle object with the specified radius.
Returns the radius of this circle.
Sets a new radius for this circle.
Returns the area of this circle.

FIGURE 9.5   The `Circle` class encapsulates circle properties and provides get/set and other functions.

LISTING 9.8   Circle2.h

```cpp
1 #ifndef CIRCLE_H
2 #define CIRCLE_H
3
4 class Circle
5 {
6 public:                                              public
7   Circle();
8   Circle(double);
9   double getArea();
10  double getRadius();                                access function
11  void setRadius(double);                            mutator function
12
13 private:                                            private
14  double radius;
15 };
16
17 #endif
```

Listing 9.9 implements the class contract specified in the header file in Listing 9.8.

LISTING 9.9   Circle2.cpp

```cpp
1 #include "Circle2.h"                                 include header file
2
3 // Construct a default circle object
4 Circle::Circle()                                     constructor
5 {
6   radius = 1;
7 }
8
9 // Construct a circle object
10 Circle::Circle(double newRadius)                     constructor
11 {
12   radius = newRadius;
13 }
14
```

get area

```
15 // Return the area of this circle
16 double Circle::getArea()
17 {
18   return radius * radius * 3.14159;
19 }
20
```

get radius

```
21 // Return the radius of this circle
22 double Circle::getRadius()
23 {
24   return radius;
25 }
26
```

set radius

```
27 // Set a new radius
28 void Circle::setRadius(double newRadius)
29 {
30   radius = (newRadius >= 0) ? newRadius : 0;
31 }
```

The **getRadius()** function (lines 22–25) returns the radius, and the **setRadius (newRadius)** function (line 28–31) sets a new radius into the object. If the new radius is negative, **0** is set to the radius in the object. Since these functions are the only ways to read and modify radius, you have total control over how the **radius** property is accessed. If you have to change the functions' implementation, you need not change the client programs. This makes the class easy to maintain.

Listing 9.10 is a client program that uses the **Circle** class to create a **Circle** object and modifies the radius using the **setRadius** function.

LISTING 9.10 TestCircle2.cpp

include header file

```
1 #include <iostream>
2 #include "Circle2.h"
3 using namespace std;
4
5 int main()
6 {
```

construct object
construct object

```
7   Circle circle1;
8   Circle circle2(5.0);
9
10  cout << "The area of the circle of radius "
```

get radius

```
11    << circle1.getRadius() << " is " << circle1.getArea() << endl;
12  cout << "The area of the circle of radius "
13    << circle2.getRadius() << " is " << circle2.getArea() << endl;
14
15  // Modify circle radius
```

set radius

```
16  circle2.setRadius(100);
17  cout << "The area of the circle of radius "
18    << circle2.getRadius() << " is " << circle2.getArea() << endl;
19
20  return 0;
21 }
```

```
The area of the circle of radius 1 is 3.14159
The area of the circle of radius 5 is 78.5397
The area of the circle of radius 100 is 31415.9
```

The data field `radius` is declared private. Private data can be accessed only within their defining class. You cannot use `circle1.radius` in the client program. A compilation error would occur if you attempted to access private data from a client.

Tip
To prevent data from being tampered with and to make the class easy to maintain, the data fields in this book will be private.

9.9 The Scope of Variables

Chapter 6, "Advanced Function Features," discussed the scope of global variables, local variables, and static local variables. Global variables are declared outside all functions and are accessible to all functions in its scope. The scope of a global variable starts from its declaration and continues to the end of the program. Local variables are defined inside functions. The scope of a local variable starts from its declaration and continues to the end of the block that contains the variable. Static local variables are permanently stored in the program so they can be used in the next call of the function.

The data fields are declared as variables and are accessible to all constructors and functions in the class. Data fields and functions can be in any order in a class. For example, all the following declarations are the same:

```
class Circle
{
public:
  Circle();
  Circle(double);
  double getArea();
  double getRadius();
  void setRadius(double);

private:
  double radius;
};
```
(a)

```
class Circle
{
public:
  Circle();
  Circle(double);

private:
  double radius;

public:
  double getArea();
  double getRadius();
  void setRadius(double);
};
```
(b)

```
class Circle
{
private:
  double radius;

public:
  double getArea();
  double getRadius();
  void setRadius(double);

public:
  Circle();
  Circle(double);
};
```
(c)

Tip
Though the class members can be in any order, the common style in C++ is to place public members first and then private members. public first

This section discusses the scope rules of all the variables in the context of a class.

You can declare a variable for data field only once, but you can declare the same variable name in a function many times in different functions.

Local variables are declared and used inside a function locally. If a local variable has the same name as a data field, the local variable takes precedence, and the data field with the same name is hidden. For example, in the program in Listing 9.11, `x` is defined as a data field and as a local variable in the function.

LISTING 9.11 `HideDataField.cpp`

```
1 #include <iostream>
2 using namespace std;
3
```

data field **x**
data field **y**

no-arg constructor

local variable

create object
invoke function

```
4 class Foo
5 {
6 public:
7   int x; // Data field
8   int y; // Data field
9
10  Foo()
11  {
12    x = 10;
13    y = 10;
14  }
15
16  void p()
17  {
18    int x = 20; // Local variable
19    cout << "x is " << x << endl;
20    cout << "y is " << y << endl;
21  }
22 };
23
24 int main()
25 {
26   Foo foo;
27   foo.p();
28
29   return 0;
30 }
```

```
x is 20
y is 10
```

Why is the printout **20** for **x** and **10** for **y**? Here is why:

■ **x** is declared as a data field in the **Foo** class, but is also defined as a local variable in the function **p()** with an initial value of **20**. The latter **x** is displayed to the console in line 19.

■ **y** is declared as a data field, so it is accessible inside function **p()**.

Tip
As demonstrated in the example, it is easy to make mistakes. To avoid confusion, do not declare the same variable name twice in a class, except for function parameters.

9.10 Class Abstraction and Encapsulation

class abstraction

class encapsulation

In Chapter 6, "Advanced Function Features," you learned about function abstraction and used it in stepwise program development. C++ provides many levels of abstraction. *Class abstraction* is the separation of class implementation from the use of a class. The creator of a class provides a description of the class and lets the user know how it can be used. The collection of functions and fields that are accessible from outside the class, together with the description of how these members are expected to behave, serves as the *class's contract*. As shown in Figure 9.6, the user of the class does not need to know how the class is implemented. The details of implementation are encapsulated and hidden from the user. This is known as *class encapsulation*. For example, you can create a **Circle** object and find the area of the circle without knowing how the area is computed.

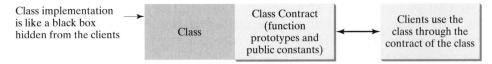

Class implementation is like a black box hidden from the clients → Class → Class Contract (function prototypes and public constants) ↔ Clients use the class through the contract of the class

FIGURE 9.6 Class abstraction separates class implementation from the use of the class.

Class abstraction and encapsulation are two sides of the same coin. Many real-life examples illustrate the concept of class abstraction. Consider, for instance, building a computer system. Your personal computer is made up of many components, such as a CPU, CD-ROM, floppy disk, motherboard, fan, and so on. Each component can be viewed as an object that has properties and functions. To get the components to work together, all you need to know is how each component is used and how it interacts with the others. You don't need to know how it works internally. The internal implementation is encapsulated and hidden from you. You can build a computer without knowing how a component is implemented.

The computer-system analogy precisely mirrors the object-oriented approach. Each component can be viewed as an object of the class for the component. For example, you might have a class that models all kinds of fans for use in a computer, with properties like fan size and speed, functions like start, stop, and so on. A specific fan is an instance of this class with specific property values.

As another example, consider getting a loan. A specific loan can be viewed as an object of a **Loan** class. Interest rate, loan amount, and loan period are its data properties, and computing monthly payment and total payment are its functions. When you buy a car, a loan object is created by instantiating the class with your loan interest rate, loan amount, and loan period. You can then use the functions to find the monthly payment and total payment of your loan. As a user of the **Loan** class, you don't need to know how these functions are implemented.

9.11 Case Study: The **Loan** Class

Video Note
the Loan class

Let us use the **Loan** class as an example to demonstrate the creation and use of classes. **Loan** has the data fields `annualInterestRate`, `numberOfYears`, and `loanAmount`, and the functions `getAnnualInterestRate`, `getNumberOfYears`, `getLoanAmount`, `setAnnualInterestRate`, `setNumberOfYears`, `setLoanAmount`, `getMonthlyPayment`, and `getTotalPayment`, as shown in Figure 9.7.

Loan	

`-annualInterestRate: double`
`-numberOfYears: int`
`-loanAmount: double`
	The annual interest rate of the loan (default: 2.5).
	The number of years for the loan (default: 1)
	The loan amount (default: 1000).

`+Loan()`
`+Loan(annualInterestRate: double,`
  `numberOfYears: int,`
  `loanAmount: double)`
`+getAnnualInterestRate(): double`
`+getNumberOfYears(): int`
`+getLoanAmount(): double`
`+setAnnualInterestRate(`
  `annualInterestRate: double): void`
`+setNumberOfYears(`
  `numberOfYears: int): void`
`+setLoanAmount(`
  `loanAmount: double): void`
`+getMonthlyPayment(): double`
`+getTotalPayment(): double`
	Constructs a default loan object.
	Constructs a loan with specified interest rate, years,
	  and loan amount.
	
	Returns the annual interest rate of this loan.
	Returns the number of the years of this loan.
	Returns the amount of this loan.
	Sets a new annual interest rate to this loan.
	
	Sets a new number of years to this loan.
	
	Sets a new amount to this loan.
	
	Returns the monthly payment of this loan.
	Returns the total payment of this loan.

FIGURE 9.7 The **Loan** class models the properties and behaviors of loans.

The UML diagram in Figure 9.7 serves as the contract for the Loan class. Throughout the book, you will play the role of both class user and class developer. The user can use the class without knowing how the class is implemented. Assume that the Loan class is available, with the header file, as shown in Listing 9.12. Let us begin by writing a test program that uses the Loan class, in Listing 9.13.

LISTING 9.12 Loan.h

```
1  #ifndef LOAN_H
2  #define LOAN_H
3
4  class Loan
5  {
6  public:
7    Loan();
8    Loan(double rate, int years, double amount);
9    double getAnnualInterestRate();
10   int getNumberOfYears();
11   double getLoanAmount();
12   void setAnnualInterestRate(double rate);
13   void setNumberOfYears(int years);
14   void setLoanAmount(double amount);
15   double getMonthlyPayment();
16   double getTotalPayment();
17
18 private:
19   double annualInterestRate;
20   int numberOfYears;
21   double loanAmount;
22 };
23
24 #endif
```

public functions — lines 6–16

private fields — lines 18–21

LISTING 9.13 TestLoanClass.cpp

```
1  #include <iostream>
2  #include <iomanip>
3  #include "Loan.h"
4  using namespace std;
5
6  int main()
7  {
8    // Enter annual interest rate
9    cout << "Enter yearly interest rate, for example 8.25: ";
10   double annualInterestRate;
11   cin >> annualInterestRate;
12
13   // Enter number of years
14   cout << "Enter number of years as an integer, for example 5: ";
15   int numberOfYears;
16   cin >> numberOfYears;
17
18   // Enter loan amount
19   cout << "Enter loan amount, for example 120000.95: ";
20   double loanAmount;
21   cin >> loanAmount;
22
23   // Create Loan object
24   Loan loan(annualInterestRate, numberOfYears, loanAmount);
25
```

include Loan header — line 3

input number of years — line 16

input loan amount — line 21

create Loan object — line 24

```
26   // Display results
27   cout << fixed << setprecision(2);
28   cout << "The monthly payment is "
29      << loan.getMonthlyPayment() << endl;                          monthly payment
30   cout << "The total payment is " << loan.getTotalPayment() << endl;   total payment
31
32   return 0;
33 }
```

The `main` function reads interest rate, payment period (in years), and loan amount (lines 8–21), creates a `Loan` object (line 24), and then obtains the monthly payment (line 29) and total payment (line 30) using the instance functions in the `Loan` class.

The `Loan` class can be implemented as in Listing 9.14.

LISTING 9.14 Loan.cpp

```
1 #include "Loan.h"
2 #include <cmath>
3 using namespace std;
4
5 Loan::Loan()                                              no-arg constructor
6 {
7    annualInterestRate = 9.5;
8    numberOfYears = 30;
9    loanAmount = 100000;
10 }
11
12 Loan::Loan(double rate, int years, double amount)         constructor
13 {
14    annualInterestRate = rate;
15    numberOfYears = years;
16    loanAmount = amount;
17 }
18
19 double Loan::getAnnualInterestRate()                      accessor function
20 {
21    return annualInterestRate;
22 }
23
24 int Loan::getNumberOfYears()                              accessor function
25 {
26    return numberOfYears;
27 }
28
29 double Loan::getLoanAmount()                              accessor function
30 {
31    return loanAmount;
32 }
33
34 void Loan::setAnnualInterestRate(double rate)             mutator function
35 {
36    annualInterestRate = rate;
37 }
38
39 void Loan::setNumberOfYears(int years)                    mutator function
40 {
41    numberOfYears = years;
42 }
43
44 void Loan::setLoanAmount(double amount)                   mutator function
```

get monthly payment

```
45 {
46   loanAmount = amount;
47 }
48
49 double Loan::getMonthlyPayment()
50 {
51   double monthlyInterestRate = annualInterestRate / 1200;
52   return loanAmount * monthlyInterestRate / (1 -
53     (pow(1 / (1 + monthlyInterestRate), numberOfYears * 12)));
54 }
55
```

get total payment

```
56 double Loan::getTotalPayment()
57 {
58   return getMonthlyPayment() * numberOfYears * 12;
59 }
```

From a class developer's perspective, a class is designed for use by many different customers. In order to be useful in a wide range of applications, a class should provide a variety of ways for customization through constructors, properties, and functions.

The Loan class contains two constructors, three *get* functions, three *set* functions, and the functions for finding monthly payment and total payment. You can construct a Loan object by using the no-arg constructor or the one with three parameters: annual interest rate, number of years, and loan amount. The three *get* functions, getAnnualInterest, getNumberO fYears, and getLoanAmount, return annual interest rate, payment years, and loan amount, respectively.

 Important Pedagogical Tip

The UML diagram for the Loan class is shown in Figure 9.7. Students should begin by writing a test program that uses the Loan class even though they don't know how the Loan class is implemented. This has three benefits:

- It demonstrates that developing a class and using a class are two separate tasks.

- It enables you to skip the complex implementation of certain classes without interrupting the sequence of the book.

- It is easier to learn how to implement a class if you are familiar with the class through using it.

For all the examples from now on, you may first create an object from the class and try to use its functions before turning your attention to its implementation.

KEY TERMS

CHAPTER SUMMARY

1. A class is a blueprint for objects.

2. A class defines the data fields for storing the properties of objects and provides constructors for creating objects and functions for manipulating them.

3. Constructors must have the same name as the class itself.

4. A non-arg constructor is a constructor that does not have arguments.

5. A class is also a data type. You can use it to declare and create objects.

6. An object is an instance of a class. You use the dot (.) operator to access members of that object through its name.

7. The *state* of an object is represented by *data fields* (also known as *properties*) with their current values.

8. The *behavior* of an object is defined by a set of functions.

9. The data fields do not have initial values. They must be initialized in constructors.

10. You can separate class declaration from class implementation by defining class declaration in a header file and class implementation in a separate file.

11. The C++ `#ifndef` directive, called *inclusion guard*, can be used to prevent a header file from being included multiple times.

12. When a function is implemented inside a class declaration, it automatically becomes an inline function.

13. Visibility keywords specify how the class, function, and data are accessed.

14. A `public` function or data is accessible to all clients.

15. A `private` function or data is accessible only inside the class.

16. You can provide a *get* function or a *set* function to enable clients to see or modify the data.

17. Colloquially, a *get* function is referred to as a *getter* (or *accessor*), and a *set* function is referred to as a *setter* (or *mutator*).

18. A *get* function has the signature

    `returnType getPropertyName()`

19. If the `returnType` is `bool`, the *get* function should be defined as

    `bool isPropertyName().`

20. A *set* function has the signature

    `void setPropertyName(dataType propertyValue)`

REVIEW QUESTIONS

Sections 9.2–9.4

9.1   Describe the relationship between an object and its defining class. How do you define a class? How do you declare and create an object?

9.2   What are the differences between constructors and functions?

9.3   How do you create an object using a no-arg constructor? How do you create an object using a constructor with arguments?

9.4   Once an object name is declared, can it be reassigned to reference another object?

9.5   Assuming that the `Circle` class is defined as in Listing 9.1, show the printout of the following code:

```cpp
Circle c1(5);
Circle c2(6);
c1 = c2;
cout << c1.radius << " " << c2.radius << endl;
```

9.6   What is wrong in the following code? (Use the `Circle` class defined in Listing 9.1, TestCircle.cpp.)

```cpp
1 int main()
2 {
3     Circle c1();
4     cout << c1.getRadius() << endl;
5
6     return 0;
7 }
```
(a)

```cpp
1 int main()
2 {
3     Circle c1(5);
4     Circle c1(6);
5
6     return 0;
7 }
```
(b)

9.7   What is wrong in the following code?

```cpp
1 class Circle
2 {
3 public:
4     Circle();
5     Circle(double);
6     double getArea();
7
8 private:
9     double radius = 1;
10 };
```

9.8   Suppose the following two are independent statements:

```cpp
Circle c;
Circle c = Circle();
```

Explain what each does.

Section 9.5

9.9   How do you separate class declaration from implementation?

9.10   What is the output of the following code? (Use the `Circle` class defined in Listing 9.8, Circle2.h.)

```
1 int main()
2 {
3   Circle c1;
4   Circle c2(6);
5   c1 = c2;
6   cout << c1.getRadius() << endl;
7   return 0;
8 }
```
(a)

```
1 int main()
2 {
3   cout << Circle(8).getRadius()
4     << endl;
5   return 0;
6 }
```
(b)

Section 9.6

9.11 What might cause multiple-declarations errors? How do you prevent multiple declarations?

9.12 What is the #define directive for?

Section 9.7

9.13 How do you implement all functions inline for Circle2.h in Listing 9.8?

Section 9.8

9.14 What is an accessor function? What is a mutator function? What are the naming conventions for such functions?

9.15 What are the benefits of data field encapsulation?

Section 9.9

9.16 Can data fields and functions be placed in any order in a class?

Sections 9.10–9.11

9.17 What is the output of the following code? (Use the Loan class defined in Listing 9.12, Loan.h.)

```
#include <iostream>
#include "Loan.h"
using namespace std;

class A
{
public:
  Loan loan;
  int i;
};

int main()
{
  A a;
  cout << a.loan.getLoanAmount() << endl;
  cout << a.i << endl;

  return 0;
}
```

PROGRAMMING EXERCISES

Pedagogical Note

three objectives

The exercises achieve three objectives:

1. Design and draw UML for classes;
2. Implement classes from the UML;
3. Use classes to develop applications.

Solutions for the UML diagrams for the even-numbered exercises can be downloaded from the Student Website and all others from the Instructor Website.

Sections 9.2–9.11

9.1 (*The* Rectangle *class*) Design a class named Rectangle to represent a rectangle. The class contains:

- Two double data fields named width and height that specify the width and height of the rectangle.
- A no-arg constructor that creates a default rectangle with width 1 and height 1.
- A constructor that creates a rectangle with the specified width and height.
- The accessor and mutator functions for all the data fields.
- A function named getArea() that returns the area of this rectangle.
- A function named getPerimeter() that returns the perimeter.

Draw the UML diagram for the class. Implement the class. Write a test program that creates two Rectangle objects. Assign width 4 and height 40 to the first object and width 3.5 and height 35.9 to the second. Display the properties of both objects and find their areas and perimeters.

Video Note
The Fan class

9.2 (*The* Fan *class*) Design a class named Fan to represent a fan. The class contains:

- An int data field named speed that specifies the speed of the fan. A fan has three speeds indicated with a value 1, 2, or 3.
- A bool data field named on that specifies whether the fan is on.
- A double data field named radius that specifies the radius of the fan.
- A no-arg constructor that creates a default fan with speed 1, on false, and radius 10.
- The accessor and mutator functions for all the data fields.

Draw the UML diagram for the class. Implement the class. Write a test program that creates two Fan objects. Assign speed 3, radius 10, and turn it on to the first object. Assign speed 2, radius 5, and turn it off to the second object. Invoke their accessor functions to display the fan properties.

9.3 (*The* Account *class*) Design a class named Account that contains:

- An int data field named id for the account.
- A double data field named balance for the account.
- A double data field named annualInterestRate that stores the current interest rate.
- A no-arg constructor that creates a default account with id 0, balance 0, and annualInterestRate 0.
- The accessor and mutator functions for id, balance, and annualInterestRate.
- A function named getMonthlyInterestRate() that returns the monthly interest rate.

■ A function named `withdraw` that withdraws a specified amount from the account.
■ A function named `deposit` that deposits a specified amount to the account.

Draw the UML diagram for the class. Implement the class. Write a test program that creates an `Account` object with an account ID of `1122`, a balance of `20000`, and an annual interest rate of `4.5%`. Use the `withdraw` function to withdraw `$2500`, use the `deposit` function to deposit `$3000`, and print the balance, the monthly interest, and the date when this account was created.

9.4   (*The* `MyPoint` *class*) Design a class named `MyPoint` to represent a point with `x` and `y`-coordinates. The class contains:

■ Two data fields `x` and `y` that represent the coordinates.
■ A no-arg constructor that creates a point (`0`, `0`).
■ A constructor that constructs a point with specified coordinates.
■ Two *get* functions for data fields `x` and `y`, respectively.
■ A function named `distance` that returns the distance from this point to another point of the `MyPoint` type.

Draw the UML diagram for the class. Implement the class. Write a test program that creates two points (`0`, `0`) and (`10`, `30.5`) and displays the distance between them.

9.5*   (*The* `Time` *class*) Design a class named `Time`. The class contains:

■ Data fields `hour`, `minute`, and `second` that represent a time.
■ A no-arg constructor that creates a `Time` object for the current time. (The data field's value will represent the current time.)
■ A constructor that constructs a `Time` object with a specified elapse time since the middle of night, Jan 1, 1970, in seconds. (The data field's value will represent this time.)
■ Three *get* functions for the data fields `hour`, `minute`, and `second`.

Draw the UML diagram for the class. Implement the class. Write a test program that creates two `Time` objects (using `Time()` and `Time(555550)`) and display their hour, minute, and second.

(*Hint:* The current time can be obtained using `time(0)`, as shown in Listing 2.11, ShowCurrentTime.cpp. The other constructor sets the hour, minute, and second for the specified elapse time. For example, if the elapse time is `555550` seconds, the hour is `10`, the minute is `19`, and the second is `9.`)

9.6*   (*Algebra: quadratic equations*) Design a class named `QuadraticEquation` for a quadratic equation $ax^2 + bx + x = 0$. The class contains:

■ Data fields `a`, `b`, and `c` that represent three coefficients.
■ A constructor for the arguments for `a`, `b`, and `c`.
■ Three `get` functions for `a`, `b`, and `c`.
■ A function named `getDiscriminant()` that returns the discriminant, which is $b^2 - 4ac$.
■ The functions named `getRoot1()` and `getRoot2()` for returning two roots of the equation:

$$r_1 = \frac{-b + \sqrt{b^2 - 4ac}}{2a} \quad \text{and} \quad r_2 = \frac{-b - \sqrt{b^2 - 4ac}}{2a}$$

These functions are useful only if the discriminant is nonnegative. Let these functions return `0` if the discriminant is negative.

Draw the UML diagram for the class. Implement the class. Write a test program that prompts the user to enter values for a, b, and c, and displays the result based on the discriminant. If the discriminant is positive, display the two roots. If the discriminant is 0, display the one root. Otherwise, display "The equation has no real roots".

CHAPTER 10

CLASS DESIGN

Objectives

- To process strings using the `string` class (§10.2).
- To develop functions with object arguments (§§10.3–10.4).
- To store and process objects in arrays (§§10.5–10.6).
- To distinguish between instance and static variables and functions (§10.7).
- To define *constant functions* to prevent data fields from being modified accidentally (§10.8).
- To explore the differences between the procedural paradigm and object-oriented paradigm (§10.9).
- To design a class for body mass index (§10.9).
- To develop classes for modeling *composition* relationships (§10.10).
- To design a class for a stack (§10.11).
- To describe the software life cycle (§10.12).
- To design classes that follow the class-design guidelines (§10.13).

10.1 Introduction

The preceding chapter introduced the important concept of objects and classes. You learned how to define classes, create objects, and use objects. This book's approach is to teach problem solving and fundamental programming techniques before object-oriented programming. This chapter addresses the transition from procedural to object-oriented programming. Students will see the benefits of object-oriented programming and use it effectively.

Our focus here is on class design. We will use several examples to illustrate the advantages of the object-oriented approach. The first example is the **string** class provided in the C++ library. The other examples involve designing new classes and using them in applications. We will also introduce some language features supporting these examples.

10.2 The **string** Class

Video Note
string class

Strings are used often in programming; you have already used string literals. In C++ there are two ways to process strings. One way is to treat them as arrays of characters ending with the null terminator (`'\0'`), as discussed in §7.10. These are known as *C-strings*. The null terminator indicates the end of the string, which is important for the C-string functions to work. The other way is to process strings using the **string** class. You can use the C-string functions to manipulate and process strings, but the **string** class is easier. Processing C-strings requires the programmer to know how characters are stored in the array. The **string** class hides the low-level storage from the programmer. The programmer is freed from implementation details. Students will see the benefits of object-oriented programming and use it effectively.

10.2.1 Constructing a String

empty string

You can create an *empty string* using **string**'s no-arg constructor. You can create a string object from a string value or from an array of characters. For example,

```
string s1; // Creates an empty string using the no-arg constructor

string message("Welcome to C++"); // Creates a string from a
                                   // string literal
```

A string literal can be assigned to a string. For example,

```
s1 = "Welcome to C++";
```

This statement creates a string and copies it to `s1`.

10.2.2 Appending a String

You can use several overloaded functions to add new contents to a string, as shown in Figure 10.1.

string
+append(s: string): string
+append(s: string, index: int, n: int): string
+append(s: string, n: int): string
+append(n: int, ch: char): string

Appends string s into this string object.
Appends n number of characters in s starting at the position index to this string.
Appends the first n number of characters in s to this string.
Appends n copies of character ch to this string.

FIGURE 10.1 The **string** class provides the functions for appending a string.

For example:

```
string s1("Welcome");
s1.append(" to C++"); // Appends " to C++" to s1
cout << s1 << endl; // s1 now becomes Welcome to C++

string s2("Welcome");
s2.append(" to C and C++", 0, 5); // Appends " to C" to s2
cout << s2 << endl; // s2 now becomes Welcome to C

string s3("Welcome");
s3.append(" to C and C++", 5); // Appends " to C" to s3
cout << s3 << endl; // s3 now becomes Welcome to C

string s4("Welcome");
s4.append(4, 'G'); // Appends "GGGG" to s4
cout << s4 << endl; // s4 now becomes WelcomeGGGG
```

10.2.3   Assigning a String

You can use several overloaded functions to assign new contents to a string, as shown in
Figure 10.2.

string
+assign(s[]: char): string
+assign(s: string, index: int, n: int): string
+assign(s: string, n: int): string
+assign(n: int, ch: char): string

Assigns array of characters or a string s to this string.

Assigns n number of characters in s starting at the position
    index to this string.

Assigns the first n number of characters in s to this string.

Assigns n copies of character ch to this string.

FIGURE 10.2   The **string** class provides the functions for assigning a string.

For example:

```
string s1("Welcome");
s1.assign("Dallas"); // Assigns "Dallas" to s1
cout << s1 << endl; // s1 now becomes Dallas

string s2("Welcome");
s2.assign("Dallas, Texas", 0, 5); // Assigns "Dalla" to s2
cout << s2 << endl; // s2 now becomes Dalla

string s3("Welcome");
s3.assign("Dallas, Texas", 5); // Assigns "Dalla" to s3
cout << s3 << endl; // s3 now becomes Dalla

string s4("Welcome");
s4.assign(4, 'G'); // Assigns "GGGG" to s4
cout << s4 << endl; // s4 now becomes GGGG
```

10.2.4   Functions at, clear, erase, and empty

You can use the **at(index)** function to retrieve a character at a specified index, **clear()** to
clear the string, **erase(index, n)** to delete part of the string, and **empty()** to test whether
a string is empty, as shown in Figure 10.3.

string
+at(index: int): char
+clear(): void
+erase(index: int, n: int): string
+empty(): bool

Returns the character at the position index from this string.

Removes all characters in this string.

Removes n characters from this string starting at position index.

Returns true if this string is empty.

FIGURE 10.3 The `string` class provides the functions for retrieving a character, clearing and erasing a string, and checking whether a string is empty.

For example:

```
string s1("Welcome");
cout << s1.at(3) << endl; // s1.at(3) returns c
cout << s1.erase(2, 3) << endl; // s1 is now Weme
s1.clear(); // s1 is now empty
cout << s1.empty() << endl; // s1.empty returns 1 (means true)
```

10.2.5 Functions `length`, `size`, `capacity`, and `c_str()`

You can use the functions `length()`, `size()`, and `capacity()` to obtain a string's length, size, and capacity and `c_str()` to return a C-string, as shown in Figure 10.4. The functions `length()` and `size()` are aliases.

string
+length(): int
+size(): int
+capacity(): int
+c_str(): char[]
+data(): char[]

Returns the number of characters in this string.

Same as length().

Returns the size of the storage allocated for this string.

Returns a C-string for this string.

Same as c_str().

FIGURE 10.4 The `string` class provides the functions for getting the length and capacity of the string.

For example, see the following code:

create string

```
1 string s1("Welcome");
2 cout << s1.length() << endl; // Length is 7
3 cout << s1.size() << endl; // Size is 7
4 cout << s1.capacity() << endl; // Capacity is 7
5
```

erase two characters

```
6 s1.erase(1, 2);
7 cout << s1.length() << endl; // Length is now 5
8 cout << s1.size() << endl; // Size is now 5
9 cout << s1.capacity() << endl; // Capacity is still 7
```

Note

capacity?

The *capacity* is set to 7 when string s1 is created in line 1. After two characters are erased in line 6, the capacity is still 7, but the length and size become 5.

10.2.6   Comparing Strings

Often, in a program, you need to compare the contents of two strings. You can use the compare function. This function returns an `int` value greater than 0, 0, or less than 0 if this string is greater than, equal to, or less than the other string, as shown in Figure 10.5.

string
+compare(s: string): int
+compare(index: int, n: int, s: string): int

Returns a value greater than 0, 0, or less than 0 if this string is greater than, equal to, or less than s.

Compares this string with s(index, index+1, ..., index + n−1).

FIGURE 10.5   The `string` class provides the functions for comparing strings.

For example:

```
string s1("Welcome");
string s2("Welcomg");
cout << s1.compare(s2) << endl; // Returns -1
cout << s2.compare(s1) << endl; // Returns 1
cout << s1.compare("Welcome") << endl; // Returns 0
```

10.2.7   Obtaining Substrings

You can obtain a single character from a string using the `at` function. You can also obtain a substring from a string using the `substr` function, as shown in Figure 10.6.

string
+substr(index: int, n: int): string
+substr(index: int): string

Returns a substring of n characters from this string starting at position index.

Returns a substring of this string starting at position index.

FIGURE 10.6   The `string` class provides the functions for obtaining substrings.

For example:

```
string s1("Welcome");
cout << s1.substr(0, 1) << endl; // Returns W
cout << s1.substr(3) << endl; // Returns come
cout << s1.substr(3, 3) << endl; // Returns com
```

10.2.8   Searching in a String

You can use the `find` function to search for a substring or a character in a string, as shown in Figure 10.7. The function returns `string::npos` (not a position) if no match is found. **npos** is a constant defined in the `string` class.

For example:

```
string s1("Welcome to HTML");
cout << s1.find("co") << endl; // Returns 3
cout << s1.find('co', 6) << endl; // Returns string::npos
cout << s1.find('o') << endl; // Returns 4
cout << s1.find('o', 6) << endl; // Returns 9
```

string	
+find(ch: char): unsigned	Returns the position of the first matching character for ch.
+find(ch: char, index: int): unsigned	Returns the position of the first matching character for ch at or from the position index.
+find(s: string): unsigned	Returns the position of the first matching substring s.
+find(s: string, index: int): unsigned	Returns the position of the first matching substring s starting at or from the position index.

FIGURE 10.7 The string class provides the functions for finding substrings.

10.2.9 Inserting and Replacing Strings

You can use the **insert** and **replace** functions to insert a substring and replace a substring in a string, as shown in Figure 10.8.

String	
+insert(index: int, s: string): string	Inserts the string s into this string at position index.
+insert(index: int, n: int, ch: char): string	Inserts the character ch n times into this string at position index.
+replace(index: int, n: int, s: string): string	Replaces the n characters starting at position index in this string with the string s.

FIGURE 10.8 The string class provides the functions for inserting and replacing substrings.

Here are examples of using the **insert** and **replace** functions:

```
string s1("Welcome to HTML");
s1.insert(11, "C++ and ");
cout << s1 << endl; // s1 becomes Welcome to C++ and HTML

string s2("AA");
s2.insert(1, 4, 'B');
cout << s2 << endl; // s2 becomes to ABBBBA

string s3("Welcome to HTML");
s3.replace(11, 4, "C++");
cout << s3 << endl; // s3 becomes Welcome to C++
```

Note

return string

A string object invokes the append, assign, erase, replace, and insert functions to change the contents of the string object. These functions also return the new string. For example, in the following code, s1 invokes the insert function to insert "C++ and" into s1, and the new string is returned and assigned to s2.

```
string s1("Welcome to HTML");
string s2 = s1.insert(11, "C++ and ");
cout << s1 << endl; // s1 becomes Welcome to C++ and HTML
cout << s2 << endl; // s2 becomes Welcome to C++ and HTML
```

Note

capacity too small?

On most compilers, the capacity is automatically increased to accommodate more characters for the functions append, assign, insert, and replace. If the capacity is fixed and is too small, the function will copy as many characters as possible.

10.2.10   String Operators

C++ supports operators to simplify string operations. Table 10.1 lists the string operators.

TABLE 10.1   String Operators

Operator	Description
[]	Accesses characters using the array subscript operators.
=	Copies the contents of one string to the other.
+	Concatenates two strings into a new string.
+=	Appends the contents of one string to the other.
<<	Inserts a string to a stream
>>	Extracts characters from a stream to a string delimited by a whitespace or the null terminator character.
==, !=, <, <=, >, >=	Six relational operators for comparing strings.

Here are the examples to use these operators:

```
string s1 = "ABC"; // The = operator                             =
string s2 = s1;  // The = operator
for (int i = s2.size() - 1; i >= 0; i--)
  cout << s2[i]; // The [] operator                              []

string s3 = s1 + "DEFG"; // The + operator                       +
cout << s3 << endl; // s3 becomes ABCDEFG                        <<

s1 += "ABC";                                                     +=
cout << s1 << endl; // s1 becomes ABCABC

s1 = "ABC";
s2 = "ABE";
cout << (s1 == s2) << endl; // Displays 0 (means false)          ==
cout << (s1 != s2) << endl; // Displays 1 (means true)           !=
cout << (s1 > s2) << endl; // Displays 0 (means false)           >
cout << (s1 >= s2) << endl; // Displays 0 (means false)          >=
cout << (s1 < s2) << endl; // Displays 1 (means true)            <
cout << (s1 <= s2) << endl; // Displays 1 (means true)           <=
```

10.2.11   Reading Strings

You can read a string from the keyboard using the `cin` object. For example, see the following code:

```
1 string city;
2 cout << "Enter a city: ";
3 cin >> city; // Read to array city
4 cout << "You entered " << city << endl;
```

Line 3 reads a string to `city`. This approach to reading a string is simple, but there is a problem. The input ends with a whitespace character. If you want to enter New York, you have to use an alternative approach. C++ provides the `getline` function in the `iostream` header file, which reads a string from the keyboard using following syntax:

```
getline(cin, s, delimitCharacter)
```

The function stops reading characters when the delimiter character is encountered. The delimiter is read but not stored into the string. The third argument `delimitCharacter` has a default value (`'\n'`).

The following code uses the `getline` function to read a string.

declare string

read a string

```
1 string city;
2 cout << "Enter a city: ";
3 getline(cin, city, '\n'); // Same as getline(cin, city)
4 cout << "You entered " << city << endl;
```

Since the default value for the third argument in the `getline` function is `'\n'`, line 3 can be replaced by

```
getline(cin, city); // Read a string
```

10.2.12 Converting Numbers to Strings

§7.10.2, "C-string Functions," introduced how to convert a string to an integer and a floating-point number using the functions `atoi` and `atof`. Sometimes you need to convert a number to a string. You can write a function to perform the conversion. However, a simple approach is to use the `stringstream` class in the `<sstream>` header. `stringstream` provides an interface to manipulate strings as if they were input/output streams. One application of `stringstream` is for converting numbers to strings. Here is an example:

number to **stringstream**
stringstream to string

```
1 stringstream ss;
2 ss << 3.1415;
3 string s = ss.str();
```

10.3 Passing Objects to Functions

So far, you have learned how to pass arguments of primitive types and array types to functions. You can also pass objects to functions. You can pass objects by value or by reference. Listing 10.1 gives an example that passes an object by value.

LISTING 10.1 PassObjectByValue.cpp

include header file

object parameter

access circle

create circle
pass object

```
 1 #include <iostream>
 2 #include "Circle2.h" // Circle2.h is defined in Listing 9.8
 3 using namespace std;
 4
 5 void printCircle(Circle c)
 6 {
 7   cout << "The area of the circle of "
 8     << c.getRadius() << " is " << c.getArea() << endl;
 9 }
10
11 int main()
12 {
13   Circle myCircle(5.0);
14   printCircle(myCircle);
15
16   return 0;
17 }
```

```
The area of the circle of 5 is 78.5397
```

The Circle class defined Circle2.h from Listing 9.8 is included in line 2. The parameter for the printCircle function is defined as Circle (line 5). The main function creates a Circle object myCircle (line 13) and passes it to the printCircle function by value (line 14). To pass an object argument by value is to copy the object to the function parameter. So the object c in the printCircle function is independent of the object myCircle in the main function, as shown in Figure 10.9(a).

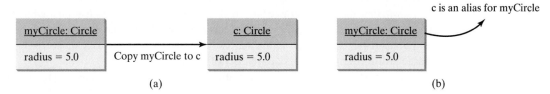

FIGURE 10.9 You can pass an object to a function (a) by value or (b) by reference.

Listing 10.2 gives an example that passes an object by reference.

LISTING 10.2 PassObjectByReference.cpp

```
 1 #include <iostream>
 2 #include "Circle2.h"                                          include header file
 3 using namespace std;
 4
 5 void printCircle(const Circle &c)                             reference parameter
 6 {
 7   cout << "The area of the circle of "
 8     << c.getRadius() << " is " << c.getArea() << endl;        access circle
 9 }
10
11 int main()
12 {
13   Circle myCircle(5.0);                                       create circle
14   printCircle(&myCircle);                                     pass reference
15
16   return 0;
17 }
```

```
The area of the circle of 5 is 78.5397
The area of the circle of 6 is 78.5397
```

A reference parameter of the Circle type is declared in the printCircle function (line 5). The main function creates a Circle object myCircle (line 13) and passes the reference of the object to the printCircle function (line 14). So the object c in the printCircle function is essentially an alias of the object myCircle in the main function, as shown in Figure 10.9(b).

Though you can pass an object to a function by value or by reference, passing by reference is preferred, because it takes time and additional memory space to pass by value. If the function does not change the object being passed, you should declare the parameter constant using the const keyword like this:

```
void printCircle(const Circle &c)
```

pass object by reference

constant parameter

defensive programming   Constant reference parameters are for *defensive programming*. If your function mistakenly changes the value of a constant parameter, a compile error will be reported.

10.4 Problem: Checking Palindromes

A string is a palindrome if it reads the same forward and backward. The words "mom," "dad," and "noon," for example, are all palindromes.

How do you write a program to check whether a string is a palindrome? One solution is to check whether the first character in the string is the same as the last character. If so, check whether the second character is the same as the second-last character. This process continues until a mismatch is found or all the characters in the string are checked, except for the middle character if the string has an odd number of characters.

To implement this idea, use two variables, say `low` and `high`, to denote the position of two characters at the beginning and the end in a string `s`, as shown in Listing 10.3 (lines 26, 29). Initially, `low` is `0` and `high` is `s.length() - 1`. If the two characters at these positions match, increment `low` by `1` and decrement `high` by `1` (lines 36–37). This process continues until (`low >= high`) or a mismatch is found.

LISTING 10.3   CheckPalindrome.cpp

```cpp
 1  #include <iostream>
 2  #include <string>
 3  using namespace std;
 4
 5  // Check whether a string is a palindrome
 6  bool isPalindrome(const string &s);
 7
 8  int main()
 9  {
10    // Prompt the user to enter a string
11    cout << "Enter a string: ";
12    string s;
13    getline(cin, s);
14
15    if (isPalindrome(s))
16      cout << s << " is a palindrome" << endl;
17    else
18      cout << s << " is not a palindrome" << endl;
19
20    return 0;
21  }
22
23  bool isPalindrome(const string &s)
24  {
25    // The index of the first character in the string
26    int low = 0;
27
28    // The index of the last character in the string
29    int high = s.length() - 1;
30
31    while (low < high)
32    {
33      if (s[low] != s[high])
34        return false; // Not a palindrome
35
36      low++;
```

include string header

function prototype

input string

check palindrome

low index

high index

update indices

```
37    high--;
38  }
39
40  return true; // The string is a palindrome
41 }
```

```
Enter a string: abccba  ↵Enter
abccba is a palindrome
Enter a string: abca  ↵Enter
abca is not a palindrome
```

The program declares a string (line 12), reads a string from the console (line 13), and invokes the isPalindrome function to check whether the string is a palindrome (line 15).

The isPalindrome function is defined in lines 23–41 to return a Boolean value. The string is passed by reference to invoke isPalindrome. The length of the string is determined by invoking s.length() in line 29.

10.5 Array of Objects

In Chapter 7, "Single-Dimensional Arrays," arrays of primitive type elements were created. You can also declare arrays of objects. For example, the following statement declares an array of ten Circle objects:

```
Circle circleArray[10]; // Declare array of ten Circle objects
```

The name of the array is circleArray, and the no-arg constructor is called to initialize each element in the array. So, circleArray[0].getRadius() returns 1, because the no-arg constructor assigns 1 to radius.

You can also use the array initializer to declare and initialize an array using a constructor with arguments. For example,

```
Circle circleArray[3] = {Circle(3), Circle(4), Circle(5)};
```

Listing 10.4 gives an example that demonstrates how to use an array of objects. The program summarizes the areas of an array of circles. It creates circleArray, an array composed of ten Circle objects; it then sets circle radii with radius 1, 2, 3, 4, ..., and 10 and displays the total area of the circles in the array.

LISTING 10.4 TotalArea.cpp

```
1 #include <iostream>
2 #include <iomanip>
3 #include "Circle2.h"                              include header file
4 using namespace std;
5
6 // Add circle areas
7 double sum(const Circle circleArray[], int size)   array of objects
8 {
9    // Initialize sum
10   double sum = 0;
11
12   // Add areas to sum
13   for (int i = 0; i < size; i++)
```

get area

```
14        sum += circleArray[i].getArea();
15
16    return sum;
17 }
18
19 // Print an array of circles and their total area
```

array of objects

```
20 void printCircleArray(const Circle circleArray[], int size)
21 {
22    cout << setw(35) << left << "Radius" << setw(8) << "Area" << endl;
23    for (int i = 0; i < size; i++)
24    {
25      cout << setw(35) << left << circleArray[i].getRadius()
26        << setw(8) <<  circleArray[i].getArea()  << endl;
27    }
28
29    cout << "-----------------------------------------------" << endl;
30
31    // Compute and display the result
32    cout << setw(35) << left << "The total area of circles is"
33        << setw(8) << sum(circleArray, size) << endl;
34 }
35
36 int main()
37 {
38    const int SIZE = 10;
39
40    // Create a Circle object with radius 1
```

create array

```
41    Circle circleArray[SIZE];
42
43    for (int i = 0; i < SIZE; i++)
44    {
```

new radius

```
45      circleArray[i].setRadius(i + 1);
46    }
47
```

pass array

```
48    printCircleArray(circleArray, SIZE);
49
50    return 0;
51 }
```

```
Radius                             Area
1                                  3.14159
2                                  12.5664
3                                  28.2743
4                                  50.2654
5                                  78.5397
6                                  113.097
7                                  153.938
8                                  201.062
9                                  254.469
10                                 314.159
-----------------------------------------------
The total area of circles is       1209.51
```

The program creates an array of ten Circle objects (line 41). Two Circle classes were introduced in this chapter. This example uses the Circle class defined in Listing 9.8.

Each object element in the array is created using the Circle's no-arg constructor. A new radius for each circle is set in lines 43–46. circleArray[i] refers to a Circle object in the array. `circleArray[i].setRadius(i + 1)` sets a new radius in the `Circle` object (line 45). The array is passed to the `printCircleArray` function, which displays the radii of the total area of the circles.

The sum of the areas of the circle is computed using the `sum` function (line 33), which takes the array of `Circle` objects as the argument and returns a `double` value for the total area.

10.6 Problem: Improving Deck-of-Cards Solution

§7.4 presented a program that picks four cards randomly from a deck of 52 cards. The program uses two functions `displayRank` and `displaySuit` to display a rank and a suit. These two functions can be replaced by defining the ranks and suits in two arrays of strings.

```
const string suits[] = {"Clubs", "Diamonds", "Hearts", "Spades"};
const string ranks[] = {"Ace", "2", "3", "4", "5", "6", "7", "8",
    "9", "10", "Jack", "Queen", "King"};
```

Listing 10.5 improves the program in §7.4.

LISTING 10.5 DeckOfCardsUsingArrayOfStrings.cpp

```cpp
 1 #include <iostream>
 2 #include <string>
 3 #include <ctime>
 4 using namespace std;
 5
 6 const int NUMBER_OF_CARDS = 52;                                    number of cards
 7
 8 // Shuffle the elements in an array
 9 void shuffle(int list[], int size)                                 shuffle an array
10 {
11   srand(time(0));
12   for (int i = 0; i < size; i++)
13   {
14     // Generate an index randomly
15     int index = rand() % NUMBER_OF_CARDS;
16     int temp = list[i];
17     list[i] = list[index];
18     list[index] = temp;
19   }
20 }
21
22 int main()
23 {
24   int deck[NUMBER_OF_CARDS];                                        create array deck
25   const string suits[] = {"Clubs", "Diamonds", "Hearts", "Spades"}; array of strings
26   const string ranks[] = {"Ace", "2", "3", "4", "5", "6", "7", "8", array of strings
27     "9", "10", "Jack", "Queen", "King"};
28
29   // Initialize cards
30   for (int i = 0; i < NUMBER_OF_CARDS; i++)                         initialize deck
31     deck[i] = i;
32
33   // Shuffle the cards
34   shuffle(deck, NUMBER_OF_CARDS);                                   shuffle deck
35
36   // Display the first four cards
37   for (int i = 0; i < 4; i++)
```

rank of a card
suit of a card

```
38   {
39     cout << ranks[deck[i] % 13] << " of "
40       << suits[deck[i] / 13] << endl;
41   }
42
43     return 0;
44 }
```

```
4 of Clubs
Ace of Diamonds
6 of Hearts
Jack of Clubs
```

The program defines an array `suits` for four suits (line 25) and an array `ranks` for 13 cards in a suits (lines 26–27). Each element in these arrays is a string. Consider the declaration for array `suits`:

```
const string suits[] = {"Clubs", "Diamonds", "Hearts", "Spades"};
```

The `suits[]` part in the declaration declares an array. The `string` part declares that each element in the array is a string. The four values to be placed in the array are `"Clubs"`, `"Diamonds"`, `"Hearts"`, and `"Spades"`. This is a constant array.

The `deck` is initialized with values `0` to `51` in lines 30–31. A deck value `0` represents card Ace of Clubs, `1` represents card 2 of Clubs, `13` represents card Ace of Diamonds, `14` represents card 2 of Diamonds.

The program invokes the `shuffle` function (line 34) to randomly shuffle the deck. After a deck is shuffled, `deck[i]` contains an arbitrary value. `deck[i] / 13` is 0, 1, 2, or 3, which determines a suit (line 40). `deck[i] % 13` is a value between 0 and 12, which determines a rank (line 39).

Video Note
static vs. instance

instance variable

10.7 Instance and Static Members

The data fields used in the classes so far are known as *instance data fields, or instance variables*. An instance variable is tied to a specific instance of the class; it is not shared among objects of the same class. For example, suppose that you create the following objects using the `Circle` class in Listing 9.8, Circle2.h:

```
Circle circle1;
Circle circle2(5);
```

The `radius` in `circle1` is independent of the `radius` in `circle2` and is stored in a different memory location. Changes made to `circle1`'s `radius` do not affect `circle2`'s `radius`, and vice versa.

static variable

If you want all the instances of a class to share data, use *static variables*, also known as *class variables*. Static variables store values for the variables in a common memory location. Accordingly, all objects of the same class are affected if one object changes the value of a static variable. C++ supports static functions as well as static variables. *Static functions* can be called without creating an instance of the class.

static function

Let us modify the `Circle` class by adding a static variable `numberOfObjects` to count the number of circle objects created. When the first object of this class is created, `numberOfObjects` is 1. When the second object is created, `numberOfObjects` becomes 2. The UML of the new circle class is shown in Figure 10.10. The `Circle` class defines the instance variable `radius` and the static variable `numberOfObjects`, the instance functions `getRadius`, `setRadius`, and `getArea`, and the static function `getNumberOfObjects`. (Note that static variables and functions are underlined in the UML diagram.)

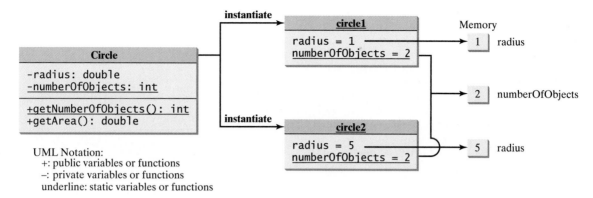

FIGURE 10.10 The instance variables, which belong to the instances, have memory storage independent of one another. The static variables are shared by all the instances of the same class.

To declare a static variable or a static function, put the modifier `static` in the variable or function declaration. So the static variable `numberOfObjects` and the static function `getNumberOfObjects()` can be declared as follows:

```
static int numberOfObjects;
```
declare static variable

```
static int getNumberOfObjects();
```
define static function

The new circle class is defined in Listing 10.6:

LISTING 10.6 Circle3.h

```
1 #ifndef CIRCLE_H
2 #define CIRCLE_H
3
4 class Circle
5 {
6 public:
7   Circle();
8   Circle(double);
9   double getArea();
10  double getRadius();
11  void setRadius(double);
12  static int getNumberOfObjects();
13
14 private:
15  double radius;
16  static int numberOfObjects;
17 };
18
19 #endif
```
static function

static variable

A static function `getNumberOfObjects` is defined in line 12 and a static variable `numberOfObjects` is declared in line 16 as a private data field in the class.

Listing 10.7 gives the implementation of the `Circle` class:

LISTING 10.7 Circle3.cpp

```
1 #include "Circle3.h"
2
3 int Circle::numberOfObjects = 0;
4
```
include header

initialize static variable

```
 5 // Construct a circle object
 6 Circle::Circle()
 7 {
 8    radius = 1;
 9    numberOfObjects++;
10 }
11
12 // Construct a circle object
13 Circle::Circle(double newRadius)
14 {
15    radius = newRadius;
16    numberOfObjects++;
17 }
18
19 // Return the area of this circle
20 double Circle::getArea()
21 {
22    return radius * radius * 3.14159;
23 }
24
25 // Return the radius of this circle
26 double Circle::getRadius()
27 {
28    return radius;
29 }
30
31 // Set a new radius
32 void Circle::setRadius(double newRadius)
33 {
34    radius = (newRadius >= 0) ? newRadius : 0;
35 }
36
37 // Return the number of circle objects
38 int Circle::getNumberOfObjects()
39 {
40    return numberOfObjects;
41 }
```

increment
 numberOfObjects

increment
 numberOfObjects

return **numberOfObjects**

The *static data field* **numberOfObjects** is initialized in line 3. When a **Circle** object is created, **numberOfObjects** is incremented (lines 9, 16).

Instance functions (e.g., **getArea()**) and instance data fields (e.g., **radius**) belong to instances and can be used only after the instances are created. They are accessed from a specific instance. Static functions (e.g., **getNumberOfObjects()**) and static data fields (e.g., **numberOfObjects**) can be accessed from any instance of the class, as well as from their class name.

The program in Listing 10.8 demonstrates how to use instance and static variables and functions and illustrates the effects of using them.

LISTING 10.8 TestCircle3.cpp

include header

```
1 #include <iostream>
2 #include "Circle3.h"
3 using namespace std;
4
5 int main()
6 {
7   cout << "Number of circle objects created: "
8     << Circle::getNumberOfObjects() << endl;
9
```

```
10      Circle circle1;
11      cout << "The area of the circle of radius "
12          << circle1.getRadius() << " is " << circle1.getArea() << endl;    invoke instance function
13      cout << "Number of circle objects created: "
14          << Circle::getNumberOfObjects() << endl;                         invoke static function
15
16      Circle circle2(5.0);
17      cout << "The area of the circle of radius "
18          << circle2.getRadius() << " is " << circle2.getArea() << endl;
19      cout << "Number of circle objects created: "
20          << Circle::getNumberOfObjects() << endl;                         invoke static function
21
22      circle1.setRadius(3.3);                                              modify radius
23      cout << "The area of the circle of radius "
24          << circle1.getRadius() << " is " << circle1.getArea() << endl;
25
26      cout << "circle1.getNumberOfObjects() returns "
27          << circle1.getNumberOfObjects() << endl;                         invoke static function
28      cout << "circle2.getNumberOfObjects() returns "
29          << circle2.getNumberOfObjects() << endl;                         invoke static function
30
31      return 0;
32  }
```

```
Number of circle objects created: 0
The area of the circle of radius 1 is 3.14159
Number of circle objects created: 1
The area of the circle of radius 5 is 78.5397
Number of circle objects created: 2
The area of the circle of radius 3.3 is 34.2119
circle1.getNumberOfObjects() returns 2
circle2.getNumberOfObjects() returns 2
```

The `main` function creates two circles, `circle1` and `circle2` (lines 10, 16). The instance variable `radius` in `circle1` is modified to become `3.3` (line 22). This change does not affect the instance variable `radius` in `circle2`, since these two instance variables are independent. The static variable `numberOfObjects` becomes `1` after `circle1` is created (line 10), and it becomes `2` after `circle2` is created (line 16).

You can access static data fields and functions from the instances of the class—e.g., `circle1.getNumberOfObjects()` in line 27 and `circle2.getNumberOfObjects()` in line 29. But it is better to access them from the class name—e.g., `Circle::`. Note that in lines 27 and 29 `circle1.getNumberOfObjects()` and `circle2.getNumberOfObjects()` could be replaced by `Circle::getNumberOfObjects()`. This improves readability, because the reader can easily recognize the static function `getNumberOfObjects()`.

Tip
Use `ClassName::functionName(arguments)` to invoke a static function and `ClassName::staticVariable` to access a static variable. This improves readability, because the user can easily recognize the static function and data in the class.

use class name

Tip
How do you decide whether a variable or function should be instance or static? A variable or function that is dependent on a specific instance of the class should be an instance variable or function. A variable or function that is not dependent on a specific instance of the class should be a static variable or function. For example, every circle has its own radius. Radius is dependent

instance or static?

on a specific circle. Therefore, `radius` is an instance variable of the `Circle` class. Since the `getArea` function is dependent on a specific circle, it is an *instance function*. Since `numberOfObjects` is not dependent on any specific instance, it should be declared static.

10.8 Constant Member Functions

You can use the `const` keyword to specify a constant parameter to tell the compiler that the parameter should not be changed in the function. C++ also enables you to specify a constant member function to tell the compiler that the function should not change the value of any data fields in the object. To do so, place the `const` keyword at the end of the function header. For example, you may redefine the `Circle` class in Listing 10.6 as shown in Listing 10.9, and the header file is implemented in Listing 10.10.

LISTING 10.9 `Circle4.h`

const function
const function

```
1 #ifndef CIRCLE_H
2 #define CIRCLE_H
3
4 class Circle
5 {
6 public:
7   Circle();
8   Circle(double);
9   double getArea() const ;
10  double getRadius() const ;
11  void setRadius(double);
12  static int getNumberOfObjects();
13
14 private:
15  double radius;
16  static int numberOfObjects;
17 };
18
19 #endif
```

LISTING 10.10 `Circle4.cpp`

```
1 #include "Circle4.h"
2
3 int Circle::numberOfObjects = 0;
4
5 // Construct a circle object
6 Circle::Circle()
7 {
8   radius = 1;
9   numberOfObjects++;
10 }
11
12 // Construct a circle object
13 Circle::Circle(double newRadius)
14 {
15   radius = newRadius;
16   numberOfObjects++;
17 }
18
19 // Return the area of this circle
```

const function

```
20 double Circle::getArea() const
```

```
21 {
22   return radius * radius * 3.14159;
23 }
24
25 // Return the radius of this circle
26 double Circle::getRadius() const
27 {
28   return radius;
29 }
30
31 // Set a new radius
32 void Circle::setRadius(double newRadius)
33 {
34   radius = (newRadius >= 0) ? newRadius : 0;
35 }
36
37 // Return the number of circle objects
38 int Circle::getNumberOfObjects()
39 {
40   return numberOfObjects;
41 }
```

const function

Like constant parameters, constant functions are for *defensive programming*. If your function mistakenly changes the value of data fields in a function, a compile error will be reported. Note that you can define only instant functions constant, not static functions.

defensive programming

Tip
You can use the `const` modifier to specify a constant reference parameter or a constant member function. You should use the `const` modifier *consistently* whenever appropriate.

use **const** consistently

10.9 Object-Oriented Thinking

This book has introduced fundamental programming techniques for problem solving using loops, functions, and arrays. The study of these techniques lays a solid foundation for object-oriented programming. Classes provide more flexibility and modularity for building reusable software. This section uses the object-oriented approach to improve the solution for a problem introduced in Chapter 3. Observing the improvements, you will gain insight on the differences between the procedural programming and object-oriented programming and see the benefits of developing reusable code using objects and classes.

Video Note
object-oriented thinking

Listing 3.3, ComputeBMI.cpp, presented a program for computing body mass index. The program cannot be reused in other programs. To make the code reusable, define a function to compute body mass index as follows:

```
double getBMI(double weight, double height)
```

This function is useful for computing body mass index for a specified weight and height. However, it has limitations. Suppose you need to associate the weight and height with a person's name and birth date. You may declare separate variables to store these values. But these values are not tightly coupled. The ideal way to couple them is to create an object that contains them. Since these values are tied to individual objects, they should be stored in instance data fields. You can define a class named BMI, as shown in Figure 10.11.

The BMI class can be defined as in Listing 10.11.

The get functions for these data fields are provided in the class, but omitted in the UML diagram for brevity.

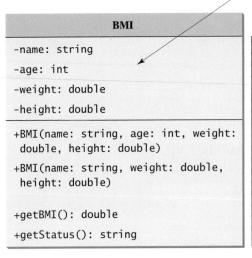

BMI
-name: string
-age: int
-weight: double
-height: double
+BMI(name: string, age: int, weight: double, height: double)
+BMI(name: string, weight: double, height: double)
+getBMI(): double
+getStatus(): string

The name of the person.

The age of the person.

The weight of the person in pounds.

The height of the person in inches.

Creates a BMI object with the specified name, age, weight, and height.

Creates a BMI object with the specified name, weight, height, and a default age 20.

Returns the BMI.

Returns the BMI status (e.g., normal, overweight, etc.)

FIGURE 10.11   The BMI class encapsulates BMI information.

LISTING 10.11   BMI.h

constructors

functions

```
1 #ifndef BMI_H
2 #define BMI_H
3
4 #include <string>
5 using namespace std;
6
7 class BMI
8 {
9 public:
10    BMI(const string &newName, int newAge,
11      double newWeight, double newHeight);
12    BMI(const string &newName, double newWeight, double newHeight);
13    double getBMI() const;
14    string getStatus() const;
15    string getName() const;
16    int getAge() const;
17    double getWeight() const;
18    double getHeight() const;
19
20 private:
21    string name;
22    int age;
23    double weight;
24    double height;
25 };
26
27 #endif
```

Tip

The **string** parameter **newName** is defined as passed-by-reference using the syntax **&newName**. This improves performance by preventing the compiler from making a copy of the object being passed into the function. Further, the reference is defined **const** to prevent newName from being modified accidentally. *You should always pass an object parameter by reference. If the object does not change in the function, define it as a const reference parameter.*

const reference parameter

 Tip

If a member function does not change data fields, define it as a const function. All member functions in the BMI class are const functions.

const function

Assume that the BMI class has been implemented. Listing 10.12 is a test program that uses this class.

LISTING 10.12 UseBMIClass.cpp

```
1  #include <iostream>
2  #include "BMI.h"
3  using namespace std;
4
5  int main()
6  {
7    BMI bmi1("John Doe", 18, 145, 70);
8    cout << "The BMI for " << bmi1.getName() << " is "
9      << bmi1.getBMI() << " " << bmi1.getStatus() << endl;
10
11   BMI bmi2("Peter King", 215, 70);
12   cout << "The BMI for " << bmi2.getName() << " is "
13     << bmi2.getBMI() << " " + bmi2.getStatus();
14
15   return 0;
16 }
```

create object
invoke instance function

create object
invoke instance function

```
The BMI for John Doe is 20.8051 normal weight
The BMI for Peter King is 30.849 seriously overweight
```

Line 7 creates an object bmi1 for John Doe and line 11 creates an object bmi2 for Peter King. You can use the instance functions getName(), getBMI(), and getStatus() to return the BMI information in a BMI object.

The BMI class can be implemented as in Listing 10.13.

LISTING 10.13 BMI.cpp

```
1  #include <iostream>
2  #include "BMI.h"
3  using namespace std;
4
5  BMI::BMI(const string &newName, int newAge,
6    double newWeight, double newHeight)
7  {
8    name = newName;
9    age = newAge;
10   weight = newWeight;
11   height = newHeight;
12 }
13
14 BMI::BMI(const string &newName, double newWeight, double newHeight)
15 {
16   name = newName;
17   age = 20;
18   weight = newWeight;
```

constructor

constructor

```
19    height = height;
20  }
21
22  double BMI::getBMI() const
23  {
24    const double KILOGRAMS_PER_POUND = 0.45359237;
25    const double METERS_PER_INCH = 0.0254;
26    double bmi = weight * KILOGRAMS_PER_POUND /
27      ((height * METERS_PER_INCH) * (height * METERS_PER_INCH));
28    return bmi;
29  }
30
31  string BMI::getStatus() const
32  {
33    double bmi = getBMI();
34    if (bmi < 16)
35      return "seriously underweight";
36    else if (bmi < 18)
37      return "underweight";
38    else if (bmi < 24)
39      return "normal weight";
40    else if (bmi < 29)
41      return "overweight";
42    else if (bmi < 35)
43      return "seriously overweight";
44    else
45      return "gravely overweight";
46  }
47
48  string BMI::getName() const
49  {
50    return name;
51  }
52
53  int BMI::getAge() const
54  {
55    return age;
56  }
57
58  double BMI::getWeight() const
59  {
60    return weight;
61  }
62
63  double BMI::getHeight() const
64  {
65    return height;
66  }
```

The mathematic formula for computing the BMI using weight and height is given in §3.8. The instance function getBMI() returns the BMI. Since the weight and height are instance data fields in the object, the getBMI() function can use these properties to compute the BMI for the object.

The instance function getStatus() returns a string that interprets the BMI. The interpretation is also given in §3.8.

This example demonstrates the advantages of using the object-oriented over the procedural paradigm. The procedural paradigm focuses on designing functions. The object-oriented paradigm couples data and functions together into objects. Software design using the object-oriented paradigm focuses on objects and operations on objects. The object-oriented approach

Procedural vs. Object-
Oriented Paradigms

combines the power of the procedural paradigm with an added dimension that integrates data with operations into objects.

In procedural programming, data and operations on the data are separate, and this methodology requires sending data to functions. Object-oriented programming places data and the operations that pertain to them within a single entity called an *object*; this approach solves many of the problems inherent in procedural programming. The object-oriented programming approach organizes programs in a way that mirrors the real world, in which all objects are associated with both attributes and activities. Using objects improves software reusability and makes programs easier to develop and easier to maintain.

10.10 Object Composition

An object can contain another object. The relationship between the two is called *composition*. In Listing 10.11, you defined the `BMI` class to contain a `string` data field. The relationship between `BMI` and `string` is composition.

Composition is actually a special case of the *aggregation* relationship. Aggregation models *has-a relationships* and represents an ownership relationship between two objects. The owner object is called an *aggregating object* and its class an *aggregating class*. The subject object is called an *aggregated object* and its class an *aggregated class*.

An object may be owned by several other aggregating objects. If an object is exclusively owned by an aggregating object, the relationship between the object and its aggregating object is referred to as *composition*. For example, "a student has a name" is a composition relationship between the `Student` class and the `Name` class, whereas "a student has an address" is an aggregation relationship between the `Student` class and the `Address` class, since an address may be shared by several students. In UML, a filled diamond is attached to an aggregating class (e.g., `Student`) to denote the composition relationship with an aggregated class (e.g., `Name`), and an empty diamond is attached to an aggregating class (e.g., `Student`) to denote the aggregation relationship with an aggregated class (e.g., `Address`), as shown in Figure 10.12.

composition

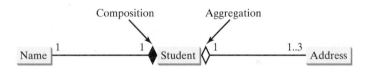

FIGURE 10.12   A student has a name and an address.

Each class involved in a relationship may specify a *multiplicity*. A multiplicity could be a number or an interval that specifies how many objects of the class are involved in the relationship. The character * means an unlimited number of objects, and the interval m..n means that the number of objects should be between m and n, inclusive. In Figure 10.12, each student has only one address, and each address may be shared by up to 3 students. Each student has one name, and a name is unique for each student.

multiplicity

An aggregation relationship is usually represented as a data field in the aggregating class. For example, the relationship in Figure 10.12 can be represented as follows:

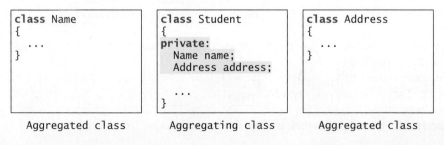

Aggregation may exist between objects of the same class. For example, a person may have a supervisor. This is illustrated in Figure 10.13.

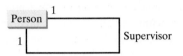

FIGURE 10.13 A person may have a supervisor.

In the relationship "a person has a supervisor," as shown in Figure 10.13, a supervisor can be represented as a data field in the **Person** class, as follows:

```
class Person
{
private:
  Person supervisor;   // The type for the data is the class itself

  ...
}
```

If a person may have several supervisors, as shown in Figure 10.14, you may use an array to store supervisors (for example, 10 supervisors).

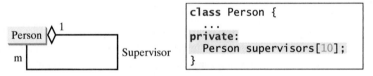

FIGURE 10.14 A person may have several supervisors.

 aggregation or composition

Note

Since aggregation and composition relationships are represented using classes in similar ways, many texts don't differentiate them and call both compositions.

10.11 Problem: The **StackOfIntegers** Class

Recall that a stack is a data structure that holds data in a last-in, first-out fashion, as shown in Figure 10.15.

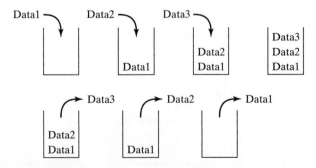

FIGURE 10.15 A stack holds data in a last-in, first-out fashion.

Stacks have many applications. For example, the compiler uses a stack to process function invocations. When a function is invoked, its parameters and local variables are pushed into a stack. When a function calls another function, the new function's parameters and local variables are pushed into the stack. When a function finishes its work and returns to its caller, its associated space is released from the stack.

stack

You can define a class to model stacks. For simplicity, assume the stack holds the `int` values. So, name the stack class `StackOfIntegers`. The UML diagram for the class is shown in Figure 10.16.

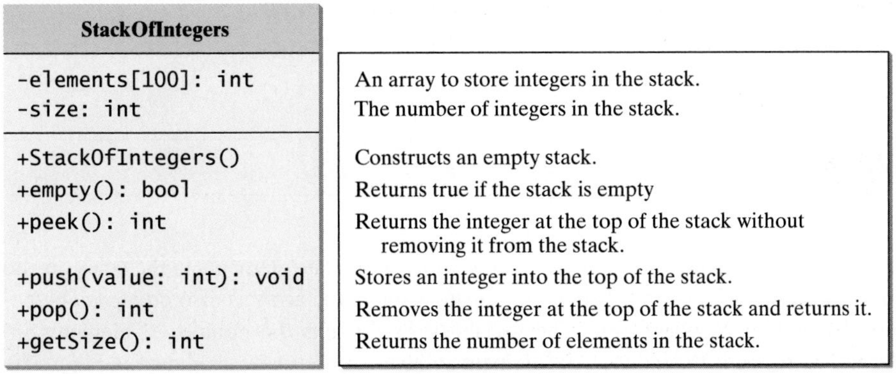

StackOfIntegers	
-elements[100]: int -size: int	An array to store integers in the stack. The number of integers in the stack.
+StackOfIntegers() +empty(): bool +peek(): int +push(value: int): void +pop(): int +getSize(): int	Constructs an empty stack. Returns true if the stack is empty Returns the integer at the top of the stack without removing it from the stack. Stores an integer into the top of the stack. Removes the integer at the top of the stack and returns it. Returns the number of elements in the stack.

FIGURE 10.16   The `StackOfIntegers` class encapsulates the stack storage and provides the operations for manipulating the stack.

Suppose that the class is available, as defined in Listing 10.14. Let us write a test program in Listing 10.15 that uses the class to create a stack (line 7), stores ten integers 0, 1, 2, ..., and 9 (lines 9–10), and displays them in reverse order (lines 12–13).

LISTING 10.14 StackOfIntegers.h

```
1 #ifndef STACK_H
2 #define STACK_H
3
4 class StackOfIntegers
5 {
6 public:                                              public members
7   StackOfIntegers();
8   bool isEmpty() const;
9   int peek() const;
10   void push(int value);
11   int pop();
12   int getSize() const;
13
14 private:                                             private members
15   int elements[100];                                 element array
16   int size;
17 };
18
19 #endif
```

LISTING 10.15 TestStackOfIntegers.cpp

```
1 #include <iostream>
2 #include "StackOfIntegers.h"                          StackOfIntegers header
```

```
 3 using namespace std;
 4
 5 int main()
 6 {
 7    StackOfIntegers stack;
 8
 9    for (int i = 0; i < 10; i++)
10      stack.push(i);
11
12    while (!stack.isEmpty())
13      cout << stack.pop() << " ";
14
15    return 0;
16 }
```

create a stack

push to stack

stack empty?
pop from stack

```
9 8 7 6 5 4 3 2 1 0
```

How do you implement the **StackOfIntegers** class? The elements in the stack are stored in an array named **elements**. When you create a stack, the array is also created. The no-arg constructor initializes **size** to **0**. The variable **size** counts the number of elements in the stack, and **size – 1** is the index of the element at the top of the stack, as shown in Figure 10.17. For an empty stack, **size** is **0**.

The **StackOfIntegers** class is implemented in Listing 10.16.

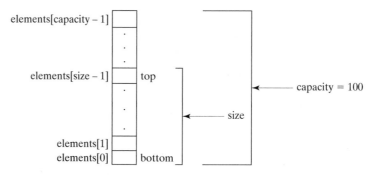

FIGURE 10.17 The StackOfIntegers class encapsulates the stack storage and provides the operations for manipulating the stack.

LISTING 10.16 StackOfIntegers.cpp

StackOfIntegers header

constructor

initialize **size**

```
 1 #include "StackOfIntegers.h"
 2
 3 StackOfIntegers::StackOfIntegers()
 4 {
 5    size = 0;
 6 }
 7
 8 bool StackOfIntegers::isEmpty() const
 9 {
10    return (size == 0);
11 }
12
13 int StackOfIntegers::peek() const
```

```
14 {
15   return elements[size - 1];
16 }
17
18 void StackOfIntegers::push(int value)
19 {
20   elements[size++] = value;
21 }
22
23 int StackOfIntegers::pop()
24 {
25   return elements[--size];
26 }
27
28 int StackOfIntegers::getSize() const
29 {
30   return size;
31 }
```

10.12 Software Life Cycle

Developing a software project is an engineering process. Software products, no matter how large or how small, have the same life cycle: requirements specification, analysis, design, implementation, testing, deployment, and maintenance, as shown in Figure 10.18.

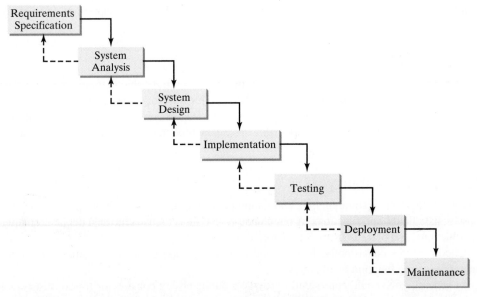

FIGURE 10.18 Developing a project involves requirements specification, system analysis, system design, implementation, testing, deployment, and maintenance.

Requirements specification is a formal process that seeks to understand the problem and to document in detail what the software system needs to do. This phase involves close interaction between users and developers. Most of the examples in this book are simple, and their requirements are clearly stated. In the real world, however, problems are not well defined. You need to work closely with your customer and study the problem carefully to identify its requirements.

System analysis seeks to analyze the business process in terms of data flow, and to identify the system's input and output. Part of the analysis entails modeling the system's behavior. The

requirements specification

system analysis

model is intended to capture the essential elements of the system and to define services to the system.

system design

System design is the process of designing the system's components. This phase involves the use of many levels of abstraction to decompose the problem into manageable components, identify classes and interfaces, and establish relationships among the classes and interfaces.

implementation

Implementation is translating the system design into programs. Separate programs are written for each component and put to work together. This phase requires the use of a programming language such as C++. The implementation involves coding, testing, and debugging.

testing

Testing ensures that the code meets the requirements specification and weeds out bugs. An independent team of software engineers not involved in the design and implementation of the project usually conducts such testing.

deployment
maintenance

Deployment makes the project available for use. *Maintenance* is concerned with changing and improving the product. A software product must continue to perform and improve in a changing environment. This requires periodic upgrades of the product to fix newly discovered bugs and incorporate changes.

This chapter is concerned mainly with object-oriented design. While there are many object-oriented methodologies, UML has become the industry-standard notation for object-oriented modeling, and itself leads to a methodology. The process of designing classes calls for identifying the classes and discovering the relationships among them.

10.13 Class Design Guidelines

You have learned how to design classes from the examples from this chapter and from many other examples in the preceding chapters. Here are some guidelines.

10.13.1 Cohesion

coherent purpose

A class should describe a single entity, and all the class operations should logically fit together to support a coherent purpose. You can use a class for students, for example, but you should not combine students and staff in the same class, because students and staff are different entities.

separating responsibilities

A single entity with too many responsibilities can be broken into several classes to separate responsibilities.

10.13.2 Consistency

naming conventions

Follow standard programming style and naming conventions. Choose informative names for classes, data fields, and functions. A popular style in C++ is to place the data declaration after the functions, and place constructors before functions.

naming consistency

Choose names consistently. It is a good practice to choose the same names for similar operations using function overloading.

no-arg constructor

In general, you should consistently provide a public no-arg constructor for constructing a default instance. If a class does not support a no-arg constructor, document the reason. If no constructors are defined explicitly, a public default no-arg constructor with an empty body is assumed.

10.13.3 Encapsulation

encapsulating data fields

A class should use the `private` modifier to hide its data from direct access by clients. This makes the class easy to maintain.

Provide a `get` function only if you want the field to be readable, and provide a `set` function only if you want the field to be updateable. A class should also hide functions not intended for client use. Such functions should be defined as private.

10.13.4   Clarity

Cohesion, consistency, and encapsulation are good guidelines for achieving design clarity. Additionally, a class should have a clear contract that is easy to explain and easy to understand.

easy to explain

Users can incorporate classes in many different combinations, orders, and environments. Therefore, you should design a class that imposes no restrictions on what the user can do with it or when, design the properties in a way that lets the user set them in any order and with any combination of values, and design functions independently of their order of occurrence. For example, the `Loan` class in Listing 9.12 contains the functions `setLoanAmount`, `setNum-berOfYears`, and `setAnnualInterestRate`. The values of these properties can be set in any order.

independent functions

You should not declare a data field that can be derived from other data fields. For example, the following `Person` class has two data fields: `birthDate` and `age`. Since `age` can be derived from `birthDate`, `age` should not be declared as a data field.

independent properties

```
class Person {
public:
  ...

private:
  Date birthDate;
  int age;
}
```

10.13.5   Completeness

Classes are designed for use by many different customers. In order to be useful in a wide range of applications, a class should provide a variety of ways for customization through properties and functions. For example, the `string` class contains more than 20 functions that are useful for a variety of applications.

10.13.6   Instance vs. Static

A variable or function that is dependent on a specific instance of the class should be an instance variable or function. A variable that is shared by all the instances of a class should be declared static. For example, the variable `numberOfObjects` in `Circle` in Listing 10.9 is shared by all the objects of the `Circle` class and therefore is declared static. A function that is not dependent on a specific instance should be defined as a static function. For instance, the `getNumberOfObjects` function in `Circle` is not tied to any specific instance, and therefore is defined as a static function.

Always reference static variables and functions from a class name (rather than an object) to improve readability and avoid errors.

A constructor is always instance, because it is used to create a specific instance. A static variable or function can be invoked from an instance function, but an instance variable or function cannot be invoked from a static function.

KEY TERMS

aggregation   331
composition   331
constant function   331
has-a relationship   331
instance data field   322
instance function   322
static data field   322
static function   322
software life cycle   335

CHAPTER SUMMARY

1. The C++ `string` class encapsulates an array of characters and provides many functions for processing strings such as `append`, `assign`, `at`, `clear`, `erase`, `empty`, `length`, `c_str`, `compare`, `substr`, `find`, `insert`, and `replace`.

2. C++ supports operators (`[]`, `=`, `+`, `+=`, `<<`, `>>`, `==`, `!=`, `<`, `<=`, `>`, `>=`) to simplify string operations.

3. You can use `cin` to read a string and use `getline(cin, s, delimiterCharacter)` to read a string ending with the specified delimiter character.

4. You can pass an object to a function by value or by reference. For performance, passing by reference is preferred.

5. If the function does not change the object being passed, declare the object parameter as a constant reference parameter to prevent the object's data being modified accidentally.

6. An instance variable or function belongs to an instance of a class. Its use is associated with individual instances.

7. A static variable is a variable shared by all instances of the same class.

8. A static function is a function that can be invoked without using instances.

9. Every instance of a class can access the class's static variables and functions. For clarity, however, it is better to invoke static variables and functions using `ClassName::staticVariable` and `ClassName::functionName(arguments)`.

10. If a function does not change the data fields of an object, define the function constant to prevent errors.

11. A constant function does not change the values of any data fields.

12. You can specify a member function to be constant by placing the `const` modifier at the end of the function declaration.

13. The object-oriented approach combines the power of the procedural paradigm with an added dimension that integrates data with operations into objects.

14. The procedural paradigm focuses on designing functions. The object-oriented paradigm couples data and functions together into objects.

15. Software design using the object-oriented paradigm focuses on objects and operations on objects.

16. An object can contain another object. The relationship between the two is called *composition*.

17. *Software life cycle* involves requirements specification, system analysis, system design, implementation, testing, deployment, *and* maintenance.

18. Some guidelines for class design are *cohesion*, *consistency*, *encapsulation*, *clarity*, and *completeness*.

REVIEW QUESTIONS

Section 10.2

10.1 To create a string `"Welcome to C++"`, you may use a statement like this:

```
string s1("Welcome to C++");
```

or this:

```
string s1 = "Welcome to C++";
```

Which one is better? Why?

10.2 Suppose that `s1` and `s2` are two strings, given as follows:

```
string s1("I have a dream");
string s2("Computer Programming");
```

Assume that each expression is independent. What are the results of the following expressions?

(1) `s1.append(s2)`
(2) `s1.append(s2, 9, 7)`
(3) `s1.append("NEW", 3)`
(4) `s1.append(3, 'N')`
(5) `s1.assign(3, 'N')`
(6) `s1.assign(s2, 9, 7)`
(7) `s1.assign("NEWNEW", 3)`
(8) `s1.assign(3, 'N')`
(9) `s1.at(0)`
(10) `s1.length()`
(11) `s1.size()`
(12) `s1.capacity()`
(13) `s1.erase(1, 2)`
(14) `s1.compare(s3)`
(15) `s1.compare(0, 10, s3)`
(16) `s1.data()`
(17) `s1.substr(4, 8)`
(18) `s1.substr(4)`
(19) `s1.find('A')`
(20) `s1.find('a', 9)`
(21) `s1.replace(2, 4, "NEW")`
(22) `s1.insert(4, "NEW")`
(23) `s1.insert(6, 8, 'N')`
(24) `s1.empty()`

10.3 Suppose that `s1` and `s2` are given as follows:

```
string s1("I have a dream");
string s2("Computer Programming");
char s3[] = "ABCDEFGHIJKLMN";
```

Assume that each expression is independent. What are the results of `s1`, `s2`, and `s3` after each of the following statements?

(1) `s1.clear()`
(2) `s1.copy(s3, 5, 2)`
(3) `s1.compare(s2)`

10.4 Suppose that `s1` and `s2` are given as follows:

```
string s1("I have a dream");
string s2("Computer Programming");
```

Assume that each expression is independent. What are the results of the following expressions?

(1) `s1[0]`
(2) `s1 = s2`
(3) `s1 = "C++ " + s2`
(4) `s2 += "C++ "`
(5) `s1 > s2`
(6) `s1 >= s2`
(7) `s1 < s2`
(8) `s1 <= s2`
(9) `s1 == s2`
(10) `s1 != s2`

10.5 Suppose you entered New York when running the following programs. What would be the printout?

```
#include <iostream>
#include <string>
using namespace std;

int main()
{
  cout << "Enter a city: ";
  string city;
  cin >> city;

  cout << city << endl;

  return 0;
}
```

(a)

```
#include <iostream>
#include <string>
using namespace std;

int main()
{
  cout << "Enter a city: ";
  string city;
  getline(cin, city);

  cout << city << endl;

  return 0;
}
```

(b)

Sections 10.3–10.4

10.6 Why is passing by reference preferred for passing an object to a function?

10.7 What is the printout of the following code?

```
#include <iostream>
using namespace std;

class Count
{
public:
  int count;

  Count(int c)
  {
    count = c;
  }

  Count()
  {
    count = 0;
  }
};

void increment(Count c, int times)
{
  c.count++;
  times++;
}

int main()
{
  Count myCount;
  int times = 0;

  for (int i = 0; i < 100; i++)
    increment(myCount, times);

  cout << "myCount.count is " << myCount.count;
```

```
    cout << " times is " << times;

    return 0;
}
```

10.8 If the highlighted code in Question 10.2 is changed to

```
void increment(Count &c, int times)
```

what will be the printout?

10.9 If the highlighted code is changed to

```
void increment(Count &c, int &times)
```

what will be the printout?

10.10 Can you change the highlighted code to the following?

```
void increment(const Count &c, int times)
```

Sections 10.5–10.6

10.11 How do you declare an array of ten `string` objects?

10.12 What is the output in the following code?

```
1 int main()
2 {
3     string cities[] = {"Atlanta", "Dallas", "Savannah"};
4     cout << cities[0] << endl;
5     cout << cities[1] << endl;
6
7     return 0;
8 }
```

Section 10.7

10.13 A data field and function can be declared as instance or static. What are the criteria for deciding?

10.14 Where do you initialize a static data field?

10.15 Suppose function `f()` is static defined in class `C` and `c` is an object of the `C` class. Can you invoke `c.f()`, `C::f()`, or `c::f()`?

Section 10.8

10.16 True or false? Only instance member functions can be declared as constant functions.

10.17 What is wrong in the following class declaration?

```
class Count
{
public:
    int count;

    Count(int c)
    {
        count = c;
    }
```

```
        Count()
        {
          count = 0;
        }

        int getCount() const
        {
          return count;
        }

        void incrementCount() const
        {
          count++;
        }
};
```

Sections 10.9–10.11

10.18 What is the output of the following code?

```
#include <iostream>
#include <string>
#include "BMI.h"
using namespace std;

int main()
{
  string name("John Doe");
  BMI bmi1(name, 18, 145, 70);
  name[0] = 'P';

  cout << "name from bml.getName() is " << bmi1.getName()
     << endl;
  cout <<  "name is " << name << endl;

  return 0;
}
```

10.19 In the following code, what will be the output from a.s and b.k in the main function?

```
 1 #include <iostream>
 2 #include <string>
 3 using namespace std;
 4
 5 class A
 6 {
 7 public:
 8   A()
 9   {
10     s = "John";
11   };
12   string s;
13 };
14
15 class B
16 {
17 public:
18   B()
```

```
19   {
20     k = 4;
21   };
22   int k;
23 };
24
25 int main()
26 {
27   A a;
28   cout << a.s << endl;
29
30   B b;
31   cout << b.k << endl;
32
33   return 0;
34 }
```

10.20 What is wrong in the following code?

```
1 #include <iostream>
2 #include <string>
3 using namespace std;
4
5 class A
6 {
7 public:
8   A() { };
9   string s("abc");
10 };
11
12 int main()
13 {
14   A a;
15   cout << a.s << endl;
16
17   return 0;
18 }
```

10.21 What is wrong in the following code?

```
1 #include <iostream>
2 #include <string>
3 using namespace std;
4
5 class A
6 {
7 public:
8   A() { };
9
10 private:
11   string s;
12 };
13
14 int main()
15 {
16   A a;
17   cout << a.s << endl;
18
19   return 0;
20 }
```

PROGRAMMING EXERCISES

Sections 10.2–10.6

10.1* *(Anagrams)* Write a function that checks whether two words are anagrams. Two words are anagrams if they contain the same letters in any order. For example, "silent" and "listen" are anagrams. The header of the function is as follows:

```
bool isAnagram(const string &s1, const string &s2)
```

Write a test program that prompts the user to enter two strings and checks whether they are anagrams. Here is a sample run of the program:

```
Enter a string s1: silent  ↵Enter
Enter a string s2: listen  ↵Enter
silent and listen are anagrams
```

```
Enter a string s1: split  ↵Enter
Enter a string s2: lisp  ↵Enter
split and lisp are not anagrams
```

10.2 *(Implementing the string class)* The `string` class is provided in the C++ library. Provide your own implementation for the following functions (name the new class `MyString1`):

```
MyString1();
MyString1(char chars[], int size);
MyString1 append(MyString1 s);
MyString1 append(MyString1 s, int index, int n);
MyString1 assign(char chars[])
MyString1 assign(MyString1 s, int index, int n)
char at(int index)
int length()
void clear()
MyString1 erase(int index, int n)
bool empty()
int compare(MyString1 s)
void copy(char s[], int index, int n)
MyString1 substr(int index, int n)
int find(char ch)
```

10.3 *(Implementing the string class)* The `string` class is provided in the C++ library. Provide your own implementation for the following functions (name the new class `MyString2`):

```
MyString2(char chars[], int size);
MyString2 append(int n, char ch)
MyString2 assign(MyString2 s, int n)
MyString2 assign(int n, char ch)
int compare(int index, int n, MyString2 s)
void copy(char s[], int index, int n)
MyString2 substr(int index)
int find(char ch, int index)
```

10.4 *(Sorting characters in a string)* Write a function that returns a sorted string using the following header:

```
string sort(string &s)
```

Write a test program that prompts the user to enter a string and displays the new sorted string. Here is a sample run of the program:

```
Enter a string s: silent  ↵Enter
The sorted string is eilnst
```

10.5* (*Checking palindrome*) Revise Listing 10.3 to check whether a string is a palindrome assuming letters are case-insensitive.

10.6** (*Checking substrings*) Rewrite the `indexOf` function in Exercise 7.22 using the `string` class as follows:

```
int indexOf(const string &s1, const string &s2)
```

Write a test program that reads two strings and checks whether one is a substring of the other. Sample runs are the same as in Exercise 7.22.

10.7* (*Occurrences of a specified character*) Rewrite the `count` function in Exercise 7.23 using the `string` class as follows:

```
int count(const string &s, char a)
```

For example, `count("Welcome", 'e')` returns `2`. Write a test program that reads a string and a character and displays the number of occurrences of the character in the string. Sample runs are the same as in Exercise 7.23.

10.8* (*Counting the letters in a string*) Rewrite the `countLetters` function in Exercise 7.24 using the string class as follows:

```
int countLetters(const string &s)
```

Write a test program that reads a string and displays the number of letters in the string. Sample runs are the same as in Exercise 7.24.

10.9* (*Hex to decimal*) Write a function that parses a hex number as a string into a decimal integer. The function header is:

```
int parseHex(const string &hexString)
```

For example, `hexString` A5 is 165 ($10 \times 16 + 5 = 165$) and FAA is 4010 ($15 \times 16^2 + 10 \times 16 + 10 = 4010$). So, `parseHex("A5")` returns 165 and `parseHex("FAA")` returns 4010. Write a test program that prompts the user to enter a hex number as a string and displays its decimal equivalent value.

10.10* (*Binary to decimal*) Write a function that parses a binary number as a string into a decimal integer. The function header is as follows:

```
int parseBinary(const string &binaryString)
```

For example, `binaryString` 10001 is 17 ($1 \times 2^4 + 0 \times 2^3 + 0 \times 2^2 + 0 \times 2 + 1 = 17$). So, `parseBinary("10001")` returns 18. Write a test program that prompts the user to enter a binary number as a string and displays its decimal equivalent value.

10.11* (*Counting occurrences of each letter in a string*) Rewrite the `count` function in Exercise 7.25 using the `string` class as follows:

```
void count(const string &s, int counts[], int size)
```

where size is the size of the `counts` array. In this case, it is `26`. Letters are not case-sensitive, i.e., letter A and a are counted the same as a.

Write a test program that reads a string, invokes the `count` function, and displays the counts. Sample runs of the program are the same as in Exercise 7.25.

10.12** (*Decimal to hex*) Write a function that parses a decimal number into a hex number as a string. The function headers are:

```
string convertDecimalToHex(int value)
```

See Appendix D, "Number Systems," for converting a decimal into a hex. Write a test program that prompts the user to enter a decimal number and displays its equivalent hex value.

10.13** (*Decimal to binary*) Write a function that parses a decimal number into a binary number as a string. The function headers are:

Video Note
Convert a decimal number into a binary number

```
string convertDecimalToBinary(int value)
```

See Appendix D, "Number Systems," for converting a decimal into a binary. Write a test program that prompts the user to enter a decimal number and displays its equivalent binary value.

10.14* (*Common prefix*) Rewrite the `prefix` function in Exercise 7.26 using the `string` class as follows:

```
string prefix(const string &s1, const string &s2)
```

Write a test program that prompts the user to enter two strings and displays their common prefix. Sample runs of the program are the same as in Exercise 7.26.

10.15** (*Guessing the capitals*) Write a program that repeatedly prompts the user to enter a capital for a state. Upon receiving the user input, the program reports whether the answer is correct. A sample output is shown below:

```
What is the capital of Alabama? Montgomery  ↵Enter
Your answer is correct.
What is the capital of Alaska? Anchorage  ↵Enter
The capital of Alaska is Juneau
```

Assume that fifty states and their capitals are stored in a two-dimensional array, as shown in Figure 10.19. The program prompts the user to enter ten states' capitals and displays the total correct count.

```
Alabama     Montgomery
Alaska      Juneau
Arizona     Phoenix
...         ...
```

FIGURE 10.19 A two-dimensional array stores states and their capitals.

10.16** (*Financial: credit card number validation*) Credit card numbers follow certain patterns. A credit card number must have between 13 and 16 digits. The number must start with:

- 4 for Visa cards
- 5 for MasterCard cards
- 37 for American Express cards
- 6 for Discover cards

In 1954, Hans Luhn of IBM proposed an algorithm for validating credit card numbers. The algorithm is useful to determine whether a card number is entered correctly or is scanned correctly by a scanner. Almost all credit card numbers are generated following this validity check, commonly known as the *Luhn check* or the *Mod 10 check*. It can be described as follows: (for illustration, consider the card number `4388576018402625`)

1. Double every second digit from right to left. If doubling of a digit results in a two-digit number, add up the two digits to get a single digit number.

   ```
   2 * 2 = 4
   2 * 2 = 4
   4 * 2 = 8
   1 * 2 = 2
   6 * 2 = 12 (1 + 2 = 3)
   5 * 2 = 10 (1 + 0 = 1)
   8 * 2 = 16 (1 + 6 = 7)
   4 * 2 = 8
   ```

2. Now add all single-digit numbers from Step 1.

   ```
   4 + 4 + 8 + 2 + 3 + 1 + 7 + 8 = 37
   ```

3. Add all digits in the odd places from right to left in the card number.

   ```
   5 + 6 + 0 + 8 + 0 + 7 + 8 + 3 = 37
   ```

4. Sum the results from Step 2 and Step 3.

   ```
   37 + 37 = 74
   ```

5. If the result from Step 4 is divisible by `10`, the card number is valid; otherwise, it is invalid. For example, the number `4388576018402625` is invalid, but the number `4388576018410707` is valid.

   Write a program that prompts the user to enter a credit card number as a string. Display whether the number is valid. Design your program to use the following functions:

   ```cpp
   /** Return true if the card number is valid */
   bool isValid(const string &cardNumber)

   /** Get the result from Step 2 */
   int sumOfEvenPlace(const string &cardNumber)

   /** Return this number if it is a single digit, otherwise,
    * return the sum of the two digits */
   int getDigit(int number)

   /** Return sum of odd-place digits in the card number */
   int sumOfOddPlace(const string &cardNumber)
   ```

10.17** (*Business: checking ISBN*) Use string operations to simplify Exercise 3.17. Enter the first 9 digits of an ISBN number as a string.

Section 10.7

10.18 (*The `MyInteger` class*) Design a class named `MyInteger`. The class contains:

- An `int` data field named `value` that stores the `int` value represented by this object.
- A constructor that creates a `MyInteger` object for the specified `int` value.

- A get function that return the `int` value.
- Functions `isEven()`, `isOdd()`, `isPrime()` that return `true` if the value is even, odd, or prime, respectively.
- Static functions `isEven(int)`, `isOdd(int)`, `isPrime(int)` that return `true` if the specified value is even, odd, or prime, respectively.
- Static functions `isEven(MyInteger)`, `isOdd(MyInteger)`, `isPrime(MyInteger)` that return `true` if the specified value is even, odd, or prime, respectively.
- Functions `equals(int)` and `equals(MyInteger)` that return `true` if the value in the object is equal to the specified value.
- A static function `parseInt(string)` that converts a string to an `int` value.

Draw the UML diagram for the class. Implement the class. Write a client program that tests all functions in the class.

10.19 (*Modifying the* `Loan` *class*) Rewrite the `Loan` class to add two static functions for computing monthly payment and total payment, as follows:

```
double getMonthlyPayment(double annualInterestRate,
  int numberOfYears, double loanAmount)

double getTotalPayment(double annualInterestRate,
  int numberOfYears, double loanAmount)
```

Write a client program to test these two functions.

Sections 10.8–10.11

10.20 (*The* `Stock` *class*) Design a class named `Stock` that contains:

- A string data field named `symbol` for the stock's symbol.
- A string data field named `name` for the stock's name.
- A `double` data field named `previousClosingPrice` that stores the stock price for the previous day.
- A `double` data field named `currentPrice` that stores the stock price for the current time.
- A constructor that creates a stock with specified symbol and name.
- The accessor functions for all data fields.
- The mutator functions for `previousClosingPrice` and `currentPrice`.
- A function named `changePercent()` that returns the percentage changed from `previousClosingPrice` to `currentPrice`.

Draw the UML diagram for the class. Implement the class. Write a test program that creates a `Stock` object with the stock symbol MSFT, the name Microsoft Corporation, and the previous closing price of `17.5`. Set a new current price to `17.6` and display the price-change percentage.

10.21 (*Geometry: n-sided regular polygon*) An n-sided regular polygon has n sides of the same length, and all its angles have the same degree (i.e., the polygon is both equilateral and equiangular). Design a class named `RegularPolygon` that contains:

- A private `int` data field named `n` that defines the number of sides in the polygon.
- A private `double` data field named `side` that stores the length of the side.
- A private `double` data field named `x` that defines the x-coordinate of the center of the polygon.
- A private `double` data field named `y` that defines the y-coordinate of the center of the polygon.

- A no-arg constructor that creates a regular polygon with n 3, side 1, x 0, and y 0.
- A constructor that creates a regular polygon with the specified number of sides and length of side, and centered at (0, 0).
- A constructor that creates a regular polygon with the specified number of sides, length of side, and x- and y-coordinates.
- The accessor and mutator functions for all data fields.
- The function getPerimeter() that returns the perimeter of the polygon.
- The function getArea() that returns the area of the polygon. The formula for computing the area of a regular polygon is

$$Area = \frac{n \times s^2}{4 \times \tan\left(\dfrac{\pi}{n}\right)}.$$

Draw the UML diagram for the class. Implement the class. Write a test program that creates three RegularPolygon objects, using the no-arg constructor, using RegularPolygon(6, 4), and using RegularPoly-gon(10, 4, 5.6, 7.8). For each object, display its perimeter and area.

10.22* (*Displaying the prime factors*) Write a program that receives a positive integer and displays all its smallest factors in decreasing order. For example, if the integer is 120, the smallest factors are displayed as 5, 3, 2, 2, 2. Use the StackOfIntegers class to store the factors (e.g., 2, 2, 2, 3, 5) and retrieve and display the factors in reverse order.

10.23*** (*Game: hangman*) Write a hangman game that randomly generates a word and prompts the user to guess one letter at a time, as shown in the sample run. Each letter in the word is displayed in an asterisk. When the user makes a correct guess, the actual letter is then displayed. When the user finishes a word, display the number of misses and ask the user whether to continue for another word. Declare an array to store words, as follows:

```
string words[] = {"write", "that", ...}; // Use any words
        // you wish
```

```
(Guess) Enter a letter in word ******* > p
(Guess) Enter a letter in word p****** > r
(Guess) Enter a letter in word pr**r** > p
      p is already in the word
(Guess) Enter a letter in word pr**r** > o
(Guess) Enter a letter in word pro*r** > g
(Guess) Enter a letter in word progr** > n
      n is not in the word
(Guess) Enter a letter in word progr** > m
(Guess) Enter a letter in word progr*m > a
The word is program. You missed 1 time

Do you want to guess for another word? Enter y or n>
```

10.24* (*Displaying the prime numbers*) Write a program that displays all the prime numbers less than 120 in decreasing order. Use the StackOfIntegers class to store the prime numbers (e.g., 2, 3, 5, ...) and retrieve and display them in reverse order.

CHAPTER 11

POINTERS AND DYNAMIC MEMORY MANAGEMENT

Objectives

- To describe what a pointer is (§11.1).
- To learn how to declare a pointer and assign a memory address to it (§11.2).
- To access values via pointers (§11.2).
- To declare constant pointers and constant data (§11.3).
- To explore the relationship between arrays and pointers (§11.4).
- To access array elements using pointers (§11.4).
- To pass arguments by reference with pointers (§11.5).
- To learn how to return a pointer from functions (§11.6).
- To use the new operator to create dynamic arrays (§11.7).
- To create objects dynamically and access objects via pointers (§11.8).
- To reference the calling object using the this pointer (§11.9).
- To implement the destructor for performing customized operations (§11.10).
- To design a class for students registering courses (§11.11).
- To create an object using the copy constructor that copies data from another object of the same type (§11.12).
- To customize the copy constructor for performing a deep copy (§11.13).

11.1 Introduction

why pointers?

Pointer is one of the most powerful features in C++. You can use a pointer to reference the address of an array, an object, or any variable. Pointers enable you to directly manipulate computer memory and manage dynamic data structures. Pointer is the heart and soul of the C++ programming language. Many of the C++ language features and library are built using pointers, including the Standard Template Library, which is covered in Chapters 22–23.

Video Note
pointer basics

11.2 Pointer Basics

Pointer variables, simply called *pointers*, are declared to hold memory addresses as their values. Normally, a variable contains a data value—e.g., an integer, a floating-point value, and a character. However, a pointer contains the memory address of a variable that in turn contains a data value. As shown in Figure 11.1, pointer **pCount** contains the memory address for variable **count**.

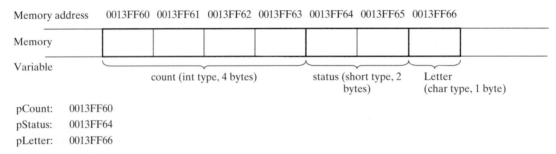

FIGURE 11.1 **pCount** contains the memory address of variable **count**.

Each byte of memory has a unique address. A variable's address is the address of the first byte allocated to that variable. As shown in Figure 11.1, variable **number** is declared as an **int** type which contains four bytes, variable **status** is declared as a **short** type which contains two bytes, and variable **letter** is declared as a **char** type which contains one byte.

Like any other variables, pointers must be declared before they can be used. To declare a pointer, use the following syntax:

declare pointer

```
dataType *pVarName;
```

Each variable being declared as a pointer must be preceded by an asterisk (*). For example, the following statements declare pointers named **pCount**, **pStatus**, and **pLetter**, which can point to an **int** variable, a **short** variable, and a **char** variable, respectively.

```
int *pCount;
short *pStatus;
char *pLetter;
```

You can now assign the address of a variable to a pointer. For example, the following code assigns the address of variable **count** to **pCount**:

assign address

```
int count = 5;

pCount = &count;
```

address operator

The ampersand (&) symbol is called the *address operator* when placed in front of a variable. It is a unary operator that returns the variable's address.

Listing 11.1 gives a complete example that demonstrates the use of the pointers.

LISTING 11.1 TestPointer.cpp

```cpp
 1 #include <iostream>
 2 using namespace std;
 3
 4 int main()
 5 {
 6   int count = 5;                                              declare variable
 7   int *pCount = &count;                                       declare pointer
 8
 9   cout << "The value of count is " << count << endl;
10   cout << "The address of count is " << &count << endl;
11   cout << "The address of count is " << pCount << endl;
12   cout << "The value of count is " << *pCount << endl;
13   cout << "The address of pCount is " << &pCount << endl;
14
15   return 0;
16 }
```

```
The value of count is 5
The address of count is 0013FF60
The address of count is 0013FF60
The value of count is 5
The address of count is 0013FF84
```

Line 6 declares a variable named **count** with an initial value **5**. Line 7 declares a pointer variable named **pCount** and initialized with the address of variable **count**. Figure 11.2 shows the relationship between **count** and **pCount**.

Memory address	0013FF60	0013FF61	0013FF62	0013FF63		0013FF84	0013FF85	0013FF86	0013FF87
Memory				5	...	00	13	FF	60
Variable	count (int type, 4 bytes)					pCount (address takes 4 bytes on my computer)			

FIGURE 11.2 **pCount** contains the address of variable **count** and *pCount references the contents of **count**.

A pointer can be initialized when it is declared or by using an assignment statement. However, if you assign an address to a pointer, the syntax is

```cpp
pCount = &count; // Correct
```

rather than

```cpp
*pCount = &count; // Wrong
```

Line 10 displays the address of **count** using **&count**. Line 11 displays the value stored in **pCount**, which is same as **&count**. The value stored in **count** is retrieved directly from **count** in line 9 and indirectly through a pointer variable using *pCount in line 12.

Referencing a value through a pointer is often called *indirection*. The syntax for referencing a value from a pointer is   indirect referencing

```cpp
*pointer
```

For example, you can increase **count** using

```cpp
count++; // Direct reference
```

or

```
(*pCount)++; // Indirect reference
```

indirection operator
dereferenced operator
dereferenced

The asterisk (*) used in the preceding statement is known as the *indirection operator* or *dereference operator* (dereference means indirect reference). When a pointer is *dereferenced*, the value at the address stored in the pointer is retrieved.

The following points on pointers are worth noting:

* in three forms

■ The asterisk (*) can be used in three different ways in C++:

  ■ As a multiplication operator, such as

  ```
  double area = radius * radius * 3.14159;
  ```

  ■ To declare a pointer variable, such as

  ```
  int *pCount = &count;
  ```

  ■ As the indirection operator, such as

  ```
  (*pCount)++;
  ```

  Don't worry. The compiler can tell what the symbol * is used for in a program.

pointer type

■ A pointer variable is declared with a type such as **int** or **double**. You have to assign the address of the variable of the same type. It is a syntax error if the type of the variable does not match the type of the pointer. For example, the following code is wrong.

```
int area = 1;
double *pArea = &area; // Wrong
```

You can assign a pointer to another pointer of the same type, but cannot assign a pointer to a non-pointer variable. For example, the following code is wrong:

```
int area = 1;
int *pArea = &area;
int i = pArea; // Wrong
```

naming pointers

■ Pointers are variables. So, the naming conventions for variables are applied to pointers. So far, we have named pointers with prefix **p**, such as **pCount** and **pArea**. However, it is impossible to enforce this convention. Soon you will realize that an array name is actually a pointer.

■ Like a local variable, a local pointer is assigned an arbitrary value if you don't initialize it. A pointer may be initialized to **0**, which is a special value to indicate that the pointer points to nothing. To prevent errors, you should always initialize pointers. Dereferencing a pointer that is not initialized could cause a fatal runtime error or it could accidentally modify important data. A number of C++ libraries including **NULL** <iostream> define NULL as **0** using the **#define** precompiler directive. It is more descriptive to use NULL than **0**.

■ You can declare two variables on the same line. For example, the following line declares two **int** variables:

```
int i = 0, j = 1;
```

Can you declare two pointer variables on the same line, as follows?

```
int* pI, pJ;
```

No, this line is equivalent to

```
int *pI,
int pJ;
```

To declare two pointers on the same line, use

```
int *pI, *pJ;
```

Suppose **pX** and **pY** are two pointer variables for variables **x** and **y**, as shown in Figure 11.3. To understand the relationships between the variables and their pointers, let us examine the effect of assigning **pY** to **pX** and *pY to *pX.

effect of assignment =

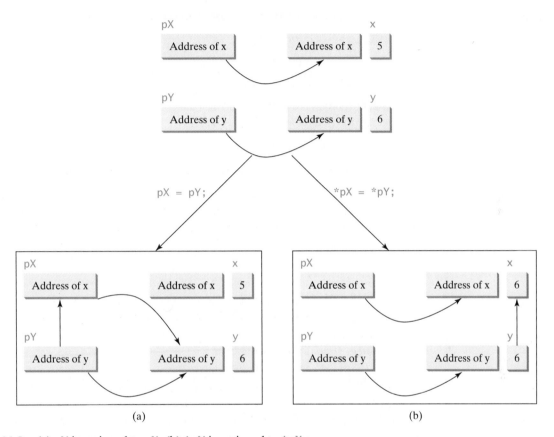

FIGURE 11.3   (a) **pY** is assigned to **pX**; (b) *pY is assigned to *pX.

The statement **pX** = **pY** assigns the content of **pY** to **pX**. The content of **pY** is the address of variable **y**. So, after this assignment, **pX** and **pY** contain the same content, as pictured in Figure 11.3(a).

Now consider *pX = *pY. With the asterisk symbol in front of **pX** and **pY**, you are dealing with the variables pointed by **pX** and **pY**. *pX refers to the contents in **x** and *pY refers to the contents in **y**. So the statement *pX = *pY assigns **6** to *pX, as pictured in Figure 11.3(b).

11.3 Using **const** with Pointers

You have learned how to declare a constant using the **const** keyword. Once it is declared, a constant cannot be changed. You can declare a *constant pointer*. For example:

constant pointer

```
double radius = 5;
double * const p = &radius;
```

Here **p** is a constant pointer. It must be declared and initialized in the same statement. You cannot assign a new address to **p** later. Though **p** is a constant, the data pointed to by p is not constant. You can change it. For example, the following statement changes radius to 10.

```
*p = 10;
```

constant data

Can you declare that dereferenced data be constant? Yes. You can add the **const** keyword in front of the data type, as follows:

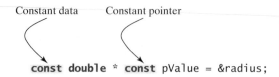

```
const double * const pValue = &radius;
```

In this case, the pointer is a constant, and the data pointed to by the pointer is also a constant. If you declare the pointer as

```
const double * p = &radius;
```

then the pointer is not a constant, but the data pointed to by the pointer is a constant. For example:

```
double radius = 5;
double * const p = &radius;
double length = 5;
*p = 6; // OK
p = &length; // Wrong because p is constant pointer

const double *p1 = &radius;
*p1 = 6; // Wrong because p1 points to a constant data
p1 = &length; // OK

const double * const p2 = &radius;
*p2 = 6; // Wrong because p2 points to a constant data
*p2 = &length; // Wrong because p2 is a constant pointer
```

11.4 Arrays and Pointers

An array without a bracket and a subscript actually represents the starting address of the array. In this sense, an array is essentially a pointer. Suppose you declare an array of **int** values as follows:

```
int list[6] = {11, 12, 13, 14, 15, 16};
```

The following statement displays the starting address of the array:

```
cout << "The starting address of the array is " << list << endl;
```

Figure 11.4 shows the array in the memory. C++ allows you to access the elements in the array using the indirection operator. To access the first element, use *list. Other elements

FIGURE 11.4 Array list points to the first element in the array.

can be accessed using *(list + 1), *(list + 2), *(list + 3), *(list + 4), and *(list + 5).

An integer may be added to or subtracted from a pointer. The pointer is incremented or decremented by that integer times the size of the element to which the pointer points. *(margin: pointer arithmetic)*

Array list points to the starting address of the array. Suppose this address is 1000. Will list + 1 be 1001? No. It is 1000 + sizeof(int). Why? Since list is declared as an array of int elements, C++ automatically calculates the address for the next element by adding sizeof(int). Recall that sizeof(type) is the size of a data type (see §2.8, "Numeric Data Types and Operations"). The size of each data type is machine dependent. On Windows, the size of the int type is usually 4. So, no matter how big each element of the list is, list + 1 points to the second element of the list, and list + 2 points to the third element, and so on.

Note

Now you see why an array index starts with 0. An array is actually a pointer. list + 0 points to the first element in the array and list[0] is an index variable for the first element in the array. *(margin: why 0-based index?)*

Listing 11.2 gives a complete program that uses pointers to access array elements.

LISTING 11.2 ArrayPointer.cpp

```cpp
1 #include <iostream>
2 using namespace std;
3
4 int main()
5 {
6   int list[6] = {11, 12, 13, 14, 15, 16};            // declare array
7
8   for (int i = 0; i < 6; i++)
9     cout << "address: " << (list + i) <<             // incrementing address
10      " value: " << *(list + i) << " " <<            // dereference operator
11      " value: " << list[i] << endl;                 // array indexed variable
12
13   return 0;
14 }
```

```
address: 0013FF4C value: 11  value: 11
address: 0013FF50 value: 12  value: 12
address: 0013FF54 value: 13  value: 13
address: 0013FF58 value: 14  value: 14
address: 0013FF5C value: 15  value: 15
address: 0013FF60 value: 16  value: 16
```

As shown in the sample output, the address of the array list is 0013FF4C. So (list + 1) is actually 0013FF4C + 4, and (list + 2) is 0013FF4C + 2 * 4 (line 9). The array elements are accessed using pointer dereference *(list + 1) (line 10). Line 11 accesses the elements using indexed variable list[i], which is equivalent to *(list + i).

Caution

*(list + 1) is different from *list + 1. The dereference operator (*) has precedence over +. So, *list + 1 adds 1 to the value of the first element in the array, while *(list + 1) dereferences the element at address (list + 1) in the array. *(margin: operator precedence)*

Note

Pointers can be compared using relational operators (==, !=, <, <=, >, >=) to determine their order. *(margin: compare pointers)*

Arrays and pointers form a close relationship. A pointer for an array can be used just like an array. You can even use indexed variables with pointers. Listing 11.3 gives such an example.

LISTING 11.3 `PointerWithIndex.cpp`

```
1  #include <iostream>
2  using namespace std;
3
4  int main()
5  {
6    int list[6] = {11, 12, 13, 14, 15, 16};
7    int *p = list;
8
9    for (int i = 0; i < 6; i++)
10     cout << "address: " << (list + i) <<
11       " value: " << *(list + i) << " " <<
12       " value: " << list[i] << " " <<
13       " value: " << *(p + i) << " " <<
14       " value: " << p[i] << endl;
15
16   return 0;
17 }
```

declare array
declare pointer

incrementing address
dereference operator
array indexed variable
dereference operator
pointer indexed variable

```
address: 0013FF4C value: 11  value: 11  value: 11  value: 11
address: 0013FF50 value: 12  value: 12  value: 12  value: 12
address: 0013FF54 value: 13  value: 13  value: 13  value: 13
address: 0013FF58 value: 14  value: 14  value: 14  value: 14
address: 0013FF5C value: 15  value: 15  value: 15  value: 15
address: 0013FF60 value: 16  value: 16  value: 16  value: 16
```

Line 7 declares an `int` pointer `p` assigned with the address of the array.

```
int *p = list;
```

Note that we do not use the address operator (`&`) to assign the address of the array to the pointer, because the name of the array is already the starting address of the array. This line is equivalent to

```
int *p = &list[0];
```

Here, `&list[0]` represents the address of `list[0]`.

As seen in this example, for array `list`, you can access an element using array syntax `list[i]` as well as pointer syntax `*(list + i)`. When a pointer such as `p` points to an array, you can use either pointer syntax or the array syntax to access an element in the array—i.e., `*(p + i)` or `p[i]`. You can use array syntax or pointer syntax to access arrays, whichever is convenient. However, there is one difference between arrays and pointers. Once an array is declared, you cannot change its address. For example, the following statement is illegal:

```
int list1[10], list2[10];
list1 = list2; // Wrong
```

In this sense, an array is a constant pointer.

pointer-based C-strings

C-strings are often referred to as *pointer-based strings*, because they can be conveniently accessed using pointers. For example, the following two declarations are both fine:

```
char city[7] = "Dallas"; // Option 1
char *pCity = "Dallas";   // Option 2
```

Each declaration creates a sequence that contains characters `'D'`, `'a'`, `'l'`, `'l'`, `'a'`, `'s'`, and `'\0'`.

You can access `city` or `pCity` using the array syntax or pointer syntax. For example, each of the following

array syntax
pointer syntax

```
cout << city[1] << endl;
cout << *(city + 1) << endl;
cout << pCity[1] << endl;
cout << *(pCity + 1) << endl;
```

displays character a (the second element in the string).

11.5 Passing Arguments by Reference with Pointers

There are two ways to pass arguments to a function in C++: *pass-by-value* and *pass-by-reference*. Pass-by-reference can be further classified into *pass-by-reference with reference arguments* and *pass-by-reference with pointers*. Listing 6.2, TestPassByValue.cpp, demonstrated the effect of pass-by-value. Listing 6.3, TestPassByReference.cpp, demonstrated the effect of pass-by reference with reference variables. Both examples used the **swap** function to demonstrate the effect. You can also implement the **swap** function using pointers. Listing 11.4 gives such an example and compares the three ways of passing arguments.

LISTING 11.4   TestPointerArgument.cpp

Video Note
pass-by-reference via pointer

```
 1 #include <iostream>
 2 using namespace std;
 3
 4 // Swap two variables using pass-by-value
 5 void swap1(int n1, int n2)
 6 {
 7    int temp = n1;
 8    n1 = n2;
 9    n2 = temp;
10 }
11
12 // Swap two variables using pass-by-reference
13 void swap2(int &n1, int &n2)
14 {
15    int temp = n1;
16    n1 = n2;
17    n2 = temp;
18 }
19
20 // Swap two variables using pass-by-pointers
21 void swap3(int *pValue1, int *pValue2)
22 {
23    int temp = *pValue1;
24    *pValue1 = *pValue2;
25    *pValue2 = temp;
26 }
27
28 int main()
29 {
30    // Declare and initialize variables
31    int num1 = 1;
32    int num2 = 2;
33
```

pass-by-value

pass-by-reference

pass-by-reference with
pointer

```
34      cout << "Before invoking the swap function, num1 is "
35         << num1 << " and num2 is " << num2 << endl;
36
37      // Invoke the swap function to attempt to swap two variables
38      swap1(num1, num2);
39
40      cout << "After invoking the swap function, num1 is " << num1 <<
41         " and num2 is " << num2 << endl;
42
43      cout << "Before invoking the swap function, num1 is "
44         << num1 << " and num2 is " << num2 << endl;
45
46      // Invoke the swap function to attempt to swap two variables
47      swap2(num1, num2);
48
49      cout << "After invoking the swap function, num1 is " << num1 <<
50         " and num2 is " << num2 << endl;
51
52      cout << "Before invoking the swap function, num1 is "
53         << num1 << " and num2 is " << num2 << endl;
54
55      // Invoke the swap function to attempt to swap two variables
56      swap3(&num1, &num2);
57
58      cout << "After invoking the swap function, num1 is " << num1 <<
59         " and num2 is " << num2 << endl;
60
61      return 0;
62 }
```

```
Before invoking the swap function, num1 is 1 and num2 is 2
After invoking the swap function, num1 is 1 and num2 is 2
Before invoking the swap function, num1 is 1 and num2 is 2
After invoking the swap function, num1 is 2 and num2 is 1
Before invoking the swap function, num1 is 2 and num2 is 1
After invoking the swap function, num1 is 1 and num2 is 2
```

Three functions swap1, swap2, and swap3 are defined in lines 5–26. Function swap1 is invoked by passing the value of num1 to n1 and the value of num2 to n2 (line 38). The swap1 function swaps the values in n1 and n2. n1, num1, n2, num2 are independent variables. After invoking the function, the values in variables num1 and num2 are not changed.

The swap2 function has two reference parameters, &n1 and &n2 (line 13). The references of num1 and num2 are passed to &n1 and &n2 (line 47), so &n1 and &num1 refer to the same memory location and &n2 and &num2 refer to the same memory location. n1 and n2 are swapped in swap2. After the function has been invoked, the values in variables num1 and num2 are also swapped.

The swap3 function has two pointer parameters, *pValue1 and *pValue2 (line 21). The references of num1 and num2 are passed to pValue1 and pValue2 (line 56), so pValue1 and &num1 refer to the same memory location and pValue2 and &num2 refer to the same memory location. *pValue1 and *pValue2 are swapped in swap3. After the function has been invoked, the values in variables num1 and num2 are also swapped.

Both pass-by-reference with reference arguments and pass-by-reference with pointer arguments are essentially the same. You can use either when you want the formal and the actual parameter to share the same memory location. In general, using pass-by-reference with reference arguments is simpler. Sometimes you need to use pass-by-reference with pointer arguments to deal with pointers.

An array parameter in a function can always be replaced using a pointer parameter. For example,

array parameter or pointer parameter

```
void m(int list[], int size)
```

can be replaced by

```
void m(int *list, int size)
```

```
void m(char c_string[])
```

can be replaced by

```
void m(char *c_string)
```

Recall that a C-string is an array of characters that ends with a *null terminator*. The size of a C-string can be detected from the C-string itself.

If a value does not change, you should declare it const to prevent it from being accidentally modified. Listing 11.5 gives an example.

const parameter

LISTING 11.5 ConstParameter.cpp

```
 1 #include <iostream>
 2 using namespace std;
 3
 4 void printArray(const int *, const int);                          function prototype
 5
 6 int main()
 7 {
 8   int list[6] = {11, 12, 13, 14, 15, 16};                         declare array
 9   printArray(list, 6);                                            invoke printArray
10
11   return 0;
12 }
13
14 void printArray(const int * list, const int size)
15 {
16   for (int i = 0; i < size; i++)
17     cout << list[i] << " ";
18 }
```

```
11 12 13 14 15 16
```

The printArray function declares an array parameter with constant data (line 4). This ensures that the contents of the array will not be changed. Note that the size parameter also is declared const. This usually is not necessary, since an int parameter is passed by value. Even though size is modified in the function, it does not affect the original size value outside this function.

11.6 Returning Pointers from Functions

You can use pointers as parameters in a function. Can you return a pointer from a function? Yes, you can.

Suppose you want to write a function that passes an array argument and returns a new array that is the reversal of the array argument. An algorithm for the function can be described as follows:

1. Let the original array be list.

2. Declare a new array named result that has the same size as the original array.

3. Write a loop to copy the first element, second, ..., and so on in the original array into the last element, second last, ..., in the new array, as shown in the following diagram.

4. Return `result` as a pointer.

The function prototype can be specified like this:

```
int *reverse(int const * list, const int size)
```

The return value type is an `int` pointer. How do you declare a new array in Step 2? You may attempt to declare it as

```
int result[size];
```

But C++ does not allow the size to be a variable. To avoid this limitation, let us assume that the array size is 6. So, you can declare it as

```
int result[6];
```

You can now implement the code in Listing 11.6, but you will soon find out that it is not working correctly.

LISTING 11.6 WrongReverse.cpp

```
 1 #include <iostream>
 2 using namespace std;
 3
 4 int *reverse(int const * list, const int size)
 5 {
 6   int result[6];
 7
 8   for (int i = 0, j = size - 1; i < size; i++, j--)
 9   {
10     result[j] = list[i];
11   }
12
13   return result;
14 }
15
16 void printArray(int const *list, const int size)
17 {
18   for (int i = 0; i < size; i++)
19     cout << list[i] << " ";
20 }
21
22 int main()
23 {
24   int list[] = {1, 2, 3, 4, 5, 6};
25   int *p = reverse(list, 6);
26   printArray(p, 6);
27
28   return 0;
29 }
```

reverse function

declare result array

reverse to result

return result

print array

invoke reverse
print array

```
6 4462476 4419772 1245016 4199126 4462476
```

The sample output is incorrect. Why? The reason is that the array `result` is a local variable. Local variables don't persist; when the function returns, the local variables are thrown away from the call stack. Attempting to use the pointer will result in erroneous and unpredictable results. To fix this problem, you have to allocate persistent storage for the `result` array so that it can be accessed after the function returns. We discuss the fix in the next section.

11.7 Dynamic Memory Allocation

C++ supports dynamic memory allocation, which enables you to allocate persistent storage dynamically. The memory is created using the new operator. For example,

```cpp
int *p = new int(4);
```

Here, new int tells the computer to allocate memory space for an int variable initialized to 4 at runtime, and the address of the variable is assigned to the pointer p. So you can access the memory through the pointer.

You can create an array dynamically. For example,

```cpp
cout << "Enter the size of the array: ";
int size;
cin >> size;
int *list = new int[size];
```

Here, new int[size] tells the computer to allocate memory space for an int array with the specified number of elements, and the address of the array is assigned to list. The array created using the new operator is also known as a *dynamic array*. Note that when you create a regular array, its size must be known at compile time. It cannot be a variable. It must be a constant. For example,

dynamic array

```cpp
int numbers[40]; // 40 is a constant value
```

When you create a dynamic array, its size is determined at runtime. It can be an integer variable. For example,

```cpp
int *list = new int[size]; // size is a variable
```

The memory allocated using the new operator is persistent and exists until it is explicitly deleted or the program exits. Now you can fix the problem in the preceding example by creating a new array dynamically in the reverse function. This array can be accessed after the function returns. Listing 11.7 gives the new program.

LISTING 11.7 CorrectReverse.cpp

```cpp
 1 #include <iostream>
 2 using namespace std;
 3
 4 int *reverse(const int * list, int size)
 5 {
 6   int *result = new int[size];
 7
 8   for (int i = 0, j = size - 1; i < size; i++, j--)
 9   {
10     result[j] = list[i];
11   }
12
13   return result;
14 }
15
16 void printArray(const int *list, int size)
17 {
18   for (int i = 0; i < size; i++)
19     cout << list[i] << " ";
20 }
21
22 int main()
23 {
24   int list[] = {1, 2, 3, 4, 5, 6};
```

reverse function

create array

reverse to result

return result

print array

invoke reverse
print array

```
25   int *p = reverse(list, 6);
26   printArray(p, 6);
27
28   return 0;
29 }
```

```
6 5 4 3 2 1
```

Listing 11.7 is almost identical to Listing 11.6 except that the new **result** array is created using the **new** operator dynamically. The size can be a variable when creating an array using the **new** operator.

C++ allocates local variables in the stack, but the memory allocated by the **new** operator is in an area of memory called the *freestore* or *heap*. The heap memory remains available until you explicitly free it or the program terminates. If you allocate heap memory for a variable while in a function, the memory is still available after the function returns. The **result** array is created in the function (line 6). After the function returns in line 25, the **result** array is intact. So, you can access it in line 26 to print all the elements in the **result** array.

freestore
heap

To explicitly free the memory created by the **new** operator, use the **delete** keyword before the pointer. For example,

```
delete p;
```

delete a dynamic array

If the memory is allocated for an array, the **[]** symbol must be placed between the **delete** keyword and the pointer to the array to release the memory properly. For example,

```
delete [] list;
```

After the memory pointed by a pointer is freed, the value of the pointer becomes undefined. Moreover, if some other pointer points to the same memory that was freed, this other pointer is also undefined. These undefined pointers are called *dangling pointers*. Don't apply the dereferencing operator * on dangling pointer. Doing so would cause serious errors.

dangling pointers

Caution

delete dynamic memory

Use the **delete** keyword only with the pointer that points to the memory created by the **new** operator. Otherwise, it may cause unexpected problems. For example, the following code is erroneous, because **p** does not point to a memory created using **new**.

```
int x = 10;
int *p = &x;
delete p; // This is wrong
```

You might inadvertently reassign a pointer before deleting the memory to which it points. Consider the following code:

```
1 int *p = new int;
2 *p = 45;
3 p = new int;
```

Line 1 declares a pointer assigned with a memory address for an **int** value, as shown in Figure 11.5(a). Line 2 assigns **45** to the variable pointed by **p**, as shown in Figure 11.5(b). Line 3 assigns a new memory address to **p**, as shown in Figure 11.5(c). The original memory space that holds value **45** is not accessible, because it is not pointed to by any pointer. This memory cannot be accessed and cannot be deleted. This is a *memory leak*.

memory leak

p   new int;

| address, e..g., 0013FF60 | 0013FF60 | not initialized yet |

(a) `int *p = new int;` allocates memory for an int
value and assigns an address to p.

p

| address, e..g., 0013FF60 | 0013FF60 | 45 |

(b) `*p = 45;` assigns 45 to the memory location pointed by p.

0013FF60 | 45 |

Memory at 0013FF60 is not referenced by any pointer. It is a leak.

p   new int;

| address, e..g., 0013FF64 | 0013FF64 | not initialized yet |

(c) `p = new int;` assigns a new address to p.

FIGURE 11.5 Unreferenced memory space causes memory leak.

11.8 Creating and Accessing Dynamic Objects

You can also create objects dynamically on the heap using the syntax shown below.

```
ClassName *pObject = new ClassName(); or
ClassName *pObject = new ClassName;
```

creates an object using the no-arg constructor and assigns the object address to the pointer.   create dynamic object

```
ClassName *pObject = new ClassName(arguments);
```

creates an object using the constructor with arguments and assigns the object address to the
pointer.

For example:

```
// Create an object using the no-arg constructor
string *p = new string(); // or string *p = new string;

// Create an object using the constructor with arguments
string *p = new string("abcdefg");
```

To access object members via a pointer, you must dereference the pointer and use the dot (`.`)
operator to object's members. For example,

```
string *p = new string("abcdefg");
cout << "The first three characters in the string are "                invoke substr()
  << (*p).substr(0, 3) << endl;
cout << "The length of the string is " << (*p).length() << endl;        invoke length()
```

C++ also provides a shorthand member selection operator for accessing object members
from a pointer: *arrow (->)* operator, which is a dash (–) immediately followed by the greater-
than (>) symbol. For example,

```
cout << "The first three characters in the string are "                invoke substr()
  << p->substr(0, 3) << endl;
cout << "The length of the string is " << p->length() << endl;          invoke length()
```

The objects are destroyed when the program is terminated. To explicitly destroy an object, invoke

delete dynamic object

```
delete p;
```

11.9 The **this** Pointer

hidden variable

Sometimes you need to reference a class's hidden data field in a function. For example, a data field name is often used as the parameter name in a set function for the data field. In this case, you need to reference the hidden data field name in the function in order to set a new value to it. A hidden data field can be accessed by using the `this` keyword, which is a special built-in pointer that references to the calling object. You can rewrite the `Circle` class defined in Circle2.h in Listing 9.8 using the `this` pointer, as shown in Listing 11.8.

LISTING 11.8 Circle5.cpp

include header file

this pointer

this pointer

```
 1 #include "Circle2.h" // Circle2.h is defined in Listing 9.8
 2
 3 // Construct a default circle object
 4 Circle::Circle()
 5 {
 6    radius = 1;
 7 }
 8
 9 // Construct a circle object
10 Circle::Circle(double radius)
11 {
12    this->radius = radius; // or (*this).radius = radius;
13 }
14
15 // Return the area of this circle
16 double Circle::getArea()
17 {
18    return radius * radius * 3.14159;
19 }
20
21 // Return the radius of this circle
22 double Circle::getRadius()
23 {
24    return radius;
25 }
26
27 // Set a new radius
28 void Circle::setRadius(double radius)
29 {
30    this->radius = (radius >= 0) ? radius : 0;
31 }
```

The parameter name `radius` in the constructor (line 10) is a local variable. To reference the data field `radius` in the object, you have to use `this->radius` (line 12). The parameter name `radius` in the `setRadius` function (line 28) is a local variable. To reference the data field `radius` in the object, you have to use `this->radius` (line 30).

11.10 Destructors

Destructors are the opposite of constructors. A constructor is invoked when an object is created and a destructor when the object is destroyed. Every class has a default destructor if the destructor is not explicitly defined. Sometimes, it is desirable to implement destructors to perform customized operations. Destructors are named the same as constructors, but you

Video Note
destructor and copy constructor

must put a tilde character (~) in front. Listing 11.9 shows a `Circle` class with a destructor defined.

LISTING 11.9 Circle6.h

```
1 #ifndef CIRCLE6_H
2 #define CIRCLE6_H
3
4 class Circle
5 {
6 public:
7   Circle();
8   Circle(double);
9   ~Circle(); // Destructor                    destructor
10  double getArea() const;
11  double getRadius() const;
12  void setRadius(double);
13  static int getNumberOfObjects();
14
15 private:
16  double radius;
17  static int numberOfObjects;
18 };
19
20 #endif
```

A destructor for the `Circle` class is defined in line 9. Destructors have no return type and no arguments.

Listing 11.10 gives the implementation of the `Circle` class defined in Circle6.h.

LISTING 11.10 Circle6.cpp

```
1 #include "Circle6.h"                          include header
2
3 int Circle::numberOfObjects = 0;
4
5 // Construct a default circle object
6 Circle::Circle()
7 {
8   radius = 1;
9   numberOfObjects++;
10 }
11
12 // Construct a circle object
13 Circle::Circle(double radius)
14 {
15  this->radius = radius;
16  numberOfObjects++;
17 }
18
19 // Return the area of this circle
20 double Circle::getArea() const
21 {
22  return radius * radius * 3.14159;
23 }
24
25 // Return the radius of this circle
26 double Circle::getRadius() const
```

```
27 {
28     return radius;
29 }
30
31 // Set a new radius
32 void Circle::setRadius(double radius)
33 {
34     this->radius = (radius >= 0) ? radius : 0;
35 }
36
37 // Return the number of circle objects
38 int Circle::getNumberOfObjects()
39 {
40     return numberOfObjects;
41 }
42
43 // Destruct a circle object
44 Circle::~Circle()
45 {
46     numberOfObjects--;
47 }
```

implement destructor

The implementation is identical to Circle3.cpp in Listing 10.7, except that the destructor is implemented to decrement **numberOfObjects** in lines 44–47.

The program in Listing 11.11 demonstrates the effects of destructors.

LISTING 11.11   TestCircle6.cpp

include header

create **pCircle1**
create **pCircle2**
create **pCircle3**

display **numberOfObjects**

destroy **pCircle1**

display **numberOfObjects**

```
1 #include <iostream>
2 #include"Circle6.h"
3 using namespace std;
4
5 int main()
6 {
7     Circle *pCircle1 = new Circle();
8     Circle *pCircle2 = new Circle();
9     Circle *pCircle3 = new Circle();
10
11     cout << "Number of circle objects created: "
12         << Circle::getNumberOfObjects() << endl;
13
14     delete pCircle1;
15
16     cout << "Number of circle objects created: "
17         << Circle::getNumberOfObjects() << endl;
18
19     return 0;
20 }
```

```
Number of circle objects created: 3
Number of circle objects created: 2
```

The program creates three **Circle** objects using the **new** operator in lines 7–9. Afterwards, **numberOfObjects** becomes **3**. The program deletes a **Circle** object in line 14. After this, **numberOfObjects** becomes **2**.

Destructors are useful for deleting memory and other resources dynamically allocated by the object, as shown in the following case study.

11.11 Case Study: The **Course** Class

Suppose you need to process course information. Each course has a name and a number of students who take the course. You should be able to add/drop a student to/from the course. You can use a class to model the courses, as shown in Figure 11.6.

Video Note
destructor and copy constructor

Course	
-courseName: string	The name of the course.
-students: string*	An array of students who take the course. students is a pointer for the array.
-numberOfStudents: int	The number of students (default: 0).
-capacity: int	The maximum number of students allowed for the course.
+Course(courseName: string, capacity: int)	Creates a Course with the specified name and maximum number of students allowed.
+~Course()	Destructor
+getCourseName(): string	Returns the course name.
+addStudent(name: string): void	Adds a new student to the course.
+dropStudent(name: string): void	Drops a student from the course.
+getStudents(): string*	Returns the array of students for the course.
+getNumberOfStudents(): int	Returns the number of students for the course.

FIGURE 11.6   The Course class models the courses.

A Course object can be created using the constructor Course(string courseName, int capacity) by passing a course name and the maximum number of students allowed. You can add a student to the course using the addStudent(string name) function, drop a student from the course using the dropStudent(string name) function, and return all the students for the course using the getStudents() function.

Suppose the class is defined as shown in Listing 11.12. Listing 11.13 gives a test class that creates two courses and adds students to them.

LISTING 11.12   Course.h

```
1 #ifndef COURSE_H
2 #define COURSE_H
3
4 #include <string>                                  using string class
5 using namespace std;
6
7 class Course                                        Course class
8 {
9 public:                                             public members
10   Course(const string &courseName, int capacity);
11   ~Course();
12   string getCourseName() const;
13   void addStudent(const string &name);
14   void dropStudent(const string &name);
15   string *getStudents() const;
16   int getNumberOfStudents() const;                  private members
17
18 private:
19   string courseName;
20   string *students;
```

```
21   int numberOfStudents;
22   int capacity;
23 };
24
25 #endif
```

LISTING 11.13 TestCourse.cpp

```
 1 #include <iostream>
 2 #include" Course.h"
 3 using namespace std;
 4
 5 int main()
 6 {
 7   Course course1("Data Structures", 10);
 8   Course course2("Database Systems", 15);
 9
10   course1.addStudent("Peter Jones");
11   course1.addStudent("Brian Smith");
12   course1.addStudent("Anne Kennedy");
13
14   course2.addStudent("Peter Jones");
15   course2.addStudent("Steve Smith");
16
17   cout << "Number of students in course1: " <<
18     course1.getNumberOfStudents() << "\n":
19   string *students = course1.getStudents();
20   for (int i = 0; i < course1.getNumberOfStudents(); i++)
21     cout << students[i] << "',";
22
23   cout << "\nNumber of students in course2: "
24     << course2.getNumberOfStudents() << "\n";
25   students = course2.getStudents();
26   for (int i = 0; i < course2.getNumberOfStudents(); i++)
27     cout << students[i] << ", ";
28
29   return 0;
30 }
```

Course header

create course1
create course2

add a student

number of students

return students

display a student

```
Number of students in course1: 3
Peter Jones, Brian Smith, Anne Kennedy,
Number of students in course2: 2
Peter Jones, Steve Smith,
```

The Course class is implemented in Listing 11.14.

LISTING 11.14 Course.cpp

```
1 #include <iostream>
2 #include" Course.h"
3 using namespace std;
4
5 Course::Course(const string &courseName, int capacity)
6 {
7   numberOfStudents = 0;
8   this->courseName = courseName ;
9   this->capacity = capacity;
```

Course header

initialize data field
set course name

```
10    students = new string[capacity];
11  }
12
13  Course::~Course()
14  {
15    delete [] students;                                          destroy dynamic array
16  }
17
18  string Course::getCourseName() const
19  {
20    return courseName;
21  }
22
23  void Course::addStudent(const string &name)                    add a student
24  {
25    if (numberOfStudents >= capacity)
26    {
27      cout << "The maximum size of array exceeded" << endl;
28      cout << "An exception is thrown" << endl;
29      throw runtime_error("maximum enrollment exceeded");
30    }
31
32    students[numberOfStudents] = name;
33    numberOfStudents++;                                          increase number of students
34  }
35
36  void Course::dropStudent(const string &name)
37  {
38    // Left as an exercise
39  }
40
41  string *Course::getStudents() const
42  {
43    return students;                                             return students
44  }
45
46  int Course::getNumberOfStudents() const
47  {
48    return numberOfStudents;
49  }
```

The **Course** constructor initializes **numberOfStudents** to **0** (line 7), sets a new course name (line 8), sets a capacity (line 9), and creates a dynamic array (line 10).

The **Course** class uses an array to store the students for the course. The array is created when a **Course** object is constructed. The array size is the maximum number of students allowed for the course. So, the array is created using **new string[capacity]**.

When a **Course** object is destroyed, the destructor is invoked to properly destroy the array (line 15).

The **addStudent** function adds a student to the array (line 23). This function first checks whether the number of students in the class exceeds the maximum capacity. If so, the program throws an exception (line 29). Exceptions will be introduced in Chapter 16, "Exception Handling."

The **getStudents** function (lines 41–44) returns the address of the array for storing the students.

The **dropStudent** function (lines 36–39) removes a student from the array. The implementation of this function is left as an exercise.

The user can create a **Course** and manipulate it through the public functions **addStudent**, **dropStudent**, **getNumberOfStudents**, and **getStudents**. However, the user doesn't need to know how these functions are implemented. The **Course** class encapsulates the internal implementation. This example uses an array to store students. You may use a different data structure to store students. The program that uses **Course** does not need to change as long as the contract of the public functions remains unchanged.

Note

When you create a **Course** object, an array of strings is created (line 10). Each element has a default string value created by the **string** class's no-arg constructor.

Caution

preventing memory leak

You should customize a destructor if the class contains a pointer data field that points to dynamically created memory. Otherwise, the program may have memory leak.

11.12 Copy Constructors

Each class may define several overloaded constructors and one destructor. Additionally, every class has a *copy constructor*, which can be used to create an object initialized with the data of another object of the same class.

The signature of the copy constructor is

```
ClassName(ClassName &)
```

For example, the copy constructor for the **Circle** class is

```
Circle(Circle &)
```

A default copy constructor is provided for each class implicitly, if it is not defined explicitly. The default copy constructor simply copies each data field in one object to its counterpart in the other object. Listing 11.15 demonstrates this.

LISTING 11.15 CopyConstructorDemo.cpp

```cpp
1  #include <iostream>
2  #include "Circle6.h" // Defined in Listing 11.9
3  using namespace std;
4
5  int main()
6  {
7    Circle circle1(5);
8    Circle circle2(circle1); // Use copy constructor
9
10   cout << "After creating circle2 from circle1:" << endl;
11   cout << "\tcircle1.getRadius() returns "
12     << circle1.getRadius() << endl;
13   cout << "\tcircle2.getRadius() returns "
14     << circle2.getRadius() << endl;
15
16   circle1.setRadius(10.5);
17   circle2.setRadius(20.5);
18
19   cout << "After modifying circle1 and circle2: " << endl;
20   cout << "\tcircle1.getRadius() returns "
21     << circle1.getRadius() << endl;
22   cout << "\tcircle2.getRadius() returns "
```

include header

create **circle1**
create **circle2**

display **circle1**

display **circle2**

modify **circle1**
modify **circle2**

display **circle1**

```
23        << circle2.getRadius() << endl;
24
25    return 0;
26 }
```
display **circle2**

```
After creating circle2 from circle1:
  circle1.getRadius() returns 5
  circle2.getRadius() returns 5

After modifying circle1 and circle2:
  circle1.getRadius() returns 10.5
  circle2.getRadius() returns 20.5
```

The program creates two **Circle** objects: **circle1** and **circle2** (lines 7–8). **circle2** is created using the copy constructor by copying **circle1**'s data.

The program then modifies the radius in **circle1** and **circle2** (lines 16–17) and displays their new radius in lines 20–23.

Note that the memberwise assignment operator and copy constructor are similar in the sense that both assign values from one object to the other. The difference is that a new object is created using a copy constructor. Using the assignment operator does not create new objects.

The default copy constructor or assignment operator for copying objects performs a *shallow copy*, rather than a *deep copy*, meaning that if the field is a pointer to some object, the address of the pointer is copied rather than its contents. Listing 11.16 demonstrates this.

shallow copy
deep copy

LISTING 11.16 ShallowCopyDemo.cpp

```
1 #include <iostream>
2 #include "Course.h" // Defined in Listing 11.12
3 using namespace std;
4
5 int main()
6 {
7   Course course1("C++", 10);
8   Course course2(course1);
9
10   course1.addStudent("Peter Pan"); // Add a student to course1
11   course2.addStudent("Lisa Ma"); // Add a student to course2
12
13   cout << "students in course1: " <<
14     course1.getStudents()[0] << endl;
15   cout << "students in course2: " <<
16     course2.getStudents()[0] << endl;
17
18   return 0;
19 }
```
include Course header

create **course1**
create **course2**

add a student
add a student

get a student

get a student

```
students in course1: Lisa Ma
students in course2: Lisa Ma
```

The **Course** class was defined in Listing 11.12. The program creates a **Course** object **course1** (line 7) and creates another **Course** object **course2** using the copy constructor (line 8). **course2** is a copy of **course1**. The **Course** class has four data fields: **courseName**, numberOfStudents, capacity, and students. The students field is a pointer type. When course1 is copied to course2 (line 8), all the data fields are copied to course2. Since students is a pointer, its value in course1 is copied to course2. Now both students in course1 and course2 point to the same array object, as shown in Figure 11.7.

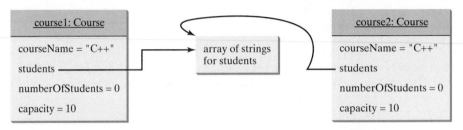

FIGURE 11.7 After course1 is copied to course2, the students data fields of course1 and course2 point to the same array.

Line 10 adds a student "Peter Pan" to course1, which is to set "Peter Pan" in the first element of the array. Line 11 adds a student "Lisa Ma" to course2 (line 11), which is to set "Lisa Ma" in the first element of the array. This in effect replaces "Peter Pan" with "Lisa Ma" in the first element of the array since both course1 and course2 use the same array to store student names. So, the student in both course1 and course2 is "Lisa Ma" (lines 13–16).

When the program terminates, course1 and course2 are destroyed. course1 and course2's destructors are invoked to delete the array from the heap (line 10 in Listing 11.14, Course.cpp). Since both course1 and course2's students pointer point to the same array, the array will be deleted twice. This will cause a runtime error.

To avoid all these problems, you should perform a deep copy so that course1 and course2 have independent arrays to store student names.

11.13 Customizing Copy Constructors

As discussed in the preceding section, the default copy constructor or assignment operator = performs a shallow copy. To perform a deep copy, you can implement the copy constructor. Listing 11.17 revises the declaration for the Course class to define a copy constructor in line 12.

LISTING 11.17 Course1.h

```
1 #ifndef COURSE_H
2 #define COURSE_H
3
4 #include <string>
5 using namespace std;
6
7 class Course
8 {
9 public:
10   Course(const string &courseName, int capacity);
11   ~Course(); // Destructor
12   Course(Course &); // Copy constructor
13   string getCourseName() const;
14   void addStudent(const string &name);
15   void dropStudent(const string &name);
16   string *getStudents() const;
17   int getNumberOfStudents() const;
18
```

copy constructor

```
19 private:
20   string courseName;
21   string *students;
22   int numberOfStudents;
23   int capacity;
24 };
25
26 #endif
```

Listing 11.18 implements the new copy constructor in lines 51–57. It copies courseName, numberOfStudents, and capacity from one course object to this course object (lines 53–55). A new array is created to hold student names in this object in line 56.

LISTING 11.18 Course1.cpp

```
 1 #include <iostream>
 2 #include "Course1.h"                                          include header file
 3
 4 Course::Course(const string &courseName, int capacity)
 5 {
 6   numberOfStudents = 0;
 7   this->courseName = courseName;
 8   this->capacity = capacity;
 9   students = new string[capacity];
10 }
11
12 Course::~Course()
13 {
14   delete [] students;
15 }
16
17 string Course::getCourseName() const
18 {
19   return courseName;
20 }
21
22 void Course::addStudent(const string &name)
23 {
24   if (numberOfStudents >= capacity)
25   {
26     cout << "The maximum size of array exceeded" << endl;
27     cout << "An exception is thrown" << endl;
28     throw runtime_error("maximum enrollment exceeded");
29   }
30
31   students[numberOfStudents] = name;
32   numberOfStudents++;
33 }
34
35 void Course::dropStudent(const string &name)
36 {
37   // Left as an exercise
38 }
39
40 string *Course::getStudents() const
41 {
42   return students;
43 }
44
```

```
45 int Course::getNumberOfStudents() const
46 {
47   return numberOfStudents;
48 }
49
50 Course::Course(Course &course) // Copy constructor
51 {
52   courseName = course.courseName;
53   numberOfStudents = course.numberOfStudents;
54   capacity = course.capacity;
55   students = new string[capacity];
56 }
```

copy constructor

create a new array

Listing 11.19 gives a program to test the custom copy constructor. The program is identical to Listing 11.16, ShallowCopyDemo.cpp, except that it uses Course1.h rather than Course.h.

LISTING 11.19 CustomCopyConstructor.cpp

include header Course1.h

```
1 #include <iostream>
2 #include "Course1.h"
3 using namespace std;
4
5 int main()
6 {
7   Course course1("C++", 10);
8   Course course2(course1);
9
10   course1.addStudent("Peter Pan"); // Add a student to course1
11   course2.addStudent("Lisa Ma"); // Add a student to course2
12
13   cout << "students in course1: " <<
14     course1.getStudents()[0] << endl;
15   cout << "students in course2: " <<
16     course2.getStudents()[0] << endl;
17
18   return 0;
19 }
```

```
students in course1: Peter Pan
students in course2: Lisa Ma
```

The copy constructor constructs a new array in **course2** for storing student names that is independent of the array in **course1**. The program adds a student **"Peter Pan"** to **course1** (line 10) and a student **"Lisa Ma"** to **course2** (line 11). As you see in the output in this example, the first student in **course1** is now **"Peter Pan"** and in **course2** is **"Lisa Ma"**. Figure 11.8 shows the two **Course** objects and two arrays of strings for students.

 Note

memberwise copy

The custom copy constructor does not change the behavior of the memberwise copy operator = by default. In Chapter 14, "Operator Overloading," will introduce how to customize the = operator.

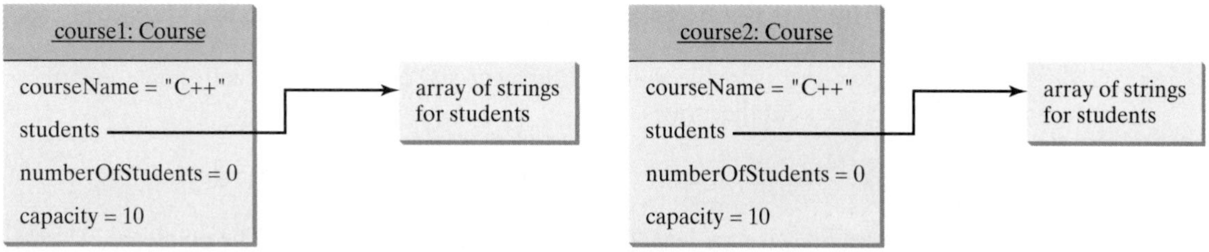

FIGURE 11.8 After `course1` is copied to `course2`, the `students` data fields of `course1` and `course2` point to two different arrays.

KEY TERMS

address operator (&)   352
arrow operator (->)   365
constant pointer   355
copy constructor   372
dangling pointer   364
deep copy   373
`delete` operator   364
dereference operator (*)   354
destructor   366

freestore   364
heap   364
indirection operator   354
memory leak   364
`new` operator   363
`NULL` pointer   354
pointer-based string   358
shallow copy   373
`this` keyword   366

CHAPTER SUMMARY

1. Pointers are variables that store the memory address of other variables.

2. The declaration

   ```
   int *pCount;
   ```

   declares `pCount` to be a pointer that can point to an `int` variable.

3. The ampersand (&) symbol is called the *address operator* when placed in front of a variable. It is a unary operator that returns the address of the variable.

4. A pointer variable is declared with a type such as `int` or `double`. You have to assign the address of the variable of the same type.

5. Like a local variable, a local pointer is assigned an arbitrary value if you don't initialize it.

6. A pointer may be initialized to `NULL` (same as `0`), which is a special value for a pointer to indicate that the pointer points to nothing.

7. The asterisk (*) placed before a pointer is known as the indirection operator or dereference operator (dereference means indirect reference).

8. When a pointer is dereferenced, the value at the address stored in the pointer is retrieved.

9. The `const` keyword can be used to declare constant pointer and constant data.

10. An array variable without a bracket and a subscript actually represents the starting address of the array.

11. You can access array elements using pointers or index variables.

12. An integer may be added or subtracted from a pointer. The pointer is incremented or decremented by that integer times the size of the element to which the pointer points.

13. Pass by reference can be further classified into *pass-by-reference with reference arguments* and *pass-by-reference with pointers*.

14. A pointer may be returned from a function. But you should not return the address of a local variable from a function, because a local variable is destroyed after the function is returned.

15. The `new` operator can be used to allocate persistent memory on the heap.

16. You should use the `delete` operator to release the memory created using the `new` operator, when the memory is no longer needed.

17. You can use pointers to reference an object and access object data fields and invoke functions using pointers.

18. You can create objects dynamically in a heap using the `new` operator.

19. The keyword `this` can be used as a pointer to the calling object.

20. Destructors are the opposite of constructors.

21. Constructors are invoked to create objects, and destructors are invoked automatically when objects are destroyed.

22. Every class has a default destructor, if the destructor is not explicitly defined.

23. The default destructor does not perform any operations.

24. Every class has a default copy constructor, if the copy constructor is not explicitly defined.

25. The default copy constructor simply copies each data field in one object to its counterpart in the other object.

REVIEW QUESTIONS

Section 11.2

11.1   How do you declare a pointer variable? Does a local pointer variable have a default value?

11.2   How do you assign a variable's address to a pointer variable? What is wrong in the following code?

```
int x = 30;
int *pX = x;
```

```
cout << "x is " << x << endl;
cout << "x is " << px;
```

11.3 What is wrong in the following code?

```
double x = 3.0;
int *pX = &x;
```

Section 11.3 Using **const** with Pointers

11.4 What is wrong in the following code:

```
int x;
int * const p = &x;
int y;
p = &y;
```

11.5 What is wrong in the following code?

```
int x;
const int *p = &x;
int y;
p = &y;
*p = 5;
```

Section 11.4

11.6 Assume you declared int *p, and p's current value is 100. What is p + 1?

11.7 Assume you declared int *p. What are the differences among p++, *p++, and (*p)++?

11.8 Assume you declared int p[4] = {1, 2, 3, 4}. What are *p, *(p+1), p[0] and p[1]?

11.9 What is wrong in the following code?

```
char *p;
cin >> p;
```

11.10 What is the printout of the following statements?

```
char * const pCity = "Dallas";
cout << pCity << endl;
cout << *pCity << endl;
cout << *(pCity + 1) << endl;
cout << *(pCity + 2) << endl;
cout << *(pCity + 3) << endl;
```

11.11 What is the output of the following code:

```
char *city = "Dallas";
cout << city[0] << endl;

char *cities[] = {"Dallas", "Atlanta", "Houston"};
cout << cities[0] << endl;
cout << cities[0][0] << endl;
```

Section 11.5

11.12 What is the output of the following code?

```
#include <iostream>
using namespace std;
```

```cpp
void f1(int x, int &y, int *z)
{
  x++;
  y++;
  (*z)++;
}

int main()
{
  int i = 1, j = 1, k = 1;
  f1(i, j, &k);

  cout << "i is " << i << endl;
  cout << "j is " << j << endl;
  cout << "k is " << k << endl;

  return 0;
}
```

Section 11.6 Returning Pointers from Functions

11.13 Can you guarantee that p[0] displays 1 and p[1] displays 2 in the following main function?

```cpp
#include <iostream>
using namespace std;

int * f()
{
  int list[] = {1, 2, 3, 4};
  return list;
}

int main()
{
  int *p = f();
  cout << p[0] << endl;
  cout << p[1] << endl;

  return 0;
}
```

Section 11.7 Dynamic Memory Allocation

11.14 How do you create the memory space for a double value? How do you access this double value? How do you release this memory?

11.15 Is the dynamic memory destroyed when the program exits?

11.16 Explain memory leak.

11.17 Suppose you create a dynamic array and later you need to release it. Identify two errors in the following code.

```cpp
double x[] = new double[30];
...
delete x;
```

Section 11.8

11.18 Are the following programs correct? If not, correct them.

```
1 int main()
2 {
3    string s1;
4    string *p = s1;
5
6    return 0;
7 }
```
(a)

```
1 int main()
2 {
3    string *p = new string;
4    string *p1 = new string();
5
6    return 0;
7 }
```
(b)

```
1 int main()
2 {
3    string *p = new string("ab");
4
5    return 0;
6 }
```
(c)

11.19 How do you create an object dynamically? How do you delete an object? Why is the code in (a) wrong and in (b) correct?

```
int main()
{
  string s1;
  string *p = s1;
  delete p;
  return 0;
}
```
(a)

```
int main()
{
  string *p = new string();
  delete p;

  return 0;
}
```
(b)

11.20 In the following code, lines 7 and 8 both create an anonymous object and print the area of the circle. Why is line 8 bad?

```
1 #include <iostream>
2 #include "Circle.h"
3 using namespace std;
4
5 int main()
6 {
7    cout << Circle(5).getArea() << endl;
8    cout << (new Circle(5))->getArea() << endl;
9
10    return 0;
11 }
```

Section 11.9

11.21 What is wrong in the following code? How can it be fixed?

```
// Construct a circle object
Circle::Circle(double radius)
{
  radius = radius;
}
```

11.22 Does every class have a destructor? How is a destructor named? Can it be overloaded? Can you redefine a destructor? Can you invoke a destructor explicitly?

11.23 What is the output of the following code?

```cpp
#include <iostream>
using namespace std;

class Employee
{
public:
  Employee(int id)
  {
    this->id = id;
  }

  ~Employee()
  {
    cout << "object with id " << id << " is destroyed" << endl;
  }

private:
  int id;
};

int main()
{
  Employee *e1 = new Employee(1);
  Employee *e2 = new Employee(2);
  Employee *e3 = new Employee(3);

  delete e3;
  delete e2;
  delete e1;

  return 0;
}
```

11.24 Why does the following class need a destructor? Add one.

```cpp
class Person
{
public:
  Person()
  {
    numberOfChildren = 0;
    children = new string[20];
  }

  void addAChild(string name)
  {
    children[numberOfChildren++] = name;
  }

  string *getChildren()
```

```
  {
    return children;
  }

  int getNumberOfChildren()
  {
    return numberOfChildren;
  }

private:
  string *children;
  int numberOfChildren;
};
```

Sections 11.12–11.13

11.25 Does every class have a copy constructor? How is a copy constructor named? Can it be overloaded? Can you redefine a copy constructor? How do you invoke one?

11.26 What is the output of the following code?

```
#include <iostream>
#include <string>
using namespace std;

int main()
{
  string s1("ABC");
  string s2("DEFG");
  s1 = string(s2);
  cout << s1 << endl;
  cout << s2 << endl;

  return 0;
}
```

11.27 Is the highlighted code in the preceding exercise the same as

```
s1 = s2;
```

Which is better?

11.28 Use the **Person** class in Review Question 11.24 to demonstrate why a deep copy is needed. Supply a customized constructor that performs a deep copy for the **children** array.

PROGRAMMING EXERCISES

Sections 11.2–11.7

11.1 (*Analyzing input*) Write a program that first reads an integer for the array size, then reads numbers into the array, computes their average, and finds out how many numbers are above the average.

11.2** (*Printing distinct numbers*) Write a program that first reads an integer for the array size, then reads numbers into the array, and displays distinct numbers (i.e., if a number appears multiple times, it is displayed only once). (*Hint:* Read a number and store it to an array if it is new. If the number is already in the array, discard it. After the input, the array contains the distinct numbers.)

11.3* (*Increasing array size*) Once an array is created, its size is fixed. Occasionally, you need to add more values to an array, but the array is full. In this case, you may create a new larger array to replace the existing array. Write a function with the following header:

```
* doubleCapacity(int *list, int size)
```

The function returns a new array that doubles the size of the parameter `list`.

11.4 (*Averaging an array*) Write two overloaded functions that return the average of an array with the following headers:

```
int average(int * array, int size);
double average(double * array, int size);
```

Write a test program that prompts the user to enter ten double values, invokes this function, and displays the average value.

11.5 (*Finding the smallest element*) Use pointers to write a function that finds the smallest element in an array of integers. Use {1, 2, 4, 5, 10, 100, 2, -22} to test the function.

Video Note
returning a pointer

11.6** (*Occurrences of each digit in a string*) Write a function that counts the occurrences of each digit in a string using the following header:

```
int * count(const string &s)
```

The function counts how many times a digit appears in the string. The return value is an array of ten elements, each of which holds the count for a digit. For example, after executing `int counts[] = count("12203AB3")`, `counts[0]` is `1`, `counts[1]` is `1`, `counts[2]` is `2`, `counts[3]` is `2`.

Write a `main` function to display the count for `"SSN is 343 32 4545 and ID is 434 34 4323"`.

Redesign the function to pass the `count` array in a parameter as follows:

```
void count(const string &s, int counts[], int size)
```

where `size` is the size of the `counts` array. In this case, it is `10`.

11.7** (*Game: ATM machine*) Use the `Account` class created in Programming Exercise 9.3 to simulate an ATM machine. Create ten accounts in an array with id 0, 1, ..., 9, and initial balance $100. The system prompts the user to enter an id. If the id is entered incorrectly, ask the user to enter a correct one. Once an id is accepted, the main menu is displayed, as shown in the sample output. You can enter a choice 1 for viewing the current balance, 2 for withdrawing money, 3 for depositing money, and 4 for exiting the main menu. Once you exit, the system will prompt for an id again. So, once the system starts, it will not stop.

```
Enter an id: 4  ↵Enter

Main menu
1: check balance
2: withdraw
3: deposit
4: exit
Enter a choice: 1  ↵Enter
The balance is 100.0
```

```
Main menu
1: check balance
2: withdraw
3: deposit
4: exit
Enter a choice: 2  ↵ Enter
Enter an amount to withdraw: 3  ↵ Enter

Main menu
1: check balance
2: withdraw
3: deposit
4: exit
Enter a choice: 1  ↵ Enter
The balance is 97.0

Main menu
1: check balance
2: withdraw
3: deposit
4: exit
Enter a choice: 3  ↵ Enter
Enter an amount to deposit: 10  ↵ Enter

Main menu
1: check balance
2: withdraw
3: deposit
4: exit
Enter a choice: 1  ↵ Enter
The balance is 107.0

Main menu
1: check balance
2: withdraw
3: deposit
4: exit
Enter a choice: 4  ↵ Enter

Enter an id:
```

11.8* (*Geometry: The `Circle2D` class*) *Define the* `Circle2D` class that contains:

- Two **double** data fields named **x** and **y** that specify the center of the circle with **get** functions.
- A data field **radius** with a **get** function.
- A no-arg constructor that creates a default circle with (**0**, **0**) for (**x**, **y**) and **1** for **radius**.
- A constructor that creates a circle with the specified **x**, **y**, and **radius**.
- A function **getArea()** that returns the area of the circle.
- A function **getPerimeter()** that returns the perimeter of the circle.
- A function **contains(double x, double y)** that returns **true** if the specified point (**x**, **y**) is inside this circle. See Figure 11.9(a).

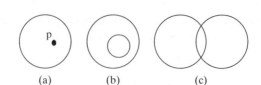

FIGURE 11.9 (a) A point is inside the circle. (b) A circle is inside another circle. (c) A circle overlaps another circle.

- A function `contains(Circle2D &circle)` that returns `true` if the specified circle is inside this circle. See Figure 11.9(b).
- A function `overlaps(Circle2D &circle)` that returns `true` if the specified circle overlaps with this circle. See Figure 11.9(c).

Draw the UML diagram for the class. Implement the class. Write a test program that creates a `Circle2D` object `c1(2, 2, 5.5)`, `c2(2, 2, 5.5)`, and `c3(4, 5, 10.5)`, displays `c1`'s area and perimeter, the result of `c1.contains(3, 3)`, `c1.contains(c2)`, and `c1.overlaps(c3)`.

11.9* (*Geometry: The Rectangle2D class*) Define the *Rectangle2D* class that contains:

- Two `double` data fields named `x` and `y` that specify the center of the rectangle with `get` and `set` functions. (Assume that the rectangle sides are parallel to `x`- or `y`-axes.)
- The data fields `width` and `height` with `get` and `set` functions.
- A no-arg constructor that creates a default rectangle with (0, 0) for (x, y) and 1 for both `width` and `height`.
- A constructor that creates a rectangle with the specified x, y, and radius.
- A function `getArea()` that returns the area of the rectangle.
- A function `getPerimeter()` that returns the perimeter of the rectangle.
- A function `contains(double x, double y)` that returns `true` if the specified point (x, y) is inside this rectangle. See Figure 11.10(a).

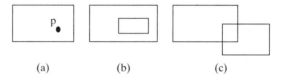

FIGURE 11.10 (a) A point is inside the rectangle. (b) A rectangle is inside another rectangle. (c) A rectangle overlaps another rectangle.

- A function `contains(Rectangle2D &r)` that returns `true` if the specified rectangle is inside this rectangle. See Figure 11.10(b).
- A function `overlaps(Rectangle2D &r)` that returns `true` if the specified rectangle overlaps with this rectangle. See Figure 11.10(c).

Draw the UML diagram for the class. Implement the class. Write a test program that creates three `Rectangle2D` objects `r1(2, 2, 5.5, 4.9)`, `r2(4, 5, 10.5, 3.2))`, and `r3(3, 5, 2.3, 5.4)`, and displays `r1`'s area and perimeter, and displays the result of `r1.contains(3, 3)`, `r1.contains(r2)`, and `r1.overlaps(r3)`.

11.10* (*Counting occurrences of each letter in a string*) Write a function that counts the occurrences of each letter in the string using the following header:

```
int * count(const string &s)
```

This function returns the counts as an array of **26** elements. For example, after invoking

```
int counts[] = count("ABcaB")
```

`counts[0]` is **2**, `counts[1]` is **2**, and `counts[2]` is **1**.

Write a main function to invoke `count("ABcaBaddeekjdfefdeg,TTew44Tt")` and display the counts.

Redesign the function to pass the **count** array in a parameter as follows:

```
void count(const string &s, int * counts, int size)
```

where size is the size of the **counts** array. In this case, it is **26**.

CHAPTER 12

TEMPLATES AND VECTORS

Objectives

- To know the motivation and benefits of templates (§12.2).
- To define a template function with type parameters (§12.2).
- To develop a generic sort function using templates (§12.3).
- To develop generic classes using class templates (§§12.4–12.5).
- To use the C++ **vector** class as a resizable array (§12.6).
- To replace arrays using vectors (§12.7).
- To evaluate expressions using stacks (§12.8).

12.1 Introduction

C++ provides functions and classes for developing reusable software. Templates provide the capability to parameterize types in functions and classes. With this capability, you can define one function or one class with a generic type that the compiler can substitute for a concrete type. For example, you may define one function for finding the maximum number between two numbers of a generic type. If you invoke this function with two `int` arguments, the generic type is replaced by the `int` type. If you invoke this function with two `double` arguments, the generic type is replaced by the `double` type.

This chapter introduces the concept of templates, and you will learn how to define function templates and class templates and use them with concrete types. You will also learn a very useful generic template `vector`, which you can use to replace arrays.

12.2 Templates Basics

Video Note
templates basics

Let us begin with a simple example to demonstrate the need for templates. Suppose you want to find the maximum of two integers, two doubles, and two characters. You might write three overloaded functions as follows:

int type

```
 1  int maxValue(int value1, int value2)
 2  {
 3    if (value1 > value2)
 4      return value1;
 5    else
 6      return value2;
 7  }
 8
```

double type

```
 9  double maxValue(double value1, double value2)
10  {
11    if (value1 > value2)
12      return value1;
13    else
14      return value2;
15  }
16
```

char type

```
17  char maxValue(char value1, char value2)
18  {
19    if (value1 > value2)
20      return value1;
21    else
22      return value2;
23  }
```

These three functions are almost identical, except that each uses a different type. The first function uses the `int` type in three places, the second the `double` type in three places, and the third the `char` type in three places. It would save typing, save space, and make the program easy to maintain if you could simply define one function with a generic type as follows:

generic type

```
GenericType maxValue(GenericType value1, GenericType value2)
{
  if (value1 > value2)
    return value1;
  else
    return value2;
}
```

This `GenericType` applies to all primitive types such as `int`, `double`, and `char`, as well as to object types.

C++ enables you to define a function template with generic types. Listing 12.1 defines a *template function* for finding a maximum value between two values of a generic type.

LISTING 12.1 GenericMaxValue.cpp

```
 1 #include <iostream>
 2 #include <string>
 3 using namespace std;
 4
 5 template<typename T>                          template prefix
 6 T maxValue(T value1, T value2)                type parameter
 7 {
 8   if (value1 > value2)
 9     return value1;
10   else
11     return value2;
12 }
13
14 int main()
15 {
16   cout << "Maximum between 1 and 3 is " << maxValue(1, 3) << endl;      invoke maxValue
17   cout << "Maximum between 1.5 and 0.3 is "
18     << maxValue(1.5, 0.3) << endl;                                      invoke maxValue
19   cout << "Maximum between 'A' and 'N' is "
20     << maxValue('A', 'N') << endl;                                      invoke maxValue
21   cout << "Maximum between \"NBC\" and \"ABC\" is "
22     << maxValue(string("NBC"), string("ABC")) << endl;                  invoke maxValue
23
24   return 0;
25 }
```

```
Maximum between 1 and 3 is 3
Maximum between 1.5 and 0.3 is 1.5
Maximum between 'A' and 'N' is N
Maximum between "NBC" and "ABC" is NBC
```

The definition for the function template begins with the keyword **template** followed by a list of parameters. Each parameter must be preceded by the interchangeable keyword **typename** or **class** in the form `<typename typeParameter>` or `<class typeParameter>`. For example, line 5

    template<typename T>

begins the definition of the function template for `maxValue`. This line is also known as the *template prefix*. Here T is a *type parameter*. By convention, a single capital letter such as T is used to denote a type parameter.

The `maxValue` function is defined in lines 6–12. A type parameter can be used in the function just like a regular type. You can use it to specify the return type of a function, declare function parameters, or declare variables in the function.

The `maxValue` function is invoked to return the maximum **int**, **double**, **char**, and **string** in lines 16–22. For the function call `maxValue(1, 3)`, the compiler recognizes that the parameter type is **int** and replaces the type parameter T with **int** to invoke the `maxValue` function with a concrete **int** type. For the function call `maxValue(string("NBC"), string("ABC"))`, the compiler recognizes that the parameter type is **string** and replaces the type parameter T with **string** to invoke the `maxValue` function with a concrete **string** type.

What happens if you replace `maxValue(string("NBC"), string("ABC"))` in line 22

C-string

with `maxValue("NBC", "ABC")`? You will be surprised to see that it returns ABC. Why? "NBC" and "ABC" are C-strings. Invoking `maxValue("NBC", "ABC")` passes the addresses of "NBC" and "ABC" to the function parameter. When comparing `value1 > value2`, the addresses of two arrays are compared, not the contents of the array!

match parameter

Caution

The generic `maxValue` function can be used to return a maximum of two values of *any type*, provided that

- The two values have the same type;
- The two values can be compared using the > operator.

For example, if one value is `int` and the other is `double` (e.g., `maxValue(1, 3.5)`), the compiler will report a syntax error because it cannot find a match for the call. If you invoke `maxValue(Circle(1), Circle(2))`, the compiler will report a syntax error because the > operator is not defined in the `Circle` class.

<typename T> preferred

Tip

You can use either `<typename T>` or `<class T>` to specify a type parameter. Using `<typename T>` is better because `<typename T>` is descriptive. `<class T>` could be confused with class declaration.

multiple type parameters

Note

Occasionally, a template function may have more than one parameter. In this case, place the parameters together inside the brackets, separated by commas, such as `<typename T1, typename T2, typename T3>`.

The parameters in the generic function in Listing 12.1 are defined as pass-by-value. You can modify it using pass-by-reference as shown in Listing 12.2.

LISTING 12.2 GenericMaxValuePassByReference.cpp

template prefix
type parameter

invoke **maxValue**

invoke **maxValue**

invoke **maxValue**

invoke **maxValue**

```
1 #include <iostream>
2 #include <string>
3 using namespace std;
4
5 template<typename T>
6 T maxValue(const T &value1, const T &value2)
7 {
8   if (value1 > value2)
9     return value1;
10  else
11    return value2;
12 }
13
14 int main()
15 {
16   cout << "Maximum between 1 and 3 is " << maxValue(1, 3) << endl;
17   cout << "Maximum between 1.5 and 0.3 is "
18     << maxValue(1.5, 0.3) << endl;
19   cout << "Maximum between 'A' and 'N' is "
20     << maxValue('A', 'N') << endl;
21   cout << "Maximum between \"NBC\" and \"ABC\" is "
22     << maxValue(string("NBC"), string("ABC")) << endl;
23
24   return 0;
25 }
```

```
Maximum between 1 and 3 is 3
Maximum between 1.5 and 0.3 is 1.5
Maximum between 'A' and 'N' is N
Maximum between "NBC" and "ABC" is NBC
```

12.3 Example: A Generic Sort

Listing 7.10, SelectionSort.h, gives a function to sort an array of **double** values. Here is a copy of the function:

```
 1 void selectionSort(double list[], int listSize)         double type
 2 {
 3   for (int i = 0; i < listSize; i++)
 4   {
 5     // Find the minimum in the list[i..listSize-1]
 6     double currentMin = list[i];                         double type
 7     int currentMinIndex = i;
 8
 9     for (int j = i + 1; j < listSize; j++)
10     {
11       if (currentMin > list[j])
12       {
13         currentMin = list[j];
14         currentMinIndex = j;
15       }
16     }
17
18     // Swap list[i] with list[currentMinIndex] if necessary;
19     if (currentMinIndex != i)
20     {
21       list[currentMinIndex] = list[i];
22       list[i] = currentMin;
23     }
24   }
25 }
```

It is easy to modify this function to write new overloaded functions for sorting an array of **int** values, **char** values, **string** values, and so on. All you need to do is to replace the word **double** by **int**, **char**, or **string** in two places (lines 1 and 6).

Instead of writing several overloaded sort functions, you can define just one template function that works for any type. Listing 12.3 defines a generic function for sorting an array of elements.

LISTING 12.3 GenericSort.cpp

```
 1 #include <iostream>
 2 #include <string>
 3 using namespace std;
 4
 5 template<typename T>                                     template prefix
 6 void sort(T list[], int listSize)                        type parameter
 7 {
 8   for (int i = 0; i < listSize; i++)
 9   {
10     // Find the minimum in the list[i..listSize-1]
11     T currentMin = list[i];                              type parameter
```

```
12        int currentMinIndex = i;
13
14        for (int j = i + 1; j < listSize; j++)
15        {
16          if (currentMin > list[j])
17          {
18            currentMin = list[j];
19            currentMinIndex = j;
20          }
21        }
22
23        // Swap list[i] with list[currentMinIndex] if necessary;
24        if (currentMinIndex != i)
25        {
26          list[currentMinIndex] = list[i];
27          list[i] = currentMin;
28        }
29      }
30 }
31
```

template prefix
type parameter

```
32 template<typename T>
33 void printArray(T list[], int listSize)
34 {
35    for (int i = 0; i < listSize; i++)
36    {
37      cout << list[i] << " ";
38    }
39    cout << endl;
40 }
41
42 int main()
43 {
44    int list1[] = {3, 5, 1, 0, 2, 8, 7};
```

invoke **sort**
invoke **printArray**

```
45    sort(list1, 7);
46    printArray(list1, 7);
47
48    double list2[] = {3.5, 0.5, 1.4, 0.4, 2.5, 1.8, 4.7};
49    sort(list2, 7);
50    printArray(list2, 7);
51
52    string list3[] = {"Atlanta", "Denver", "Chicago", "Dallas"};
53    sort(list3, 4);
54    printArray(list3, 4);
55
56    return 0;
57 }
```

```
0 1 2 3 5 7 8
0.4 0.5 1.4 1.8 2.5 3.5 4.7
Atlanta Chicago Dallas Denver
```

Two template functions are defined in this program. The template function **sort** (lines 5–30) uses the type parameter T to specify the element type in an array. This function is identical to the **selectionSort** function except that the parameter **double** is replaced by a generic type T.

The template function **printArray** (lines 32–40) uses the type parameter T to specify the element type in an array. This function displays all the elements in the array to the console.

The `main` function invokes the `sort` function to sort an array of `int`, `double`, and `string` values (lines 45, 49, 53) and invokes the `printArray` function to display these arrays (lines 46, 50, 54).

Tip
When you define a generic function, it is better to start with a nongeneric function, debug and test it, and then convert it to a generic function.

developing generic function

12.4 Class Templates

In the preceding sections, you defined template functions with type parameters for the function. You also can define template classes with type parameters for the class. The type parameters can be used everywhere in the class where a regular type appears.

Recall that the `StackOfIntegers` class, defined in §10.11, can be used to create a *stack* for `int` values. Here is a copy of the class with its UML class diagram, as shown in Figure 12.1(a).

Video Note
template class

StackOfIntegers
-elements[100]: int
-size: int
+StackOfIntegers()
+empty(): bool
+peek(): int
+push(value: int): void
+pop(): int
+getSize(): int

(a)

Stack\<T\>
-elements[100]: T
-size: int
+Stack()
+empty(): bool
+peek(): T
+push(value: T): void
+pop(): T
+getSize(): int

(b)

FIGURE 12.1 Stack\<T\> is a generic version of the Stack class.

```
1 #ifndef STACK_H
2 #define STACK_H
3
4 class StackOfIntegers
5 {
6 public:
7   StackOfIntegers();
8   bool empty() const;
9   int peek() const;                        int type
10  void push(int value);                    int type
11  int pop();                               int type
12  int getSize() const;
13
14 private:
15  int elements[100];
16  int size;                                int type
17 };
18
19 StackOfIntegers::StackOfIntegers()
```

```
20 {
21   size = 0;
22 }
23
24 bool StackOfIntegers::empty() const
25 {
26   return (size == 0);
27 }
28
29 int StackOfIntegers::peek() const
30 {
31   return elements[size - 1];
32 }
33
34 void StackOfIntegers::push(int value)
35 {
36   elements[size++] = value;
37 }
38
39 int StackOfIntegers::pop()
40 {
41   return elements[--size];
42 }
43
44 int StackOfIntegers::getSize() const
45 {
46   return size;
47 }
48
49 #endif
```

By replacing the highlighted int in the preceding code with double, char, or string, you easily can modify this class to define classes such as StackOfDouble, StackOfChar, and StackOfString for representing a stack of int, double, and string values. But, instead of writing almost identical code for these classes, you can define just one *template class* that works for the element of any type. Figure 12.1(b) shows the UML class diagram for the new generic Stack class. Listing 12.4 defines a generic stack class for storing elements of certain types.

LISTING 12.4 GenericStack.h

```
1 #ifndef STACK_H
2 #define STACK_H
3
4 template<typename T>
5 class Stack
6 {
7 public:
8   Stack();
9   bool empty() const;
10  T peek() const;
11  void push(T value);
12  T pop();
13  int getSize() const;
14
15 private:
16  T elements[100];
17  int size;
18 };
19
```

template prefix *(line 4)*

type parameter *(line 10)*
type parameter *(line 11)*

type parameter *(line 16)*

```
20 template<typename T>                                          function template
21 Stack<T>::Stack()
22 {
23   size = 0;
24 }
25
26 template<typename T>                                          function template
27 bool Stack<T>::empty() const
28 {
29   return (size == 0);
30 }
31
32 template<typename T>                                          function template
33 T Stack<T>::peek() const
34 {
35   return elements[size - 1];
36 }
37
38 template<typename T>                                          function template
39 void Stack<T>::push(T value)
40 {
41   elements[size++] = value;
42 }
43
44 template<typename T>                                          function template
45 T Stack<T>::pop()
46 {
47   return elements[--size];
48 }
49
50 template<typename T>                                          function template
51 int Stack<T>::getSize() const
52 {
53   return size;
54 }
55
56 #endif
```

The syntax for class templates is basically the same as that for function templates. You place the *template prefix* before the class declaration (line 4), just as you place the template prefix before the function template.

```
template<typename T>
```

The type parameter can be used in the class just like any regular data type. Here, the type T is used to define functions **peek()** (line 10), **push(T value)** (line 11), and **pop()** (line 12). T also is used in line 16 to declare array **elements**.

The constructors and functions are defined the same way for regular classes, except that the constructors and functions themselves are templates. So, you have to place the template prefix before the constructor and function header. For example,

```
template<typename T>
Stack<T>::Stack()
{
  size = 0;
}

template<typename T>
bool Stack<T>::empty()
{
```

```
    return (size == 0);
  }

  template<typename T>
  T Stack<T>::peek()
  {
    return elements[size - 1];
  }
```

Note also that the class name before the scope resolution operator `::` is `Stack<T>`, not `Stack`.

 Tip

compile issue

GenericStack.h combines class declaration and class implementation into one file. Normally, you put class declaration and class implementation into two separate files. For class templates, however, it is safer to put them together, because some compliers cannot compile them separately.

Listing 12.5 gives a test program that creates a stack for `int` values in line 9 and a stack for strings in line 18.

LISTING 12.5 TestGenericStack.cpp

generic **Stack**

int stack

string stack

```
 1 #include <iostream>
 2 #include <string>
 3 #include "GenericStack.h"
 4 using namespace std;
 5
 6 int main()
 7 {
 8   // Create a stack of int values
 9   Stack<int> intStack;
10   for (int i = 0; i < 10; i++)
11     intStack.push(i);
12
13   while (!intStack.empty())
14     cout << intStack.pop() << " ";
15   cout << endl;
16
17   // Create a stack of strings
18   Stack<string> stringStack;
19   stringStack.push("Chicago");
20   stringStack.push("Denver");
21   stringStack.push("London");
22
23   while (!stringStack.empty())
24     cout << stringStack.pop() << " ";
25   cout << endl;
26
27   return 0;
28 }
```

```
9 8 7 6 5 4 3 2 1 0
London Denver Chicago
```

declaring objects

To declare an object from a template class, you have to specify a concrete type for the type parameter `T`. For example,

```
Stack<int> intStack;
```

This declaration replaces the type parameter T with int. So, intStack is a stack for int values. The object intStack is just like any other object. The program invokes the push function on intStack to add ten int values to the stack (line 11), and displays the elements from the stack (lines 13–14).

The program declares a stack object for storing strings in line 18, adds three strings in the stack (lines 19–21), and displays the strings from the stack (line 24).

Note the code in lines 9–11:

```
while (!intStack.empty())
  cout << intStack.pop() << " ";
cout << endl;
```

and in lines 23–25:

```
while (!stringStack.empty())
  cout << stringStack.pop() << " ";
cout << endl;
```

These two fragments are almost identical. The difference is that the former operates on intStack and the latter on stringStack. You can define a function with a stack parameter to display the elements in the stack. The new program is shown in Listing 12.6.

LISTING 12.6 TestGenericStack1.cpp

```
1 #include <iostream>
2 #include <string>
3 #include "GenericStack.h"            generic Stack
4 using namespace std;
5
6 template<typename T>
7 void printStack(Stack<T> &stack)     Stack<T> parameter
8 {
9   while (!stack.empty())
10     cout << stack.pop() << " ";
11   cout << endl;
12 }
13
14 int main()
15 {
16   // Create a stack of int values
17   Stack<int> intStack;
18   for (int i = 0; i < 10; i++)
19     intStack.push(i);
20   printStack(intStack);              invoke printStack
21
22   // Create a stack of strings
23   Stack<string> stringStack;
24   stringStack.push("Chicago");
25   stringStack.push("Denver");
26   stringStack.push("London");
27   printStack(stringStack);           invoke printStack
28
29   return 0;
30 }
```

The generic class name Stack<T> is used as a parameter type in a template function (line 7).

default type

Note

C++ allows you to assign a *default type* for a type parameter in a class template. For example, you may assign `int` as a default type in the generic **Stack** class as follows:

```
template<typename T = int>
class Stack
{
  . . .
};
```

You now can declare an object using the default type like this:

```
Stack<> stack;  // stack is a stack for int values
```

You can use default type only in class templates, not in function templates.

nontype parameter

Note

You also can use *nontype parameters* along with type parameters in a template prefix. For example, you may declare the array capacity as a parameter for the **Stack** class as follows:

```
template<typename T, int capacity>
class Stack
{
  . . .
private:
  T elements[capacity];
  int size;
};
```

So, when you create a stack, you can specify the capacity for the array. For example,

```
Stack<string, 500> stack;
```

declares a stack that can hold up to **500** strings.

static members

Note

You can define static members in a template class. Each template specialization has its own copy of a static data field.

12.5 Improving the **Stack** Class

There is a problem in the **Stack** class. The elements of the stack are stored in an array with a fixed size **100** (see line 16 in Listing 12.4). So, you cannot store more than **100** elements in a stack. You could change **100** to a larger number, but if the actual stack is small, this would waste space. One way to resolve this dilemma is to allocate more memory dynamically when needed.

The `size` property in the Stack<T> class represents the number of elements in the stack. Let us add a new property named `capacity` that represents the current size of the array for storing the elements. The no-arg constructor of Stack<T> creates an array with capacity **12**. When you add a new element to the stack, you may need to increase the array size in order to store the new element if the current capacity is full.

How do you increase the array capacity? You cannot do so, once the array is declared. To circumvent this restriction, you may create a new, larger array, copy the contents of the old array to this new one, and delete the old array.

The improved Stack<T> class is shown in Listing 12.7.

LISTING 12.7   ImprovedStack.h

```
1  #ifndef IMPROVEDSTACK_H
2  #define IMPROVEDSTACK_H
3
4  template<typename T>                                          define Stack class
5  class Stack
6  {
7  public:
8     Stack();
9     Stack(const Stack &);
10    ~Stack();
11    bool empty() const;
12    T peek() const;
13    void push(T value);
14    T pop();
15    int getSize() const;
16
17 private:
18    T *elements;
19    int size;
20    int capacity;
21    void ensureCapacity();
22 };
23
24 template<typename T>                                          implement Stack class
25 Stack<T>::Stack(): size(0), capacity(16)                      no-arg constructor
26 {
27    elements = new T[capacity];
28 }
29
30 template<typename T>
31 Stack<T>::Stack(const Stack &stack)                           copy constructor
32 {
33    elements = new T[stack.capacity];
34    size = stack.size;
35    capacity = stack.capacity;
36    for (int i = 0; i < size; i++)
37    {
38       elements[i] = stack.elements[i];
39    }
40 }
41
42 template<typename T>                                          destructor
43 Stack<T>::~Stack()
44 {
45    delete [] elements;
46 }
47
48 template<typename T>
49 bool Stack<T>::empty() const
50 {
51    return (size == 0);
52 }
53
54 template<typename T>
55 T Stack<T>::peek() const
```

```
56 {
57   return elements[size - 1];
58 }
59
60 template<typename T>
61 void Stack<T>::push(T value)
62 {
63   ensureCapacity();
64   elements[size++] = value;
65 }
66
67 template<typename T>
68 void Stack<T>::ensureCapacity()
69 {
70   if (size >= capacity)
71   {
72     T *old = elements;
73     capacity = 2 * size;
74     elements = new T[size * 2];
75
76     for (int i = 0; i < size; i++)
77       elements[i] = old[i];
78
79     delete [] old;
80   }
81 }
82
83 template<typename T>
84 T Stack<T>::pop()
85 {
86   return elements[--size];
87 }
88
89 template<typename T>
90 int Stack<T>::getSize() const
91 {
92   return size;
93 }
94
95 #endif
```

increase capacity if needed

create a new array

copy to the new array

destroy the old array

Since the internal array `elements` is dynamically created, a destructor must be provided to properly destroy the array to avoid memory leak (lines 42–46). Note that the array elements in Listing 12.4, GenericStack.h, are not allocated dynamically, so there is no need to provide a destructor in that case.

The `push(T value)` function (lines 60–65) adds a new element to the stack. This function first invokes `ensureCapacity()` (line 63), which ensures that there is a space in the array for the new element.

The `ensureCapacity()` function (lines 67–81) checks whether the array is full. If it is, create a new array that doubles the current array size, set the new array as the current array, copy the old array to the new array, and delete the old array (line 79).

Please note that the syntax to destroy a dynamically created array is

```
delete [] elements; // Line 45
delete [] old; // Line 79
```

What happens if you mistakenly write the following?

```
delete elements; // Line 45
delete old; // Line 79
```

The program will compile and run fine for a stack of primitive-type values, but it is not correct for a stack of objects. The statement `delete [] elements` first calls the destructor on each object in the `elements` array and then destroys the array, whereas the statement `delete elements` calls the destructor only on the first object in the array.

12.6 The C++ **vector** Class

You can use an array to store a collection of data such as strings and `int` values. There is a serious limitation: the array size is fixed when the array is created. C++ provides the *vector* class, which is more flexible than arrays. You can use a `vector` object just like an array, but a vector's size can grow automatically if needed.

Video Note
the vector class

To create a vector, use the syntax:

```
vector<elementType> vectorName;
```

For example,

```
vector<int> intVector;
```

creates a vector to store `int` values.

```
vector<string> stringVector;
```

creates a vector to store `string` objects.

Figure 12.2 lists several frequently used functions in the vector class in a UML class diagram.

vector<elementType>	
+vector<elementType>()	Constructs an empty vector with the specified element type.
+vector<elementType>(size: int)	Constructs a vector with the initial size, filled with default values.
+push_back(element: elementType): void	Appends the element in this vector.
+pop_back(): void	Removes the last element from this vector.
+size(): unsigned int	Returns the number of the elements in this vector.
+at(index: int): elementType	Returns the element at the specified index in this vector.
+empty(): bool	Returns true if this vector is empty.
+clear(): void	Removes all elements from this vector.
+swap(v2: vector): void	Swaps the contents of this vector with the specified vector.

FIGURE 12.2   The `vector` class functions as a resizable array.

You can also create a vector with the initial size, filled with default values. For example, the following code creates a vector of initial size **10** with default values **0**.

```
vector<int> intVector(10);
```

A vector can be accessed using the array subscript operator `[]`. For example,

```
cout << intVector[0];
```

displays the first element in the vector.

Caution

To use the array subscript operator `[]`, the element must already exist in the vector. Like array, the index is **0**-based in a vector—i.e., the index of the first element in the vector is **0** and the last one is `v.size()` – **1**. To use an index beyond this range would cause errors.

vector index range

Listing 12.8 gives an example of using vectors.

LISTING 12.8 TestVector.cpp

vector header
string header

create a vector

append **int** value
append **string**

vector size
vector subscript

create a vector

vector size
vector subscript

remove element

create vector
swap vector
assign string

vector size
at function

```cpp
1 #include <iostream>
2 #include <vector>
3 #include <string>
4 using namespace std;
5
6 int main()
7 {
8   vector<int> intVector;
9
10  // Store numbers 1, 2, 3, 4, 5, ..., 10 to the vector
11  for (int i = 0; i < 10; i++)
12    intVector.push_back(i + 1);
13
14  // Display the numbers in the vector
15  cout << "Numbers in the vector: ";
16  for (int i = 0; i < intVector.size(); i++)
17    cout << intVector[i] << " ";
18
19  vector<string> stringVector;
20
21  // Store strings into the vector
22  stringVector.push_back("Dallas");
23  stringVector.push_back("Houston");
24  stringVector.push_back("Austin");
25  stringVector.push_back("Norman");
26
27  // Display the string in the vector
28  cout << "\nStrings in the string vector: ";
29  for (int i = 0; i < stringVector.size(); i++)
30    cout << stringVector[i] << " ";
31
32  stringVector.pop_back(); // Remove the last element
33
34  vector<string> v2;
35  v2.swap(stringVector);
36  v2[0] = "Atlanta";
37
38  // Redisplay the string in the vector
39  cout << "\nStrings in the vector v2: ";
40  for (int i = 0; i < v2.size(); i++)
41    cout << v2.at(i) << " ";
42
43  return 0;
44 }
```

```
Numbers in the vector: 1 2 3 4 5 6 7 8 9 10
Strings in the string vector: Dallas Houston Austin Norman
Strings in the vector v2: Atlanta Houston Austin
```

Since the **vector** class is used in the program, line 2 includes its header file. Since the **string** class is also used, line 3 includes the **string** class header file.

A vector for storing **int** values is created in line 8. The **int** values are appended to the vector in line 11. There is no limit on the size of the vector. The size grows automatically as more elements are added into the vector. The program displays all the `int` values in the vector in lines 15–17. Note the array subscript operator [] is used to retrieve an element in line 17.

A vector for storing strings is created in line 19. Four strings are added to the vector (lines 22–25). The program displays all the strings in the vector in lines 29–30. Note the array subscript operator [] is used to retrieve an element in line 30.

Line 32 removes the last string from the vector. Line 34 creates another vector v2. Line 35 swaps v2 with `stringVector`. Line 36 assigns a new string to the v2[0]. The program displays the strings in v2. Note that the `at` function is used to retrieve the elements. You can also use the subscript operator [] to retrieve the elements.

The `size()` function returns the size of the vector as an `unsigned int`, not `int`. Some compilers may warn you because an unsigned value is used with a signed `int` value in variable `i` (lines 16, 29, 40). This is just a warning and should not cause any problems, because the unsigned value is automatically promoted to a signed value when it is needed. To get rid of the warning, declare `i` to be `unsigned int` in line 16 as follows:

`unsigned int`

```
for (unsigned int i = 0; i < intVector.size(); i++)
```

12.7 Replacing Arrays Using the **vector** Class

A vector is a resizable array. Using vectors is more flexible than using arrays. All the examples in the preceding chapters that use arrays can be modified using vectors. This section rewrites Listing 7.2, DeckOfCards.cpp, and Listing 8.1, PassTwoDimensionalArray, using vectors.

Recall that Listing 7.2 is a program that picks four cards randomly from a deck of 52 cards. We use a vector to store the 52 cards with initial values 0 to 51, as follows:

```
const int NUMBER_OF_CARDS = 52;
vector<int> deck(NUMBER_OF_CARDS);

// Initialize cards
for (int i = 0; i < NUMBER_OF_CARDS; i++)
  deck[i] = i;
```

`deck[0]` to `deck[12]` are Clubs, `deck[13]` to `deck[25]` are Diamonds, `deck[26]` to `deck[38]` are Hearts, and `deck[39]` to `deck[51]` are Spades. Listing 12.9 gives the solution to the problem.

LISTING 12.9 DeckOfCardsUsingVector.cpp

```
 1 #include <iostream>
 2 #include <vector>
 3 #include <ctime>
 4 using namespace std;
 5
 6 const int NUMBER_OF_CARDS = 52;
 7
 8 void displayRank(int rank)
 9 {
10   if (rank == 0)
11     cout << "Ace of ";
12   else if (rank == 10)
13     cout << "Jack of ";
14   else if (rank == 11)
15     cout << "Queen of ";
16   else if (rank == 12)
17     cout << "King of ";
```

include **vector**

display rank

display suit

```
18   else
19     cout << rank << " of ";
20 }
21
22 void displaySuit(int suit)
23 {
24   if (suit == 0)
25     cout << "Clubs" << endl;
26   else if (suit == 1)
27     cout << "Diamonds" << endl;
28   else if (suit == 2)
29     cout << "Hearts" << endl;
30   else if (suit == 3)
31     cout << "Spades" << endl;
32 }
33
34 int main()
35 {
36   vector<int> deck(NUMBER_OF_CARDS);
37
38   // Initialize cards
39   for (int i = 0; i < NUMBER_OF_CARDS; i++)
40     deck[i] = i;
41
42   // Shuffle the cards
43   srand(time(0));
44   for (int i = 0; i < NUMBER_OF_CARDS; i++)
45   {
46     // Generate an index randomly
47     int index = rand() % NUMBER_OF_CARDS;
48     int temp = deck[i];
49     deck[i] = deck[index];
50     deck[index] = temp;
51   }
52
53   // Display the first four cards
54   for (int i = 0; i < 4; i++)
55   {
56     displayRank(deck[i] % 13);
57     displaySuit(deck[i] / 13);
58   }
59
60   return 0;
61 }
```

create vector **deck**

initialize **deck**

shuffle **deck**

display rank
display suit

```
4 of Clubs
Ace of Diamonds
6 of Hearts
Jack of Clubs
```

This program is identical to Listing 7.2, except that line 2 includes the vector class and line 36 creates a vector instead of an array. Interestingly, the syntax for using arrays and vectors is very similar, because you can use indexes in the brackets to access the elements in a vector, which is the same as for accessing array elements.

Recall that Listing 8.1 creates a two-dimensional array and invokes a function to return the sum of all elements in the array. A vector of vectors can be used to represent a two-dimensional array. Here is an example to represent an array with four rows and three columns:

```cpp
vector<vector<int> > matrix(4); // Four rows

for (int i = 0; i < 4; i++)
  matrix[i] = vector<int>(3);

matrix[0][0] = 1; matrix[0][1] = 2; matrix[0][2] = 3;
matrix[1][0] = 4; matrix[1][1] = 5; matrix[1][2] = 6;
matrix[2][0] = 7; matrix[2][1] = 8; matrix[2][2] = 9;
matrix[3][0] = 10; matrix[3][1] = 11; matrix[3][2] = 12;
```

Note

There is a space separating > and > in the line

```cpp
vector<vector<int> > matrix(4); // Four rows
```

Without the space, some old C++ compilers may not compile.

Listing 12.10 revises Listing 8.1, PassTwoDimensionalArray.cpp, using vectors.

LISTING 12.10 TwoDArrayUsingVector.cpp

```cpp
1 #include <iostream>
2 #include <vector>
3 using namespace std;
4
5 int sum(const vector<vector<int> > &matrix)
6 {
7   int total = 0;
8   for (int row = 0; row < matrix.size(); row++)
9   {
10    for (int column = 0; column < matrix[row].size(); column++)
11    {
12      total += matrix[row][column];
13    }
14  }
15
16  return total;
17 }
18
19 int main()
20 {
21   vector< vector<int> > matrix(4); // Four rows
22
23   for (int i = 0; i < 4; i++)
24     matrix[i] = vector<int>(3); // Each row has three columns
25
26   matrix[0][0] = 1; matrix[0][1] = 2; matrix[0][2] = 3;
27   matrix[1][0] = 4; matrix[1][1] = 5; matrix[1][2] = 6;
28   matrix[2][0] = 7; matrix[2][1] = 8; matrix[2][2] = 9;
29   matrix[3][0] = 10; matrix[3][1] = 11; matrix[3][2] = 12;
30
31   cout << "Sum of all elements is " << sum(matrix) << endl;
32
33   return 0;
34 }
```

include **vector**

function with vector

vector for 2-D array

assign values

> Sum of all elements is 78

The variable `array` is declared as a vector. Each element of the vector `matrix[i]` is another vector. So, `matrix[i][j]` represents the ith row and jth column in a two-dimensional array.

The `sum` function returns the sum of all elements in the vector. The size of the vector can be obtained from the `size()` function in the `vector` class. So, you don't have to specify the vector's size when invoking the `sum` function. The same function for two-dimensional array requires two parameters as follows:

```
int sum(const int a[][COLUMN_SIZE], int rowSize)
```

Using vectors for representing two-dimensional arrays simplifies coding.

12.8 Case Study: Evaluating Expressions

compound expression

Stacks have many applications. This section gives an application of using stacks. You can enter an arithmetic expression from Google to evaluate the expression as shown in Figure 12.3.

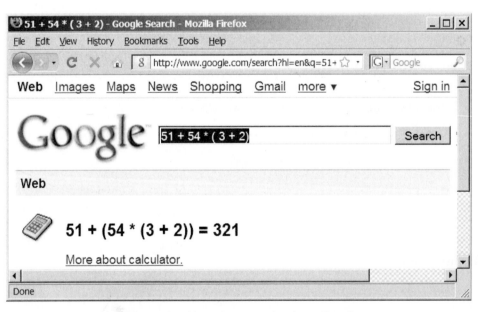

FIGURE 12.3 You can evaluate an arithmetic expression from Google.

How does Google evaluate an expression? This section presents a program that evaluates a *compound expression* with multiple operators and parentheses (e.g., $(15 + 2) * 34 - 2$). For simplicity, assume that the operands are integers and operators are of four types: +, -, *, and /.

process an operator

The problem can be solved using two stacks, named `operandStack` and `operatorStack`, for storing operands and operators, respectively. Operands and operators are pushed into the stacks before they are processed. When an *operator is processed*, it is popped from `operatorStack` and applied on the first two operands from `operandStack` (the two operands are popped from `operandStack`). The resultant value is pushed back to `operandStack`.

The algorithm takes two phases:

Phase I: Scanning expression

The program scans the expression from left to right to extract operands, operators, and the parentheses.

- If the extracted item is an operand, push it to **operandStack**.
- If the extracted item is a + or – operator, process all the operators at the top of **operatorStack** with higher or equal precedence (i.e., +, –, *, /), push the extracted operator to **operatorStack**.
- If the extracted item is a * or / operator, process all the operators at the top of **operatorStack** with higher or equal precedence (i.e., *, /), push the extracted operator to **operatorStack**.
- If the extracted item is a (symbol, push it to **operatorStack**.
- If the extracted item is a) symbol, repeatedly process the operators from the top of **operatorStack** until seeing the (symbol on the stack.

Phase II: Clearing stack

Repeatedly process the operators from the top of **operatorStack** until **operatorStack** is empty.

The following diagram shows how the algorithm is applied to evaluate the expression **(1 + 2) * 4 – 3**.

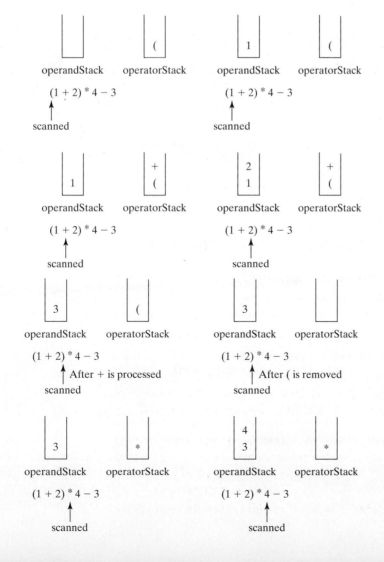

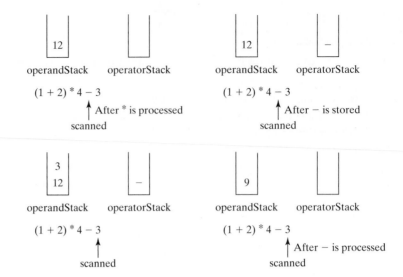

Listing 12.11 gives the program.

LISTING 12.11 EvaluateExpression.cpp

```
1  #include <iostream>
2  #include <vector>
3  #include <string>
4  #include <cctype>
5  #include "ImprovedStack.h"
6
7  using namespace std;
8
9  // Split an expression into numbers, operators, and parentheses
10 vector<string> split(const string &expression);
11
12 // Evaluate an expression and return the result
13 int evaluateExpression(const string &expression);
14
15 // Perform an operation
16 void processAnOperator(
17   Stack<int> &operandStack, Stack<char> &operatorStack);
18
19 int main()
20 {
21   string expression;
22   cout << "Enter an expression: ";
23   getline(cin, expression);
24
25   cout << expression << " = "
26     << evaluateExpression(expression) << endl;
27
28   return 0;
29 }
30
31 vector<string> split(const string &expression)
32 {
33   vector<string> v; // A vector to store split items as strings
34   string numberString; // A numeric string
35
36   for (int i = 0; i < expression.length(); i++)
```

split expression

evaluate expression

perform an operation

read an expression

evaluate expression

split expression

```
37    {
38      if (isdigit(expression[i]))
39        numberString.append(1, expression[i]); // Append a digit        append numeral
40      else
41      {
42        if (numberString.size() > 0)
43        {
44          v.push_back(numberString); // Store the numeric string         store number
45          numberString.erase(); // Empty the numeric string
46        }
47
48        if (!isspace(expression[i]))
49        {
50          string s;
51          s.append(1, expression[i]);
52          v.push_back(s); // Store an operator and parenthese            store operator/parenthese
53        }
54      }
55    }
56
57    // Store the last numeric string
58    if (numberString.size() > 0)
59      v.push_back(numberString);                                        store last number
60
61    return v;
62 }
63
64 /** Evaluate an expression */
65 int evaluateExpression(const string &expression)
66 {
67    // Create operandStack to store operands
68    Stack<int> operandStack;                                            operandStack
69
70    // Create operatorStack to store operators                          + or - scanned
71    Stack<char> operatorStack;                                          operatorStack
72
73    // Extract operands and operators
74    vector<string> tokens = split(expression);                          split expression
75
76    // Phase 1: Scan tokens
77    for (int i = 0; i < tokens.size(); i++)                             scan each token
78    {
79      if (tokens[i][0] == '+' || tokens[i][0] == '-')
80      {
81        // Process all +, -, *, / in the top of the operator stack
82        while (!operatorStack.empty() && (operatorStack.peek() == '+'
83         || operatorStack.peek() == '-' || operatorStack.peek() == '*'
84         || operatorStack.peek() == '/'))
85        {
86          processAnOperator(operandStack, operatorStack);
87        }
88
89        // Push the + or - operator into the operator stack
90        operatorStack.push(tokens[i][0]);
91      }
92      else if (tokens[i][0] == '*' || tokens[i][0] == '/')              * or / scanned
93      {
94        // Process all *, / in the top of the operator stack
95        while (!operatorStack.empty() && (operatorStack.peek() == '*'
96          || operatorStack.peek() == '/'))
```

```
 97      {
 98        processAnOperator(operandStack, operatorStack);
 99      }
100
101      // Push the * or / operator into the operator stack
102      operatorStack.push(tokens[i][0]);
103    }
104    else if (tokens[i][0] == '(')
105    {
106      operatorStack.push('('); // Push '(' to stack
107    }
108    else if (tokens[i][0] == ')')
109    {
110      // Process all the operators in the stack until seeing '('
111      while (operatorStack.peek() != '(')
112      {
113        processAnOperator(operandStack, operatorStack);
114      }
115
116      operatorStack.pop(); // Pop the '(' symbol from the stack
117    }
118    else
119    { // An operand scanned. Push an operand to the stack as integer
120      operandStack.push(atoi(tokens[i].c_str()));
121    }
122  }
123
124  // Phase 2: process all the remaining operators in the stack
125  while (!operatorStack.empty())
126  {
127    processAnOperator(operandStack, operatorStack);
128  }
129
130  // Return the result
131  return operandStack.pop();
132 }
133
134 /** Process one opeator: Take an operator from operatorStack and
135  * apply it on the operands in the operandStack */
136 void processAnOperator(
137    Stack<int> &operandStack, Stack<char> &operatorStack)
138 {
139    char op = operatorStack.pop();
140    int op1 = operandStack.pop();
141    int op2 = operandStack.pop();
142    if (op == '+')
143      operandStack.push(op2 + op1);
144    else if (op == '-')
145      operandStack.push(op2 - op1);
146    else if (op == '*')
147      operandStack.push(op2 * op1);
148    else if (op == '/')
149      operandStack.push(op2 / op1);
150 }
```

(with left-margin annotations:)
(scanned — line 104
) scanned — line 108
an operand scanned — line 120
clear **operatorStack** — line 127
return result — line 131
process + — line 143
process - — line 145
process * — line 147
process / — line 149

```
Enter an expression: (13 + 2) * 4 - 3  ↵Enter
(13 + 2) * 4 - 3 = 57
```

```
Enter an expression: 5 / 4 + (2 - 3) * 5 ⏎Enter
5 / 4 + (2 - 3) * 5 = -4
```

The program reads an expression as a string (line 23) and invokes the `evaluateExpression` function (line 26) to evaluate the expression.

The `evaluateExpression` function creates two stacks `operandStack` and `operatorStack` (lines 68, 71) and invokes the `split` function to extract numbers, operators, and parentheses from the expression (line 74) into tokens. The tokens are stored in a vector of strings. For example, if the expression is `(13 + 2) * 4 - 3)`, the tokens are `(, 13, +, 2, ), *, 4, -`, and `3`.

The `evaluateExpression` function scans each token in the `for` loop (lines 77–122). If a token is an operand, push it to `operandStack` (line 120). If a token is a + or – operator (line 79), process all the operators from the top of `operatorStack` if any (lines 81–87) and push the newly scanned operator to the stack (line 90). If a token is a * or / operator (line 92), process all the * and / operators from the top of `operatorStack` if any (lines 95–99) and push the newly scanned operator to the stack (line 102). If a token is a `(` symbol (line 104), push it to `operatorStack`. If a token is a `)` symbol (line 108), process all the operators from the top of `operatorStack` until seeing the `)` symbol (lines 111–114) and pop the `)` symbol from the stack (line 116).

After all tokens are considered, the program processes the remaining operators in `operatorStack` (lines 125–128).

The `processAnOperator` function (lines 136–150) processes an operator. The function pops the operator from `operatorStack` (line 139) and pops two operands from `operandStack` (lines 140–141). Depending on the operator, the function performs an operation and pushes the result of the operation back to `operandStack` (lines 143, 145, 147, 149).

KEY TERMS

template class 396	type parameter 391
template function 391	vector 403
template prefix 391	stack 395

CHAPTER SUMMARY

1. Templates provide the capability to parameterize types in functions and classes.

2. You can define functions or classes with generic types that can be substituted for concrete types by the compiler.

3. The definition for the function template begins with the keyword `template` followed by a list of parameters. Each parameter must be preceded by the interchangeable keywords `class` or `typename` in the form `<typename typeParameter>` or `<class typeParameter>`

4. When you define a generic function, it is better to start with a nongeneric function, debug and test it, and then convert it to a generic function.

5. The syntax for class templates is basically the same as that for function templates. You place the template prefix before the class declaration, just as you place the template prefix before the function template.

6. If the elements need to be processed in a last-in first-out fashion, use a stack to store the elements.

7. The array size is fixed after it is created. C++ provides the `vector` class, which is more flexible than arrays.

8. The `vector` class is a generic class. You can use it to create objects for concrete types.

9. You can use a `vector` object just like an array, but a vector's size can grow automatically if needed.

REVIEW QUESTIONS

Sections 12.2–12.3

12.1 For the `maxValue` function in Listing 12.1, can you invoke it with two arguments of different types, such as `maxValue(1, 1.5)`?

12.2 For the `maxValue` function in Listing 12.1, can you invoke it with two arguments of strings, such as `maxValue("ABC", "ABD")`? Can you invoke it with two arguments of circles, such as `maxValue(Circle(2), Circle(3))`?

12.3 Can `template<typename T>` be replaced by `template<class T>`?

12.4 Can a type parameter be named using any identifier other than a keyword?

12.5 Can a type parameter be of a primitive type or an object type?

12.6 What is wrong in the following code?

```
1 #include <iostream>
2 #include <string>
3 using namespace std;
4
5 template<typename T>
6 T maxValue(T value1, T value2)
7 {
8     int result;
9     if (value1 > value2)
10       result = value1;
11    else
12       result = value2;
13    return result;
14 }
15
16 int main()
17 {
18    cout << "Maximum between 1 and 3 is "
19      << maxValue(1, 3) << endl;
20    cout << "Maximum between 1.5 and 0.3 is "
21      << maxValue(1.5, 0.3) << endl;
22    cout << "Maximum between 'A' and 'N' is "
23     << maxValue('A', 'N') << endl;
24    cout << "Maximum between \"ABC\" and \"ABD\" is "
25      << maxValue("ABC", "ABD") << endl;
26
27    return 0;
28 }
```

12.7 Suppose you define the maxValue function as follows:

```
template<typename T1, typename T2>
T1 maxValue(T1 value1, T2 value2)
{
  if (value1 > value2)
    return value1;
  else
    return value2;
}
```

What would be the return value from invoking maxValue(1,   2.5), maxValue(1.4, 2.5), and maxValue(1.5, 2)?

12.8 Suppose you define the swap function as follows:

```
template<typename T>
void swap(T &var1, T &var2)
{
  T temp = var1;
  var1 = var2;
  var2 = temp;
}
```

What is wrong in the following code?

```
1 int main()
2 {
3   int v1 = 1;
4   int v2 = 2;
5   swap(v1, v2);
6
7   double d1 = 1;
8   double d2 = 2;
9   swap(d1, d2);
10
11  swap(v1, d2);
12  swap(1, 2);
13
14  return 0;
15 }
```

Sections 12.4–12.5

12.9 Do you have to use the template prefix for each function in the class declaration? Do you have to use the template prefix for each function in the class implementation?

12.10 What is wrong in the following code?

```
template<typename T = int>
void printArray(T list[], int arraySize)
{
  for (int i = 0; i < arraySize; i++)
  {
    cout << list[i] << " ";
  }
  cout << endl;
}
```

12.11 What is wrong in the following code?

```
1 template<typename T>
2 class Foo
3 {
4 public:
5    Foo();
6    T f1(T value);
7    T f2();
8 };
9
10 Foo::Foo()
11 {
12    ...
13 }
14
15 T Stack::f1(T value)
16 {
17    ...
18 }
19
20 T Stack::f2()
21 {
22    ...
23 };
```

12.12 Suppose the template prefix for the **Stack** class is

```
template<typename T = string>
```

Can you create a stack of strings using the following?

```
Stack stack;
```

12.13 What is wrong if line 79 in Listing 12.7 ImprovedStack.h is replaced by

```
delete old;
```

Section 12.6

12.14 How do you declare a vector to store **double** values? How do you append a **double** to a vector? How do you find the size of a vector? How do you remove an element from a vector?

12.15 Why is the code in (a) wrong, but the code in (b) correct?

```
vector<int> v;
v[0] = 4;
```
(a)

```
vector<int> v(5);
v[0] = 4;
```
(b)

12.16 Write the code that represents the following array using a vector:

```
int list[4] = {1, 2, 3, 4};
```

12.17 Write the code that represents the following array using a vector:

```
int matrix[4][4] =
  {{1, 2, 3, 4},
```

```
{5, 6, 7, 8},
{9, 10, 11, 12},
{13, 14, 15, 16}};
```

PROGRAMMING EXERCISES

12.1 (*Maximum in array*) Design a generic function that returns a maximum element from an array. The function should have two parameters. One is the array of a generic type, and the other is the size of the array. Test the function with the array of `int`, `double`, and `string` values.

12.2 (*Linear search*) Rewrite the linear search function in Listing 7.8, LinarySearch.h, to use a generic type for array elements. Test the function with array of `int`, `double`, and `string` values.

12.3 (*Binary search*) Rewrite the binary search function in Listing 7.9, BinarySearch.h, to use a generic type for array elements. Test the function with array of `int`, `double`, and `string` values.

12.4 (*Insertion sort*) Rewrite the insertion search function in Listing 7.11, InsertionSort.h, to use a generic type for array elements. Test the function with array of `int`, `double`, and `string` values.

12.5 (*Swap values*) Write a generic function that swaps values in two variables. Your function should have two parameters of the same type. Test the function with `int`, `double`, and `string` values.

12.6* (*Function `printStack`*) Add the `printStack` function into the `Stack` class as an instance function to display all the elements in the stack. The `Stack` class was introduced in Listing 12.4, GenericStack.h.

12.7* (*Function `contains`*) Add the `contains(T element)` function into the `Stack` class as an instance function to check whether the element is in the stack. The `Stack` class was introduced in Listing 12.4, GenericStack.h.

12.8** (*Implementing `vector` class*) The `vector` class is provided in the standard C++ library. Implement the `vector` class as an exercise. The standard vector class has many functions. For this exercise, implement only the functions defined in the UML class diagram, as shown in Figure 12.2.

12.9 (*Implementing a stack class using a vector*) In Listing 12.4, `GenericStack` is implemented using arrays. Implement it using a vector.

12.10 (*The `Course` class*) Rewrite the `Course` class in Listing 11.17, Course1.h. Use a `vector` to replace an array to store students.

12.11** (*Simulation: coupon collector's problem*) Rewrite Exercise 7.21 using vectors to represent arrays.

12.12** (*Geometry: same line?*) Rewrite Exercise 8.16 using vectors to represent arrays.

Video Note
Use vector to replace arrays

12.13** (*Splitting an expression*) Suppose an expression is represented in a string (i.e., `35 * 4 + 5 / (4 + 5)`). Write a function that splits the expression into numbers, operators, and parentheses. The function takes an expression as the argument and returns a vector of strings. Each string represents a number, an operand, or a parenthesis. The header of the function is given as follows:

```
vector<string> split(const string &expression)
```

For example, `split("35 * 4 + 5 / (4 + 5)")` returns a vector that contains the strings 35, *, 4, +, 5, /, (, 4, +, 5,).

Write a test program that prompts the user to enter an expression and displays the split items in reverse order. For example, if the user enters 4 + 50, the program displays 50, +, and 4 in three lines in this order.

12.14 (*Closest pair*) Listing 8.3 finds a closest pair of two points. The program prompts the user to enter 8 points. The number 8 is fixed. Rewrite the program. First prompt the user to enter the number of points, and then prompt the user to enter all the points.

12.15** (*Matching grouping symbols*) A C++ program contains various pairs of grouping symbols, such as:

Parentheses: (and).
Braces: { and }.
Brackets: [and].

Note that the grouping symbols cannot overlap. For example, (a{b)} is illegal. Write a program that prompts the user to enter a C++ source-code file name and checks whether the file has correct pairs of grouping symbols.

12.16** (*Postfix notation*) Postfix notation is a way of writing expressions without using parentheses. For example, the expression (1 + 2) * 3 would be written as 1 2 + 3 *. A postfix expression is evaluated using a stack. Scan a postfix expression from left to right. A variable or constant is pushed to the stack. When an operator is encountered, apply the operator with the top two operands in the stack and replace the two operands with the result. The following diagram shows how to evaluate 1 2 + 3 *.

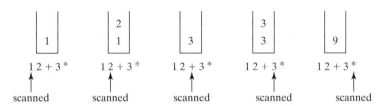

Write a program that prompts the user to enter a postfix expression and evaluates it.

12.17**** (*Game: the 24-point card game*) The 24-point card game is to pick any four cards from 52 cards (note two Jokers are excluded). Each card represents a number. A King, Queen, and Jack represent 13, 12, and 11, respectively. Enter an expression that uses the four numbers for the selected cards. Each number must be used once and only once. You can use the operators (addition, subtraction, multiplication, and division) and parentheses in any combination in the expression. The expression must evaluate to 24. If such an expression does not exist, enter 0. Here is a sample run of the program:

```
4 of Clubs
Ace of Diamonds
6 of Hearts
Jack of Clubs
Enter an expression: (11 + 1 - 6) * 4  ↵Enter
Congratulations! You got it!
```

```
Ace (1) of Diamonds
5 of Diamonds
9 of Spades
Queen (12) of Hearts
Enter an expression: (13 - 9) * (1 + 5)  ↵Enter
Congratulations! You got it!
```

```
6 of Clubs
5 of Clubs
Jack (11) of Clubs
5 of Spades
Enter an expression: 0  ↵Enter
Sorry, one correct expression would be (5 * 6) - (11 - 5)
```

```
6 of Clubs
5 of Clubs
Queen (12) of Clubs
5 of Spades
Enter an expression: 0  ↵Enter
Yes. No 24 points
```

12.18** (*Converting infix to postfix*) Write a function that converts an infix expression into a postfix expression using the following header.

```
string infixToPostfix(const string &expression)
```

For example, the function should convert the infix expression $(1 + 2) * 3$ to $1 \; 2 \; + \; 3 \; *$ and $2 * (1 + 3)$ to $2 \; 1 \; 3 \; + \; *$.

CHAPTER 13

FILE INPUT AND OUTPUT

Objectives

- To use `ofstream` for output (§13.2.1) and `ifstream` for input (§13.2.2).
- To test whether a file exists (§13.2.3).
- To test the end of a file (§13.2.4).
- To write data in a desired format (§13.3).
- To read and write data using the `getline`, `get`, and `put` functions (§13.4).
- To use an `fstream` object to read and write data (§13.5).
- To open a file with specified modes (§13.5).
- To use the `eof()`, `fail()`, `bad()`, and `good()` functions to test stream states (§13.6).
- To understand the difference between text I/O and binary I/O (§13.7).
- To write binary data using the `write` function (§13.7.1).
- To read binary data using the `read` function (§13.7.2).
- To cast primitive type values and objects to character arrays using the `reinterpret_cast` operator (§13.7).
- To read/write arrays and objects (§§13.7.3–13.7.4).
- To use the `seekp` and `seekg` functions to move the file pointers for random file access (§13.8).
- To open a file for both input and output to update files (§13.9).

13.1 Introduction

Data stored in variables, arrays, and objects are temporary; they are lost when the program terminates. To permanently store the data created in a program, you need to save them in a file on a permanent storage medium, such as a disk. The file can be transported and can be read later by other programs.

C++ provides the `ifstream`, `ofstream`, and `fstream` classes for processing and manipulating files. These classes are all defined in the `<fstream>` header file. The `ifstream` class is for reading data from a file, the `ofstream` class is for writing data to a file, and the `fstream` class can be used for both reading and writing data in a file.

C++ uses the term *stream* to describe a flow of data. If it flows to your program, the stream is called an *input stream*. If it flows out from your program, it is called an *output stream*. C++ uses objects to read/write a stream of data. For convenience, an input object is called an *input stream* and an output object is called an *output stream*.

input stream

output stream

You have already used the input stream and output stream in your programs. `cin` (console input) is a predefined object for reading input from the keyboard, and `cout` (console output) is a predefined object for outputting characters to the console. These two objects are defined in the `<iostream>` header file. In this chapter, you will learn how to read/write data from/to files.

cin stream

cout stream

13.2 Text I/O

Video Note
simple text I/O

This section demonstrates how to perform simple text input and output. Let us first consider output.

13.2.1 Writing Data to a File

The `ofstream` class can be used to write primitive data-type values, arrays, strings, and objects to a text file. Listing 13.1 demonstrates how to write data. The program creates an instance of `ofstream` and writes two lines to the file "scores.txt". Each line consists of first name (a string), middle name initial (a character), last name (a string), and score (an integer).

LISTING 13.1 TextFileOutput.cpp

include **fstream** header

declare object

open file

output to file

close file

```
1 #include <iostream>
2 #include <fstream>
3 using namespace std;
4
5 int main()
6 {
7   ofstream output;
8
9   // Create a file
10  output.open("scores.txt");
11
12  // Write two lines
13  output << "John" << " " << "T" << " " << "Smith"
14    << " " << 90 << endl;
15  output << "Eric" << " " << "K" << " " << "Jones"
16    << " " << 85 << endl;
17
18  output.close();
19
20  cout << "Done" << endl;
21
22  return 0;
23 }
```

scores.txt

```
John T Smith 90
Eric K Jones 85
```

Since the `ofstream` class is defined in the `fstream` header file, line 2 includes this header file.

Line 7 creates an object, `output`, from the `ofstream` class using its no-arg constructor.

Line 10 opens a file named scores.txt for the `output` object. If the file does not exist, a new file is created. If the file already exists, its contents are destroyed without warning.

You can write data to the `output` object using the stream insertion operator (`<<`) in the same way that you send data to the `cout` object. Lines 13–16 write strings and numeric values to `output`, as shown in Figure 13.1.

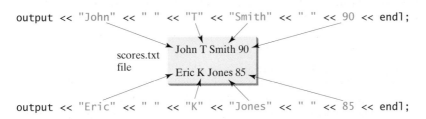

FIGURE 13.1 The output stream sends data to the file.

The `close()` function (line 18) must be used to close the stream for the object. If this function is not invoked, the data may not be saved properly in the file.

You may open an output stream using the following constructor:

```
ofstream output("scores.txt");
```

This statement is equivalent to

```
ofstream output;
output.open("scores.txt");
```

Caution
If a file already exists, its contents will be destroyed without warning.

Note
Every file is placed in a directory in the file system. An *absolute file name* contains a file name with its complete path and drive letter. For example, **c:\example\scores.txt** is the absolute file name for the file **scores.txt** on the Windows operating system. Here **c:\example** is referred to as the *directory path* for the file. Absolute file names are machine dependent. On UNIX, the absolute file name may be **/home/liang/example/scores.txt**, where **/home/liang/example** is the directory path for the file **scores.txt**.

Caution
The directory separator for Windows is a backslash (\). The backslash is a special character in C++ and should be written as \\ in a string literal (see Table 2.5). For example,

```
output.open("c:\\example\\scores.txt");
```

Note
An absolute file name is platform dependent. It is better to use a *relative file name* without drive letters. If you use an IDE to run C++, the directory of the relative file name can be specified in the IDE. For example, the default directory for data files is the same directory with the source code in Visual C++.

Margin notes:
including **<fstream>** header

create object

open file

cout

close file

alternative syntax

file exists?

absolute file name

\ in file names

relative file name

13.2.2 Reading Data from a File

The `ifstream` class can be used to read data from a text file. Listing 13.2 demonstrates how to read data. The program creates an instance of `ifstream` and reads data from the file scores.txt, which was created in the preceding example.

LISTING 13.2 TextFileInput.cpp

```
1 #include <iostream>
2 #include <fstream>
3 #include <string>
4 using namespace std;
5
6 int main()
7 {
8     ifstream input("scores.txt");
9
10    // Read data
11    string firstName;
12    char mi;
13    string lastName;
14    int score;
15    input >> firstName >> mi >> lastName >> score;
16    cout << firstName << " " << mi << " " << lastName << " "
17      << score << endl;
18
19    input >> firstName >> mi >> lastName >> score;
20    cout << firstName << " " << mi << " " << lastName << " "
21      << score << endl;
22
23    input.close();
24
25    cout << "Done" << endl;
26
27    return 0;
28 }
```

*include **fstream** header* — line 2
input object — line 8
input from file — line 15
input from file — line 19
close file — line 23

```
John T Smith 90
Eric K Jones 85
Done
```

*including **<fstream>** header*

Since the `ifstream` class is defined in the `fstream` header file, line 2 includes this header file.

Line 8 creates an object, `input`, from the `ifstream` class for file "scores.txt".

cin

You can read data from the `input` object using the stream extraction operator (>>) in the same way that you read data from the `cin` object. Lines 15 and 19 read strings and numeric values from the input file, as shown in Figure 13.2.

input >> firstName >> mi >> lastName >> score;

scores.txt
file

John T Smith 90

Eric K Jones 85

input >> firstName >> mi >> lastName >> score;

FIGURE 13.2 The input stream reads data from the file.

The `close()` function (line 23) must be used to close the stream for the object. It is not necessary to close the input file, but doing so is a good practice in order to release the resources occupied by the file.

close file

You may open an input stream using the following constructor:

alternative syntax

```
ifstream input("scores.txt");
```

This statement is equivalent to

```
ifstream input;
input.open("scores.txt");
```

Caution

To read data correctly, you need to know exactly how data are stored. For example, the program in Listing 13.2 would not work if the file contained number as a **double** value with a decimal point.

know data format

13.2.3 Testing File Existence

If the file does not exist, your program will run and produce incorrect results. Can your program check whether a file exists? Yes. You can invoke the `fail()` function immediately after invoking the **open** function. If `fail()` returns **true**, it indicates that the file does not exist.

file not exist?

```
 1 // Open a file
 2 input.open("scores.txt");
 3
 4 if (input.fail())
 5 {
 6    cout << "File does not exist" << endl;
 7    cout << "Exit program" << endl;
 8
 9    return 0;
10 }
```

check file operation

13.2.4 Testing End of File

Listing 13.2 reads two lines from the data file. If you don't know how many lines are in the file and want to read them all, how do you recognize the end of file? You can invoke the `eof()` function on the input object to detect it.

eof function

Suppose a file named **number.txt** contains the numbers shown in Figure 13.3.

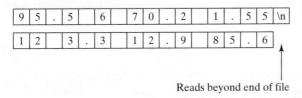

Reads beyond end of file

FIGURE 13.3   The input stream reads data from the file.

Listing 13.3 gives a program that reads numbers from the file and displays their sum.

LISTING 13.3 `TestEndOfFile.cpp`

```
1 #include <iostream>
2 #include <fstream>
3 using namespace std;
4
```

include **fstream** header

```
5  int main()
6  {
7      // Open a file
8      ifstream input("number.txt");
9
10     if (input.fail())
11     {
12         cout << "File does not exist" << endl;
13         cout << "Exit program" << endl;
14         return 0;
15     }
16
17     double sum = 0;
18     double number;
19     while (!input.eof()) // Continue if not end of file
20     {
21         input >> number;  // Read data
22         cout << number << " ";  // Display data
23         sum += number;
24     }
25
26     input.close();
27
28     cout << "\nSum is " << sum << endl;
29
30     return 0;
31 }
```

create input object (line 8)

file exists? (line 10)

end of file? (line 19)

input from file (line 21)

close file (line 26)

display data (line 28)

```
95.5 6 70.2 1.55 12 3.3 12.9 85.6
sum is 287.05
```

The program reads data in a loop (lines 19–24). Each iteration of the loop reads one number and adds it to sum. The loop terminates when the input reaches the end of file.

end of file?

How does the program recognize the end of file? When there is nothing more to read, eof() returns true. How does the program know there is nothing to read? This information is obtained from the operating system. When the program reads the last number 85.6 in the file, it attempts to read beyond 6, as shown in Figure 13.3. The operating system notifies the program that the end of file is reached. When you invoke eof() immediately after reading the last number, it returns true.

Caution

Ctrl+Z or Ctrl+D

If the data are read from the console, you can use *Ctrl+Z* on Windows or *Ctrl+D* on UNIX to signify the end of file.

13.3 Formatting Output

You have used the stream manipulators to format output to the console in §3.16, "Formatting Output." You can use the same stream manipulator to format output to a file. Listing 13.4 gives an example that formats the student records to the file named formattedscores.txt.

LISTING 13.4 WriteFormatData.cpp

include **iomanip** header
include **fstream** header

```
1 #include <iostream>
2 #include <iomanip>
3 #include <fstream>
4 using namespace std;
5
```

```
 6 int main()
 7 {
 8   ofstream output;                                                           declare object
 9
10   // Create a file
11   output.open("formattedscores.txt");
12
13   // Write two lines
14   output << setw(6) << "John" << setw(2) << "T" << setw(6) << "Smith"        output with format
15      << " " << setw(4) << 90 << endl;
16   output << setw(6) << "Eric" << setw(2) << "K" << setw(6) << "Jones"        output with format
17      << " " << setw(4) << 85;
18
19   output.close();                                                            close file
20
21   cout << "Done" << endl;
22
23   return 0;
24 }
```

The contents of the file are shown below:

		J	o	h	n		T		S	m	i	t	h			9	0	\n
		E	r	i	c		K		J	o	n	e	s			8	5	

13.4 Functions: **getline**, **get**, and **put**

There is a problem in reading data using the stream extraction operator (>>). Data are delimited by whitespace. What happens if the whitespace characters are part of a string? In §10.2.11, "Reading Strings," you learned how to use the **getline** function to read a string with whitespace. You can use the same function to read strings from a file. Recall that the syntax for the **getline** function is

```
getline(ifstream &input, int string s, char delimitChar)
```

The function stops reading characters when the delimiter character or end-of-file mark is encountered. If the delimiter is encountered, it is read but not stored in the array. The third argument **delimitChar** has a default value ('\n'). The **getline** function is defined in the **iostream** header file.   **getline**

Suppose a file named state.txt is created that contains the state names delimited by the pound (#) symbol. The following diagram shows the contents in the file:

N	e	w		Y	o	r	k	#	N	e	w		M	e	x	i	c	o
#	T	e	x	a	s	#	I	n	d	i	a	n	a					

Listing 13.5 gives a program that reads the states from the file.

LISTING 13.5   ReadCity.cpp

```
1 #include <iostream>
2 #include <fstream>                                                           include fstream header
3 #include <string>
4 using namespace std;
5
```

```
 6 int main()
 7 {
 8   // Open a file
 9   ifstream input("state.txt");
10
11   if (input.fail())
12   {
13     cout << "File does not exist" << endl;
14     cout << "Exit program" << endl;
15     return 0;
16   }
17
18   // Read data
19   string city;
20
21   while (!input.eof()) // Continue if not end of file
22   {
23     getline(input, city, '#');
24     cout << city << endl;
25   }
26
27   input.close();
28
29   cout << "Done" << endl;
30
31   return 0;
32 }
```

input object *(line 9)*

file exist? *(line 11)*

string city *(line 19)*

end of file? *(line 21)*

input from file *(line 23)*
display data *(line 24)*

close file *(line 27)*

```
New York
New Mexico
Texas
Indiana
Done
```

Invoking `getline(input, state, '#')` (line 23) reads characters to the array `state` until it encounters the # character or the end-of-file.

Two other useful functions are `get` and `put`. You can invoke the `get` function on an input object to read a character and invoke the `put` function on an output object to write a character.

get function

The `get` function has two versions:

```
char get() // Return a char
ifstream * get(char &ch) // Read a character to ch
```

The first version returns a character from the input. The second version passes a character reference argument, reads a character from the input, and stores it in `ch`. This function also returns the reference to the input object being used.

put function

The header for the `put` function is

```
void put(char ch)
```

It writes the specified character to the output object.

Listing 13.6 gives an example of using these two functions. The program prompts the user to enter a file and copies it to a new file.

LISTING 13.6 CopyFile.cpp

include **fstream** header

```
1 #include <iostream>
2 #include <fstream>
3 #include <string>
```

```
 4 using namespace std;
 5
 6 int main()
 7 {
 8   // Enter a source file
 9   cout << "Enter a source file name: ";
10   string inputFilename;
11   cin >> inputFilename;                                      enter input filename
12
13   // Enter a target file
14   cout << "Enter a target file name: ";
15   string outputFilename;
16   cin >> outputFilename;                                     enter output filename
17
18   // Create input and output streams
19   ifstream input(inputFilename.c_str());                     input object
20   ofstream output(outputFilename.c_str());                   output object
21
22   if (input.fail())                                          file exist?
23   {
24     cout << inputFilename << " does not exist" << endl;
25     cout << "Exit program" << endl;
26     return 0;
27   }
28
29   char ch = input.get();
30   while (!input.eof()) // Continue if not end of file         end of file?
31   {
32     output.put(ch);                                          put function
33     ch = input.get(); // Read next character                 get function
34   }
35
36   input.close();                                             close file
37   output.close();                                            close file
38
39   cout << "\nCopy Done" << endl;
40
41   return 0;
42 }
```

```
Enter a source file name: c:\example\CopyFile.cpp  ⏎Enter
Enter a target file name: c:\example\temp.txt  ⏎Enter
Copy Done
```

The program prompts the user to enter a source file name in line 11 and a target file name in line 16. An input object for **inputFilename** is created in line 19 and an output object for **outputFilename** in line 20. File names must be C-strings. **inputFilename.c_str()** returns a C-string from string **inputFilename**.

Lines 22–27 check whether the input file exists. Lines 30–34 read characters repeatedly one at a time using the **get** function and write the character to the output file using the **put** function.

Suppose lines 29–34 are replaced by the following code:

```
while (!input.eof()) // Continue if not end of file
{
  output.put(input.get());
}
```

What will happen? If you run the program with this new code, you will see that the new file is one byte larger than the original one. The new file contains an extra garbage character at the end. The reason is that, when the last character is read from the input file using `input.get()`, `input.eof()` is still `false`. Afterward, the program attempts to read another character; `input.eof()` now becomes `true`. However, the extraneous garbage character has already been sent to the output file.

The correct code in Listing 13.6 reads a character (line 29) and checks `eof()` (line 30). If `eof()` is `true`, the character is not put to `output`; otherwise, it is copied (line 32). This process continues until `eof()` returns `true`.

13.5 `fstream` and File Open Modes

In the preceding sections, you used the `ofstream` to write data and the `ifstream` to read data. Alternatively, you can use the `fstream` class to create an input or output stream. It is convenient to use `fstream` if your program needs to use the same stream object for both input and output. To open an `fstream` file, you have to specify a file mode to tell C++ how the file will be used. The file modes are listed in Table 13.1.

TABLE 13.1 File Modes

Mode	Description
`ios::in`	Opens a file for input.
`ios::out`	Opens a file for output.
`ios::app`	Appends all output to the end of the file.
`ios::ate`	Opens a file for output. If the file already exists, move to the end of the file. Data can be written anywhere in the file.
`ios::truct`	Discards the file's contents if the file already exists. (This is the default action for `ios:out`.)
`ios::binary`	Opens a file for binary input and output.

Note

Some of the file modes also can be used with `ifstream` and `ofstream` objects to open a file. For example, you may use the `ios:app` mode to open a file with an `ofstream` object so that you can append data to the file. However, for consistency and simplicity, it is better to use the file modes with the `fstream` objects.

Note

combining modes

Several modes can be combined using the | operator. This is a bitwise inclusive-OR operator. See Supplement IV.J, "Bit Operations," for more details. For example, to open an output file named city.txt for appending data, you can use the following statement:

```
stream.open("city.txt", ios::out | ios::app);
```

Listing 13.7 gives a program that creates a new file named city.txt (line 11) and writes data to the file. The program then closes the file and reopens it to append new data (line 19), rather than overriding it. Finally, the program reads all data from the file.

LISTING 13.7 AppendFile.cpp

include **fstream** header

```
1 #include <iostream>
2 #include <fstream>
3 #include <string>
4 using namespace std;
5
```

```
 6 int main()
 7 {
 8   fstream inout;                                                    fstream object
 9
10   // Create a file
11   inout.open("city.txt", ios::out);                                open output file
12
13   // Write cities
14   inout << "Dallas" << " " << "Houston" << " " << "Atlanta" << " ";  write data
15
16   inout.close();                                                    close stream
17
18   // Append to the file
19   inout.open("city.txt", ios::out | ios::app);                     open output for append
20
21   // Write cities
22   inout << "Savannah" << " " << "Austin" << " " << "Chicago";        write data
23
24   inout.close();                                                    close stream
25
26   string city;
27
28   // Open the file
29   inout.open("city.txt", ios::in);                                 open for input
30   while (!inout.eof()) // Continue if not end of file               end of file?
31   {
32     inout >> city;                                                 read data
33     cout << city << " ";
34   }
35
36   inout.close();                                                    close stream
37
38   return 0;
39 }
```

```
Dallas Houston Atlanta Savannah Austin Chicago
```

The program creates an `fstream` object in line 8 and opens the file city.txt for output using the file mode `ios::out` in line 11. After writing data in line 14, the program closes the stream in line 16.

The program uses the same stream object to reopen the text file with the combined modes `ios::out | ios::app` in line 19. The program then appends new data to the end of the file in line 22 and closes the stream in line 24.

Finally, the program uses the same stream object to reopen the text file with the input mode `ios::in` in line 29. The program then reads all data from the file (lines 30–34).

13.6 Testing Stream States

Video Note
testing stream states

You have used the `eof()` function and `fail()` function to test the states of a stream. C++ provides several more functions in a stream for testing *stream states*. Each stream object contains a set of bits that act as flags. These bit values (0 or 1) indicate the state of a stream. Table 13.2 lists these bits.

The states of the I/O operations are represented in these bits. It is not convenient to directly access these bits. C++ provides member functions in the IO stream object to test them. These functions are listed in Table 13.3.

TABLE 13.2 Stream State Bit Values

Bit	Description
`ios::eofbit`	Set when the end of an input stream is reached.
`ios::failbit`	Set when an operation has failed.
`ios::hardfail`	Set when an unrecoverable error has occurred.
`ios::badbit`	Set when an invalid operation has been attempted.
`ios::goodbit`	Set when an operation is successful.

TABLE 13.3 Stream State Functions

Function	Description
`eof()`	Returns `true` if the `eofbit` flag is set.
`fail()`	Returns `true` if the `failbit` or `hardfail` flag is set.
`bad()`	Returns `true` if the `badbit` is set.
`good()`	Returns `true` if the `goodbit` is set.
`clear()`	Clears all flags.

Listing 13.8 gives an example to detect the stream states.

LISTING 13.8 ShowStreamState.cpp

```
 1 #include <iostream>
 2 #include <fstream>
 3 #include <string>
 4 using namespace std;
 5
 6 void showState(fstream &);
 7
 8 int main()
 9 {
10   fstream inout;
11
12   // Create an output file
13   inout.open("temp.txt", ios::out );
14   inout << "Dallas";
15   cout << "Normal operation (no errors)" << endl;
16   showState(inout);
17   inout.close();
18
19   // Create an output file
20   inout.open("temp.txt", ios::in );
21
22   // Read a string
23   string city;
24   inout >> city;
25   cout << "End of file (no errors)" << endl;
26   showState(inout);
27
28   inout.close();
29
30   // Attempt to read after file closed
31   inout >> city;
32   cout << "Bad operation (errors)" << endl;
33   showState(inout);
34
```

include **fstream** header

function prototype

input object

open input file

show state
close file

open output file

read city

show state

close file

show state

```
35    return 0;
36 }
37
38 void showState(fstream & stream)                                    show state
39 {
40    cout << "Stream status: " << endl;
41    cout << "  eof(): " << stream.eof() << endl;
42    cout << "  fail(): " << stream.fail() << endl;
43    cout << "  bad(): " << stream.bad() << endl;
44    cout << "  good(): " << stream.good() << endl;
45 }
```

```
Normal operation (no errors)
Stream status:
  eof(): 0
  fail(): 0
  bad(): 0
  good(): 1
End of file (no errors)

Stream status:
  eof(): 1
  fail(): 0
  bad(): 0
  good(): 0

Bad operation (errors)
Stream status:
  eof(): 1
  fail(): 1
  bad(): 0
  good(): 0
```

The program creates a `fstream` object using its no-arg constructor in line 10, opens temp.txt for output in line 13, and writes a string Dallas in line 14. The state of the stream is displayed in line 16. There are no errors so far.

The program then closes the stream in line 17, reopens temp.txt for input in line 20, and reads a string Dallas in line 24. The state of the stream is displayed in line 26. There are no errors so far, but the end of file is reached.

Finally the program closes the stream in line 28 and attempts to read data after the file is closed in line 31, which causes an error. The state of the stream is displayed in line 33.

When invoking the `showState` function in lines 16, 26, and 33, the stream object is passed to the function by reference.

13.7 Binary I/O

Video Note
binary I/O

So far you have used text files. Data stored in a *text file* are represented in human-readable form. Data stored in a *binary file* are represented in binary form. You cannot read binary files. They are designed to be read by programs. For example, the C++ source programs are stored in text files and can be read by a text editor, but the C++ executable files are stored in binary files and are read by the operating system. The advantage of binary files is that they are more efficient to process than text files.

text file
binary file

Although it is not technically precise and correct, you can envision a text file as consisting of a sequence of characters and a binary file as consisting of a sequence of bits. For example, the decimal integer **199** is stored as the sequence of three characters, `'1'`, `'9'`, `'9'`, in a text file, and the same integer is stored as a **byte**-type value C7 in a binary file, because decimal **199** equals hex C7 ($199 = 12 \times 16^1 + 7$).

> **Note**
>
> Computers do not differentiate binary files and text files. All files are stored in binary format, and thus all files are essentially binary files. *Text I/O* is built upon *binary I/O* to provide a level of abstraction for character encoding and decoding.

text vs. binary I/O

Binary I/O does not require conversions. If you write a numeric value to a file using binary I/O, the exact value in the memory is copied into the file. To perform binary I/O in C++, you have to open a file using the binary mode **ios::binary**. By default, a file is opened in text mode.

ios::binary

You used the << operator and **put** function to write data to a text file and the >> operator, **get**, and **getline** functions to read data from a text file. To read/write data from/to a binary file, you have to use the **read** and **write** functions on a stream.

13.7.1 The **write** Function

The syntax for the **write** function is

write function

```
streamObject.write(char *s, int size)
```

which writes a C-string **s** to the file.

Listing 13.9 shows an example of using the **write** function.

LISTING 13.9 BinaryCharOutput.cpp

```
1 #include <iostream>
2 #include <fstream>
3 #include <string>
4 using namespace std;
5
6 int main()
7 {
8     fstream binaryio;
9     binaryio.open("city.dat", ios::out | ios::binary);
10    string s = "Atlanta";
11    binaryio.write(s.c_str(), s.size()); // Write s to file
12    binaryio.close();
13
14    cout << "Done" << endl;
15
16    return 0;
17 }
```

fstream object
open binary file
string
write data
close file

Line 8 opens the binary file city.dat for output. Invoking binaryio.write(s.c_str(), s.size()) (line 11) writes string **s** to the file.

Often you need to write data other than characters. How can you accomplish this? You can use the **reinterpret_cast** operator to cast data to characters and then write the characters to the file. The **reinterpret_cast** operator can cast any pointer type to another pointer type of unrelated classes. It simply performs a binary copy of the value from one type to the other without altering the data. The syntax of using the **reinterpret_cast** operator is as follows:

```
reinterpret_cast<dataType>(address)
```

Here, **address** is the starting address of the data (primitive, array, or object) and **dataType** is the data type you are casting to. In this case for binary I/O, it is **char***.

For example, see the code in Listing 13.10.

LISTING 13.10 BinaryIntOutput.cpp

```
 1 #include <iostream>
 2 #include <fstream>
 3 using namespace std;
 4
 5 int main()
 6 {
 7   fstream binaryio;
 8   binaryio.open("temp.dat", ios::out | ios::binary);
 9   int value = 199;
10   binaryio.write(reinterpret_cast<char*>(&value), sizeof(value));
11   binaryio.close();
12
13   cout << "Done" << endl;
14
15   return 0;
16 }
```

fstream object
open binary file
int value
binary output
close file

Line 10 writes the content in variable **value** to the file. **reinterpret_cast<char*>**
(&value) (line 10) cast the address of the **int** value to the type **char***. **sizeof(value)**
returns the storage size for the value variable, which is **4**, since it is an **int** type variable.

Note

For consistency, this book uses the extension **.txt** to name text files and **.dat** to name binary
files.

.txt and .dat

13.7.2   The read Function

The syntax for the **read** function is

```
streamObject.read(char *address, int size)
```

read function

The **size** parameter indicates the maximum number of characters read. The actual number of characters read can be obtained from a member function **gcount**.

Assume the file city.dat was created in Listing 13.9. Listing 13.11 reads the characters
using the **read** function.

LISTING 13.11 BinaryCharInput.cpp

```
 1 #include <iostream>
 2 #include <fstream>
 3 using namespace std;
 4
 5 int main()
 6 {
 7   fstream binaryio;
 8   binaryio.open("city.dat", ios::in | ios::binary );
 9   char s[10];
10   binaryio.read(s, 10);
11   cout << "number of chars read: " << binaryio.gcount() << endl;
12   s[binaryio.gcount()] = '\0';
13   cout << s;
14   binaryio.close();
15
16   return 0;
17 }
```

fstream object
open binary file
character array
read data
gcount()

close file

```
Atlan
```

Line 8 opens the binary file city.dat for input. Invoking `binaryio.read(s, 10)` (line 10) reads up to **10** characters from the file to the array. The actual number of characters read can be determined by invoking `binaryio.gcount()` (line 11).

Assume that the file temp.dat was created in Listing 13.10. Listing 13.12 reads the integer using the **read** function.

LISTING 13.12 BinaryIntInput.cpp

```cpp
1  #include <iostream>
2  #include <fstream>
3  using namespace std;
4
5  int main()
6  {
7    fstream binaryio;
8    binaryio.open("temp.dat", ios::in | ios::binary);
9    int value;
10   binaryio.read(reinterpret_cast<char*>(&value), sizeof(value));
11   cout << value;
12   binaryio.close();
13
14   return 0;
15 }
```

fstream object
open binary file
int value
binary output

close file

```
199
```

The data in the file temp.dat were created in Listing 13.10. The data consisted of an integer and were cast to characters before stored. This program first read the data as characters and then used the `reinterpret_cast` operator to cast characters into an **int** value (line 10).

13.7.3 Example: Binary Array I/O

You can use the `reinterpret_cast` operator to cast data of any type to characters and vice versa. This section gives an example in Listing 13.13 to write an array of **double** values to a binary file and read it back from the file.

LISTING 13.13 BinaryArrayIO.cpp

```cpp
1  #include <iostream>
2  #include <fstream>
3  using namespace std;
4
5  int main()
6  {
7    const int SIZE = 5;  // Array size
8
9    fstream binaryio; // Create stream object
10
11   // Write array to the file
12   binaryio.open("array.dat", ios::out | ios::binary);
13   double array[SIZE] = {3.4, 1.3, 2.5, 5.66, 6.9};
14   binaryio.write(reinterpret_cast<char*>(&array), sizeof(array));
15   binaryio.close();
16
```

constant array size

fstream object

open binary file
create array
write to file
close file

```
17   // Read array from the file
18   binaryio.open("array.dat", ios::in | ios::binary );          open input file
19   double result[SIZE];                                          create array
20   binaryio.read(reinterpret_cast<char*>(&result), sizeof(result));   read from file
21   binaryio.close();                                             close file
22
23   // Display array
24   for (int i = 0; i < SIZE; i++)
25     cout << result[i] << " ";
26
27   return 0;
28 }
```

```
3.4 1.3 2.5 5.66 6.9
```

The program creates a stream object in line 9, opens the file array.dat for binary output in line 12, writes an array of **double** values to the file in line 14, and closes the file in line 15.

The program then opens the file array.dat for binary input in line 18, reads an array of **double** values from the file in line 20, and closes the file in line 21.

Finally, the program displays the contents in the array **result** (lines 24–25).

13.7.4   Example: Binary Object I/O

You can use the **reinterpret_cast** operator to cast data of any object type to characters and vice versa. This section gives an example of writing objects to a binary file and reading the objects back from the file.

Listing 13.1 writes student records into a text file. A student record consists of first name, middle initial, last name, and score. These fields are written to the file separately. A better way of processing is to define a class to model records. Each record is an object of the **Student** class.

Note

C++ object I/O is compiler-dependent. Most compilers can perform object I/O for the objects   compiler-dependent
whose data fields are of primitive types. Some compilers can handle objects with string data fields
with certain restrictions. Visual C++ requires that a string be less than 15 characters.

Let the class be named **Student** with the data fields **firstName**, **mi**, **lastName**, and **score**, their supporting accessors and mutators, and two constructors. The class UML diagram is shown in Figure 13.4.

> The *get* and *set* functions for these data fields are provided in the class but for brevity omitted in the UML diagram.

Student
-firstName: string
-mi: char
-lastName: string
-score: int
+Student()
+Student(firstName: string, mi: char, lastName: string, score: int)

The first name of this student.

The middle initial of this student.

The last name of this student.

The score of this student.

Constructs a default Student object.

Constructs a student with specified first name, mi, last name, and score

FIGURE 13.4   The **Student** class describes student information.

Listing 13.14 defines the **Student** class in the header file, and Listing 13.15 implements the class.

LISTING 13.14 Student.h

public members
no-arg constructor
constructor

mutator function

accessor function

private data fields

```cpp
1 #ifndef STUDENT_H
2 #define STUDENT_H
3 #include <string>
4 using namespace std;
5
6 class Student
7 {
8 public:
9    Student();
10   Student(const string &firstName, char mi,
11      const string &lastName, int score);
12   void setFirstName(const string &s);
13   void setMi(char mi);
14   void setLastName(const string &s);
15   void setScore(int score);
16   string getFirstName() const;
17   char getMi() const;
18   string getLastName() const;
19   int getScore() const;
20
21 private:
22   string firstName;
23   char mi;
24   string lastName;
25   int score;
26 };
27
28 #endif
```

LISTING 13.15 Student.cpp

include header file

no-arg constructor

constructor

setFirstName

```cpp
1 #include "Student.h"
2
3 // Construct a default student
4 Student::Student()
5 {
6 }
7
8 // Construct a Student object with specified data
9 Student::Student(const string &firstName, char mi,
10   const string &lastName, int score)
11 {
12   setFirstName(firstName);
13   setMi(mi);
14   setLastName(lastName);
15   setScore(score);
16 }
17
18 void Student::setFirstName(const string &s)
19 {
20   firstName = s;
21 }
22
23 void Student::setMi(char mi)
```

```
24 {
25   this->mi = mi;
26 }
27
28 void Student::setLastName(const string &s)
29 {
30   lastName = s;
31 }
32
33 void Student::setScore(int score)
34 {
35   this->score = score;
36 }
37
38 string Student::getFirstName() const
39 {
40   return firstName;
41 }
42
43 char Student::getMi() const
44 {
45   return mi;
46 }
47
48 string Student::getLastName() const
49 {
50   return lastName;
51 }
52
53 int Student::getScore() const
54 {
55   return score;
56 }
```

getFirstName

Listing 13.16 gives a program that creates two **Student** objects, writes them to a file named object.dat, and reads them back from the file.

LISTING 13.16 BinaryObjectIO.cpp

```
 1 #include <iostream>
 2 #include <fstream>
 3 #include "Student.h"
 4 using namespace std;
 5
 6 void displayStudent(const Student &student)
 7 {
 8   cout << student.getFirstName() << " ";
 9   cout << student.getMi() << " ";
10   cout << student.getLastName() << " ";
11   cout << student.getScore() << endl;
12 }
13
14 int main()
15 {
16   fstream binaryio; // Create stream object
17   binaryio.open("object.dat", ios::out | ios::binary);
18
19   Student student1("John", 'T', "Smith", 90);
20   Student student2("Eric", 'K', "Jones", 85);
21
```

include **Student** header

display **Student** data

fstream object
open output file

create student1
create student2

```
write student1          22    binaryio.write(reinterpret_cast<char*>
                        23      (&student1), sizeof(Student));
write student2          24    binaryio.write(reinterpret_cast<char*>
                        25      (&student2), sizeof(Student));
                        26
close file              27    binaryio.close();
                        28
                        29    // Read student back from the file
open input file         30    binaryio.open("object.dat", ios::in | ios::binary);
                        31
create student          32    Student studentNew;
                        33
read from file          34    binaryio.read(reinterpret_cast<char*>
                        35      (&studentNew), sizeof(Student));
                        36
display student         37    displayStudent(studentNew);
                        38
                        39    binaryio.read(reinterpret_cast<char*>
                        40      (&studentNew), sizeof(Student));
                        41
                        42    displayStudent(studentNew);
                        43
                        44    binaryio.close();
                        45
                        46    return 0;
                        47 }
```

```
John T Smith 90
Eric K Jones 85
```

The program creates a stream object in line 16, opens the file object.dat for binary output in line 17, creates two **Student** objects in lines 19–20, writes them to the file in lines 22–25, and closes the file in line 27.

The statement to write an object to the file is

```
binaryio.write(reinterpret_cast<char*>
  (&student1), sizeof(Student));
```

The address of object `student1` is cast into the type `char*`. The size of an object is determined by the data fields in the object.

The program opens the file object.dat for binary input in line 30, creates a **Student** object using its no-arg construction in line 32, reads a **Student** object from the file in lines 34–35, and displays the object's data in line 37. The program continues to read another object (lines 39–40) and displays its data in line 42.

Finally the program closes the file in line 44.

13.8 Random Access File

file pointer

A file consists of a sequence of bytes. A special marker called *file pointer* is positioned at one of these bytes. A read or write operation takes place at the location of the file pointer. When a file is opened, the file pointer is set at the beginning of the file. When you read or write data to the file, the file pointer moves forward to the next data item. For example, if you read a character using the `get()` function, C++ reads one byte from the file pointer, and now the file pointer is 1 byte ahead of the previous location, as shown in Figure 13.5.

All the programs you have developed so far read/write data sequentially. That is, the file pointer always moves forward. If a file is open for input, it starts to read data from the beginning

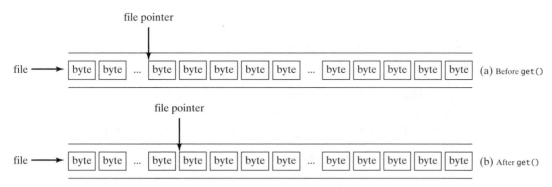

FIGURE 13.5 After a character is read, the file pointer is moved one byte ahead.

to the end. If a file is open for output, it writes data one item after the other from the beginning or from the end (with the append mode `ios::app`).

The problem with *sequential access* is that in order to read a byte in a specific location, all the bytes that precede it must be read. This is not efficient. C++ enables the file pointer to jump backward or forward freely using the **seekp** and **seekg** member functions on a stream object. This capability is known as *random file access*.

The **seekp** ("seek put") function is for the output stream, and the **seekg** ("seek get") function is for the input stream. Each function has two versions with one argument or two arguments. With one argument, the argument is the absolute location. For example,

```
input.seekg(0);
output.seekp(0);
```

moves the file pointer to the beginning of the file.

With two arguments, the first argument is a long integer that indicates an offset, and the second argument, known as the *seek base*, specifies where to calculate the offset from. Table 13.4 lists the three possible seek base arguments.

seekp function
seekg function

TABLE 13.4   Seek Base

Seek Base	Description
`ios::beg`	Calculates the offset from the beginning of the file.
`ios::end`	Calculates the offset from the end of the file.
`ios::cur`	Calculates the offset from the current file pointer.

Table 13.5 gives some examples of using the **seekp** and **seekg** functions.

TABLE 13.5   seekp and seekg Examples

Statement	Description
`seekg(100L, ios::beg);`	Moves the file pointer to the 100th byte from the beginning of the file.
`seekg(-100L, ios::end);`	Moves the file pointer to the 100th byte backward from the end of the file.
`seekp(42L, ios::cur);`	Moves the file pointer to the 42nd byte forward from the current file pointer.
`seekp(-42L, ios::cur);`	Moves the file pointer to the 42nd byte backward from the current file pointer.
`seekp(100L);`	Moves the file pointer to the 100th byte in the file.

tellp function
tellg function

You can also use the `tellp` and `tellg` functions to return the position of the file pointer in the file.

Listing 13.17 demonstrates how to access a file randomly. The program first stores 10 student objects into the file and then retrieves the third student from the file.

LISTING 13.17 RandomAccessFile.cpp

```cpp
1 #include <iostream>
2 #include <fstream>
3 #include "Student.h"
4 using namespace std;
5
6 void displayStudent(Student student)
7 {
8   cout << student.getFirstName() << " ";
9   cout << student.getMi() << " ";
10   cout << student.getLastName() << " ";
11   cout << student.getScore() << endl;
12 }
13
14 int main()
15 {
16   fstream binaryio; // Create stream object
17   binaryio.open("object1.dat", ios::out | ios::binary);
18
19   Student student1("Student1", 'T', "Smith", 90);
20   Student student2("Student2", 'T', "Smith", 90);
21   Student student3("Student3", 'T', "Smith", 90);
22   Student student4("Student4", 'T', "Smith", 90);
23   Student student5("Student5", 'T', "Smith", 90);
24   Student student6("Student6", 'T', "Smith", 90);
25   Student student7("Student7", 'T', "Smith", 90);
26   Student student8("Student8", 'T', "Smith", 90);
27   Student student9("Student9", 'T', "Smith", 90);
28   Student student10("Student10", 'T', "Smith", 90);
29
30   binaryio.write(reinterpret_cast<char*>
31     (&student1), sizeof(Student));
32   binaryio.write(reinterpret_cast<char*>
33     (&student2), sizeof(Student));
34   binaryio.write(reinterpret_cast<char*>
35     (&student3), sizeof(Student));
36   binaryio.write(reinterpret_cast<char*>
37     (&student4), sizeof(Student));
38   binaryio.write(reinterpret_cast<char*>
39     (&student5), sizeof(Student));
40   binaryio.write(reinterpret_cast<char*>
41     (&student6), sizeof(Student));
42   binaryio.write(reinterpret_cast<char*>
43     (&student7), sizeof(Student));
44   binaryio.write(reinterpret_cast<char*>
45     (&student8), sizeof(Student));
46   binaryio.write(reinterpret_cast<char*>
47     (&student9), sizeof(Student));
48   binaryio.write(reinterpret_cast<char*>
49     (&student10), sizeof(Student));
50
51   binaryio.close();
52
53   // Read student back from the file
```

```
54    binaryio.open("object1.dat", ios::in | ios::binary);           open input file
55
56    Student studentNew;                                            create student
57
58    binaryio.seekg(2 * sizeof(Student));                           move to third student
59
60    cout << "Current position is " << binaryio.tellg() << endl;
61
62    binaryio.read(reinterpret_cast<char*>                          read student
63      (& studentNew), sizeof(Student));
64
65    displayStudent(studentNew);                                    display student
66
67    cout << "Current position is " << binaryio.tellg() << endl;
68
69    binaryio.close();
70
71    return 0;
72 }
```

```
Current position is 144
Student3 T Smith 90
Current position is 216
```

The program creates a stream object in line 16, opens the file object1.dat for binary output in line 17, creates ten **Student** objects in lines 19–28, writes them to the file in lines 30–49, and closes the file in line 51.

The program opens the file object1.dat for binary input in line 54, creates a **Student** object using its no-arg construction in line 56, and moves the file pointer to the address of the third student in the file in line 58. The current position is now at **136**. (Note that the size of each **Student** object is 72.) After the third object is read, the file pointer is moved to the fourth object. So, the current position becomes **204**.

C++ object I/O is compiler-dependent. The sample output is produced from Visual C++. If you run it from other compilers, you may encounter problems or produce different output.

13.9 Updating Files

Often you need to update the contents of the file. You can open a file for both input and output. For example,

```
binaryio.open("object1.dat", ios::in | ios::out | ios::binary);
```

This statement opens the binary file object1.dat for both input and output.

Listing 13.18 demonstrates how to update a file. Suppose file object1.dat already has been created with ten **Student** objects from Listing 13.17. The program first reads the third student from the file, changes the last name, writes the revised object back to the file, and reads the new object back from the file.

LISTING 13.18 UpdateFile.cpp

```
1 #include <iostream>
2 #include <fstream>                                                 include header file
3 #include "Student.h"
4 using namespace std;
5
6 void displayStudent(Student student)
7 {
```

```
 8     cout << student.getFirstName() << " ";
 9     cout << student.getMi() << " ";
10     cout << student.getLastName() << " ";
11     cout << student.getScore() << endl;
12  }
13
14  int main()
15  {
16     fstream binaryio; // Create stream object
17
18     // Open file for input and output
19     binaryio.open("object1.dat", ios::in | ios::out | ios::binary);
20
21     Student student1;
22     binaryio.seekg(2 * sizeof(Student));
23     binaryio.read(reinterpret_cast<char*>
24       (&student1), sizeof(Student));
25     displayStudent(student1);
26
27     student1.setLastName("Peterson");
28     binaryio.seekp(2 * sizeof(Student));
29     binaryio.write(reinterpret_cast<char*>
30       (&student1), sizeof(Student));
31
32     Student student2;
33     binaryio.seekg(2 * sizeof(Student));
34     binaryio.read(reinterpret_cast<char*>
35       (&student2), sizeof(Student));
36     displayStudent(student2);
37
38     binaryio.close();
39
40     return 0;
41  }
```

- open input/output — line 19
- student1 — line 21
- read student1 — lines 23
- display student1 — line 25
- update student1 — line 29
- student2 — line 32
- read student2 — line 34
- display student2 — line 36

```
Student3 T Smith 90
Student3 T Peterson 90
```

The program creates a stream object in line 16 and opens the file object1.dat for binary input and output in line 19.

The program first reads the third object from the file (lines 23–24), displays it (line 25), changes its last name (line 27), and writes the revised object back to the file (lines 29–30).

The program then reads the third object back from the file (lines 34–35) and displays it (line 36). You will see that the last name of this object has been changed in the sample output.

KEY TERMS

absolute file name 423	stream 422
binary I/O 434	random access file 441
file open mode 430	relative file name 423
file pointer 440	sequential access file 441
fstream 422	stream state 431
ifstream 422	text I/O 434
ofstream 422	

CHAPTER SUMMARY

1. C++ provides the classes `ofstream`, `ifstream`, and `fstream` for facilitating file input and output.

2. You can use the `ofstream` class to write data to a file, use `ifstream` to read data from a file, and use the `fstream` class to read and write data.

3. You can use the `open` function to open a file, the `close` function to close a file, the `fail` function to test whether a file exists, the `eof` function to test whether the end of the file is reached.

4. The stream manipulators (e.g., `setw`, `setprecision`, `fixed`, `showpoint`, `left`, and `right`) can be used to format output.

5. You can use the `getline` function to read a line from a file, the `get` function to read a character from a file, and the `put` function to write a character to a file.

6. The file open modes (`iso::in`, `iso::out`, `iso::app`, `iso::truct`, and `iso::binary`) can be used to specify how a file is opened.

7. File I/O can be classified into text I/O and binary I/O.

8. Text I/O interprets data in sequences of characters. How text is stored in a file is dependent on the encoding scheme for the file. C++ automatically performs encoding and decoding for text I/O.

9. Binary I/O interprets data as raw binary values. To perform binary I/O, open the file using the `iso::binary` mode.

10. For binary output, use the `write` function. For binary input, use the `read` function.

11. You can use the `reinterpret_cast` operator to cast any type of data into an array of bytes for binary input and output.

12. You can process a file sequentially or in a random manner.

13. The `seekp` and `seekg` functions can be used to move the file-access pointer anywhere in the file before invoking the `put` and `get` functions.

REVIEW QUESTIONS

Section 13.2

13.1 How do you declare and open a file for output? How do you declare and open a file for input?

13.2 Why should you always close a file after it is processed?

13.3 How do you detect whether a file exists?

13.4 How do you detect whether the end of file is reached?

Section 13.3

13.5 Can you use the stream manipulators to format text output?

Section 13.4

13.6 What are the differences between `getline` and `get` functions?

13.7 What function do you use to write a character?

Section 13.5

13.8 How do you open a file so that you can append data into the file?

13.9 What is the file open mode `ios::truct`?

Section 13.6

13.10 How do you determine the state of I/O operations?

Section 13.7

13.11 What is a text file, and what is a binary file? Can you view a text file or a binary file using a text editor?

13.12 How do you open a file for binary I/O?

13.13 The `write` function can write only an array of bytes. How do you write a primitive-type value or an object into a binary file?

13.14 If you write string `"ABC"` to an ASCII text file, what values are stored in a file?

13.15 If you write string `"100"` to an ASCII text file, what values are stored in a file? If you write a numeric byte-type value `100` using binary I/O, what values are stored in a file?

Section 13.8 Random Access File

13.16 What is the file pointer?

13.17 What are the differences between `seekp` and `seekg`?

PROGRAMMING EXERCISES

Sections 13.2–13.6

13.1* (*Creating a text file*) Write a program to create a file named **Exercise13_1.txt** if it does not exist. If it does exist, append new data to it. Write `100` integers created randomly into the file using text I/O. Integers are separated by a space.

13.2* (*Counting characters*) Write a program that prompts the user to enter a file name and displays the number of characters in the file.

13.3* (*Processing scores in a text file*) Suppose that a text file **Exercise13_3.txt** contains an unspecified number of scores. Write a program that reads the scores from the file and displays their total and average. Scores are separated by blanks.

13.4* (*Writing/Reading data*) Write a program to create a file named **Exercise13_4.txt** if it does not exist. If it does exist, append new data to it. Write `100` integers created randomly into the file using text I/O. Integers are separated by spaces in the file. Read the data back from the file and display the sorted data.

Section 13.7

13.5* (*Creating a binary data file*) Write a program to create a file named **Exercise13_5.dat** if it does not exist. If it does exist, append new data to it. Write `100` integers created randomly into the file using binary I/O.

13.6* (*Storing Loan objects*) Write a program that creates five **Loan** objects and stores them in a file named **Exercise13_6.dat**. The **Loan** class was introduced in Listing 9.12.

13.7* (*Restoring objects from a file*) Suppose a file named **Exercise13_6.dat** has been created from the preceding exercise. Write a program that reads the **Loan** objects from the file and computes the total of the loan amount. Suppose you don't know how many **Loan** objects are in the file. Use the **eof()** to detect the end of the file.

13.8* (*Copying files*) Listing 13.6, CopyFile.cpp, copies files using text I/O. Revise the program that copies files using binary I/O. Here is a sample run of the program:

```
Enter a source file name: c:\exercise.zip
Enter a target file name: c:\exercise.bak
Copy Done
```

13.9* (*Splitting files*) Suppose you wish to back up a huge file (e.g., a 10-GB AVI file) to a CD-R. You can achieve it by splitting the file into smaller pieces and backing up these pieces separately. Write a utility program that splits a large file into smaller ones. You program should prompt the user to enter a source file and the number of bytes in each smaller file. Here is a sample run of the program:

Video Note
splitting a large file

```
Enter a source file name: c:\exercise.zip
Enter the number of bytes in each smaller file: 9343400
File c:\exercise.zip.0 produced
File c:\exercise.zip.1 produced
File c:\exercise.zip.2 produced
File c:\exercise.zip.3 produced
Split Done
```

13.10*(*Combining files*) Write a utility program that combines the files into a new file. Your program should prompt the user to enter the number of source files, each source-file name, and the target file name. Here is a sample run of the program:

```
Enter the number of source files: 4
Enter a source file: c:\exercise.zip.0
Enter a source file: c:\exercise.zip.1
Enter a source file: c:\exercise.zip.2
Enter a source file: c:\exercise.zip.3
Enter a target file: c:\temp.zip
Combine Done
```

13.11 (*Encrypting files*) Encode the file by adding 5 to every byte in it. Write a program that prompts the user to enter an input file name and an output file name and saves the encrypted version of the input file to the output file.

13.12 (*Decrypting files*) Suppose a file is encrypted using the scheme in Programming Exercise 13.11. Write a program to decode an encrypted file. Your program should prompt the user to enter an input file name and an output file name and should save the unencrypted version of the input file to the output file.

13.13*** (*Game: hangman*) Rewrite Programming Exercise 10.23. The program reads the words stored in a text file, named Exercise13_13.txt. Words are delimited by spaces. Hint: Read the words from the file and store them in a vector.

Section 13.8

13.14* (*Updating count*) Suppose you want to track how many times a program has been executed. You may store an `int` to count the file. Increase the count by 1 each time this program is executed. Let the program be **Exercise13_14** and store the count in **Exercise13_14.dat**.

CHAPTER 14

OPERATOR OVERLOADING

Objectives

- To define the `Rational` class for creating rational numbers (§14.2).
- To discover how an operator can be overloaded in C++ using a function (§14.3).
- To overload the relational operators (<, <=, =, !=, >=, >) and arithmetic operators (+, -, *, /) (§14.3).
- To overload the subscript operator [] (§14.4).
- To overload the shorthand assignment operators +=, -=, *=, and /= (§14.5).
- To overload the unary operators + and - (§14.6).
- To overload the prefix and postfix ++ and -- operators (§14.7).
- To enable friend functions and friend classes to access a class's private members (§14.8).
- To overload the stream insertion and extraction operators << and >> as friend nonmember functions (§14.9).
- To define operator functions to perform object conversions to a primitive type (§14.10.1).
- To define appropriate constructors to perform conversions from a numeric value to an object type (§14.10.2).
- To define a new `Rational` class with overloaded operators (§14.11).
- To overload the = operator to perform a deep copy (§14.12).

Video Note

what is operator overloading?

14.1 Introduction

In §10.2.10, "String Operators," you learned how to use operators to simplify string operations. You can use the + operator to concatenate two strings, the relational operators (==, !=, <, <=, >, >=) to compare two strings, and the array subscript operator [] to access a character. In §12.6, "The C++ vector Class," you learned how to use the [] operator to access an element in a vector. For example, the following code uses the [] operator to return a character from a string (line 3), the + operator to combine two strings (line 4), the < operator to compare two strings (line 5), the [] operator to return an element from a vector (line 10).

[] operator
+ operator
< operator

```
1 string s1("Washington");
2 string s2("California");
3 cout << "The first character in s1 is "  << s1[0] << endl;
4 cout << "s1 + s2 is "  << (s1 + s2 ) << endl;
5 cout << "s1 < s2? " << (s1 < s2 ) << endl;
6
7 vector<int> v;
8 v.push_back(3);
9 v.push_back(5);
```

[] operator

```
10 cout << "The first element in v is " << v[0] << endl;
```

The operators are actually functions defined in a class. These functions are named with keyword **operator** followed by the actual operator. For example, you can rewrite the preceding code using the function syntax as follows:

```
1 string s1("Washington");
2 string s2("California");
```

[] operator function

```
3 cout << "The first character in s1 is " << s1.operator[](0)
    << endl;
```

+ operator function
< operator function

```
4 cout << "s1 + s2 is " << operator+(s1, s2) << endl;
5 cout << "s1 < s2? " << operator<(s1, s2) << endl;
6
7 vector<int> v;
8 v.push_back(3);
9 v.push_back(5);
```

[] operator function

```
10 cout << "The first element in v is " << v.operator[](0) << endl;
```

The **operator[]** function is a member function in the **string** class, and the **vector** class and **operator+** and **operator<** are nonmember functions in the **string** class. Note that a member function must be invoked by an object using the syntax **objectName.functionName(...)**, such as **s1.operator[](0)**. Obviously, it is more intuitive and convenient to use the operator syntax **s1[0]** than the function syntax **s1.operator[](0)**.

operator overloading

Defining functions for operators is called *operator overloading*. Operators such as +, ==, !=, <, <=, >, >=, and [] are overloaded in the **string** class. How do you overload operators in your custom classes? This chapter uses the **Rational** class as an example to demonstrate how to overload a variety of operators. First you will learn how to design a **Rational** class for supporting rational-number operations and then overload the operators to simplify these operations.

14.2 The **Rational** Class

Video Note

the Rational class

A rational number has a numerator and a denominator in the form a/b, where a is the numerator and b is the denominator. For example, 1/3, 3/4, and 10/4 are rational numbers.

A rational number cannot have a denominator of 0, but a numerator of 0 is fine. Every integer i is equivalent to a rational number i/1. Rational numbers are used in exact computations involving fractions—for example, 1/3 = 0.33333.... This number cannot be precisely represented in floating-point format using data type **double** or **float**. To obtain the exact result, we must use rational numbers.

C++ provides data types for integers and floating-point numbersz but not for rational numbers. This section shows how to design a class to represent rational numbers.

A `Rational` number can be represented using two data fields: `numerator` and `denominator`. You can create a `Rational` number with specified numerator and denominator or create a default `Rational` number with numerator `0` and denominator `1`. You can add, subtract, multiply, divide, and compare rational numbers. You can also convert a rational number into an integer, floating-point value, or string. The UML class diagram for the `Rational` class is given in Figure 14.1.

Rational	
-numerator: int	The numerator of this rational number.
-denominator: int	The denominator of this rational number.
+Rational()	Creates a rational number with numerator 0 and denominator 1.

+Rational(numerator: int,
  denominator: int)
	Creates a rational number with specified numerator and
	  denominator.

+getNumerator(): int	Returns the numerator of this rational number.
+getDenominator(): int	Returns the denominator of this rational number.
+add(secondRational: Rational): Rational	Returns the addition of this rational with another.
+subtract(secondRational: Rational): Rational	Returns the subtraction of this rational with another.
+multiply(secondRational: Rational): Rational	Returns the multiplication of this rational with another.
+divide(secondRational: Rational): Rational	Returns the division of this rational with another.

+compareTo(secondRational:
  Rational): int
	Returns an int value -1, 0, or 1 to indicate whether this rational
	  number is less than, equal to, or greater than the specified
	  number.

+equals(secondRational: Rational): bool	Returns true if this rational number is equal to the specified number.
+intValue(): int	Returns the numerator / denominator.
+doubleValue(): double	Returns the 1.0 * numerator / denominator.
+toString(): string	Returns a string in the form "numerator / denominator." Returns numerator if denominator is 1.
-gcd(n: int, d: int): int	Returns the greatest common divisor between n and d.

FIGURE 14.1 The properties, constructors, and functions of the `Rational` class are illustrated in UML.

A rational number consists of a numerator and a denominator. There are many equivalent rational numbers; for example, $1/3 = 2/6 = 3/9 = 4/12$. For convenience, $1/3$ is used in this example to represent all rational numbers that are equivalent to $1/3$. The numerator and the denominator of $1/3$ have no common divisor except 1, so $1/3$ is said to be in *lowest terms*.

lowest term

To reduce a rational number to its lowest terms, you need to find the greatest common divisor (GCD) of the absolute values of its numerator and denominator and then divide both numerator and denominator by this value. You can use the function for computing the GCD of two integers `n` and `d`, as suggested in Listing 4.8, GreatestCommonDivisor.cpp. The numerator and denominator in a `Rational` object are reduced to their lowest terms.

As usual, we first write a test program to create `Rational` objects and test the functions in the `Rational` class. Listing 14.1 shows the header file for the `Rational` class, and Listing 14.2 is a test program.

LISTING 14.1 Rational.h

include guard
define constant

```cpp
 1 #ifndef RATIONL_H
 2 #define RATIONL_H
 3 #include <string>
 4 using namespace std;
 5
 6 class Rational
 7 {
 8 public:
 9   Rational();
10   Rational(int numerator, int denominator);
11   int getNumerator() const;
12   int getDenominator() const;
13   Rational add(const Rational &secondRational) const;
14   Rational subtract(const Rational &secondRational) const;
15   Rational multiply(const Rational &secondRational) const;
16   Rational divide(const Rational &secondRational) const;
17   int compareTo(const Rational &secondRational) const;
18   bool equals(const Rational &secondRational) const;
19   int intValue() const;
20   double doubleValue() const;
21   string toString() const;
22
23 private:
24   int numerator;
25   int denominator;
26   static int gcd(int n, int d);
27 };
28
29 #endif
```

public members

private members

static function

LISTING 14.2 TestRationalClass.cpp

include **Rational**

create **Rational**

invoke **toString**
invoke **add**

invoke **subtract**

invoke **multiply**

invoke **divide**

```cpp
 1 #include <iostream>
 2 #include "Rational.h"
 3 using namespace std;
 4
 5 int main()
 6 {
 7   // Create and initialize two rational numbers r1 and r2.
 8   Rational r1(4, 2);
 9   Rational r2(2, 3);
10
11   // Test toString, add, subtract, multiply, and divide
12   cout << r1.toString() << " + " << r2.toString() << " = "
13     << r1.add(r2).toString() << endl;
14   cout << r1.toString() << " - " << r2.toString() << " = "
15     << r1.subtract(r2).toString() << endl;
16   cout << r1.toString() << " * " << r2.toString() << " = "
17     << r1.multiply(r2).toString() << endl;
18   cout << r1.toString() << " / " << r2.toString() << " = "
19     << r1.divide(r2).toString() << endl;
20
```

```
21   // Test intValue and double
22   cout << "r2.intValue()" << " is " << r2.intValue() << endl;         invoke intValue
23   cout << "r2.doubleValue()" << " is " << r2.doubleValue() << endl;    invoke doubleValue
24
25   // Test compareTo and equal
26   cout << "r1.compareTo(r2) is " << r1.compareTo(r2) << endl;          invoke compareTo
27   cout << "r2.compareTo(r1) is " << r2.compareTo(r1) << endl;
28   cout << "r1.compareTo(r1) is " << r1.compareTo(r1) << endl;
29   cout << "r1.equals(r1) is "                                          invoke equal
30        << (r1.equals(r1) ? "true" : "false") << endl;
31   cout << "r1.equals(r2) is "
32        << (r1.equals(r2) ? "true" : "false") << endl;
33
34   return 0;
35 }
```

```
2 + 2/3 = 8/3
2 - 2/3 = 4/3
2 * 2/3 = 4/3
2 / 2/3 = 3
r2.intValue() is 0
r2.doubleValue() is 0.666667
r1.compareTo(r2) is 1
r2.compareTo(r1) is -1
r1.compareTo(r1) is 0
r1.equals(r1) is true
r1.equals(r2) is false
```

The `main` function creates two rational numbers, `r1` and `r2` (lines 8–9), and displays the results of `r1 + r2`, `r1 - r2`, `r1 x r2`, and `r1 / r2` (lines 12–19). To perform `r1 + r2`, invoke `r1.add(r2)` to return a new `Rational` object. Similarly, `r1.subtract(r2)` returns a new `Rational` object for `r1 - r2`, `r1.multiply(r2)` for `r1 x r2`, and `r1.divide(r2)` for `r1 / r2`.

The `intValue()` function displays the `int` value of `r1` (line 22). The `doubleValue()` function displays the `double` value of `r2` (line 23).

Invoking `r1.compareTo(r2)` (line 26) returns `1`, since `r1` is greater than `r2`. Invoking `r2.compareTo(r1)` (line 27) returns `-1`, since `r2` is less than `r1`. Invoking `r1.compareTo(r1)` (line 28) returns `0`, since `r1` is equal to `r1`. Invoking `r1.equals(r1)` (line 29) returns `true`, since `r1` is equal to `r1`. Invoking `r1.equals(r2)` (line 30) returns `false`, since `r1` are `r2` are not equal.

The `Rational` class is implemented in Listing 14.3.

LISTING 14.3 Rational.cpp

```
1 #include "Rational.h"                                                  Rational header
2 #include <sstream> // Used in toString to convert numbers to strings
3
4 Rational::Rational()                                                   no-arg constructor
5 {
6   numerator = 0;                                                       initialize data fields
7   denominator = 1;
8 }
9
```

constructor	
initialize data fields	
gcd	
add	
$\frac{a}{b} + \frac{c}{d} = \frac{ad + bc}{bd}$	
subtract	
$\frac{a}{b} - \frac{c}{d} = \frac{ad - bc}{bd}$	
multiply	
$\frac{a}{b} \times \frac{c}{d} = \frac{ac}{bd}$	
divide	
$\frac{a}{b} \div \frac{c}{d} = \frac{ad}{bc}$	

```
10  Rational::Rational(int numerator, int denominator)
11  {
12    int factor = gcd(numerator, denominator);
13    this->numerator = ((denominator > 0) ? 1 : -1) * numerator / factor;
14    this->denominator = abs(denominator) / factor;
15  }
16
17  int Rational::getNumerator() const
18  {
19    return numerator;
20  }
21
22  int Rational::getDenominator() const
23  {
24    return denominator;
25  }
26
27  // Find GCD of two numbers
28  int Rational::gcd(int n, int d)
29  {
30    int n1 = abs(n);
31    int n2 = abs(d);
32    int gcd = 1;
33
34    for (int k = 1; k <= n1 && k <= n2; k++)
35    {
36      if (n1 % k == 0 && n2 % k == 0)
37        gcd = k;
38    }
39
40    return gcd;
41  }
42
43  Rational Rational::add(const Rational &secondRational) const
44  {
45    int n = numerator * secondRational.getDenominator() +
46      denominator * secondRational.getNumerator();
47    int d = denominator * secondRational.getDenominator();
48    return Rational(n, d);
49  }
50
51  Rational Rational::subtract(const Rational &secondRational) const
52  {
53    int n = numerator * secondRational.getDenominator()
54      - denominator * secondRational.getNumerator();
55    int d = denominator * secondRational.getDenominator();
56    return Rational(n, d);
57  }
58
59  Rational Rational::multiply(const Rational &secondRational) const
60  {
61    int n = numerator * secondRational.getNumerator();
62    int d = denominator * secondRational.getDenominator();
63    return Rational(n, d);
64  }
65
66  Rational Rational::divide(const Rational &secondRational) const
67  {
68    int n = numerator * secondRational.getDenominator();
69    int d = denominator * secondRational.numerator;
```

```
70     return Rational(n, d);
71 }
72
73 int Rational::compareTo(const Rational &secondRational) const          compareTo
74 {
75     Rational temp = subtract(secondRational);
76     if (temp.getNumerator() < 0)
77       return -1;
78     else if (temp.getNumerator() == 0)
79       return 0;
80     else
81       return 1;
82 }
83
84 bool Rational::equals(const Rational &secondRational) const             equals
85 {
86     if (compareTo(secondRational) == 0)
87       return true;
88     else
89       return false;
90 }
91
92 int Rational::intValue() const                                          intValue
93 {
94     return getNumerator() / getDenominator();
95 }
96
97 double Rational::doubleValue() const                                    doubleValue
98 {
99     return 1.0 * getNumerator() / getDenominator();
100 }
101
102 string Rational::toString() const                                      toString
103 {
104    stringstream ss1, ss2;
105    ss1 << numerator;
106    ss2 << denominator;
107
108    if (denominator == 1)
109      return ss1.str() + "";
110    else
111      return ss1.str() + "/" + ss2.str();
112 }
```

The rational number is encapsulated in a `Rational` object. Internally, a rational number is represented in its lowest terms (lines 13–14), and the numerator determines its sign (line 13). The denominator is always positive (line 14).

The `gcd()` function (lines 28–41) is private; it is not intended for use by clients. The `gcd()` function is only for internal use by the `Rational` class. The `gcd()` function is also static, since it is not dependent on any particular `Rational` object.

The `abs(x)` function (lines 30–31) is defined in the standard C++ library that returns the absolute value of `x`.

Two `Rational` objects can interact with each other to perform add, subtract, multiply, and divide operations. These functions return a new `Rational` object (lines 43–71).

The `compareTo(&secondRational)` function (lines 73–82) compares this rational number to the other rational number. It first subtracts the second rational from this rational and saves the result in `temp` (line 75). Return `-1`, `0`, or `1`, if `temp`'s numerator is less than, equal to, or greater than `0`.

The `equals(&secondRational)` function (lines 84–90) utilizes the `compareTo` function to compare this rational number to the other one. If this function returns 0, the `equals` function returns `true`; otherwise, it returns `false`.

The functions `intValue` and `doubleValue` return an `int` and a `double` value, respectively, for this rational number (lines 92–100).

The `toString()` function (lines 102–112) returns a string representation of a `Rational` object in the form `numerator/denominator` or simply `numerator` if `denominator` is 1.

Tip

The numerator and denominator are represented using two variables. We can represent them also using an array of two integers. See Programming Exercise 14.2. The signatures of the public functions in the `Rational` class are not changed, although the internal representation of a rational number is changed. This is a good illustration of the idea that the data fields of a class should be kept private so as to *encapsulate* the implementation of the class from the use of the class.

encapsulation

Video Note
overload the < operators

14.3 Operator Functions

It is convenient to compare two string objects using an intuitive syntax like

```
string1 < string2
```

Can you compare two `Rational` objects using a similar syntax like the following?

```
r1 < r2
```

how to overload operators?

Yes. You can define a special function called the *operator function* in the class. The operator function is just like a regular function except that it must be named with keyword `operator` followed by the actual operator. For example, the following function header

```
bool operator< (const Rational &secondRational) const
```

defines the < operator function that returns `true` if this `Rational` object is less than `secondRational`. You can invoke the function using

```
r1.operator< (r2)
```

or simply

```
r1 < r2
```

overload **operator<**

To use this operator, you have to add the function header for `operator<` in the public section in Listing 14.1 Rational.h and implement the function in the Rational.cpp in Listing 14.3 as follows:

function operator

invoke **compareTo**

```
1 bool Rational::operator< (const Rational &secondRational) const
2 {
3   // compareTo is already defined Rational.h
4   if (compareTo(secondRational) < 0)
5     return true;
6   else
7     return false;
8 }
```

The following code

```
Rational r1(4, 2);
Rational r2(2, 3);
```

```
cout << "r1 < r2 is " << (r1.operator<(r2) ? "true" : "false");
cout << "\nr1 < r2 is " << ((r1 < r2) ? "true" : "false");
cout << "\nr2 < r1 is " << (r2.operator<(r1) ? "true" : "false");
```

displays

```
r1 < r2 is false
r1 < r2 is false
r2 < r1 is true
```

Note that `r1.operator<(r2)` is same as `r1 < r2`. The latter is simpler and therefore preferred.

C++ allows you to overload the operators listed in Table 14.1. Table 14.2 shows the four operators that cannot be overloaded. C++ does not allow you to create new operators. 　　　overloadable operators

TABLE 14.1   Operators That Can Be Overloaded

+	–	*	/	%	^	&	|	~	!	=
<	>	+=	-=	*=	/=	%=	^=	&=	|=	<<
>>	>>=	<<=	==	!=	<=	>=	&&	||	++	--
->*	,	->	[]	()	new	delete				

TABLE 14.2   Operators That Cannot Be Overloaded

?:	.	.*	::

Note

C++ defines the operator precedence and associativity (see §3.17, "Operator Precedence and Associativity"). You cannot change the operator precedence and associativity by overloading. 　　　precedence and associativity

Note

Most operators are binary operators. Some are unary. You cannot change the number of operands by overloading. For example, the / divide operator is binary and ++ is unary. 　　　number of operands

Here is another example that overloads the binary + operator in the **Rational** class. Add the following function header in Rational.h in Listing 14.1. 　　　overload binary +

```
Rational operator+ (const Rational &secondRational) const
```

Implement the function in Rational.cpp in Listing 14.3 as follows:

```
1 Rational Rational::operator+ (const Rational &secondRational) const
2 {
3   // add is already defined Rational.h
4   return add(secondRational);
5 }
```

+ function operator

invoke **add**

The following code

```
Rational r1(4, 2);
Rational r2(2, 3);
cout << "r1 + r2 is " << (r1 + r2).toString() << endl;
```

displays

```
r1 + r2 is 8/3
```

Video Note
overload the **[]** operators

subscript operator

14.4 Overloading the **[]** Operator

In C++, the pair of square brackets **[]** is called the *subscript operator*. You have used this operator to access array elements and the elements in a **string** object and a **vector** object. You can overload this operator to access the contents of the object if desirable. For example, you may wish to access the numerator and denominator of a **Rational** object **r** using **r[0]** and **r[1]**.

We first give an incorrect solution to overload the **[]** operator. We will then identify the problem and give a correct solution. To enable a **Rational** object to access its numerator and denominator using the **[]** operator, define the following function header in the Rational.h header file:

```
int operator[](int index);
```

Implement the function in Rational.cpp as follows:

[] function operator

access numerator

access denominator

throw exception

```
 1 int Rational::operator[](int index)    ◄───────── Partially correct
 2 {
 3    if (index == 0)
 4      return numerator;
 5    else if (index == 1)
 6      return denominator;
 7    else
 8    {
 9      throw runtime_error("subscript out of range");
10    }
11 }
```

The following code

```
Rational r(2, 3);
cout << "r[0] is " << r[0] << endl;
cout << "r[1] is " << r[1] << endl;
```

displays

```
r[0] is 2
r[1] is 3
```

Line 9 throws an exception. Exceptions will be introduced in Chapter 16, "Exception Handling." For now, just accept that this is the way of throwing an exception.

Can you set a new numerator or denominator like an array assignment such as the following?

```
r[0] = 5;
r[1] = 6;
```

If you compile it, you will get the following error:

```
Lvalue required in function main()
```

In C++, *Lvalue* (short for left value) refers to anything that can appear on the left side of   Lvalue
the assignment operator (=) and *Rvalue* (short for right value) refers to anything that can   Rvalue
appear on the right side of the assignment operator (=). How can you make r[0] and r[1] an
Lvalue so that you can assign a value to r[0] and r[1]? The answer is that you can define
the [] operator to return a reference of the variable.
    Add the following correct function header in Rational.h:

```
int &operator[](int index);
```

Implement the function in Rational.cpp:

```
int &Rational::operator[](int index)  ◄──────── Correct
{
  if (index == 0)
    return numerator;
  else if (index == 1 )
    return denominator;
  else
  {
    throw runtime_error("subscript out of range");
  }
}
```

correct function header

You are familiar with pass-by-reference. *Return-by-reference* and pass-by-reference are   return-by-reference
the same concept. In pass-by-reference, the formal parameter and the actual parameter are
aliases. In return-by-reference, the function returns an alias to a variable.
    In this function, if index is 0, the function returns an alias of variable numeration. If
index is 1, the function returns an alias of variable denominator.
    The following code

```
1 Rational r(2, 3);
2 r[0] = 5; // Set numerator to 5
3 r[1] = 6; // Set denominator to 6
4 cout << "r[0] is " << r[0] << endl;
5 cout << "r[1] is " << r[1] << endl;
6 cout << "r.doubleValue() is " << r.doubleValue() << endl;
```

assign to r[0]
assign to r[1]

displays

```
r[0] is 5
r[1] is 6
r.doubleValue() is 0.833333
```

In r[0], r is an object and 0 is the argument to the member function []. When r[0] is used
as an expression, it returns a value for the numerator. When r[0] is used on the left side of
the assignment operator, it is an alias for the variable numerator. So, r[0] = 5 assigns 5 to
numerator.
    The [] operator functions as both accessor and mutator. For example, you use r[0] as an   [] accessor and mutator
accessor to retrieve the numerator in an expression, and you use r[0] = value as a mutator.

Lvalue operator

For convenience, we call a function operator that returns a reference an *Lvalue operator*. Several other operators such as +=, -=, *=, /=, and %= are also Lvalue operators.

14.5 Overloading Shorthand Assignment Operators

C++ has shorthand assignment operators +=, -=, *=, /=, and %= for adding, subtracting, multiplying, dividing, and modulus a value in a variable. You can overload these operators in the `Rational` class.

Note that the shorthand operators can be used as Lvalues. For example, the code

```
int x = 0;
(x += 2) += 3;
```

is legal. So shorthand assignment operators are Lvalue operators and you should overload them to return by reference.

Here is an example that overloads the addition assignment operator +=. Add the function header in Listing 14.1, Rational.h.

```
Rational &operator+= (const Rational &secondRational)
```

Implement the function in Listing 14.2, Rational.cpp.

+= function operator

add to calling object
return calling object

```
1 Rational &Rational::operator+= (const Rational &secondRational)
2 {
3   *this = add(secondRational);
4   return *this;
5 }
```

Line 3 invokes the `add` function to add the calling `Rational` object with the second `Rational` object. The result is copied to the calling object `*this` in line 3. The calling object is returned in line 4.

For example, the following code

+= function operator

```
1 Rational r1(2, 4);
2 Rational r2 = r1 += Rational(2, 3);
3 cout << "r1 is " << r1.toString() << endl;
4 cout << "r2 is " << r2.toString() << endl;
```

displays

```
r1 is 7/6
r2 is 7/6
```

14.6 Overloading the Unary Operators

The + and - are unary operators. They can be overloaded, too. Since the unary operator operates on one operand that is the calling object itself, the unary function operator has no parameters.

Here is an example that overloads the - operator. Add the function header in Listing 14.1, Rational.h.

```
Rational operator-()
```

Implement the function in Listing 14.2, Rational.cpp.

```
1 Rational Rational::operator-()
2 {
3   return Rational(-numerator, denominator);
4 }
```

negate numerator
return calling object

Negating a `Rational` object is the same as negating its numerator (line 3). Line 4 returns the calling object. Note that the negating operator returns a new `Rational`. The calling object itself is not changed.

The following code

```
1 Rational r2(2, 3);
2 Rational r3 = -r2;  // Negate r2
3 cout << "r3 is " << r2.toString() << endl;
4 cout << "r3 is " << r3.toString() << endl;
```

unary − operator

displays

```
r2 is 2/3
r3 is -2/3
```

14.7 Overloading the ++ and −− Operators

The `++` and `−−` operators may be prefix or postfix. The prefix `++var` or `−−var` first adds or subtracts `1` from the variable and then evaluates to the new value in the `var`. The postfix `var++` or `var−−` adds or subtracts `1` from the variable, but evaluates to the old value in the `var`.

If the `++` and `−−` are implemented correctly, the following code

```
1 Rational r2(2, 3);
2 Rational r3 = ++r2 ; // Prefix increment
3 cout << "r3 is " << r3.toString() << endl;
4 cout << "r2 is " << r2.toString() << endl;
5
6 Rational r1(2, 3);
7 Rational r4 = r1++ ; // Postfix increment
8 cout << "r1 is " << r1.toString() << endl;
9 cout << "r4 is " << r4.toString() << endl;
```

assign to **r2[0]**
assign to **r2[1]**

should display

```
r3 is 5/3
r2 is 5/3
r1 is 5/3
r4 is 2/3   ⏎Enter  ←──────  r4 stores the original value of r1
```

How does C++ distinguish the prefix `++` or `−−` function operators from the postfix `++` or `−−` function operators? C++ defines postfix `++`/`−−` function operators with a special dummy parameter of the `int` type and defines the prefix `++` function operator with no parameters as follows:

```
Rational &operator++();
```

prefix ++ operator

```
Rational operator++(int dummy)
```

postfix ++ operator

Note that the prefix ++ and -- operators are Lvalue operators, but the postfix ++ and -- operators are not. These prefix and postfix ++ operator functions can be implemented as follows:

```
1  // Prefix increment
2  Rational &Rational::operator++()
3  {
4     numerator += denominator;
5     return *this;
6  }
7
8  // Postfix increment
9  Rational Rational::operator++(int dummy)
10 {
11    Rational temp(numerator, denominator);
12    numerator += denominator;
13    return temp;
14 }
```

$\frac{a}{b} + 1 = \frac{a+b}{b}$

return calling object

create temp

$\frac{a}{b} + 1 = \frac{a+b}{b}$

return temp object

In the prefix ++ function, line 4 adds the denominator to the numerator. This is the new numerator for the calling object after adding 1 to the Rational object. Line 5 returns the calling object.

In the postfix ++ function, line 11 creates a temporary Rational object to store the original calling object. Line 12 increments the calling object. Line 13 returns the original calling object.

14.8 `friend` Functions and `friend` Classes

Some operators such as + and > are better implemented as friend non-member functions. C++ allows you to overload the stream insertion operator (<<) and the stream extraction operator (>>). These operators must be implemented as friend non-member functions. This section introduces friend functions and friend classes to prepare you to overload these operators.

Private members of a class cannot be accessed from outside the class. Occasionally, it is convenient to allow some trusted functions and classes to access a class's private members. C++ enables you to use the `friend` *keyword* to define `friend` functions and `friend` classes so that these trusted functions and classes can access another class's private members.

friend class

Listing 14.4 gives an example that defines a *friend class*.

a friend class

LISTING 14.4 Date.h

```
1  class Date
2  {
3  public:
4     Date(int year, int month, int day)
5     {
6        this->year = year;
7        this->month = month;
8        this->day = day;
9     }
10
11    friend class AccessDate;
12
13 private:
14    int year;
15    int month;
16    int day;
17 };
```

The `AccessDate` class (line 4) is defined as a friend class. So, you can directly access private data fields `year`, `month`, and `day` from the `AccessDate` class in Listing 14.5.

LISTING 14.5 TestFriendClass.cpp

```
1  #include <iostream>
2  #include "Date.h"                                    header Date1.h
3  using namespace std;
4
5  class AccessDate
6  {
7  public:
8    static void p()                                    static function
9    {
10     Date birthDate(2010, 3, 4);                       create a Date
11     birthDate.year = 2000;                            modify private data
12     cout << birthDate.year;                           access private data
13   }
14 };
15
16 int main()
17 {
18   AccessDate::p();                                    invoke static function
19
20   return 0;
21 }
```

The `AccessDate` class is defined in lines 5–14. A `Date` object is created in the class. Since `AccessDate` is a friend class of the `Date` class, the private data in `Date` object can be accessed from a `Date` object in the `AccessDate` class (lines 11–12). The main function invokes the static function `AccessDate::p()` in line 18.

Listing 14.6 gives an example of how to use a *friend function*. The program defines the `Date` class with a friend function `p` (line 13). Function `p` is not a member of the `Date` class but can access the private data in `Date`. In function `p`, a `Date` object is created in line 23, and the private field data `year` is modified in line 24 and retrieved in line 25.

friend function

LISTING 14.6 TestFriendFunction.cpp

```
1  #include <iostream>
2  using namespace std;
3
4  class Date
5  {
6  public:
7    Date(int year, int month, int day)
8    {
9      this->year = year;
10     this->month = month;
11     this->day = day;
12   }
13   friend void p();                                    define friend function
14
15 private:
16   int year;
17   int month;
18   int day;
19 };
20
```

```
21 void p()
22 {
23   Date date(2010, 5, 9);
24   date.year = 2000;
25   cout << date.year;
26 }
27
28 int main()
29 {
30   p();
31
32   return 0;
33 }
```

modify private data
access private data

invoke friend function

14.9 Overloading the << and >> Operators

So far, in order to display a `Rational` object, you invoke the `toString()` function to return a string representation for the `Rational` object and then display the string. For example, to display a `Rational` object `r`, you write

```
cout << r.toString();
```

Wouldn't it be nice to be able to display a `Rational` object directly using a syntax like the following?

```
cout << r;
```

The stream insertion operator (`<<`) and the stream extraction operator (`>>`) are just like other binary operators in C++. `cout << r` is actually the same as `<<(cout, r)` or `operator<<(cout, r)`.

Consider the following statement:

```
r1 + r2;
```

The operator is `+` with two operands `r1` and `r2`. Both are instances of the `Rational` class. So, you can overload the `+` operator as a member function with `r2` as the parameter. However, for the statement

```
cout << r;
```

why nonmember function
for <<?

the operator is `<<` with two operands `cout` and `r`. The first operand is an instance of the `ostream` class, not the `Rational` class. So, you cannot overload the `<<` operator as a member function in the `Rational` class. However, you can define the function as a friend function of the `Rational` class in the Rational.h header file:

```
friend ostream &operator<<(ostream &out, const Rational &rational);
```

chains of <<

Note that this function returns a reference of `ostream`, because you may use the `<<` operator in a chain of expressions. Consider the following statement:

```
cout << r1 << " followed by " << r2;
```

This is equivalent to

```
((cout << r1) << " followed by ") << r2;
```

For this to work, `cout << r1` must return a reference of `ostream`.

So, the function << can be implemented as follows:

```
ostream &operator<<(ostream &out, const Rational &rational)
{
  out << rational.numerator << "/" << rational.denominator;
  return out;
}
```

Similarly, to overload the >> operator, define the following function header in the Rational.h header file:

```
friend istream &operator>>(istream &in, Rational &rational);
```

Implement this function in Rational.cpp as follows:

```
istream &operator>>(istream &in, Rational &rational)
{
  cout << "Enter numerator: ";
  in >> rational.numerator;

  cout << "Enter denominator: ";
  in >> rational.denominator;
  return in;
}
```

The following code gives a test program that uses the overloaded << and >> functions operators.

```
1 Rational r1, r2;
2 cout << "Enter first rational number" << endl;
3 cin >> r1;                                              >> operator
4
5 cout << "Enter second rational number" << endl;
6 cin >> r2;                                              >> operator
7
8 cout << r1 << " + " << r2 << " = " << r1 + r2 << endl;  << operator
```

```
Enter first rational number
Enter numerator: 1  ↵Enter
Enter denominator: 2  ↵Enter
Enter second rational number
Enter numerator: 3
Enter denominator: 4
1/2 + 3/4 is 5/4
```

Line 3 reads values to a rational object from `cin`. In line 8, `r1 + r2` is evaluated to a new rational number, which is then sent to `cout`.

14.10 Automatic Type Conversions

C++ can perform certain type conversions automatically. You can define functions to enable conversions from a `Rational` object to a primitive type value or vice versa.

14.10.1 Converting to a Primitive Data Type

You can add an `int` value with a `double` value such as

```
4 + 5.5
```

In this case, C++ performs automatic type conversion to convert an `int` value `4` to a double value `4.0`.

Can you add a rational number with an `int` or a `double` value? Yes. You have to define a function operator to convert an object into `int` or `double`. Here is the implementation of the function to convert a `Rational` object to a `double` value.

```
Rational::operator double()
{
    return doubleValue(); // doubleValue() already in Rational.h
}
```

Don't forget that you have to add the member function header in the Rational.h header file.

```
operator double();
```

conversion function syntax

This is a special syntax for defining conversion functions to a primitive type in C++. There is no return type. The function name is the type that you want the object to be converted to.

So, the following code

add rational with double

```
1 Rational r1(1, 4);
2 double d = r1 + 5.1;
3 cout << "r1 + 5.1 is " << d << endl;
```

displays

```
r1 + 5.1 is 5.35
```

The statement in line 2 adds a rational number `r1` with a `double` value `5.1`. Since the conversion function is defined to convert a rational number to a `double`, `r1` is converted to a `double` value `0.25`, which is then added with `5.1`.

14.10.2 Converting to an Object Type

A `Rational` object can be automatically converted to a numeric value. Can a numeric value be automatically converted to a `Rational` object? Yes, it can.

To achieve this, define the following constructor in the header file:

```
Rational(int numerator);
```

and implement it in the implementation file as follows:

```
Rational::Rational(int numerator)
{
    this->numerator = numerator;
    this->denominator = 1;
}
```

Provided that the + operator is also overloaded (see §14.3), the following code

```
Rational r1(2, 3);
Rational r = r1 + 4; // Automatically converting 4 to Rational

cout << r << endl;
```

displays

14 / 3

When C++ sees `r1 + 4`, it first checks to see if the + operator has been overloaded to add a `Rational` with an integer. Since no such function is defined, the system next searches for the + operator to add a `Rational` with another `Rational`. Since 4 is an integer, C++ uses the constructor that constructs a `Rational` object from an integer argument. In other words, C++ performs an automatic conversion to convert an integer to a `Rational` object. This automatic conversion is possible because the suitable constructor is available. Now two `Rational` objects are added using the overloaded + operator to return a new `Rational` object (14 / 3).

You can add a `Rational` object with an integer like this:

```
r1 + 4
```

Can you add an integer with a `Rational` object like this?

```
4 + r1
```

Naturally you would think the + operator is symmetric. However, it does not work, because the left operand is the calling object for the + operator and the left operand must be a `Rational` object. Here 4 is an integer, not a `Rational` object. C++ does not perform automatic conversion in this case. To circumvent this problem, define the + operator as a nonmember function in the Rational.h header file as follows:

```
Rational operator+ (const Rational &r1, const Rational &r2)
```

Implement the function in Rational.cpp as follows:

```
1 Rational operator+ (const Rational &r1, const Rational &r2)
2 {
3   return r1.add(r2) ;
4 }
```

+ function operator

invoke **add**

Automatic type conversion to the user-defined object also works for comparison operators (<, <=, ==, !=, >, >=).

Note that the examples for the `operator<` and `operator+` are defined as member functions in §14.3, "Operator Functions." From now on, we will define them as nonmember functions.

14.11 The **Rational** Class with Overloaded Operators

The preceding sections introduced how to overload function operators. The following points are worth noting:

- Conversion functions from a class type to a primitive type or from a primitive type to a class type cannot both be defined in the same class. Doing so would cause ambiguity errors, because the compiler cannot decide which conversion to perform. Often converting from a primitive type to a class type is more useful. So, we will define our `Rational` class to support automatic conversion from a primitive type to the `Rational` type.

  automatic type conversion

- Most operators can be overloaded either as member or non-member functions. However, the =, [], ->, and () operators must be overloaded as member functions and << and >> operators must be overloaded as nonmember functions.

  member vs. nonmember

- If an operator (i.e., +, -, %, /, %, <, <=, ==, !=, >, and >=) can be implemented either as a member or nonmember function, it is better to overload it as a nonmember function to enable automatic type conversion with symmetric operands.

  nonmember preferred

Lvalue

■ If you want the returned object to be used as an Lvalue (i.e., used on the left-hand side of the assignment statement), you need to define the function to return a reference. The shorthand assignment operators +=, -=, *=, /=, and %=, the prefix ++ and -- operators, the subscript operator [], and the assignment operators = are Lvalue operators.

&&, ||, comma

■ You should avoid overloading &&, ||, and , (comma) operators. The && and || operators perform short-circuit evaluation. When overloaded, these operators perform complete evaluation. This is contrary to the behavior of these operators. The , operator guarantees a left-to-right evaluation. When it is overloaded, there is no such guarantee.

Listing 14.7 gives a new header file named RationalWithOperators.h for the **Rational** class with function operators. Lines 10–22 in the new file are the same as in Listing 14.1 Rational.h. The functions for shorthand assignment operators (+=, -=, *=, /=), subscript operator [], prefix ++, and prefix -- are defined to return a reference (lines 27–37). The stream extraction << and stream insertion >> operators are defined in lines 48–49. The nonmember functions for comparison operators (<, <=, >, >=, ==, !=) and arithmetic operators (+, -, *, /) are defined in lines 57–69.

LISTING 14.7 RationalWithOperators.h

```
1 #ifndef RATIONALWITHOPERATORS_H
2 #define RATIONALWITHOPERATORS_H
3 #include <string>
4 #include <iostream>
5 using namespace std;
6
7 class Rational
8 {
9 public:
10   Rational();
11   Rational(int numerator, int denominator);
12   int getNumerator() const;
13   int getDenominator() const;
14   Rational add(const Rational &secondRational) const;
15   Rational subtract(const Rational &secondRational) const;
16   Rational multiply(const Rational &secondRational) const;
17   Rational divide(const Rational &secondRational) const;
18   int compareTo(const Rational &secondRational) const;
19   bool equals(const Rational &secondRational) const;
20   int intValue() const;
21   double doubleValue() const;
22   string toString() const;
23
24   Rational(int numerator); // Suitable for type conversion
25
26   // Define function operators for shorthand operators
27   Rational &operator+=(const Rational &secondRational);
28   Rational &operator-=(const Rational &secondRational);
29   Rational &operator*=(const Rational &secondRational);
30   Rational &operator/=(const Rational &secondRational);
31
32   // Define function operator []
33   int &operator[](int index);
34
35   // Define function operators for prefix ++ and --
36   Rational &operator++();
```

constructor for type conversion

shorthand operators

subscript operator

prefix ++ operator

```
37    Rational &operator--();                                          postfix ++ operator
38
39    // Define function operators for postfix ++ and --
40    Rational operator++(int dummy);
41    Rational operator--(int dummy);
42
43    // Define function operators for unary + and -
44    Rational operator+();                                            unary + operator
45    Rational operator-();
46
47    // Define the << and >> operators
48    friend ostream &operator<<(ostream &, const Rational &);         << operator
49    friend istream &operator>>(istream &, Rational &);               >> operator
50
51 private:
52    int numerator;
53    int denominator;
54    static int gcd(int n, int d);
55 };
56
57 // Define nonmember function operators for relational operators
58 bool operator<(const Rational &r1, const Rational &r2);             nonmember functions
59 bool operator<=(const Rational &r1, const Rational &r2);
60 bool operator>(const Rational &r1, const Rational &r2);
61 bool operator>=(const Rational &r1, const Rational &r2);
62 bool operator==(const Rational &r1, const Rational &r2);
63 bool operator!=(const Rational &r1, const Rational &r2);
64
65 // Define nonmember function operators for arithmetic operators
66 Rational operator+(const Rational &r1, const Rational &r2);         nonmember functions
67 Rational operator-(const Rational &r1, const Rational &r2);
68 Rational operator*(const Rational &r1, const Rational &r2);
69 Rational operator/(const Rational &r1, const Rational &r2);
70
71 #endif
```

Listing 14.8 implements the header file. The member functions for shorthand assignment operators +=, -=, *=, and /= change the contents of the calling object (lines 121–143). You have to assign the result of the operation to **this**. The comparison operators are implemented by invoking **r1.compareTo(r2)** (lines 218–246). The arithmetic operators +, -, *, and / are implemented by invoking the functions **add**, **subtract**, **multiply**, and **divide** (lines 249–267).

LISTING 14.8   RationalWithOperators.cpp

```
 1 #include "RationalWithOperators.h"                                 include header
 2 #include <sstream>
 3
 4 Rational::Rational()
 5 {
 6    numerator = 0;
 7    denominator = 1;
 8 }
 9
10 Rational::Rational(int numerator, int denominator)
11 {
12    int factor = gcd(numerator, denominator);
13    this->numerator = (denominator > 0 ? 1 : -1) * numerator / factor;
14    this->denominator = abs(denominator) / factor;
15 }
16
```

```
17 int Rational::getNumerator() const
18 {
19   return numerator;
20 }
21
22 int Rational::getDenominator() const
23 {
24   return denominator;
25 }
26
27 // Find GCD of two numbers
28 int Rational::gcd(int n, int d)
29 {
30   int n1 = abs(n);
31   int n2 = abs(d);
32   int gcd = 1;
33
34   for (int k = 1; k <= n1 && k <= n2; k++)
35   {
36     if (n1 % k == 0 && n2 % k == 0)
37       gcd = k;
38   }
39
40   return gcd;
41 }
42
43 Rational Rational::add(const Rational &secondRational) const
44 {
45   int n = numerator * secondRational.getDenominator() +
46     denominator * secondRational.getNumerator();
47   int d = denominator * secondRational.getDenominator();
48   return Rational(n, d);
49 }
50
51 Rational Rational::subtract(const Rational &secondRational) const
52 {
53   int n = numerator * secondRational.getDenominator()
54     - denominator * secondRational.getNumerator();
55   int d = denominator * secondRational.getDenominator();
56   return Rational(n, d);
57 }
58
59 Rational Rational::multiply(const Rational &secondRational) const
60 {
61   int n = numerator * secondRational.getNumerator();
62   int d = denominator * secondRational.getDenominator();
63   return Rational(n, d);
64 }
65
66 Rational Rational::divide(const Rational &secondRational) const
67 {
68   int n = numerator * secondRational.getDenominator();
69   int d = denominator * secondRational.numerator;
70   return Rational(n, d);
71 }
72
73 int Rational::compareTo(const Rational &secondRational) const
74 {
75   Rational temp = subtract(secondRational);
76   if (temp.getNumerator() < 0)
```

```
77        return -1;
78      else if (temp.getNumerator() == 0)
79        return 0;
80      else
81        return 1;
82  }
83
84  bool Rational::equals(const Rational &secondRational) const
85  {
86      if (compareTo(secondRational) == 0)
87        return true;
88      else
89        return false;
90  }
91
92  int Rational::intValue() const
93  {
94      return getNumerator() / getDenominator();
95  }
96
97  double Rational::doubleValue() const
98  {
99      return 1.0 * getNumerator() / getDenominator();
100 }
101
102 string Rational::toString() const
103 {
104     stringstream ss1, ss2;
105     ss1 << numerator;
106     ss2 << denominator;
107
108     if (denominator == 1)
109       return ss1.str() + "";
110     else
111       return ss1.str() + "/" + ss2.str();
112 }
113
114 Rational::Rational(int numerator) // Suitable for type conversion          constructor
115 {
116     this->numerator = numerator;
117     this->denominator = 1;
118 }
119
120 // Define function operators for shorthand operators                       shorthand assignment
121 Rational &Rational::operator+=(const Rational &secondRational)                   operators
122 {
123     *this = add(secondRational);
124     return *this;
125 }
126
127 Rational &Rational::operator-=(const Rational &secondRational)
128 {
129     *this = subtract(secondRational);
130     return *this;
131 }
132
133 Rational &Rational::operator*=(const Rational &secondRational)
134 {
135     *this = multiply(secondRational);
136     return *this;
```

```
137 }
138
139 Rational &Rational::operator/=(const Rational &secondRational)
140 {
141    *this = divide(secondRational);
142    return *this;
143 }
144
```

[] operator

```
145 // Define function operator []
146 int &Rational::operator[](int index)
147 {
148    if (index == 0)
149       return numerator;
150    else if (index == 1)
151       return denominator;
152    else
153    {
154       throw runtime_error("subscript out of range");
155    }
156 }
157
```

prefix ++

```
158 // Define function operators for prefix ++ and --
159 Rational &Rational::operator++()
160 {
161    numerator += denominator;
162    return *this;
163 }
164
165 Rational &Rational::operator--()
166 {
167    numerator -= denominator;
168    return *this;
169 }
170
```

postfix ++

```
171 // Define function operators for postfix ++ and --
172 Rational Rational::operator++(int dummy)
173 {
174    Rational temp(numerator, denominator);
175    numerator += denominator;
176    return temp;
177 }
178
179 Rational Rational::operator--(int dummy)
180 {
181    Rational temp(numerator, denominator);
182    numerator -= denominator;
183    return temp;
184 }
185
```

unary + operator

```
186 // Define function operators for unary + and -
187 Rational Rational::operator+()
188 {
189    return *this;
190 }
191
192 Rational Rational::operator-()
193 {
194    return Rational(-numerator, denominator);
195 }
196
```

```
197  // Define the output and input operator                              << operator
198  ostream &operator<<(ostream &out, const Rational &rational)
199  {
200    if (rational.denominator == 1)
201      out << rational.numerator;
202    else
203      out << rational.numerator << "/" << rational.denominator;
204    return out;
205  }
206
207  istream &operator>>(istream &in, Rational &rational)
208  {
209    cout << "Enter numerator: ";
210    in >> rational.numerator;
211
212    cout << "Enter denominator: ";
213    in >> rational.denominator;
214    return in;
215  }
216
217  // Define function operators for relational operators               relational operators
218  bool operator<(const Rational &r1, const Rational &r2)
219  {
220    return (r1.compareTo(r2) < 0);
221  }
222
223  bool operator<=(const Rational &r1, const Rational &r2)
224  {
225    return (r1.compareTo(r2) <= 0);
226  }
227
228  bool operator>(const Rational &r1, const Rational &r2)
229  {
230    return (r1.compareTo(r2) > 0);
231  }
232
233  bool operator>=(const Rational &r1, const Rational &r2)
234  {
235    return (r1.compareTo(r2) >= 0);
236  }
237
238  bool operator==(const Rational &r1, const Rational &r2)
239  {
240    return (r1.compareTo(r2) == 0);
241  }
242
243  bool operator!=(const Rational &r1, const Rational &r2)
244  {
245    return (r1.compareTo(r2) != 0);
246  }
247
248  // Define non-member function operators for arithmetic operators     arithmetic operators
249  Rational operator+(const Rational &r1, const Rational &r2)
250  {
251    return r1.add(r2);
252  }
253
254  Rational operator-(const Rational &r1, const Rational &r2)
255  {
256    return r1.subtract(r2);
```

```
257 }
258
259 Rational operator*(const Rational &r1, const Rational &r2)
260 {
261   return r1.multiply(r2);
262 }
263
264 Rational operator/(const Rational &r1, const Rational &r2)
265 {
266   return r1.divide(r2);
267 }
```

Listing 14.9 gives a program for testing the new **Rational** class.

LISTING 14.9 TestRationalWithOperators.cpp

```
 1 #include <iostream>
 2 #include <string>
 3 #include "RationalWithOperators.h"
 4 using namespace std;
 5
 6 int main()
 7 {
 8   // Create and initialize two rational numbers r1 and r2.
 9   Rational r1(4, 2);
10   Rational r2(2, 3);
11
12   // Test relational operators
13   cout << r1 << " > " << r2 << " is " <<
14     ((r1 > r2) ? "true" : "false") << endl;
15   cout << r1 << " < " << r2 << " is " <<
16     ((r1 < r2) ? "true" : "false") << endl;
17   cout << r1 << " == " << r2 << " is " <<
18     ((r1 == r2) ? "true" : "false") << endl;
19   cout << r1 << " != " << r2 << " is " <<
20     ((r1 != r2) ? "true" : "false") << endl;
21
22   // Test toString, add, subtract, multiply, and divide operators
23   cout << r1 << " + " << r2 << " = " << r1 + r2 << endl;
24   cout << r1 << " - " << r2 << " = " << r1 - r2 << endl;
25   cout << r1 << " * " << r2 << " = " << r1 * r2 << endl;
26   cout << r1 << " / " << r2 << " = " << r1 / r2 << endl;
27
28   // Test shorthand operators
29   Rational r3(1, 2);
30   r3 += r1;
31   cout << "r3 is " << r3 << endl;
32
33   // Test function operator []
34   Rational r4(1, 2);
35   r4[0] = 3; r4[1] = 4;
36   cout << "r4 is " << r4 << endl;
37
38   // Test function operators for prefix ++ and --
39   r3 = r4++;
40   cout << "r3 is " << r3 << endl;
41   cout << "r4 is " << r4 << endl;
42
43   // Test function operator for conversion
44   cout << "1 + " << r4 << " is " << (1 + r4) << endl;
```

include new **Rational**

relational operator

arithmetic operator

array subscript []

postfix ++

type conversion

```
45
46   return 0;
47 }
```

```
2 > 2/3 is true
2 < 2/3 is false
2 == 2/3 is false
2 != 2/3 is true
2 + 2/3 = 8/3
2 - 2/3 = 4/3
2 * 2/3 = 4/3
2 / 2/3 = 3
r3 is 5/2
r4 is 3/4
r3 is 3/4
r4 is 7/4
1 + 7/4 is 11/4
```

14.12 Overloading the = Operators

By default, the = operator performs a memberwise copy from one object to the other. For example, the following code copies **r2** to **r1**.

```
1 Rational r1(1, 2);
2 Rational r2(4, 5);
3 r1 = r2;
4 cout << "r1 is " << r1 << endl;
5 cout << "r2 is " << r2 << endl;
```

copy **r2** to **r1**

So, the output is

```
r1 is 4/5
r2 is 4/5
```

The behavior of the = operator is the same as that of the default copy constructor. It performs a *shallow copy*, meaning that if the data field is a pointer to some object, the address of the pointer is copied rather than its contents. In §11.13, "Customizing Copy Constructors," you learned how to customize the copy constructor to perform a deep copy. However, customizing the copy constructor does not change the default behavior of the assignment copy operator =. For example, the Course class defined in Listing 11.17, Course1.h, has a pointer data field named **students** which points to an array of **string** object. If you run the following code using the assignment operator to assign **course1** to **course2**, as shown in line 9 in Listing 14.10, you will see that both **course1** and **course2** point to the same array.

shallow copy

LISTING 14.10 DefaultAssignmentDemo.cpp

```
1 #include <iostream>
2 #include "Course1.h" // Defined in Listing 11.17
3 using namespace std;
4
5 int main()
```

include Course header

```
 6 {
 7     Course course1("Java Programming", 10);
 8     Course course2("C++ Programming", 14);
 9     Course course2 = course1;
10
11     course1.addStudent("Peter Pan"); // Add a student to course1
12     course2.addStudent("Lisa Ma"); // Add a student to course2
13
14     cout << "students in course1: " <<
15       course1.getStudents()[0].data() << endl;
16     cout << "students in course2: " <<
17       course2.getStudents()[0].data() << endl;
18
19     return 0;
20 }
```

create **course1**
create **course2**
assign to **course2**

add a student
add a student
get a student

get a student

```
students in course1: Lisa Ma
students in course2: Lisa Ma
```

To change the way the default assignment operator = works, you need to overload the = operator. In the Course1.h file in Listing 11.17, define

```
const Course &operator= (const Course &course);
```

Why is the return type **Course** not **void**? C++ allows expressions with multiple assignments, such as:

```
course1 = course2 = course3;
```

In this statement, **course3** is copied to **course2**, and then returns **course2**, and then **course2** is copied to **course1**. So the = operator must have a valid return value type.

In the Course1.cpp in Listing 11.18, add the following function implementation:

```
1 Course &operator=(const Course &course)
2 {
3     courseName = course.courseName;
4     numberOfStudents = course.numberOfStudents;
5     capacity = course.capacity;
6     students = new string[capacity];
7
8     return *this;
9 }
```

copy **courseName**
copy **numberofStudetns**
copy **capacity**
create array

return calling object

Line 8 returns the calling object using *this. Note that this is the pointer to the calling object, so *this refers to the calling object.

If you run Listing 14.10 now, **course1** and **course2** will have their independent array objects for **students**.

Note

the rule of three

The copy constructor, the = assignment operator, and the destructor are called the *rule of three*, or *the Big Three*. If they are not defined explicitly, all three are created by the compiler automatically. You should customize them if a data field in the class is a pointer that points to a dynamic generated array or object. If you have to customize one of the three, you should customize the other two as well.

KEY TERMS

friend class 462	Lvalue operator 460
friend function 463	return-by-reference 459
`friend` keyword 462	rule of three 476

CHAPTER SUMMARY

1. C++ allows you to overload operators to simplify operations for objects.

2. You can overload nearly all operators except `?:`, `.`, `.*`, and `::`.

3. You cannot change the operator precedence and associativity by overloading.

4. In C++, the array subscript `[]` is an operator. You can overload this operator to access the contents of the object using the arraylike syntax if desirable.

5. A C++ function may return a reference, which is an alias for the returned variable.

6. The shorthand assignment operators (`+=`, `-=`, `*=`, `/=`), subscript operator `[]`, prefix `++`, and prefix `--` operators are Lvalue operators. The functions for overloading these operators should return a reference.

7. The `friend` keyword can be used to give the trusted functions and classes access to a class's private members.

8. The operators `[]`, `++`, `--`, and `[]` should be overloaded as member functions.

9. The `<<` and `>>` operators should be overloaded as nonmember friend functions.

10. The arithmetic operators (`+`, `-`, `*`, `/`) and comparison operators (`>`, `>=`, `==`, `!=`, `<`, `<=`) should be implemented as nonmember functions.

11. C++ can perform certain type conversions automatically if appropriate functions and constructors are defined.

REVIEW QUESTIONS

Section 14.3

14.1 How do you define an operator function for overloading an operator?

14.2 List the operators that cannot be overloaded.

14.3 Can you change the operator precedence or associativity by overloading?

Section 14.4

14.4 What is an Lvalue? What is an Rvalue?

14.5 Explain pass-by-reference and return-by-reference.

14.6 What should be the function signature for the `[]` operator?

Section 14.5

14.7 When you overload a shorthand operator such as +=, should the function be void or nonvoid?

14.8 Why should the functions for shorthand assignment operators return a reference?

Section 14.6

14.9 What should be the function signature for the unary + operator?

14.10 Why is the following implementation for the unary – operator wrong?

```
Rational Rational::operator-()
{
  numerator *= -1;
  return *this;
}
```

Section 14.7

14.11 What should be the function signature for the prefix ++ operator? for the postfix ++ operator?

14.12 Suppose you implement the postfix ++ as follows

```
Rational Rational::operator++(int dummy)
{
  Rational temp(*this);
  add(Rational(1, 0));
  return temp;
}
```

Is this implementation correct? If so, compare it with the implementation in the text; which one is better?

Section 14.8

14.13 How do you define a friend function to access a class's private members?

14.14 How do you define a friend class to access a class's private members?

Section 14.9

14.15 What should be the function signature for the << operator? for the >> operator?

14.16 Why the << and >> operators should be defined as nonmember functions?

14.17 Suppose you overload the << operator as follows:

```
ostream &operator<<(ostream &stream, const Rational &rational)
{
  stream << rational.getNumerator() << " / "
    << rational.getDenominator();
  return stream;
}
```

Do you still need to define

```
friend ostream &operator<<(ostream &stream, Rational &rational)
```

in the Rational class?

Section 14.10

14.18 What should be the function signature for converting an object to the int type?

14.19   Can a class define the conversion function to convert an object to a primitive type value and define a conversion constructor to convert a primitive type value to an object simultaneously in the class?

PROGRAMMING EXERCISES

14.1   (*Using the `Rational` class*) Write a program that computes the following summation series using the `Rational` class:

$$\frac{1}{2} + \frac{2}{3} + \frac{3}{4} + \ldots + \frac{98}{99} + \frac{99}{100}$$

14.2*   (*Demonstrating the benefits of encapsulation*) Rewrite the `Rational` class in §14.2 using a new internal representation for the numerator and denominator. Declare an array of two integers as follows:

```
int r[2];
```

Use `r[0]` to represent the numerator and `r[1]` to represent the denominator. The signatures of the functions in the `Rational` class are not changed, so a client application that uses the previous `Rational` class can continue to use this new `Rational` class without any modification.

14.3*   (*The `Circle` class*) Implement the relational operators (`<`, `<=`, `==`, `!=`, `>`, `>=`) in the `Circle` class in Listing 9.8, Circle2.h, to order the `Circle` objects according to their radii.

14.4*   (*The `StackOfIntegers` class*) §10.14 defined the `StackOfIntegers` class. Implement the subscript operator `[]` in this class to access the elements via the `[]` operator.

14.5**   (*Implementing string operators*) The `string` class in the C++ standard library supports the overloaded operators, as shown in Table 10.1. Implement the following operators: `[]`, `+`, `<<`, `<`, `<=` in the `MyString1` class in Programming Exercise 10.2.

14.6**   (*Implementing string operators*) The `string` class in the C++ standard library supports the overloaded operators, as shown in Table 10.1. Implement the following operators: `+=`, `>>`, `==`, `!=`, `>`, `>=` in the `MyString1` class in Programming Exercise 10.3.

14.7*   (*Math: The `Complex` class*) A complex number has the form $a + bi$, where a and b are real numbers and i is $\sqrt{-1}$. You can perform addition, subtraction, multiplication, and division for complex numbers using the following formulas:

Video Note
the Complex class

$$a + bi + c + di = (a + c) + (b + d)i$$

$$a + bi - (c + di) = (a - c) + (b - d)i$$

$$(a + bi)*(c + di) = (ac - bd) + (bc + ad)i$$

$$(a + bi)/(c + di) = (ac + bd)/(c^2 + d^2) + (bc - ad)i/(c^2 + d^2)$$

Design a class named `Complex` for representing complex numbers and the functions `add`, `subtract`, `multiply`, `divide` for performing complex-number operations, and the `toString` function for returning a string representation for a complex number. The `toString` function returns `a + bi` as a string. If b is `0`, it simply returns `a`.

Provide three constructors `Complex(a, b)`, `Complex(a)`, and `Complex()`. `Complex()` creates a `Complex` object for number 0 and `Complex(a)` creates a `Complex` object with 0 for b.

Overload the operators +, -, *, /, +=, -=, *=, /=, [], unary + and -, prefix ++ and --, postfix ++ and --, <<, >>.

Overload the operators +, -, *, / as nonmember functions. Overload [] so that [0] returns a and [1] returns b.

CHAPTER 15

INHERITANCE AND POLYMORPHISM

Objectives

- To develop a derived class from a base class through inheritance (§15.2).

- To enable generic programming by passing objects of a derived type to a parameter of a base class type (§15.3).

- To understand constructor and destructor chaining (§15.4).

- To know how to invoke the base class's constructors with arguments (§15.4).

- To redefine functions in the derived class (§15.5).

- To distinguish between redefining and overloading (§15.5).

- To enable polymorphism and dynamic binding using virtual functions (§15.6).

- To distinguish between redefining and overriding functions (§15.6).

- To distinguish between static matching and dynamic binding (§15.6).

- To access protected members of a base class from derived classes (§15.7).

- To define abstract classes with pure virtual functions (§15.8).

- To cast an object of a base class type to a derived type using the `dynamic_cast` operator (§15.9).

15.1 Introduction

Object-oriented programming allows you to derive new classes from existing ones. This is called *inheritance*. It is an important and powerful feature in C++ for reusing software. Suppose you are to define classes to model circles, rectangles, and triangles. These classes have many common features. What is the best way to design them to avoid redundancy? The answer is to use inheritance—the subject of this chapter.

Video Note
define derived classes

15.2 Base Classes and Derived Classes

You use a class to model objects of the same type. Different classes may have some common properties and behaviors, which can be generalized in a class that can be shared by other classes. Inheritance enables you to define a general class and later extend it to more specialized ones. The specialized classes inherit properties and functions from the general class.

Consider geometric objects. Suppose you want to design the classes to model geometric objects like circles and rectangles. Geometric objects have many common properties and behaviors. They can be drawn in a certain color, filled or unfilled. Thus, a general class `GeometricObject` can be used to model all geometric objects. This class contains the properties `color` and `filled` and their appropriate `get` and `set` functions. Assume that this class also contains the `toString()` function, which returns a string representation for the object. Since a circle is a special type of geometric object, it shares common properties and functions with other geometric objects. Thus, it makes sense to define the `Circle` class that extends the `GeometricObject` class. Likewise, `Rectangle` can also be defined as a derived class of `GeometricObject`. Figure 15.1 shows the relationships among these classes. An arrow pointing to the *base class* is used to denote the inheritance relationship between the two classes involved.

derived class
base class

In C++ terminology, a class `C1` extended from another class `C2` is called a *derived class*, and `C2` is called a *base class*. We also refer to a base class as a *parent class* and to a derived class as an *extended class*. A derived class inherits accessible data fields and functions from its base class and may also add new data fields and functions.

The `Circle` class inherits all accessible data fields and functions from the `GeometricObject` class. In addition, it has a new data field, `radius`, and its associated `get` and `set` functions. It also contains the `getArea()`, `getPerimeter()`, and `getDiameter()` functions for returning the area, perimeter, and diameter of the circle.

The `Rectangle` class inherits all accessible data fields and functions from the `GeometricObject` class. In addition, it has data fields `width` and `height` and its associated `get` and `set` functions. It also contains the `getArea()` and `getPerimeter()` functions for returning the area and perimeter of the rectangle.

The class declaration for `GeometricObject` is shown in Listing 15.1. The preprocessor directives in lines 1 and 2 guard against multiple declarations. The C++ `string` class header is included in line 3 to support the use of the `string` class in `GeometricObject`. The `isFilled()` function is the accessor for the `filled` data field. Since this data field is the `bool` type, the accessor function is named `isFilled()` by convention.

LISTING 15.1 `GeometricObject.h`

inclusion guard

```
1 #ifndef GEOMETRICOBJECT_H
2 #define GEOMETRICOBJECT_H
3 #include <string>
4 using namespace std;
5
6 class GeometricObject
```

```
 7 {
 8 public:                                                    public members
 9   GeometricObject();
10   GeometricObject(const string &color, bool filled);
11   string getColor() const;
12   void setColor(const string &color);
13   bool isFilled() const;
14   void setFilled(bool filled);
15   string toString() const;
16
17 private:                                                   private members
18   string color;
19   bool filled;
20 }; // Must place semicolon here
21
22 #endif
```

```
         GeometricObject
┌────────────────────────────────┐     ┌──────────────────────────────────────────────┐
│ -color: string                 │     │ The color of the object (default: white).      │
│ -filled: bool                  │     │ Indicates whether the object is filled with a  │
│                                │     │   color (default: false).                      │
│ +GeometricObject()             │     │ Creates a GeometricObject.                     │
│ +GeometricObject(color: string,│     │ Creates a GeometricObject with the specified   │
│   filled: bool)                │     │   color and filled values.                     │
│ +getColor(): string            │     │ Returns the color.                             │
│ +setColor(color: string): void │     │ Sets a new color.                              │
│ +isFilled(): bool              │     │ Returns the filled property.                   │
│ +setFilled(filled: bool): void │     │ Sets a new filled property.                    │
│ +toString(): string            │     │ Returns a string representation of this object.│
└────────────────────────────────┘     └──────────────────────────────────────────────┘
```

```
              Circle                                    Rectangle
┌────────────────────────────────┐     ┌──────────────────────────────────────────────┐
│ -radius: double                │     │ -width: double                                 │
│                                │     │ -height: double                                │
│ +Circle()                      │     │                                                │
│ +Circle(radius: double)        │     │ +Rectangle()                                   │
│ +Circle(radius: double, color: │     │ +Rectangle(width: double, height: double)      │
│   string, filled: bool)        │     │ +Rectangle(width: double, height: double,      │
│ +getRadius(): double           │     │   color: string, filled: bool)                 │
│ +setRadius(radius: double): void│    │ +getWidth(): double                            │
│ +getArea(): double             │     │ +setWidth(width: double): void                 │
│ +getPerimeter(): double        │     │ +getHeight(): double                           │
│ +getDiameter(): double         │     │ +setHeight(height: double): void               │
└────────────────────────────────┘     │ +getArea(): double                             │
                                        │ +getPerimeter(): double                        │
                                        └──────────────────────────────────────────────┘
```

FIGURE 15.1 The GeometricObject class is the base class for Circle and Rectangle.

The GeometricObject class is implemented in Listing 15.2. The toString function (lines 35–38) returns a string that describes the object. The string operator + is used to concatenate two strings and returns a new string object.

LISTING 15.2 GeometricObject.cpp

header file

```
1 #include "GeometricObject.h"
2
```

no-arg constructor

```
3 GeometricObject::GeometricObject()
4 {
5   color = "white";
6   filled = false;
7 }
8
```

no-arg constructor

```
9 GeometricObject::GeometricObject(const string &color, bool filled)
10 {
11   this->color = color;
12   this->filled = filled;
13 }
14
```

getColor

```
15 string GeometricObject::getColor() const
16 {
17   return color;
18 }
19
```

setColor

```
20 void GeometricObject::setColor(const string &color)
21 {
22   this->color = color;
23 }
24
```

isFilled

```
25 bool GeometricObject::isFilled() const
26 {
27   return filled;
28 }
29
```

setFilled

```
30 void GeometricObject::setFilled(bool filled)
31 {
32   this->filled = filled;
33 }
34
```

toString

```
35 string GeometricObject::toString() const
36 {
37   return "GeometricObject";
38 }
```

The class declaration for `Circle` is shown in Listing 15.3. Line 5 defines that the `Circle` class is derived from the base class `GeometricObject`. The syntax

Derived class   Base class

class Circle: public GeometricObject

tells the compiler that the class is derived from the base class. So, all public members in `GeometricObject` are inherited in `Circle`.

LISTING 15.3 DerivedCircle.h

inclusion guard

```
1 #ifndef DERIVEDCIRCLE_H
2 #define DERIVEDCIRCLE_H
3 #include "GeometricObject.h"
4
```

extends **GeometricObject**

```
5 class Circle: public GeometricObject
```

```
 6 {
 7 public:                                                          public members
 8   Circle();
 9   Circle(double);
10   Circle(double radius, const string &color, bool filled);
11   double getRadius() const;
12   void setRadius(double);
13   double getArea() const;
14   double getPerimeter() const;
15   double getDiameter() const;
16   string toString() const;
17
18 private:                                                         private members
19   double radius;
20 }; // Must place semicolon here
21
22 #endif
```

The `Circle` class is implemented in Listing 15.4.

LISTING 15.4 DerivedCircle.cpp

```
 1 #include "DerivedCircle.h"                                       Circle header
 2
 3 // Construct a default circle object
 4 Circle::Circle()                                                 no-arg constructor
 5 {
 6   radius = 1;
 7 }
 8
 9 // Construct a circle object with specified radius
10 Circle::Circle(double radius)                                    constructor
11 {
12   this->radius = radius;
13 }
14
15 // Construct a circle object with specified radius,              constructor
16 //   color and filled values
17 Circle::Circle(double radius, const string &color, bool filled)
18 {
19   this->radius = radius;
20   setColor(color);
21   setFilled(filled);
22 }
23                                                                  getRadius
24 // Return the radius of this circle
25 double Circle::getRadius() const
26 {
27   return radius;
28 }
29                                                                  setRadius
30 // Set a new radius
31 void Circle::setRadius(double radius)
32 {
33   this->radius = (radius >= 0) ? radius : 0;
34 }
35                                                                  getArea
36 // Return the area of this circle
37 double Circle::getArea() const
```

getPerimeter

```
38 {
39    return radius * radius * 3.14159;
40 }
41
42 // Return the perimeter of this circle
43 double Circle::getPerimeter() const
44 {
45    return 2 * radius * 3.14159;
46 }
```

getDiameter

```
47
48 // Return the diameter of this circle
49 double Circle::getDiameter() const
50 {
51    return 2 * radius;
52 }
53
54 // Redefine the toString function
55 string Circle::toString() const
56 {
57    return "Circle object";
58 }
```

The constructor `Circle(double radius, const string &color, bool filled)` is implemented by invoking the `setColor` and `setFilled` functions to set the `color` and `filled` properties (lines 17–22). These two public functions are defined the base class `GeometricObject` and are inherited in `Circle`. So, they can be used in the derived class.

You might attempt to use the data fields `color` and `filled` directly in the constructor as follows:

private member in base class

```
Circle::Circle(double radius, const string &c, bool f)
{
   this->radius = radius;
   color = c; // Illegal since color is private in the base class
   filled = f; // Illegal since filled is private in the base class
}
```

This is wrong, because the private data fields `color` and `filled` in the `GeometricObject` class cannot be accessed in any class other than the `GeometricObject` class itself. The only way to read and modify `color` and `filled` is through their `get` and `set` functions.

The class declaration for `Rectangle` is shown in Listing 15.5. Line 5 defines that the `Rectangle` class is derived from the base class `GeometricObject`. The syntax

Derived class   Base class

`class Rectangle: public GeometricObject`

tells the compiler that the class is derived from the base class. So, all public members in `GeometricObject` are inherited in `Rectangle`.

LISTING 15.5   DerivedRectangle.h

inclusion guard

```
1 #ifndef DERIVEDRECTANGLE_H
2 #define DERIVEDRECTANGLE_H
3 #include "GeometricObject.h"
4
```

```
 5 class Rectangle: public GeometricObject                          extends GeometricObject
 6 {
 7 public:                                                          public members
 8   Rectangle();
 9   Rectangle(double width, double height);
10   Rectangle(double width, double height,
11     const string &color, bool filled);
12   double getWidth() const;
13   void setWidth(double);
14   double getHeight() const;
15   void setHeight(double);
16   double getArea() const;
17   double getPerimeter() const;
18   string toString() const;
19
20 private:                                                         private members
21   double width;
22   double height;
23 };  // Must place semicolon here
24
25 #endif
```

The Rectangle class is implemented in Listing 15.6.

LISTING 15.6 DerivedRectangle.cpp

```
 1 #include "DerivedRectangle.h"                                    Rectangle header
 2
 3 // Construct a default rectangle object
 4 Rectangle::Rectangle()                                           no-arg constructor
 5 {
 6   width = 1;
 7   height = 1;
 8 }
 9
10 // Construct a rectangle object with specified width and height
11 Rectangle::Rectangle(double width, double height)                constructor
12 {
13   this->width = width;
14   this->height = height;
15 }
16
17 Rectangle::Rectangle(                                            constructor
18   double width, double height, const string &color, bool filled)
19 {
20   this->width = width;
21   this->height = height;
22   setColor(color);
23   setFilled(filled);
24 }
25
26 // Return the width of this rectangle
27 double Rectangle::getWidth() const                               getWidth
28 {
29   return width;
30 }
31
32 // Set a new radius
33 void Rectangle::setWidth(double width)                           setWidth
```

```
34 {
35   this->width = (width >= 0) ? width : 0;
36 }
37
```

getHeight
```
38 // Return the height of this rectangle
39 double Rectangle::getHeight() const
40 {
41   return height;
42 }
43
```

setHeight
```
44 // Set a new height
45 void Rectangle::setHeight(double height)
46 {
47   this->height = (height >= 0) ? height : 0;
48 }
49
```

getArea
```
50 // Return the area of this rectangle
51 double Rectangle::getArea() const
52 {
53   return width * height;
54 }
55
```

getPerimeter
```
56 // Return the perimeter of this rectangle
57 double Rectangle::getPerimeter() const
58 {
59   return 2 * (width + height);
60 }
61
62 // Redefine the toString function, to be covered in Section 15.5
63 string Rectangle::toString() const
64 {
65   return "Rectangle object";
66 }
```

Listing 15.7 gives a test program that uses these three classes—GeometricObject, Circle, and Rectangles.

LISTING 15.7 TestGeometricObject.cpp

GeometricObject header
Circle header
Rectangle header

create a GeometricObject

create a Circle

```
 1 #include "GeometricObject.h"
 2 #include "DerivedCircle.h"
 3 #include "DerivedRectangle.h"
 4 #include <iostream>
 5 using namespace std;
 6
 7 int main()
 8 {
 9   GeometricObject shape;
10   shape.setColor("red");
11   shape.setFilled(true);
12   cout << shape.toString() << endl
13     << " color: " << shape.getColor()
14     << " filled: " << (shape.isFilled() ? "true" : "false") << endl;
15
16   Circle circle(5);
17   circle.setColor("black");
18   circle.setFilled(false);
19   cout << circle.toString()<< endl
20     << " color: " << shape.getColor()
21     << " filled: " << (shape.isFilled() ? "true" : "false")
```

```
22        << " radius: " << circle.getRadius()
23        << " area: " << circle.getArea()
24        << " perimeter: " << circle.getPerimeter() << endl;
25
26    Rectangle rectangle(2, 3);                                    create a Rectangle
27    rectangle.setColor("orange");
28    rectangle.setFilled(true);
29    cout << rectangle.toString()<< endl
30        << " color: " << shape.getColor()
31        << " filled: " << (shape.isFilled() ? "true" : "false")
32        << " width: " << rectangle.getWidth()
33        << " height: " << rectangle.getHeight()
34        << " area: " << rectangle.getArea()
35        << " perimeter: " << rectangle.getPerimeter() << endl;
36
37    return 0;
38 }
```

```
Geometric object
  color: red filled: true
Circle object
  color: red filled: true radius: 5 area: 78.5397 perimeter: 31.4159
Rectangle object
  color: red filled: true width: 2 height: 3 area: 6 perimeter: 10
```

The program creates a `GeometricObject` and invokes its functions `setColor`, `setFilled`, `toString`, `getColor`, and `isFilled` in lines 9–14.

The program creates a `Circle` object and invokes its functions `setColor`, `setFilled`, `toString`, `getColor`, `isFilled`, `getRadius`, `getArea`, and `getPerimeter` in lines 16–24. Note that the `setColor` and `setFilled` functions are defined in the `Geometric-Object` class and inherited in the `Circle` class.

The program creates a `Rectangle` object and invokes its functions `setColor`, `setFilled`, `toString`, `getColor`, `isFilled`, `getWidth`, `getHeight`, `getArea`, and `getPerimeter` in lines 26–35. Note that the `setColor` and `setFilled` functions are defined in the `GeometricObject` class and inherited in the `Rectangle` class.

Note the following points about inheritance:

■ Private data fields in a base class are not accessible outside the class. Therefore, they cannot be used directly in a derived class. They can, however, be accessed/mutated through public accessor/mutator if defined in the base class.   *private data fields*

■ Not all *is-a relationships* should be modeled using inheritance. For example, a square is a rectangle, but you should not define a `Square` class to extend a `Rectangle` class, because there is nothing to extend (or supplement) from a rectangle to a square. Rather you should define a `Square` class to extend the `GeometricObject` class. For class `A` to extend class `B`, `A` should contain more detailed information than `B`.   *nonextensible is-a*

■ Inheritance is used to model the *is-a* relationship. Do not blindly extend a class just for the sake of reusing functions. For example, it makes no sense for a `Tree` class to extend a `Person` class, even though they share common properties such as height and weight. A derived class and its base class must have the *is-a* relationship.   *no blind extension*

■ C++ allows you to derive a derived class from several classes. This capability is known as *multiple inheritance*, which is discussed in Supplement IV.A, "Multiple Inheritance."   *multiple inheritance*

15.3 Generic Programming

An object of a derived class can be passed wherever an object of a base type parameter is required. Thus a function can be used generically for a wide range of object arguments. This is known as *generic programming*. If a function's parameter type is a base class (e.g., GeometricObject), you may pass an object to this function of any of the parameter's derived classes (e.g., Circle or Rectangle).

For example, suppose you define a function as follows:

```
void displayGeometricObject(GeometricObject &shape)
{
  cout << shape.getColor() << endl;
}
```

The parameter type is GeometricObject. You can invoke this function in the following code:

```
displayGeometricObject(GeometricObject("black", true));
displayGeometricObject(Circle(5));
displayGeometricObject(Rectangle(2, 3));
```

Each statement creates an anonymous object and passes it to invoke display-GeometricObject. Since Circle and Rectangle are derived from GeometricObject, you can pass a Circle object or a Rectangle object to the GeometricObject parameter type in the displayGeometricObject function.

15.4 Constructors and Destructors

A derived class inherits accessible data fields and functions from its base class. Does it inherit constructors or destructors? Can base class constructors and destructors be invoked from derived classes? We now consider these questions and their ramification.

15.4.1   Calling Base Class Constructors

A constructor is used to construct an instance of a class. Unlike data fields and functions, the constructors of a base class are not inherited in the derived class. They can only be invoked from the constructors of the derived classes to initialize the data fields in the base class. You can invoke the base class's constructor from the constructor initializer list of the derived class. The syntax is as follows:

```
DerivedClass(parameterList): BaseClass()
{
  // Perform initialization
}
```

or

```
DerivedClass(parameterList): BaseClass(argumentList)
{
  // Perform initialization
}
```

The former invokes the no-arg constructor of its base class, and the latter invokes the base class constructor with the specified arguments.

A constructor in a derived class always invokes a constructor in its base class explicitly or implicitly. If a base constructor is not invoked explicitly, the base class's no-arg constructor is invoked by default. For example,

The `Circle(double radius, const string &color, bool filled)` constructor (lines 7–22) in Listing 15.4, DerivedCircle.cpp, can also be implemented by invoking the base class's constructor `GeometricObject(const string &color, bool filled)` as follows:

```
1 // Construct a circle object with specified radius, color and filled
2 Circle::Circle(double radius, const string &color, bool filled)
3   : GeometricObject(color, filled)                                    invoke base constructor
4 {
5   this->radius = radius;
6 }
```

or

```
1 // Construct a circle object with specified radius, color and filled
2 Circle::Circle(double radius, const string &color, bool filled)
3   : GeometricObject(color, filled), radius(radius)                    initialize data field
4 {
5 }
```

The latter also initializes the data field `radius` in the constructor initializer. `radius` is a data field defined in the `Circle` class.

15.4.2 Constructor and Destructor Chaining

Constructing an instance of a class invokes the constructors of all the base classes along the inheritance chain. When constructing an object of a derived class, the derived class constructor first invokes its base class constructor before performing its own tasks. If a base class is derived from another class, the base class constructor invokes its parent class constructor before performing its own tasks. This process continues until the last constructor along the inheritance hierarchy is called. This is called *constructor chaining*. Conversely, the destructors are automatically invoked in reverse order. When an object of a derived class is destroyed, the derived class destructor is called. After it finishes its tasks, it invokes its base class destructor. This process continues until the last destructor along the inheritance hierarchy is called. This is called *destructor chaining*.

Consider the following code in Listing 15.8:

LISTING 15.8 ChainingDemo.cpp

```
1 #include <iostream>
2 using namespace std;
3
4 class Person
5 {
6 public:
7   Person()
```

Person class

```
 8    {
 9      cout << "Performs tasks for Person's constructor" << endl;
10    }
11
12    ~Person()
13    {
14      cout << "Performs tasks for Person's destructor" << endl;
15    }
16 };
17
```

Employee class

```
18 class Employee: public Person
19 {
20 public:
21    Employee()
22    {
23      cout << "Performs tasks for Employee's constructor" << endl;
24    }
25
26    ~Employee()
27    {
28      cout << "Performs tasks for Employee's destructor" << endl;
29    }
30 };
31
```

Faculty class

```
32 class Faculty: public Employee
33 {
34 public:
35    Faculty()
36    {
37      cout << "Performs tasks for Faculty's constructor" << endl;
38    }
39
40    ~Faculty()
41    {
42      cout << "Performs tasks for Faculty's destructor" << endl;
43    }
44 };
45
46 int main()
47 {
```

create a **Faculty**

```
48    Faculty faculty;
49
50    return 0;
51 }
```

```
Performs tasks for Person's constructor
Performs tasks for Employee's constructor
Performs tasks for Faculty's constructor
Performs tasks for Faculty's destructor
Performs tasks for Employee's destructor
Performs tasks for Person's destructor
```

The program creates an instance of **Faculty** in line 48. Since **Faculty** is derived from **Employee** and **Employee** is derived from **Person**, **Faculty**'s constructor invokes **Employee**'s constructor before it performs its own task. **Employee**'s constructor invokes **Person**'s constructor before it performs its own task, as shown in the following figure:

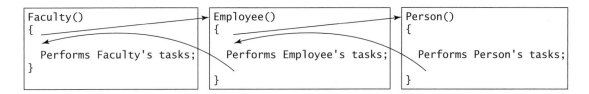

When the program exits, the **Faculty** object is destroyed. So the **Faculty**'s destructor is called, then **Employee**'s, and finally **Person**'s, as shown in the following figure:

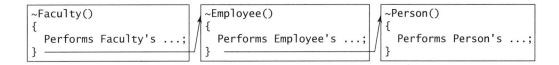

Caution

If a class is designed to be extended, it is better to provide a *no-arg constructor* to avoid programming errors. Consider the following code:

no-arg constructor

```
1 class Fruit
2 {
3 public:
4   Fruit(int id)
5   {
6   }
7 };
8
9 class Apple: public Fruit
10 {
11 public:
12   Apple()
13   {
14   }
15 };
```

Since no constructor is explicitly defined in **Apple**, **Apple**'s default no-arg constructor is defined implicitly. Since **Apple** is a derived class of **Fruit**, **Apple**'s default constructor automatically invokes **Fruit**'s no-arg constructor. However, **Fruit** does not have a no-arg constructor, because **Fruit** has an explicit constructor defined. Therefore, the program cannot be compiled.

Note

If the base class has a customized copy constructor and assignment operator, you should customize these in the derived classes to ensure that the data fields in the base class are properly copied. Suppose class **Child** is derived from **Parent**. The code for the copy constructor in **Child** would typically look like this:

copy constructor
assignment operator

```
Child::Child(const Child &object): Parent(object)
{
  // Write the code for copying data fields in Child
}
```

The code for the assignment operator in **Child** would typically look like this:

```
Child& Child::operator=(const Child &object)
{
  Parent::operator=(object);
  // Write the code for copying data fields in Child
}
```

destructor

When a destructor for a derived class is invoked, it automatically invokes the destructor in the base class. So, there is no need to explicitly invoke the destructor in the base class. The destructor in the derived class only needs to destroy the dynamically created memory in the derived class.

15.5 Redefining Functions

The `toString()` function is defined in the `GeometricObject` class to return a string `"Geometric object"` (lines 35–38 in Listing 15.2) as follows:

```
string GeometricObject::toString() const
{
  return "Geometric object";
}
```

To *redefine* a base class's function in the derived class, you need to add the function's prototype in the derived class's header file, and provide a new implementation for the function in the derived class's implementation file.

The `toString()` function is redefined in the `Circle` class (lines 55–58 in Listing 15.4) as follows:

```
string Circle::toString() const
{
  return "Circle object";
}
```

The `toString()` function is redefined in the `Rectangle` class (lines 63–66 in Listing 15.6) as follows:

```
string Rectangle::toString() const
{
  return "Rectangle object";
}
```

So, the following code

create **GeometricObject**
invoke **toString**

create **Circle**
invoke **toString**

create **Rectangle**

invoke **toString**

```
1 GeometricObject shape;
2 cout << "shape.toString() returns " << shape.toString() << endl;
3
4 Circle circle(5);
5 cout << "circle.toString() returns " << circle.toString() << endl;
6
7 Rectangle rectangle(4, 6);
8 cout << "rectangle.toString() returns "
9   << rectangle.toString() << endl;
```

displays:

```
shape.toString() returns Geometric object
circle.toString() returns Circle object
rectangle.toString() returns Rectangle object
```

The code creates a `GeometricObject` in line 1. The `toString` function defined in `GeometricObject` is invoked in line 2, since `shape`'s type is `GeometricObject`.

The code creates a `Circle` object in line 4. The `toString` function defined in `Circle` is invoked in line 5, since `circle`'s type is `Circle`.

The code creates a `Rectangle` object in line 7. The `toString` function defined in `Rectangle` is invoked in line 9, since `rectangle`'s type is `Rectangle`.

If you wish to invoke the `toString` function defined in the `GeometricObject` class on the calling object `circle`, use the scope resolution operator (`::`) with the base class name. For example, the following code

Invoke function in the base

```
Circle circle(5);
cout << "circle.toString() returns " << circle.toString() << endl;
cout << "invoke the base class's toString() to return "
  << circle.GeometricObject::toString();
```

displays

```
circle.toString() returns Circle object
invoke the base class's toString() to return Geometric object
```

Note

In §5.7, "Overloading Functions," you learned about overloading functions. Overloading a function is a way to provide more than one function with the same name but with different signatures to distinguish them. To redefine a function, the function must be defined in the derived class using the same signature and same return type as in its base class.

redefining vs. overloading

15.6 Polymorphism and Virtual Functions

Before introducing *polymorphism*, let us begin with an example in Listing 15.9 to demonstrate the need for it.

Video Note
polymorphism and virtual functions

LISTING 15.9   WhyPolymorphismDemo.cpp

```
1 #include <iostream>
2 #include "GeometricObject.h"
3 #include "DerivedCircle.h"
4 #include "DerivedRectangle.h"
5
6 using namespace std;
7
8 void displayGeometricObject(GeometricObject &g)
9 {
10   cout << g.toString() << endl;
11 }
12
13 int main()
14 {
15   displayGeometricObject(GeometricObject());
16   displayGeometricObject(Circle(5));
17   displayGeometricObject(Rectangle(4, 6));
18
19   return 0;
20 }
```

displayGeometricObject

invoke **toString**

invoke **displayGeometric-Object**

invoke **displayGeometric-Object**

invoke **displayGeometric-Object**

```
Geometric object
Geometric object
Geometric object
```

This program defines the `displayGeometricObject` function that invokes the `toString` function on a `GeometricObject` (line 10).

The `displayGeometricObject` function is invoked in lines 15–17 by passing the anonymous objects `GeometricObject()`, `Circle(5)`, and `Rectangle(4, 6)`, respectively. As shown in the output, the `toString()` function defined in class `GeometricObject` is invoked.

Can you invoke the `toString()` function defined in `Circle` when executing `displayGeometricObject(Circle(5))`, the `toString()` function defined in `Rectangle` when executing `displayGeometricObject(Rectangle(4, 6))`, and the `toString()` function defined in `GeometricObject` when executing `displayGeometricObject(GeometricObject())`? You can do so simply by declaring `toString` as a *virtual function* in the base class `GeometricObject`.

Suppose you replace line 15 in Listing 15.1 with the following function declaration:

why virtual function?

define virtual function

```
virtual string toString() const;
```

Now if you rerun Listing 15.9, you will see the following output:

```
Geometric object
Circle object
Rectangle object
```

virtual

With the `toString()` function defined as `virtual` in the base class, C++ dynamically determines which `toString()` function to invoke at runtime. When invoking `displayGeometricObject(Circle(5))`, `Circle(5)` is passed to `g` by reference. Since `g` refers to an object of the `Circle` type, the `toString` function defined in class `Circle` is invoked. The capability of determining which function to invoke at runtime is known as *dynamic binding*. It is also commonly known as *polymorphism* (from a Greek word meaning "many forms"), because one generic base type can have many derived types.

dynamic binding
polymorphism

Note

overriding a function

In C++, *redefining* a virtual function in a derived class is called *overriding a function*.

To enable dynamic binding for a function, you need to do two things:

■ The function must be defined `virtual` in the base class.

■ The variable that references the object must be passed by reference to the virtual function.

Listing 15.9 passes the object to a parameter by reference (line 8); alternatively, you can rewrite lines 8–11 by passing reference via pointer, as in Listing 15.10:

LISTING 15.10 WhyPolymorphismDemoUsingPointer.cpp

pass-by-reference via pointer

invoke **toString**

```
 1 #include <iostream>
 2 #include "GeometricObject.h"
 3 #include "DerivedCircle.h"
 4 #include "DerivedRectangle.h"
 5
 6 using namespace std;
 7
 8 void displayGeometricObject(GeometricObject *g)
 9 {
10   cout << (*g).toString() << endl;
11 }
12
13 int main()
```

```
14 {
15   displayGeometricObject(&GeometricObject());
16   displayGeometricObject(&Circle(5));
17   displayGeometricObject(&Rectangle(4, 6));
18
19   return 0;
20 }
```

invoke **displayGeometric-Object**

invoke **displayGeometric-Object**

invoke **displayGeometric-Object**

```
Geometric object
Circle object
Rectangle object
```

However, if the object argument is passed by value, the virtual functions are not bound dynamically. As shown in Listing 15.11, even though the function is defined to be virtual, the output is the same as it would be without using the virtual function.

LISTING 15.11   WhyPolymorphismDemoPassByValue.cpp

```
 1 #include <iostream>
 2 #include "GeometricObject.h"
 3 #include "DerivedCircle.h"
 4 #include "DerivedRectangle.h"
 5
 6 using namespace std;
 7
 8 void displayGeometricObject(GeometricObject g)
 9 {
10   cout << g.toString() << endl;
11 }
12
13 int main()
14 {
15   displayGeometricObject(GeometricObject());
16   displayGeometricObject(Circle(5));
17   displayGeometricObject(Rectangle(4, 6));
18
19   return 0;
20 }
```

pass-by-value

invoke **toString**

invoke **displayGeometric-Object**

invoke **displayGeometric-Object**

invoke **displayGeometric-Object**

```
Geometric object
Geometric object
Geometric object
```

Note the following points regarding virtual functions:

■ If a function is defined **virtual** in a base class, it is automatically **virtual** in all its derived classes. The keyword **virtual** need not be added in the function declaration in the derived class.

■ Matching a function signature and binding a function implementation are two separate issues. The *declared type* of the variable decides which function to match at compile time. The compiler finds a matching function according to parameter type, number of parameters, and order of the parameters at compile time. A virtual function may be implemented in several derived classes. C++ dynamically binds the implementation of the function at runtime, decided by the *actual class* of the object referenced by the variable.

virtual

static matching vs. dynamic binding

15.7 The **protected** Keyword

So far you have used the `private` and `public` keywords to specify whether data fields and functions can be accessed from outside the class. Private members can be accessed only from inside the class, and public members can be accessed from any other classes.

why **protected**?

Often it is desirable to allow derived classes to access data fields or functions defined in the base class but not allow nonderived classes to do so. For this purpose you can use the `protected` keyword. A protected data field or a protected function in a base class can be accessed in its derived classes.

visibility keyword

The keywords `private`, `protected`, and `public` are known as *visibility* or *accessibility* *keywords* because they specify how class and class members are accessed. Their visibility increases in this order:

$$\xrightarrow{\text{Visibility increases}}$$
private, protected, public

Listing 15.12 demonstrates the use of `protected` keywords.

LISTING 15.12 `VisibilityDemo.cpp`

```cpp
1  #include <iostream>
2  using namespace std;
3
4  class B
5  {
6  public:
7    int i;
8
9  protected:
10   int j;
11
12 private:
13   int k;
14 };
15
16 class A: public B
17 {
18 public:
19   void display() const
20   {
21     cout << i << endl; // Fine, can access it
22     cout << j << endl; // Fine, can access it
23     cout << k << endl; // Wrong, cannot access it
24   }
25 };
26
27 int main()
28 {
29   A a;
30   cout << a.i << endl; // Fine, can access it
31   cout << a.j << endl; // Wrong, cannot access it
32   cout << a.k << endl; // Wrong, cannot access it
33
34   return 0;
35 }
```

public
protected
private

Since A is derived from B and j is protected, j can be accessed from class A in line 22. Since k is private, k cannot be accessed from class A.

Since i is public, i can be accessed from a.i in line 30. Since j and k are not public, they cannot be accessed from the object a in lines 31–32.

15.8 Abstract Classes and Pure Virtual Functions

In the inheritance hierarchy, classes become more specific and concrete *with each new derived class*. If you move from a derived class back up to its parent and ancestor classes, the classes become more general and less specific. Class design should ensure that a base class contains common features of its derived classes. Sometimes a base class is so abstract that it cannot have any specific instances. Such a class is referred to as an *abstract class*.

abstract class

In §15.2, "Base Classes and Derived Classes," `GeometricObject` was defined as the base class for `Circle` and `Rectangle`. `GeometricObject` models common features of geometric objects. Both `Circle` and `Rectangle` contain the `getArea()` and `getPerimeter()` functions for computing the area and perimeter of a circle and a rectangle. Since you can compute areas and perimeters for all geometric objects, it is better to define the `getArea()` and `getPerimeter()` functions in the `GeometricObject` class. However, these functions cannot be implemented in the `GeometricObject` class, because their implementation is dependent on the specific type of geometric object. Such functions are referred to as *abstract functions*. After you define the abstract functions in `GeometricObject`, `GeometricObject` becomes an abstract class. The new `GeometricObject` class is shown in Figure 15.2. In UML graphic notation, the names of abstract classes and their abstract functions are italicized, as shown in Figure 15.2.

abstract function

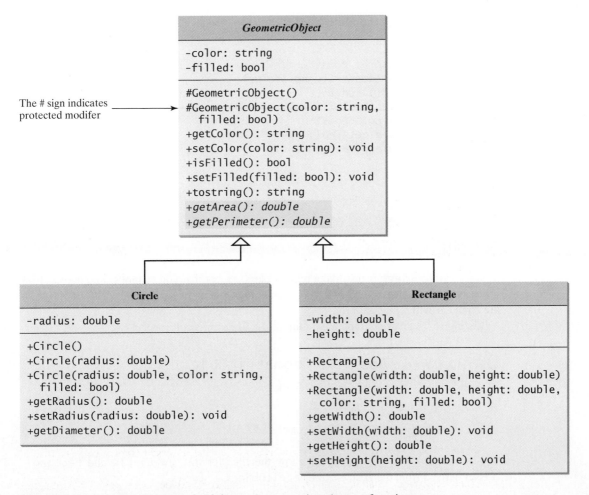

The # sign indicates protected modifer

FIGURE 15.2 The new `GeometricObject` class contains abstract functions.

pure virtual function

In C++, abstract functions are called *pure virtual functions*. A class that contains pure virtual functions becomes an abstract class. A pure virtual function is defined this way:

——— Indicating pure virtual function

```
virtual double getArea() = 0;
```

The = 0 notation indicates that getArea is a pure virtual function. A pure virtual function does not have a body or implementation in the base class.

Listing 15.13 defines the new abstract GeometricObject class with two pure virtual functions in lines 18–19.

LISTING 15.13 AbstractGeometricObject.h

```
1  #ifndef ABSTRACTGEOMETRICOBJECT_H
2  #define ABSTRACTGEOMETRICOBJECT_H
3  #include <string>
4  using namespace std;
5
6  class GeometricObject
7  {
8  protected:
9     GeometricObject();
10    GeometricObject(const string &color, bool filled);
11
12 public:
13    string getColor() const;
14    void setColor(const string &color);
15    bool isFilled() const;
16    void setFilled(bool filled);
17    string toString() const;
18    virtual double getArea() = 0;
19    virtual double getPerimeter() = 0;
20
21 private:
22    string color;
23    bool filled;
24 }; // Must place semicolon here
25
26 #endif
```

pure virtual function
pure virtual function

GeometricObject is just like a regular class, except that you cannot create objects from it because it is an abstract class. If you attempt to create an object from GeometricObject, the compiler will report an error.

Listing 15.14 gives an implementation of the GeometricObject class.

LISTING 15.14 AbstractGeometricObject.cpp

include header

```
1  #include "AbstractGeometricObject.h"
2
3  // Omitted
4  // Same as lines 3-38 in GeometricObject.cpp in Listing 15.2
```

Listings 15.15, 15.16, and 15.17 show the files for the new Circle and Rectangle classes derived from the abstract GeometricObject.

LISTING 15.15 DerivedCircleFromAbstractGeometricObject.h

```
1 #ifndef DERIVEDCIRCLEFROMABSTRACTGEOMETRICOBJECT_H
2 #define DERIVEDCIRCLEFROMABSTRACTGEOMETRICOBJECT_H
3 #include "AbstractGeometricObject.h"
4
5 // Omitted
6 // Same as lines 5-21 in DerivedCircle.h in Listing 15.3
7
8 #endif
```

inclusion guard

AbstractGeometricObject header

LISTING 15.16 DerivedCircleFromAbstractGeometric-Object.cpp

```
1 #include" DerivedCircleFromAbstractGeometricObject.h"
2
3 // Omitted
4 // Same as lines 3-58 in DerivedCircle.cpp in Listing 15.4
```

inclusion guard

AbstractGeometricObject header

LISTING 15.17 DerivedRectangleFromAbstractGeometric-Object.h

```
1 #ifndef DERIVEDRECTANGLEFROMGEOMETRICOBJECT_H
2 #define DERIVEDRECTANGLEFROMGEOMETRICOBJECT_H
3 #include "AbstractGeometricObject.h"
4
5 // Omitted
6 // Same as lines 5-23 in DerivedRectangle.h in Listing 15.5
7
8 #endif
```

inclusion guard

AbstractGeometricObject header

LISTING 15.18 DerivedRectangleFromAbstractGeometric-Object.cpp

```
1 #include "DerivedRectangleFromAbstractGeometricObject.h"
2
3 // Omitted
4 // Same as lines 3-66 in DerivedRectangle.cpp in Listing 15.6
```

inclusion guard

AbstractGeometric-Object header

You may be wondering whether the abstract functions **getArea** and **getPerimeter** should be removed from the **GeometricObject** class. The following example in Listing 15.19 shows the benefits of defining them in the **GeometricObject** class.

This example presents a program that creates two geometric objects (a circle and a rectangle), invokes the **equalArea** function to check whether the two objects have equal areas, and invokes the **displayGeometricObject** function to display the objects.

LISTING 15.19 TestAbstractGeometricObject.cpp

```
1 #include "AbstractGeometricObject.h"
2 #include "DerivedCircleFromAbstractGeometricObject.h"
3 #include "DerivedRectangleFromAbstractGeometricObject.h"
4 #include <iostream>
5 using namespace std;
6
7 // A function for comparing the areas of two geometric objects
8 bool equalArea(GeometricObject &g1,
9   GeometricObject &g2)
```

include header file

dynamic binding

```
10 {
11   return g1.getArea() == g2.getArea();
12 }
13
14 // A function for displaying a geometric object
15 void displayGeometricObject(GeometricObject &g)
16 {
17   cout << "The area is " << g.getArea() << endl;
18   cout << "The perimeter is " << g.getPerimeter() << endl;
19 }
20
21 int main()
22 {
23   Circle circle(5);
24   Rectangle rectangle(5, 3);
25
26   cout << "Circle info: " << endl;
27   displayGeometricObject(circle);
28
29   cout << "\nRectangle info: " << endl;
30   displayGeometricObject(rectangle);
31
32   cout << "\nThe two objects have the same area? " <<
33     (equalArea(circle, rectangle) ? "Yes" : "No") << endl;
34
35   return 0;
36 }
```

dynamic binding
dynamic binding

```
Circle info:
The area is 78.5397
The perimeter is 31.4159

Rectangle info:
The area is 15
The perimeter is 16

The two objects have the same area? No
```

The program creates a `Circle` object and a `Rectangle` object in lines 23–24.

The pure virtual functions `getArea()` and `getPerimeter()` defined in the `GeometricObject` class are overridden in the `Circle` class and the `Rectangle` class.

When invoking `displayGeometricObject(circle1)` (line 27), the functions `getArea` and `getPerimeter` defined in the `Circle` class are used, and when invoking `displayGeometricObject(rectangle)` (line 30), the functions `getArea` and `getPerimeter` defined in the `Rectangle` class are used. C++ dynamically determines which of these functions to invoke at runtime, depending on the type of object.

Similarly, when invoking `equalArea(circle, rectangle)` (line 33), the `getArea` function defined in the `Circle` class is used for `g1.getArea()`, since `g1` is a circle. Also, the `getArea` function defined in the `Rectangle` class is used for `g2.getArea()`, since `g2` is a rectangle.

why abstract functions?

Note that if the `getArea` and `getPerimeter` functions were not defined in `GeometricObject`, you cannot define the `equalArea` and `displayObject` functions in this program. So, you now see the benefits of defining the abstract functions in `GeometricObject`.

15.9 Casting: `static_cast` vs. `dynamic_cast`

Suppose you wish to rewrite the `displayGeometricObject` function in Listing 15.18, TestAbstractGeometricObject.cpp, to display the radius and diameter for a circle object and the width and height for a rectangle object. You may attempt to implement the function as follows:

```
void displayGeometricObject(GeometricObject &g)
{
  cout << "The raidus is " << g.getRadius() << endl;
  cout << "The diameter is " << g.getDiameter() << endl;

  cout << "The width is " << g.getWidth() << endl;
  cout << "The height is " << g.getHeight() << endl;

  cout << "The area is " << g.getArea() << endl;
  cout << "The perimeter is " << g.getPerimeter() << endl;
}
```

This code cannot be compiled because `g`'s type is `GeometricObject`, but the `GeometricObject` class does not contain the `getRadius()`, `getDiameter()`, `get-Width()`, and `getHeight()` functions.

To fix the problem, we will need to cast `g` into `Circle` or `Rectangle`, as shown in the following code:

`static_cast` operator

```
 1 void displayGeometricObject(GeometricObject &g)
 2 {
 3   GeometricObject *p = &g;
 4   cout << "The raidus is " <<
 5     static_cast<Circle*>(p)->getRadius() << endl;
 6   cout << "The diameter is " <<
 7     static_cast<Circle*>(p)->getDiameter() << endl;
 8
 9   cout << "The width is " <<
10     static_cast<Rectangle*>(p)->getWidth() << endl;
11   cout << "The height is " <<
12     static_cast<Rectangle*>(p)->getHeight() << endl;
13
14   cout << "The area is " << g.getArea() << endl;
15   cout << "The perimeter is " << g.getPerimeter() << endl;
16 }
```

casting to Circle*

Casting must be performed on the reference of the object, not the object itself. So a pointer `p` is used to point to a `GeometricObject` `g` (line 3). This new function can compile but is not correct. For a `Circle` object, it is cast to `Rectangle` to invoke `getWidth()` in line 10. Likewise, for a `Rectangle` object, it is cast to `Circle` to invoke `getRadius()` in line 5. We need to ensure that the object is indeed a `Circle` object before invoking `getRadius()`. This can be done using `dynamic_cast`.

why dynamic casting

The `dynamic_cast` works like the `static_cast`. Additionally, it performs runtime checking to ensure that casting is successful. If casting fails, it returns NULL. So, if you run the following code,

`dynamic_cast` operator

```
1 Rectangle rectangle(5, 3);
2 GeometricObject *p = &rectangle;
3 Circle *p1 = dynamic_cast<Circle*>(p);
4 cout << (*p1).getRadius() << endl;
```

`p1` will be NULL. A runtime error will occur when running the code in line 4. Recall that NULL is defined as 0, which indicates that a pointer does not point to any object. The

NULL

definition of NULL is in a number of standard libraries including <iostream> and <cstddef>.

Note

upcasting and downcasting

Assigning a pointer of a derived class type to a pointer of its base class type is called *upcasting*, and assigning a pointer of a base class type to a pointer of its derived class type is called *downcasting*. Upcasting can be performed implicitly without using the static_cast or dynamic_cast operator. For example, the following code is correct:

```cpp
GeometricObject *p = new Circle(1);
Circle *p1 = new Circle(2);
p = p1;
```

However, downcasting must be performed explicitly. For example, to assign **p** to **p1**, you have to use

```cpp
p1 = static_cast<Circle*>(p); or p1 = dynamic_cast<Circle*>(p);
```

Note

dynamic_cast for virtual function

dynamic_cast can be performed only on the pointer of a polymorphic type; i.e., the type contains a virtual function.

Now you can rewrite the displayGeometricObject function using dynamic casting, as in Listing 15.20, to check whether casting is successful at runtime.

LISTING 15.20   DynamicCastingDemo.cpp

include header file

```cpp
1 #include "AbstractGeometricObject.h"
2 #include "DerivedCircleFromAbstractGeometricObject.h"
3 #include "DerivedRectangleFromAbstractGeometricObject.h"
4 #include <iostream>
5 using namespace std;
6
7 // A function for displaying a geometric object
8 void displayGeometricObject(GeometricObject &g)
9 {
10   cout << "The area is " << g.getArea() << endl;
11   cout << "The perimeter is " << g.getPerimeter() << endl;
12
13   GeometricObject *p = &g;
14   Circle *p1 = dynamic_cast<Circle*>(p);
15   Rectangle *p2 = dynamic_cast<Rectangle*>(p);
16
17   if (p1 != NULL)
18   {
19     cout << "The radius is " << p1->getRadius() << endl;
20     cout << "The diameter is " << p1->getDiameter() << endl;
21   }
22
23   if (p2 != NULL)
24   {
25     cout << "The width is " << p2->getWidth() << endl;
26     cout << "The height is " << p2->getHeight() << endl;
27   }
28 }
29
30 int main()
31 {
32   Circle circle(5);
33   Rectangle rectangle(5, 3);
34
```

casting to **Circle**
casting to **Rectangle**

```
35    cout << "Circle info: " << endl;
36    displayGeometricObject(circle);
37
38    cout << "\nRectangle info: " << endl;
39    displayGeometricObject(rectangle);
40
41    return 0;
42 }
```

```
Circle info:
The area is 78.5397
The perimeter is 31.4159
The radius is 5
The diameter is 10

Rectangle info:
The area is 15
The perimeter is 16
The width is 5
The height is 3
```

Line 13 creates a pointer for a `GeometricObject g`. The **dynamic_cast** operator (line 14) checks whether pointer **p** points to a `Circle` object. If so, the object's address is assigned to **p1**; otherwise **p1** is NULL. If **p1** is not NULL, the **getRadius()** and **getDiameter()** functions of the `Circle` object (pointed by **p1**) are invoked in lines 19–20. Similarly, if the object is a rectangle, its width and height are displayed in lines 25–26.

The program invokes the **displayGeometricObject** function to display a `Circle` object in line 36 and a `Rectangle` object in line 39. The function casts the parameter **g** into a `Circle` pointer **p1** in line 14 and a `Rectangle` pointer **p2** in line 15. If it is a `Circle` object, the object's **getRadius()** and **getDiameter()** functions are invoked in lines 19–20. If it is a `Rectangle` object, the object's **getWidth()** and **getHeight()** functions are invoked in lines 25–26.

The function also invokes `GeometricObject`'s **getArea()** and **getPerimeter()** functions in lines 10–11. Since these two functions are defined in the `GeometricObject` class, there is no need to downcast the object parameter to `Circle` or `Rectangle` in order to invoke them.

Tip

Occasionally, it is useful to obtain information about the class of the object. You can use the **typeid** operator to return a reference to an object of class **type_info**. For example, you can use the following statement to display the class name for object **x**:

typeid operator

```
string x;
cout << typeid(x).name() << endl;
```

It displays string, because **x** is an object of the **string** class. To use the **typeid** operator, the program must include the **<typeinfo>** header file.

Tip

It is good practice to always define destructors virtual. Suppose class **Child** is derived from class **Parent** and destructors are not virtual. Consider the following code:

define destructor virtual

```
Parent *p = new Child;
...
delete p;
```

When **delete** is invoked with **p**, **Parent**'s destructor is called, since **p** is declared a pointer for **Parent**. **p** actually points to an object of **Child**, but **Child**'s destructor is never called. To fix the problem, define the destructor virtual in class **Parent**. Now, when **delete** is invoked with **p**, **Child**'s destructor is called and then **Parent**'s destructor is called, since constructors are virtual.

KEY TERMS

abstract class 499	inheritance 482
abstract function 499	*is-a* relationship 489
base class 482	override function 496
constructor chaining 491	polymorphism 495
derived class 482	protected 498
destructor chaining 491	pure virtual function 500
downcasting 504	redefine function 494
dynamic binding 496	upcasting 504
generic programming 490	virtual function 496

CHAPTER SUMMARY

1. You can derive a new class from an existing class. This is known as *class inheritance*. The new class is called a *derived class*, *child class*, or *extended class*. The existing class is called a *base class* or *parent class*.

2. An object of a derived class can be passed wherever an object of a base type parameter is required. Then a function can be used generically for a wide range of object arguments. This is known as *generic programming*.

3. A constructor is used to construct an instance of a class. Unlike data fields and functions, the constructors of a base class are not inherited in the derived class. They can only be invoked from the constructors of the derived classes to initialize the data fields in the base class.

4. A child class constructor always invokes its base class constructor. If a base constructor is not invoked explicitly, the base class no-arg constructor is invoked by default.

5. Constructing an instance of a class invokes the constructors of all the base classes along the inheritance chain.

6. A base class constructor is called from a derived class constructor. Conversely, the destructors are automatically invoked in reverse order, with the derived class's destructor invoked first. This is called *constructor and destructor chaining*.

7. A function defined in the base class may be redefined in the derived class. A redefined function must match the signature and return type of the function in the base class.

8. A virtual function enables dynamic binding. A virtual function is often redefined in the derived classes. The compiler decides which function implementation to use dynamically at runtime.

9. If a function defined in a base class needs to be redefined in its derived classes, you should define it virtual to avoid confusions and mistakes. On the other hand, if a function

will not be redefined, it is more efficient not to declare it virtual, because more time and system resource are required to bind virtual functions dynamically at runtime.

10. A protected data field or a protected function in a base class can be accessed in its derived classes.

11. A pure virtual function is also called an abstract function.

12. If a class contains a pure virtual function, the class is called an abstract class.

13. You cannot create instances from an abstract class, but abstract classes can be used as data types for parameters in a function to enable generic programming.

14. You can use the `dynamic_cast` operator to cast an object of a base class type to a pointer of a derived class type in order to invoke the functions defined in the derived classes.

REVIEW QUESTIONS

Sections 15.2–15.5

15.1 What is the printout of running the program in (a)? What problem arises in compiling the program in (b)?

```cpp
#include <iostream>
using namespace std;

class Parent
{
public:
  Parent()
  {
    cout <<
      "Parent's no-arg constructor is invoked";
  }
};

class Child: public Parent
{
};

int main()
{
  Child c;

  return 0;
}
```
(a)

```cpp
#include <iostream>
using namespace std;

class Parent
{
public:
  Parent(int x)
  {
  }
};

class Child: public Parent
{
};

int main()
{
  Child c;

  return 0;
}
```
(b)

15.2 True or false? (1) A derived class is a subset of a base class. (2) When invoking a constructor from a derived class, its base class's no-arg constructor is always invoked. (3) You can *override* a private function defined in a base class. (4) You can override a static function defined in a base class. (5) You can override a constructor.

15.3 Identify the problems in the following classes.

```cpp
1 class Circle
2 {
3 public:
4   Circle(double radius)
```

```
5   {
6      radius = radius;
7   }
8
9      double getRadius()
10  {
11     return radius;
12  }
13
14     double getArea()
15  {
16     return radius * radius * 3.14159;
17  }
18
19 private:
20    double radius;
21 };
22
23 class B : Circle
24 {
25 public:
26   B(double radius, double length): Circle(radius)
27   {
28      length = length;
29   }
30
31   // Returns Circle's getArea * length
32   double getArea()
33   {
34      return getArea() * length;
35   }
36
37 private:
38    double length;
39 };
```

15.4 Explain the difference between function overloading and function overriding.

15.5 Show the output of the following code:

```cpp
#include <iostream>
using namespace std;

class Parent
{
public:
  Parent()
  {
    cout << "Parent's no-arg constructor is invoked" << endl;
  }

  ~Parent()
  {
    cout << "Parent's destructor is invoked" << endl;
  }
};

class Child: public Parent
{
public:
  Child()
```

```
  {
    cout << "Child's no-arg constructor is invoked" << endl;
  }

  ~Child()
  {
    cout << "Child's destructor is invoked" << endl;
  }
};

int main()
{
  Child c1;
  Child c2;

  return 0;
}
```

15.6 If a base class has a customized copy constructor and assignment operator, how should you define the copy constructor and the assignment operator in the derived class?

15.7 If a base class has a customized destructor, are you required to implement the destructor in the derived class?

Section 15.6

15.8 Show the output of the following code:

```
#include <iostream>
using namespace std;

class Parent
{
public:
  void f()
  {
    cout << "invoke f from Parent" << endl;
  }
};

class Child: public Parent
{
public:
  void f()
  {
    cout << "invoke f from Child" << endl;
  }
};

void p(Parent a)
{
  a.f();
}

int main()
{
  Parent a;
  a.f();
  p(a);
```

```
            Child b;
            b.f();
            p(b);

            return 0;
        }
```

15.9   Show the output of the following code:

```
#include <iostream>
using namespace std;

class Parent
{
public:
  virtual void f()
    {
      cout << "invoke f from Parent" << endl;
    }
};

class Child: public Parent
{
public:
  void f()
    {
      cout << "invoke f from Child" << endl;
    }
};

void p(Parent a)
{
  a.f();
}

int main()
{
  Parent a;
  a.f();
  p(a);

  Child b;
  b.f();
  p(b);

  return 0;
}
```

If you replace void p(Parent a) by void p(Parent &a), what will be the output?

15.10 Is declaring virtual functions enough to enable dynamic binding?

15.11 Is it a good practice to define all functions virtual?

Sections 15.7

15.12 If a member is declared private in a class, can it be accessed from other classes? If a member is declared protected in a class, can it be accessed from other classes? If a member is declared public in a class, can it be accessed from other classes?

Section 15.8

15.13 How do you define a pure virtual function?

15.14 What is wrong in the following code?

```
class A
{
public:
  virtual void f() = 0;
};

int main()
{
  A a;

  return 0;
}
```

15.15 Can you compile and run the following code? What will be the output?

```
#include <iostream>
using namespace std;

class A
{
public:
  virtual void f() = 0;
};

class B: public A
{
public:
  void f()
  {
    cout << "invoke f from B" << endl;
  }
};

class C: public B
{
public:
  virtual void m() = 0;
};

class D: public C
{
public:
  virtual void m()
  {
    cout << "invoke m from D" << endl;
  }
};

void p(A &a)
{
  a.f();
}

int main()
```

```
  {
    D d;
    p(d);
    d.m();

    return 0;
  }
```

15.16 The `getArea` and `getPerimeter` functions may be removed from the `Geo-metricObject` class. What are the benefits of defining `getArea` and `get-Perimeter` as abstract functions in the `GeometricObject` class?

15.17 What is upcasting? What is downcasting?

15.18 When do you need to downcast an object from a base class type to a derived class type?

15.19 What will be the value in `p1` after the following statements?

```
GeometricObject *p = new Rectangle(2, 3);
Circle *p1 = new Circle(2);
p1 = dynamic_cast<Circle*>(p);
```

15.20 Analyze the following code:

```cpp
#include <iostream>
using namespace std;

class Parent
{
};

class Child: public Parent
{
public:
  void m()
  {
    cout << "invoke m" << endl;
  }
};

int main()
{
  Parent *p = new Child();

  // To be replaced;

  return 0;
}
```

(a) What compile errors will you get if the highlighted line is replaced by the following code?

```
(*p).m();
```

(b) What compile errors will you get if the highlighted line is replaced by the following code?

```
Child *p1 = dynamic_cast<Child*>(p);
(*p1).m();
```

(c) Will the program compile and run if the highlighted line is replaced by the following code?

```
Child *p1 = static_cast<Child*>(p);
(*p1).m();
```

15.21 Why should you define a destructor virtual?

PROGRAMMING EXERCISES

15.1 (*The Triangle class*) Design a class named `Triangle` that extends `GeometricObject`. The class contains:

- Three `double` data fields named `side1`, `side2`, and `side3` to denote three sides of the triangle.
- A no-arg constructor that creates a default triangle with each side `1.0`.
- A constructor that creates a rectangle with the specified `side1`, `side2`, and `side3`.
- The accessor functions for all three data fields.
- A function named `getArea()` that returns the area of this triangle.
- A function named `getPerimeter()` that returns the perimeter of this triangle.

Draw the UML diagram that involves the classes `Triangle` and `GeometricObject`. Implement the class. Write a test program that creates a `Triangle` object with sides 1, 1.5, 1, setting color `yellow` and filled `true`, and displaying the area, perimeter, color, and whether filled or not.

15.2 (*The Person, Student, Employee, Faculty, and Staff classes*) Design a class named `Person` and its two derived classes named `Student` and `Employee`. Make `Faculty` and `Staff` derived classes of `Employee`. A person has a name, address, phone number, and e-mail address. A student has a class status (freshman, sophomore, junior, or senior). An employee has an office, salary, and date-hired. Define a class named `MyDate` that contains the fields `year`, `month`, and `day`. A faculty member has office hours and a rank. A staff member has a title. Override the `toString` function in each class to display the class name and the person's name.

Draw the UML diagram for the classes. Implement the classes. Write a test program that creates a `Person`, `Student`, `Employee`, `Faculty`, and `Staff`, and invokes their `toString()` functions.

15.3 (*Extending MyPoint*) In Exercise 9.4, the `MyPoint` class was created to model a point in a two-dimensional space. The `MyPoint` class has the properties `x` and `y` that represent `x`- and `y`-coordinates, two `get` functions for `x` and `y`, and the function for returning the distance between two points. Create a class named `ThreeDPoint` to model a point in a three-dimensional space. Let `ThreeDPoint` be derived from `MyPoint` with the following additional features:

Video Note
the MyPoint class

- A data field named `z` that represents the `z`-coordinate.
- A no-arg constructor that constructs a point with coordinates (0, 0, 0).
- A constructor that constructs a point with three specified coordinates.
- A `get` function that returns the `z` value.
- Override of the `distance` function to return the distance between two points in the three-dimensional space.

Draw the UML diagram for the classes involved. Implement the classes. Write a test program that creates two points (0, 0, 0) and (10, 30, 25.5) and displays the distance between them.

15.4   (*Derived classes of Account*) In Exercise 9.3, the `Account` class was created to model a bank account. An account has the properties account number, balance, and annual interest rate, date created, and functions to deposit and withdraw. Create two derived classes for checking and saving accounts. A checking account has an overdraft limit, but a savings account cannot be overdrawn. Override the `toString` function in the derived classes.

Draw the UML diagram for the classes. Implement the classes. Write a test program that creates objects of `Account`, `SavingsAccount`, and `CheckingAccount` and invokes their `toString()` functions.

15.5   (*Implementing a stack class using inheritance*) In Listing 12.4, `GenericStack` is implemented using arrays. Create a new stack class that extends `vector`. Draw the UML diagram for the classes. Implement it.

CHAPTER 16

EXCEPTION HANDLING

Objectives

- To get an overview of exceptions and exception handling (§16.2).
- To know how to throw an exception and how to catch it (§16.2).
- To explore the advantages of using exception handling (§16.3).
- To create exceptions using C++ standard exception classes (§16.4).
- To define custom exception classes (§16.5).
- To catch multiple exceptions (§16.6).
- To explain how an exception is propagated (§16.7).
- To rethrow exceptions in a catch block (§16.8).
- To define functions with an exception throw list (§16.9).
- To use exception handling appropriately (§16.10).

16.1 Introduction

An *exception* indicates an unusual situation that may occur during a program's execution. For example, suppose your program uses a vector v to store elements. The program accesses an element in the vector using v[i], assuming that the element at the index i exists. The exceptional situation occurs when the element at the index i does not exist. You should write the code in the program to deal with this exceptional case. This chapter introduces the concept of exception handling in C++. You will learn how to throw, catch, and process an exception.

16.2 Exception-Handling Overview

To demonstrate exception handling, let us begin with an example that reads in two integers and displays their quotient, as shown in Listing 16.1.

LISTING 16.1 Quotient.cpp

```
 1 #include <iostream>
 2 using namespace std;
 3
 4 int main()
 5 {
 6   // Read two integers
 7   cout << "Enter two integers: ";
 8   int number1, number2;
 9   cin >> number1 >> number2;
10
11   cout << number1 << " / " << number2 << " is "
12     << (number1 / number2) << endl;
13
14   return 0;
15 }
```

reads two integers

integer division

```
Enter two integers: 5 2 ↵Enter
5 / 2 is 2
```

If you enter 0 for the second number, a runtime error occurs, because you cannot divide an integer by 0. (*Recall that a floating-point number divided by 0 does not raise an exception.*) A simple way to fix the error is to add an if statement to test the second number, as shown in Listing 16.2.

LISTING 16.2 QuotientWithIf.cpp

```
 1 #include <iostream>
 2 using namespace std;
 3
 4 int main()
 5 {
 6   // Read two integers
 7   cout << "Enter two integers: ";
 8   int number1, number2;
 9   cin >> number1 >> number2;
10
11   if (number2 != 0)
12   {
13     cout << number1 << " / " << number2 << " is "
14       << (number1 / number2) << endl;
15   }
```

reads two integers

test number2

```
16    else
17    {
18      cout << "Divisor cannot be zero" << endl;
19    }
20
21    return 0;
22 }
```

```
Enter two integers: 5 0 ↵Enter
Divisor cannot be zero
```

Listing 16.2 can be rewritten using exception handling, as shown in Listing 16.3. Listing 16.2 is simpler, so in this case you should not use exception handling. The purpose of Listing 16.3 is simply to demonstrate the concept of exception handling. Later you will see the advantages of using exception handling.

LISTING 16.3 QuotientWithException.cpp

```
1 #include <iostream>
2 using namespace std;
3
4 int main()
5 {
6   // Read two integers
7   cout << "Enter two integers: ";
8   int number1, number2;
9   cin >> number1 >> number2;                              reads two integers
10
11   try                                                     try block
12   {
13     if (number2 == 0)
14       throw number1;
15
16     cout << number1 << " / " << number2 << " is "
17       << (number1 / number2) << endl;
18   }
19   catch (int e)                                           catch block
20   {
21     cout << "Exception: an integer " << e <<
22       " cannot be divided by zero" << endl;
23   }
24
25   cout << "Execution continues ..." << endl;
26
27   return 0;
28 }
```

```
Enter two integers: 5 3 ↵Enter
5 / 3 is 1
Execution continues ...
```

```
Enter two integers: 5 0 ↵Enter
Exception: an integer 5 cannot be divided by zero
Execution continues ...
```

The program contains a `try` block and a `catch` block. The `try` block (lines 11–18) contains the code that is executed in normal circumstances. The `catch` block contains the code that is executed when `number2` is zero. When `number2` is zero, the program throws an exception by executing

throw statement

```
throw number1;
```

exception
throwing exception

The value thrown, in this case `number1`, is called an *exception*. The execution of a throw statement is called *throwing an exception*. You can throw a value of any type. In this case, the value is of the `int` type.

handle exception

When an exception is thrown, the normal execution flow is interrupted. As the name suggests, to "throw an exception" is to pass the exception from one place to another. The exception is caught by the `catch` block. The code in the `catch` block is executed to *handle the exception*. Afterward, the statement (line 25) after the `catch` block is executed.

The `throw` statement is analogous to a function call, but instead of calling a function, it calls a `catch` block. In this sense, a `catch` block is like a function definition with a parameter that matches the type of the value being thrown. However, after the `catch` block has been executed, the program control does not return to the `throw` statement; instead, it executes the next statement after the `catch` block.

The identifier `e` in the `catch` block header

```
catch (int e)
```

catch block parameter

acts very much like a parameter in a function. So, it is referred to as a `catch` block parameter. The type (e.g., `int`) preceding `e` specifies the kind of exception the `catch` block can catch. Once the exception is caught, you can access the thrown value from this parameter in the body of a catch block.

In summary, a template for a `try-throw-catch` block may look like this:

```
try
{
  Code to try;
  Throw an exception with a throw statement or
    from function if necessary;
  More code to try;
}
catch (type e)
{
  Code to process the exception;
}
```

An exception may be thrown directly using a `throw` statement in a `try` block, or a function may be invoked that throws an exception.

omit catch block parameter

 Note

If you are not interested in the contents of an exception object, the `catch` block parameter may be omitted. For example, the following `catch` block is legal.

```
try
{
  // ...
}
catch (int)
{
  cout << "Error occurred " << endl;
}
```

16.3 Exception-Handling Advantages

Video Note
exception handling advantage

Listing 16.3 gives a simple example to demonstrate exception handling. It does not show any real advantages. Now, to demonstrate the advantages of using exception handling, we look at an example of throwing an exception in a function.

Listing 16.4 rewrites Listing 16.3 to compute a quotient using a function.

LISTING 16.4 QuotientWithFunction.cpp

```cpp
 1 #include <iostream>
 2 using namespace std;
 3
 4 int quotient(int number1, int number2)          quotient function
 5 {
 6   if (number2 == 0)
 7     throw number1;                               throw exception
 8
 9   return number1 / number2;
10 }
11
12 int main()
13 {
14   // Read two integers
15   cout << "Enter two integers: ";
16   int number1, number2;
17   cin >> number1 >> number2;                     reads two integers
18
19   try                                            try block
20   {
21     int result = quotient(number1, number2);     invoke function
22     cout << number1 << " / " << number2 << " is "
23       << result << endl;
24   }
25   catch (int e)                                  catch block
26   {
27     cout << "Exception from function: an integer " << e <<
28       " cannot be divided by zero" << endl;
29   }
30
31   cout << "Execution continues ..." << endl;
32
33   return 0;
34 }
```

```
Enter two integers: 5 3 ⏎Enter
5 / 3 is 1
Execution continues ...
```

```
Enter two integers: 5 0 ⏎Enter
Exception from function: an integer 5 cannot be divided by zero
Execution continues ...
```

Function **quotient** (lines 4–10) returns the quotient of two integers. If **number2** is **0**, it cannot return a value. So, an exception is thrown in line 7.

The main function invokes the **quotient** function (line 21). If the quotient function executes normally, it returns a value to the caller. If the **quotient** function encounters an exception, it throws the exception back to its caller. The caller's **catch** block handles the exception.

advantage

Now you see the *advantages* of using exception handling. It enables a function to throw an exception to its caller. Without this capability, a function must handle the exception or terminate the program.

Video Note
C++ exception classes

16.4 Exception Classes

The **catch** block parameter in the preceding examples is the **int** type. A class type is often more useful, because an object can contain more information that you want to throw to a **catch** block. C++ provides a number of predefined classes that can be used for creating exception objects. These classes are shown in Figure 16.1.

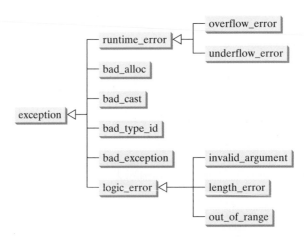

FIGURE 16.1 You can use standard library classes to create exception objects.

exception
what()
runtime_error

The root class in this hierarchy is **exception** (defined in header **<exception>**). It contains the virtual function **what()** that returns an exception object's error message.

The **runtime_error** class (defined in header **<stdexcept>**) is a base class for several *standard exception* classes that describes runtime errors. Class **overflow_error** describes an arithmetic overflow—i.e., a value is too large to be stored. Class **underflow_error** describes an arithmetic underflow—i.e., a value is too small to be stored.

logic_error

The **logic_error** class (defined in header **<stdexcept>**) is a base class for several standard exception classes that describes logic errors. Class **invalid_argument** indicates that an invalid argument has been passed to a function. Class **length_error** indicates that an object's length has exceeded the maximum allowed length. Class **out_of_range** indicates that a value has exceeded its allowed range.

bad_alloc
bad_cast
bad_typeid
bad_exception

Classes **bad_alloc**, **bad_cast**, **bad_type_id**, and **bad_exception** describe the exceptions thrown by C++ operators. For example, a **bad_alloc** exception is thrown by the **new** operator if the memory cannot be allocated. A **bad_cast** exception is thrown by the **dynamic_cast** operator as the result of a failed cast to a reference type. A **bad_typeid** exception is thrown by the **typeid** operator when the operand for **typeid** is a **NULL** pointer. The **bad_exception** class describes an exception that can be thrown from an unexpected handler. C++ requires that **unexpected** is called when a function throws an exception that is not on its *throw list*.

These classes are used by some functions in the C++ standard library to *throw exceptions*. You also can use these classes to throw exceptions in your programs. Listing 16.5 rewrite Listing 16.4, QuotientWithFunction.cpp, by throwing a `runtime_error`.

LISTING 16.5 QuotientThrowRuntimeError.cpp

```
 1 #include <iostream>
 2 using namespace std;
 3
 4 int quotient(int number1, int number2)                    quotient function
 5 {
 6   if (number2 == 0)
 7     throw runtime_error("Divisor cannot be zero");         throw exception
 8
 9   return number1 / number2;
10 }
11
12 int main()
13 {
14   // Read two integers
15   cout << "Enter two integers: ";
16   int number1, number2;
17   cin >> number1 >> number2;                               reads two integers
18
19   try                                                      try block
20   {
21     int result = quotient(number1, number2);               invoke function
22     cout << number1 << " / " << number2 << " is "
23       << result << endl;
24   }
25   catch (runtime_error &e)                                 catch block
26   {
27     cout << e.what() << endl;
28   }
29
30   cout << "Execution continues ..." << endl;
31
32   return 0;
33 }
```

```
Enter two integers: 5 3  ↵Enter
5 / 3 is 1
Execution continues ...
```

```
Enter two integers: 5 0  ↵Enter
Divisor cannot be zero
Execution continues ...
```

The `quotient` function in Listing 16.4 throws an `int` value, but the function in this program throws a `runtime_error` object (line 7). You can create a `runtime_error` object by passing a string that describes the exception.

The catch block catches a `runtime_error` exception and invokes the `what` function to return a string description of the exception (line 27).

Listing 16.6 shows an example of handling the bad_alloc exception.

LISTING 16.6 ExceptionDemo1.cpp

```cpp
1 #include <iostream>
2 using namespace std;
3
4 int main()
5 {
6   try
7   {
8     for (int i = 1; i <= 100; i++)
9     {
10      new int[70000000];
11      cout << i << " arrays have been created" << endl;
12    }
13  }
14  catch (bad_alloc &e)
15  {
16    cout << "Exception: " << e.what() << endl;
17  }
18
19  return 0;
20 }
```

try block

create a large array

catch block

invoke e.what()

```
1 arrays have been created
2 arrays have been created
3 arrays have been created
4 arrays have been created
5 arrays have been created
6 arrays have been created
Exception: bad alloc exception thrown
```

The output shows that the program creates six arrays before it fails on the seventh new operator. When it fails, a bad_alloc exception is thrown and caught in the catch block, which displays the message returned from e.what().

Listing 16.7 shows an example of handling the bad_cast exception.

LISTING 16.7 ExceptionDemo2.cpp

include typeinfo
see Listing 15.15
see Listing 15.17

```cpp
1 #include <typeinfo>
2 #include "DerivedCircleFromAbstractGeometricObject.h"
3 #include "DerivedRectangleFromAbstractGeometricObject.h"
4 #include <iostream>
5 using namespace std;
6
7 int main()
8 {
9   try
10  {
11    Rectangle r(3, 4);
12    Circle & c = dynamic_cast<Circle&>(r);
13  }
14  catch (bad_cast &e)
```

try block

cast

catch block

```
15  {
16    cout << "Exception: " << e.what() << endl;
17  }
18
19  return 0;
20 }
```

invoke **e.what()**

```
Exception: Bad Dynamic_cast!
```

Dynamic casting was introduced in §15.9. In line 12, a reference of a `Rectangle` object is cast to a `Circle` reference type, which is illegal, and a `bad_cast` exception is thrown. The exception is caught in the `catch` block in line 16.

Listing 16.8 shows an example of throwing and handling an `invalid_argument` exception.

LISTING 16.8 ExceptionDemo3.cpp

```
1 #include <iostream>
2 #include <stdexcept>
3 using namespace std;
4
5 double getArea(double radius)
6 {
7   if (radius < 0)
8     throw invalid_argument("Radius cannot be negative");
9
10    return radius * radius * 3.14159;
11 }
12
13 int main()
14 {
15   // Prompt the user to enter radius
16   cout << "Enter radius: ";
17   double radius;
18   cin >> radius;
19
20   try
21   {
22     double result = getArea(radius);
23     cout << "The area is " << result << endl;
24   }
25   catch (exception &e)
26   {
27     cout << e.what() << endl;
28   }
29
30   cout << "Execution continues ..." << endl;
31
32   return 0;
33 }
```

getArea function

throw exception

reads radius

try block

invoke function

catch block

```
Enter radius: 5 ⏎Enter
The area is 78.5397
Execution continues ...
```

```
Enter radius: -5  ↵Enter
Radius cannot be negative
Execution continues ...
```

In the sample output, the program prompts the user to enter radius, `5` and `-5`. Invoking `getArea(-5)` (line 22) causes a `invalid_error` exception to be thrown (line 8). This exception is caught in the `catch` block in line 25. Note that the catch-block parameter type `exception` is a base class for `invalid_argument`. So, it can catch an `invalid_argument`.

16.5 Custom Exception Classes

Video Note
creating custom exception classes

C++ provides the exception classes listed in Figure 16.1. Use them whenever possible instead of creating your own exception classes. However, if you run into a problem that cannot be adequately described by the predefined exception classes, you can create your own exception class. This class is just like any C++ class, but often it is desirable to derive it from `exception` or a derived class of `exception` so you can utilize the common features (e.g., the `what()` function) in the `exception` class.

Let us consider the `Triangle` class for modeling triangles. The class UML diagram is shown in Figure 16.2. The class is derived from the `GeometricObject` class, which is an abstract class introduced in §15.8.

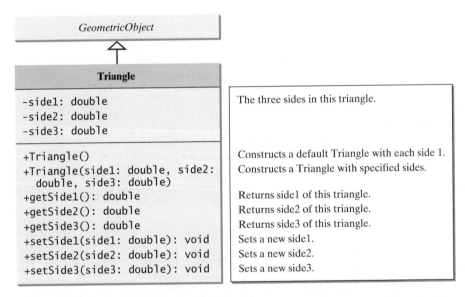

FIGURE 16.2 The `Triangle` class models triangles.

A triangle is valid if the sum of any two sides is greater than the third side. When you attempt to create a triangle, or change a side of a triangle, you need to ensure that this property is not violated. Otherwise, an exception should be thrown. You can define the `TriangleException` class as in Listing 16.9 to model this exception.

LISTING 16.9 TriangleException.h

```
 1 #include <stdexcept>                                          include stdexcept
 2 using namespace std;
 3
 4 class TriangleException: public logic_error               extend logic_error
 5 {
 6 public:
 7   TriangleException(double side1, double side2, double side3)
 8     : logic_error("Invalid triangle")                   invoke base constructor
 9   {
10     this->side1 = side1;
11     this->side2 = side2;
12     this->side3 = side3;
13   }
14
15   double getSide1() const
16   {
17     return side1;
18   }
19
20   double getSide2() const
21   {
22     return side2;
23   }
24
25   double getSide3() const
26   {
27     return side3;
28   }
29
30 private:
31   double side1, side2, side3;
32 }; // Semicolon required
```

The `TriangleException` class describes a logic error, so it is appropriate to define this class to extend the standard `logic_error` class in line 4. Since `logic_error` is in the `<stdexcept>` header file, this header is included in line 1.

Recall that if a base constructor is not invoked explicitly, the base class's no-arg constructor is invoked by default. However, since the base class `logic_error` does not have a no-arg constructor, you must invoke a base class's constructor to avoid compile errors in line 8. Invoking `logic_error("Invalid triangle")` sets an error message, which can be returned from invoking `what()` on an `exception` object.

Note

A custom exception class is just like a regular class. Extending from a base class is not necessary, but it is a good practice to extend from the standard `exception` or a derived class of `exception` so your custom exception class can use the functions from the standard classes.

Note

The header file TriangleException.h contains the implementation for the class. Recall that this is the inline implementation. For short functions, using inline implementation is efficient.

The `Triangle` class can be implemented as follows.

LISTING 16.10 Triangle.h

<table>
<tr><td>header for
  GeometricObject</td><td>

```cpp
1 #include "AbstractGeometricObject.h" // Defined in Listing 15.13
2 #include "TriangleException.h"
3 #include <cmath>
```
</td></tr>
</table>

header for **TriangleException**	
header for **cmath**	
extend **GeometricObject**	
no-arg constructor	
constructor	
throw **TriangleException**	
throw **TriangleException**	
throw **TriangleException**	

```cpp
 4
 5 class Triangle: public GeometricObject
 6 {
 7 public:
 8   Triangle()
 9   {
10     side1 = side2 = side3 = 1;
11   }
12
13   Triangle(double side1, double side2, double side3)
14   {
15     if (!isValid(side1, side2, side3))
16       throw TriangleException(side1, side2, side3);
17
18     this->side1 = side1;
19     this->side2 = side2;
20     this->side3 = side3;
21   }
22
23   double getSide1() const
24   {
25     return side1;
26   }
27
28   double getSide2() const
29   {
30     return side2;
31   }
32
33   double getSide3() const
34   {
35     return side3;
36   }
37
38   void setSide1(double side1)
39   {
40     if (!isValid(side1, side2, side3))
41       throw TriangleException(side1, side2, side3);
42
43     this->side1 = side1;
44   }
45
46   void setSide2(double side2)
47   {
48     if (!isValid(side1, side2, side3))
49       throw TriangleException(side1, side2, side3);
50
51     this->side2 = side2;
52   }
53
54   void setSide3(double side3)
55   {
56     if (!isValid(side1, side2, side3))
```

```
57          throw TriangleException(side1, side2, side3);
58
59      this->side3 = side3;
60    }
61
62    double getPerimeter() const
63    {
64      return side1 + side2 + side3;
65    }
66
67    double getArea() const
68    {
69      double s = getPerimeter() / 2;
70      return sqrt(s * (s - side1) * (s - side2) * (s - side3));
71    }
72
73 private:
74    double side1, side2, side3;
75
76    bool isValid(double side1, double side2, double side3) const
77    {
78      return (side1 < side2 + side3) && (side2 < side1 + side3) &&
79
80        (side3 < side1 + side2);
81    }
82 };
```

throw **TriangleException**

override **getPerimeter()**

override **getArea()**

check sides

The `Triangle` class extends `GeometricObject` (line 5) and overrides the pure virtual functions `getPerimeter` and `getArea` defined in the `GeometricObject` class (lines 62–71).

The `isValid` function (lines 76–81) checks whether a triangle is valid. This function is defined private for use inside the `Triangle` class.

When constructing a `Triangle` object with three specified sides, the constructor invokes the `isValid` function (line 15) to check validity. If not valid, a `TriangleException` object is created and thrown in line 16. Validity also is checked when the functions `setSide1`, `setSide2`, and `setSide3` are invoked. When invoking `setSide1(side1)`, `isValid(side1, side2, side3)` is invoked. Here `side1` is the new `side1` to be set, not the current `side1` in the object.

Listing 16.11 gives a test program that creates a `Triangle` object using its no-arg constructor (line 9), displays its perimeter and area (lines 10–11), and changes its `side3` to 4 (line 13), which causes a `TriangleException` to be thrown. The exception is caught in the `catch` block (lines 17–22).

LISTING 16.11 TestTriangle.cpp

```
1 #include <iostream>
2 #include "Triangle.h"
3 using namespace std;
4
5 int main()
6 {
7   try
8   {
9     Triangle triangle;
10    cout << "Perimeter is " << triangle.getPerimeter() << endl;
11    cout << "Area is " << triangle.getArea() << endl;
12
13    triangle.setSide3(4);
```

Triangle header

create object

set new side

```
14       cout << "Perimeter is " << triangle.getPerimeter() << endl;
15       cout << "Area is " << triangle.getArea() << endl;
16     }
17     catch (TriangleException &ex)
18     {
19       cout << ex.what();
20       cout << " three sides are " << ex.getSide1() << " "
21         << ex.getSide2() << " " << ex.getSide3() << endl;
22     }
23
24     return 0;
25 }
```

catch block

invoke **ex.what()**
invoke **ex.getSide1()**

```
Perimeter is 3
Area is 0.433013
Invalid triangle three sides are 1 1 4
```

The `what()` function is defined in the `exception` class. Since `TriangleException` is derived from `logic_error`, which is derived from `exception`, you can invoke `what()` (line 19) to display an error message on a `TriangleException` object. The Triangle-Exception object contains the information pertinent to a triangle. This information is useful for handling the exception.

16.6 Multiple Catches

Usually a `try` block should run without exceptions. Occasionally, though, it may throw an exception of one type or another. For example, a nonpositive value for a side in a triangle in Listing 16.11 may be considered a type of exception different from a `TriangleException`. So, the `try` block may throw a nonpositive-side exception or a `TriangleException`, depending on the occasion. One `catch` block can catch only one type of exception. C++ allows you to add multiple `catch` blocks after a `try` block in order to catch multiple types of exceptions.

Let us revise the example in the preceding section by creating a new exception class named `NonPositiveSideException` and incorporating it in the `Triangle` class. The `NonPositiveSideException` class is shown in Listing 16.12 and the new `Triangle` class in Listing 16.13.

LISTING 16.12 NonPositiveSideException.h

include **stdexcept**

extend **logic_error**

invoke base constructor

```
1 #include <stdexcept>
2 using namespace std;
3
4 class NonPositiveSideException : public logic_error
5 {
6 public:
7   NonPositiveSideException(double side)
8     : logic_error("Nonpositive side")
9   {
10    this->side = side;
11  }
12
13  double getSide() const
14  {
15    return side;
16  }
17
```

```
18 private:
19   double side;
20 };
```

The NonPositiveSideException class describes a logic error, so it is appropriate to define this class to extend the standard **logic_error** class in line 4.

LISTING 16.13 NewTriangle.h

```
 1 #include "AbstractGeometricObject.h"
 2 #include "TriangleException.h"
 3 #include "NonPositiveSideException.h"
 4 #include <cmath>
 5
 6 class Triangle: public GeometricObject
 7 {
 8 public:
 9   Triangle()
10   {
11     side1 = side2 = side3 = 1;
12   }
13
14   Triangle(double side1, double side2, double side3)
15   {
16     check(side1);
17     check(side2);
18     check(side3);
19
20     if (!isValid(side1, side2, side3))
21       throw TriangleException(side1, side2, side3);
22
23     this->side1 = side1;
24     this->side2 = side2;
25     this->side3 = side3;
26   }
27
28   double getSide1() const
29   {
30     return side1;
31   }
32
33   double getSide2() const
34   {
35     return side2;
36   }
37
38   double getSide3() const
39   {
40     return side3;
41   }
42
43   void setSide1(double side1)
44   {
45     check(side1);
46     if (!isValid(side1, side2, side3))
47       throw TriangleException(side1, side2, side3);
48
49     this->side1 = side1;
50   }
51
```

header for **GeometricObject**
header for
  TriangleException
NonPositiveSideException
header for **cmath**
extend **GeometricObject**

no-arg constructor

constructor

check **side1**

throw **TriangleException**

check **side1**

check **side1**

```
52    void setSide2(double side2)
53    {
54      check(side2);
55      if (!isValid(side1, side2, side3))
56        throw TriangleException(side1, side2, side3);
57
58      this->side2 = side2;
59    }
60
61    void setSide3(double side3)
62    {
63      check(side3);
64      if (!isValid(side1, side2, side3))
65        throw TriangleException(side1, side2, side3);
66
67      this->side3 = side3;
68    }
69
70    double getPerimeter() const
71    {
72      return side1 + side2 + side3;
73    }
74
75    double getArea() const
76    {
77      double s = getPerimeter() / 2;
78      return sqrt(s * (s - side1) * (s - side2) * (s - side3));
79    }
80
81  private:
82    double side1, side2, side3;
83
84    bool isValid(double side1, double side2, double side3) const
85    {
86      return (side1 < side2 + side3) && (side2 < side1 + side3) &&
87        (side3 < side1 + side2);
88    }
89
90    void check(double side) const
91    {
92      if (side <= 0)
93        throw NonPositiveSideException(side);
94    }
95  };
```

throw **NonPositiveSide-Exception**

The new `Triangle` class is identical to the one in Listing 16.10, except that it also checks nonpositive sides. When a `Triangle` object is created, all of its sides are checked by invoking the `check` function (lines 16–18). The `check` function checks whether a side is nonpositive (line 92); it throws a `NonPositiveSideException` (line 93).

Listing 16.14 gives a test program that prompts the user to enter three sides (lines 9–11) and creates a `Triangle` object (line 12).

LISTING 16.14 MultipleCatchDemo.cpp

new **Triangle** class

```
1  #include <iostream>
2  #include "NewTriangle.h"
3  using namespace std;
4
```

```
 5 int main()
 6 {
 7   try
 8   {
 9     cout << "Enter three sides: ";
10     double side1, side2, side3;
11     cin >> side1 >> side2 >> side3;
12     Triangle triangle(side1, side2, side3);        create object
13     cout << "Perimeter is " << triangle.getPerimeter() << endl;
14     cout << "Area is " << triangle.getArea() << endl;
15   }
16   catch (NonPositiveSideException &ex)              catch block
17   {
18     cout << ex.what();
19     cout << " the side is " << ex.getSide() << endl;
20   }
21   catch (TriangleException &ex)                     catch block
22   {
23     cout << ex.what();
24     cout << " three sides are " << ex.getSide1() << " "
25       << ex.getSide2() << " " << ex.getSide3() << endl;
26   }
27
28   return 0;
29 }
```

```
Enter three sides: 2 2.5 2.5  ↵Enter  ←——— Normal execution
Perimeter is 7
Area is 2.29129

Enter three sides: -1 1 1  ↵Enter  ←——— Nonpositive side -1
Nonpositive side the side is -1

Enter three sides: 1 2 1  ↵Enter  ←——— Invalid triangle
Invalid triangle three sides are 1 2 1
```

As shown in the sample output, if you enter three sides 2, 2.5, and 2.5, it is a legal triangle. The program displays the perimeter and area of the triangle (lines 13–14). If you enter -1, 1, and 1, the constructor (line 12) throws a NonPositiveSideException. This exception is caught by the catch block in line 16 and processed in lines 18–19. If you enter 1, 2, and 1, the constructor (line 12) throws a TriangleException. This exception is caught by the catch block in line 21 and processed in lines 23–25.

Note

Various exception classes can be derived from a common base class. If a catch block catches exception objects of a base class, it can catch all the exception objects of the derived classes of that base class.

catch block

Note

The order in which exceptions are specified in catch blocks is important. A catch block for a base class type should appear after a catch block for a derived class type. Otherwise, the exception of a derived class is always caught by the catch block for the base class. For example, the ordering in (a) below is erroneous, because TriangleException is a derived class of logic_error. The correct ordering should be as shown in (b). In (a), a TriangleException occurred in the try block is caught by the catch block for logic_error.

order of exception handlers

```
try
{
    ...
}
catch (logic_error &ex)
{
    ...
}
catch (TriangleException &ex)
{
    ...
}
```

```
try
{
    ...
}
catch (TriangleException &ex)
{
    ...
}
catch (logic_error &ex)
{
    ...
}
```

(a) Wrong order   (b) Correct order

16.7 Exception Propagation

You now know how to declare an exception and how to throw an exception. When an exception is thrown, it can be caught and handled in a **try-catch** block, as follows:

```
try
{
    statements;   // Statements that may throw exceptions
}
catch (Exception1 &exVar1)
{
    handler for exception1;
}
catch (Exception2 &exVar2)
{
    handler for exception2;
}
...
catch (ExceptionN &exVar3)
{
    handler for exceptionN;
}
```

If no exceptions arise during the execution of the **try** block, the **catch** blocks are skipped.

If one of the statements inside the **try** block throws an exception, C++ skips the remaining statements in the **try** block and starts the process of finding the code to handle the exception. This code, called the *exception handler*, is found by propagating the exception backward through a chain of function calls, starting from the current function. Each **catch** block is examined in turn, from first to last, to see whether the type of the exception object is an instance of the exception class in the **catch** block. If so, the exception object is assigned to the variable declared, and the code in the **catch** block is executed. If no handler is found, C++ exits this function, passes the exception to the function that invoked the function, and continues the same process to find a handler. If no handler is found in the chain of functions being invoked, the program prints an error message on the console and terminates. The process of finding a handler is called *catching an exception*.

Suppose the **main** function invokes **function1**, **function1** invokes **function2**, **function2** invokes **function3**, and **function3** throws an exception, as shown in Figure 16.3. Consider the following scenario:

exception handler

catching exception

- If the exception type is **Exception3**, it is caught by the **catch** block for handling exception **ex3** in **function2**. **statement5** is skipped, and **statement6** is executed.

- If the exception type is `Exception2`, `function2` is aborted, the control is returned to `function1`, and the exception is caught by the `catch` block for handling exception `ex2` in `function1`. `statement3` is skipped, and `statement4` is executed.

- If the exception type is `Exception1`, `function1` is aborted, the control is returned to the `main` function, and the exception is caught by the `catch` block for handling exception `ex1` in the `main` function. `statement1` is skipped, and `statement2` is executed.

- If the exception is not caught in `function2`, `function1`, and `main`, the program terminates. `statement1` and `statement2` are not executed.

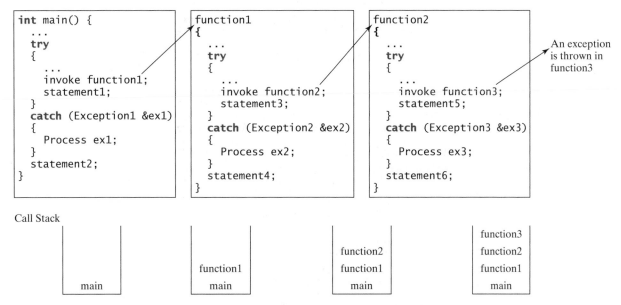

FIGURE 16.3 If an exception is not caught in the current function, it is passed to its caller. The process is repeated until the exception is caught or passed to the `main` function.

16.8 Rethrowing Exceptions

C++ allows an exception handler to rethrow the exception if it cannot process it or simply wants to let its caller be notified. The syntax may look like this:

```
try
{
  statements;
}
catch (TheException &ex)
{
  perform operations before exits;
  throw;
}
```

The statement **throw** rethrows the exception so that other handlers get a chance to process it.

Listing 16.15 gives an example that demonstrates how to *rethrow exceptions*.

LISTING 16.15 RethrowExceptionDemo.cpp

```cpp
1 #include <iostream>
2 #include <stdexcept>
3 using namespace std;
4
5 int f1()
6 {
7   try
8   {
9     throw runtime_error("Exception in f1");
10  }
11  catch (exception &ex)
12  {
13    cout << "Exception caught in function f1" << endl;
14    cout << ex.what() << endl;
15    throw; // Rethrow the exception
16  }
17 }
18
19 int main()
20 {
21   try
22   {
23     f1();
24   }
25   catch (exception &ex)
26   {
27     cout << "Exception caught in function main" << endl;
28     cout << ex.what() << endl;
29   }
30
31   return 0;
32 }
```

throw an exception

catch block

rethrow exception

invoke **f1**

catch block

```
Exception caught in function f1     ←——— Handler in function f1
Exception in f1

Exception caught in function main   ←——— Handler in function main
Exception in f1
```

The program invokes function **f1** in line 23, which throws an exception in line 9. This exception is caught in the **catch** block in line 11, and it is rethrown to the main function in line 15. The **catch** block in the main function catches the rethrown exception and processes it in lines 27–28.

16.9 Exception Specification

throw list

An *exception specification*, also known as *throw list*, lists exceptions that a function can throw. So far, you have seen the function defined without a throw list. In this case, the function can throw any exception. So, it is tempting to omit exception specification. However, this is not a good practice. A function should give warning of any exceptions it might throw, so that programmers can write a robust program to deal with these potential exceptions in a **try-catch** block.

The syntax for exception specification is as follows:

```
returnType functionName(parameterList) throw (exceptionList)
```

The exceptions are declared in the function header. For example, you should revise the `check` function and the `Triangle` constructor in Listing 16.13 to specify appropriate exceptions as follows:

```
 1 void check(double side) throw (NonPositiveSideException)
 2 {
 3   if (side <= 0)
 4     throw NonPositiveSideException(side);
 5 }
 6
 7 Triangle(double side1, double side2, double side3)
 8   throw (NonPositiveSideException, TriangleException)
 9 {
10   check(side1);
11   check(side2);
12   check(side3);
13
14   if (!isValid(side1, side2, side3))
15     throw TriangleException(side1, side2, side3);
16
17   this->side1 = side1;
18   this->side2 = side2;
19   this->side3 = side3;
20 }
```

throw list

throw **NonPositiveSide-
Exception**

throw list

throw **TriangleException**

Function **check** declares that it throws `NonPositiveSideException` and constructor `Triangle` declares that it throws `NonPositiveSideException` and `TriangleException`.

Note
Placing **throw()** after a function header, known as an *empty exception specification*, declares that the function does not throw any exceptions. If a function attempts to throw an exception, a standard C++ function **unexpected** is invoked, which normally terminates the program.

empty exception specification

Note
Throwing an exception that is not declared in the throw list will cause the function **unexpected** to be invoked. However, a function without exception specification can throw any exception and will not cause **unexpected** to be invoked.

undeclared exception

16.10 When to Use Exceptions

The **try** block contains the code that is executed in normal circumstances. The **catch** block contains the code that is executed in exceptional circumstances. Exception handling separates error-handling code from normal programming tasks, thus making programs easier to read and to modify. Be aware, however, that exception handling usually requires more time and resources, because it requires instantiating a new exception object, rolling back the call stack, and propagating the exception through the chain of functions invoked to search for the handler.

An exception occurs in a function. If you want the exception to be processed by its caller, you should throw it. If you can handle the exception in the function where it occurs, there is no need to throw or use exceptions.

In general, common exceptions that may occur in multiple classes in a project are candidates for exception classes. Simple errors that may occur in individual functions are best handled locally without throwing exceptions.

Exception handling is for dealing with unexpected error conditions. Do not use a **try-catch** block to deal with simple, expected situations. Which situations are exceptional and which are expected is sometimes difficult to decide. The point is not to abuse exception handling as a way to deal with a simple logic test.

A general paradigm for exception handling is that you declare to throw an exception in a function as shown in (a) below, and use the function in a **try-catch** block as shown in (b).

```
returnType function1(parameterList)
  throw (exceptionList)
{
  ...
  if (an exception condition)
    throw AnException(arguments);
  ...
}
```

```
returnType function2(parameterList)
{
  try
  {
    ...
    function1 (arguments);
    ...
  }
  catch (AnException &ex)
  {
    Handler;
  }
  ...
}
```

(a)   (b)

KEY TERMS

exception   516
exception specification   534
function unexpected   535
rethrow exception   533

standard exception   520
throw exception   521
throw list   534

CHAPTER SUMMARY

1. Exception handling makes programs robust. Exception handling separates error-handling code from normal programming tasks, thus making programs easier to read and to modify. Another important advantage of exception handling is that it enables a function to throw an exception to its caller.

2. C++ allows you to use the **throw** statement to throw a value of any type (primitive or class type) when an exception occurs. This value is passed to a **catch** block as an argument so that the **catch** block can utilize this value to process the exception.

3. When an exception is thrown, the normal execution flow is interrupted. If the exception value matches a **catch** block parameter type, the control is transferred to a **catch** block. Otherwise, the function is exited and the exception is thrown to the function's caller. If the exception is not handled in the **main** function, the program is aborted.

4. C++ provides a number of predefined classes that can be used for creating exception objects. You can use the **exception** class or its derived classes **runtime_error** and **logic_error** to create exception objects.

5. You also can create a custom exception class if the predefined classes cannot adequately describe exceptions. This class is just like any C++ class, but often it is desirable to derive it from **exception** or a derived class of **exception** so you can utilize the common features (e.g., the **what()** function) in the **exception** class.

6. A **try** block may be followed by multiple **catch** blocks. The order in which exceptions are specified in **catch** blocks is important. A **catch** block for a base class type should appear after a **catch** block for a derived class type.

7. If a function throws an exception, you should declare the exception's type in the function header to warn programmers to deal with potential exceptions.

8. Exception handling should not be used to replace simple tests. You should test simple exceptions whenever possible and reserve exception handling for dealing with situations that cannot be handled with `if` statements.

REVIEW QUESTIONS

Sections 16.2–16.3

16.1 Show the output of the following code with input `120`.

```cpp
#include <iostream>
using namespace std;

int main()
{
  cout << "Enter a temperature: ";
  double temperature;
  cin >> temperature;

  try
  {
    cout << "Start of try block ..." << endl;

    if (temperature > 95)
      throw temperature;

    cout << "End of try block ..." << endl;
  }
  catch (double temperature)
  {
    cout << "The temperature is " << temperature << endl;
    cout << "It is too hot" << endl;
  }

  cout << "Continue ..." << endl;

  return 0;
}
```

16.2 What would be the output for the preceding code if the input were `80`?

16.3 Would it be an error if you changed

```cpp
catch (double temperature)
{
  cout << "The temperature is " << temperature << endl;
  cout << "It is too hot" << endl;
}
```

in the preceding code to the following?

```cpp
catch (double)
{
  cout << "It is too hot" << endl;
}
```

Sections 16.4–16.5

16.4 Describe the C++ `exception` class and its derived classes. Give examples of using `bad_alloc` and `bad_cast`. Why is it a good practice to define custom exception classes derived from a standard exception class?

16.5 Show the output of the following code with input 10, 60, and 120, respectively.

```cpp
#include <iostream>
using namespace std;

int main()
{
  cout << "Enter a temperature: ";
  double temperature;
  cin >> temperature;

  try
  {
    cout << "Start of try block ..." << endl;

    if (temperature > 95)
      throw runtime_error("Exceptional temperature");

    cout << "End of try block ..." << endl;
  }
  catch (runtime_error &ex)
  {
    cout << ex.what() << endl;
    cout << "It is too hot" << endl;
  }

  cout << "Continue ..." << endl;

  return 0;
}
```

Sections 16.6–16.10

16.6 Can you throw multiple exceptions in one `throw` statement? Can you have multiple `catch` blocks in a `try-catch` block?

16.7 Suppose that `statement2` causes an exception in the following `try-catch` block:

```cpp
try
{
  statement1;
  statement2;
  statement3;
}
catch (Exception1 ex1)
{
}
catch (Exception2 ex2)
{
}

statement4;
```

Answer the following questions:

■ Will `statement3` be executed?
■ If the exception is not caught, will `statement4` be executed?
■ If the exception is caught in the `catch` block, will `statement4` be executed?
■ If the exception is passed to the caller, will `statement4` be executed?

16.8 Suppose that `statement2` causes an exception in the following statement:

```
try
{
  statement1;
  statement2;
  statement3;
}
catch (Exception1 ex1)
{
}
catch (Exception2 ex2)
{
}
catch (Exception3 ex3)
{
  statement4;
  throw;
}
statement5;
```

Answer the following questions:

■ Will `statement5` be executed if the exception is not caught?
■ If the exception is of type `Exception3`, will `statement4` be executed, and will `statement5` be executed?

16.9 What is the purpose of exception specifications? How do you declare a throw list? Can you declare multiple exceptions in a function declaration?

PROGRAMMING EXERCISES

16.1* (*runtime_error*) Exercise 10.9 specifies the `parseHex(const string & hexString)` function that converts a hex string into a decimal number. Implement the `parseHex` function to throw a `runtime_error` exception if the string is not a hex string. Write a test program that prompts the user to enter a hex number as a string and display the number in decimal.

16.2* (*runtime_error*) Exercise 10.10 specifies the `parseBinary(const string & bianryString)` function that converts a binary string into a decimal number. Implement the `parseBinary` function to throw a `runtime_error` exception if the string is not a binary string. Write a test program that prompts the user to enter a binary number as a string and displays the number in decimal.

16.3* (Modify *Rational class*) §14.4, "Overloading the [] Operators," introduced how to overload the [] array subscript operator in the `Rational` class. If the subscript is neither 0 nor 1, the function throws a `runtime_error` exception. Define a custom exception called `IllegalSubscriptException` and let the function operator throw an `IllegalSubscriptException` if the subscript is neither 0 nor 1. Write a test program with a try-catch block to handle this type of exception.

16.4* (Modify *StackOfIntegers class*) In §10.11, "Problem: The StackOfIntegers Class," you defined a stack class for integers. Define a custom exception class named EmptyStackException and let the pop function throw an EmptyStackException if the stack is empty. Write a test program with a try-catch block to handle this type of exception.

Video Note
the HexFormatException class

16.5* (*HexFormatException*) Implement the parseHex function in Exercise 16.1 to throw a HexFormatException if the string is not a hex string. Define a custom exception class named HexFormatException. Write a test program that prompts the user to enter a hex number as a string and displays the number in decimal.

16.6* (*BinaryFormatException*) Implement the parseBinary function in Exercise 16.2 to throw a BinaryFormatException if the string is not a binary string. Define a custom exception class named BinaryFormatException. Write a test program that prompts the user to enter a binary number as a string and displays the number in decimal.

PART 3

ALGORITHMS AND DATA STRUCTURES

The design and implementation of efficient algorithms and data structures is an important subject in computer science. Data structures such as lists, stacks, queues, sets, maps, heaps, and binary trees have many applications in compiler construction, computer operating systems, and file management. C++ provides vectors, deques, lists, stacks, queues, sets, and maps in the Standard Template Library (STL). This part of the book introduces the main subjects in a typical data structures course.

Prerequisites for Part 3

Chapters 21–26 are bonus chapters available from the companion Website.

bonus chapters

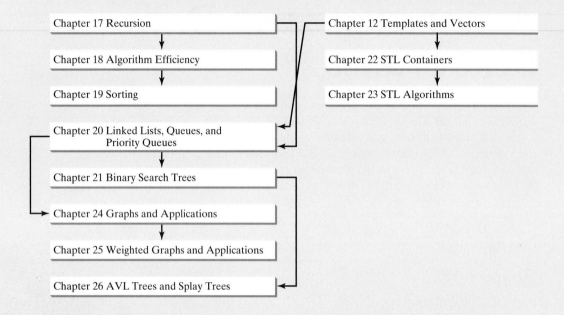

CHAPTER 17

RECURSION

Objectives

- To describe what a recursive function is and the benefits of using recursion (§17.1).
- To develop recursive programs for recursive mathematical functions (§§17.2–17.3).
- To explain how recursive function calls are handled in a call stack (§§17.2–17.3).
- To think recursively (§17.4).
- To use an overloaded helper function to derive a recursive function (§17.5).
- To solve selection sort using recursion (§17.5.1).
- To solve binary search using recursion (§17.5.2).
- To solve the Towers of Hanoi problem using recursion (§17.6).
- To solve the Eight Queens problem using recursion (§17.7).
- To understand the relationship and difference between recursion and iteration (§17.8).

17.1 Introduction

Suppose you wish to print all permutations of a string. For example, for a string abc, its permutations are abc, acb, bac, bca, cab, and cba. How do you solve this problem? There are several ways to do so. An intuitive and effective solution is to use recursion.

The classic Eight Queens puzzle is to place eight queens on a chessboard such that no two can attack each other (i.e., no two queens are on the same row, same column, or same diagonal), as shown in Figure 17.1. How do you write a program to solve this problem? There are several ways to solve this problem. An intuitive and effective solution is to use recursion.

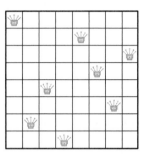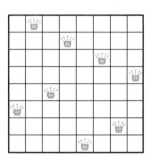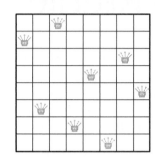

FIGURE 17.1 The Eight Queens problem can be solved using recursion.

To use recursion is to program using *recursive functions*—functions that directly or indirectly invoke themselves. Recursion is a useful programming technique. In some cases, it enables you to develop a natural, straightforward, simple solution to an otherwise difficult problem. This chapter introduces the concepts and techniques of recursive programming and illustrates by examples how to "think recursively."

17.2 Example: Factorials

Many mathematical functions are defined using recursion. We begin with a simple example that illustrates recursion.

The factorial of a number n can be recursively defined as follows:

```
0! = 1;
n! = n × (n - 1)!; n > 0
```

How do you find n! for a given n? It is easy to find 1! because you know that 0! is 1 and 1! is 1 × 0!. Assuming you know that (n - 1)!, n! can be obtained immediately using n × (n - 1)!. Thus, the problem of computing n! is reduced to computing (n - 1)!. When computing (n - 1)!, you can apply the same idea recursively until n is reduced to 0.

Let `factorial(n)` be the function for computing n!. If you call the function with n = 0, it immediately returns the result. The function knows how to solve the simplest case, which is referred to as the *base case* or the *stopping condition*. If you call the function with n > 0, it reduces the problem into a subproblem for computing the factorial of n - 1. The subproblem is essentially the same as the original problem but is simpler or smaller than the original. Because the subproblem has the same property as the original, you can call the function with a different argument, which is referred to as a *recursive call*.

The recursive algorithm for computing `factorial(n)` can be simply described as follows:

```
if (n == 0)
  return 1;
else
  return n * factorial(n - 1);
```

A recursive call can result in many more recursive calls, because the function is dividing a subproblem into new subproblems. For a recursive function to terminate, the problem must eventually be reduced to a stopping case. At this point the function returns a result to its caller. The caller then performs a computation and returns the result to its own caller. This process continues until the result is passed back to the original caller. The original problem can now be solved by multiplying **n** by the result of `factorial(n - 1)`.

Listing 17.1 is a complete program that prompts the user to enter a nonnegative integer and displays the factorial for the number.

LISTING 17.1   ComputeFactorial.cpp

```cpp
1 #include <iostream>
2 using namespace std;
3
4 // Return the factorial for a specified number
5 int factorial(int);
6
7 int main()
8 {
9   // Prompt the user to enter an integer
10   cout << "Please enter a nonnegative integer: ";
11   int n;
12   cin >> n;
13
14   // Display factorial
15   cout << "Factorial of " << n << " is " << factorial(n);
16
17   return 0;
18 }
19
20 // Return the factorial for a specified number
21 int factorial(int n)
22 {
23   if (n == 0) // Base case                              base case
24     return 1;
25   else
26     return n * factorial(n - 1); // Recursive call      recursion
27 }
```

```
Please enter a nonnegative integer: 5 ⏎Enter
Factorial of 5 is 120
```

The `factorial` function (lines 21–27) is essentially a direct translation of the recursive mathematical definition for the factorial into C++ code. The call to `factorial` is recursive because it calls itself. The parameter passed to `factorial` is decremented until it reaches the base case of 0.

Figure 17.2 illustrates the execution of the recursive calls, starting with **n = 4**. The use of stack space for recursive calls is shown in Figure 17.3.

Caution

Infinite recursion can occur if recursion does not reduce the problem in a manner that allows it to   infinite recursion
eventually converge into the base case. For example, suppose you mistakenly write the
`factorial` function as follows:

```cpp
int factorial(int n)
{
  return n * factorial(n - 1);
}
```

The function runs infinitely and causes the stack overflow.

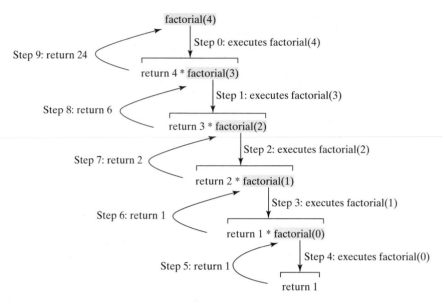

FIGURE 17.2 Invoking `factorial(4)` spawns recursive calls to `factorial`.

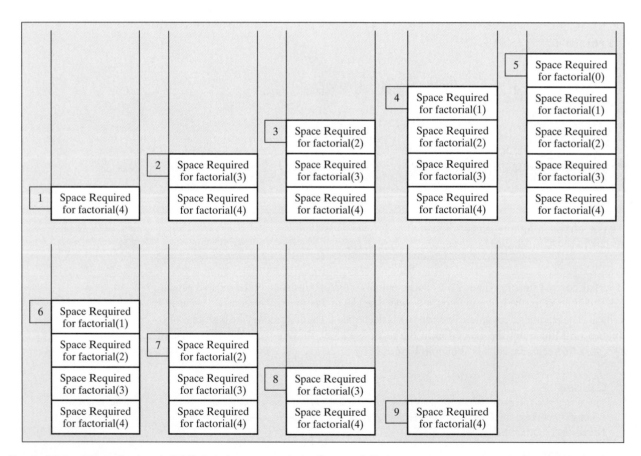

FIGURE 17.3 When `factorial(4)` is being executed, the `factorial` function is called recursively, causing memory space to dynamically change.

Pedagogical Note

It is simpler and more efficient to implement the `factorial` function using a loop. However, the recursive `factorial` function is a good example to demonstrate the concept of recursion.

17.3 Problem: Fibonacci Numbers

The `factorial` function in the preceding section easily could be rewritten without using recursion. In some cases, however, using recursion enables you to give a natural, straightforward, simple solution to a program that would otherwise be difficult to solve. Consider the well-known Fibonacci series problem, as follows:

The series: 0   1   1   2   3   5   8   13   21   34   55   89 ...

Indices: 0   1   2   3   4   5   6   7   8   9   10   11

The Fibonacci series begins with 0 and 1, and each subsequent number is the sum of the preceding two numbers in the series. The series can be defined recursively as follows:

```
fib(0) = 0;
fib(1) = 1;
fib(index) = fib(index - 2) + fib(index - 1); index >= 2
```

The Fibonacci series was named for Leonardo Fibonacci, a medieval mathematician, who originated it to model the growth of the rabbit population. It can be applied in numeric optimization and in various other areas.

How do you find `fib(index)` for a given `index`? It is easy to find `fib(2)` because you know `fib(0)` and `fib(1)`. Assuming that you know `fib(index - 2)` and `fib(index - 1)`, `fib(index)` can be obtained immediately. Thus, the problem of computing `fib(index)` is reduced to computing `fib(index - 2)` and `fib(index - 1)`. When computing `fib(index - 2)` and `fib(index - 1)`, you apply the idea recursively until `index` is reduced to 0 or 1.

The base case is `index = 0` or `index = 1`. If you call the function with `index = 0` or `index = 1`, it immediately returns the result. If you call the function with `index >= 2`, it divides the problem into two subproblems for computing `fib(index - 1)` and `fib(index - 2)` using recursive calls. The recursive algorithm for computing `fib(index)` can be simply described as follows:

```
if (index == 0)
  return 0;
else if (index == 1)
  return 1;
else
  return fib(index - 1) + fib(index - 2);
```

Listing 17.2 is a complete program that prompts the user to enter an index and computes the Fibonacci number for the index.

LISTING 17.2   ComputeFibonacci.cpp

```cpp
1 #include <iostream>
2 using namespace std;
3
4 // The function for finding the Fibonacci number
5 int fib(int);
6
7 int main()
8 {
9    // Prompt the user to enter an integer
```

```
10    cout <<  "Enter an index for the Fibonacci number: ";
11    int index;
12    cin >> index;
13
14    // Display factorial
15    cout << "Fibonacci number at index " << index << " is "
16      << fib(index) << endl;
17
18    return 0;
19 }
20
21 // The function for finding the Fibonacci number
22 int fib(int index)
23 {
24    if (index == 0) // Base case
25      return 0;
26    else if (index == 1) // Base case
27      return 1;
28    else // Reduction and recursive calls
29      return fib(index - 1) + fib(index - 2);
30 }
```

base case → line 24
base case → line 26
recursion → line 29

```
Enter an index for the Fibonacci number: 7  ↵Enter
Fibonacci number at index 7 is 13
```

The program does not show the considerable amount of work done behind the scenes by the computer. Figure 17.4, however, shows successive recursive calls for evaluating `fib(4)`. The original function, `fib(4)`, makes two recursive calls, `fib(3)` and `fib(2)`, and then returns `fib(3)` + `fib(2)`. But in what order are these functions called? In C++, operands for the binary + operator may be evaluated in any order. Assume it is evaluated from the left to right. The labels in Figure 17.4 show the order in which functions are called.

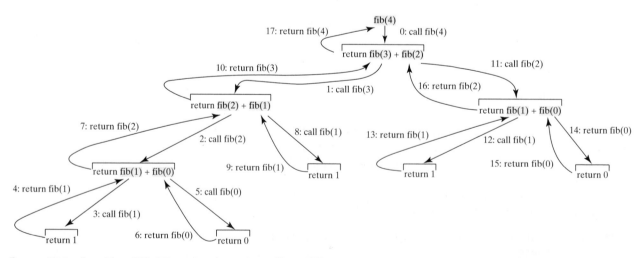

FIGURE 17.4 Invoking `fib(4)` spawns recursive calls to `fib`.

As shown in Figure 17.4, there are many duplicated recursive calls. For instance, `fib(2)` is called twice, `fib(1)` three times, and `fib(0)` twice. In general, computing `fib(index)` requires twice as many recursive calls as are needed for computing `fib(index - 1)`. As you try larger index values, the number of calls substantially increases.

Besides the large number of recursive calls, the computer requires more time and space to run recursive functions.

 Pedagogical Note

The recursive implementation of the `fib` function is very simple and straightforward, but not efficient. See Exercise 17.2 for an efficient solution using loops. The recursive `fib` function is a good example to demonstrate how to write recursive functions, though it is not practical.

17.4 Problem Solving Using Recursion

The preceding sections presented two classic recursion examples. All recursive functions have the following characteristics:

recursion characteristics

- The function is implemented using an `if-else` or a `switch` statement that leads to different cases.

if-else

- One or more base cases (the simplest case) are used to stop recursion.

base cases

- Every recursive call reduces the original problem, bringing it increasingly closer to a base case until it becomes that case.

reduction

In general, to solve a problem using recursion, you break it into subproblems. If a subproblem resembles the original problem, you can apply the same approach to solve the subproblem recursively. This subproblem is almost the same as the original problem in nature with a smaller size.

Let us consider a simple problem of printing a message for n times. You can break the problem into two subproblems: one is to print the message one time and the other is to print the message n - 1 times. The second problem is the same as the original problem with a smaller size. The base case for the problem is n == 0. You can solve this problem using recursion as follows:

```
void nPrintln(const string &message, int times)
{
  if (times >= 1)
  {
    cout << message << endl;
    nPrintln(message, times - 1);
  } // The base case is times == 0
}
```

recursive call

Note that the `fib` function in the preceding example returns a value to its caller, but the `nPrintln` function is `void` and does not return a value to its caller.

Many of the problems presented in the early chapters can be solved using recursion if you *think recursively*. Consider the palindrome problem in Listing 10.3. Recall that a string is a palindrome if it reads the same from the left and from the right. For example, mom and dad are palindromes, but uncle and aunt are not. The problem to check whether a string is a palindrome can be divided into two subproblems:

think recursively

- Check whether the first character and the last character of the string are equal.

- Ignore these two end characters and check whether the rest of the substring is a palindrome.

The second subproblem is the same as the original problem with a smaller size. There are two base cases: (1) the two end characters are not same; (2) the string size is 0 or 1. In case 1, the string is not a palindrome; and in case 2, the string is a palindrome. The recursive function for this problem can be implemented in Listing 17.3.

LISTING 17.3 RecursivePalindrome1.cpp

include header file

function header

string length

recursive call

input string

```
 1 #include <iostream>
 2 #include <string>
 3 using namespace std;
 4
 5 bool isPalindrome(const string &s)
 6 {
 7   if (s.size() <= 1) // Base case
 8     return true;
 9   else if (s[0] != s[s.size() - 1]) // Base case
10     return false;
11   else
12     return isPalindrome(s.substr(1, s.size() - 2));
13 }
14
15 int main()
16 {
17   cout << "Enter a string: ";
18   string s;
19   getline(cin, s);
20
21   if (isPalindrome(s))
22     cout << s << " is a palindrome" << endl;
23   else
24     cout << s << " is not a palindrome" << endl;
25
26   return 0;
27 }
```

```
Enter a string: aba  ↵Enter
aba is a palindrome
```

```
Enter a string: abab  ↵Enter
abab is not a palindrome
```

The isPalindrome function checks whether the size of the string is less than or equal to 1 (line 7). If so, the string is a palindrome. The function checks whether the first and the last elements of the string are the same (line 9). If not, the string is not a palindrome. Otherwise, obtain a substring of s using s.substr(1, s.size() - 2) and recursively invoke isPalindrome with the new string (line 12).

17.5 Recursive Helper Functions

The preceding recursive isPalindrome function is not efficient, because it creates a new string for every recursive call. To avoid creating new strings, you can use the low and high indices to indicate the range of the substring. These two indices must be passed to the recursive function. Since the original function is isPalindrome(const string &s), you have to create a new function isPalindrome(const string &s, int low, int high) to accept additional information on the string, as shown in Listing 17.4.

LISTING 17.4 RecursivePalindrome2.cpp

```
1 #include <iostream>
2 #include <string>
3 using namespace std;
4
5 bool isPalindrome(const string &s, int low, int high)          helper function
6 {
7   if (high <= low) // Base case
8     return true;
9   else if (s[low] != s[high]) // Base case
10    return false;
11  else
12    return isPalindrome(s, low + 1, high - 1);               recursive call
13 }
14
15 bool isPalindrome(const string &s)                            function header
16 {
17   return isPalindrome(s, 0, s.size() - 1);                    invoke helper function
18 }
19
20 int main()
21 {
22   cout << "Enter a string: ";
23   string s;
24   getline(cin, s);                                            input string
25
26   if (isPalindrome(s))
27     cout << s << " is a palindrome" << endl;
28   else
29     cout << s << " is not a palindrome" << endl;
30
31   return 0;
32 }
```

```
Enter a string: aba  ↵Enter
aba is a palindrome

Enter a string: abab  ↵Enter
abab is not a palindrome
```

Two overloaded isPalindrome functions are defined. The function isPalindrome(const string &s) (line 15) checks whether a string is a palindrome, and the second function isPalindrome(const string &s, int low, int high) (line 5) checks whether a substring s(low..high) is a palindrome. The first function passes the string s with low = 0 and high = s.size() − 1 to the second function. The second function can be invoked recursively to check a palindrome in an ever-shrinking substring. It is a common design technique in recursive programming to define a second function that receives additional parameters. Such a function is known as a *recursive helper function*.

recursive helper function

Helper functions are very useful to design recursive solutions for problems involving strings and arrays. The sections that follow present two more examples.

17.5.1 Selection Sort

Selection sort was introduced in §7.9.1. Now we introduce a recursive selection sort for characters in a string. A variation of selection sort works as follows. It finds the largest element in the list and places it last. It then finds the largest element remaining and places it next to last, and so on until the list contains only a single element. The problem can be divided into two subproblems:

- Find the largest element in the list and swap it with the last element.

- Ignore the last element and sort the remaining smaller list recursively.

The base case is that the list contains only one element. Listing 17.5 gives the recursive sort function.

LISTING 17.5 RecursiveSelectionSort.cpp

```
 1 #include <iostream>
 2 #include <string>
 3 using namespace std;
 4
 5 void sort(string &s, int high)          // helper sort function
 6 {
 7   if (high > 0)
 8   {
 9     // Find the largest element and its index
10     int indexOfMax = 0;
11     char max = s[0];
12     for (int i = 1; i <= high; i++)
13     {
14       if (s[i] > max)
15       {
16         max = s[i];
17         indexOfMax = i;
18       }
19     }
20
21     // Swap the largest with the last element in the list
22     s[indexOfMax] = s[high];
23     s[high] = max;
24
25     // Sort the remaining list
26     sort(s, high - 1);                  // recursive call
27   }
28 }
29
30 void sort(string &s)                    // sort function
31 {
32   sort(s, s.size() - 1);                // invoke helper function
33 }
34
35 int main()
36 {
37   cout << "Enter a string: ";
38   string s;
39   getline(cin, s);                      // input string
40
41   sort(s);
42
43   cout << "The sorted string is " << s << endl;
44
45   return 0;
46 }
```

Labels in left margin:
- helper sort function (line 5)
- recursive call (line 26)
- sort function (line 30)
- invoke helper function (line 32)
- input string (line 39)

```
Enter a string: ghfdacb  ↵Enter
The sorted string is abcdfgh
```

Two overloaded `sort` functions are defined. The function `sort(string &s)` sorts characters in `s[0..s.size() - 1]` and the second function `sort(string &s, int high)` sorts characters in `s[0..high]`. The helper function can be invoked recursively to sort an ever-shrinking substring.

17.5.2 Binary Search

Binary search was introduced in §7.8.2. For binary search to work, the elements in the array must already be ordered. The binary search first compares the key with the element in the middle of the array. Consider the following three cases:

- **Case 1:** If the key is less than the middle element, recursively search the key in the first half of the array.

- **Case 2:** If the key is equal to the middle element, the search ends with a match.

- **Case 3:** If the key is greater than the middle element, recursively search the key in the second half of the array.

Case 1 and Case 3 reduce the search to a smaller list. Case 2 is a base case when there is a match. Another base case is that the search is exhausted without a match. Listing 17.6 gives a clear, simple solution for the binary search problem using recursion.

LISTING 17.6 `RecursiveBinarySearch.cpp`

```cpp
 1  #include <iostream>
 2  using namespace std;
 3
 4  int binarySearch(const int list[], int key, int low, int high)          // helper function
 5  {
 6    if (low > high)  // The list has been exhausted without a match
 7      return -1; // key not found                                          // base case
 8
 9    int mid = (low + high) / 2;
10    if (key < list[mid])
11      return binarySearch(list, key, low, mid - 1);                        // recursive call
12    else if (key == list[mid])
13      return mid;                                                          // base case
14    else
15      return binarySearch(list, key, mid + 1, high);                       // recursive call
16  }
17
18  int binarySearch(const int list[], int key, int size)                    // binarySearch function
19  {
20    int low = 0;
21    int high = size - 1;
22    return binarySearch(list, key, low, high);                             // call helper function
23  }
24
25  int main()
26  {
27    int list[] = {2, 4, 7, 10, 11, 45, 50, 59, 60, 66, 69, 70, 79};
28    int i = binarySearch(list, 2, 13); // Returns 0
29    int j = binarySearch(list, 11, 13); // Returns 4
30    int k = binarySearch(list, 12, 13); // Returns -1
31
32    cout << "binarySearch(list, 2, 13) returns " << i << endl;
33    cout << "binarySearch(list, 11, 13) returns " << j << endl;
34    cout << "binarySearch(list, 12, 13) returns " << k << endl;
35
36    return 0;
37  }
```

```
binarySearch(list, 2, 13) returns 0
binarySearch(list, 11, 13) returns 4
binarySearch(list, 12, 13) returns -1
```

The `binarySearch` function in line 18 finds a key in the whole list. The helper `binarySearch` function in line 4 finds a key in the list with index from `low` to `high`.

The `binarySearch` function in line 18 passes the initial array with `low = 0` and `high = size - 1` to the helper `binarySearch` function. The helper function is invoked recursively to find the key in an ever-shrinking subarray.

Video Note

Towers of Hanoi

17.6 Towers of Hanoi

The Towers of Hanoi problem is a classic recursion example. It can be solved easily using recursion but is difficult to solve otherwise.

The problem involves moving a specified number of disks of distinct sizes from one tower to another while observing the following rules:

■ There are *n* disks labeled 1, 2, 3, ..., *n*, and three towers labeled A, B, and C.

■ No disk can be on top of a smaller disk at any time.

■ All the disks are initially placed on tower A.

■ Only one disk can be moved at a time, and it must be the top disk on the tower.

The objective is to move all the disks from A to B with the assistance of C. For example, if you have three disks, the steps to move all of the disks from A to B are shown in Figure 17.5.

Note

The Towers of Hanoi is a classic computer science problem. Many websites are devoted to this problem. The website www.cut-the-knot.com/recurrence/hanoi.html is worth a look.

In the case of three disks, you can find the solution manually. For a larger number of disks, however—even for four—the problem is quite complex. Fortunately, the problem has an inherently recursive nature, which leads to a straightforward recursive solution.

The base case for the problem is `n = 1`. If `n == 1`, you could simply move the disk from A to B. When `n > 1`, you could split the original problem into three subproblems and solve them sequentially.

1. Move the first `n - 1` disks from A to C with the assistance of tower B, as shown in Step 1 in Figure 17.6.

2. Move disk `n` from A to B, as shown in Step 2 in Figure 17.6.

3. Move `n - 1` disks from C to B with the assistance of tower A, as shown in Step 3 in Figure 17.6.

The following function moves *n* disks from the `fromTower` to the `toTower` with the assistance of the `auxTower`:

```
void moveDisks(int n, char fromTower, char toTower, char auxTower)
```

The algorithm for the function can be described as follows:

```
if (n == 1) // Stopping condition
  Move disk 1 from the fromTower to the toTower;
else
```

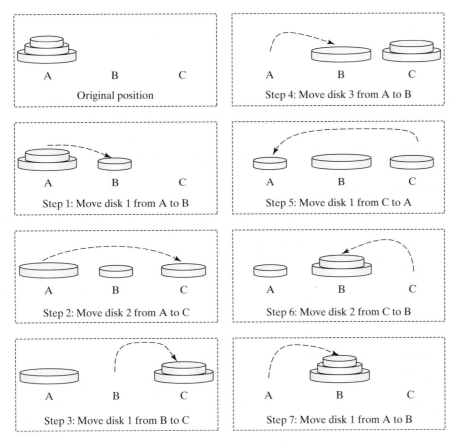

FIGURE 17.5   The goal of the Towers of Hanoi problem is to move disks from tower A to tower B without breaking the rules.

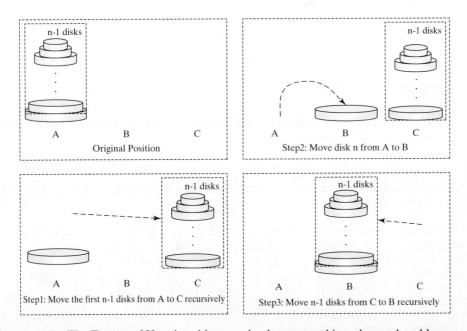

FIGURE 17.6   The Towers of Hanoi problem can be decomposed into three subproblems.

```
{
  moveDisks(n - 1, fromTower, auxTower, toTower);
  Move disk n from the fromTower to the toTower;
  moveDisks(n - 1, auxTower, toTower, fromTower);
}
```

Listing 17.7 is a program that prompts the user to enter the number of disks and invokes the recursive function **moveDisks** to display the solution for moving the disks.

LISTING 17.7 TowersOfHanoi.cpp

```
 1 #include <iostream>
 2 using namespace std;
 3
 4 /* The function for finding the solution to move n disks
 5    from fromTower to toTower with auxTower */
 6 void moveDisks(int n, char fromTower,
 7     char toTower, char auxTower)
 8 {
 9   if (n == 1) // Stopping condition
10     cout << "Move disk " << n << " from " <<
11       fromTower << " to " << toTower << endl;
12   else
13   {
14     moveDisks(n - 1, fromTower, auxTower, toTower);
15     cout << "Move disk " << n << " from " <<
16       fromTower << " to " << toTower << endl;
17     moveDisks(n - 1, auxTower, toTower, fromTower);
18   }
19 }
20
21 int main()
22 {
23   // Read number of disks, n
24   cout << "Enter number of disks: ";
25   int n;
26   cin >> n;
27
28   // Find the solution recursively
29   cout << "The moves are: " << endl;
30   moveDisks(n, 'A', 'B', 'C');
31
32   return 0;
33 }
```

recursive function (line 6)
recursion (line 14)
recursion (line 17)

```
Enter number of disks: 4 ⏎Enter
The moves are:
Move disk 1 from A to C
Move disk 2 from A to B
Move disk 1 from C to B
Move disk 3 from A to C
Move disk 1 from B to A
Move disk 2 from B to C
Move disk 1 from A to C
Move disk 4 from A to B
Move disk 1 from C to B
Move disk 2 from C to A
Move disk 1 from B to A
```

```
Move disk 3 from C to B
Move disk 1 from A to C
Move disk 2 from A to B
Move disk 1 from C to B
```

This problem is inherently recursive. Using recursion makes it possible to find a natural, simple solution. It would be difficult to solve the problem without using recursion.

Consider tracing the program for n = 3. The successive recursive calls are shown in Figure 17.7. As you can see, writing the program is easier than tracing the recursive calls. The system uses stacks to trace the calls behind the scenes. To some extent, recursion provides a level of abstraction that hides iterations and other details from the user.

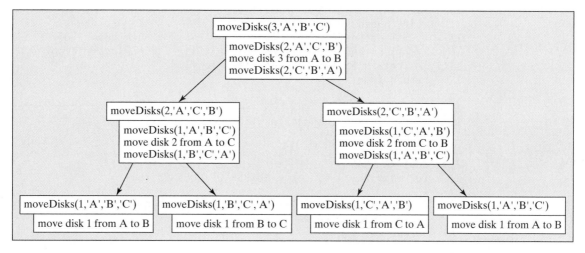

FIGURE 17.7 Invoking `moveDisks(3, 'A', 'B', 'C')` spawns calls to `moveDisks` recursively.

17.7 Eight Queens

This section gives a recursive solution to the Eight Queens problem presented earlier. The task is to place a queen in each row on a chessboard in such a way that no two queens can attack each other. You may use a two-dimensional array to represent a chessboard. However, since each row can have only one queen, it is sufficient to use a one-dimensional array to denote the position of the queen in the row. So, let us declare array **queens** as follows:

```
int queens[8];
```

Assign **j** to **queens[i]** to denote that a queen is placed in row **i** and column **j**. Figure 17.8(a) shows the contents of array **queens** for the chessboard in Figure 17.8(b).

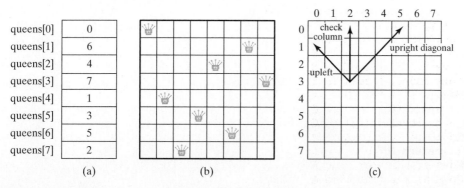

FIGURE 17.8 `queens[i]` denotes the position of the queen in row i.

Listing 17.8 is a program that finds a solution for the Eight Queens problem.

LISTING 17.8 EightQueen.cpp

```cpp
 1 #include <iostream>
 2 using namespace std;
 3
 4 const int NUMBER_OF_QUEENS = 8; // Constant: eight queens
 5 int queens[NUMBER_OF_QUEENS];
 6
 7 /** Check whether a queen can be placed at row i and column j */
 8 bool isValid(int row, int column)
 9 {
10   for (int i = 1; i <= row; i++)
11     if (queens[row - i] == column      // Check column
12       || queens[row - i] == column - i  // Check upper left diagonal
13       || queens[row - i] == column + i) // Check upper right diagonal
14       return false; // There is a conflict
15   return true; // No conflict
16 }
17
18 /** Display the chessboard with eight queens */
19 void printResult()
20 {
21   cout << "\n-------------------------------\n";
22   for (int row = 0; row < NUMBER_OF_QUEENS; row++)
23   {
24     for (int column = 0; column < NUMBER_OF_QUEENS; column++)
25       printf(column == queens[row] ? "| Q " : "|   ");
26     cout << "|\n-------------------------------\n";
27   }
28 }
29
30 /** Search to place a queen at the specified row */
31 void search(int row)
32 {
33   static bool found = false; // Set true when one solution is found
34
35   for (int column = 0; column < NUMBER_OF_QUEENS && !found; column++)
36   {
37     if (isValid(row, column))
38     {
39       queens[row] = column; // Place a queen at (row, column)
40       if (row < NUMBER_OF_QUEENS - 1)
41         search(row + 1); // Search the next row
42       else
43         found = true; // One solution found
44     }
45   }
46 }
47
48 int main()
49 {
50   search(0); // Start search from row 0. Note row indices are 0 to 7
51   printResult(); // Display result
52
53   return 0;
54 }
```

check if valid

search this row

search columns

search next row

found

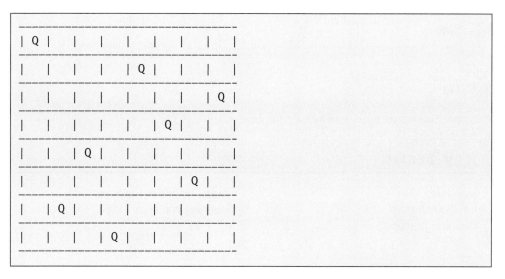

The program invokes `search(0)` (line 50) to start a search for a solution at row `0`, which recursively invokes `search(1)`, `search(2)`, . . . , and `search(7)` (line 41).

The `search(row)` function checks whether a queen can be placed in column `0`, `1`, `2`, . . . , and `7` in a `for` loop (line 35). If a valid position is found (line 37), place a queen in the column (line 39) and continue to search for the next row (line 41). If all rows are searched, set found to `true`. Note that `found` is declared a static local variable (line 33). Once found becomes `true`, no further search is needed (see `!found` condition in line 35).

The `isValid(row, column)` function checks whether placing a queen at the specified position causes a conflict with the queens placed before this row. It ensures that no queen is placed in the same column (line 11), no queen is placed in the upper left diagonal (line 12), and no queen is placed in the upper right diagonal (line 13).

17.8 Recursion versus Iteration

Recursion is an alternative form of program control. It is essentially repetition without a loop control. When you use loops, you specify a loop body. The repetition of the loop body is controlled by the loop-control structure. In recursion, the function itself is called repeatedly. A selection statement must be used to control whether to call the function recursively or not.

Recursion bears substantial overhead. Each time the program calls a function, the system must assign space for all of the function's local variables and parameters. This can consume considerable memory and requires extra time to manage the additional space.

Any problem that can be solved recursively can be solved nonrecursively with iterations. Recursion has some negative aspects: it uses up too much time and too much memory. Why, then, should you use it? In some cases, using recursion enables you to specify a clear, simple solution for an inherent recursive problem that would otherwise be difficult to obtain. The Towers of Hanoi problem is such an example, which is rather difficult to solve without using recursion.

The decision whether to use recursion or iteration should be based on the nature of the problem you are trying to solve and your understanding of the problem. The rule of thumb is to use whichever of the two approaches can best develop an intuitive solution that naturally mirrors the problem. If an iterative solution is obvious, use it. It generally will be more efficient than the recursive option.

recursion overhead

recursion advantages

recursion or iteration?

stack overflow

> **Note**
> Your recursive program could run out of memory, causing a *stack overflow* runtime error.

performance concern

> **Tip**
> If you are concerned about your program's performance, avoid using recursion, because it takes more time and consumes more memory than iteration.

KEY TERMS

base case   544
infinite recursion   545
recursive function   544

recursive helper function   551
stopping condition   544

CHAPTER SUMMARY

1. A recursive function is one that invokes itself directly or indirectly. For a recursive function to terminate, there must be one or more base cases.

2. Recursion is an alternative form of program control. It is essentially repetition without a loop control. It can be used to specify simple, clear solutions for inherently recursive problems that would otherwise be difficult to solve.

3. Sometimes the original function needs to be modified to receive additional parameters in order to be invoked recursively. A recursive helper function can be defined for this purpose.

4. Recursion bears substantial overhead. Each time the program calls a function, the system must assign space for all of the function's local variables and parameters. This can consume considerable memory and requires extra time to manage the additional space.

REVIEW QUESTIONS

Sections 17.1–17.3

17.1   What is a recursive function? Describe the characteristics of recursive functions. What is an infinite recursion?

17.2   Write a recursive mathematical definition for computing 2^n for a positive integer n.

17.3   Write a recursive mathematical definition for computing x^n for a positive integer n and a real number x.

17.4   Write a recursive mathematical definition for computing $1 + 2 + 3 + \ldots + n$ for a positive integer.

17.5   How many times is the `factorial` function in Listing 17.1 invoked for `factorial(6)`?

17.6   How many times is the `fib` function in Listing 17.2 invoked for `fib(6)`?

17.7   Show the output of the following program:

```cpp
#include <iostream>
using namespace std;

int f(int n)
{
  if (n == 1)
    return 1;
  else
    return n + f(n - 1);
}

int main()
{
  cout << "Sum is " << f(5) << endl;

  return 0;
}
```

```cpp
#include <iostream>
using namespace std;

void f(int n)
{
  if (n > 0)
  {
    cout << n % 10;
    f(n / 10);
  }
}

int main()
{
  f(1234567);

  return 0;
}
```

17.8 Show the output of the following two programs:

```cpp
#include <iostream>
using namespace std;

void f(int n)
{
  if (n > 0)
  {
    cout << n << " ";
    f(n - 1);
  }
}

int main()
{
  f(5);

  return 0;
}
```

```cpp
#include <iostream>
using namespace std;

void f(int n)
{
  if (n > 0)
  {
    f(n - 1);
    cout << n << " ";
  }
}

int main()
{
  f(5);

  return 0;
}
```

17.9 What is wrong in the following function?

```cpp
#include <iostream>
using namespace std;

void f(double n)
{
  if (n != 0)
  {
    cout << n;
    f(n / 10);
  }
}

int main()
{
  f(1234567);

  return 0;
}
```

Sections 17.4–17.5

17.10 Show the call stack for `isPalindrome("abcba")` using the functions defined in Listings 17.3 and 17.4, respectively.

17.11 Show the call stack for `sort("abcba")` using the function defined in Listing 17.5.

17.12 What is a recursive helper function?

Section 17.6

17.13 How many times is the `moveDisks` function in Listing 17.7 invoked for `moveDisks(5, 'A', 'B', 'C')`?

Section 17.8

17.14 Which of the following statements are true?

- Any recursive function can be converted into a nonrecursive function.
- A recursive function takes more time and memory to execute than a nonrecursive function.
- Recursive functions are *always* simpler than nonrecursive functions.
- There is always a condition statement in a recursive function to check whether a base case is reached.

17.15 What is the cause for the stack overflow exception?

PROGRAMMING EXERCISES

Sections 17.2–17.3

17.1 (*Computing factorials*) Rewrite the `factorial` function in Listing 17.1 using iterations.

17.2* (*Fibonacci numbers*) Rewrite the `fib` function in Listing 17.2 using iterations.

Hint

To compute `fib(n)` without recursion, yo obtain `fib(n - 2)` and `fib(n - 1)` first. Let `f0` and `f1` denote the two previous Fibonacci numbers. The current Fibonacci number would then be `f0 + f1`. The algorithm can be described as follows:

```
f0 = 0; // For fib(0)
f1 = 1; // For fib(1)

for (int i = 1; i <= n; i++)
{
  currentFib = f0 + f1;
  f0 = f1;
  f1 = currentFib;
}

// After the loop, currentFib is fib(n)
```

Video Note
the GCD problem

17.3* (*Computing greatest common divisor using recursion*) The `gcd(m, n)` can also be defined recursively as follows:

- If `m % n` is `0`, `gcd (m, n)` is `n`.
- Otherwise, `gcd(m, n)` is `gcd(n, m % n)`.

Write a recursive function to find the GCD. Write a test program that computes `gcd(24, 16)` and `gcd(255, 25)`.

17.4   (*Summing series*) Write a recursive function to compute the following series:

$$m(i) = 1 + \frac{1}{2} + \frac{1}{3} + \dots + \frac{1}{i}$$

17.5   (*Summing series*) Write a recursive function to compute the following series:

$$m(i) = \frac{1}{3} + \frac{2}{5} + \frac{3}{7} + \frac{4}{9} + \frac{5}{11} + \frac{6}{13} + \dots + \frac{i}{2i + 1}$$

17.6**   (*Summing the series*) Write a recursive function to compute the following series:

$$m(i) = \frac{1}{2} + \frac{2}{3} + \dots + \frac{i}{i + 1}$$

17.7*   (*Fibonacci series*) Modify Listing 17.2, ComputeFibonacci.cpp, so that the program finds the number of times the `fib` function is called. (*Hint:* Use a global variable and increment it every time the function is called.)

Section 17.4

17.8**   (*Printing the digits in an integer reversely*) Write a recursive function that displays an `int` value reversely on the console using the following header:

```
void reverseDisplay(int value)
```

For example, `reverseDisplay(12345)` displays `54321`.

17.9**   (*Printing the characters in a string reversely*) Write a recursive function that displays a string reversely on the console using the following header:

```
void reverseDisplay(const string &s)
```

For example, `reverseDisplay("abcd")` displays `dcba`.

17.10*   (*Occurrences of a specified character in a string*) Write a recursive function that finds the number of occurrences of a specified letter in a string using the following function header.

Video Note
counting occurrence

```
int count(const string &s, char a)
```

For example, `count("Welcome", 'e')` returns `2`.

17.11** (*Summing the digits in an integer using recursion*) Write a recursive function that computes the sum of the digits in an integer. Use the following function header:

```
int sumDigits(long n)
```

For example, `sumDigits(234)` returns 2 + 3 + 4 = 17.

Section 17.5

17.12** (*Printing the characters in a string reversely*) Rewrite Exercise 17.9 using a helper function to pass the substring high index to the function. The helper function header is:

```
void reverseDisplay(const string &s, int high)
```

17.13** (*Finding the largest number in an array*) Write a recursive function that returns the largest integer in an array.

17.14* (*Finding the number of uppercase letters in a string*) Write a recursive function to return the number of uppercase letters in a string.

17.15* (*Occurrences of a specified character in a string*) Rewrite Exercise 17.10 using a helper function to pass the substring high index to the function. You need to define the following two functions. The second one is a recursive helper function.

```
int count(const string &s, char a)
int count(const string &s, char a, int high)
```

Section 17.6

17.16* (*Towers of Hanoi*) Modify Listing 17.7, TowersOfHanoi.cpp, so that the program finds the number of moves needed to move *n* disks from tower A to tower B. (*Hint:* Use a global variable and increment it every time the function is called.)

Comprehensive

17.17*** (*String permutations*) Write a recursive function to print all permutations of a string. For example, for a string abc, the printout is

```
abc
acb
bac
bca
cab
cba
```

(*Hint:* Define the following two functions. The second is a helper function.)

```
void displayPermuation(const string &s)
void displayPermuation(const string &s1, const string &s2)
```

The first function simply invokes displayPermuation("", s). The second function uses a loop to move a character from s2 to s1 and recursively invoke it with a new s1 and s2. The base case is that s2 is empty and prints s1 to the console.

17.18*** (*Game: Sudoku*) Rewrite Listing 8.4, Sudoku.cpp, using recursion. A Sudoku puzzle may have multiple solutions. Display only one solution in this exercise.

17.19*** (*Game: multiple Eight Queens solutions*) Rewrite Programming Exercise 7.20 using recursion.

17.20*** (*Game: multiple Sudoku solutions*) Modify Exercise 8.17 to display all possible solutions for a Sudoku puzzle.

CHAPTER 18

ALGORITHM EFFICIENCY

Objectives

- To estimate algorithm efficiency using the Big O notation (§18.2).

- To explain growth rates and why constants and nondominating terms can be ignored in the estimation (§18.2).

- To determine the complexity of various types of algorithms (§18.3).

- To analyze the binary search algorithm (§18.4.1).

- To analyze the selection sort algorithm (§18.4.2).

- To analyze the insertion sort algorithm (§18.4.3).

- To analyze the Towers of Hanoi algorithm (§18.4.4).

- To describe common growth functions (constant, logarithmic, log-linear, quadratic, cubic, exponential) (§18.4.5).

- To design efficient algorithms for finding Fibonacci numbers (§18.5).

- To design efficient algorithms for finding GCD (§18.6).

- To design efficient algorithms for finding prime numbers (§18.7).

- To design efficient algorithms for finding a closest pair of points (§18.8).

18.1 Introduction

Suppose two algorithms perform the same task, such as search (linear search vs. binary search) or sort (selection sort vs. insertion sort). Which one is better? To answer this question, we might implement these algorithms and run the programs to get execution time. But there are two problems with this approach:

1. First, many tasks run concurrently on a computer. The execution time of a particular program depends on the system load.

2. Second, the execution time depends on specific input. Consider, for example, linear search and binary search. If an element to be searched happens to be the first in the list, linear search will find the element quicker than binary search.

It is very difficult to compare algorithms by measuring their execution time. To overcome these problems, a theoretical approach was developed to analyze algorithms independent of computers and specific input. This approach approximates the effect of a change on the size of the input. In this way, you can see how fast an algorithm's execution time increases as the input size increases, so you can compare two algorithms by examining their *growth rates*.

18.2 Big *O* Notation

Consider linear search. The linear search algorithm compares the key with the elements in the array sequentially until the key is found or the array is exhausted. If the key is not in the array, it requires n comparisons for an array of size n. If the key is in the array, it requires $n/2$ comparisons on average. The algorithm's execution time is proportional to the size of the array. If you double the size of the array, you will expect the number of comparisons to double. The algorithm grows at a linear rate. The growth rate has an order of magnitude of n. Computer scientists use the *Big O notation* to represent "order of magnitude." Using this notation, the complexity of the linear search algorithm is $O(n)$, pronounced as "*order of n.*"

For the same input size, an algorithm's execution time may vary, depending on the input. An input that results in the shortest execution time is called the *best-case* input, and an input that results in the longest execution time is called the *worst-case* input. Best case and worst case are not representative, but worst-case analysis is very useful. You can be sure that the algorithm will never be slower than the worst case. An *average-case analysis* attempts to determine the average amount of time among all possible inputs of the same size. Average-case analysis is ideal, but difficult to perform, because for many problems it is hard to determine the relative probabilities and distributions of various input instances. Worst-case analysis is easier to perform, so the analysis is generally conducted for the worst case.

The linear search algorithm requires n comparisons in the worst-case and $n/2$ comparisons in the average case. Using the Big *O* notation, both cases require $O(n)$ time. The multiplicative constant (1/2) can be omitted. Algorithm analysis is focused on growth rate. The multiplicative constants have no impact on growth rates. The growth rate for $n/2$ or $100n$ is the same as for n, as illustrated in Table 18.1. Therefore, $O(n) = O(n/2) = O(100n)$.

TABLE 18.1 Growth Rates

n ╲ $f(n)$	n	$n/2$	$100n$	
100	100	50	10000	
200	200	100	20000	
	2	2	2	$f(200)\,/\,f(100)$

Consider the algorithm for finding the maximum number in an array of n elements. To find the maximum number if n is 2, it takes one comparison; if n is 3, two comparisons. In general, it takes $n - 1$ comparisons to find the maximum number in a list of n elements. Algorithm analysis is for large input size. If the input size is small, there is no significance in estimating an algorithm's efficiency. As n grows larger, the n part in the expression $n - 1$ dominates the complexity. The Big O notation allows you to ignore the nondominating part (e.g., -1 in the expression $n - 1$) and highlight the important part (e.g., n in the expression $n - 1$). So, the complexity of this algorithm is $O(n)$.

The Big O notation estimates the execution time of an algorithm in relation to the input size. If the time is not related to the input size, the algorithm is said to take *constant time* with the notation $O(1)$. For example, a function that retrieves an element at a given index in an array takes constant time, because the time does not grow as the size of the array increases.

The following mathematical summations are often useful in algorithm analysis:

large input size

ignoring nondominating terms

constant time

useful summations

$$1 + 2 + 3 + \dots + (n - 1) + n = \frac{n(n + 1)}{2} = O(n^2)$$

$$a^0 + a^1 + a^2 + a^3 + \dots + a^{(n-1)} + a^n = \frac{a^{n+1} - 1}{a - 1} = O(a^n)$$

$$2^0 + 2^1 + 2^2 + 2^3 + \dots + 2^{(n-1)} + 2^n = \frac{2^{n+1} - 1}{2 - 1} = 2^{n+1} - 1 = O(2^n)$$

18.3 Examples: Determining Big O

This section gives several examples of determining Big O for repetition, sequence, and selection statements.

Example 1

Consider the time complexity for the following loop:

```
for (i = 1; i <= n; i++)
{
  k = k + 5;
}
```

It is a constant time, c, for executing

```
k = k + 5;
```

Since the loop is executed n times, the time complexity for the loop is

$$T(n) = (\text{a constant } c) * n = O(n).$$

Example 2

What is the time complexity for the following loop?

```
for (i = 1; i <= n; i++)
{
  for (j = 1; j <= n; j++)
  {
    k = k + i + j;
  }
}
```

It is a constant time, c, for executing

```
k = k + i + j;
```

The outer loop executes n times. For each iteration in the outer loop, the inner loop is executed n times. So, the time complexity for the loop is

$$T(n) = (\text{a constant } c) * n * n = O(n^2)$$

quadratic time

An algorithm with the $O(n^2)$ time complexity is called a *quadratic algorithm*. The quadratic algorithm grows quickly as the problem size increases. If you double the input size, the time for the algorithm is quadrupled. Algorithms with a nested loop are often quadratic.

Example 3

Consider the following loop:

```
for (i = 1; i <= n; i++)
{
  for (j = 1; j <= i; j++)
  {
    k = k + i + j;
  }
}
```

The outer loop executes n times. For $i = 1, 2, \ldots$, the inner loop is executed one time, two times, and n times. So, the time complexity for the loop is

$$T(n) = c + 2c + 3c + 4c + \ldots + nc = cn(n + 1)/2 = (c/2)n^2 + (c/2)n = O(n^2)$$

Example 4

Consider the following loop:

```
for (i = 1; i <= n; i++)
{
  for (j = 1; j <= 20; j++)
  {
    k = k + i + j;
  }
}
```

The inner loop executes 20 times, and the outer loop n times. So, the time complexity for the loop is

$$T(n) = 20 * c * n = O(n)$$

Example 5

Consider the following sequences:

```
for (j = 1; j <= 10; j++)
{
  k = k + 4;
}

for (i = 1; i <= n; i++)
{
  for (j = 1; j <= 20; j++)
  {
    k = k + i + j;
  }
}
```

The first loop executes 10 times, and the second loop $20 * n$ times. So, the time complexity for the loop is

$$T(n) = 10 * c + 20 * c * n = O(n)$$

Example 6

Consider the computation of a^n for an integer n. A simple algorithm would multiply a n times, as follows:

```
result = 1;
for (int i = 1; i <= n; i++)
  result *= a;
```

The algorithm takes $O(n)$ time. Without loss of generality, assume $n = 2^k$. You can improve the algorithm using the following scheme:

```
result = a;
for (int i = 1; i <= k; i++)
  result = result * result;
```

The algorithm takes $O(\log n)$ time. For an arbitrary n, you can revise the algorithm and prove that the complexity is still $O(\log n)$ (Review Question 18.7).

Note

For simplicity, since $O(\log n) = O(\log_2 n) = O(\log_a n)$, the constant base is omitted.

omitting base

18.4 Analyzing Algorithm Time Complexity

You have used many algorithms in this book. This section will analyze the complexity of several well-known algorithms: binary search, selection sort, insertion sort, and Towers of Hanoi.

18.4.1 Analyzing Binary Search

The binary search algorithm presented in Listing 7.9, BinarySearch.h, searches a key in a sorted array. Each iteration in the algorithm contains a fixed number of operations, denoted by c. Let $T(n)$ denote the time complexity for a binary search on a list of n elements. Without loss of generality, assume n is a power of 2 and $k = \log n$. Since binary search eliminates half of the input after two comparisons,

$$T(n) = T\left(\frac{n}{2}\right) + c = T\left(\frac{n}{2^2}\right) + c + c = T\left(\frac{n}{2^k}\right) + kc$$

$$= T(1) + c \log n = 1 + (\log n)c$$

$$= O(\log n)$$

Ignoring constants and nondominating terms, the complexity of the binary search algorithm is $O(\log n)$. An algorithm with the $O(\log n)$ time complexity is called a *logarithmic algorithm*. The base of the log is 2, but the base does not affect a logarithmic growth rate, so it can be omitted. The logarithmic algorithm grows slowly as the problem size increases. If you square the input size, you only double the time for the algorithm.

logarithmic time

18.4.2 Analyzing Selection Sort

The selection sort algorithm presented in Listing 7.10, SelectionSort.h, finds the smallest number in the list and places it first. It then finds the smallest number remaining and places it next to first, and so on until the list contains only a single number. The number of comparisons is $n - 1$ for the first iteration, $n - 2$ for the second iteration, and so on. Let $T(n)$ denote the complexity for selection sort and c denote the total number of other operations such as assignments and additional comparisons in each iteration. So,

$$T(n) = (n - 1) + c + (n - 2) + c + \ldots + 2 + c + 1 + c$$

$$= \frac{(n - 1)(n - 1 + 1)}{2} + c(n - 1) = \frac{n^2}{2} - \frac{n}{2} + cn - c$$

$$= O(n^2)$$

Therefore, the complexity of the selection sort algorithm is $O(n^2)$.

18.4.3 Analyzing Insertion Sort

The insertion sort algorithm presented in Listing 7.11, InsertionSort.h, sorts a list of values by repeatedly inserting a new element into a sorted partial array until the whole array is sorted. At the kth iteration, to insert an element into an array of size k, it may take k comparisons to find the insertion position, and k moves to insert the element. Let $T(n)$ denote the complexity for insertion sort and c denote the total number of other operations such as assignments and additional comparisons in each iteration. So,

$$T(n) = (2 + c) + (2 \times 2 + c) + \ldots + (2 \times (n - 1) + c)$$

$$= 2(1 + 2 + \ldots + n - 1) + c(n - 1)$$

$$= 2\frac{(n - 1)n}{2} + cn - c = n^2 - n + cn - c$$

$$= O(n^2)$$

Therefore, the complexity of the insertion sort algorithm is $O(n^2)$. So, the selection sort and insertion sort are of the same time complexity.

18.4.4 Analyzing the Towers of Hanoi Problem

The Towers of Hanoi problem presented in Listing 17.7, TowersOfHanoi.cpp, moves n disks from tower A to tower B with the assistance of tower C recursively as follows:

1. Move the first $n - 1$ disks from A to C with the assistance of tower B.

2. Move disk n from A to B.

3. Move $n - 1$ disks from C to B with the assistance of tower A.

Let $T(n)$ denote the complexity for the algorithm that moves n disks and c denote the constant time to move one disk; i.e., $T(1)$ is c. So,

$$T(n) = T(n - 1) + c + T(n - 1)$$

$$= 2T(n - 1) + c$$

$$= 2(2T(n - 2) + c) + c$$

$$= 2(2(2T(n - 3) + c) + c) + c$$

$$= 2^{n-1} T(1) + 2^{n-2} c + \ldots + 2c + c$$

$$= 2^{n-1} c + 2^{n-2} c + \ldots + 2c + c = (2^n - 1)c = O(2^n)$$

An algorithm with $O(2^n)$ time complexity is called an *exponential algorithm*. As the input size increases, the time for the exponential algorithm grows exponentially. Exponential algorithms are not practical for large input size.

$O(2^n)$
exponential time

18.4.5 Comparing Common Growth Functions

The preceding sections analyzed the complexity of several algorithms. Table 18.2 lists some common growth functions and shows how growth rates change as the input size doubles from $n = 25$ to $n = 50$.

TABLE 18.2   Change of Growth Rates

Function	Name	$n = 25$	$n = 50$	$f(50)/f(25)$
$O(1)$	Constant time	1	1	1
$O(\log n)$	Logarithmic time	4.64	5.64	1.21
$O(n)$	Linear time	25	50	2
$O(n\log n)$	Log-linear time	116	282	2.43
$O(n^2)$	Quadratic time	625	2500	4
$O(n^3)$	Cubic time	15625	125000	8
$O(2^n)$	Exponential time	3.36×10^7	1.27×10^{15}	3.35×10^7

These functions are ordered as follows, as illustrated in Figure 18.1.

$$O(1) < O(\log n) < O(n) < O(n \log n) < O(n^2) < O(n^3) < O(2^n)$$

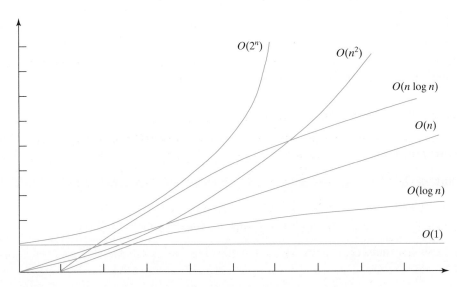

FIGURE 18.1   As the size n increases, the function grows.

18.5 Case Studies: Finding Fibonacci Numbers

§17.3, "Problem: Computing Fibonacci Numbers," gave a recursive function for finding the Fibonacci number, as follows:

Video Note
Algorithms for finding Fibonacci numbers

```
/** The function for finding the Fibonacci number */
long fib(long index)
```

```
    {
      if (index == 0) // Base case
        return 0;
      else if (index == 1) // Base case
        return 1;
      else  // Reduction and recursive calls
        return fib(index - 1) + fib(index - 2);
    }
```

We can now prove that the complexity of this algorithm is $O(2^n)$. For convenience, let the index be n. Let $T(n)$ denote the complexity for the algorithm that finds fib(n) and c denote the constant time for comparing the index with 0 and 1; i.e., $T(1)$ is c. So,

$$T(n) = T(n - 1) + T(n - 2) + c$$

$$\leq 2T(n - 1) + c$$

$$\leq 2(2T(n - 2) + c) + c$$

$$= 2^2\, T(n - 2) + 2c + c$$

Similar to the analysis of the Towers of Hanoi problem, we can show that $T(n)$ is $O(2^n)$.

This algorithm is not efficient. Is there an efficient algorithm for finding a Fibonacci number? The trouble in the recursive `fib` function is that it is invoked redundantly with the same arguments. For example, to compute `fib(4)`, `fib(3)` and `fib(2)` are invoked. To compute `fib(3)`, `fib(2)` and `fib(1)` are invoked. Note that `fib(2)` is redundantly invoked. We can improve the procedure by avoiding repeated calling of the `fib` function with the same argument. Note that a new Fibonacci number is obtained by adding the preceding two numbers in the sequence. If you use two variables `f0` and `f1` to store the two preceding numbers, the new number can be immediately obtained by adding `f0` with `f1`. Now you should update `f0` and `f1` by assigning `f1` to `f0` and assigning the new number to `f1`. The new function is presented in Listing 18.1.

LISTING 18.1 ImprovedFibonacci.cpp

```
 1 #include <iostream>
 2 using namespace std;
 3
 4 // The function for finding the Fibonacci number
 5 int fib(int);
 6
 7 int main()
 8 {
 9   // Prompt the user to enter an integer
10   cout <<  "Enter an index for the Fibonacci number: ";
11   int index;
12   cin >> index;
13
14   // Display factorial
15   cout << "Fibonacci number at index " << index << " is "
16     << fib(index) << endl;
17
18   return 0;
19 }
20
21 // The function for finding the Fibonacci number
22 int fib(int n)
23 {
24   if (n == 0 || n == 1)
```

input

invoke **fib**

simple case

```
25       return n;
26
27    long f0 = 0; // For fib(0)
28    long f1 = 1; // For fib(1)
29    long currentFib = 1; // For fib(2)
30
31    for (int i = 2; i <= n; i++)
32    {
33      currentFib = f0 + f1;
34      f0 = f1;
35      f1 = currentFib;
36    }
37
38    return currentFib;
39 }
```

f0
f1

get a new **fib**

```
Enter an index for the Fibonacci number: 6 ↵Enter
Fibonacci number at index 6 is 8
```

```
Enter an index for the Fibonacci number: 7 ↵Enter
Fibonacci number at index 7 is 13
```

Obviously, the complexity of this new algorithm is $O(n)$. This is a tremendous improvement over the recursive $O(2^n)$ algorithm.

$O(n)$

18.6 Case Studies: Finding Greatest Common Divisors

This section presents several algorithms, seeking an efficient one for finding the greatest common divisor between two integers.

Video Note
Algorithms for finding GCD

GCD

The greatest common divisor of two integers is the largest number that can evenly divide both integers. Listing 4.8, GreatestCommonDivisor.cpp, presented a brute-force algorithm for finding the greatest common divisor (gcd) of two integers m and n. The algorithm checks whether k (for k = 2, 3, 4, and so on) is a common divisor for n1 and n2, until k is greater than n1 or n2. The algorithm can be described as follows:

```
int gcd(int m, int n)
{
  int gcd = 1;

  for (int k = 2; k <= m && k <= n; k++)
  {
    if (m % k == 0 && n % k == 0)
      gcd = k;
  }

  return gcd;
}
```

Assume $m \geq n$, the complexity of this algorithm is obviously $O(n)$.

Is there any better algorithm for finding the gcd? Rather than searching for a possible divisor from 1 up, it is more efficient to search from n down. Once a divisor is found, it is the gcd. So, you can improve the algorithm using the following loop:

$O(n)$
assume $m \geq n$

improved solutions

```
for (int k = n; k >= 1; k--)
{
  if (m % k == 0 && n % k == 0)
```

```
        {
          gcd = k;
          break;
        }
    }
```

This algorithm is better than the preceding one, but its worst-case time complexity is still $O(n)$.

A divisor for a number n cannot be greater than n / 2. So you can further improve the algorithm using the following loop:

```
    for (int k = n / 2; k >= 1; k--)
    {
      if (m % k == 0 && n % k == 0)
      {
        gcd = k;
        break;
      }
    }
```

However, this algorithm is incorrect, because n can be a divisor for m. This case must be considered. The correct algorithm is shown in Listing 18.2.

LISTING 18.2   GCD1.cpp

```
 1 #include <iostream>
 2 using namespace std;
 3
 4 /** Return the gcd of two integers */
 5 int gcd(int m, int n)
 6 {
 7   int gcd = 1;
 8
 9   if (m % n == 0) return n;
10
11   for (int k = n / 2; k >= 1; k--)
12   {
13     if (m % k == 0 && n % k == 0)
14     {
15       gcd = k;
16       break;
17     }
18   }
19
20   return gcd;
21 }
22
23 int main()
24 {
25   // Prompt the user to enter two integers
26   cout << "Enter first integer: ";
27   int n1;
28   cin >> n1;
29
30   cout << "Enter second integer: ";
31   int n2;
32   cin >> n2;
33
34   cout << "The greatest common divisor for " << n1 <<
```

check divisor (line 13)

gcd found (line 15)

input (line 27)

input (line 31)

```
35      " and " << n2 << " is " << gcd(n1, n2);
36
37    return 0;
38 }
```

```
Enter first integer: 2525 ↵Enter
Enter second integer: 125 ↵Enter
The greatest common divisor for 2525 and 125 is 25
```

```
Enter first integer: 3 ↵Enter
Enter second integer: 3 ↵Enter
The greatest common divisor for 3 and 3 is 3
```

Assuming $m \geq n$, the **for** loop is executed at most n/2 times, which cuts the time by half from the previous algorithm. The time complexity of this algorithm is still $O(n)$, but practically, it is much faster than the algorithm in Listing 4.8.

O(n)

 Note

The Big *O* notation provides a good theoretical estimate of algorithm efficiency. However, two algorithms of the same time complexity are not necessarily equally efficient. As shown in the preceding example, both algorithms in Listings 4.8 and 18.2 have the same complexity, but in practice the one in Listing 18.2 is obviously better.

practical consideration

A more efficient algorithm for finding gcd was discovered by Euclid around 300 B.C. This is one of the oldest known algorithms. It can be described recursively as follows:

improved solutions

Let `gcd(m, n)` denote the gcd for integers `m` and `n`:

■ If `m % n` is 0, `gcd (m, n)` is `n`.

■ Otherwise, `gcd(m, n)` is `gcd(n, m % n)`.

It is not difficult to prove the correctness of the algorithm. Suppose `m % n = r`. So, `m = qn + r`, where `q` is the quotient of `m / n`. Any number that is divisible by `m` and `n` must also be divisible by `r`. Therefore, `gcd(m, n)` is same as `gcd(n, r)`, where `r = m % n`. The algorithm can be implemented as in Listing 18.3.

LISTING 18.3 GCD2.cpp

```cpp
1 #include <iostream>
2 using namespace std;
3
4 /** Return the gcd of two integers */
5 int gcd(int m, int n)
6 {
7   if (m % n == 0)
8     return n;
9   else
10     return gcd(n, m % n);
11 }
12
13 int main()
14 {
15   // Prompt the user to enter two integers
16   cout << "Enter first integer: ";
17   int n1;
18   cin >> n1;
```

base case

reduction

input

input

invoke **gcd**

```
19
20    cout << "Enter second integer: ";
21    int n2;
22    cin >> n2;
23
24    cout << "The greatest common divisor for " << n1 <<
25        " and " << n2 << " is " << gcd(n1, n2) << endl;
26
27    return 0;
28 }
```

```
Enter first integer: 2525  ↵Enter
Enter second integer: 125  ↵Enter
The greatest common divisor for 2525 and 125 is 25
```

```
Enter first integer: 3  ↵Enter
Enter second integer: 3  ↵Enter
The greatest common divisor for 3 and 3 is 3
```

best case
average case
worst case

In the best case when m % n is 0, the algorithm takes just one step to find the gcd. It is difficult to analyze the average case. However, we can prove that the worst-case time complexity is $O(\log n)$.

Assuming $m \geq n$, we can show that m % n < m / 2, as follows:

- If n <= m / 2, m % n < m / 2, since the remainder of m divided by n is always less than n.

- If n > m / 2, m % n = m – n < m / 2. Therefore, m % n < m / 2.

Euclid's algorithm recursively invokes the **gcd** function. It first calls gcd(m, n), then calls gcd(n, m % n), and gcd(m % n, n % (m % n)), and so on, as follows:

```
    gcd(m, n)
=   gcd(n, m % n)
=   gcd(m % n, n % (m % n))
=   ...
```

Since m % n < m / 2 and n % (m % n) < n / 2, the argument passed to the gcd function is reduced by half after every two iterations. After invoking gcd two times, the second parameter is less than $n/2$. After invoking gcd four times, the second parameter is less than $n/4$. After invoking gcd six times, the second parameter is less than $\frac{n}{2^3}$. Let k be the number of times the gcd function is invoked. After invoking gcd k times, the second parameter is less than $\frac{n}{2^{(k/2)}}$, which is greater than or equal to 1. That is,

$$\frac{n}{2^{(k/2)}} \geq 1 \quad => \quad n \geq 2^{(k/2)} \quad => \quad \log n \geq k/2 \quad => \quad k \leq 2 \log n$$

Therefore, $k \leq 2 \log n$. So, the time complexity of the gcd function is $O(\log n)$.

The worst case occurs when the two numbers result in most divisions. It turns out that two successive Fibonacci numbers will result in most divisions. Recall that the Fibonacci series begins with 0 and 1, and each subsequent number is the sum of the preceding two numbers in the series:

$$0 \quad 1 \quad 1 \quad 2 \quad 3 \quad 5 \quad 8 \quad 13 \quad 21 \quad 34 \quad 55 \quad 89 \quad \cdots$$

The series can be recursively defined as

```
fib(0) = 0;
fib(1) = 1;
fib(index) = fib(index - 2) + fib(index - 1); index >= 2
```

For two successive Fibonacci numbers `fib(index)` and `fib(index -1)`,

```
gcd(fib(index), fib(index - 1))
= gcd(fib(index - 1), fib(index - 2))
= gcd(fib(index - 2), fib(index - 3))
= gcd(fib(index - 3), fib(index - 4))
= ...
= gcd(fib(2), fib(1))
= 1
```

For example,

```
gcd(21, 13)
= gcd(13, 8)
= gcd(8, 5)
= gcd(5, 3)
= gcd(3, 2)
= gcd(2, 1)
= 1
```

So, the number of times the gcd function is invoked is the same as the index. We can prove that *index* $\leq 1.44 \log n$, where `n` = `fib(index - 1)`. This is a tighter bound than *index* $\leq 2 \log n$.

Table 18.3 summarizes the complexity of three algorithms for finding the gcd:

TABLE 18.3 Comparisons of GCD Algorithms

	Listing 4.8	Listing 18.2	Listing 18.3
Complexity	$O(n)$	$O(n)$	$O(\log n)$

18.7 Case Studies: Finding Prime Numbers

A $100,000 award awaits the first individual or group that discovers a prime number with at least 10,000,000 decimal digits (www.eff.org/awards/coop.php). This section presents several algorithms in the search for an efficient algorithm for finding the prime numbers.

An integer greater than 1 is *prime* if its only positive divisor is 1 or itself. For example, 2, 3, 5, and 7 are prime numbers, but 4, 6, 8, and 9 are not.

what is prime?

How do you determine whether a number n is prime? Listing 4.14 presented a brute-force algorithm for finding prime numbers. The algorithm checks whether 2, 3, 4, 5, . . ., or n - 1 is divisible by n. If not, n is prime. This algorithm takes $O(n)$ time to check whether n is prime. Note that you need only check whether 2, 3, 4, 5, . . ., or n/2 is divisible by n. If not, n is prime. The algorithm is slightly improved, but it is still of the order of $O(n)$.

In fact, we can prove that if n is not a prime, n must have a factor that is greater than 1 and less than or equal to $\sqrt{n}$. Here is the proof. Since n is not a prime, there exist two numbers p and q such that n = pq with $1 \leq p \leq q$. Note that $n = \sqrt{n}\sqrt{n}$. p must be less than or equal to $\sqrt{n}$. Hence, you need only check whether 2, 3, 4, 5, . . ., or $\sqrt{n}$ is divisible by n. If not, n is prime. This significantly reduces the time complexity of the algorithm to $O(\sqrt{n})$.

Now consider the algorithm for finding all the prime numbers up to n. A straightforward implementation is to check whether i is prime for i = 2, 3, 4, . . ., n. The program is given in Listing 18.4.

LISTING 18.4 PrimeNumbers.cpp

```cpp
 1 #include <iostream>
 2 #include <cmath>
 3 using namespace std;
 4
 5 int main()
 6 {
 7   cout << "Find all prime numbers <= n, enter n: ";
 8   int n;
 9   cin >> n;
10
11   const int NUMBER_PER_LINE = 10; // Display 10 per line
12   int count = 0; // Count the number of prime numbers
13   int number = 2; // A number to be tested for primeness
14
15   cout << "The prime numbers are:" << endl;
16
17   // Repeatedly find prime numbers
18   while (number <= n)
19   {
20     // Assume the number is prime
21     bool isPrime = true; // Is the current number prime?
22
23     // Test if number is prime
24     for (int divisor = 2; divisor <= sqrt(number * 1.0); divisor++)
25     {
26       if (number % divisor == 0)
27       { // If true, number is not prime
28         isPrime = false; // Set isPrime to false
29         break; // Exit the for loop
30       }
31     }
32
33     // Print the prime number and increase the count
34     if (isPrime)
35     {
36       count++; // Increase the count
37
38       if (count % NUMBER_PER_LINE == 0)
39       {
40         // Print the number and advance to the new line
41         cout << number << endl;
42       }
43       else
44         cout << number << " ";
45     }
46
47     // Check whether the next number is prime
48     number++;
49   }
50
51   cout << "\n" << count << " number of primes <= " << n << endl;
52
53   return 0;
54 }
```

check prime — line 21

increase count — line 36

check next number — line 48

```
Find all prime numbers <= n, enter n: 1000  ↵Enter
The prime numbers are:
       2       3       5       7      11      13      17      19      23      29
      31      37      41      43      47      53      59      61      67      71
...
...
168 number of primes <= 1000
```

The program is not efficient if you have to compute `Math.sqrt(number)` for every iteration of the for loop (line 21). A good compiler should evaluate `Math.sqrt(number)` only once for the entire for loop. To make sure this happens, you may explicitly replace line 21 by the following two lines:

```
int squareRoot = sqrt(number * 1.0);
for (int divisor = 2; divisor <= squareRoot; divisor++)
```

In fact, there is no need to actually compute `Math.sqrt(number)` for every `number`. You need only look for the perfect squares such as 4, 9, 16, 25, 36, 49, and so on. Note that for all the numbers between 36 and 48, their `(int)(Math.sqrt(number))` is 6. With this insight, you can replace the code in lines 18–31 with the following code:

```
...
int squareRoot = 1;

// Repeatedly find prime numbers
while (number <= n)
{
  // Assume the number is prime
  boolean isPrime = true; // Is the current number prime?

  if (squareRoot * squareRoot < number) squareRoot++;

  // Test whether number is prime
  for (int divisor = 0; divisor <= squareRoot; divisor++)
  {
    if (number % divisor == 0) // If true, number is not prime
    {
      isPrime = false; // Set isPrime to false
      break; // Exit the for loop
    }
  }
}
...
```

Now we turn our attention to analyzing the complexity of this program. Since it takes $\sqrt{i}$ steps in the for loop (lines 21–26) to check whether number i is prime, the algorithm takes $\sqrt{2} + \sqrt{3} + \sqrt{4} + \ldots + \sqrt{n}$ steps to find all the prime numbers less than or equal to n. Observe that

$$\sqrt{2} + \sqrt{3} + \sqrt{4} + \ldots + \sqrt{n} \leq n\sqrt{n}$$

Therefore, the time complexity for this algorithm is $O(n\sqrt{n})$.

To determine whether i is prime, the algorithm checks whether 2, 3, 4, 5, ..., and $\sqrt{i}$ is divisible by i. This algorithm can be further improved. In fact, you need only check whether the prime numbers from 2 to $\sqrt{i}$ are possible divisors for i.

We can prove that if i is not prime, there must exist a prime number p such that $i = pq$ and $p \leq q$. Here is the proof. Assume that i is not prime; let p be the smallest factor of i. p must be prime, otherwise, p has a factor k with $2 \leq k < p$. k is also a factor of i, which contradicts that p be the smallest factor of i. Therefore, if i is not prime, you can find a prime number from 2 to $\sqrt{i}$ that is divisible by i. This leads to a more efficient algorithm for finding all prime numbers up to n, as shown in Listing 18.5.

LISTING 18.5 EfficientPrimeNumbers.cpp

```cpp
 1 #include <iostream>
 2 #include <cmath>
 3 #include <vector>
 4 using namespace std;
 5
 6 int main()
 7 {
 8   cout << "Find all prime numbers <= n, enter n: ";
 9   int n;
10   cin >> n;
11
12   const int NUMBER_PER_LINE = 10; // Display 10 per line
13   int count = 0; // Count the number of prime numbers
14   int number = 2; // A number to be tested for primeness
15   // A vector to hold prime numbers
16   vector<int> primeVector;
17   int squareRoot = 1; // Check whether number <= squareRoot
18
19   cout << "The prime numbers are:"  << endl;
20
21   // Repeatedly find prime numbers
22   while (number <= n)
23   {
24     // Assume the number is prime
25     bool isPrime = true; // Is the current number prime?
26
27     if (squareRoot * squareRoot < number) squareRoot++;
28
29     // Test if number is prime
30     for (int k = 0; k < primeVector.size()
31                 && primeVector.at(k) <= squareRoot; k++)
32     {
33       if (number % primeVector.at(k) == 0) // If true, not prime
34       {
35         isPrime = false; // Set isPrime to false
36         break; // Exit the for loop
37       }
38     }
39
40     // Print the prime number and increase the count
41     if (isPrime)
42     {
43       count++; // Increase the count
44       primeVector.push_back(number); // Add a new prime to the list
45       if (count % NUMBER_PER_LINE == 0)
46       {
47         // Print the number and advance to the new line
```

check prime

increase count

```
48            cout << number << endl;
49          }
50        else
51            cout << number << " ";
52      }
53
54      // Check if the next number is prime
55      number++;
56    }
57
58    cout << "\n" << count << " number of primes <= " << n << endl;
59    return 0;
60 }
```

check next number

```
Find all prime numbers <= n, enter n: 1000  ↵Enter
The prime numbers are:
         2        3        5        7       11       13       17       19       23       29
        31       37       41       43       47       53       59       61       67       71
...
...
168 number of primes <= 1000
```

Let $\pi(i)$ denote the number of prime numbers less than or equal to i. The primes under **20** are **2, 3, 5, 7, 11, 13, 17,** and **18**. So, $\pi(2)$ is **1**, $\pi(3)$ is **2**, $\pi(6)$ is **3**, and $\pi(20)$ is **8**. It has been proved that $\pi(i)$ is approximately $\dfrac{i}{\log i}$ (see primes.utm.edu/howmany.shtml).

For each number **i**, the algorithm checks whether a prime number less than or equal to $\sqrt{i}$ is divisible by i. The number of prime numbers less than or equal to $\sqrt{i}$ is $\dfrac{\sqrt{i}}{\log \sqrt{i}} = \dfrac{2\sqrt{i}}{\log i}$. Thus, the complexity for finding all prime numbers up to n is

$$\frac{2\sqrt{2}}{\log 2} + \frac{2\sqrt{3}}{\log 3} + \frac{2\sqrt{4}}{\log 4} + \frac{2\sqrt{5}}{\log 5} + \frac{2\sqrt{6}}{\log 6} + \frac{2\sqrt{7}}{\log 7} + \frac{2\sqrt{8}}{\log 8} + \dots + \frac{2\sqrt{n}}{\log n}$$

Since $\dfrac{\sqrt{i}}{\log i} < \dfrac{\sqrt{n}}{\log n}$ for $i < n$ and $n \geq 16$,

$$\frac{2\sqrt{2}}{\log 2} + \frac{2\sqrt{3}}{\log 3} + \frac{2\sqrt{4}}{\log 4} + \frac{2\sqrt{5}}{\log 5} + \frac{2\sqrt{6}}{\log 6} + \frac{2\sqrt{7}}{\log 7} + \frac{2\sqrt{8}}{\log 8} + \dots + \frac{2\sqrt{n}}{\log n}$$

$$< \frac{2n\sqrt{n}}{\log n}$$

Therefore, the complexity of this algorithm is $O\left(\dfrac{n\sqrt{n}}{\log n}\right)$.

Is there an algorithm that is better than $O\left(\dfrac{n\sqrt{n}}{\log n}\right)$? Let us examine the well-known Eratosthenes algorithm for finding prime numbers. Eratosthenes (276–194 B.C.) was a Greek mathematician who devised a clever algorithm, known as the *Sieve of Eratosthenes*, for finding all prime numbers $\leq n$. His algorithm is to use an array named **primes** of n Boolean values. Initially, all elements in **primes** are set **true**. Since the multiples of **2** are not prime,

Sieve of Eratosthenes

set `primes[2 * i]` to `false` for all $2 \le i \le n/2$, as shown in Figure 18.2. Since we don't care about `primes[0]` and `primes[1]`, these values are marked $\times$ in the figure.

primes array

index	0	1	2	3	4	5	6	7	8	9	10	11	12	13	14	15	16	17	18	19	20	21	22	23	24	25	26	27
initial	×	×	T	T	T	T	T	T	T	T	T	T	T	T	T	T	T	T	T	T	T	T	T	T	T	T	T	T
$k = 2$	×	×	T	T	F	T	F	T	F	T	F	T	F	T	F	T	F	T	F	T	F	T	F	T	F	T	F	T
$k = 3$	×	×	T	T	F	T	F	T	F	F	F	T	F	T	F	F	F	T	F	T	F	F	F	T	F	T	F	F
$k = 5$	×	×	Ⓣ	Ⓣ	F	Ⓣ	F	Ⓣ	F	F	F	Ⓣ	F	Ⓣ	F	F	F	Ⓣ	F	Ⓣ	F	F	F	Ⓣ	F	F	F	F

FIGURE 18.2 The values in `primes` are changed with each prime number `k`.

Since the multiples of 3 are not prime, set `primes[3 * i]` to `false` for all $3 \le i \le n/3$. Since the multiples of 5 are not prime, set `primes[5 * i]` to `false` for all $5 \le i \le n/5$. Note that you don't need to consider the multiples of 4, because they are also multiples of 2, which have already been considered. Similarly, multiples of 6, 8, 9 need not be considered. You need only consider the multiples of a prime number `k` = 2, 3, 5, 7, 11, ..., and set the corresponding element in `primes` to `false`. Afterward, if `primes[i]` is still true, then `i` is a prime number. As shown in Figure 18.2, 2, 3, 5, 7, 11, 13, 17, 19, 23 are prime numbers. Listing 18.6 gives the program for finding the prime numbers using the *Sieve of Eratosthenes* algorithm.

LISTING 18.6 SieveOfEratosthenes.cpp

```cpp
1 #include <iostream>
2 using namespace std;
3
4 int main()
5 {
6   cout << "Find all prime numbers <= n, enter n: ";
7   int n;
8   cin >> n;
9
10  bool *primes = new bool[n + 1];    // Prime number sieve
11
12  // Initialize primes[i] to true
13  for (int i = 0; i < n + 1; i++)
14  {
15    primes[i] = true;
16  }
17
18  for (int k = 2; k <= n / k; k++)
19  {
20    if (primes[k])
21    {
22      for (int i = k; i <= n / k; i++)
23      {
24        primes[k * i] = false; // k * i is not prime
25      }
26    }
27  }
28
```

create sieve (line 10)

initialize sieve (line 15)

nonprime (line 24)

```
29   const int NUMBER_PER_LINE = 10; // Display 10 per line
30   int count = 0; // Count the number of prime numbers found so far
31   // Print prime numbers
32   for (int i = 2; i < n + 1; i++)
33   {
34     if (primes[i])
35     {
36       count++;
37       if (count % 10 == 0)
38         cout << i << endl;
39       else
40         cout << i << " ";
41     }
42   }
43
44   cout << "\n" << count << " number of primes <= " << n << endl;
45
46   delete [] primes;                                              delete sieve
47
48   return 0;
49 }
```

```
Find all prime numbers <= n, enter n: 1000  ↵Enter
The prime numbers are:
    2     3     5     7    11    13    17    19    23    29
   31    37    41    43    47    53    59    61    67    71
...
...
168 number of primes <= 1000
```

Note that k <= n / k (line 18). Otherwise, k * i would be greater than n (line 20). What is the time complexity of this algorithm?

For each prime number k (line 20), the algorithm sets primes[k * i] to false (line 24). This is performed n / k - k + 1 times in the for loop (line 22). Thus, the complexity for finding all prime numbers up to n is

$$\frac{n}{2} - 2 + 1 + \frac{n}{3} - 3 + 1 + \frac{n}{5} - 5 + 1 + \frac{n}{7} - 7 + 1 + \frac{n}{11} - 11 + 1 \ldots$$

$$= O\left(\frac{n}{2} + \frac{n}{3} + \frac{n}{5} + \frac{n}{7} + \frac{n}{11} + \ldots\right) < O(n\pi(n))$$

$$= O\left(n\frac{\sqrt{n}}{\log n}\right)$$

This upper bound $O\left(\frac{n\sqrt{n}}{\log n}\right)$ is very loose. The actual time complexity is much better than $O\left(\frac{n\sqrt{n}}{\log n}\right)$. The Sieve of Eratosthenes algorithm is good for a small n such that the array primes can fit in the memory.

Table 18.4 summarizes the complexity of three algorithms for finding all prime numbers up to n.

	Listing 4.14	Listing 18.4	Listing 18.5	Listing 18.6
TABLE 18.4 Comparison of Prime Number Algorithms				
Complexity	$O(n^2)$	$O(n\sqrt{n})$	$O\left(\dfrac{n\sqrt{n}}{\log n}\right)$	$O\left(\dfrac{n\sqrt{n}}{\log n}\right)$

18.8 Case Studies: Closest Pair of Points

Given a set of points, the closest-pair problem is to find the two points that are nearest to each other. §8.6, "Problem: Finding a Closest Pair," presented an intuitive algorithm for finding a closest pair of points. The algorithm computes the distances between all pairs of points and finds the pair with the minimum distance. Clearly, the algorithm takes $O(n^2)$ time. Can you beat this algorithm?

One strategy is to use a divide-and-conquer approach, as described in Listing 18.7:

LISTING 18.7 Algorithm for Finding a Closest Pair

Step 1: Sort the points in increasing order of x-coordinates. For the points with the same x-coordinates, sort on y-coordinates. This results in a sorted list S of points.

Step 2: Divide S into two subsets S_1 and S_2 of the equal size using the midpoint in the sorted list. Let the midpoint be in S_1. Recursively find the closest pair in S_1 and S_2. Let d_1 and d_2 denote the distance of the closest pairs in the two subsets, respectively.

Step 3: Find the closest pair between a point in S_1 and a point in S_2 and denote their distance to be d_3. The closest pair is the one with the distance $\min(d_1, d_2, d_3)$.

Selection sort and insertion sort take $O(n^2)$ time. In Chapter 26, we will introduce merge sort and heap sort. These sorting algorithms take $O(n \log n)$ time. So, Step 1 can be done in $O(n \log n)$ time.

Step 3 can be done in $O(n)$ time. Let $d = \min(d_1, d_2)$. We already know that the closest-pair distance cannot be larger than d. For a point in S_1 and a point in S_2 to form a closest pair in S, the left point must be in **stripL** and the right point in **stripR**, as pictured in Figure 18.3(a).

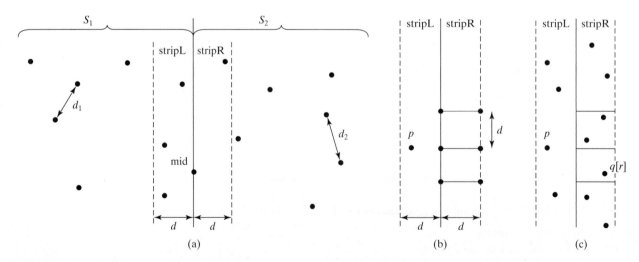

FIGURE 18.3 The midpoint divides the points into two sets of equal size.

Further, for a point p in `stripL`, you need only consider a right point within the $d \times 2d$ rectangle, as shown in Figure 18.3(b). Any right point outside the rectangle cannot form a closest pair with p. Since the closest-pair distance in S_2 is greater than or equal to d, there can be at most six points in the rectangle. So, for each point in `stripL`, at most six points in `stripR` need to be considered.

For each point p in `stripL`, how do you locate the points in the corresponding $d \times 2d$ rectangle area in `stripR`? This can be done efficiently if the points in `stripL` and `stripR` are sorted in increasing order of their y-coordinates. Let `pointsOrderedOnY` be the list of the points presorted in increasing order of y-coordinates. `pointsOrderedOnY` can be obtained beforehand in the algorithm. `stripL` and `stripR` can be obtained from `pointsOrderedOnY` in Step 3 as follows:

LISTING 18.8 Algorithm for obtaining stripL and stripR

```
1 for each point p in pointsOrderedOnY
2   if (p is in S1 and mid.x - p.x <= d)
3     append p to stripL;                                       stripL
4   else if (p is in S2 and p.x - mid.x <= d)
5     append p to stripR;                                       stripR
```

Let the points in `stripL` and `stripR` be $\{p_0, p_1, \dots, p_k\}$ and $\{q_0, q_1, \dots, q_t\}$. A closest pair between a point in `stripL` and a point in `stripR` can be found using the algorithm described in Listing 18.9.

LISTING 18.9 Algorithm for Finding a Closest Pair in Step 3

```
1 d = min(d1, d2);
2 r = 0; // r is the index in stripR
3 for (each point p in stripL)
4 {
5   // Skip the points below the rectangle area
6   while (r < size of stripR && q[r].y <= p.y - d)
7     r++;
8
9   let r1 = r;
10  while (r1 < size of stripR && |q[r1].y - p.y| <= d)
11  {
12    // Check if (p, q[r1]) is a possible closest pair          update closest pair
13    if (distance(p, q[r1]) < d)
14    {
15      d = distance(p, q[r1]);
16      (p, q[r1]) is now the current closed pair;
17    }
18
19    r1 = r1 + 1;
20  }
21 }
```

The points in `stripL` are considered from $p_0, p_1, \dots, p_k$ in this order. For a point `p` in `stripL`, skip the points in `stripR` that are below `p.y` - `d` (lines 6–7). Once a point is skipped, it will no longer be considered. The `while` loop (lines 10–20) checks whether (`p`, `q[r1]`) is a possible closest pair. There are at most six such `q[r1]`'s. So, the complexity for finding a closest pair in Step 3 is $O(n)$.

Let $T(n)$ denote the time complexity for the algorithm. So,

$$T(n) = 2T(n/2) + O(n) = O(n \log n)$$

Therefore, a closest pair of points can be found in $O(n \log n)$ time. The complete implementation of this algorithm is left as an exercise (see Exercise 18.9).

18.9 Preview of Other Algorithms

The examples in this chapter demonstrated how to analyze and design efficient algorithms for several well-known problems. Chapter 19 will introduce efficient algorithms for internal and external sorting. Chapter 20 will introduce efficient algorithms for implementing lists, queues, and priority queues. Chapters 21 and 26 will introduce efficient algorithms for implementing binary search trees, AVL trees, and Splay trees. Chapters 22–23 will introduce STL containers and algorithms. Chapters 24 and 25 will introduce efficient algorithms and data structures for graph problems.

For the algorithms in the rest of the book, we will also analyze their complexities. Recurrence relations are a useful tool for analyzing algorithm complexity. Table 18.5 summarizes the common recurrence relations.

TABLE 18.5 Common Recurrence Relations

Recurrence Relation	Result	Example
$T(n) = T(n/2) + O(1)$	$T(n) = O(\log n)$	Binary search, Euclid's GCD
$T(n) = T(n - 1) + O(1)$	$T(n) = O(n)$	Linear search
$T(n) = 2T(n/2) + O(1)$	$T(n) = O(n)$	
$T(n) = 2T(n/2) + O(n)$	$T(n) = O(n \log n)$	Merge sort (Chapter 19)
$T(n) = 2T(n/2) + O(n \log n)$	$T(n) = O(n \log^2 n)$	
$T(n) = T(n - 1) + O(n)$	$T(n) = O(n^2)$	Selection sort, insertion sort
$T(n) = 2T(n - 1) + O(1)$	$T(n) = O(2^n)$	Towers of Hanoi
$T(n) = T(n - 1) + T(n - 2) + O(1)$	$T(n) = O(2^n)$	Recursive Fibonacci algorithm

KEY TERMS

average-time analysis   566
best-time analysis   566
Big O notation   566
constant time   567
exponential time   571

growth rate   566
logarithmic time   569
quadratic time   568
worst-time analysis   566

CHAPTER SUMMARY

1. The Big O notation is a theoretical approach for analyzing the performance of an algorithm. It estimates how fast an algorithm's execution time increases as the input size increases. So, you can compare two algorithms by examining their *growth rates*.

2. An input that results in the shortest execution time is called the *best-case* input, and an input that results in the longest execution time is called the *worst-case* input.

3. Best case and worst case are not representative, but worst-case analysis is very useful. You can be sure that the algorithm will never be slower than the worst case.

4. An average-case analysis attempts to determine the average amount of time among all possible inputs of the same size.

5. Average-case analysis is ideal, but difficult to perform, because for many problems it is hard to determine the relative probabilities and distributions of various input instances.

6. If the time is not related to the input size, the algorithm is said to take *constant time* with the notation $O(1)$.

7. Linear search takes $O(n)$ time. An algorithm with the $O(n)$ time complexity is called a *linear algorithm.*

8. Binary search takes $O(\log n)$ time. An algorithm with the $O(\log n)$ time complexity is called a *logarithmic algorithm.*

9. The worst-time complexity for selection sort and insertion sort is $O(n^2)$.

10. An algorithm with the $O(n^2)$ time complexity is called a *quadratic algorithm.*

11. The time complexity for the Towers of Hanoi problem is $O(2^n)$.

12. An algorithm with the $O(2^n)$ time complexity is called an *exponential algorithm.*

13. A Fibonacci number at a given index can be found in $O(n)$ time.

14. Euclid's GCD algorithm takes $O(\log n)$ time.

15. All prime numbers less than or equal to n can be found in $O\left(\dfrac{n\sqrt{n}}{\log n}\right)$ time.

REVIEW QUESTIONS

Sections 18.2

18.1   Put the following growth functions in order:

$$\frac{5n^3}{4032}, \quad 44 \log n, \quad 10n \log n, \quad 500, \quad 2n^2, \quad \frac{2^n}{45}, \quad 3n$$

18.2   Count the number of iterations in the following loops.

```
int count = 1;
while (count < 30)
{
    count = count * 2;
}
```
(a)

```
int count = 15;
while (count < 30)
{
    count = count * 3;
}
```
(b)

```
int count = 1;
while (count < n)
{
    count = count * 2;
}
```
(c)

```
int count = 15;
while (count < n)
{
    count = count * 3;
}
```
(d)

18.3   How many stars are displayed in the following code if **n** is **10**? How many if **n** is 20? Use the Big *O* notation to estimate the time complexity.

```
for (int i = 0; i < n; i++)
{
  cout << '*';
}
```

```
for (int i = 0; i < n; i++)
{
  for (int j = 0; j < n; j++)
  {
    cout << '*';
  }
}
```

```
for (int k = 0; k < n; k++)
{
  for (int i = 0; i < n; i++)
  {
    for (int j = 0; j < n; j++)
    {
      cout << '*';
    }
  }
}
```

```
for (int k = 0; k < 10; k++)
{
  for (int i = 0; i < n; i++)
  {
    for (int j = 0; j < n; j++)
    {
      cout << '*';
    }
  }
}
```

18.4   Use the Big *O* notation to estimate the time complexity of the following functions:

```
void mA (int n)
{
  for (int i = 0; i < n; i++)
  {
    cout << rand();
  }
}
```

```
void mB (int n)
{
  for (int i = 0; i < n; i++)
  {
    for (int j = 0; j < i; j++)
      cout << rand();
  }
}
```

```
void mC (int m, int size)
{
  for (int i = 0; i < size; i++)
  {
    cout << m[i];
  }

  for (int i = size - 1; i >= 0; )
  {
    cout << m[i];
    i--;
  }
}
```

```
void mD (int m[], int size)
{
  for (int i = 0; i < size; i++)
  {
    for (int j = 0; j < i; j++)
      cout << m[i] * m[j];
  }
}
```

18.5   Estimate the time complexity for adding two $n \times m$ matrices, and for multiplying an $n \times m$ matrix by an $m \times k$ matrix.

18.6   Analyze the following sorting algorithm:

```
for (int i = 0; i < SIZE; i++)
{
  if (list[i] > list[i + 1])
  {
    swap list[i] with list[i + 1];
    i = 0;
  }
}
```

18.7   Example 7 in §18.3 assumes $n = 2^k$. Revise the algorithm for an arbitrary n and prove that the complexity is still $O(\log n)$.

PROGRAMMING EXERCISES

18.1* (*Maximum consecutive sorted substring*) Write an efficient algorithm to find the maximum consecutive sorted substring in a string. For example, the maximum consecutive sorted substring in `"abacdefkabfh"` is `acdefk`. Analyze the time complexity of your algorithm. Your program should prompt the user to enter a string and display its maximum consecutive sorted substring.

18.2** (*Maximum sorted subsequence*) Write an efficient algorithm to find the maximum sorted subsequence in a string. For example, the maximum sorted subsequence in `"abacdefkabfhxy"` is `acdefkxy`. Analyze the time complexity of your algorithm. Your program should prompt the user to enter a string and display its maximum sorted subsequence.

18.3* (*Pattern matching*) Write an efficient algorithm to check whether a string is in a text. *Assume that all characters in the string are distinct.* Analyze the time complexity of your algorithm. For simplicity, assume that the text is stored in a string, too. Your program should prompt the user to enter two strings; it should display the index of the matching string if the second string is a substring in the first string, otherwise display unmatched.

18.4* (*Pattern matching*) Write an efficient algorithm to check whether a string is in a text. Analyze the time complexity of your algorithm. For simplicity, assume the text is stored in a string, too. Your program should prompt the user to enter two strings; it should display the index of the matching string if the second string is a substring in the first string, otherwise display unmatched.

Video Note
Pattern matching

18.5* (*Execution time for GCD*) Write a program that obtains the execution time for finding the GCD of every two consecutive Fibonacci numbers from index 40 to index 45 using the algorithms in Listings 18.2 and 18.3. Your program should print a table like this:

	40	41	42	43	44	45
Listing 18.2 GCD1						
Listing 18.3 GCD2						

(*Hint*: You can use the following code template to obtain the execution time.)

```
long startTime = time(0);
perform the task;
long endTime = time(0);
long executionTime = endTime - startTime;
```

18.6** (*Execution time for prime numbers*) Write a program that obtains the execution time for finding all the prime numbers less than 8,000,000, 10,000,000, 12,000,000, 14,000,000, 16,000,000, and 18,000,000 using the algorithms in Listings 18.4–18.6. Your program should print a table like this:

	8000000	10000000	12000000	14000000	16000000	18000000
Listing 18.4						
Listing 18.5						
Listing 18.6						

18.7** (*All prime numbers up to* 1,000,000,000) Write a program that finds all prime numbers up to 1,000,000,000. There are approximately 50,847,534 such prime numbers. Your program should meet the following requirements:

- Your program should store the prime numbers in a binary data file, named Exercise18_7.dat. When a new prime number is found, the number is appended to the file.
- To find whether a new number is prime, your program should load the prime numbers from the file to an array of the **long** type of size 100000. If no number in the array is a divisor for the new number, continue to read the next 100000 prime numbers from the data file, until a divisor is found or all numbers in the file are read. If no divisor is found, the new number is prime.
- Since this program takes a long time to finish, you should run it as a batch job from a UNIX machine. If the machine is shut down and rebooted, your program should resume by using the prime numbers stored in the binary data file rather than starting over from the scratch.

18.8 (*Number of prime numbers*) The preceding exercise stores the prime numbers in a file named Exercise18_7.dat. Write a program that finds the number of prime numbers less than or equal to 10, 100, 1,000, 10,000, 100,000, 1,000,000, and 10,000,000. Your program should read the data from Exercise18_7.dat. Note that the data file may continue to grow as more prime numbers are stored to it.

18.9*** (*Closest pair of points*) §18.8 introduced an algorithm for finding a closest pair of points using a divide-and-conquer approach. Implement the algorithm to meet the following requirements:

- Define a class named **Pair** with data fields **p1** and **p2** to represent two points, and a function named **getDistance()** that returns the distance of the two points.
- Implement the following functions:

```
/** Return the closest pair of points */
Pair * getClosestPair(vector<vector<double> > points)
```

```
/** Return the closest pair of points */
Pair * getClosestPair(vector<Point> points)
```

```
/** Return the distance of the closest pair of points
 * in pointsOrderedOnX[low..high]. This is a recursive
 * function. pointsOrderedOnX and pointsOrderedOnY are
 * not changed in the subsequent recursive calls.
 */
double distance(vector<Point> pointsOrderedOnX,
  int low, int high, vector<Point> pointsOrderedOnY)
```

```
/** Return the distance between two points p1 and p2 */
double distance(Point &p1, Point &p2)
```

```
/** Return the distance between points (x1, y1)
   and (x2, y2) */
double distance(double x1, double y1, double x2, double y2)
```

18.10 (*Last 10 prime numbers*) Exercise 18.7 stores the prime numbers in a file named Exercise18_7.dat. Write an efficient program that reads the last 10 numbers in the file. (*Hint*: Don't read every number. Skip all before the last 10 numbers in the file.)

CHAPTER 19

SORTING

Objectives

- To study and analyze time efficiency of various sorting algorithms (§§19.2–19.8).
- To design, implement, and analyze bubble sort (§19.3).
- To design, implement, and analyze merge sort (§19.4).
- To design, implement, and analyze quick sort (§19.5).
- To design, implement, and analyze heap sort (§19.6).
- To design, implement, and analyze bucket sort and radix sort (§19.7).
- To sort large data in a file (§19.8).

19.1 Introduction

why study sorting?

Sorting is a classic subject in computer science. We study sorting algorithms for three reasons. First, they illustrate many creative approaches to problem solving, which can be applied to other problems. Second, they are good for practicing fundamental programming techniques using selection statements, loops, functions, and arrays. Third, they are excellent examples to demonstrate algorithm performance.

what data to sort?

The data to be sorted might be integers, doubles, characters, or any generic element type. In §7.9, "Sorting Arrays," we looked at selection sort and insertion sort for numeric values. In §12.3, "Example: A Generic Sort," the selection sort algorithm was extended to sort an array of the generic element type. For simplicity, the present section assumes:

1. Data to be sorted are integers,

2. Data are sorted in ascending order, and

3. Data are stored in an array.

The programs can be easily modified to sort other types of data, to sort in descending order, or to sort data in a vector or a linked list.

There are many algorithms for sorting. You have already learned selection sort and insertion sort. This chapter introduces bubble sort, merge sort, quick sort, bucket sort, radix sort, and external sort.

 Note
The whole chapter is optional. No chapter in the book depends on this chapter.

19.2 Bubble Sort

The bubble sort algorithm makes several passes through the array. On each pass, successive neighboring pairs are compared. If a pair is in decreasing order, its values are swapped; otherwise, the values remain unchanged. This technique is called a *bubble sort* or *sinking sort*, because the smaller values gradually "bubble" their way to the top and the larger values sink to the bottom. After the first pass, the last element becomes the largest in the array. After the second pass, the second-to-last element becomes the second-largest in the array. The process continues until all the elements are sorted.

bubble sort illustration

Figure 19.1(a) shows the first pass of a bubble sort of an array of six elements (2 9 5 4 8 1). Compare the elements in the first pair (2 and 9), and no swap is needed, because they are already in order. Compare the elements in the second pair (9 and 5), and swap 9 with 5, because 9 is greater than 5. Compare the elements in the third pair (9 and 4), and swap 9 with 4. Compare the elements in the fourth pair (9 and 8), and swap 9 with 8. Compare the elements in the fifth pair (9 and 1), and swap 9 with 1. The pairs being compared are highlighted and the numbers already sorted are italicized.

The first pass places the largest number (9) as the last in the array. The second pass, as shown in Figure 19.1(b), compares and orders pairs of elements sequentially. There is no need

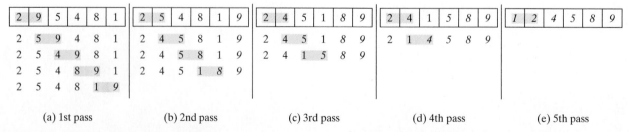

(a) 1st pass   (b) 2nd pass   (c) 3rd pass   (d) 4th pass   (e) 5th pass

FIGURE 19.1   Each pass compares and orders the pairs of elements sequentially.

to consider the last pair, because the last element in the array is already the largest. The third pass, as shown in Figure 19.1(c), compares and orders pairs of elements sequentially, excepting the last two elements, which are already ordered. So in the *k*th pass, there is no need to consider the last $k - 1$ elements, which are already ordered.

The algorithm for bubble sort can be described as follows:

algorithm

LISTING 19.1 Bubble Sort Algorithm

```
1 for (int k = 1; k < arraySize; k++)
2 {
3    // Perform the kth pass
4    for (int i = 0; i < arraySize - k; i++)
5    {
6       if (list[i] > list[i + 1])
7          swap list[i] with list[i + 1];
8    }
9 }
```

Note that if no swap takes place in a pass, there is no need to perform the next pass, because all the elements are already sorted. You may use this property to improve the algorithm, as in Listing 19.2.

LISTING 19.2 Improved Bubble Sort Algorithm

```
1 bool needNextPass = true;
2 for (int k = 1; k < arraySize && needNextPass; k++)
3 {
4    // Array may be sorted and next pass not needed
5    needNextPass = false;
6    // Perform the kth pass
7    for (int i = 0; i < arraySize - k; i++)
8    {
9       if (list[i] > list[i + 1])
10      {
11         swap list[i] with list[i + 1];
12         needNextPass = true; // Next pass still needed
13      }
14   }
15 }
```

The algorithm can be implemented as follows:

LISTING 19.3 BubbleSort.h

```
1 /* The function for sorting the numbers */
2 void bubbleSort(int list[], int arraySize)
3 {
4    bool needNextPass = true;
5
6    for (int k = 1; k < arraySize && needNextPass; k++)
7    {
8       // Array may be sorted and next pass not needed
9       needNextPass = false;
10      for (int i = 0; i < arraySize - k; i++)
11      {
12         if (list[i] > list[i + 1])
13         {
14            // Swap list[i] with list[i + 1]
15            int temp = list[i];
```

```
16              list[i] = list[i + 1];
17              list[i + 1] = temp;
18
19              needNextPass = true; // Next pass still needed
20          }
21      }
22  }
23 }
```

19.2.1 Bubble Sort Time

In the best case, the bubble sort algorithm needs just the first pass to find out that the array is already sorted. No next pass is needed. Since the number of comparisons is $n - 1$ in the first pass, the best-case time for bubble sort is $O(n)$.

In the worst case, the bubble sort algorithm requires $n - 1$ passes. The first pass takes $n - 1$ comparisons, the second pass $n - 2$ comparisons, and so on. The last pass takes one comparison. So, the total number of comparisons is:

$$(n - 1) + (n - 2) + \ldots + 2 + 1$$

$$= \frac{(n - 1)n}{2} = \frac{n^2}{2} - \frac{n}{2} = O(n^2)$$

Therefore, the worst-case time for bubble sort is $O(n^2)$.

19.3 Merge Sort

Video Note
Merge sort

The *merge sort* algorithm can be described recursively as follows. The algorithm divides the array into two halves and applies merge sort on each half recursively. After the two halves are sorted, they are merged. The algorithm is described in Listing 19.4.

LISTING 19.4 Merge Sort Algorithm

base condition

sort first half
sort second half
merge two halves

```
 1 void mergeSort(int list[], int arraySize)
 2 {
 3    if (arraySize > 1)
 4    {
 5      mergeSort on list[0 ... arraySize / 2];
 6      mergeSort on list[arraySize / 2 + 1 ... arraySize]);
 7      merge list[0 ... arraySize / 2] with
 8         list[arraySize / 2 + 1 ... arraySize];
 9    }
10 }
```

merge sort illustration

Figure 19.2 illustrates a merge sort of an array of eight elements (2 9 5 4 8 1 6 7). The original array is split into (2 9 5 4) and (8 1 6 7). Apply merge sort on these two subarrays recursively to split (2 9 5 4) into (2 9) and split (5 4) and (8 1 6 7) into (8 1) and (6 7). This process continues until the subarray contains only one element. For example, array (2 9) is split into subarrays (2) and (9). Since array (2) contains a single element, it cannot be further split. Now merge (2) with (9) into a new sorted array (2 9), merge (5) with (4) into a new sorted array (4 5). Merge (2 9) with (4 5) into a new sorted array (2 4 5 9), and finally merge (2 4 5 9) with (1 6 7 8) into a new sorted array (1 2 4 5 6 7 8 9).

The recursive call continues dividing the array into subarrays until each subarray contains only one element. The algorithm then merges these small subarrays into larger sorted subarrays until one sorted array results. The function for merging two sorted arrays is given in Listing 19.5.

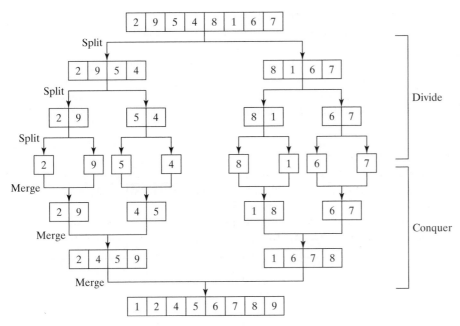

FIGURE 19.2 Merge sort employs a divide-and-conquer approach to sort the array.

LISTING 19.5 Function for Merging Two Arrays

```
1 void merge(int list1[], int list1Size,
2   int list2[], int list2Size, int temp[])
3 {
4   int current1 = 0; // Index in list1
5   int current2 = 0; // Index in list2
6   int current3 = 0; // Index in temp
7
8   while (current1 < list1Size && current2 < list2Size)
9   {
10    if (list1[current1] < list2[current2])
11      temp[current3++] = list1[current1++];          move to temp
12    else
13      temp[current3++] = list2[current2++];          move to temp
14  }
15
16  while (current1 < list1Size)
17    temp[current3++] = list1[current1++];            rest to temp
18
19  while (current2 < list2Size)
20    temp[current3++] = list2[current2++];            rest to temp
21 }
```

This function merges arrays `list1` and `list2` into a new array `temp`. So, the size of `temp` should be `list1Size + list2Size`. `current1` and `current2` point to the current element to be considered in `list1` and `list2` (lines 4–5). The function repeatedly compares the current elements from `list1` and `list2` and moves the smaller one to `temp`. If the smaller one is in `list1`, `current1` is increased by 1 (line 11). If the smaller one is in `list2`, `current2` is increased by 1 (line 13). Finally, all the elements in one of the lists are moved to `temp`. If there are still unmoved elements in `list1`, copy them to `temp` (lines 16–17). If there are still unmoved elements in `list2`, copy them to `temp` (lines 19–20).

Figure 19.3 illustrates how to merge two arrays `list1` (2 4 5 9) and `list2` (1 6 7 8). Initially, the current elements to be considered in the arrays are 2 and 1. Compare them and move the smaller element 1 to `temp`, as shown in Figure 19.3(a). `current2` and `current3` are increased by 1. Continue to compare the current elements in the two arrays and move the smaller one to `temp` until one of the arrays is completely moved. As shown in Figure 19.3(b), all the elements in `list2` are moved to `temp`, and `current1` points to element 9 in `list1`. Copy 9 to `temp`, as shown in Figure 19.3(c).

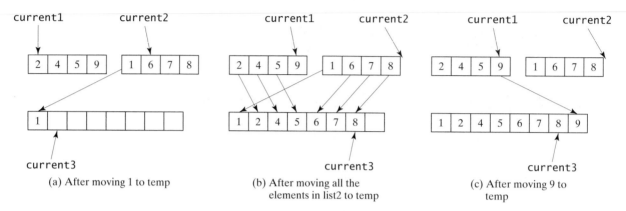

(a) After moving 1 to temp   (b) After moving all the elements in list2 to temp   (c) After moving 9 to temp

FIGURE 19.3 Two sorted arrays are merged into one sorted array.

The merge sort algorithm is implemented in Listing 19.6.

LISTING 19.6 MergeSort.h

```
1  // Function prototype
2  void arraycopy(int source[], int sourceStartIndex,
3    int target[], int targetStartIndex, int length);
4
5  void merge(int list1[], int list1Size,
6    int list2[], int list2Size, int temp[]);
7
8  /* The function for sorting the numbers */
9  void mergeSort(int list[], int arraySize)
10 {
11   if (arraySize > 1)
12   {
13     // Merge sort the first half
14     int *firstHalf = new int[arraySize / 2];
15     arraycopy(list, 0, firstHalf, 0, arraySize / 2);
16     mergeSort(firstHalf, arraySize / 2);
17
18     // Merge sort the second half
19     int secondHalfLength = arraySize - arraySize / 2;
20     int *secondHalf = new int[secondHalfLength];
21     arraycopy(list, arraySize / 2, secondHalf, 0, secondHalfLength);
22     mergeSort(secondHalf, secondHalfLength);
23
24     // Merge firstHalf with secondHalf
25     int *temp = new int[arraySize];
26     merge(firstHalf,  arraySize / 2, secondHalf, secondHalfLength,
27       temp);
28     arraycopy(temp, 0, list, 0, arraySize);
29     delete [] temp;
30     delete [] firstHalf;
```

mergeSort

create **firstHalf**

sort **firstHalf**

create **secondHalf**

sort **secondHalf**

merge two halves

copy to original array
delete

```
31      delete [] secondHalf;
32   }
33 }
34
35 void merge(int list1[], int list1Size,
36    int list2[], int list2Size, int temp[])
37 {
38    // Same as in Listing 19.5, so omitted
39 }
40
41 void arraycopy(int source[], int sourceStartIndex,
42    int target[], int targetStartIndex, int length)
43 {
44    for (int i = 0; i < length; i++)
45    {
46       target[i + targetStartIndex] = source[i + sourceStartIndex];
47    }
48 }
```

The algorithm creates a new array `firstHalf`, which is a copy of the first half of `list` (line 14). The algorithm invokes `mergeSort` recursively on `firstHalf` (line 16). The length of the `firstHalf` is `arraySize / 2` and that of the `secondHalf` is `arraySize - array-Size / 2`. The new array `secondHalf` was created to contain the second part of the original array `list`. The algorithm invokes `mergeSort` recursively on `secondHalf` (line 22). After `firstHalf` and `secondHalf` are sorted, they are merged to become a new sorted array in `temp` (line 26). Finally, `temp` is copied to the original array `list` (line 28). So, array `list` is now sorted.

19.3.1 Merge Sort Time

Let $T(n)$ denote the time required for sorting an array of n elements using merge sort. Without loss of generality, assume n is a power of 2. The merge sort algorithm splits the array into two subarrays, sorts them using the same algorithm recursively, and then merges the subarrays. So,

time analysis

$$T(n) = T\left(\frac{n}{2}\right) + T\left(\frac{n}{2}\right) + mergetime$$

The first $T\left(\frac{n}{2}\right)$ is the time for sorting the first half of the array and the second $T\left(\frac{n}{2}\right)$ is the time for sorting the second half. To merge two subarrays, it takes at most $n - 1$ comparisons to compare the elements from the two subarrays and n moves to move elements to the temporary array. So, the total time is $2n - 1$. Therefore,

$$T(n) = T\left(\frac{n}{2}\right) + T\left(\frac{n}{2}\right) + mergetime$$

$$= 2T\left(\frac{n}{2}\right) + 2n - 1$$

$$= 2\left(2T\left(\frac{n}{4}\right) + 2\frac{n}{2} - 1\right) + 2n - 1$$

$$= 2\left(2\left(2T\left(\frac{n}{8}\right) + 2\frac{n}{4} - 1\right) + 2\frac{n}{2} - 1\right) + 2n - 1$$

$$= 2\left(2\left(2T\left(\frac{n}{2^3}\right) + 2\frac{n}{2^2} - 1\right) + 2\frac{n}{2} - 1\right) + 2n - 1$$

$$= 2^k T\left(\frac{n}{2^k}\right) + 2n - 2^{k-1} + \ldots + 2n - 2 + 2n - 1$$

$$= 2^k T\left(\frac{n}{2^k}\right) + \overbrace{2n + 2n + \ldots + 2n}^{k} - 2^{k-1} + \ldots - 2 - 1$$

$$= 2^k T\left(\frac{n}{2^k}\right) + 2nk - (2^k - 1)$$

$$= 2^{\log n} T(1) + 2n(\log n) - (2^{\log n} - 1)$$

$$= n + 2n \log n - n + 1$$

$$= 2n \log n + 1 = O(n \log n)$$

O(nlogn) merge sort

The complexity of merge sort is $O(nlogn)$. This algorithm is better than selection sort, insertion sort, and bubble sort.

Video Note
Quick sort

19.4 Quick Sort

Quick sort, developed by C. A. R. Hoare (1962), works as follows: Select an element, called the *pivot*, in the array. Divide the array into two parts, such that all the elements in the first part are less than or equal to the pivot, and all the elements in the second part are greater than the pivot. Recursively, apply the quick sort algorithm to the first part and then the second part. The algorithm is described in Listing 19.7.

LISTING 19.7 Quick Sort Algorithm

base condition

select the pivot
partition the list

sort first part
sort second part

```
 1 void quickSort(int list[], int arraySize)
 2 {
 3    if (arraySize > 1)
 4    {
 5      select a pivot;
 6      partition list into list1 and list2 such that
 7        all elements in list1 <= pivot and all elements
 8        in list2 > pivot;
 9      quickSort on list1;
10      quickSort on list2;
11    }
12 }
```

Pivot

| list1 | | list2 |

how to partition

Each partition places the pivot in the right place. The selection of the pivot affects the performance of the algorithm. Ideally, you should choose the pivot that divides the two parts evenly. For simplicity, assume the first element in the array is chosen as the pivot. Exercise 19.4 proposes an alternative strategy for selecting the pivot.

quick sort illustration

Figure 19.4 illustrates how to sort an array (5 2 9 3 8 4 0 1 6 7) using quick sort. Choose the first element 5 as the pivot. The array is partitioned into two parts, as shown in Figure 19.4(b). The highlighted pivot is placed in the right place in the array. Apply quick sort on two partial arrays (4 2 1 3 0) and then (8 9 6 7). The pivot 4 partitions (4 2 1 3 0) into just one partial array (0 2 1 3), as shown in Figure 19.4(c). Apply quick sort on (0 2 1 3). The pivot 0 partitions it to just one partial array (2 1 3), as shown in Figure 19.4(d). Apply quick sort on (2 1 3). The

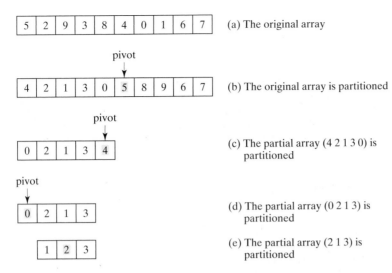

FIGURE 19.4 The quick sort algorithm is recursively applied to partial arrays.

pivot 2 partitions it to (1) and (3), as shown in Figure 19.4(e). Apply quick sort on (1). Since the array contains just one element, no further partition is needed.

Now we turn our attention to partition. To partition an array or a partial array, search for the first element from left forward in the array that is greater than the pivot, then search for the first element from right backward in the array that is less than or equal to the pivot. Swap these two elements. Repeat the same search and swap operations until all the elements are searched. Listing 19.8 gives a function that partitions a partial array `list[first..last]`. The first element in the partial array is chosen as the pivot (line 4). Initially, `low` points to the second element in the partial array, and `high` points to the last element in the partial array. The function returns the new index for the pivot that divides the partial array into two parts.

LISTING 19.8 Partition Function

```
 1  /* Partition the array list[first..last] */
 2  int partition(int list[], int first, int last)
 3  {
 4    int pivot = list[first]; // Choose the first element as the pivot
 5    int low = first + 1; // Index for forward search
 6    int high = last; // Index for backward search
 7
 8    while (high > low)
 9    {
10      // Search forward from left
11      while (low <= high && list[low] <= pivot)              forward
12        low++;
13
14      // Search backward from right
15      while (low <= high && list[high] > pivot)              backward
16        high--;
17
18      // Swap two elements in the list
19      if (high > low)                                        swap
20      {
21        int temp = list[high];
22        list[high] = list[low];
23        list[low] = temp;
24      }
25  }
26
```

```
27   while (high > first && list[high] >= pivot)
28     high--;
29
30     // Swap pivot with list[high]
31   if (pivot > list[high])
32   {
33     list[first] = list[high];
34     list[high] = pivot;
35     return high;
36   }
37   else
38   {
39     return first;
40   }
41 }
```

place pivot

pivot's new index

pivot's new index

partition illustration

Figure 19.5 illustrates how to partition an array (5 2 9 3 8 4 0 1 6 7). Choose the first element 5 as the pivot. Initially, `low` is the index that points to element 2 and `high` points to element 7, as shown in Figure 19.5(a). Advance index `low` forward to search for the first element (9) that is greater than the pivot, and move index `high` backward to search for the first element (1) that is less than or equal to the pivot, as shown in Figure 19.5(b). Swap 9 with 1, as shown in Figure 19.5(c). Continue the search, and move `low` to point to element 8 and `high`

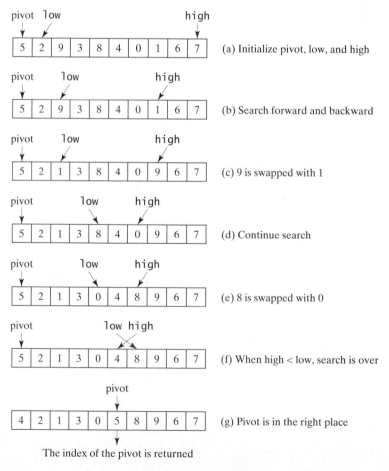

(a) Initialize pivot, low, and high

(b) Search forward and backward

(c) 9 is swapped with 1

(d) Continue search

(e) 8 is swapped with 0

(f) When high < low, search is over

(g) Pivot is in the right place

The index of the pivot is returned

FIGURE 19.5 The partition function returns the index of the pivot after it is put in the right place.

to point to element 0, as shown in Figure 19.5(d). Swap element 8 with 0, as shown in Figure 19.5(e). Continue to move `low` until it passes `high`, as shown in Figure 19.5(f). Now all the elements are examined. Swap the pivot with element 4 at index `high`. The final partition is shown in Figure 19.5(g). The index of the pivot is returned when the function is finished.

The quick sort algorithm is implemented in Listing 19.9 with two overloaded `quickSort` functions. The first function (line 2) is used to sort an array. The second is a helper function (line 6) that sorts a partial array with a specified range.

LISTING 19.9 QuickSort.h

```
 1 // Function prototypes
 2 void quickSort(int list[], int arraySize);
 3 void quickSort(int list[], int first, int last);
 4 int partition(int list[], int first, int last);
 5
 6 void quickSort(int list[], int arraySize)
 7 {
 8   quickSort(list, 0, arraySize - 1);
 9 }
10
11 void quickSort(int list[], int first, int last)
12 {
13   if (last > first)
14   {
15     int pivotIndex = partition(list, first, last);
16     quickSort(list, first, pivotIndex - 1);
17     quickSort(list, pivotIndex + 1, last);
18   }
19 }
20
21 /* Partition the array list[first..last] */
22 int partition(int list[], int first, int last)
23 {
24   // Same as in Listing 19.8, so omitted
25 }
26
```

sort function
helper function
partition function

helper function

call helper function

recursion base

find pivot
recursive call
recursive call

19.4.1 Quick Sort Time

To partition an array of n elements, it takes n comparisons and n moves in the worst case. So, the time required for partition is $O(n)$.

In the worst case, the pivot divides the array each time into one big subarray with the other empty. The size of the big subarray is one less than the one previously divided. The algorithm requires $(n - 1) + (n - 2) + \ldots + 2 + 1 = O(n^2)$ time.

In the best case, the pivot divides the array each time into two parts of about the same size. Let $T(n)$ denote the time required for sorting an array of n elements using quick sort. So,

$O(n)$ partition time
$O(n^2)$ worst-case time

$O(n\log n)$ best-case time

recursive quick sort on subarrays   partition time

$$T(n) = T\left(\frac{n}{2}\right) + T\left(\frac{n}{2}\right) + n.$$

Similar to the merge sort analysis, $T(n) = O(n \log n)$.

On the average, the pivot will not divide the array each time into two parts of the same size or into one empty part. Statistically, the sizes of the two parts will be very close. So the average time is $O(n\log n)$. The exact average-case analysis is beyond the scope of this book.

$O(n\log n)$ average-case time

quick sort vs. merge sort

Both merge sort and quick sort employ the divide-and-conquer approach. For merge sort, the bulk of work is to merge two sublists, which takes place *after* the sublists are sorted. For quick sort, the bulk of work is to partition the list into two sublists, which takes place *before* the sublists are sorted. Merge sort is more efficient than quick sort in the worst case, but in the average case the two are equally efficient. Merge sort requires a temporary array for merging two subarrays. Quick sort does not need additional array space. So, quick sort is more space efficient than merge sort.

19.5 Heap Sort

root
left subtree
right subtree
length
depth

Heap sort uses a binary heap, which is a complete binary tree. A binary tree is a hierarchical structure. It either is empty or consists of an element, called the *root*, and two distinct binary trees, called the *left subtree* and *right subtree*. The *length* of a path is the number of the edges in the path. The *depth* of a node is the length of the path from the root to the node.

A *heap* is a binary tree with the following properties:

- It is a complete binary tree.

- Each node is greater than or equal to any of its children.

complete binary tree

A binary tree is *complete* if each of its levels is full, except that the last level may not be full and all the leaves on the last level are placed leftmost. For example, in Figure 19.6, the binary trees in (a) and (b) are complete, but the binary trees in (c) and (d) are not complete. Further, the binary tree in (a) is a heap, but the binary tree in (b) is not a heap, because the root (39) is less than its right child (42).

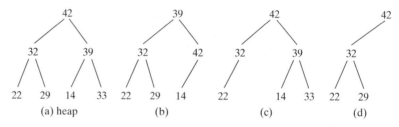

FIGURE 19.6 A heap is a special complete binary tree.

binary tree animation

> **Pedagogical Note**
> A heap can be implemented efficiently for inserting keys and for deleting the root. Follow the link www.cs.armstrong.edu/liang/cpp2e/animation/HeapAnimation.html to see how a heap works, as shown in Figure 19.7.

19.5.1 Representing a Heap

A heap can be stored in a vector or an array if the heap size is known in advance. The heap in Figure 19.8(a) can be represented using an array, as in Figure 19.8(b). The root is at position 0, and its two children are at positions 1 and 2. For a node at position i, its left child is at position $2i + 1$ and its right child at position $2i + 2$, and its parent is $(i - 1)/2$. For example, the node for element 39 is at position 4, so its left child (element 14) is at 9 ($2 \times 4 + 1$), its right child (element 33) is at 10 ($2 \times 4 + 2$), and its parent (element 42) is at 1 ($(4 - 1)/2$).

If the heap size is not known in advance, it is better to use a vector to store a heap.

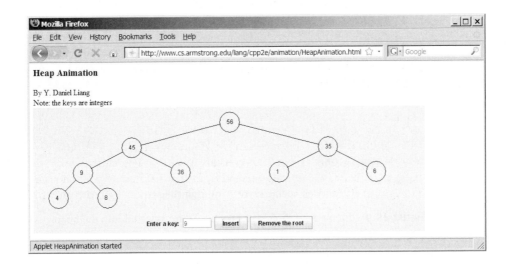

FIGURE 19.7 The animation tool enables you to insert a key and delete the root visually.

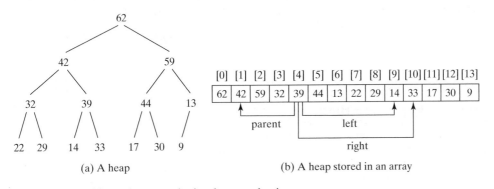

(a) A heap   (b) A heap stored in an array

FIGURE 19.8 A binary heap can be implemented using an array.

19.5.2 Adding a New Node

To add a new node to the heap, first add it to the end of the heap and then rebuild the tree as follows:

```
Let the last node be the current node;
while (the current node is greater than its parent)
{
  Swap the current node with its parent;
  Now the current node is one level up;
}
```

Suppose the heap is initially empty. The heap is shown in Figure 19.9, after adding numbers 3, 5, 1, 19, 11, and 22 in this order.

Now consider adding 88 into the heap. Place the new node 88 at the end of the tree, as in Figure 19.10(a). Swap 88 with 19, as in Figure 19.10(b). Swap 88 with 22, as in Figure 19.10(c).

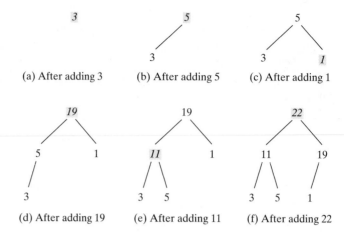

(a) After adding 3   (b) After adding 5   (c) After adding 1

(d) After adding 19   (e) After adding 11   (f) After adding 22

FIGURE 19.9 Elements 3, 5, 1, 19, 11, and 22 are inserted into the heap.

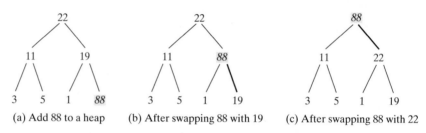

(a) Add 88 to a heap   (b) After swapping 88 with 19   (c) After swapping 88 with 22

FIGURE 19.10 Rebuild the heap after adding a new node.

19.5.3   Removing the Root

Often, you need to remove the max element which is the root in a heap. After the root is removed, the tree must be rebuilt to maintain the heap property. The algorithm for building the tree can be described as follows:

```
Move the last node to replace the root;
Let the root be the current node;
while (the current node has children and the current node is
       smaller than one of its children)
{
  Swap the current node with the larger of its children;
  Now the current node is one level down;
}
```

Figure 19.11 shows the process of rebuilding a heap after the root 62 is removed from Figure 19.8(a). Move the last node 9 to the root as in Figure 19.11(a). Swap 9 with 59 as in Figure 19.11(b). Swap 9 with 44 as in Figure 19.11(c). Swap 9 with 30 as in Figure 19.11(d).

Figure 19.12 shows the process of rebuilding a heap after the root 59 is removed from Figure 19.11(d). Move the last node 17 to the root as in Figure 19.12(a). Swap 17 with 44 as in Figure 19.12(b). Swap 17 with 30 as in Figure 19.12(c).

19.5.4   The Heap Class

Now you are ready to design and implement the Heap class. The class diagram is shown in Figure 19.13. Its implementation is given in Listing 19.10

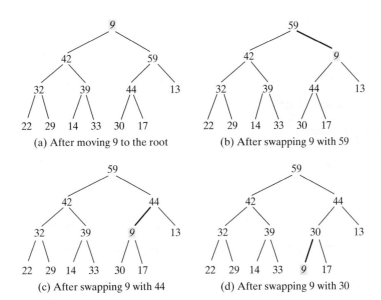

Figure 19.11   Rebuild the heap after the root 62 is removed.

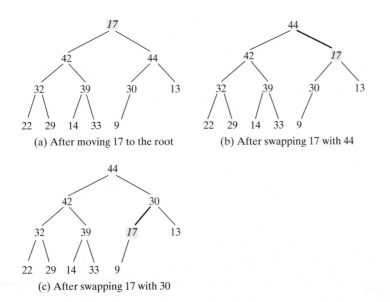

Figure 19.12   Rebuild the heap after the root 59 is removed.

Heap<T>	
-vector: vector<T>	Stores the elements in the vector.
+Heap()	Creates a default heap.
+Heap(elements[]: T, arraySize: int)	Creates a heap with the specified objects.
+remove(): T	Removes the root from the heap and returns it.
+add(element: T): void	Adds a new object to the heap.
+getSize(): int	Returns the size of the heap.

Figure 19.13   Heap provides operations for manipulating a heap.

LISTING 19.10 Heap.h

```
1 #ifndef HEAP_H
2 #define HEAP_H
3 #include <vector>
4 #include <stdexcept>
5 using namespace std;
6
7 template<typename T>
8 class Heap
9 {
10 public:
11   Heap();
12   Heap(T elements[], int arraySize);
13   T remove() throw (runtime_error);
14   void add(T element);
15   int getSize();
16
17 private:
18   vector<T> v;
19 };
20
21 template <typename T>
22 Heap<T>::Heap()
23 {
24 }
25
26 template <typename T>
27 Heap<T>::Heap(T elements[], int arraySize)
28 {
29   for (int i = 0; i < arraySize; i++)
30   {
31     add(elements[i]);
32   }
33 }
34
35 /* Remove the root from the heap */
36 template <typename T>
37 T Heap<T>::remove() throw (runtime_error)
38 {
39   if (v.size() == 0)
40     throw runtime_error("Heap is empty");
41
42   T removedElement = v[0];
43   v[0] = v[v.size() - 1]; // Copy the last element to root
44   v.pop_back(); // Remove the last element
45
46   // Maintain the heap property
47   int currentIndex = 0;
48   while (currentIndex < v.size())
49   {
50     int leftChildIndex = 2 * currentIndex + 1;
51     int rightChildIndex = 2 * currentIndex + 2;
52
53     // Find the maximum between two children
54     if (leftChildIndex >= v.size()) break; // The tree is a heap
55     int maxIndex = leftChildIndex;
56     if (rightChildIndex < v.size())
57     {
58       if (v[maxIndex] < v[rightChildIndex])
```

Margin notes:
- include **vector**
- include **stdexcept**
- **Heap** class
- public constructor
- public function
- internal heap representation
- no-arg constructor
- constructor
- add a new element
- remove the root
- empty heap
- new root
- remove the last
- adjust the tree

```
59          {
60            maxIndex = rightChildIndex;
61          }
62        }
63
64        // Swap if the current node is less than the maximum
65        if (v[currentIndex] < v[maxIndex])
66        {
67          T temp = v[maxIndex];
68          v[maxIndex] = v[currentIndex];
69          v[currentIndex] = temp;
70          currentIndex = maxIndex;
71        }
72        else
73          break; // The tree is a heap
74      }
75
76      return removedElement;
77  }
78
79  /* Insert element into the heap and maintain the heap property */
80  template <typename T>
81  void Heap<T>::add(T element)
82  {
83      v.push_back(element); // Append element to the heap
84      int currentIndex = v.size() - 1; // The index of the last node
85
86      // Maintain the heap property
87      while (currentIndex > 0)
88      {
89        int parentIndex = (currentIndex - 1) / 2;
90        // Swap if the current element is greater than its parent
91        if (v[currentIndex] > v[parentIndex])
92        {
93          T temp = v[currentIndex];
94          v[currentIndex] = v[parentIndex];
95          v[parentIndex] = temp;
96        }
97        else
98          break; // the tree is a heap now
99
100       currentIndex = parentIndex;
101     }
102 }
103
104 /* Get the number of element in the heap */
105 template <typename T>
106 int Heap<T>::getSize()
107 {
108     return v.size();
109 }
110
111 #endif
```

- line 76: return removed element
- line 81: add element
- line 83: append element
- line 87: adjust the tree
- line 106: get size

A heap is represented using a vector internally (line 18). You may change it to other data structures, but the **Heap** class contract will remain unchanged.

The **remove()** function (lines 36–77) removes and returns the root. To maintain the heap property, the function moves the last element to the root position and swaps it with its larger child if it is less than the larger child. This process continues until the last element becomes a leaf or is not less than its children.

The add(T element) function (lines 80–102) appends the element to the tree and then swaps it with its parent if it is greater than its parent. This process continues until the new element becomes the root or is not greater than its parent.

19.5.5   Sorting Using the Heap Class

To sort an array using a heap, first create an object using the Heap class, add all the elements to the heap using the add function, and remove all the elements from the heap using the remove function. The elements are removed in descending order. Listing 19.11 is an algorithm for sorting an array of a generic type using a heap.

LISTING 19.11   HeapSort.h

include **Heap.h**

generic type
sort function

create a heap

add element

remove element

```
 1 #include "Heap.h"
 2
 3 template <typename T>
 4 void heapSort(T list[], int arraySize)
 5 {
 6   Heap<T> heap;
 7
 8   for (int i = 0; i < arraySize; i++)
 9     heap.add(list[i]);
10
11   for (int i = 0; i < arraySize; i++)
12     list[i] = heap.remove();
13 }
```

19.5.6   Heap Sort Time Complexity

height of a heap

Let us turn our attention to analyzing the time complexity for the heap sort. Let h denote the height for a heap of n elements. Since a heap is a complete binary tree, the first level has 1 node, the second level has 2 nodes, the kth level has 2^{k-1} nodes, the $(h-1)$th level has 2^{h-2} nodes, and the hth level has at least 1 and at most 2^{h-1} nodes. Therefore,

$$1 + 2 + \ldots + 2^{h-2} < n \le 1 + 2 + \ldots + 2^{h-2} + 2^{h-1}$$

i.e.,

$$2^{h-1} - 1 < n \le 2^h - 1$$
$$2^{h-1} < n + 1 \le 2^h$$
$$h - 1 < \log(n + 1) \le h$$

Thus, $h < \log(n + 1) + 1$ and $\log(n + 1) \le h$. Therefore, $\log(n + 1) \le h < \log(n + 1) + 1$. Hence, the height of the heap is $O(\log n)$.

$O(n\log n)$ worst–case time

Since the add function traces a path from a leaf to a root, it takes at most h steps to add a new element to the heap. So, the total time for constructing an initial heap is $O(n\log n)$ for an array of n elements. Since the remove function traces a path from a root to a leaf, it takes at most h steps to rebuild a heap after removing the root from the heap. Since the remove function is invoked n times, the total time for producing a sorted array from a heap is $O(n\log n)$.

heap sort vs. merge sort

Both merge sort and heap sort requires $O(n\log n)$ time. Merge sort requires a temporary array for merging two subarrays. Heap sort does not need additional array space. So, heap sort is more space efficient than merge sort.

19.6 Bucket Sort and Radix Sort

Video Note
bucket sort and radix sort

All sort algorithms discussed so far are general sorting algorithms that work for keys of any type (e.g., integers, strings, and any comparable objects). These algorithms sort the elements by comparing their keys. The lower bound for general sorting algorithms is $O(n\log n)$. So, no sorting algorithms based on comparisons can perform better than $O(n\log n)$. However, if the keys are small integers, you can use *bucket sort* without having to compare the keys.

The bucket sort algorithm works as follows. Assume the keys are in the range from 0 to N-1. We need N buckets labeled 0, 1, ..., and N-1. If an element's key is i, the element is put into the bucket i. Each bucket holds the elements with the same key value. You can use a vector to implement a bucket.

Clearly, it takes $O(n + N)$ time to sort the list and uses $O(n + N)$ space, where n is the list size.

Note that if N is too large, bucket sort is not desirable. You can use *radix sort*. Radix sort is based on bucket sort, but it is more efficient than bucket sort.

Note that bucket sort is *stable*, meaning that if two elements in the original list have the same key value, their order is not changed in the sorted list. That is, if element e_1 and element e_2 have the same key and e_1 precedes e_2 in the original list, e_1 still precedes e_2 in the sorted list.

stable

Again assume that the keys are positive integers. The idea of the radix sort is to divide the keys into subgroups based on their radix positions. For example, 934 is divided into $\{9, 3, 4\}$ and 1344 is divided into $\{1, 3, 4, 4\}$. Radix sort applies the bucket sort repeatedly for the key values on radix positions, starting with the least-significant position from the left to right. Each time when you apply the bucket sort, you need only ten buckets.

Consider sorting the elements with the keys:

331, 454, 230, 34, 343, 45, 59, 453, 345, 231, 9

Apply the bucket sort on the last radix position. The elements are put into the buckets as follows:

buckets[0]	buckets[1]	buckets[2]	buckets[3]	buckets[4]	buckets[5]	buckets[6]	buckets[7]	buckets[8]	buckets[9]
230	331 231		343 453	454 34	45 345				59 9

After being removed from the buckets, the elements are in the following order:

230, 331, 231, 343, 453, 454, 34, 45, 345, 59, 9

Apply the bucket sort on the second-last radix position. The elements are put into the buckets as follows:

buckets[0]	buckets[1]	buckets[2]	buckets[3]	buckets[4]	buckets[5]	buckets[6]	buckets[7]	buckets[8]	buckets[9]
9			230 331 231 34	343 45 345	453 454 59				

After being removed from the buckets, the elements are in the following order:

9, 230, 331, 231, 34, 343, 45, 345, 453, 454, 59

(Note that 9 is 009.)

Apply the bucket sort on the third-last radix position. The elements are put into the buckets as follows:

buckets[0]	buckets[1]	buckets[2]	buckets[3]	buckets[4]	buckets[5]	buckets[6]	buckets[7]	buckets[8]	buckets[9]
9 34 45 59		230 231	331 343 345	453					

After being removed from the buckets, the elements are in the following order:

9, 34, 45, 59, 230, 231, 331, 43, 45, 453

The elements are now sorted.

In general, radix sort takes $O(dn)$ time to sort n elements with integer keys, where d is the maximum number of radix positions among all keys.

19.7 External Sort

All the sort algorithms discussed in the preceding sections assume that all data to be sorted is available at one time in internal memory, such as an array. To sort data stored in an external file, you may first bring it to the memory, then sort it internally. However, if the file is too large, all data in the file cannot be brought to memory at one time. This section discusses how to sort data in a large external file.

For simplicity, assume that two million `int` values are stored in a binary file named large-data.dat. This file was created using the following program:

LISTING 19.12 CreateLargeFile.cpp

```cpp
 1 #include <iostream>
 2 #include <fstream>
 3 #include <cstdlib>
 4 using namespace std;
 5
 6 int main()
 7 {
 8   fstream output;
 9   output.open("largedata.dat", ios::out | ios::binary);
10
11   for (int i = 0; i < 2000000; i++)
12   {
13     int value = rand();
14     output.write(reinterpret_cast<char *>(&value), sizeof (value));
15   }
16
17   output.close();
18   cout << "File created" << endl;
19
20   fstream input;
21   input.open("largedata.dat", ios::in | ios::binary);
22   int value;
23
24   cout << "The first 10 numbers in the file are " << endl;
25   for (int i = 0; i < 10; i++)
26   {
27     input.read(reinterpret_cast<char *>(& value), sizeof (value));
28     cout << value << " ";
29   }
30
31   input.close();
32
33   return 0;
34 }
```

a binary output stream (line 9)
random value (line 13)
output an **int** value (line 14)
close output (line 17)
a binary output stream (line 21)
read input (line 27)
close input (line 31)

```
File created
The first 10 numbers in the file are
130 10982 1090 11656 7117 17595 6415 22948 31126 9004
```

A variation of merge sort can be used to sort this file in two phases:

Phase I:

Repeatedly bring data from the file to an array, sort the array using an internal sorting algorithm, and output the data from the array to a temporary file. This process is shown in Figure 19.14. Ideally, you want to create a large array, but the maximum size of the array is limited. Assume that the maximum array size is of 100000 `int` values. In the temporary file, every 100000 `int` values are sorted. They are denoted as S_1, S_2, ..., and S_k, where the last segment, S_k, may contain less than 100000 values.

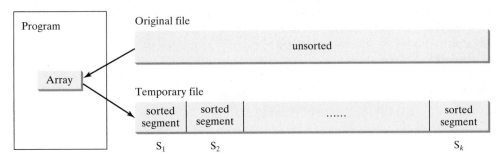

FIGURE 19.14 The original file is sorted in segments.

Phase II:

Merge every pair of sorted segments (e.g., S_1 with S_2, S_3 with S_4, ..., and so on) into a larger sorted segment and save the new segment into a new temporary file. Continue the same process until one sorted segment results. Figure 19.15 shows how to merge eight segments.

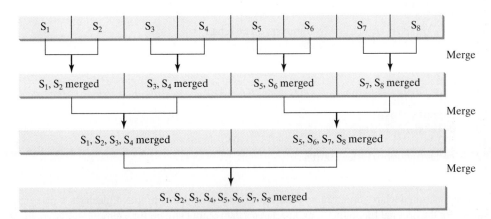

FIGURE 19.15 Sorted segments are merged iteratively.

(*Note:* It is not necessary to merge two successive segments. For example, you may merge S_1 with S_5, S_2 with S_6, S_3 with S_7, and S_4 with S_8, in the first merge step. This observation is useful to implement Phase II efficiently.)

19.7.1 Implementing Phase I

Listing 19.13 gives the function that reads each segment of data from a file, sorts the segment, and stores the sorted segment into a new file. The function returns the number of segments.

LISTING 19.13 Creating Initial Sorted Segments

```
 1   /* Sort original file into sorted segments */
 2   int initializeSegments(int segmentSize, char* originalFile, char* f1)
 3   {
 4     int *list = new int[segmentSize];
 5
 6     fstream input;
 7     input.open(originalFile, ios::in | ios::binary);
 8     fstream output;
 9     output.open(f1, ios::out | ios::binary);
10
11     int numberOfSegments = 0;
12     while (!input.eof())
13     {
14       int i = 0;
15       for ( ; !input.eof() && i < segmentSize; i++)
16       {
17         input.read(reinterpret_cast<char *>
18           (&list[i]), sizeof(list[i]));
19       }
20
21       if (input.eof()) i--;
22       if (i <= 0)
23         break;
24       else
25         numberOfSegments++;
26
27       // Sort an array list[0..i-1]
28       quickSort(list, i);
29
30       // Write the array to f1.dat
31       for (int j = 0; j < i; j++)
32       {
33         output.write(reinterpret_cast<char *>
34           (&list[j]), sizeof(list[j]));
35       }
36     }
37
38     input.close();
39     output.close();
40     delete [] list;
41
42     return numberOfSegments;
43   }
```

Margin notes:
- a dynamic array (line 4)
- a binary input stream (line 7)
- a binary output stream (line 9)
- end of file? (line 12)
- read an **int** value (line 17)
- discard a garbage character (line 21)
- sort segment (line 28)
- output an **int** value (line 33)
- close the file (line 38)
- return # of segments (line 42)

The function declares an array with the specified segment size in line 4, declares a data input stream for the original file in line 7, and declares a data output stream for a temporary file in line 9.

Lines 15–19 read a segment of data from the file into the array. Line 28 sorts the array. Lines 31–35 write the data in the array to the temporary file.

The number of the segments is returned in line 42. Note that every segment has segmentSize number of elements except the last segment, which may have a smaller number of elements.

19.7.2 Implementing Phase II

In each merge step, two sorted segments are merged to form a new segment. The size of the new segment is doubled. The number of segments is reduced by half after each merge step. A segment is too large to be brought to an array in memory. To implement a merge step, copy half the number of segments from file f1.dat to a temporary file f2.dat. Then merge the first remaining segment in f1.dat with the first segment in f2.dat into a temporary file named f3.dat, as shown in Figure 19.16.

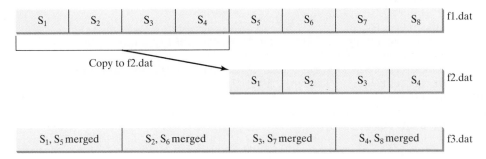

FIGURE 19.16 Sorted segments are merged iteratively.

(*Note:* f1.dat may have one segment more than f2.dat. If so, move the last segment into f3.dat after the merge.)

Listing 19.14 gives a function that copies the first half of the segments in f1.dat to f2.dat. Listing 19.15 gives a function that merges a pair of segments in f1.dat and f2.dat. Listing 19.16 gives a function that merges two segments.

LISTING 19.14 Copying First Half Segments

```
1  /* Copy the first half the number of segments from f1.dat to f2.dat */
2  void copyHalfToF2(int numberOfSegments, int segmentSize,        input stream f1
3    fstream &f1, fstream &f2)                                      output stream f2
4  {
5    for (int i = 0; i < (numberOfSegments / 2) * segmentSize; i++)  segments copied
6    {
7      int value;
8      f1.read(reinterpret_cast<char *>(& value), sizeof(value));
9      f2.write(reinterpret_cast<char *>(& value), sizeof(value));
10   }
11 }
```

LISTING 19.15 Merging All Segments

```
1  /* Merge all segmentss */
2  void mergeSegments(int numberOfSegments, int segmentSize,       input stream f1 and f2
3    fstream &f1, fstream &f2, fstream &f3)                         output stream f3
4  {
5    for (int i = 0; i < numberOfSegments; i++)                     merge two segments
6    {
7      mergeTwoSegments(segmentSize, f1, f2, f3);
8    }
9
10   // f1 may have one extra segment; copy it to f3
11   while (!f1.eof())                                              extra segment in f1
12   {
13     int value;
14     f1.read(reinterpret_cast<char *>(&value), sizeof(value));
15     if (f1.eof()) break;
16     f3.write(reinterpret_cast<char *>(&value), sizeof(value));
17   }
18 }
```

LISTING 19.16 Merging Two Segments

```
1  /* Merge two segments */
2  void mergeTwoSegments(int segmentSize, fstream &f1, fstream &f2,
3    fstream &f3)
4  {
5    int intFromF1;
6    f1.read(reinterpret_cast<char *>(&intFromF1), sizeof(intFromF1));
7    int intFromF2;
8    f2.read(reinterpret_cast<char *>(&intFromF2), sizeof(intFromF2));
9    int f1Count = 1;
10   int f2Count = 1;
11
12   while (true)
13   {
14     if (intFromF1 < intFromF2)
15     {
16       f3.write(reinterpret_cast<char *>
17         (&intFromF1), sizeof(intFromF1));
18       if (f1.eof() || f1Count++ >= segmentSize)
19       {
20         if (f1.eof()) break;
21         f3.write(reinterpret_cast<char *>
22           (&intFromF2), sizeof(intFromF2));
23         break;
24       }
25       else
26       {
27         f1.read(reinterpret_cast<char *>
28           (& intFromF1), sizeof(intFromF1));
29       }
30     }
31     else
32     {
33       f3.write(reinterpret_cast<char *>
34         (&intFromF2), sizeof(intFromF2));
35       if (f2.eof() || f2Count++ >= segmentSize)
36       {
37         if (f2.eof()) break;
38         f3.write(reinterpret_cast<char *>
39           (&intFromF1), sizeof(intFromF1));
40         break;
41       }
42       else
43       {
44         f2.read(reinterpret_cast<char *>
45           (&intFromF2), sizeof(intFromF2));
46       }
47     }
48   }
49
50   while (!f1.eof() && f1Count++ < segmentSize)
51   {
52     int value;
53     f1.read(reinterpret_cast<char *>
54       (&value), sizeof(value));
55     if (f1.eof()) break;
56     f3.write(reinterpret_cast<char *>
57       (&value), sizeof(value));
58   }
```

Margin notes:

input streams f1 and f2 (lines 2–3)
output stream f3

read from f1 (line 6)

read from f2 (line 8)

write to f3 (line 16)

segment in f1 finished (line 18)

write to f3 (line 21)

segment in f2 finished (line 35)

remaining f1 segment (line 50)

```
59
60   while (!f2.eof() && f2Count++ < segmentSize)          remaining f2 segment
61   {
62     int value;
63     f2.read(reinterpret_cast<char *>
64       (&value), sizeof(value));
65     if (f2.eof()) break;
66     f3.write(reinterpret_cast<char *>
67       (&value), sizeof(value));
68   }
69 }
```

19.7.3   Combining Two Phases

Listing 19.17 gives the complete program for sorting int values in largedata.dat and storing the sorted data in sortedlargedata.dat.

LISTING 19.17   SortLargeFile.cpp

```
 1 #include <iostream>
 2 #include <fstream>                                        include fstream
 3 #include "QuickSort.h"                                    include quick sort
 4 using namespace std;
 5
 6 // Function prototype
 7 int initializeSegments(int segmentSize,                   function prototype
 8   char* originalFile, char* f1);
 9 void mergeTwoSegments(int segmentSize, fstream &f1, fstream &f2,
10   fstream &f3);
11 void merge(int numberOfSegments, int segmentSize,
12   char* f1, char* f2, char* f3) ;
13 void copyHalfToF2(int numberOfSegments, int segmentSize,
14   fstream &f1, fstream &f2);
15 void mergeOneStep(int numberOfSegments, int segmentSize,
16   char* f1, char* f2, char* f3);
17 void mergeSegments(int numberOfSegments, int segmentSize,
18   fstream &f1, fstream &f2, fstream &f3);
19 void copyFile(char * f1, char * target);
20
21 int main()
22 {
23   const int MAX_ARRAY_SIZE = 100000;                      max array size
24
25   // Implement Phase 1: Create initial segments
26   int numberOfSegments =
27     initializeSegments(MAX_ARRAY_SIZE, "largedata.dat", "f1.dat");   create segments
28
29   // Implement Phase 2: Merge segments recursively
30   merge(numberOfSegments, MAX_ARRAY_SIZE,                 merge recursively
31     "f1.dat", "f2.dat", "f3.dat");
32 }
33
34 /* Sort original file into sorted segments */
35 int initializeSegments(int segmentSize, char* originalFile, char* f1)
36 {
37   // Same as Listing 19.13, so omitted
38 }
39
40 /* Recursively merge sorted segments */
41 void merge(int numberOfSegments, int segmentSize,        recursive merge
```

```
42    char* f1, char* f2, char* f3)
43  {
44    if (numberOfSegments > 1)
45    {
46      mergeOneStep(numberOfSegments, segmentSize, f1, f2, f3);
47      merge((numberOfSegments + 1) / 2, segmentSize * 2, f3, f1, f2);
48    }
49    else
50    {
51      // rename f1 as the final sorted file
52      copyFile(f1, "sortedlargedata.dat");
53      cout << "\nSorted into the file sortedlargedata.dat" << endl;
54    }
55  }
56
57  /* Copy file from f1 to target */
58  void copyFile(char * f1, char * target)
59  {
60    fstream input;
61    input.open(f1, ios::in | ios::binary);
62
63    fstream output;
64    output.open(target, ios::out | ios::binary);
65
66    while (!input.eof()) // Continue if not end of file
67    {
68      int value;
69      input.read(reinterpret_cast<char *> (& value), sizeof(value));
70      if (input.eof()) break;
71      output.write(reinterpret_cast<char *> (& value), sizeof(value));
72    }
73
74    input.close();
75    output.close();
76  }
77
78  /* Merge every pair of two segments */
79  void mergeOneStep(int numberOfSegments, int segmentSize, char* f1,
80    char* f2, char* f3)
81  {
82    fstream f1Input;
83    f1Input.open(f1, ios::in | ios::binary);
84
85    fstream f2Output;
86    f2Output.open(f2, ios::out | ios::binary);
87
88    // Copy half the number of segments from f1.dat to f2.dat
89    copyHalfToF2(numberOfSegments, segmentSize, f1Input, f2Output);
90    f2Output.close();
91
92    // Merge remaining segments in f1 with segments in f2 into f3
93    fstream f2Input;
94    f2Input.open(f2, ios::in | ios::binary);
95    fstream f3Output;
96    f3Output.open(f3, ios::out | ios::binary);
97
98    mergeSegments(numberOfSegments / 2, segmentSize,
```

copy file

merge one time

```
99          f1Input, f2Input, f3Output);
100
101     f1Input.close();
102     f2Input.close();
103   f3Output.close();
104 }
105
106 /* Copy the first half the number of segments from f1.dat to f2.dat */
107 void copyHalfToF2(int numberOfSegments, int segmentSize,
108     fstream &f1, fstream &f2)
109 {
110    // Same as Listing 19.14, so omitted
111 }
112
113 /* Merge all segments */
114 void mergeSegments(int numberOfSegments, int segmentSize,
115     fstream &f1, fstream &f2, fstream &f3)
116 {
117    // Same as Listing 19.15, so omitted
118 }
119
120 /* Merge two segments */
121 void mergeTwoSegments(int segmentSize, fstream &f1, fstream &f2,
122     fstream &f3)
123 {
124    // Same as Listing 19.16, so omitted
125 }
```

Assume MAX_ARRAY_SIZE is 100000 (line 23), which is also the initial segment size. Line 27 creates initial segments from the original array and stores the sorted segments in a new file f1.dat. Lines 30–31 produce a sorted file in sortedlargedata.dat. The merge function

```
merge(int numberOfSegments,
    int segmentSize, char * f1, char * f2, char * f3)
```

merges the segments in f1 into f3, using f2 to assist the merge. The merge function is invoked recursively with many merge steps. Each merge step reduces the numberOfSegments by half and doubles the sorted segment size. After completing one merge step, the next merge step merges the new segments in f3 to f2, using f1 to assist the merge. So the statement to invoke the new merge function is (line 18)

```
merge((numberOfSegments + 1) / 2, segmentSize * 2, f3, f1, f2);
```

The numberOfSegments for the next merge step is (numberOfSegments + 1) / 2. For example, if numberOfSegments is 5, numberOfSegments is 3 for the next merge step, because every two segments are merged but there is one left unmerged.

The recursive merge function ends when numberOfSegments is 1. In this case, f1 contains sorted data. File f1 is copied to sortedlargedata.dat in line 52.

19.7.4 External Sort Analysis

In the external sort, the dominating cost is that of I/O. Assume n is the number of the elements to be sorted in the file. In Phase I, n elements are read from the original file and output to a temporary file. So, the I/O for Phase I is $O(n)$.

In Phase II, before the first merge step, the number of sorted segments is $\frac{n}{c}$, where c is `MAX_ARRAY_SIZE`. Each merge step reduces the number of segments by half. So, after the first merge step, the number of segments is $\frac{n}{2c}$. After the second merge step, the number of segments is $\frac{n}{2^2 c}$. After the third merge step, the number of segments is $\frac{n}{2^3 c}$. After $\log\left(\frac{n}{c}\right)$ merge steps, the number of segments is reduced to 1. Therefore, the total number of merge steps is $\log\left(\frac{n}{c}\right)$.

In each merge step, half the number of segments are read from file `f1` and then written into a temporary file `f2`. The remaining segments in `f1` are merged with the segments in `f2`. The number of I/Os in each merge step is $O(n)$. Since the total number of merge steps is $\log\left(\frac{n}{c}\right)$, the total number of I/Os is

$$O(n) \times \log\left(\frac{n}{c}\right) = O(n \log n)$$

Therefore, the complexity of the external sort is $O(n\log n)$.

KEY TERMS

CHAPTER SUMMARY

1. The worst-time complexity for selection sort, insertion sort, bubble sort, and quick sort is $O(n^2)$.

2. The average-time and worst-time complexity for merge sort is $O(n\log n)$. The average time for quick sort is also $O(n\log n)$.

3. The time complexity for heap sort is $O(n\log n)$.

4. Bucket sort and radix sort are specialized sorting algorithms for integer keys. These algorithms sort keys using buckets rather than comparing keys. They are more efficient than general sorting algorithms.

5. Heap is a useful data structure for designing efficient sorting algorithms and priority queues. A *heap* is a binary tree with two properties: (1) It is a complete binary tree; (2) Each node is greater than or equal to any of its children.

6. You can implement a heap using an array or a vector.

7. A variation of merge sort can be applied to sort large data from external files.

REVIEW QUESTIONS

Sections 19.2–19.4

19.1 Use Figure 19.1 as an example to show how to apply bubble sort on {45, 11, 50, 59, 60, 2, 4, 7, 10}.

19.2 Use Figure 19.2 as an example to show how to apply merge sort on {45, 11, 50, 59, 60, 2, 4, 7, 10}.

19.3 Use Figure 19.4 as an example to show how to apply quick sort on {45, 11, 50, 59, 60, 2, 4, 7, 10}.

Section 19.5

19.4 What is a complete binary tree? What is a heap? Describe how to remove the root from a heap and how to add a new object to a heap.

19.5 What is the return value from invoking the `remove` function if the heap is empty?

19.6 Add the elements 4, 5, 1, 2, 9, 3 into a heap in this order. Draw the diagrams to show the heap after each element is added.

19.7 Show the heap after the root in the heap in Figure 19.12(c) is removed.

Sections 19.6–19.7

19.8 Show how to apply radix sort on {232, 353, 344, 20, 35, 326, 767, 679, 678, 671, 343}.

19.9 There are 10 numbers {2, 3, 4, 0, 5, 6, 7, 9, 8, 1} stored in the external file large-data.dat. Trace the SortLargeFile program by hand with `MAX_ARRAY_SIZE` 2.

PROGRAMMING EXERCISES

19.1 (*Generic bubble sort*) Write a generic function for bubble sort.

19.2 (*Generic merge sort*) Write a generic function for merge sort.

19.3 (*Generic quick sort*) Write a generic function for quick sort.

19.4 (*Improving quick sort*) The quick sort algorithm presented in the book selects the first element in the list as the pivot. Revise it by selecting the medium among the first, middle, and last elements in the list.

Video Note
Improve quick sort

19.5 (*Generic heap sort*) Write a test program that invokes the generic sort function to sort an array of `int` values, an array of `double` values, and an array of strings.

19.6 (*Checking order*) Write the following overloaded functions that check whether an array is ordered in ascending order or descending order. By default, the function checks ascending order. To check descending order, pass `false` to the ascending argument in the function.

```
// T is a generic type
bool ordered(T list[], int size)
```

```
// T is a generic type
bool ordered(T list[], int size, bool ascending)
```

19.7* (*Radix sort*) Write a program that randomly generates 1,000,000 integers and sorts them using radix sort.

19.8 (*Execution time for sorting*) Write a program that obtains the execution time of selection sort, insertion sort, bubble sort, merge sort, quick sort, and heap sort for input size 500,000, 1,000,000, 1,500,000, 2,000,000, 2,500,000, and 3,000,000. Your program should print a table like this:

Array size	Selection Sort	Insertion Sort	Bubble Sort	Merge Sort	Quick Sort	Heap Sort
500000						
1000000						
1500000						
2000000						
2500000						
3000000						

(*Hint:* You can use the following code template to obtain the execution time.)

```
long startTime = time(0);
perform the task;
long endTime = time(0);
long executionTime = endTime - startTime;
```

19.9 (*Execution time for external sorting*) Write a program that obtains the execution time of external sort for integers of size 5,000,000, 10,000,000, 15,000,000, 20,000,000, 25,000,000, and 30,000,000. Your program should print a table like this:

File size	5000000	10000000	15000000	20000000	25000000	30000000
Time						

CHAPTER 20

LINKED LISTS, QUEUES, AND PRIORITY QUEUES

Objectives

- To create nodes to store elements in a linked list (§20.2).

- To access the nodes in a linked list via pointers (§20.3).

- To define a `LinkedList` class for storing and processing data in a list (§20.4).

- To add an element to the head of a list (§20.4.1).

- To add an element to the end of a list (§20.4.2).

- To insert an element into a list (§20.4.3).

- To remove the first element from a list (§20.4.4).

- To remove the last element from a list (§20.4.5).

- To remove an element at a specified position in a list (§20.4.6).

- To implement iterators for traversing the elements in various types of containers (§20.5).

- To explore the variations of linked lists (§20.6).

- To implement the `Queue` class using a linked list (§20.7).

- To implement the `PriorityQueue` class using a heap (§20.8).

20.1 Introduction

§12.4, "Class Templates," introduced a generic **Stack** class. The elements in the stack are stored in an array. The array size is fixed. If the array is too small, the elements cannot be stored in the stack; if it is too large, a lot of space will be wasted. A possible solution was proposed in §12.5, "Improving the **Stack** Class." Initially, the stack uses a small array. When there is no room to add a new element, the stack creates a new array that doubles the size of the old array, copies the contents from the old array to this new one, and discards the old array. It is time consuming to copy the array.

linked list

This chapter introduces a new data structure, called *linked list*. A linked list is efficient for storing and managing a varying number of elements. This chapter also discusses how to implement queues using linked lists.

20.2 Nodes

In a linked list, each element is contained in a structure called the *node*. When a new element is added, a node is created to contain it. All the nodes are chained through pointers, as shown in Figure 20.1.

FIGURE 20.1   A linked list consists of any number of nodes chained together.

Nodes can be defined using a class, as follows:

template class

```
 1  template<typename T>
 2  class Node
 3  {
 4  public:
```

element type
node pointer

```
 5    T element;   // Element contained in the node
 6    Node *next;  // Pointer to the next node
 7
```

no-arg constructor

```
 8    Node()  // No-arg constructor
 9    {
10      next = NULL;
11    }
12
```

no-arg constructor

```
13    Node(T element)  // Constructor
14    {
15      this->element = element;
16      next = NULL;
17    }
18  };
```

Node is defined as a template class with a type parameter **T** for specifying the element type.

NULL is 0

By convention, pointer variables named **head** and **tail** are used to point to the first and the last node in the list. If the list is empty, both **head** and **tail** should be **NULL**. Recall that **NULL** is a C++ constant for **0**, which indicates that a pointer does not point to any node. The definition of **NULL** is in a number of standard libraries including **<iostream>** and **<cstddef>**. Here is an example that creates a linked list to hold three nodes. Each node stores a string element.

Step 1: Declare `head` and `tail`:

```
Node<string> *head = NULL, *tail = NULL;
```

The list is empty now.
head is NULL and tail is NULL

`head` and `tail` are both `NULL`. The list is empty.

Step 2: Create the first node and insert it to the list:

After the first node is inserted

```
head = new Node<string>("Chicago");
tail = head;
```

head ⟶ "Chicago" ⟵ tail
next: NULL

FIGURE 20.2 Append the first node to the list.

After the first node is inserted in the list, `head` and `tail` point to this node, as shown in Figure 20.2.

Step 3: Create the second node and append it to the list:

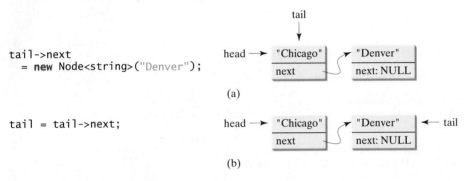

```
tail->next
  = new Node<string>("Denver");
```

(a)

```
tail = tail->next;
```

(b)

FIGURE 20.3 Append the second node to the list.

To append the second node to the list, link it with the first node, as shown in Figure 20.3(a). The new node is now the tail node. So you should move tail to point to this new node, as shown in Figure 20.3(b).

Step 4: Create the third node and append it to the list:

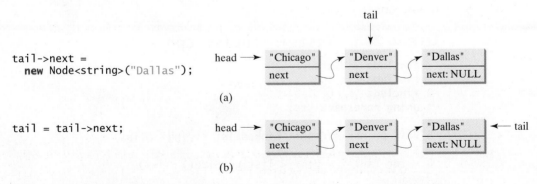

```
tail->next =
  new Node<string>("Dallas");
```

(a)

```
tail = tail->next;
```

(b)

FIGURE 20.4 Append the third node to the list.

To append the new node to the list, link it with the last node, as shown in Figure 20.4(a). The new node is now the tail node. So you should move tail to point to this new node, as shown in Figure 20.4(b).

Each node contains the element and a pointer that points to the next element. If the node is the last in the list, its pointer data field `next` contains the value `NULL`. You can use this property to detect the last node. For example, you may write the following loop to traverse all the nodes in the list.

current pointer
check last node

next node

```
1 Node<string> *current = head;
2 while (current != NULL )
3 {
4   cout << current->element << endl;
5   current = current->next;
6 }
```

The `current` pointer points to the first node in the list initially (line 1). In the loop, the element of the current node is retrieved (line 4), and then `current` points to the next node (line 5). The loop continues until the current node is `NULL`.

20.3 The `LinkedList` Class

Video Note
Implementing LinkedList

Linked list is a popular data structure for storing data in sequential order. For example, a list of students, a list of available rooms, a list of cities, and a list of books all can be stored using lists. The operations listed here are typical of most lists:

- Retrieve an element from a list.
- Insert a new element to a list.
- Delete an element from a list.
- Find how many elements are in a list.
- Find whether an element is in a list.
- Find whether a list is empty.

Figure 20.5 gives the class diagram for `LinkedList`. `LinkedList` is a class template with type parameter `T` that represents the type of the elements stored in the list.

You can get an element from the list using `get(int index)`. The index is 0-based; i.e., the node at the head of the list has index `0`. Assume that the `LinkedList` class is available in the header file LinkedList.h. Let us begin by writing a test program that uses the `LinkedList` class, as shown in Listing 20.1. The program creates a list using `LinkedList` (line 18). It uses the `add` function to add strings to the list and the `remove` function to remove strings.

LISTING 20.1 TestLinkedList.cpp

include class

print list

list size

get element

```
1 #include <iostream>
2 #include <string>
3 #include "LinkedList.h"
4 using namespace std;
5
6 void printList(const LinkedList<string> &list)
7 {
8   for (int i = 0; i < list.getSize() ; i++)
9   {
10    cout << list.get(i) << " ";
11  }
12  cout << endl;
13 }
14
15 int main()
```

```
16 {
17    // Create a list for strings
18    LinkedList<string> list;                                              create list
19
20    // Add elements to the list
21    list.add("America"); // Add it to the list                           append element
22    cout << "(1) ";
23    printList(list);                                                      invoke printList
24
25    list.add(0, "Canada"); // Add it to the beginning of the list         insert element
26    cout << "(2) ";
27    printList(list);
28
29    list.add("Russia"); // Add it to the end of the list                 append element
30    cout << "(3) ";
31    printList(list);
32
33    list.add("France"); // Add it to the end of the list                 append element
34    cout << "(4) ";
35    printList(list);
36
37    list.add(2, "Germany"); // Add it to the list at index 2              insert element
38    cout << "(5) ";
39    printList(list);
40
41    list.add(5, "Norway"); // Add it to the list at index 5               insert element
42    cout << "(6) ";
43    printList(list);
44
45    list.add(0, "Netherlands"); // Same as list.addFirst("Netherlands")   insert element
46    cout << "(7) ";
47    printList(list);
48
49    // Remove elements from the list
50    list.removeAt(0); // Same as list.remove("Netherlands ") in this case remove element
51    cout << "(8) ";
52    printList(list);
53
54    list.removeAt(2); // Remove the element at index 2                    remove element
55    cout << "(9) ";
56    printList(list);
57
58    list.removeAt(list.getSize() - 1); // Remove the last element         remove element
59    cout << "(10) ";
60    printList(list);
61
62    return 0;
63 }
```

```
 (1) America
 (2) Canada America
 (3) Canada America Russia
 (4) Canada America Russia France
 (5) Canada America Germany Russia France
 (6) Canada America Germany Russia France Norway
 (7) Netherlands Canada America Germany Russia France Norway
 (8) Canada America Germany Russia France Norway
 (9) Canada America Russia France Norway
(10) Canada America Russia France
```

LinkedList<T>	
-head: Node<T>*	The head of the list.
-tail: Node<T>*	The tail of the list.
-size: int	The size of the list.
+LinkedList()	(no-arg constructor) Creates a default linked list.
+LinkedList(&list: LinkedList<T>)	(copy constructor) Copies the list to this list.
+~LinkedList()	(destructor) Destructs a linked list.
+addFirst(element: T): void	Adds the element to the head of the list.
+addLast(element: T): void	Adds the element to the tail of the list.
+getFirst(): T	Returns the first element in the list.
+getLast(): T	Returns the last element in the list.
+removeFirst(): T	Removes the first element from the list.
+removeLast(): T	Removes the last element from the list.
+add(element: T) : void	Appends a new element at the end of this list.
+add(index: int, element: T) : void	Adds a new element at the specified index in this list.
+clear(): void	Removes all the elements from this list.
+contains(element: T): bool	Returns true if this list contains the specified element.
+get(index: int) : T	Returns the element from this list at the specified index.
+indexOf(element: T) : int	Returns the index of the first matching element in this list.
+isEmpty(): bool	Returns true if this list contains no elements.
+lastIndexOf(element: T) : int	Returns the index of the last matching element in this list.
+remove(element: T): void	Removes the specified element from this list.
+getSize(): int	Returns the number of elements in this list.
+removeAt(index: int) : T	Removes the element at the specified index and returns the removed element.
+set(index: int, element: T) : T	Sets the element at the specified index and returns the element being replaced.
+begin(): Iterator<T>	Returns an iterator for the first element in the list.
+end(): Iterator<T>	Returns an iterator that passes the last element in the list.

Node<T>	
element: T	The element contained in the node.
*next: Node<T>	Pointer to the next node.
+Node(element: T)	Creates an empty node.
+Node(element: T)	Creates a Node with the specified element.

FIGURE 20.5 LinkedList implements a list using a linked list of nodes.

20.4 Implementing LinkedList

Now let us turn our attention to implementing the LinkedList class. Some functions are easy to implement. For example, the isEmpty() function simply returns head == NULL, and the clear() function simply destroys all nodes in the list and sets head and tail to NULL.

The **addLast(T element)** function is same as the **add(T element)** function. The reason for defining both is convenience.

20.4.1 Implementing **addFirst(T element)**

The **addFirst(T element)** function can be implemented as follows:

```
1 template<typename T>
2 void LinkedList<T>::addFirst(T element)
3 {
4   Node<T> *newNode = new Node<T>(element);    create a node
5   newNode->next = head;                       link with head
6   head = newNode;                             head to new node
7   size++;                                     increase size
8
9   if (tail == NULL)                           was empty?
10    tail = head;
11 }
```

The **addFirst(T element)** function creates a new node (line 4) to store the element and insert the node to the beginning of the list (line 5), as shown in Figure 20.6(a). After the insertion, **head** should point to this new element node (line 6), as shown in Figure 20.6(b).

If the list is empty (line 9), both **head** and **tail** will point to this new node (line 10). After the node is created, the size should be increased by 1 (line 7).

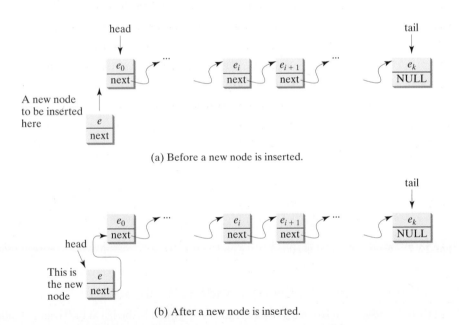

(a) Before a new node is inserted.

(b) After a new node is inserted.

FIGURE 20.6 A new element is inserted to the beginning of the list.

20.4.2 Implementing **addLast(T element)**

The **addLast(T element)** function creates a node to hold an element and appends the node at the end of the list. It can be implemented as follows:

```
1 template<typename T>
2 void LinkedList<T>::addLast(T element)
3 {
4   if (tail == NULL)
```

create a node

create a node

increase size

```
 5  {
 6    head = tail = new Node<T>(element);
 7  }
 8  else
 9  {
10    tail->next = new Node<T>(element);
11    tail = tail->next;
12  }
13
14  size++;
15 }
```

Consider two cases:

1. if the list is empty (line 4), both **head** and **tail** will point to this new node (line 6);

2. otherwise, insert the node at the end of the list (line 10). After the insertion, **tail** should refer to this new element node (line 11), as shown in Figure 20.7. In any case, after the node is created, the size should be increased by **1** (line 14).

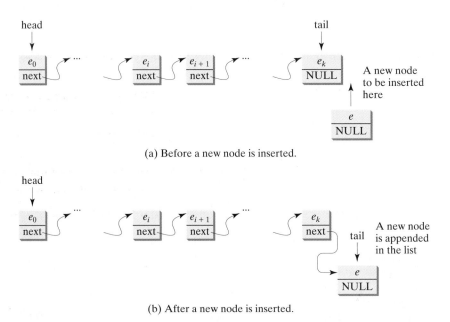

(a) Before a new node is inserted.

(b) After a new node is inserted.

FIGURE 20.7 A new element is added at the end of the list.

20.4.3 Implementing add(int index, T element)

The **add(int index, T element)** function adds an element to the list at the specified index. It can be implemented as follows:

```
 1 template<typename T>
 2 void LinkedList<T>::add(int index, T element)
 3 {
 4   if (index == 0)
 5     addFirst(element);
 6   else if (index >= size)
 7     addLast(element);
 8   else
 9   {
10     Node<T> *current = head;
```

insert first

insert last

```
11      for (int i = 1; i < index; i++)
12        current = current->next;
13      Node<T> *temp = current->next;
14      current->next = new Node<T>(element);                    create a node
15      (current->next)->next = temp;
16      size++;                                                   increase size
17    }
18 }
```

Consider three cases:

1. If **index** is **0**, invoke **addFirst(element)** (line 5) to insert the element at the beginning of the list;

2. If **index** is greater than or equal to **size**, invoke **addLast(element)** (line 7) to insert the element at the end of the list;

3. Otherwise, create a new node to store the new element and locate where to insert it. As shown in Figure 20.8(a), the new node is to be inserted between the nodes **current** and **temp**. The function assigns the new node to **current->next** and assigns **temp** to the new node's **next**, as shown in Figure 20.8(b). The size is now increased by **1** (line 16).

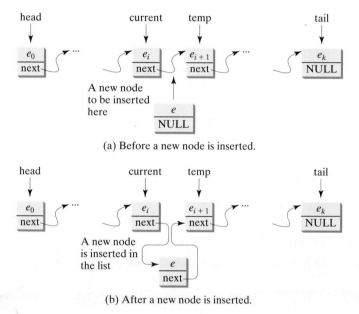

(a) Before a new node is inserted.

(b) After a new node is inserted.

FIGURE 20.8 A new element is inserted in the middle of the list.

20.4.4 Implementing removeFirst()

The **removeFirst()** function can be implemented as follows:

```
1 template<typename T>
2 T LinkedList<T>::removeFirst() throw (runtime_error)
3 {
4    if (size == 0)
5      throw runtime_error("No elements in the list");          throw exception
6    else
7    {
8      Node<T> *temp = head;                                     keep old head
9      head = head->next;                                        new head
```

decrease **size**

destroy the node

```
10    size--;
11    if (head == NULL) tail = NULL;
12    T element = temp->element;
13    delete temp;
14    return element;
15  }
16 }
```

Consider three cases:

1. If the list is empty, an exception is thrown (line 5);

2. Otherwise, remove the first node from the list by pointing **head** to the second node, as shown in Figure 20.9. The size is reduced by **1** after the deletion (line 10);

3. If the list has just one node, then after removing it, **tail** should be set to **NULL** (line 11).

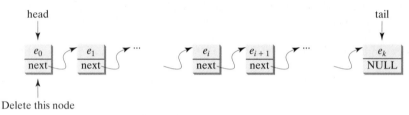

(a) Before the node is deleted.

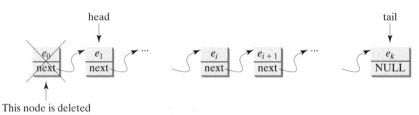

(b) After the node is deleted.

FIGURE 20.9   The first node is deleted from the list.

20.4.5   Implementing removeLast()

The removeLast() function can be implemented as follows:

throw exception
size 1?

head and tail NULL
size is 1

destroy the node
return element

size > 1

```
1 template<typename T>
2 T LinkedList<T>::removeLast() throw (runtime_error)
3 {
4   if (size == 0)
5     throw runtime_error("No elements in the list");
6   else if (size == 1)
7   {
8     Node<T> *temp = head;
9     head = tail = NULL;
10    size = 0;
11    T element = temp->element;
12    delete temp;
13    return element;
14  }
15  else
16  {
17    Node<T> *current = head;
18
```

```
19      for (int i = 0; i < size - 2; i++)
20        current = current->next;
21
22      Node<T> *temp = tail;
23      tail = current;                            move tail
24      tail->next = NULL;
25      size--;                                    reduce size
26      T element = temp->element;
27      delete temp;                               destroy the node
28      return element;                            return element
29    }
30 }
```

Consider three cases:

1. If the list is empty, an exception is thrown (line 5);

2. If the list contains only one node, this node is destroyed; `head` and `tail` both become `NULL` (line 9);

3. Otherwise, the last node is destroyed and the `tail` is repositioned to point to the second-to-last node, as shown in Figure 20.10. For the last two cases, the size is reduced by 1 after the deletion (lines 10, 25), and the element value of the deleted node is returned (lines 13, 28).

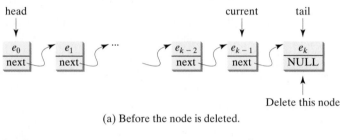

(a) Before the node is deleted.

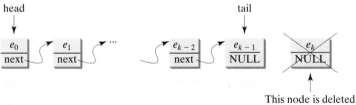

(b) After the node is deleted.

FIGURE 20.10 The last node is deleted from the list.

20.4.6 Implementing `removeAt(int index)`

The `removeAt(int index)` function finds the node at the specified index and then removes it. It can be implemented as follows:

```
1 template<typename T>
2 T LinkedList<T>::removeAt(int index) throw (runtime_error)
3 {
4   if (index < 0 || index >= size)
5     throw runtime_error("Index out of range");        throw exception
6   else if (index == 0)
7     return removeFirst();                             remove first
8   else if (index == size - 1)
```

remove last

locate previous

locate current
remove from list
reduce size

destroy the node
return element

```
 9        return removeLast();
10    else
11    {
12      Node<T> *previous = head;
13
14      for (int i = 1; i < index; i++)
15      {
16        previous = previous->next;
17      }
18
19      Node<T> *current = previous->next;
20      previous->next = current->next;
21      size--;
22      T element = current->element;
23      delete current;
24      return element;
25    }
26 }
```

Consider four cases:

1. If `index` is beyond the range of the list (i.e., `index < 0 || index >= size`), throw an exception (line 5);

2. If `index` is `0`, invoke `removeFirst()` to remove the first node (line 7);

3. If `index` is `size - 1`, invoke `removeLast()` to remove the last node (line 9);

4. Otherwise, locate the node at the specified `index`. Let `current` denote this node and `previous` denote the node before it, as shown in Figure 20.11(a). Assign `current->next` to `previous->next` to eliminate the current node, as shown in Figure 20.11(b).

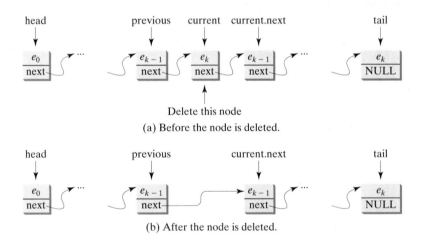

(a) Before the node is deleted.

(b) After the node is deleted.

FIGURE 20.11 A node is deleted from the list.

20.4.7 The source code for `LinkedList`

Listing 20.2 gives the implementation of `LinkedList`.

LISTING 20.2 `LinkedList.h`

`runtime_error` header

```
1 #ifndef LINKEDLIST_H
2 #define LINKEDLIST_H
3 #include <stdexcept>
4 using namespace std;
5
```

```
 6 template<typename T>
 7 class Node
 8 {
 9 public:
10   T element;   // Element contained in the node
11   Node<T> *next; // Pointer to the next node
12
13   Node() // No-arg constructor
14   {
15     next = NULL;
16   }
17
18   Node(T element) // Constructor
19   {
20     this->element = element;
21     next = NULL;
22   }
23 };
24
25 template<typename T>
26 class Iterator : public std::iterator<std::forward_iterator_tag, T>
27 {
28 public:
29   Iterator(Node<T> *p)
30   {
31     current = p;
32   };
33
34   Iterator operator++()
35   {
36     current = current -> next;
37     return *this;
38   }
39
40   T &operator*()
41   {
42     return current -> element;
43   }
44
45   bool operator==(const Iterator<T> &iterator)
46   {
47     return current == iterator.current;
48   }
49
50   bool operator!=(const Iterator<T> &iterator)
51   {
52     return current != iterator.current;
53   }
54
55 private:
56   Node<T> *current;
57 };
58
59 template<typename T>
60 class LinkedList
61 {
62 public:
63   LinkedList();
64   LinkedList(LinkedList<T> &list);
65   ~LinkedList();
66   void addFirst(T element);
```

class **Node**

class **Iterator**
discussed in §20.5

class **LinkedList**

```
67    void addLast(T element);
68    T getFirst() const;
69    T getLast() const;
70    T removeFirst() throw (runtime_error);
71    T removeLast();
72    void add(T element);
73    void add(int index, T element);
74    void clear();
75    bool contains(T element) const;
76    T get(int index) const;
77    int indexOf(T element) const;
78    bool isEmpty() const;
79    int lastIndexOf(T element) const;
80    void remove(T element);
81    int getSize() const;
82    T removeAt(int index);
83    T set(int index, T element);
84
85    Iterator<T> begin()
86    {
87      return Iterator<T>(head);
88    };
89
90    Iterator<T> end()
91    {
92      return Iterator<T>(tail->next);
93    };
94
95  private:
96    Node<T> *head, *tail;
97    int size;
98  };
99
100 template<typename T>
101 LinkedList<T>::LinkedList()
102 {
103    head = tail = NULL;
104    size = 0;
105 }
106
107 template<typename T>
108 LinkedList<T>::LinkedList(LinkedList<T> &list)
109 {
110    head = tail = NULL;
111    size = 0;
112
113    Node<T> *current = list.head;
114    while (current != NULL)
115    {
116      this->add(current->element);
117      current = current->next;
118    }
119 }
120
121 template<typename T>
122 LinkedList<T>::~LinkedList()
123 {
124    clear();
125 }
126
```

no-arg constructor

copy constructor

destructor

```
127  template<typename T>
128  void LinkedList<T>::addFirst(T element)                          addFirst
129  {
130    // Same as in §20.4.1, so omitted
131  }
132
133  template<typename T>
134  void LinkedList<T>::addLast(T element)                           addLast
135  {
136    // Same as in §20.4.2, so omitted
137  }
138
139  template<typename T>
140  T LinkedList<T>::getFirst() const                                getFirst
141  {
142    if (size == 0)
143      throw runtime_error("Index out of range");
144    else
145      return head->element;
146  }
147
148  template<typename T>
149  T LinkedList<T>::getLast() const                                 getLast
150  {
151    if (size == 0)
152      throw runtime_error("Index out of range");
153    else
154      return tail->element;
155  }
156
157  template<typename T>
158  T LinkedList<T>::removeFirst() throw (runtime_error)             removeFirst
159  {
160    // Same as in §20.4.4, so omitted
161  }
162
163  template<typename T>
164  T LinkedList<T>::removeLast()                                    removeLast
165  {
166    // Same as in §20.4.5, so omitted
167  }
168
169  template<typename T>
170  void LinkedList<T>::add(T element)                               add
171  {
172    addLast(element);
173  }
174
175  template<typename T>
176  void LinkedList<T>::add(int index, T element)                   add
177  {
178    // Same as in §20.4.3, so omitted
179  }
180
181  template<typename T>
182  void LinkedList<T>::clear()                                      clear
183  {
184    while (head != NULL)
185    {
186      Node<T> *temp = head;
```

```
187       head = head->next;
188       delete temp;
189     }
190
191     tail = NULL;
192 }
193
194 template<typename T>
195 T LinkedList<T>::get(int index) const
196 {
197     if (index < 0 || index > size - 1)
198       throw runtime_error("Index out of range");
199
200     Node<T> *current = head;
201     for (int i = 0; i < index; i++)
202       current = current->next;
203
204     return current->element;
205 }
206
207 template<typename T>
208 int LinkedList<T>::indexOf(T element) const
209 {
210     // Implement it in this exercise
211     Node<T> *current = head;
212     for (int i = 0; i < size; i++)
213     {
214       if (current->element == element)
215         return i;
216       current = current->next;
217     }
218
219     return -1;
220 }
221
222 template<typename T>
223 bool LinkedList<T>::isEmpty() const
224 {
225     return head == NULL;
226 }
227
228 template<typename T>
229 int LinkedList<T>::getSize() const
230 {
231     return size;
232 }
233
234 template<typename T>
235 T LinkedList<T>::removeAt(int index)
236 {
237     // Same as in §20.4.6, so omitted
238 }
239
240     // The functions remove(T element), lastIndexOf(T element),
241     // contains(T element), and set(int index, T element) are
242     // left as an exercise
243
244 #endif
```

get

indexOf

isEmpty

getSize

removeAt

A linked list contains nodes defined in the Node class (lines 6–23). You can obtain iterators for traversing the elements in a linked list. The `Iterator` class (lines 25–57) will be discussed in §20.5.

The header of the `LinkedList` class is defined in lines 59–98. The no-arg constructor (lines 100–105) constructs an empty linked list with **head** and **tail NULL** and **size 0**.

The copy constructor (lines 107–119) creates a new linked list by copying the contents from an existing list. This is done by inserting the elements from the existing linked list to the new one (lines 113–118).

The destructor (lines 121–125) removes all nodes from the linked list by invoking the `clear` function (lines 181–192), which deletes all the nodes from the list (line 188).

The implementation for functions `addFirst(T element)` (lines 127–131), `addLast(T element)` (lines 133–137), `removeFirst()` (lines 157–161), `removeLast()` (lines 163–167), `removeFirst()` (lines 157–161), `removeLast()` (lines 163–167), `add(int index, T element)` (lines 175–179), and `removeAt(int index)` (lines 234–238) is discussed in §20.4.1–20.4.6.

The functions `getFirst()` and `getLast()` (lines 139–155) return the first and last elements in the list, respectively.

The `get(int index)` function returns the element at the specified index (lines 194–205).

The implementation of `lastIndexOf(T element)`, `remove(T element)`, `contains(T element)`, and `set(int index, Object o)` (lines 240–242) is omitted and left as an exercise.

20.4.8   The time complexity of `LinkedList`

Table 20.1 summarizes the complexities of the functions in `LinkedList`.

TABLE 20.1   Time Complexities for functions in `LinkedList`

Functions	LinkedList
add(e: T)	$O(1)$
add(index: int, e: T)	$O(n)$
clear()	$O(n)$
contains(e: T)	$O(n)$
get(index: int)	$O(n)$
indexOf(e: T)	$O(n)$
isEmpty()	$O(1)$
lastIndexOf(e: T)	$O(n)$
remove(e: T)	$O(n)$
size()	$O(1)$
remove(index: int)	$O(n)$
set(index: int, e: T)	$O(n)$
addFirst(e: T)	$O(1)$
removeFirst()	$O(1)$

You can use an array, a vector, or a linked list to store elements. If you don't know the number of elements in advance, it is more efficient to use a vector or a linked list, because these can grow and shrink dynamically. If your application requires frequent insertion and deletion anywhere, it is more efficient to store elements using a linked list, because inserting an element into an array or a vector would require all the elements in the array after the insertion point to be moved. If the number of elements in an application is fixed and the application does not require random insertion and deletion, it is simple and efficient to use an array to store the elements.

20.5 Iterators

Iterator is an important advanced construct in C++. It provides a uniform way for traversing elements in various types of containers. The Standard Template Library (STL) uses iterators to access the elements in the containers. The STL will be introduced in Chapters 22 and 23. The present section creates an iterator class for traversing the elements in a linked list. The objectives here are twofold: (1) to look at an example of how to create an iterator class; (2) to become familiar with iterators and how to use them to traverse the elements in a container.

Iterators can be viewed as encapsulated pointers. In a linked list, you can use pointers to traverse the list. But iterators have more functions than pointers. Iterators are objects. Iterators contain functions for accessing and manipulating elements. The **Iterator** class for traversing the elements in a linked list is defined in Figure 20.12.

Iterator<T>	
-*current: Node<T>	Current pointer in the iterator.
+Iterator(*p: Node<T>)	Constructs an iterator with a specified pointer.
+operator++(): Iterator<T>	Obtains the iterator for the next pointer.
+operator*(): T	Returns the element from the node pointed by the iterator.
+operator==(&itr: Iterator<T>): bool	Returns true if this iterator is the same as the iterator itr.
+operator!=(&itr: Iterator<T>): bool	Returns true if this iterator is different from the iterator itr.

FIGURE 20.12 **Iterator** encapsulates pointers with additional functions.

This class is implemented in lines 25–57 in Listing 20.2. Since constructors and functions are short, they are implemented as inline functions.

The **Iterator** class uses the data field **current** to point to the node being traversed (line 56).

The constructor (lines 29–32) creates an iterator that points to a specified node.

The **operator++()** function moves current to point to the next node in the list (line 34).

To obtain iterators from a **LinkedList**, the following two functions are defined and implemented in lines 85–93 in Listing 20.2.

```
Iterator<T> begin();
Iterator<T> end();
```

The **begin()** function returns the iterator for the first element in the list, and the **end()** function returns the iterator that represents a position pastthe last element in the list.

Listing 20.3 gives an example that uses iterators to traverse the elements in a linked list and displays the strings in uppercase. The program creates a **LinkedList** for strings in line 17, adds four strings to the list (lines 20–23), and traverses all the elements in the list using iterators and displays them in uppercase (lines 26–30).

LISTING 20.3 TestIterator.cpp

```
1 #include <iostream>
2 #include <string>
3 #include "LinkedList.h"
4 using namespace std;
5
6 string toUpperCase(string s)
```

```
 7 {
 8    for (int i = 0; i < s.length(); i++)
 9      s[i] = toupper(s[i]);
10
11    return s;
12 }
13
14 int main()
15 {
16    // Create a list for strings
17    LinkedList<string> list;                                    create list
18
19    // Add elements to the list
20    list.add("America");                                        add string
21    list.add("Canada");
22    list.add("Russia");
23    list.add("France");
24
25    // Traverse a list using iterators
26    for (Iterator<string> iterator = list.begin();             traverse list
27      iterator != list.end(); iterator++)
28    {
29      cout << toUpperCase(*iterator) << " ";                   access element
30    }
31
32    return 0;
33 }
```

```
AMERICA CANADA RUSSIA FRANCE
```

Note

An iterator functions like a pointer. It may be implemented using pointers, array indexes, or other   benefits of iterators
data structures. The abstraction of iterators spares you the details of implementation. Chapter 22,
"STL Containers," will introduce iterators in STL. STL iterators provide a uniform interface for
accessing the elements in a container, so you can use iterators to access the elements in a vector
or a set just as in a linked list.

Note that the `Iterator` class is derived from `std::iterator<std::forward_iterator_tag, T>`. It is not necessary to make `Iterator` a child class of `std::iterator<std::forward_iterator_tag, T>`, but doing so enables you to invoke the C++ STL library functions for `LinkedList` elements. These functions use iterators to traverse elements in the container. Listing 20.4 gives an example that uses the C++ STL library functions `max_element` and `min_element` to return the maximum and minimum elements in a linked list.

LISTING 20.4 TestSTLAlgorithm.cpp

```
1 #include <iostream>
2 #include <algorithm>                                          library for STL algorithms
3 #include <string>
4 #include "LinkedList.h"
5 using namespace std;
6
7 int main()
8 {
9    // Create a list for strings
```

create list

```
10    LinkedList<string> list;
11
12    // Add elements to the list
```

add string

```
13    list.add("America");
14    list.add("Canada");
15    list.add("Russia");
16    list.add("France");
17
18    cout << "The max element in the list is: " <<
```

max_element function

```
19       *max_element(list.begin(), list.end()) << endl;
20
21    cout << "The min element in array1: " <<
```

min_element function

```
22       *min_element(list.begin(), list.end()) << endl;
23
24    return 0;
25 }
```

```
The max element in the list is: Russia
The min element in array1: America
```

The `max_element(iterator1, iterator2)` returns the iterator for the maximum element between `iterator1` and `iterator2 - 1`. Iterators are like pointers. You can call an iterator just as a pointer for convenience.

20.6 Variations of Linked Lists

The linked list introduced in the preceding section is known as a *singly linked list*. It contains a pointer to the list's first node, and each node contains a pointer to the next node sequentially. Several variations of the linked list are useful in certain applications.

A *circular, singly linked list* differs in that the pointer of the last node points back to the first node, as shown in Figure 20.13(a).

A *doubly linked list* contains the nodes with two pointers. One points to the next node and the other to the previous node, as shown in Figure 20.13(b). These two pointers are conveniently

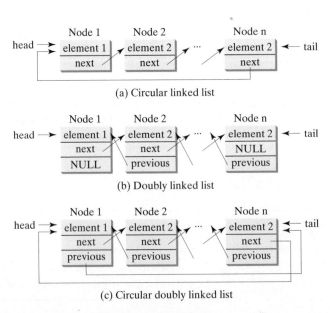

FIGURE 20.13 Linked lists may appear in various forms.

called *a forward pointer* and *a backward pointer*. So, a doubly linked list can be traversed forward and backward.

A *circular, doubly linked list* has the property that the forward pointer of the last node points to the first node and the backward pointer of the first pointer points to the last node, as shown in Figure 20.13(b).

The implementation of these linked lists is left to the exercises.

20.7 Queues

A *queue* represents a waiting list. It can be viewed as a special type of list whose elements are inserted into the end (tail) and are accessed and deleted from the beginning (head), as shown in Figure 20.14.

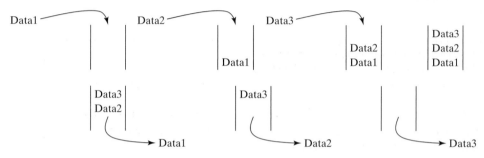

FIGURE 20.14 A queue holds objects in a first-in, first-out fashion.

There are two ways to design the queue class:

- Using composition: You can declare a linked list as a data field in the queue class, as shown in Figure 20.15(a).   composition

- Using inheritance: You can define a queue class by extending the linked list class, as shown in Figure 20.15(b).   inheritance

(a) Using composition   (b) Using inheritance

FIGURE 20.15 Queue may be implemented using composition or inheritance.

Both designs are fine, but using composition is better, because it enables you to define a completely new queue class without inheriting the unnecessary and inappropriate functions from the linked list. Figure 20.16 shows the UML class diagram for the queue. Its implementation is shown in Listing 20.5.

Queue\<T>	
-list: LinkedList\<T>	Stores the elements in the queue.
+enqueue(element: T): void	Adds an element to this queue.
+dequeue(): T	Removes an element from this queue.
+getSize(): int	Returns the number of elements from this queue.

FIGURE 20.16 Queue uses a linked list to provide a first-in, first-out data structure.

LISTING 20.5   Queue.h

include **LinkedList**

class template

linked list

constructor

enqueue

dequeue

getSize

```cpp
1 #ifndef QUEUE_H
2 #define QUEUE_H
3 #include "LinkedList.h"
4 #include <stdexcept>
5 using namespace std;
6
7 template<typename T>
8 class Queue
9 {
10 public:
11   Queue();
12   void enqueue(T element);
13   T dequeue() throw (runtime_error);
14   int getSize() const;
15
16 private:
17   LinkedList<T> list;
18 };
19
20 template<typename T>
21 Queue<T>::Queue()
22 {
23 }
24
25 template<typename T>
26 void Queue<T>::enqueue(T element)
27 {
28   list.addLast(element);
29 }
30
31 template<typename T>
32 T Queue<T>::dequeue() throw (runtime_error)
33 {
34   return list.removeFirst();
35 }
36
37 template<typename T>
38 int Queue<T>::getSize() const
39 {
40   return list.getSize();
41 }
42
43 #endif
```

A linked list is created to store the elements in a queue (line 17). The enqueue(T element) function (lines 25–29) adds elements into the tail of the queue. The dequeue() function (lines 31–35) removes an element from the head of the queue and returns the removed element. The getSize() function (lines 37–41) returns the number of elements in the queue.

Listing 20.6 gives an example that creates a queue for int values (line 17) and a queue for strings (line 24) using the Queue class. It uses the enqueue function to add elements to the queues (lines 19, 25–27) and the dequeue function to remove int values and strings from the queue.

LISTING 20.6   TestQueue.cpp

include **Queue**

```cpp
1 #include <iostream>
2 #include "Queue.h"
3 #include <string>
```

```
 4 using namespace std;
 5
 6 template<typename T>
 7 void printQueue(Queue<T> &queue)
 8 {
 9   while (queue.getSize() > 0)
10     cout << queue.dequeue() << " ";
11   cout << endl;
12 }
13
14 int main()
15 {
16   // Queue of int values
17   Queue<int> intQueue;
18   for (int i = 0; i < 10; i++)
19     intQueue.enqueue(i);
20
21   printQueue(intQueue);
22
23   // Queue of strings
24   Queue<string> stringQueue;
25   stringQueue.enqueue("New York");
26   stringQueue.enqueue("Boston");
27   stringQueue.enqueue("Denver");
28
29   printQueue(stringQueue);
30
31   return 0;
32 }
```

class template

printQueue function

queue size?
dequeue

create a queue

enqueue int

invoke **printQueue**

create a queue
enqueue

invoke **printQueue**

```
0 1 2 3 4 5 6 7 8 9
New York Boston Denver
```

20.8 Priority Queues

A regular queue is a first-in, first-out data structure. Elements are appended to the end of the queue and are removed from the beginning. In a *priority queue*, elements are assigned with priorities. The element with the highest priority is accessed or removed first. A priority queue has a largest-in, first-out behavior. For example, the emergency room in a hospital assigns patients with priority numbers; the patient with the highest priority is treated first.

A priority queue can be implemented using a heap, where the root is the element with the highest priority in the queue. Heap was introduced in §19.5, "Heap Sort." The class diagram for the priority queue is shown in Figure 20.17. Its implementation is given in Listing 20.7.

Video Note
Implementing priority queue

PriorityQueue<T>	
-heap: Heap<T>	Stores the element in the priority queue.
+enqueue(element: T): void	Adds an element to this queue.
+dequeue(): T	Removes an element from this queue.
+getSize(): int	Returns the number of elements from this queue.

FIGURE 20.17 `PriorityQueue` uses a heap to provide a largest-in, first-out data structure.

LISTING 20.7 PriorityQueue.h

heap for priority queue

```
 1 #ifndef PRIORITYQUEUE_H
 2 #define PRIORITYQUEUE_H
 3 #include "Heap.h" // Defined in Listing 19.10
 4
 5 template<typename T>
 6 class PriorityQueue
 7 {
 8 public:
```

constructor

```
 9   PriorityQueue();
10   void enqueue(T element);
11   T dequeue() throw (runtime_error);
12   int getSize() const;
13
14 private:
```

heap

```
15   Heap<T> heap;
16 };
17
18 template<typename T>
19 PriorityQueue<T>::PriorityQueue()
20 {
21 }
22
23 template<typename T>
```

add to queue

```
24 void PriorityQueue<T>::enqueue(T element)
25 {
26   heap.add(element);
27 }
28
29 template<typename T>
```

remove from queue

```
30 T PriorityQueue<T>::dequeue() throw (runtime_error)
31 {
32   return heap.remove();
33 }
34
35 template<typename T>
```

queue size

```
36 int PriorityQueue<T>::getSize() const
37 {
38   return heap.getSize();
39 }
40
41 #endif
```

Listing 20.8 gives an example of using a priority queue for patients. The **Patient** class is defined in lines 5–37. Line 42 creates a priority queue. Four patients with associated priority values are created and enqueued in lines 43–46. Line 50 dequeues a patient from the queue.

LISTING 20.8 TestPriorityQueue.cpp

```
 1 #include <iostream>
```

include **PriorityQueue**

```
 2 #include "PriorityQueue.h"
 3 using namespace std;
 4
```

Patient class

```
 5 class Patient
 6 {
 7 public:
```

Patient constructor

```
 8   Patient(string name, int priority)
```

```
 9    {
10      this->name = name;
11      this->priority = priority;
12    }
13
14    bool operator<(Patient &secondPatient)                          overload < operator
15    {
16      return (this->priority < secondPatient.priority);
17    }
18
19    bool operator>(Patient &secondPatient)                          overload > operator
20    {
21      return (this->priority > secondPatient.priority);
22    }
23
24    string getName()                                                getName
25    {
26      return name;
27    }
28
29    int getPriority()                                               getPriority
30    {
31      return priority;
32    }
33
34 private:
35    string name;
36    int priority;
37 };
38
39 int main()
40 {
41    // Queue of patients
42    PriorityQueue<Patient> patientQueue;                            create a priority queue
43    patientQueue.enqueue(Patient("John", 2));                       add to queue
44    patientQueue.enqueue(Patient("Jim", 1));
45    patientQueue.enqueue(Patient("Tim", 5));
46    patientQueue.enqueue(Patient("Cindy", 7));
47
48    while (patientQueue.getSize() > 0)
49    {
50      Patient element = patientQueue.dequeue();                     remove from queue
51      cout << element.getName() << " (priority: " <<
52        element.getPriority() << ") ";
53    }
54
55    return 0;
56 }
```

```
Cindy(priority: 7) Tim(priority: 5) John(priority: 2) Jim(priority: 1)
```

The < and > operators are defined the **Patient** class, so two patients can be compared. You can use any class type for the elements in the heap, provided that the elements can be compared using the < and > operators.

KEY TERMS

circular doubly linked list 641
circular singly linked list 640
dequeue 642
doubly linked list 640
enqueue 642

linked list 622
priority queue 643
queue 641
singly linked list 640

CHAPTER SUMMARY

1. A linked list grows and shrinks dynamically. Nodes in a linked list are dynamically created using the **new** operator, and they are destroyed using the **delete** operator.

2. A queue represents a waiting list. It can be viewed as a special type of list whose elements are inserted into the end (tail) and are accessed and deleted from the beginning (head).

3. If you don't know the number of elements in advance, it is more efficient to use a linked list, which can grow and shrink dynamically.

4. If your application requires frequent insertion and deletion anywhere, it is more efficient to store elements using a linked list, because inserting an element into an array would require moving all the elements in the array after the insertion point.

5. If the elements need to be processed in a first-in, first-out fashion, use a queue to store the elements.

6. A priority queue can be implemented using a heap, where the root is the element with the highest priority in the queue.

REVIEW QUESTIONS

Section 20.2

20.1 Are the following class declarations correct?

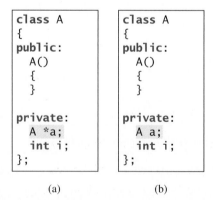

```
class A
{
public:
  A()
  {
  }

private:
  A *a;
  int i;
};
```
(a)

```
class A
{
public:
  A()
  {
  }

private:
  A a;
  int i;
};
```
(b)

20.2 What is NULL for?

20.3 When a node is created using the Node class, is the next pointer of this new node NULL?

Section 20.3

20.4 Which of the following statements are used to insert a string `s` to the head of the list? Which ones are used to append a string `s` to the end of the list?

```
list.addFirst(s);
list.add(s);
list.add(0, s);
list.add(1, s);
```

20.5 Which of the following statements are used to remove the first element from the list? Which ones are used to remove the last element from the list?

```
list.removeFirst(s);
list.removeLast(s);
list.removeFirst();
list.removeLast();
list.remove(0);
list.removeAt(0);
list.removeAt(list.getSize() - 1);
list.removeAt(list.getSize());
```

20.6 Suppose the `removeAt` function is renamed as `remove` so that there are two overloaded functions, `remove(T element)` and `remove(int index)`. This is incorrect. Explain the reason.

Section 20.4

20.7 If a linked list does not contain any nodes, what are the values in `head` and `tail`?

20.8 If a linked list has only one node, is `head == tail` true? List all cases in which `head == tail` is true.

20.9 When a new node is inserted to the head of a linked list, will the `head` pointer and the `tail` pointer be changed?

20.10 When a new node is inserted to the end of a linked list, will the `head` pointer and the `tail` pointer be changed?

20.11 When a node is removed from a linked list, what will happen if you don't explicitly use the `delete` operator to release the node?

20.12 Under what circumstances would the functions `removeFirst`, `removeLast`, and `removeAt` throw an exception?

20.13 Discuss the pros and cons of using arrays and linked lists.

20.14 If the number of elements in the program is fixed, what data structure should you use? If the number of elements in the program changes, what data structure should you use?

20.15 If you have to add or delete the elements anywhere in a list, should you use an array or a linked list?

20.16 If you change the function signature for `printList` in line 6 in Listing 20.1 to

void printList(LinkedList<string> list)

will the program work? So, what is the difference between the two signatures?

20.17 What will happen when you run the following code?

```
1 #include <iostream>
2 #include <string>
3 #include "LinkedList.h"
4 using namespace std;
```

```
 5
 6 int main()
 7 {
 8   LinkedList<string> list;
 9   list.add("abc");
10   cout << list.removeLast() << endl;
11   cout << list.removeLast() << endl;
12
13   return 0;
14 }
```

20.18 Show the output of the following code:

```
 1 #include <iostream>
 2 #include <string>
 3 #include "LinkedList.h"
 4 using namespace std;
 5
 6 int main()
 7 {
 8   LinkedList<string> list;
 9   list.add("abc");
10
11   try
12   {
13     cout << list.removeLast() << endl;
14     cout << list.removeLast() << endl;
15   }
16   catch (runtime_error ex)
17   {
18     cout << "The list size is " <<  list.getSize() << endl;
19   }
20
21   return 0;
22 }
```

Section 20.5

20.19 What is a circular, singly linked list? What is a doubly linked list? What is a circular, doubly linked list?

Sections 20.6–20.7

20.20 You can use inheritance or composition to design the data structures for queues. Discuss the pros and cons of these two approaches.

20.21 Show the output of the following code:

```
 1 #include <iostream>
 2 #include <string>
 3 #include "ImprovedStack.h" // Defined in Listing 12.7
 4 #include "Queue.h"
 5 using namespace std;
 6
 7 int main()
 8 {
 9   Stack<string> stack;
10   Queue<int> queue;
11
12   stack.push("Georgia");
13   stack.push("Indiana");
14   stack.push("Oklahoma");
```

```
15
16   cout << stack.pop() << endl;
17   cout << "Stack's size is " << stack.getSize() << endl;
18
19   queue.enqueue(1);
20   queue.enqueue(2);
21   queue.enqueue(3);
22
23   cout << queue.dequeue() << endl;
24   cout << "Queue's size is " << queue.getSize() << endl;
25
26   return 0;
27 }
```

20.22 What is a priority queue?

PROGRAMMING EXERCISES

Sections 20.2–20.4

20.1* (*Implementing* remove(T element)) The implementation of remove(T element) is omitted in Listing 20.2, LinkedList.h. Implement it.

20.2* (*Implementing* lastIndexOf(T element)) The implementation of lastIndexOf(T element) is omitted in Listing 20.2, LinkedList.h. Implement it.

20.3* (*Implementing* contains(T element)) The implementation of contains(T element) is omitted in Listing 20.2, LinkedList.h. Implement it.

20.4* (*Implementing* set(int index, T element)) The implementation of contains(T element) is omitted in Listing 20.2, LinkedList.h. Implement it.

Video Note
Implementing lastIndexOf function

20.5 (*Adding set-like operations in* LinkedList) Add and implement the following functions in LinkedList:

```
/* Add the elements in otherList to this list.
 */
void addAll(const LinkedList<T> &otherList)

/* Remove all the elements in otherList from this list
 */
void removeAll(const LinkedList<T> &otherList)

/* Retain the elements in this list if they are also in oth-
erList
 */
void retainAll(const LinkedList<T> &otherList)
```

Write a test program that creates two linked lists, list1 and list2, with the initial values {"Beijing", "Tokyo", "New York", "London", "Paris"} and {"Beijing", "Shanghai", "Paris", "Berlin", "Rome"}, then invokes list1.addAll(list2), list1.removeAll(list2), and list1.retainAll(list2), and displays the resulting new list1.

Section 20.5

20.6* (*Creating a doubly linked list*) The LinkedList class in the text is a singly linked list that enables one-way traversal of the list. Modify the Node class to add the new field name **previous** to refer to the previous node in the list, as follows:

template<typename T>

```
class Node
{
public:
  T element;  // Element contained in the node
  Node<T> *previous; // Pointer to the previous node
  Node<T> *next; // Pointer to the next node

  Node() // No-arg constructor
  {
    previous = NULL;
    next = NULL;
  }

  Node(T element) // Constructor
  {
    this->element = element;
    previous = NULL;
    next = NULL;
  }
};
```

Simplify the implementation of the add(T element, int index) and removeAt(int index) functions to take advantage of the doubly linked list.

Sections 20.6–20.7

20.7 (*Implementing Stack using inheritance*) In Listing 12.7, ImprovedStack.h, Stack is implemented using composition. Create a new stack class that extends LinkedList.

20.8 (*Implementing Queue using inheritance*) In Listing 20.5 Queue.h, Queue is implemented using composition. Create a new queue class that extends LinkedList.

APPENDIXES

C++ Keywords

The following keywords are reserved for use by the C++ language. They should not be used for anything other than their predefined purposes in C++.

asm	do	inline	return	typedef
auto	double	int	short	typeid
bool	dynamic_cast	log	signed	typename
break	else	long	sizeof	union
case	enum	mutable	static	unsigned
catch	explicit	namespace	static_cast	using
char	extern	new	struct	virtual
class	false	operator	switch	void
const	float	private	template	volatile
const_cast	for	protected	this	wchar_t
continue	friend	public	throw	while
default	goto	register	true	
delete	if	reinterpret_cast	try	

APPENDIX B

The ASCII Character Set

Tables B.1 and B.2 show ASCII characters and their respective decimal and hexadecimal codes. The decimal or hexadecimal code of a character is a combination of its row index and column index. For example, in Table B.1, the letter A is at row 6 and column 5, so its decimal equivalent is 65; in Table B.2, letter A is at row 4 and column 1, so its hexadecimal equivalent is 41.

TABLE B.1 ASCII Character Set in the Decimal Index

	0	1	2	3	4	5	6	7	8	9
0	nul	soh	stx	etx	eot	enq	ack	bel	bs	ht
1	nl	vt	ff	cr	so	si	dle	dc1	dc2	dc3
2	dc4	nak	syn	etb	can	em	sub	esc	fs	gs
3	rs	us	sp	!	"	#	$	%	&	'
4	(	)	*	+	,	-	.	/	0	1
5	2	3	4	5	6	7	8	9	:	;
6	<	=	>	?	@	A	B	C	D	E
7	F	G	H	I	J	K	L	M	N	O
8	P	Q	R	S	T	U	V	W	X	Y
9	Z	[	\	]	^	_	`	a	b	c
10	d	e	f	g	h	i	j	k	l	m
11	n	o	p	q	r	s	t	u	v	w
12	x	y	z	{	|	}	~	del		

TABLE B.2 ASCII Character Set in the Hexadecimal Index

	0	1	2	3	4	5	6	7	8	9	A	B	C	D	E	F
0	nul	soh	stx	etx	eot	enq	ack	bel	bs	ht	nl	vt	ff	cr	so	si
1	dle	dc1	dc2	dc3	dc4	nak	syn	etb	can	em	sub	esc	fs	gs	rs	us
2	sp	!	"	#	$	%	&	'	(	)	*	+	,	-	.	/
3	0	1	2	3	4	5	6	7	8	9	:	;	<	=	>	?
4	@	A	B	C	D	E	F	G	H	I	J	K	L	M	N	O
5	P	Q	R	S	T	U	V	W	X	Y	Z	[	\	]	^	_
6	`	a	b	c	d	e	f	g	h	i	j	k	l	m	n	o
7	p	q	r	s	t	u	v	w	x	y	z	{	|	}	~	del

APPENDIX C

Operator Precedence Chart

The operators are shown in decreasing order of precedence from top to bottom. Operators in the same group have the same precedence, and their associativity is shown in the table.

Operator	Type	Associativity
::	binary scope resolution	left to right
::	unary scope resolution	
.	object member access via object	left to right
->	object member access via pointer	
()	function call	
[]	array subscript	
++	postfix increment	
--	postfix decrement	
typeid	runtime type information	
dynamic_cast	dynamic cast (runtime)	
static_cast	static cast (compile time)	
reinterpret_cast	cast for nonstandard conversion	
++	prefix increment	right to left
--	prefix decrement	
+	unary plus	
-	unary minus	
!	unary logical negation	
~	bitwise negation	
sizeof	size of a type	
&	address of a variable	
*	pointer of a variable	
new	dynamic memory allocation	
new[]	dynamic array allocation	
delete	dynamic memory deallocation	
delete[]	dynamic array deallocation	
(type)	C-Style cast	right to left
*	multiplication	left to right
/	division	
%	modulus	

Operator	Type	Associativity
+	addition	left to right
-	subtraction	
<<	output or bitwise left shift	left to right
>>	input or bitwise right shift	
<	less than	left to right
<=	less than or equal to	
>	greater than	
>=	greater than or equal to	
==	equal	left to right
!=	not equal	
&	bitwise AND	left to right
^	bitwise exclusive OR	left to right
|	bitwise inclusive OR	left to right
&&	Boolean AND	left to right
||	Boolean OR	left to right
?:	ternary operator	right to left
=	assignment	right to left
+=	addition assignment	
-=	subtraction assignment	
*=	multiplication assignment	
/=	division assignment	
%=	modulus assignment	
&=	bitwise AND assignment	
^=	bitwise exclusive OR assignment	
|=	bitwise inclusive OR assignment	
<<=	bitwise left-shift assignment	
>>=	bitwise right-shift assignment	

Appendix D

Number Systems

I Introduction

binary numbers

The binary number system has two digits, 0 and 1. Computers use binary numbers internally, because storage devices like memory and disks are made to store 0s and 1s. A number or character is stored as a sequence of 0s and 1s. Each 0 or 1 is called a *bit*.

decimal numbers

In our daily life we use decimal numbers. When we write a number like 20 in a program, it is assumed to be a decimal number. Internally, computer software is used to convert decimal numbers into binary numbers, and vice versa.

We write computer programs using decimal numbers. However, to deal with an operating system, we need to reach down to the "machine level" by using binary numbers. Binary numbers tend to be very long and cumbersome. Often hexadecimal numbers are used to abbreviate them, with each hexadecimal digit representing four binary digits. The hexadecimal number system has sixteen digits: 0–9, A–F. The letters A, B, C, D, E, and F correspond to the decimal numbers 10, 11, 12, 13, 14, and 15.

hexadecimal number

The digits in the decimal number system are 0, 1, 2, 3, 4, 5, 6, 7, 8, and 9. A decimal number is represented using a sequence of one or more of these digits. The value that each digit represents depends on its position, which denotes an integral power of 10. For example, the digits 7, 4, 2, and 3 in decimal number 7423 represent 7000, 400, 20, and 3, respectively, as shown below:

$$\boxed{7 \mid 4 \mid 2 \mid 3} = 7 \times 10^3 + 4 \times 10^2 + 2 \times 10^1 + 3 \times 10^0$$

$$10^3 \ 10^2 \ 10^1 \ 10^0 \quad = 7000 + 400 + 20 + 3 = 7423$$

base

radix

The decimal number system has ten digits, and the position values are integral powers of 10. We say that 10 is the *base* or *radix* of the decimal number system. Similarly, since the binary number system has two digits, the base of the binary number system is 2, and since the hex number system has sixteen digits, the base of the hex number system is 16.

If 1101 is a binary number, the digits 1, 1, 0, and 1 represent $1 \times 2^3, 1 \times 2^2, 0 \times 2^1$, and 1×2^0, respectively:

$$\boxed{1 \mid 1 \mid 0 \mid 1} = 1 \times 2^3 + 1 \times 2^2 + 0 \times 2^1 + 1 \times 2^0$$

$$2^3 \ 2^2 \ 2^1 \ 2^0 \quad = \quad 8 \quad + \quad 4 \quad + \quad 0 \quad + \quad 1 \quad = \quad 13$$

If 7423 is a hex number, the digits 7, 4, 2, and 3 represent $7 \times 16^3, 4 \times 16^2, 2 \times 16^1$, and 3×16^0, respectively:

$$\boxed{7 \mid 4 \mid 2 \mid 3} = 7 \times 16^3 + 4 \times 16^2 + 2 \times 16^1 + 3 \times 16^0$$

$$16^3 \ 16^2 \ 16^1 \ 16^0 \quad = 28672 \ + 1024 \ + 32 + 3 = 29731$$

2 Conversions Between Binary and Decimal Numbers

Given a binary number $b_n b_{n-1} b_{n-2} \ldots b_2 b_1 b_0$, the equivalent decimal value is

binary to decimal

$$b_n \times 2^n + b_{n-1} \times 2^{n-1} + b_{n-2} \times 2^{n-2} + \ldots + b_2 \times 2^2 + b_1 \times 2^1 + b_0 \times 2^0$$

The following are examples of converting binary numbers to decimals:

Binary	Conversion Formula	Decimal
10	$1 \times 2^1 + 0 \times 2^0$	2
1000	$1 \times 2^3 + 0 \times 2^2 + 0 \times 2^1 + 0 \times 2^0$	8
10101011	$1 \times 2^7 + 0 \times 2^6 + 1 \times 2^5 + 0 \times 2^4 + 1 \times 2^3 + 0 \times 2^2 + 1 \times 2^1 + 1 \times 2^0$	171

To convert a decimal number d to a binary number is to find the bits $b_n, b_{n-1},$ *decimal to binary* $b_{n-2}, \ldots, b_2, b_1,$ and b_0 such that

$$d = b_n \times 2^n + b_{n-1} \times 2^{n-1} + b_{n-2} \times 2^{n-2} + \ldots + b_2 \times 2^2 + b_1 \times 2^1 + b_0 \times 2^0$$

These bits can be found by successively dividing d by 2 until the quotient is 0. The remainders are $b_0, b_1, b_2, \ldots, b_{n-2}, b_{n-1},$ and b_n.

For example, the decimal number 123 is 1111011 in binary. The conversion is done as follows:

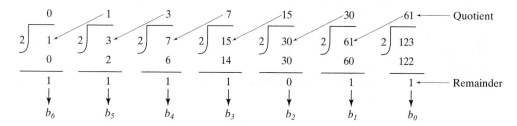

Tip

The Windows Calculator, as shown in Figure 1, is a useful tool for performing number conversions. To run it, choose *Programs*, *Accessories*, and *Calculator* from the Start button.

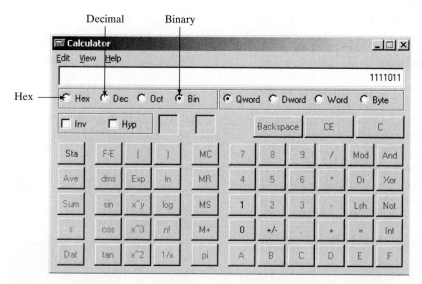

FIGURE 1 You can perform number conversions using the Windows Calculator.

3 Conversions Between Hexadecimal and Decimal Numbers

hex to decimal

Given a hexadecimal number $h_n h_{n-1} h_{n-2} \ldots h_2 h_1 h_0$, the equivalent decimal value is

$$h_n \times 16^n + h_{n-1} \times 16^{n-1} + h_{n-2} \times 16^{n-2} + \ldots + h_2 \times 16^2 + h_1 \times 16^1 + h_0 \times 16^0$$

The following are examples of converting hexadecimal numbers to decimals:

Hexadecimal	Conversion Formula	Decimal
7F	$7 \times 16^1 + 15 \times 16^0$	127
FFFF	$15 \times 16^3 + 15 \times 16^2 + 15 \times 16^1 + 15 \times 16^0$	65535
431	$4 \times 16^2 + 3 \times 16^1 + 1 \times 16^0$	1073

decimal to hex

To convert a decimal number d to a hexadecimal number is to find the hexadecimal digits $h_n, h_{n-1}, h_{n-2}, \ldots, h_2, h_1$, and h_0 such that

$$d = h_n \times 16^n + h_{n-1} \times 16^{n-1} + h_{n-2} \times 16^{n-2} + \ldots$$
$$+ h_2 \times 16^2 + h_1 \times 16^1 + h_0 \times 16^0$$

These numbers can be found by successively dividing d by 16 until the quotient is 0. The remainders are $h_0, h_1, h_2, \ldots, h_{n-2}, h_{n-1}$, and h_n.

For example, the decimal number 123 is 7B in hexadecimal. The conversion is done as follows:

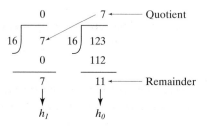

4 Conversions Between Binary and Hexadecimal Numbers

hex to binary

To convert a hexadecimal to a binary number, simply convert each digit in the hexadecimal number into a four-digit binary number, using Table 1.

For example, the hexadecimal number 7B is 1111011, where 7 is 111 in binary, and B is 1011 in binary.

binary to hex

To convert a binary number to a hexadecimal, convert every four binary digits from right to left in the binary number into a hexadecimal number.

For example, the binary number 1110001101 is 38D, since 1101 is D, 1000 is 8, and 11 is 3, as shown below.

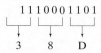

TABLE I Converting Hexadecimal to Binary

Hexadecimal	Binary	Decimal
0	0000	0
1	0001	1
2	0010	2
3	0011	3
4	0100	4
5	0101	5
6	0110	6
7	0111	7
8	1000	8
9	1001	9
A	1010	10
B	1011	11
C	1100	12
D	1101	13
E	1110	14
F	1111	15

(*Note:* Octal numbers are also useful. The octal number system has eight digits, 0 to 7. A decimal number 8 is represented in the octal system as 10.)

REVIEW QUESTIONS

1 Convert the following decimal numbers into hexadecimal and binary numbers.

100; 4340; 2000

2 Convert the following binary numbers into hexadecimal and decimal numbers.

1000011001; 100000000; 100111

3 Convert the following hexadecimal numbers into binary and decimal numbers.

FEFA9; 93; 2000

INDEX